FOREWORD BY BILLY J. KRAMER
PREFACE BY BOB HARRIS, OBE

THE SONGS THE BEATLES I GAVE AWAY

By COLIN HALL

Featuring original words of wisdom from

Peter Asher
John Askew aka Johnny Gentle aka Darren Young
Cilla Black OBE
John Clay (The Black Dyke Mills Band)
Megan Davies (The Applejacks)
Colin Hanton (Quarry Man)
Billy Hatton (The Fourmost)
Mary Hopkin
Freda Kelly
Astrid Kirchherr
Billy J. Kramer
Jackie Lomax
Sir Paul McCartney
Sir George Martin
Chas Newby
Klaus Voormann
Alan White

GREAT NORTHERN

Great Northern Books
PO Box 1380, Bradford,
West Yorkshire, BD5 5FB

www.greatnorthernbooks.co.uk

© Colin Hall 2022

Every effort has been made to acknowledge correctly and contact the copyright holders of material in this book. Great Northern Books Ltd apologises for any unintentional errors or omissions, which should be notified to the publisher.

All rights reserved. No part of this book may be reproduced in any form or by any means without permission in writing from the publisher, except by a reviewer who may quote brief passages in a review.

ISBN: 978-1-912101-45-0

Design by David Burrill

Front cover design: Gavin Askew

CIP Data
A catalogue for this book is available from the British Library

Print managed by Jellyfish Print Solutions

Printed and bound by CPI Group (UK) Ltd, Croydon, CR0 4YY

For my wife Sylvia, my daughter Hannah, sons Alex and James, their respective spouses Toby, Vanessa and Pavlina and my grandchildren Dylan, Riber, Charlotte and Sebastian. Love you always ...

For Bob Harris and Trudie Myerscough-Harris whose support and inspiration have made this book possible.

Also for my mother, Elsie Stevens, whom I never knew but has always been a part of my life.

*"Like a running blaze on a plain,
like a flash of lightning in the clouds.
We live in the flicker."*

Joseph Conrad, *Heart of Darkness*, April 1899

CONTENTS

FOREWORD BY BILLY J. KRAMER — 9
PREFACE BY BOB HARRIS, OBE — 10
INTRODUCTION — 12
PREQUEL: A BRIEF HISTORY OF HOW (AND BY WHOM) THE UK — 14
RECORD CHARTS WERE COMPILED BETWEEN 1952–69 (and beyond)

Part 1 Liverpool: He Saw Him Standing There

1: JOHN WINSTON LENNON: the early years 1940–1956 — 18
2: THE GUITAR … AS A HOBBY — 24
3: JAMES PAUL McCARTNEY: the early years 1942–56 — 31
4: PLAY BY HIS EARS — 34
5: 1957 … AND WE'D NEVER HAD IT SO GOOD — 37
6: I SAW HIM STANDING THERE — 43
7: THE TWO OF THEM — 47
8: AND THEN THERE WERE FOUR — 50
9: LENNON AND McCARTNEY ORIGINALS — 52
10: 1960: THE FUTURE STARTS HERE — 57
11: THE JACARANDA — 59
12: THE SECOND 'E' — 61
13: ALLAN AND LARRY MAKE PLANS — 63
14: WHAT THE HELL HAVE YOU SENT ME HERE, LARRY? — 67

Part 2 Hamburg

15: PETE BEST TO THE RESCUE — 82
16: DIRECT FROM HAMBURG … THE SENSATIONAL BEATLES! — 88
17: 1961 – CHAS NEWBY AND THE ECLECTIC SONG SET — 92
18: BACK TO REALITY — 97
19: GUITARS, GROUPS AND GIGS — 104
20: BILL HARRY, 'MERSEY BEAT' AND BRIAN EPSTEIN — 107
21: WITH OR WITHOUT A BARGEPOLE — 112
22: THE TWIST AND THE STORY OF HANK BALLARD — 115
23: THE BALLAD OF GRAHAM FISHER — 118
24: RIGHT THEN, BRIAN – MANAGE US (Passing the Decca Audition) — 124
25: THE DECCA TAPES — 128
26: THE CAVERN CLUB: THE LUNCHTIME SESSIONS — 136
27: THE BALLAD OF DICK ROWE — 141
28: A SIMPLE TWIST OF FATE — 144
29: THE CLOSED DOOR OPENS — 147
30: EYEBALL TO EYEBALL: SONGWRITING — 150
31: IN A DIFFERENT KEY, THE RETURN OF 'LOVE ME DO' — 158
32: GEORGE MARTIN'S TIE — 160
33: THE BALLAD OF PETE BEST — 163
34: INJECTING VIGOUR — 169
35: LOVE ME DO: A UK Chart History — 172
36: PLEASE PLEASE ME — 174

Part 3 Northern Songs

37:	PUBLISHING	178
38:	DICK JAMES HAS A GREAT NOTION	182
39:	CATSWALK	187
40:	SHAKE IT UP BABY	191
41:	THE HIT MACHINE TURNS ON	193
42:	WRITING A SWIMMING POOL	196
43:	A SONG THEY WERE SINGING	197
44:	THE POWER OF SONG	201
45:	A GIVEAWAY SPURNED …	207
46:	EPPY GETS IT WRONG	209
47:	1963, BILLY J. GETS ON HIS WAY …	212
48:	*WITH* THE DAKOTAS	219
49:	PAUL THROUGH AND THROUGH	225
50:	BILLY J. IN THE USA	228
51:	GOOD TO ME	231
52:	KEEPING BILLY J. SATISFIED	240
53:	BILLY J. BOUNCES BACK	245
54:	TOMMY QUIGLEY	247
55:	TOMMY QUICKLY, SOLO STAR	249
56:	LETTING TOMMY GO	252
57:	SUCCESS LIKE FAILURE	254
58:	1963, A BEATLEBUDDY SPARES A TUNE	259
59:	ONLY SO MANY BEATLES SONGS TO GO ROUND	263
60:	A LIVER BIRD SINGS	268
61:	THE SOUND OF SCOUSE	273
62:	1963, ONE OF THE IN-CROWD	278
63:	A HORRIBLE, MOURNFUL DIRGE	281
64:	1964, AND THE BEAT GOES ON	285
65:	THE SONGWRITER OF WIMPOLE STREET	288
66:	PETER ASHER AND THE ELVIS MANIAC	290
67:	MAGIC IS STILL THERE	295
68:	1964 ELSEWHERE AND AT OTHER TIMES	300
69:	1964, DIAMONDS, RHODESIANS AND STRANGERS …	302
70:	1964, BRUM BEAT AND THE SOUND OF SOLIHULL	313
71:	1964, FIVE O'CLOCK CLUB	318
72:	1964, BILLY J. SEEN … FROM A WINDOW	325
73:	THIS ONE'S FOR YOU CILLA!	330
74:	1965 AND A CHANGING OF THE GUARD	334
75:	BEING A SHORT DIVERSION INTO 'YESTERDAY'	340
76:	A MAN IN NEED OF A DECENT TAILOR	346
77:	P.J. GETS A LITTLE HELP FROM HIS FRIENDS	351
78:	BERNARD WEBB LENDS A HAND	354
79:	1966, Part 1 – BLOODY TRIBAL RITES	356
80:	1966, Part 2 – MAKING PROMOS	360
81:	1966, Part 3 – BACK ON THE ROAD AGAIN	361
82:	1966, Part 4 – ON BEING MORE POPULAR THAN JESUS	365
83:	1966, Part 5 – INDICA	368
84:	1966, Part 6 – WHAT PAUL DID ON HIS HOLIDAYS	371
85:	1966, Part 7 – GEORGE MARTIN AND THE SAGA OF THE TUDOR MINSTRELS	375
86:	1966, Part 8 – YOU CAN'T PLEASE EVERYBODY …	383
	PAUL ON TRYING TO KEEP IT IN THE FAMILY (WAY)	

87:	1967, Part 1 – 'SERGEANT PEPPER' AND FRIENDS	387
88:	1967, Part 2 – MUSIC THE BEATLES RECORDED AND GAVE AWAY NEVER TO BE HEARD AGAIN …	389
89:	1967, Part 3 – 'OUR WORLD'	391
90:	1967, Part 4 – A CATCALL FROM THE PAST	395
91:	1967, Part 5 – THE MAHARISHI MAHESH YOGI AND TRANSCENDENTAL MEDITATION	400
92:	1967, Part 6 – BRIAN EPSTEIN AND APPLE	404

Part 4 Apple

93:	WONDERWALL	410
94:	1968 – BLUE MEANIES IN SIGHT	414
95:	A NEW SONG FOR CILLA	416
96:	CILLA AND THE SONGS GEORGE AND RINGO WROTE FOR HER	421
97:	RINGO, EMMANUEL AND A GIRL CALLED CANDY	424
98:	1968, GIVING IT ALL AWAY: BUSINESS BITES FROM THE APPLE AND BEYOND	425
99:	APPLE RECORDS AND OL' BLUE EYES	429
100:	'Z' IS FOR ZAPPLE	431
101:	LIVERPOOL SLIM	434
102:	APPLE 3, A SONG FROM RISHIKESH	438
103:	THE FURTHER ADVENTURES OF JACKIE LOMAX	445
104:	APPLE 4, PAUL GOES TO YORKSHIRE	450
105:	A DAY OUT IN SALTAIRE	453
106:	JOHN FOSTER AND SONS LTD BLACK DYKE MILLS BAND	456
107:	1968 … THOSE WERE THE DAYS …	458
108:	1969, GETTING BACK	463
109:	FOR MARY HOPKIN OF PONTARDAWE, SOUTH WALES …	466
110:	MARY HOPKIN BIDS APPLE GOODBYE	473
111:	GEORGE STEPS OUT	478
112:	THE CONTINUING ADVENTURES OF GEORGE AND ERIC, 1969	483
113:	PAUL AND LINDA ENJOY A WINTER BREAK	487
114:	MORTIMER AND THE ILL-FATED STORY OF APPLE 16	491
115:	ENTER THE IVEYS …	496
116:	AND, IN THE END	504
117:	GEORGE AND DORIS	511
118:	SORRY, BUT IT'S TIME TO GO	519

POSTSCRIPT: WE LOVE YOU BEATLES – OH YES WE DO!	521
Sources: Bibliography, Discography (selective)	524
Thank you	526

"John and Paul were opposite sides of the same coin. They had distinctive talents but they managed to mesh them. They were equal in their talents. Paul had this incredible gift for melody and harmony, John had an incredible gift with words and with quirky harmony changes, with quirky chords and they formed their songs in that way."

Sir George Martin 2008

FOREWORD

It's an honour to have been asked to write the foreword for Colin's book. I am eternally grateful to have recorded so many Lennon-McCartney songs. Growing up, I always felt people from Liverpool had something special. We shared our tea, milk and sugar together while getting over the aftermath of World War II on ration books and our great sense of humour.

It took the persistence of Brian Epstein and the amazing talents of John, Paul, George and Ringo to change the world. I am proud to have been a part of the greatest chapter in rock and roll history.

When I first saw the Beatles, they were only playing carefully chosen cover songs which blew me away. Nobody was aware of their amazing songwriting talents at that point. But then, at the Majestic Ballroom in Birkenhead, there was a Mersey Beat Poll Winners concert that I was a part of due to being the highest placed non-professional. It was the first time I witnessed the Beatles performing one of their original songs, 'Please Please Me', before it was released. I was amazed! Little did I know how that night would change my life.

'Do You Want to Know a Secret', 'I'll Keep You Satisfied', 'From a Window', 'I Call Your Name', and, of course, 'Bad to Me', are songs that John and Paul wrote especially for me.

They raised the bar so high that nobody has even come close and never will.

BILLY J. KRAMER
October 2020

PREFACE BY BOB HARRIS

I believe that all the best things grow out of friendship and this book is a beautiful demonstration of that ideal.

I first met Colin Hall more than 15 years ago at the Cambridge Folk Festival. During our first conversation he told me that, on behalf of the National Trust, he and his wife Sylvia were the custodians of the Liverpool houses where two of the Beatles had spent their formative years. He explained that he was the keeper of 'Mendips' on Menlove Avenue, the house where John Lennon had lived with his Auntie Mimi, while Sylvia looked after Paul McCartney's childhood home on nearby Forthlin Road. It was a fascinating conversation. It was like Colin was re-telling my early teenage years.

I found myself being swept up by his passion and knowledge and by the memories he was triggering in my mind of an era that, for so many people of my generation, still echoes as one of the best times of our lives. It was a moment of fabulous energy – a glorious Rock 'n' Roll fuelled-transition as the austere, ration-book, post-war age of the monochrome Fifties burst into the new, exciting culture explosion of the technicolour Sixties.

Colin invited me to visit him and Sylvia in Liverpool to experience their own private 'Magical Mystery Tour', taking in all the major Beatle landmarks and visiting the houses. It was an invitation I couldn't possibly turn down and what a day it turned out to be.

We went into the bowels of the Cavern Club on Matthew Street, drove up Penny Lane past the bank that stands on the corner and stood gazing out over Strawberry Fields. Nothing to get hung about. It was a very special day. But of all the sensory excitement, it was John's childhood home Mendips that had by far the biggest impact on me. Stepping across the threshold of that modest 1930s semi-detached dwelling was literally like stepping back into a portal of my own childhood.

Yoko Ono had bought the house in 2002 and immediately donated it to the National Trust who, with the aid of photographs and first-hand accounts, restored it to a state which exactly recreated the way it was when John had lived there 50 years before. I was spellbound.

It was like walking into my mum and dad's house in the Fifties. The first thing that struck me was the sun dappling through the leaded lights of the bay windows, casting colours across the carpet of the prim and pristine front room. Every house of the time had a room just like it – rarely used by the family, but kept spotless for special days, Sundays, or when someone important like the local vicar or a teacher from school came to call.

As I explored further into the house, I came across a black-and-white photograph in the family album that deeply resonated with me. It was a picture of John in his school uniform, his cap askew on his head, blazer unbuttoned over a V-necked pullover, tie half undone, grey trousers not quite down below his knees, almost meeting his pulled-up long school socks, satchel over his shoulder. That young lad was me … and every other schoolboy of the mid-1950s. We all looked exactly like that.

There was a big old electric radio in the morning room with a lovely, shiny dial. It is said that, at the time, it had a flex coming out of the back of it which was pinned to the skirting board that led up the side of the stairs and into John's bedroom, where it was plugged into a speaker on a shelf at the top of the bed above his head. There were posters of Elvis on the walls and old 45s scattered on the bedspread – Little Richard, Lonnie Donegan and Roy Orbison. I could not believe how I felt when I saw all this stuff. This was manna from heaven.

To complete the day, Colin and I travelled the short journey from 'Mendips' to St Peter's Church in Woolton village, scene of the historic moment when John and Paul met for the first time. It was the day that a church fete was taking place and Paul accompanied his school friend Ivan Vaughan to watch a performance by John's band the Quarry Men, who played an afternoon skiffle set in the field next to the church graveyard.

As we gazed over the fence and across the open land, I half closed my eyes. I could literally visualise it all, like a scene from my own childhood – summer marquees, stalls, sunshine, music playing. So evocative. I asked Colin to remind me of the date the fete took place. It was 6th July 1957. The 50th anniversary of that moment was only a few months away. I couldn't believe what had fallen into my lap. This was the perfect idea for a radio programme.

A few days later I was at the BBC suggesting to the Radio 2 controller, Lesley Douglas, that the network should mark this amazing anniversary with a special documentary. She agreed, on the understanding that we record a brand-new and exclusive interview with Paul McCartney. Paul said yes and the resulting programme became one of the proudest moments of my entire broadcasting career.

The Day John Met Paul was broadcast on Radio 2 in the week of the 50th anniversary, recreating and celebrating that historical moment. The programme featured rare live recordings, studio sessions and interviews with Paul, his brother Mike and the Quarry Men. We also recorded a magical conversation with Cynthia Lennon. All the elements were woven together by our brilliant editor Neil Myners, while Colin poured his huge knowledge into the mix.

The process of scripting and mixing was enjoyable beyond belief. We made great art between us and the reaction to the programme was incredible. The show has been repeated multiple times on Radio 2 and 6 Music and went on to win us a Silver Award in the Best Documentary category of the Sony Radio Awards that year, a wonderful accolade.

We didn't want to let it go. We'd all had so much fun making the programme that Colin, Neil and I began to look for other ideas and ways to work together again. Neil and I broke off for a few months to make a Rolling Stones documentary, instigated by my wife Trudie, and *The Sandy Denny Story* for Radio 2, which won us another Sony, before Colin came up with the proposal for our next major project – *The Songs the Beatles Gave Away*, such a great idea. Compiling it became a dream job, a labour of love and a major epic, all rolled into one.

Paul McCartney gave us another wonderful interview at his MPL office in Soho. We spent a beautiful afternoon with Sir George Martin and his wife Judy, at their home in Coleshill. Colin compiled interviews in Liverpool with Billy J. Kramer, Billy Hatton from the Fourmost, and Jackie Lomax, while Olivia Harrison kindly gave us an incredible star-studded recording of Jackie's 'Soul Milk Sea'. I located a brilliant BBC archive recording of George Harrison, explaining the story of how he wrote the song 'Badge' with Eric Clapton for supergroup Cream, and we located rare singles from across the world.

Additionally, I recorded interviews with Mary Hopkin, Johnny Gentle and Cilla Black and we unearthed the charming, original recording of the McCartney song 'Step Inside Love', a demo recorded by Cilla, Paul and Sir George Martin in a tiny Soho studio in 1968.

The Songs the Beatles Gave Away turned out to be an even bigger project than *The Day John Met Paul*, and the feeling of camaraderie between Colin, Neil and myself made it an incredibly special process for all of us. When all the pieces of the audio jigsaw had been put together it was broadcast as part of a Beatle weekend on Radio 2 and it's the material we compiled between us for the programme that forms the basis of this book.

As you read on, Colin will take you through the stories, the adventures, the interviews and the histories of all the songs we featured on the show.

These are magic moments we have been privileged to share, getting to the heart of relatively neglected aspects of the songwriting history of the biggest band the world has ever known.

Who knew, when Colin and I first started talking at the Cambridge Folk Festival all those years ago, that all this would have happened. But it has, and these programmes have been a wonderful experience of friendship, excitement and creative energy.

I'm thrilled to have been a part of it all.

BOB HARRIS OBE

Introduction: THE REASON WHY

Throughout the Sixties it seemed that everything the Beatles touched turned to gold. John Lennon and Paul McCartney's compositional talents got better and better all the time, as did George Harrison's. Every new single and album marked a startling progression that took the group and its fans in new, different and always exciting directions. New songs. New sounds. New thrills. Onwards and upwards, it was an amazing journey. And, as they tested the boundaries of popular music by continually taking daring compositional and artistic risks, their listeners stayed tuned, enthralled by what they heard.

No group has been quite so attuned to the zeitgeist of their time. It was an intuitive gift: where the Beatles went others eagerly followed.

Through it all Lennon and McCartney rarely wasted a song. Tunes that somehow didn't work for the Beatles themselves would be stored away, either on tape or in the memory, to be returned to at some time in the future, and more often than not to offer to other artists for whom they were deemed better suited. And once the Beatles were up and running, John and Paul were occasionally moved to compose brand new songs specifically intended for *other* artists, *not* for themselves.

They were encouraged in this endeavour by their manager Brian Epstein, who knew this would keep the Beatles brand on the charts beyond the time enjoyed by the group's own releases. John and Paul were more than happy to oblige, knowing that, as writers, a hit for someone else, but written by themselves, would always be a hit for their individual bank balances.

Beyond the pride of having a song on the charts John and Paul were only too well aware that the 'pop' music scene of the late Fifties and early Sixties was notoriously fickle. In their experience the big 'stars of today' had a tendency to become the 'have-beens of tomorrow'. Journalists would frequently pose the question to them of how long they thought the Beatles would last. John, Paul, George and Ringo's replies were always modest, realistic and based on their experience of who and what had gone before, acknowledging that they knew the good fortune they were experiencing was unlikely to last very long. Privately they may have hoped they would prove the exception to the rule, but not possessed of a crystal ball they knew only too well that while they were cresting their own wave of popularity they needed to make the most of it financially as well as artistically. With this in mind, as songwriters, John and Paul understood they could not afford to rest on their laurels.

Right from the start, the additional income from composing meant that John and Paul earned more than Ringo and George. John and Paul knew this, but they also recognised that all four Beatles would benefit from the more hits they provided for the group.

As the Beatles began to top music charts around the world, Lennon and McCartney were eager to establish their reputation as composers, so that when the bubble finally burst (and they fully expected it would) they could continue to earn a healthy income as writers. To quote Sir Paul McCartney: "And let's not forget the commercial aspect, if you wrote another hit that was more money and you could maybe get a car or something and we weren't averse to that kind of conversation."

During the Sixties, many artists 'covered' songs written by John and Paul that the Beatles had already recorded and released on their own LPs or EPs, but had decided not to release as singles. As a consequence, Beatles albums were eagerly seized upon and songs composed by John and Paul, but not issued as singles by the group itself, were turned into UK Top 10 or Top 20 hits by acts such as Marmalade with 'Ob-la-di, Ob-la-da', Joe Cocker with 'With a Little Help from My Friends', the Overlanders with 'Michelle',

David and Jonathan also with 'Michelle', the Silkie with 'You've Got to Hide Your Love Away', Matt Monro with 'Yesterday' and Cliff Bennett and the Rebel Rousers with 'Got to Get You into My Life'. Beyond these notable hits, there were countless other 'cover' versions of Beatles songs recorded by such a myriad of diverse artists across the musical spectrum and around the world that it truly beggared belief.

For this volume my focus has been those heady days of the Sixties when the 45rpm single record bossed the world of 'pop' music and the charts. The singles featured here, however, were not 'covers' of Beatles songs such as those mentioned above; the singles that grace my book were first-time editions of songs that had not been commercially released by the Beatles themselves. For want of a better expression, they are tunes John, Paul and George 'gave away'. They were either never issued officially by the Beatles themselves during the existence of the group as an active recording unit, or were tunes which they did not take beyond the 'demo' stage.

They are, therefore, unique recordings, a separate Beatles songbook: a body of work released by other artists fortunate enough to be gifted original tunes, some specifically composed for them, others originally written with the Beatles in mind, but not actually released by the group themselves. As such the tunes were eagerly accepted by others, no doubt in the hope that some of that special Beatles magic would rub off and propel them into the charts …

My story also encapsulates the amazing journey the Beatles made from the early days as the Quarry Men and Silver Beatles, when they struggled to get gigs, through to the heady days of Beatlemania and beyond, to the years when they ceased touring.

Inevitably, at the point of coming off the road, John, Paul, George and Ringo began to move beyond their perceived Beatles personae to become individual artists in their own right. Thus, as they individually sought inspiration and opportunities with which to express their restless and still burgeoning creativity, they often moved in different directions. For a few more years, they were able to co-exist within the protective shelter provided by the collective identity of the Beatles, but the day was fast approaching when even this shell would fracture and they would break free, no longer Beatles, but artistically and creatively solo artists restless to prove themselves.

My book is set strictly within the parameters of the Beatles years, and the stories it tells took place more on the fringes of Beatlemania rather than at its core. It is very much about the post-war 'pop' music scene in the UK. Unlike the overwhelmingly corporate and slick 'pop' music industry of today, these were male-run, male-dominated, incredibly less politically correct times when the rules were still being written. Coming out of the suffering, deprivation and rationing of the war years, they were fuelled by an energy the like of which we are unlikely to experience again.

Significantly, it was a time bereft of social media and the unrelenting demand for instant gratification. Some might say, 'We made our own entertainment'. In the case of skiffle they'd be pretty much on the money. These were the days when the discovery of what young people thought was 'new' music brought an entire generation together on a shared journey into an uncertain future. Back then music exerted a powerful energy that, for huge numbers of young people, became a unifying force that many believed could help change the world for the better. It provided an identity and/or rallying call with which young people could mark their place in society. The cerebral and physical excitement experienced during the Sixties by the 'discovery' and celebration of a new singer or group, especially one that, at first, very few others seemed to know about, is hard to convey to children of the 21st century. Reputations spread mostly by word of mouth (usually after having read mentions in music newspapers, such as *NME, Melody Maker* and *Disc*). Sonic outlets for music were few and so it became our mission as teenagers to investigate and spread the word wherever and whenever we could … In the process we were greatly assisted and guided by Radio Luxembourg and the emergent pirate radio stations. A core requirement of this mission was always to 'shake it up, baby' and 'have some fun tonight', which we did without hesitation and always with great glee and as much abandon we thought we could get away with! And, of course, looking hip at all times was all part of the scene.

Colin Hall
Menlove Avenue, Liverpool, October 2021

PREQUEL

A BRIEF HISTORY OF HOW (AND BY WHOM) THE UK RECORD CHARTS WERE COMPILED BETWEEN 1952–69 (and beyond)

In the 1950s, and for most of the 1960s, the UK Official Charts Company Limited (or its equivalent) did not exist. Originally, music charts in the UK had been dedicated to the sales of sheet music which appeared in specialty music journals, such as the *Accordion Times and Music Express*. This was because back then people were more inclined to perform music themselves at home, hence the significance of sales of sheet music. Most ordinary folk did not own a record player and so the sales of records were small. Throughout the 1930s the accordion enjoyed incredible popularity as an instrument played not only by professionals but also by people in their own homes. However, after the end of the Second World War (1939–45) the instrument's popularity declined.*

(*John Lennon's mother Julia was an accomplished piano accordion player. Her daughter Julia has very fond memories of her mum entertaining the family by playing her beloved accordion and singing to them.)

By 1951, sales of the *Accordion Times and Musical Express* were in such decline that just 15 minutes before it was due to be officially closed an offer from music promoter and agent Maurice Kinn to purchase the paper for £1,000 was readily accepted. Kinn immediately set about turning the broadsheet's fortunes around. He began the process by re-naming it the *New Musical Express* and it was under this name the paper was re-launched in March 1952. (By the 1960s the *New Musical Express*, or *NME*, as it became more popularly known, was 'the bible' for most music fans who each week would eagerly scour its pages to read about new records, discover new artists, tours and most importantly which records were either going up, down, or just entering the 'charts'.)

Kinn was a fan of the American record charts published in the US broadsheet *Billboard* (the newspaper in which music charts had originated in 1940). He decided to start publishing a UK single record sales charts in the *New Musical Express*, believing that this would broaden the paper's appeal and help boost its sales. After a lot of planning, on 14 November 1952, the *New Musical Express* published the UK's first ever record sales chart. It was only 12 pages long and at the top of the pile in its first singles chart was American actor and singer Al Martino with his recording of 'Here In My Heart', which remained at number 1 for a staggering 9 weeks.

Kinn's instinct proved sound: as sales of records increased during the Fifties so music fans loved studying the *NME* chart to discover which new songs and artists were proving popular. Accordingly, sales of the *New Musical Express* boomed to the point they rivalled those of its rival publication *Melody Maker*.

To compile the *NME*, chart staff would telephone record shops (mainly in the Greater London area) asking them to keep a note of the number of records they sold each week.

From this very limited source (only 20 shops were contacted for the first chart), a weekly chart would be compiled and published. The number of shops participating in the collection of sales figures would later rise to 52 and on 1 October 1954 *NME* published its first Top 20 chart.

Other publications could see what was happening at *NME* and, in 1955, they also began compiling their own charts. Thus, in January 1955, *Record Mirror* printed a Top 10 Singles Chart based on postal returns from record shops (financed by the *Record Mirror* itself). By October of the same year *Record Mirror* expanded its chart into a Top 20. In April, *NME*'s charts expanded to a Top 30. *Melody Maker* published its own Top 20 for the first time on 7 April 1956, based on telephone calls to 19 record stores. It was the first music paper to include Northern Ireland in its poll.

Disc (and at times known as *Disc Weekly* and *Disc and Music Echo*) was another weekly UK music paper. Renowned for its up-to-date and numerous news stories, lively readers' page, plus its focus on both artists and the weekly charts, it was more 'pop' orientated than either *NME* or *MM*, but always a very good read. Launched in 1958 it compiled its own charts based, initially, on a figure culled from approximately just 25 shops, but by the mid-Sixties this had expanded to 100. Based on figures received from record companies between 1959 and 1973, it also awarded Silver and Gold Discs for sales of 250,000 and 1,000,000 discs. Contributors included Jack Good, John Peel and its most famous singles reviewer was Penny Valentine. In August 1975 it was merged with *Record Mirror* and Paul McCartney was one of many musicians who wrote to the publication to express his regret at its demise.

The author has found *Disc*'s single reviews, as penned by Don Nicholl and Penny Valentine, a marvellous resource in tracking the critical reception of most of the songs the Beatles 'gave away'.

In August 1959, *Record Retailer*, a monthly trade newspaper for the UK record industry, was launched. Its title was expanded to *Record Retailer and Music Industry News* and in March 1960 it published a Top 50 singles chart. It was more accurate than those being published by the aforementioned music weeklies. Accordingly, in March 1963, *Record Mirror* quit compiling its own charts and instead began publishing the *Record Retailer* chart.

Despite this, *NME* continued to be the most popular music paper in the 1960s. Its charts were keenly followed by fans, but *Record Retailer*'s chart was gaining the edge for its accuracy. In 1960 it published a Top 50. The fact that it had been set up by independent record shops, and had no funding or associations with the record companies themselves, *Record Retailer*'s independence meant its charts were less prone to accusations of 'hyping' than *NME*'s.

NME continued to publish its own chart, but by 1969 the British Market Research Bureau (BMRB) had started to collect sales figures from over 250 record retailers around the UK to compile the UK 'Official' Singles Chart. That word 'Official' was crucial and it was this listing that would be used by the BBC and *Record Retailer*. Over the years, BMRB was replaced by Gallup, who in 1990 was replaced as the official compiler of the UK music charts by Chart Information Network Limited, or CIN (re-named as the Official UK Charts Company in 2001). The UK OCC has been responsible for the UK Official Music Charts ever since.

The UK Charts from 1969 onwards, as published by the Official UK Charts Company, are regarded as definitive. The period from 1952 up to 1969 is more problematic due to the number of different charts available at the time and whose listings did not always correspond and did not come from the same sources. To determine chart placings for that period, both the Official UK Charts Company and the *Guinness Book of Records* rely on the *NME* charts for the period 1952 to 1960, and the *Record Retailer* charts from 1960 to 1969.

But to return to the 1960s, on which my book focuses, every week the new singles and long player 'charts' printed in music newspapers such as *NME*, *Disc*, *Record Mirror* or *Melody Maker* were what we relied upon to get up-to-date information on the latest chart activity. As noted, chart placings could differ from music newspaper to newspaper depending from which music stores they received their sales figures.

Consequently, if you were a reader of *NME*, *Disc* or *Melody Maker*, in their charts 'Please Please Me' reached the coveted number 1 position. As most teenagers in the 1960s referred to these newspapers as their pop music 'bibles', they always remember reading in 1963 that 'Please Please Me' had become the first Beatles single to reach number 1. And so 'Please Please Me' entered our memory banks as the group's first chart topper.

However, in *Record Retailer*, 'Please Please Me' peaked at number 2. Consequently, as *Record Retailer* evolved into the Official UK Charts Company, nowadays 'Please Please Me' is no longer officially credited as a UK number 1 single and therefore has lost its status as the Beatles' first UK number 1. (It does not appear on the Beatles' compilation album *1* released in 2000.) Instead that honour now goes to the Beatles' follow-up single, 'From Me to You', which hit the number 1 spot in *Record Retailer* throughout May and into June 1963. (This is why in pub quizzes the elderly members of your team should not be relied upon to answer correctly the question, 'What was the Beatles' first UK number 1?'. If they are so old, like this author, they were actually alive at the time, and were devotees of *NME*, they will inevitably plump for 'Please Please Me', and in turn blow your chances of winning.)

In *The Songs The Beatles Gave Away*, all UK singles chart details quoted are taken from the 'Official Charts, Official Singles' compiled by the Official UK Charts Company, www.officialcharts.com.

Along the way there has also been a little help from *The Guinness Book of British Hit Singles* by Jo and Tim Rice with Paul Gambaccini and Mike Read (1977 edition).

Another essential resource that has helped fill in the blanks, provided easily observed details of an individual single's progress, and which contains a series of brilliant year-by-year nutshell observations that tell it how it was (in *Record Mirror*), has been *20 Years of British Record Charts 1955-1975*, with commentary by Peter Jones and Tony Jasper and edited by Tony Jasper (Queen Anne Press, 1975).

The timings for all the Beatles' singles/giveaway songs are taken from the marvellous *All Together Now, The First Complete Beatles Discography 1961–1975* by Harry Castleman and Walter J. Podrazik (Ballantine Books, New York, 1976).

All USA singles chart details in *The Songs The Beatles Gave Away* are taken from *Billboard*'s records archive.

THE BEATLES
George Harrison: born on Thursday 25 February 1943, in the upstairs front bedroom of the family home 12 Arnold Grove, Wavertree, Liverpool.
Died aged 58 on Thursday 29 November 2001 at a friend's house in Los Angeles, California, USA.
John Winston Ono Lennon: born on Wednesday 9 October 1940 in Liverpool Maternity Hospital on Oxford Street, Liverpool.
Died aged 40 on Monday 8 December 1980 after he was shot and fatally wounded as he entered the archway of The Dakota, his home with his wife Yoko Ono, in New York City, New York, USA.
James Paul McCartney: born on Thursday 18 June 1942 in a private room in Walton Hospital, Rice Lane, Liverpool.
Richard Starkey aka 'Richy', 'Ringo Starr': born on Sunday 7 July 1940 in an upstairs bedroom at 9 Madryn Street, the Dingle, Liverpool.

PART 1

LIVERPOOL

HE SAW HIM STANDING THERE

Chapter 1:
JOHN WINSTON LENNON: the early years 1940–1956

Born on 9 October 1940, John Lennon was the only child of Julia Stanley and Alfred Lennon. Although the couple had only married on 3 December 1938, they had actually met some ten years earlier, as teenagers, in 1928. By the time war broke out Alfred was working as a merchant sailor – a perilous occupation indeed – and during the following years of conflict would spend more time at sea than at home in Liverpool. On one occasion he was gone for approximately 18 months with neither word nor money sent home. Such a turn of events left Julia with very good reason to believe her husband was one of many mariners tragically 'lost' at sea. She carried on with her life, but had very little money and had to move from a rented house where she lived with John to return to live with her father, George 'Pop' Stanley at 9 Newcastle Road, near the roundabout at the top of Penny Lane.

At her father's house, Julia began a relationship with a soldier who was lodging there and she became pregnant. 'Pop' Stanley was a man in his seventies and steeped in Victorian values. From the moment he realised his daughter was pregnant to a man who was clearly *not* her husband, he put Julia under intense pressure to give up her unborn child or expect no further support from him. The soldier offered to marry Julia, but apparently would not consider looking after John. Outraged, Julia would not countenance that proposal.

Meanwhile, in November 1944, Alfred Lennon turned up – very unexpectedly. Despite Alfred's counter-declaration that he would care for both John and her unborn child, Julia knew she could not rely on what she viewed as a hollow promise given her husband's frequent absences and dismal track record of support. Plus, in her head, she knew their marriage was over even if Alfred chose to blindly hope it could still be saved. And so, with her father intransigent and Alfred already back at sea, Julia had virtually no choice but to succumb to family pressure and allow her baby to be taken for adoption. Julia was left forlorn. A little girl, whom she named Victoria Elizabeth, was born on 19 June 1945. (Julia's baby was adopted after six weeks by Peder and Margaret Pedersen who gave her the name Ingrid Maria. The family lived in Crosby, just north of Liverpool.)[1]

Through these times John had mostly been with his mum, but in December 1944 and the early months of 1945 he'd also lived with Alfred's brother Sydney and his family in Maghull. Apart from her father 'Pop', significant others who helped out from time to time with John were Julia's eldest sister Mary, or 'Mimi' as she was known within the family, and her husband George Smith. Mimi and George lived in the pleasant, leafy, middle-class, south-Liverpool suburb of Woolton, just a few miles from Penny Lane. (Mimi was the eldest of five girls, the 'Stanley sisters' as they were known before each married, and the matriarchal figure within the family after the sisters' mother Annie had died in 1941.)

Not long after the birth of Victoria, Julia met John Albert Dykins whom she would call 'Bobby' but whose family knew him as Jack … someone with whom she *did* most definitely want to be and he with her.

By late March 1946, Julia, together with John, moved out of her father's home, 9 Newcastle Road, Wavertree, to live in Gateacre Village (close to Woolton) with Bobby, where home was a small one-bedroom flat.

Once more victim of his ingrained 'Victorian' values, 'Pop' Stanley was outraged by the fact that Julia had left him to cohabit with a man to whom she was not legally married. On a practical level he no doubt also missed having his daughter around to help care for him.

Much more to the point, a highly significant detail of Julia and Bobby's new accommodation had come to light and this was that it was furnished with only one double-bed in which all three occupants were sleeping. However temporary Julia intended this arrangement to be, once Mimi got wind of the fact her shock and outright disapproval were instant: in her mind such a situation could not be allowed to continue. Encouraged by Pop's displeasure she visited Julia and Bobby to see for herself and no doubt set things right.

Her initial inquiry met with a tetchy rebuke from Bobby and so she responded by initiating the intervention of Liverpool's Public Assistance Committee (Social Services) requesting that they specifically investigate the sleeping arrangements the couple had in place for the little boy. That the situation could not have been resolved in some other way is astonishing and suggests the level of ill will felt by the family towards Bobby. As a result, John was moved to live with Mimi and her husband George in the more spacious accommodation of their semi-detached house 'Mendips', number 251 Menlove Avenue, Woolton.

Whether this was intended initially by the authorities as just a temporary arrangement until Julia and Bobby found more suitable accommodation of their own, it soon became permanent: John never lived with his mum again on a full-time basis. He stayed with Mimi and George who did not have children of their own, cared for John 'in loco parentis' and never adopted him.

On a return to Liverpool in late May 1946, and fully aware that Julia and Bobby Dykins were living together, Alfred was concerned to learn that John was living with Mimi and George in Woolton. Never Mimi's greatest fan (likewise she was none too keen on him) it was on this occasion that Alfred visited John, Mimi and George at Mendips where he stayed the night before whisking his son off for what has become their famous sojourn in Blackpool. In that famous holiday resort, father and son resided with Billy Hall, a seafaring friend of Alfred's, in Billy's parents' home, Alfred clearly harbouring concerns for his son's future.

Some three weeks later, Julia and Bobby tracked Alfred and John down. After a meeting between Julia and Alfred (with Bobby present) it was agreed Julia would care for John and take him with her and Bobby back to Liverpool while Alfred would return to sea.

Once back in the city, the couple took John to 'Mendips' and handed him into the care of Mimi and George. It became his home until October 1963 ... the longest he would ever live in any one place.

Mimi had first seen John in the Oxford Street Maternity Hospital on the day he was born. From the moment she laid eyes upon him she was apparently smitten, telling Hunter Davies, the Beatles biographer, "The minute I saw John that was it. I was lost forever."[2] Without alluding to the events leading up to John's coming to live with her, Mimi also told Davies that, "I wanted him of course ... it did seem the best thing to do ... he already looked upon my house as a second home anyway." Significantly, Mimi also told Davies that both Fred and Julia wanted her to adopt their son, but she was never able to "get them both down to the office together to sign the forms."[3]

Mimi's view of events is strongly contested by John's sister, Julia. In her 2007 autobiography *Imagine This*, she describes in considerable detail (in Chapter 7 'The Too-Small Flat' in particular) her mother's desperate attempts to keep her son and Mimi's fierce reluctance to countenance any such thing.[4]

There is no doubt that the first five or six years of John Lennon's life had been irregular in terms of his parents' relationship. He barely saw his father and spent only weeks in a home where both Mum and Dad were together with him at the same time. Going to live with his Aunt Mary/Mimi and Uncle George in 'Mendips' would have brought security and calm into his world, somewhere he would come to call home and where he would always have his very own room, a private space all to himself in which he would say he did his 'dreaming' as he grew up. Mimi and her husband George were adults on whom he came to strongly rely and who he knew genuinely cared for him. There is no doubt Mimi could be strict, she had rules by which he was expected to abide and of the two George was the 'soft' one who put him to bed and sang him nursery rhymes ... Mimi worked hard, for 16 years she took in lodgers at Mendips to help pay the way and made sure that, materially, John lacked for very little.

The war exacted a harsh price on many families all over Britain and many children were brought up, not by their parents but, for various reasons, by other members of their family. Economics dictated that parents had to make hard, heartbreaking decisions.

Such arrangements weren't unusual, but it didn't mean that in later years, as they entered their teens and twenties, those children didn't ask why they hadn't been brought up by their real parents. Equally it did not mean parents ever forgave themselves for parting with children even when they had absolutely no other choice.

At first, Mimi discouraged Julia from visiting John frequently so that the little boy could settle into his new home and become accustomed to his new circumstances. As he grew older and into his teens Julia began to see him on a regular basis, and even before then John always knew exactly who 'Mum' was. He never referred to Mimi as his parent. Julia was a warm, loving person with a zest for life that was infectious. She was a talented musician who could sing, dance, play the piano, banjo and ukulele, and who particularly loved to entertain her children, Julia, Jacqueline and John by playing her beloved piano accordion for them. She lit up the room and for a sensitive young boy such as John, the contrast between her and his more serious and strict aunt could not have been more acute. How often he must have wondered to himself, "Why don't I live with Mum?"

Colin Hanton, the drummer with John's first band, the Quarry Men skiffle group, told the author that "Julia was unlike any of our mums, she looked younger, dressed more stylishly, had a zany sense of humour, loved Elvis and behaved more like an older sister than a mum."[5]

No wonder John missed her.

John: "I moved in with my auntie who lived in the suburbs in a nice semi-detached place with a small garden and doctors and lawyers and that ilk living around – not the poor slummy kind of image that was projected in all the Beatles stories. In the class system, it was about half a class higher than Paul, George and Ringo, who lived in government-subsidised housing. We owned our house and had a garden. They didn't have anything like that."[6]

As a youngster, John enjoyed reading, writing, drawing and painting. In particular, he loved the stories of 'Just William' by Richmal Crompton and adored Lewis Carroll's poetry and stories of 'Alice'.

Aunt Mimi: "He never showed the slightest interest in games and toys. I had twenty volumes of the world's best short stories and we had a love of books in common. John used to go back and read them over and over again, particularly Balzac. I thought there was a lot of Balzac in his songwriting later on. Anyway, he'd read most of the classics by the time he was ten."[7]

By the time he was a teenager, Julia, her partner Bobby, and their girls Julia and Jacqueline, had moved to live on the Springwood Estate in Allerton, just about a mile or so away from Woolton and 'Mendips'. Thanks to the intervention of his cousin Stanley (circa 1953), John was alerted to this fact and was soon spending weekends and school holidays with his mum, Bobby and his sisters Julia and Jacqueline in their family home of 1 Blomfield Road.

Very quickly Julia became a defining influence on and *in* his life.

Not only was Julia a very good singer, dancer and instrumentalist, who had from time to time contemplated a musical career, his father Alfred could hold a tune, play the harmonica and at heart had always wanted to be an entertainer. As a schoolboy in 1927, improbable as it sounds, Alfred, or 'Freddie' as he was known, ran away from school to join 'Will Murray's Gang' a children's music hall act. He was 13 going on 14 at the time and in 1927 children usually left school at 14.

This was not a sudden rush of blood to the head on Freddie's part, as apparently he had passed an audition for the 'Gang' when they were appearing in Liverpool. As 'a special treat' Alfred's older brother Sydney had taken him to see the show and at the end, when Murray invited parents whose children had any talent to visit him backstage, Sydney duly took Freddie to meet the man himself. Backstage, Freddie accompanied himself on piano and sang 'We All Like to Be Beside the Seaside'. Murray was suitably impressed and invited him to join the Gang. On behalf of their mother Polly, whom Sydney explained could neither read not write, Sydney duly signed a form releasing Freddie to join the troupe.

Unfortunately for Freddie, he was also a pupil at the Bluecoat Orphanage school. He wasn't an orphan but when Freddie was just seven his father Jack had died leaving Polly with six children to bring up on her own. In order to survive and ensure her children had a good start in life, Polly had been forced to let Freddie and his sister Edith become boarders at the Bluecoat which meant that the orphanage shared the custody of both children. For Freddie to join Will Murray's Gang, as his legal guardians, the Bluecoat also had to give permission, which they refused to do.

Undeterred, Freddie left a farewell letter and ran off to join the show regardless. By the time the troupe reached Glasgow the authorities caught up with him and he was returned to Liverpool. The urge to entertain never left Freddie, and later, in his days as a merchant sailor, on whichever vessel he sailed, he loved to entertain the ship's crew. In particular, he liked to impersonate popular singers of the day, such as Al Jolson and Charlie Chaplin.

At 'Mendips', John's Uncle George could hold a tune and was well known around the village as a good whistler. The villagers could testify to his prowess as a whistler because for a time before the war, George and his brother owned the local dairy farm and as he rode/led his horse and cart around the village to deliver milk George loved to whistle. When, as a toddler, it was John's bedtime, Uncle George would sing nursery rhymes with his nephew. And, like his beloved Uncle George, John also loved to whistle.

From the autumn of 1947 (John turned seven in October) until Christmas 1962, to help ends meet, Aunt Mimi took in student lodgers at Mendips. The bombing of Liverpool during WWII had left the city with an acute shortage of student accommodation and so good lodgings were in great demand. For those becoming landlords or landladies it was a good way of making extra, much-needed cash. One of the very first student lodgers at Mendips in the autumn of 1947 was a student of education named Harold Phillips who could play harmonica. Harold responded to John's fascination with the instrument and generously bought the little boy his first harmonica which became the first instrument John learned.

(Aunt Mimi and Uncle George held Harold's gift back until Christmas and put it in John's Christmas stocking as a special present. In September 2021, previously unheard tapes of John speaking to Canadian journalist Ken Zeilig on three separate occasions in 1969 and 1970 were sold at auction. On one of these John recalled reaching into his Christmas stocking in 1947 to find the instrument, commenting, "That was one of the greatest moments of my life, when I got my first harmonica.")[8]

In general terms, while John's talents for drawing, painting, reading and writing were approved of and encouraged by his aunt, (she bought him *How to Draw* tutors) his appreciation of popular music was not championed in the same way. The little boy clearly had an aptitude for music and could carry a tune, but Mimi was neither impressed nor swayed by John's gifts. For Mimi her nephew's fascination with music and singing carried worrisome echoes of the fanciful ways of his mother Julia and his wayward father Alfred. Viewing popular music as no more than a trifling distraction and fearing John might follow in his father's footsteps, Mimi's focus was always John's education, no more so than when he entered his teens. Success at school is what mattered, for down that path lay the prospect of a well paid 'career for life' and a good pension. Mimi was determined her nephew would not deviate from that path.

Mimi would not have been alone in her focus on education as the way forward. Most post-war parents would have been very much on her wavelength for they were of the generation who had fought in the Second World War. For the majority of them growing up in the 1920s and 30s, education had ended at age 14 when they left school without any qualifications and with correspondingly low career expectations. Considered as mere 'factory fodder', low paid work in factories, mills, mines, docks or menial office jobs was the most children from the working classes could expect, while during wars they doubled as 'cannon fodder'.

This dreadful social order in Britain was untenable but it took the devastating loss of life and the traumatic impact of the First and Second World Wars to bring about hesitant moves towards meaningful change. As the Second World War drew to a close and the monumental sacrifices the country had exacted from the 'ordinary' people of Britain was recognised, it became a national imperative that in the future their children should receive a better deal in life.

The euphoria of peace-time appeared to herald that the days of the 'Establishment' viewing the working classes as mere factory and cannon fodder were over. The Welfare State was born, headed by the formation of the National Health Service. The chance of gaining something better for themselves when they went to work was established through an improved education system, a system that, in theory, would deliver greater opportunities for all. It began in 1944 with the 'Butler' Education Act, which extended the school leaving age to 15 for all pupils. More time spent at school was one of the key tenets for post-war social 'revolution'.

Crucially, the Education Act of 1944 introduced the eleven-plus examination. If a pupil passed this then, potentially, the world became their oyster. Passing the eleven-plus meant a pupil could stay at school not just to age 15, but to 16, and maybe even beyond! Passing the exam meant a pupil became a 'grammar school' boy or girl who would be educated to 16 when, after successfully taking exams called O levels, they could continue at school until age 18. At 18 pupils could take a further series of exams called A levels. Success at A level would provide the opportunity to attend university, obtain a degree and enter a profession. If a pupil's parents were not rich or financially capable of supporting them at university a pupil would be able to apply for a grant.

What all this meant was that, in theory, suddenly working-class children had been gifted by a grateful government the opportunity to rise above such a lowly social status to possibly become a doctor, lawyer, banker ... one of the very pillars of British society. This was a golden ticket of educational opportunity unheard of before the war.

The only drawback was that on average only 20% of the school population passed the eleven-plus (even lower in Liverpool), leaving the rest to attend a 'secondary modern' (or a technical school, i.e., for those who were 'good with their hands') and the prospect of becoming factory fodder just like their parents before them.

Even for those who passed, despite the availability of grants, it was not always easy to leave a family who were struggling to get by and attend university. The pressure was still great to leave school and get a job to help out at home. Not only that, but university was almost an alien concept, if not an alien world, for working-class children to contemplate. They would be entering the world of the middle and upper classes which was a massive, quite daunting psychological barrier to be crossed that not all could manage even if they had the right grades.

Aside from any financial concerns, the psychological challenge of crossing this barrier for children from a working-class background cannot be over-estimated. It meant entering a world that was totally alien from anything they had ever experienced before: it was the world of the 'Establishment', a world of privilege, populated by young people who were far wealthier, better educated and spoke differently to them. More often than not they looked down on the working class. They also behaved differently, taking privilege for granted.

Such students had been brought up to believe that the world was theirs to own and to rule. Born with a silver spoon in their mouths, it was a given that their destiny was to be in charge and run the country … breaking into that world for a boy or girl from either a two-up, two-down terraced house, or a tiny concrete council house in the middle of a vast council estate, took some doing.

Nevertheless, a window of opportunity had opened, most parents recognised this and eagerly hoped their child would pass the eleven-plus and at least have the opportunity to enjoy a 'better life' than them.

Mimi set her sights high. She wanted John to work hard at school and go to university. He was bright and capable and in 1952 had passed the eleven-plus, and so by the summer of 1957 he was a 16-year-old grammar school boy attending Quarry Bank High School for Boys. Already possessed of the golden ticket of educational opportunity, by 1957 John faced his O level examinations and the prospect of entering the sixth form, the very portal to university. In her view of the world, John was standing on the edge of destiny. With university on the horizon, all he had to do was pass his exams. She was determined it was an opportunity her nephew would not squander.

Unfortunately for Mimi, John did not share her educational ambitions and was looking towards a different horizon.

This was because by then, like so many other British teenagers, he was in the thrall of noisy American rock 'n' roll music and some equally tuneless homemade hybrid racket called 'skiffle'. He was obsessed by both, but particularly by rock 'n' roll. For Aunt Mimi, puerile distractions such as Lonnie Donegan, 'the king of skiffle music', and Elvis Presley, 'the king rock 'n' roll', were miscreant purveyors of five-minute fads that threatened to derail her nephew's educational progress. Visions of that feckless Freddie must have filled her mind on a daily basis.

And so it was that John's obsession with these tuneless aberrations were not to be encouraged at all. And at Mendips they weren't. However, by 1957 John was spending time with Julia who had a record player and bought rock 'n' roll records for herself: indeed, she called her cat, Elvis …

---

1 'The Sister John Lennon Never Knew,' *My Weekly*, 29 March 2008: Interview with Ingrid Pedersen by Rosie Edser p.16 In this interview Ingrid says, "I've heard that Julia and Margaret (her adoptive mother) knew one another, but how they were connected I don't know. Julia's family, by all accounts unhappy at my birth, pressurised Julia to give me up." Ingrid also says of her biological father, that Julia "had a relationship with my father, Taffy Williams, from early 1944, falling pregnant in the autumn. I've heard that he'd wanted them to live together, but wouldn't accept John."
2 & 3 *The Beatles: The Authorised Biography* by Hunter Davies, (Heinemann, 1968) p.6 and p.7.
4 *Imagine This: Growing up With My Brother John Lennon* by Julia Baird, (Hodder & Stoughton, 2007) my text includes no specific quotations from Julia's biography but Chapter 7 'The Too-Small Flat' pages 32–36 provides an insight into Julia's reaction to John being cared for by Mimi.
5 Colin Hanton in conversation with the author for *Pre:Fab!* by Colin Hanton with Colin Hall, (The Book Guild, 2018)
6 John Lennon, *Playboy* magazine, published January 1981. (Interviewed by David Sheff, September 1980.)
7 *John Lennon*, Ray Coleman, (Futura Publications, 1984) p.25.
8 John Lennon in conversation with Canadian journalist Ken Zeilig, 1969/70. Tapes re-discovered and sold for auction in September 2021.

Chapter 2:
THE GUITAR … AS A HOBBY

The first instrument John requested at 'Mendips' was a piano. For a woman who was so aspirational middle-class it might seem odd that Mimi would not run with this and at least send him for lessons to see how he responded. Maybe it was the expense such lessons would incur that caused her to deny him. More likely was its association with the fickle world of music and entertainment, a liking for which both his parents had shared and therefore one *not* to be encouraged in John. And so his request was declined with words to the effect that, "There will be none of that common sing-a-long stuff in this house …"

As has already been noted, unlike his Aunt Mimi, his mother Julia *was* a musician and a huge fan of popular music. She owned a banjo, ukulele, piano accordion and a piano … all of which she often played. She and Bobby enjoyed a shared love of popular music, owned a record player and Julia bought Elvis Presley records for herself. Not too many mothers did that in 1950s Britain.

Rock 'n' roll music was in its infancy and its purveyors were viewed with disdain by most parents. They feared the wild, and what was to them, tuneless music that had so inexplicably captivated their sons and daughters. Many considered it to be the work of the Devil. In their minds it threatened the moral turpitude of British teenagers. For many British parents just knowing it came from the USA was enough to damn it forever. This came from the tendency among Brits in the early to mid-twentieth century to believe the UK set the standards in all walks of life and the rest of the world struggled to meet them. Consequently, sections of British society were not slow to turn up their noses at American popular culture, considering it to be brash and aimed at the masses … the epitome of trash.

Brits who had fought in, or in other ways experienced the Second World War, retained a largely ambivalent view of the USA. They might reluctantly acknowledge the debt owed by Britain to the States for finally getting on board and helping turn the tide against Hitler and the Nazis, but ingrained into the British subconscious was the notion that America had waited too long to do so and was an upstart nation born originally from largely European misfits, criminals and rejects. Both the country and too many of its people were viewed as flash and fickle, tacky and trite. 'Yanks', as Brits called these 'Johnnies-come-lately', had no class and were simply too full of themselves. So, what hope for the country's latest offering to a poor unsuspecting post-war world: this outrageously noisy, blatantly crude, barely articulate, shamelessly sexual, tuneless thing called rock 'n' roll?

For most of the UK's adult population in the 1950s, the howls of rock 'n' roll as it crested a burgeoning wave of an emergent teen culture was something quite alien, an aberration – and the insane popularity of Elvis Presley was considered a passing but worrisome craze. Here was an entertainer parents believed to be of little or no inner substance, but nevertheless one capable of wreaking irreparable psychological damage on their children. They sought in vain to understand just what was going on. For a generation who had fought a world war, rock 'n' roll seemed trivial and crude in the extreme. Knowing that it emanated from the USA and had its roots in black culture was all most Brits needed to damn it without question.

And so they did.

In September 1956, acclaimed British conductor, Sir Malcolm Sargent had this to say about this new musical phenomenon: 'The amazing thing about rock 'n' roll is that youngsters who go into such ecstasies sincerely believe that there is something new and wonderful about the music. There is nothing new or wonderful about it. Rock 'n' roll has been played in the jungle for centuries. It is nothing more than an exhibition of primitive tom-tom thumping."[1]

The amazing thing is that back then, no jaws dropped, no voice was raised in protest. Instead heads simply nodded in agreement, for Sir Malcolm had hit the nail on the head for most of that conservative generation with what was a generally held opinion.

American rock 'n' roll, a form of 'dance music' aimed at teenagers, arrived in the UK during 1954–55. Records by Bill Haley – 'Shake Rattle & Roll' and 'Rock Around the Clock' – had taken the fledgling UK record sales charts by storm. Haley's presence on the British popular music scene was an awakening for John Lennon. He'd hear Bill's records down at his mother's house and be fully aware of the new sound she was enjoying on her record player, but of much more musical significance for him and for many, many other future stars of British rock 'n' roll was the emergence of the UK's Lonnie Donegan in January 1956, some six months ahead of the earth-shattering arrival of Elvis on the UK charts with 'Heartbreak Hotel'.

Although John's life turned forever in the instant he first heard Elvis Presley sing, and he would famously declare 'Before Elvis there was nothing', there had in fact been one other. And that other was Lonnie. John tuned in to Lonnie to the extent of even buying a copy of Lonnie's debut hit single 'Rock Island Line' and so was fully aware that Lonnie was the purveyor of a new form of music called 'Skiffle', an acoustic kissing cousin of rock 'n' roll steeped in Americana. Indeed, John became quite a fan of Lonnie, purchasing several of Lonnie's early singles, but nothing and no one was to touch him in quite the way as did hearing the lonesome, blues-honed vocals of that supremely handsome hillbilly boy from Tupelo, Mississippi, USA, Mr Elvis Aaron Presley.

Mimi: "It was Elvis Presley all day long. I got very tired of him talking about this new singer. I was particularly upset because suddenly he wouldn't let me into his bedroom. If I opened the door he'd say: 'Leave it, I'll tidy it up.' He became a mess, almost overnight, and all because of Elvis Presley. He had a poster of him in his bedroom. There was a pyjama top in the bathroom, the trousers in the bedroom, socks somewhere else, shirts flung on the floor."[2]

Mimi was not alone: parents up and down the land were being confronted by such previously unheard of behaviour in their teenage sons and daughters.

And it wasn't just British parents who feared the influence of Elvis. Before them rock 'n' roll had had the adult population of the USA quaking in their shoes, fearing it to be the enemy of all that was decent and morally correct. For many, Elvis was the emissary of the Devil sent to turn their children onto the path of delinquency.

Typical of many adults, Frank Sinatra was evangelical in his opposition to this new form of music (and Elvis in particular). In an article for the US magazine *Western World* published in 1958 he referred "to the bulk of rock 'n' roll" with these words: "It fosters almost totally negative and destructive reactions in young people. It smells phoney and false. It is sung, played and written for the most part by cretinous goons and by means of its almost imbecilic reiterations and sly, lewd – in plain fact – dirty lyrics, it manages to be the martial music of every side-burned delinquent on the face of the earth."[3]

Vehement and extreme views for sure (and very careful not to actually mention Elvis by name!), Frank's hysteria tapped directly into the unease most American parents felt about the emergence of rock 'n' roll.

Aunt Mimi was an intelligent, well-read, well-spoken woman who, had she been born into a later age, most probably would have attended university. For her a place at university was the epitome of success and the key to a successful and rewarding future. Julia was equally bright, but compared to Mimi far more vivacious and outward-going, although both were possessed with a sharp sense of humour. Unlike her elder sister, Julia was a free spirit unconfined by the conventions of the time. The eldest of five sisters, Mimi took her role as matriarch seriously. To her, appearances and good behaviour mattered very much. She was socially aspirational for herself and her nephew and like so many other people, whether they were parents or not, when it came down to it, 'What *would* the neighbours think?' was of great concern to Mimi Smith.

And it must never be forgotten that, although Mimi and George lived in a very pleasant home in the middle-class suburb of Woolton, they were not wealthy. From 1947 until the Christmas of 1962, John's aunt took in student lodgers from the University of Liverpool (and also from the nearby all-girl F.L. Calder Teacher Training College) to supplement her husband's meagre post-war income. After George's premature death in 1955, she had to increase the number of lodgers she cared for to compensate for the loss of his income. So she worked very hard, physically, to maintain the home and standard of living both she and John enjoyed.

No wonder then that Mimi's main and understandable preoccupations in the summer of 1957 were to get her nephew not to dress outrageously, to behave himself and to make good on his success in the eleven-plus. In other words, she wanted him to pass enough O levels to be able to enter the sixth form so that he could study for university and hopefully pursue a professional career. Such an ambition for her nephew was laudable, good parenting.

There is no doubt that John had the potential and opportunity to do well. A coveted (by parents) place at university was not beyond him. If only he had wanted it half as much as his Aunt Mimi wanted it for him then there would have been no problem whatsoever … but he didn't.

To Aunt Mimi's absolute dismay, almost from the moment he walked through the doors at Quarrybank, John had been a reluctant student. Negative school report followed negative report as John's slide from A to C stream never lost momentum. The advent of skiffle and rock 'n' roll and John's immersion in these national 'crazes' added to Mimi's woes and her constant struggle to keep him focused on school. Even so, as the evidence mounted on an almost daily basis to the contrary, Mimi kept alive the hope that, when it mattered, John would buckle down and pass just enough O levels in the summer of 1957 to see him over the line …

He didn't.

Never one to miss what was happening in her nephew's life – especially where school was concerned – Mimi had been quick to realise that Presley's arrival in John's life had become the major barrier to success in his O levels (along with *that* guitar his mother had helped him acquire). Failure in these exams would leave him to the mercies of an 'ordinary' job. Mimi knew only too well that John was possibly allergic to physical work and not at all practical, and so the idea that he could leave school to undertake menial work was, in her mind, an absolute non-starter. Her fear for what would become of him *long-term* should this nightmare scenario become a reality was a concern she shared with most parents for whom a good education and qualifications were the passports to solid futures, greater prospects and prosperity for their children.

John: "It was Elvis who really got me buying records. I thought that early stuff of his was great. The Bill Haley era passed me by, in a way. When his records came on the wireless, my mother used to hear them, but they didn't do anything for me. It was Elvis who got me hooked to beat music. When I heard 'Heartbreak Hotel' I thought, 'This is it', and I started to grow side-boards and all that gear … I was just drifting. I wouldn't study at school."[4]

As the exams approached, adding to Mimi's increasing dismay and growing despondency, she saw the distractions working upon John were multiplying.

Lonnie's hit record 'Rock Island Line' (number 8, January 1956) was a real game changer. Before Elvis broke onto the scene, this was the single that inspired and enabled British teenagers like John to make a noise all of their own.

'Rock Island Line' introduced 'skiffle music' into British teen consciousness and allowed them to form music groups of their own because 'skiffle' was performed without the all-important electric guitars that were integral to performing rock 'n' roll. As such, skiffle surmounted the barrier that prevented British youths from playing rock 'n' roll for themselves. Electric guitars, those essential and defining instruments of the genre, were very, very expensive. Mostly they came from the USA and as such were very, very expensive to import. (The British guitar manufacturer Grimshaw's debuted their first purpose-made, semi-acoustic electric instrument, the SS Deluxe in 1957.) In the Fifties to even think of importing an electric guitar from the USA and playing rock 'n' roll for themselves was an absolute non-starter for cash-strapped British wannabies. They could dream all they wanted but turning that dream into a practical reality was thwarted at the very first hurdle: the price tag.

And this is why Lonnie Donegan played *the* crucial role: at the very moment of absolute UK teenage desperation, along came skiffle … from that moment on there would be no turning back.

Essentially, 'skiffle' utilised acoustic and homemade instruments the like of which any kid in Britain could easily lay their hands. Like the poor black folk in the USA from whom skiffle had originated, the music's reliance on homemade instruments served poor British white kids in just the same way. It was cheap and open to all. No expense incurred, no expensive lessons, and in the space of an afternoon a group could be formed. In this way 'skiffle' was totally accessible and fun. It shared the same roots as rock 'n' roll and was as close as Brits could get to rock 'n' roll without plugging in. Very soon it became a national craze, a homemade substitute for rock: over the next two and a half years it is estimated tens of thousands of UK teenagers formed at least 10,000 skiffle groups.

For a while the craze for skiffle more than matched the relentless growth in the popularity of rock 'n' roll. Stars such as Little Richard, Gene Vincent (Vincent's 'Be Bop A Lula' was the first record Paul ever bought) and Eddie Cochran very quickly captured John's and Paul's interest and imagination but, crucially, so had Lonnie Donegan. (As noted, John had bought Donegan's seminal 'Rock Island Line'.) There was also a skiffle group called the Vipers who bothered the Top 20 a couple of times during 1957 when they scored two Top 10 hits with 'Don't You Rock Me Daddy-O' (number 10 on 14 February) and 'Cumberland Gap' (number 10 on 18 March). Their records were produced by a chap at Parlophone called George Martin …

John's passion and pre-occupation with the music of rock 'n' roll and skiffle filled a void in his life: once he heard Elvis sing, he had found something that he understood implicitly and which connected directly to his creative heart. Unlike school and academia, he had discovered something that spoke to him at source to give his life purpose. He desperately wanted to become a singer in his own right. In his mind a vision of the future was forming, one that inspired and excited him, but at the same time horrified Mimi.

Further exasperating her efforts to get John focused on his studies was the growing influence in his life of Julia. By 1955/56 John was a regular visitor to her home in Springwood which was just a mile or so from his home in Woolton. He loved spending time with her and his sisters. His bond with his mum was strengthened by her love of popular music. An excellent musician, she taught John how to play banjo versions of favourite songs from her youth: 'Little White Lies', 'Don't Blame Me', 'Ramona' and 'Girl of My Dreams'. She and her partner Bobby owned a record player and Julia bought Elvis records for herself. She also taught John 'Ain't That a Shame' (Fats Domino, a Top 30 UK hit for him in early 1957).

John's sister Julia captured exactly what was happening when she wrote: "As John entered his teens and spent more time with us, she started to teach him music and he loved it. Their inborn, shared artistic talent became their renewed umbilical cord and it was soul-strong."[5]

In his mum, John had found a kindred spirit, an adult who actively encouraged his musical endeavours and did not dismiss them as irrelevant. Despite the imminence of his O levels, Julia went further and helped him to acquire a cheap mail-order acoustic guitar expressly so that he could play in a skiffle group. Up to this point John had been borrowing a cheap acoustic guitar from Geoff Lee, a friend at Quarry Bank High School, who could not play it himself but was happy for John to use it. Thus it was that, by the end of March 1957, John Lennon was the proud owner of a Gallotone Champion acoustic guitar, a mail-order instrument of such inestimable quality its manufacturers assured prospective purchasers that it was 'guaranteed not to split'.

John: "I started with a banjo when I was 15, when my mother taught me some banjo chords. I played the guitar when I was young, like a banjo, with the sixth string hanging loose! I always thought Lonnie and Elvis were great, and all I ever wanted to do was to vamp. I got some banjo things off okay, then George and Paul came along and taught me other things. My first guitar cost me ten pounds – it was one advertised in a paper you send away for. Why did I get it? Oh, the usual kid's desire to get up on stage, I suppose. And also my mother said she could play any stringed instrument. She did teach me a bit ..."[6]

John's Gallotone guitar was delivered to Julia's home and when he finally dared to take it home to 'Mendips', Mimi was singularly unimpressed. Thereafter her growing anxiety for his future was frequently expressed when she would caution her errant nephew with the words: "The guitar's all very well, John, but you'll never make a living out of it!"[7]

Almost from the moment the Gallotone took up residency in John's small bedroom, Aunt Mimi must have not just *seen* the writing on the wall but on a daily basis *heard* it loud and clear. Alongside learning the rock and skiffle tunes of the day, John even attempted to write tunes of his own, one of which he referred to as 'Calypso Rock'. Unfortunately, he could not remember how such tunes went when he woke up the next day, but they signalled a desire not just to copy but to originate.

John now had the means to sing and make a noise all of his own. He could do what Elvis did. He might not be able to plug in – no kid in Britain could – but that was no barrier: Lonnie had delivered skiffle into the lives of British youth and so John knew just what to do next. As 1957 progressed, any token studying he had been doing went completely out of the window when John and like-minded friends at school formed 'The Quarry Men,' skiffle group.

As Elvis, Lonnie and the Quarry Men vied for John's attention, Mimi became desperate. In a last-gasp attempt to draw her nephew back from the brink of academic catastrophe, Mimi acceded to his request that when it was his turn within the Quarry Men to host a rehearsal he could bring them to 'Mendips'. In return to placate his aunt's growing anxieties, John apparently promised to do some work in order to pass enough exams to remain at school. Mimi must have known this was highly unlikely, but by now it was all she had and so she clung to this merest of possibilities.

Living just behind Mendips, on Vale Road, was a boy called Ivan Vaughan, whom John had known ever since he had come to live in Woolton. Some 20 months younger than John, Ivan had attended Dovedale Primary School with him and was a member of John's gang, 'The Outlaws'. Like John, Ivan was a bright boy who also passed his eleven-plus, but did not join his friend at Quarry Bank. Instead, from 1953 Ivan attended a prestigious Liverpool grammar school called the Liverpool Institute for Boys which stood in front of the Anglican Cathedral on St. James's Mount overlooking Liverpool city centre and the River Mersey. On the very first day at the Institute, even before the boys had gone into school to be put into their class groups, Ivan had befriended Paul McCartney. As they stood chatting together in the playground, they learned that they had been born on exactly the same day. This shared personal detail bonded the two boys who went on to forge a lifelong friendship. By attending the 'Inny', as the Institute was nicknamed, Ivan became the schoolboy who effectively knew both John Lennon and Paul McCartney and, as such, was destined to become the mutual friend who later introduced them to one other.

Addendum: *Julia and her role in John's life in 1957: you may say I'm a dreamer ...*

John's mother, Julia, played a crucial role in his musical development. A vivacious, talented person, she was someone who had a mind of her own and possessed a zany sense of fun.

On one level, assisting John to acquire a guitar of his own could be interpreted as an act of rebellion because it went against Mimi and Mimi's attempts to persuade him to focus on his forthcoming O level exams (and Julia would have known that). But it was not a conscious act of opposition on Julia's part. Mimi had all the reponsibilities of John as a teenager, something Julia didn't, instead she could indulge him. It was undeniably a tough time for his Aunt. What helping John acquire the Gallotone most surely underlines is Julia embracing her role as 'Mum' and the close bond that was rapidly developing between her and her son by the mid-Fifties. By then John was connecting with his mother in ways he never could or ever did with his aunt: this was a 'Mother and Child reunion' of special resonance. His sister Julia says it was a bond strengthened by the fact that they were both musicians. This particular aspect of their reunion was something Mimi just did not get. He could never have had this sort of relationship with Mimi.

John and Julia acted in common purpose and that purpose was to make music and have fun. As such, helping John acquire his guitar was not so much a conscious act of rebellion on Julia's part, but the natural action of a mother in support of her son. By sharing in this venture with him she was not only showing she loved him but that she believed in him and in what he was doing. John had never experienced such a relationship with anyone else before.

His mum had been mostly absent from his day-to-day life, but at this point she was back and recognising something within him of which Mimi was fearful and would rather have denied because it did not fit in with her aspirations for him. As such, music was a shared passion that allowed mother and son to navigate those missing years and grow close again very quickly. And what Julia recognised in John she liked and understood.

Up to this point Mimi had pulled the strings in John's life, but here in these all-important mid-teenage years, Mum was spontaneously asserting her position and bonding with her son as only a mother could. John would have recognised that he now had an ally – and a powerful one at that. And like all children he was not averse to playing one adult off against another if it suited his purpose!

Nevertheless, Mimi's role in John's life was critical and he recognised what she had done for him. She had helped care for him when he needed it most: from being just a small boy when he had been moved from one place to another during the years of the war when Julia's relationship with her husband Alfred was breaking down, mainly because he was rarely around. Mimi provided stability in John's life and she and her husband George cared for him deeply. Mimi's love was not demonstrative but practical and focused on always being there for him. She could be harsh but he knew he could rely on her. She always believed she had his best interests at heart and this was to give him the best start in life which was a good home, sound values in life and a good education.

In this respect Mimi believed she knew best. And, to be fair, many parents both then and now feel exactly the same. She knew John may not have appreciated her point ofview at the time, but believed he would thank her in the long run. She may have passed on to her nephew her love of Literature which undoubtedly influenced his love of words, wordplay and flair for creative writing but she saw rock 'n' roll as a flash in the pan, a five-minute craze from the USA, its proponents here today and gone tomorrow. From her perspective the whole shebang was something of no lasting value, certainly not a career path for her nephew to pursue. Her goal was for him to follow a career with a solid future, not to waste time on something that, in her opinion, was clearly not going to happen and was of no value in the first place.

Such was the strength of her convictions, Mimi believed she knew John better than he did himself. For her it was all-important for John to do the right thing. Anything that smacked of 'Bohemia' (or risk) was to be denied and so his love of music was not encouraged.

On the other hand, by doing what she did, Julia was **not** actively encouraging John to fail his exams per se or to go against Mimi, but she was most definitely saying, 'I believe in you and what you want to do and I support you in those ventures, they do have value'. She'd been missing for a long while and had not had day to day parental responsibilities (nor the costs) of John's upbringing that Mimi had had, but at this moment in time Julia became the most important person in his life, she could indulge him, and was telling him it was okay to pursue his dreams. She was giving credence and value to John's own ideas about himself and his future, whereas Mimi was more or less saying, 'Do as I tell you, or else you could seriously regret it when you are older'. In this way, Julia did help to liberate her son from conventionality ... not just in her words but in her actions ... she was saying your dreams and what you want for yourself in life are as important as what others want for you or tell you that you should be doing.

The different ways in which his aunt and his mother displayed their love for him must have been confusing for John to take on board ... and Julia's more carefree outlook most definitely appealed to John at a point in his life when most youngsters feel the pressure from adults to look to the future and form some sort of plan for what they are going to do.

Before this, John had not enjoyed such support from either of his parents because they had been absent from his day-to-day life. But now Mum was back and she was there for him. He had found someone who understood him and believed in him.

John would have recognised that in her way Mimi wanted the best for him. He would have understood that for many years she had worked extremely hard as landlady to the succession of students who had passed through the portals of 'Mendips' to ensure he had enjoyed a good standard of living and that all she was asking was for him to make the most of his opportunities. Despite all this and the strength of her arguments, he also knew that there was something inside that would make him resist the best of her interventions and intentions.

What Julia gave him was different, it spoke to him at the very core of his being. It must have made him very happy that at last he felt loved for himself and the person he was becoming. In Julia, briefly, John had the best mum he could have wished for.

For John Lennon, from now on there would never be a safety net and convention would no longer be his guide.

He would never forget what Mimi had done for him and he would never stop loving his mother.

---

1 & 3 'I Hate Rock 'N' Roll: Squares Knock The Rock Not Everyone Was A Fan'. Quotations from an article by Spencer Leigh for the magazine *Now Dig This*, No. 332, November 2010, p.8 and p.9.
2 & 7 *John Lennon*, Ray Coleman, (Futura Publications, 1984) p.49 and p.55.
4 & 6 *John Lennon in His Own Words*, compiled by Miles, (Omnibus Press, 1980) p.15 and p.17.
5 *Imagine This*, Julia Baird, (Hodder & Stoughton, 2007) p.88.

Chapter 3:
JAMES PAUL McCARTNEY: the early years 1942–56

James Paul McCartney was born on 18 June 1942. His mother and father, Jim and Mary McCartney, had married on 15 April 1941 when Jim was 39 and Mary 31. They had two sons: Paul, their eldest, and Michael born on 7 January 1944. Mary was a Roman Catholic and Jim was Church of England (although he later became agnostic). Keeping to a pre-marital agreement the boys were christened Roman Catholic but raised non-denominationally. They were not enrolled in Catholic schools because Jim believed the pupils there spent too much time on religion at the expense of their education.

Just like John's Aunt Mimi, Paul McCartney's parents put great stead in the importance of education.

Before the war, Jim worked for A. Hannay & Co, a cotton broker in Chapel Street, Liverpool. He was too old to be called up for the armed services during World War II (he was also disqualified on medical grounds due to a childhood injury to his left eardrum) and so, when the cotton exchange closed during the war, Jim became a lathe-turner at Napier's engineering works which made shell cases for bombs. At nights he also served as a volunteer fireman. When the war ended Jim returned to work for Hannay's as a salesman in the Cotton Exchange, but the war had adversely affected the cotton trade and he rarely brought home more than £6 a week. Throughout his life Jim cherished playing the piano and it was this that gave him succour in the dark times he encountered. Jim was self-taught and very good, what might be called a 'natural'.

In 1923, aged just 14, Mary began her training at Walton Hospital to become a state registered nurse and worked there as a midwife.

Shortly after her marriage to Jim, Mary left her post in Walton Hospital because at that time nurses could not continue to work in hospitals if they married. Instead she became a district health visitor caring for families who were either living in Blitz-damaged houses often bereft of water or electricity or with those in emergency (usually equally dire) accommodation.

In 1947, when Paul was 5 and Michael 3, Mary became a domiciliary midwife. Throughout the city, housing was desperately scarce and so a major 'perk' of her new post was that it entitled Mary and her family to accommodation. However, this also meant that the McCartneys were constantly on the move during Paul and Michael's early years, as Mary would be regularly re-located to live on the next of the new 'council estates' (social housing) nearing completion and which, after the devastation of the Second World War, were springing up on the edges of Liverpool. Such estates were built to help re-house the vast number of Liverpool's dispossessed citizens from the war. Over two-thirds of all the homes in the city had been damaged or destroyed during the 'Blitz'. As a consequence of her work, Mary was on call to help deliver the many babies being born in the city after the war. Once an estate began to fill with residents a 'baby boom' would quickly follow and Mary was in constant demand.

Paul: "The first house I remember was at 72 Western Avenue in Speke, which we moved to when I was four. The road was still being built and roadside grass was being sown and trees were being planted. The city always ran out where we lived, there was always a field next to us. The minute they built more houses on that field, we moved to another place where there was another field…"[1]

Mary's job meant that she earned more than her husband, but even so nurses were not well paid and money was always a concern for the family. In his official memoir written by

Barry Miles, Paul recollected that while his family was not poor, by the same token they were not rich, and so they did not own a car and it was not until the coronation of Queen Elizabeth II in 1953 that they owned a television set. Mary rode a bicycle to and from work. Paul became the first one in the family to own a car when he purchased a Ford Consul Classic (four door) with his 'Beatles earnings'.

Paul and Michael were bright, intelligent boys who, like John Lennon, passed their eleven-plus exams. In 1953, Paul was one of four from 90 pupils at the Joseph William School to obtain high enough marks to be offered a place at Liverpool's top grammar school, the Liverpool Institute. This prestigious institution regularly sent more of its students to Oxford and Cambridge universities than any other state school in Britain. Mary and Jim's happiness and pride in Paul's achievement was matched just two years later when Michael was equally successful and passed his eleven-plus to join his brother at the Institute.

(In 1954, George Harrison passed his eleven-plus with high enough marks to also attend 'the Inny'. He and Paul shared the same bus to school and on these daily journeys the two boys struck up a friendship based on a shared passion for electric guitars.)

In 1956, just as Michael turned 12, Mary and Jim moved from Speke on the very edge of the city to live in the pleasant south Liverpool suburb of Allerton. Their new home would be number 20 Forthlin Road, a mid-terrace house on the newly constructed Mather Avenue council estate. It lay just a mile or so down the hill from Woolton and John's home 'Mendips'.

Paul: "My mother was always on the lookout for a better place for us to live. It was a bit of an uproot but we soon settled there and it was a reasonable area. Her idea was to get us out of a bad area into a slightly posh area so that perhaps some of the posh might rub off on us. It was also a safer area; in fact, it was quite a middle-class area where we were, but they'd built a council estate in the middle of all the posh houses, much to the chagrin of the local residents, I'm sure, though we never heard anything about that."[2]

20 Forthlin Road, Allerton became the McCartney family home until the end of 1964 when Paul, who had moved away in late 1963, bought his father a new home on The Wirral on 'the other side of the water' (i.e., Mersey Estuary).

For Mary and Jim, 20 Forthlin Road was intended to be the family home for the foreseeable future, a place where they could put down some roots and end the moving around every couple of years that had become a major feature of family life. At this stage in their lives both parents believed their boys needed stability in order to fully focus on their studies at the Liverpool Institute where they were now both pupils.

Paul: "My parents aspired for us, very much indeed … My mum wanted me to be a doctor … And my dad, who left school at fourteen, would have loved me to be a great scientist, a great university graduate. I always feel grateful for that."[3]

Tragically, Mary never got to see her boys grow up, for shortly after moving into 20 Forthlin Road she was diagnosed with cancer. Despite the presence of a lump in her breast and being in great pain she carried on working without mentioning her symptoms to her colleagues. By the time she did, it was too late. Mary was diagnosed with cancer, but the illness was too advanced and, although a mastectomy was performed, after the operation she succumbed to an embolism on 31 October 1956.

Paul: "She was great. She was a really wonderful woman and really did pull the family along, which is probably why in the end she died of a stress-related illness. She was, as so many women are, the unsung leader of the family."[4]

Addendum: *20 Forthlin Road and Mendips*

20 Forthlin Road
Paul and Michael's former home was one of 330 houses built as part of the Mather

Avenue estate between 1949 and 1952. Designed by Sir Lancelot Keay (as 'Intermediate Type Standard Building 5') number 20 Forthlin Road is a two-storey, three-bedroomed, mid-terrace property. Built with traditional wooden sash-windows by Costains at a cost of £1,369, 9 shillings and 1 pence, the National Trust have owned the property since 1995 after being first informed by John Birt, the then Director-General of the BBC and Liverpudlian, that it was up for sale. Lord Birt, as he is now, believed the house ought to be preserved because it was "the birthplace of the Beatles". Fortunately, the National Trust agreed with him.

Prior to the war much of Liverpool's social housing had been criticised for being substandard ('jerry-built') and so it was stipulated that the Mather Avenue estate was to be built from the best materials, which included ebony door-knobs and solid brass fittings. The property was not fitted with central heating and so was heated by an 'Era' coal fire in the living room, while upstairs the bedrooms were installed with 'Falco' electric fires. Luxury for the times! Maybe the biggest 'luxury' of all was that the property enjoyed a bathroom and 'an inside toilet'. All the houses on the estate were owned by the local council and so their occupants paid rent to the council which also maintained the properties.

Mendips

John Lennon's former home, 'Mendips' (number 251 Menlove Avenue, Woolton, Liverpool) is a three-bedroomed, semi-detached house. Built in 1933, it is typical of the thousands and thousands of such homes that were built on the outskirts of Britain's towns and cities during that decade. Middle-class, as opposed to working-class (like 20 Forthlin), such properties created what we now call 'suburbia'. Such houses were bigger, but their design not much different to Paul's home. Privately owned, not rented, residents usually took out a mortgage to purchase such houses. The exteriors varied in style and 'Mendips' is distinguished by its art nouveau-style glass windows at the front of the house and inside by its art deco fireplaces. 'Mendips' even has a bell board in the morning room which could be used to call the maid. (John's Aunt Mimi, whose house it was, most definitely never employed a maid.)

'Mendips' cost its first owner £810 in 1933. Originally named 'Anton Roy', it was its second owner, one Ernest Bridon Harrop, a bank official, who re-named it 'Mendips', a name retained by Mimi and George Smith who moved into the property circa 1943. George died in 1955, leaving Mary or 'Mimi' to continue living in the property until 1965 when she moved to Sandbanks, Dorset, to live in a bungalow purchased for her by John. George and Mimi's nephew, John, lived with them from age 5 in the spring of 1946 until 1963 when he, his wife Cynthia, and their baby son Julian, moved to live in London.

Yoko Ono Lennon purchased 'Mendips' in 2002 and very generously immediately donated the house to the National Trust. (Most of the information about 'Mendips' and 20 Forthlin Road has been sourced from the National Trust's souvenir booklets for each property.)

The blue plaque on the front of 'Mendips' was placed there in 2000 by English Heritage some two years before Yoko bought the property to give to the Trust. It says John lived there from 1945. There's no doubt he spent some time living in the house during that year, most probably around the time Julia gave birth to Victoria but, after spending the early months of 1945 living in Maghull with his Uncle Sydney Lennon's family, he mostly lived with his mother Julia during 1945 at number 9 Newcastle Road and was still doing so in the early months of 1946 before moving briefly with Mum and Bobby into a flat in Gateacre Village and did not move into 'Mendips' permanently until the spring of 1946.

1, 2, 3, 4 *Paul McCartney: Many Years from Now*, Barry Miles, (Vintage, 1998) pp.5, 15, 12, 20.

Chapter 4:
PLAY BY HIS EARS

From the moment they were born, both John and Paul were exposed to music and songs from a variety of sources that included film and show tunes, musicals, popular songs from the radio, songs from the war, jazz tunes, television theme tunes, hymns (both boys sang in church choirs).

Whereas John did not receive encouragement from his Aunt Mimi to pursue his musical talent, Paul did. Paul and Michael's father was a terrific pianist who, as a young man, had played trumpet in his own band, the Jim Mac Band. Their grandfather, Joe, had played E-flat bass in his work's brass band (Cope's, tobacco manufacturers). Music – especially playing music for themselves – was integral to McCartney family life.

Like Mimi with John, Jim and Mary were very keen for their boys Paul and Michael to succeed academically. They were proud that their sons were Institute boys and encouraged them with their studies. They were also happy for them to enjoy outside interests such as music and learn an instrument for themselves. For Paul's 13th birthday when the family were still living in Speke, his parents bought him a nickel-plated trumpet and around the same time Michael received a set of drums which he says, "fell off the back of a lorry".[1]

Situated at the heart of the home in the family living room at 20 Forthlin Road was Jim's beloved and much played upright piano. At family gatherings, such as New Year, Jim would become ensconced at the keyboard while the family stood around and sang. Paul's father was self-trained or, as Auntie Mill used to say, "Oooh, listen to our Jim, he can play by his ears. He's a great pianist."[2]

From this shared family enjoyment of popular songs no doubt came Paul's ear for melody and love of harmony. Younger brother Michael recalled that, at family parties, "Gathered around the piano we'd all take different parts of the harmony. Dad was like a human juke box, put a pint on top of the piano and he'd play your request."[3]

Favourites oft performed by Jim included 'Lullaby of the Leaves', 'After You've Gone', 'Chicago' and 'Stairway to Paradise', and he also composed tunes of his own, such as 'Walking in the Park with Eloise'. One of Paul's early memories was of sitting under the piano, as his father played, from where he could feel the vibrations of Jim's feet on the pedals.

Paul: "He had a lot of music in him, my dad. He taught me and my brother harmony; not the concept, not written down, but he would say, 'This tune is the harmony to that tune,' so I learned very early to sing harmony which was one of my big roles in the Beatles. Whenever John sang I automatically sang in harmony with him, and that's due to my dad's teaching."[4]

Jim was a fan of Scott Joplin. In Paul's song, 'When I'm Sixty-Four', the tune (the words came much later) which was written in Forthlin as he sat at his dad's piano aged just 14, echoes of Joplin's most famous tune 'The Entertainer' can be heard. Despite requests from Paul to teach him to play piano, Jim declined. He wanted Paul to learn the instrument correctly.

Paul: "My dad was the original. To us kids he was a pretty good player, he could play a lot of tunes on the piano. I was very influenced by him. I used to ask him to teach me but he said, 'No, you must take lessons,' like all parents do … He thought he wasn't good enough to teach me … but it would have done me because he was pretty good."[5]

Two attempts were made to send Paul to piano lessons, but he did not stick with either. First, when the family were still living in Speke and Paul had just started at the Liverpool

Institute, Mary and Jim thought he should take lessons and arranged for him to study with an elderly lady who lived nearby. These did not last long for Paul quickly railed against being set five-finger exercises to practise at home, which he likened to being set 'homework'.

Aged 16, Paul made a second attempt to learn 'properly', but these lessons were also doomed because by then other considerations had come into play which made him a reluctant student. His new tutor was a young man (aged about 19) who lived nearby on Mather Avenue and attempted to teach Paul as if he was a beginner. The problem was that by then Paul was not a beginner and had actually started to attempt to write tunes at the piano (including what became 'When I'm Sixty-Four'). By teaching himself at home, Paul had found a way of playing which suited his creative drive and he was reluctant to abandon this for a return to basics. As a consequence, he quit the lessons.

After the death of Mary in 1956, Mike McCartney remembers that his father Jim bought him a banjo and Paul a Spanish guitar. Mike said his dad had enjoyed playing the piano as a child and it had helped him escape the strictures of his family's poverty, so, in the same way, Jim believed music might help his boys deal with the tragedy of their mother's death. It was good thinking.[6]

The suddenness of Mary's death was a devastating blow for her boys. In an instant the rock of their young lives had gone. Home life could never be the same. Paul reacted by retreating within himself, distancing himself from those around him. When he eventually acquired his Zenith guitar it became a refuge, his absolute focus. He played it constantly, everywhere he went – on the bus, in the bath, sitting on the toilet seat – everywhere!

Rock 'n' roll had exploded into British teen consciousness in 1954–55 with Bill Haley and His Comets, but when Elvis hit the UK charts in June 1956 with 'Heartbreak Hotel' everything changed. In later life, Paul referred to Presley as 'the Messiah'. Like John Lennon, Paul McCartney was irrevocably smitten. He simply wanted to be Elvis.

Interestingly, in conversation with Colin and Sylvia Hall, Mike McCartney said he believed that, had their mother Mary not died, she would have never allowed Paul to pursue music over his studies and would have insisted he put schoolwork and exams first. Most certainly she would not have allowed him to travel to Hamburg …

POSTSCRIPT: THE UK'S TOP 30 POPULAR HITS OF 1956
01 Doris Day: Whatever Will Be Will Be (Que Sera Sera)
02 Pat Boone: I'll Be Home
03 Frankie Laine: A Woman in Love
04 The Dream Weavers: It's Almost Tomorrow
05 Johnnie Ray: Just Walkin' in the Rain
06 Kay Starr: Rock and Roll Waltz
07 Winifred Atwell: The Poor People of Paris
08 Elvis Presley: Heartbreak Hotel
09 Teenagers featuring Frankie Lymon: Why Do Fools Fall in Love
10 Ronnie Hilton: No Other Love
11 The Hilltoppers: Only You
12 Anne Shelton: Lay Down Your Arms
13 Dean Martin: Memories Are Made of This
14 Elvis Presley: Hound Dog
15 Lou Busch: Zambezi
16 Bill Haley & His Comets: Rock Around the Clock
17 Tennessee Ernie Ford: Sixteen Tons
18 Lonnie Donegan: Lost John / Stewball
19 David Whitfield: My September Love
20 Bill Haley & His Comets: Rockin' through the Rye

21 Bill Haley & His Comets: The Saints Rock 'n' Roll
22 Tony Martin: Walk Hand in Hand
23 Mel Torme: Mountain Greenery
24 Teresa Brewer: A Tear Fell
25 Teresa Brewer: Sweet Old-Fashioned Girl
26 Bill Haley & His Comets: See You Later Alligator
27 Lonnie Donegan: Rock Island Line
28 Frankie Vaughan: The Green Door
29 Dave King with the Keynotes: Memories Are Made of This
30 Bill Hayes: The Ballad of Davy Crockett

1, 2 & 3 Mike McCartney as told to Sylvia Hall, National Trust custodian at 20 Forthlin Road, Allerton, Liverpool circa 2010.
4 & 5 *Paul McCartney: Many Years from Now*, Barry Miles (Vintage, 1998) p.23 & p.22.
6 Mike McCartney in conversation with Sylvia and Colin Hall, 2019.

Chapter 5:
1957 ... AND WE'D NEVER HAD IT SO GOOD

This was *the* year that John and Paul met but, as the Fifties went, it was in many ways a *very* significant year in its own right. Much that occurred during its 12 months shaped what would happen in the Sixties.

In the city of Liverpool, the ravages of World War II cast a long shadow, every street bore the scars of that terrible conflict. Bomb sites and bomb damage proliferated, rationing had only just ended ... the euphoria that greeted the end of the war in Europe had been replaced by a sense of growing disillusionment among many who had originally anticipated better times and greater prosperity for all.

Internationally the drive for peace had been subverted by something called the 'Cold War' as 'the West' (Democracy) set itself against the 'Eastern bloc' (Communism). Forever in the background, something dubbed the 'Third World' perpetually sang for its supper. For all, although most people had more pressing matters to attend to on a daily basis, the possibility of global nuclear fallout was an ever-present threat.

Amid all this, Britain was trying to keep up. It may have 'won' the war, but the country's role and influence as a world power was in decline. It was struggling economically and in the wake of the Suez Crisis of 1956 the USA formally assumed the UK's mantle of 'Leader of the Free World'. Ideologically, economically and militarily the USA believed its role was to save the universe from the abomination of Communism. To succeed in this goal, it believed that first and foremost it had to dominate (annihilate would have been a preferable option), defeat and prevent the USSR in *its* fiendish design to spread the red tide of socialism around the globe. 'Better dead than red' was the soundbite of the day.

Equally the USSR was determined to better the USA and emerge victorious from this ideological struggle. Wherever you looked in the world it was doing all it could to combat American intentions and win supporters to its cause. Locked in such bitter opposition, both sides began to stockpile nuclear weapons in the hope that they would have more than the other and that as a result the other side would *not* attack it, knowing that if they did so they were likely to be obliterated themselves. The daily march towards such mutually assured destruction was relentless as both sides determined not to fall behind the other in the 'arms race' to oblivion.

If they thought about it too much this horrific scenario *could* scare and shock the average citizen at home, but mostly it did not stop anyone in their tracks. Life went on as it always had done. Everyday life was usually enough of a struggle for most people, and resolving the nuclear impasse could always wait until another day. There was always a bill to be paid, a mouth to be fed, a new kid on the block to check out, a new record on the juke box ... there was simply no time for standing around, moaning and complaining: it was a case of grab what you could for now, enjoy it or let it go forever.

To ease readers into the life and times of teenagers Lennon, McCartney, Harrison and Starkey, it may be interesting (if not fascinating) to peruse a list of events and happenings that filled the newspapers and radio news broadcasts of the day and formed the backdrop to the world of teenage guitarists and singers John, Paul and George during the year that they all met and in which future bandmate Ringo Starr got his first set of drums ...

The bomb may have been about to drop, but as UK Prime Minister Harold Macmillan proudly reminded us all, economically (although many would heartily disagree), 'we'd never had it so good!'

Jan 1: An Irish Republican Army (IRA) unit attacks Brookeborough RUC barracks in one of the most famous incidents of the IRA's Operation Harvest.
Jan 3: 1st electric watch introduced, Lancaster, Pennsylvania, USA.
Jan 5: US President Eisenhower asks Congress to send troops to the Middle East.
Jan 6: Elvis Presley makes his 7th and final appearance on *The Ed Sullivan Show* (USA).
Jan 7: Algerian militant and National Liberation Front member Djamila Bouhired sets off a bomb in an Algiers cafe killing 11 civilians, precipitating the Battle of Algiers.
Jan 10: As a result of the Suez Crisis the UK Prime Minister Anthony Eden resigns. He is succeeded by Harold Macmillan.
Jan 12: Southern Christian Leadership Council founded with Martin Luther King Jr. as leader at Ebenezer Church in Atlanta.
Jan 13: *All That Fall*, first radio play by Samuel Beckett, airs on BBC Third Programme.
Jan 14: Humphrey Bogart dies aged 57.
Jan 16: The Cavern Club opens on Matthews Street in Liverpool, England.
Jan 19: USSR performs atmospheric nuclear test (one of many during the year).
Jan 25: FBI arrests Jack and Myra Soble, charged with spying for USSR.
Jan 29: Graham Greene's *Potting Shed* premieres in NYC.
Jan 31: Trans-Iranian oil pipe line finished.
Feb 1: 1st black pilot (PH Young) on a US scheduled passenger airline.
Feb 2: UN adopts a resolution calling for Israeli troops to leave Egypt.
Feb 4: 1st electric portable typewriter placed on sale (Syracuse, NY).
Feb 14: Georgia Senate unanimously approves Senator Leon Butts' bill barring blacks from playing baseball with whites.
Feb 16: The "Toddlers' Truce", a controversial television closedown between 6.00pm and 7.00pm is abolished in the United Kingdom.
Feb 25: Buddy Holly, as one of the Crickets, records 'That'll Be the Day', which will be released as a group single.
Feb 27: Mao's famous speech to the Supreme State Conference "On Correct Handling of Contradictions Among People" expounding Maoist ideals.
Mar 3: 2nd Eurovision Song Contest: Corry Brokken for Netherlands wins singing "Net als toen" in Frankfurt.
Mar 5: Eamon de Valera's Fianna Fail party wins election in Ireland.
Mar 6: Ghana (formerly Gold Coast) declares independence from the UK.
Mar 8: Egypt reopens the Suez Canal after Israel withdraws from occupied Egyptian territory.
Mar 10: Thousands of soccer fans riot in Italy.
Mar 10: Osama bin Laden born Riyadh, Saudi Arabia.
Mar 13: Bloody battles follow anti-Batista demonstration in Havana, Cuba.
Mar 15: Great Britain becomes the third nation to explode a nuclear bomb.
Mar 17: Dutch ban on Sunday driving lifted.
Mar 20: Britain accepts NATO offer to mediate in Cyprus, but Greece rejects it.
Mar 21: Tennessee Williams' *Orpheus Descending* premieres in NYC.
Mar 22: Elvis Presley releases 'All Shook Up'
Mar 23: US Army sells its last homing pigeons.
Mar 27: 29th Academy Awards: *Around the World in 80 Days* is Best Film, Ingrid Bergman (for her role as Anna Koreff/Anastasia in *Anastasia*) and Yul Brynner (for his role as King Mongkut in *The King and I*) are best actors.
Apr 3: Samuel Beckett's *Endgame* premieres in London.
Apr 10: John Osborne's *Entertainer* premieres in London.
Apr 11: Britain agrees to Singaporean self-rule.
May 4: Alan Freed hosts *Rock 'n' Roll Show*, the 1st prime-time network rock show.
May 4: Anne Frank Foundation forms in Amsterdam.

May 6: Pulitzer Prize awarded to John F. Kennedy for *Profiles in Courage*.
May 8: South Vietnamese President, Ngo Dinh Diem, arrives in the United States on a state visit.
May 15: 'Operation Grapple': Britain tests its first hydrogen bomb near Christmas Island in the Indian Ocean.
May 22: South Africa's government approves race separation in universities.
May 27: Toronto's CHUM-AM, (1050 kHz) becomes Canada's first radio station to broadcast only top 40 rock 'n' roll music format.
May 28: US performs nuclear test at Nevada Test Site.
May 30: The Second European Cup Final, Madrid: Alfredo Di Stéfano and Francisco Gento score as defending champions Real Madrid beat Fiorentina 2-0 in the Santiago Bernabéu Stadium, Madrid.
May 31: Great Britain performs nuclear test at Christmas Island (atmospheric).
Jun 4: First Test: Peter May and Colin Cowdrey make 411 stand v West Indies at Edgbaston, Birmingham. Sonny Ramadhin bowls 98 overs for the West Indies. The match was a draw.
Jun 5: NY narcotics investigator, Dr Herbert Berger, urges AMA to investigate use of stimulating drugs by athletes.
Jun 24: The U.S. Supreme Court rules that obscenity is *not* protected by the First Amendment in Roth v. United States.
Jun 27: The British Medical Research Council publishes a report suggesting a direct link between smoking and lung cancer.
Jul 2: 1st submarine designed to fire guided missiles launched, Grayback.
Jul 5: Wimbledon's Men's Final: Australian Lew Hoad retains his title by beating fellow countryman Ashley Cooper 6-2, 6-1, 6-2.
Jul 6: Wimbledon Women's Tennis (considered at the time as the World Championship of tennis): Althea Gibson became the first black female athlete (in its 80-year history) to win Wimbledon, beating Darlene Hard 6-3, 6-2 (Althea won it again in 1958). Gibson was the first champion of Wimbledon to receive the trophy personally from Queen Elizabeth II, of which she commented, "Shaking hands with the queen of England was a long way from being forced to sit in the colored section of the bus."
Jul 6: John Lennon (16) and Paul McCartney (15) met for the first time at St. Peter's Annual Church Fete in Woolton, Liverpool, where Lennon was performing with his skiffle group, the Quarry Men (John, Rod Davis, Len Garry, Eric Griffiths, Colin Hanton, Pete Shotton).
Jul 8: Irish Premier Eamon de Valera arrests Sinn Fein leaders.
Jul 12: US Surgeon General Leroy Burney connects smoking with lung cancer.
Jul 16: US Marine Major John Glenn orbits the Earth.
Jul 19: 1st rocket with nuclear warhead fired, Yucca Flat, Nevada.
Jul 20: **British Prime Minister, Harold Macmillan, tells a Tory rally in Bedford, "Let us be frank about it, *most of our people have never had it so good*. Go around the country, go to the industrial towns, go to the farms and you will see a state of prosperity such as we have never had in my lifetime – nor indeed in the history of this country."** *He had obviously never visited the backstreets of Liverpool ...*
Jul 21: Althea Gibson wins the US Nationals (the precursor of the US Open). She is the first black player to win a major US tennis tournament. She repeated her triumph in 1958.
Jul 21: PGA Championship Men's Golf, Miami Valley GC: Lionel Hebert wins 2 & 1 from Dow Finsterwald; last time event played under match-play format.
Jul 26: Baseball legend Mickey Mantle hits career Home Run number 200.
Jul 28: Jerry Lee Lewis makes his 1st TV appearances on *The Steve Allen Show*.

Jul 29: Floyd Patterson wins the World Heavyweight Boxing title.
Aug 1: US and Canada create North American Air Defense Command (NORAD).
Aug 3: British offensive against imam Galeb Ben Ali of Oman.
Aug 4: Argentine Maserati driver Juan Manuel Fangio clinches his record 5th F1 World Drivers Championship (his 4th consecutive) by winning the German Grand Prix at the Nürburgring.
Aug 5: *American Bandstand* premieres on network TV (ABC).
Aug 5: Comic strip *Andy Capp* makes its debut in the UK.
Aug 7: Congress passes the Civil Rights Act of 1957.
Aug 7: Oliver Hardy dies aged 65.
Aug 31: Federation of Malaya gains independence from Great Britain.
Sep 4: Governor of Arkansas, Orval Faubus, calls out the National Guard to prevent 9 black students from entering Little Rock's Central High School. Faubus was in contravention of a U.S. Supreme Court ruling in 'Brown vs. Board of Education of Topeka' of 17 May 1954 that unanimously (9-0) decided that individual U.S. state laws that permitted/allowed racial segregation in public schools were unconstitutional even if the segregated schools were otherwise equal in quality. The ruling of 1954 did not establish any sort of timescale or way of ending segregation and a second ruling in 1955 had only ordered states to end segregation with 'all deliberate speed'. Little Rock was the first attempt to implement the Supreme Court's ruling. It put the racism of America's Deep South on view for the whole world to see.
Sep 3: Allen Ginsberg's *Howl and Other Poems* is ruled not obscene.
Sep 5: *On the Road* by Jack Kerouac is published by Viking Press in New York.
Sep 8: US National Championship Men's Tennis, Forest Hills, New York: in an all-Australian final Mal Anderson beats Ashley Cooper 10-8, 7-5, 6-4 to win his only Grand Slam event.
Sep 8: US National Championship Women's Tennis, Forest Hills, NY: Althea Gibson beats Louise Brough Clapp 6-3, 6-2 for the first of her 2 home singles crowns.
Sep 9: US President Eisenhower signs 1st Civil Rights bill since Reconstruction.
Sep 9: 'Diana' by Paul Anka reaches number 1 in the USA.
Sep 15: Konrad Adenauer's CDU wins parliamentary election in West Germany.
Sep 19: 1st underground nuclear explosion at Las Vegas, Nevada.
Sep 23: 'That'll Be the Day' by the Crickets (of whom Buddy Holly was a member) reaches number 1 on the *Billboard* Hot 100.
Sep 23: White mob forces 9 black students enrolled at Little Rock's Central High School in Arkansas to withdraw.
Sep 25: 300 US Army troops guard 9 black children's return to Central High School in Arkansas.
Sep 25: Great Britain performs nuclear test at Maralinga, Australia.
Sep 23: President Dwight D. Eisenhower orders US troops to support integration of 9 black students at Little Rock Central High School in Arkansas.
Sep 24: Elvis Presley releases 'Jailhouse Rock' (*Billboard* Song of the Year 1957).
Sep 25: 18th Venice Film Festival: Influential Indian film *Aparajito* directed by Satyajit Ray is first film to win the Golden Lion and the Critics Award.
Sep 28: 'Honeycomb' by Jimmie F. Rodgers hits *Billboard* number 1.
Sep 29: An explosion at the Mayak plutonium production plant in the Soviet Union spreads radiation over 20,000 square miles (52,000 km^2).
Sep 29: The Crickets release their second single 'Oh Boy!' / 'Not Fade Away'.
Oct 1: B-52 bombers begin full-time flying alert in case of USSR attack.
Oct 1: First appearance of "In God We Trust" on U.S. paper currency.
Oct 2: David Lean's *The Bridge on the River Kwai* is released (Academy Awards Best Picture, 1958).

Oct 3: German statesman Willy Brandt is elected mayor of West Berlin (1957–1966).
Oct 4: Soviet Union launches Sputnik 1, the 1st artificial Earth satellite into elliptical low Earth orbit.
Oct 10: A fire at the Windscale nuclear plant in Cumbria, England becomes the world's first major nuclear accident.
Oct 12: First commercial flight between California and Antarctica.
Oct 12: Canadian Prime Minister Lester Bowles Pearson wins Nobel Peace Prize for his work in helping to resolve the Suez Crisis.
Oct 14: The Everly Brothers reach number 1 on the *Billboard* Hot 100 with 'Wake Up Little Susie'.
Oct 17: French author Albert Camus awarded the Nobel Prize for Literature.
Oct 21: *Jailhouse Rock*, the movie, starring Elvis Presley opens in Memphis, Tennessee.
Oct 23: Christian Dior dies aged 52.
Oct 29: Hand grenade explodes in Israel's Knesset (Parliament).
Oct 30: Dmitri Shostakovich's 11th Symphony premieres in Moscow.
Nov 3: USSR launches Sputnik 2 with space dog Laika aboard, the first animal in space. She was left to die in space.
Nov 7: Cold War: the Gaither Report calls for more American missiles and fallout shelters.
Nov 8: Great Britain performs atmospheric nuclear test at Christmas Island.
Nov 16: BBC's first pop music show, *Six-Five Special*, is broadcast from the tiny 2i's Coffee Bar in Soho, London, the birthplace of UK rock 'n' roll. On Saturday evenings it fills the space previously occupied by the 'Toddler's Truce'.
Nov 22: Simon and Garfunkel appear on *American Bandstand* as 'Tom and Jerry'.
Nov 22: Miles Davis Quintet debuts a jazz concert at Carnegie Hall in New York.
Nov 27: US Army withdraws from Little Rock, Arkansas, after Central High School integration.
Dec 1: Sam Cooke, Buddy Holly and the Crickets debut on *The Ed Sullivan Show*.
Dec 2: Sam Cooke's single 'You Send Me' reaches *Billboard* number 1.
Dec 7: Wilson Hall, Garston, Liverpool: at the behest of Paul McCartney 14-year-old George Harrison attends a Quarry Men show and on the bus home afterwards is introduced to John Lennon for whom he performs the instrumental, 'Raunchy'.
Dec 12: Willem J. Kolff and his team at Ohio's Cleveland Clinic remove the heart from a dog and replace it with a pneumatic pump which keeps the dog alive for 90 minutes, proving the viability of the artificial heart.
Dec 13: Rock 'n' roll pianist Jerry Lee Lewis marries 13-year-old Myra Gale Brown, the daughter of his cousin, a union that was to cause a storm of outrage. He did so despite the fact he was still married to his 1st wife Jane Mitcham.
Dec 17: US successfully test-fires Atlas intercontinental ballistic missile.
Dec 17: Ballon d'Or: Real Madrid forward Alfredo Di Stéfano wins award for best football player in Europe ahead of Englishmen Billy Wright and Duncan Edwards.
Dec 19: *Music Man* featuring the song "Til There Was You' opens at Majestic Theatre, NYC. It ran for 1375 performances.
Dec 20: Elvis Presley receives his draft notice to join the US Army for National Service.
Dec 25: 17-year-old Richard Starkey of the Dingle, Liverpool, receives his first drum kit (snare, bass and homemade cymbal) from his mother Elsie's partner Harold Graves.
Significant publication of 1957: Bert Weedon's *Play in a Day* guitar guide (Chappell & Co Ltd) Price 5/-

THE UK'S TOP 30 MOST POPULAR HIT SONGS IN 1957

01 Paul Anka: Diana
02 Elvis Presley: All Shook Up
03 Tab Hunter: Young Love
04 Pat Boone: Love Letters in the Sand
05 Guy Mitchell: Singing the Blues
06 Lonnie Donegan: Gamblin' Man / Putting on the Style
07 Harry Belafonte: Island in the Sun
08 Johnnie Ray: Yes Tonight Josephine
09 Pat Boone: Don't Forbid Me
10 Frankie Vaughan: The Garden of Eden
11 Harry Belafonte: Mary's Boy Child
12 Nat 'King' Cole: When I Fall in Love
13 Lonnie Donegan: Cumberland Gap
14 Harry Belafonte: The Banana Boat Song
15 Andy Williams: Butterfly
16 The Crickets: That'll Be the Day
17 Bing Crosby & Grace Kelly: True Love
18 Johnny Duncan & The Bluegrass Boys: Last Train to San Fernando
19 Elvis Presley: Party
20 Russ Hamilton: We Will Make Love
21 Debbie Reynolds: Tammy
22 Elvis Presley: (Let Me Be Your) Teddy Bear
23 The Diamonds: Little Darlin'
24 Guy Mitchell: Rock-a-Billy
25 Lonnie Donegan: Don't You Rock Me Daddy-O
26 Ronnie Hilton: Around the World
27 Pat Boone: Friendly Persuasion
28 Little Richard: Long Tall Sally
29 Petula Clark: With All My Heart
30 Guy Mitchell: Knee Deep in the Blues

30 FILMS POPULAR IN THE UK IN 1957
(not in any order of popularity/box office success)

12 Angry Men
The Bridge on the River Kwai
3:10 to Yuma
The Seventh Seal
Old Yeller
Jailhouse Rock
Gunfight at the OK Corral
Wild Strawberries
The Spirit of St Louis
Witness for the Prosecution
Lucky Jim
The Admirable Crichton
Doctor at Large
Carry On Admiral
Blue Murder at St Trinian's
The Curse of Frankenstein
The Barretts of Wimpole Street
The Prince and the Showgirl
Ill Met by Moonlight
Tarzan and the Lost Safari
The Enemy Below
Sweet Smell of Success
Woman in a Dressing Gown
Saint Joan
A King in New York
Campbell's Kingdom
Fire Down Below
Hell Drivers
Interpol
Silk Stockings

Various news sources

Chapter 6:
I SAW HIM STANDING THERE

John's neighbour Ivan Vaughan was the mutual friend who brought John and Paul together. One of Paul's best friends at the Liverpool Institute, Ivan was John's neighbour in Woolton, and so he knew both boys and that they played guitars and sang. Consequently, Ivan thought it would be a good idea to introduce them. The occasion he deemed appropriate for this was the annual St. Peter's Church Garden Fete held in Woolton on Saturday afternoon 6 July 1957 at which Ivan knew John was scheduled to perform with his skiffle group, the Quarry Men.

Lest it be forgotten these were teenage boys: in July 1957 John was 16 going on 17 while both Ivan and Paul had just turned 15. They were young boys at the very start of life's great adventure and so, while it doesn't always get a mention, it wasn't all about music, there was an ulterior motive behind Ivan and Paul's decision to visit the fete that day: Ivan had apparently told his friend that it was 'a good place to meet girls'. That in itself would have been sufficient reason for Ivan and Paul to visit the fete, never mind the presence of a skiffle group. To this end Paul turned up to the event with his hair Brylcreemed back into a 'Tony Curtis' or DA (duck's arse), very tight black 'drainies' (narrow/drainpipe trousers) and a light coloured sports jacket replete with metallic threads which sparkled in the sunshine.[1] This was all very much in the style of 'A White Sport Coat and a Pink Carnation' which had a been UK pop hit earlier that summer for both the King Brothers and Terry Dene.

The Quarry Men on the back of a lorry as part of the pre-St.Peter's Church Fete celebrations on Saturday, 6 July 1957. (James L. Davis)

Ivan and Paul arrived at the fete some time after it had started. Sometime prior to the Quarry Men's appearance at the fete, Colin Hanton, the Quarry Men's drummer, recalls that while the other members of the group were still out and about enjoying the attractions of the event, he had retired to the scout hut on the field where they had all secured their equipment. Colin was passing time jamming with a scout who played bugle when John arrived back at the hut with Ivan and a boy whom Colin had never seen before. Although not introduced at that moment, Colin would soon get to know Ivan's mystery friend as a lad called Paul McCartney. They did not linger long, for the Quarry Men were due on 'stage' (actually this was a low, concrete plinth situated on the church field and *not* the back of a lorry as popular legend has it: earlier, as part of a procession around Woolton prior to the opening of the fete, the group *had* sat on the back of a lorry).

It was around tea-time as the fete was drawing to a close and folk were beginning to exit the event when the Quarry Men were performing. Paul stood alongside Ivan to listen to them. The song Paul distinctly remembers hearing John sing that day was 'Come Go with Me' by the Dell-Vikings. He knew the song well and soon realised that John was not singing the correct words.

Paul: "He was making them up. He was singing 'Come, come, come go with me down to the penitentiary'. I thought they are kind of bluesy but they're not the words. But that is enterprising. That was my first introduction to seeing them, liking them as a band and liking John's ingenuity, liking his voice and his stage presence."[2]

'Come Go with Me' had been written by Clarence Quick. The line sung by the Dell-Vikings' Norman Wright that John had misheard was, 'Come go with me, Way beyond the sea.'

After witnessing the Quarry Men's performance on the church field, Ivan and Paul strolled over to the church hall where the Quarry Men had re-located to take a break before playing again at the evening's Grand Dance.

Once inside the hall in the small 'green room' at the back of the main room, Ivan briefly introduced Paul to a wary John and a couple of the Quarry Men, Len Garry (tea chest bass) and Pete Shotton (washboard). (Apparently Colin Hanton the drummer and guitarist Eric Griffiths had both 'nipped home' for their teas while banjo player Rod Davis thinks he had either also gone home for his tea or had simply slipped out to the toilet.) John, Pete, Len and Ivan were impressed when, after having invited Paul to "show them what he could do", the new boy picked up a guitar and effortlessly reeled off Eddie Cochran's 'Twenty Flight Rock'. This was a song Pete says the Quarry Men "thought too difficult for our band to even attempt."[3]

Paul: "One of the guys had a guitar – it could've been John's – which I borrowed ... All my mates (like Ian James and George Harrison) were right-handed so I'd learned to play – just about – upside down. And the song I could do was 'Twenty Flight Rock' by Eddie Cochran. I remember John being very impressed – I think mainly because I knew the words – that was like the currency in those days. It wasn't so much how you sang but it was, 'He knows all the words!' So that was impressive..."[4]

Knowing all the words was a key point that would have mightily impressed a not easily impressed John Lennon, especially when, as Shotton notes, "Paul further ingratiated himself by writing out from memory the complete lyrics to some of John's favourite rock 'n' roll numbers".[5]

For several reasons Paul's knowledge of the lyrics would have been very impressive for budding skifflers and rock 'n' rollers because this was not always easy to do. For a start, records were only awarded limited air-time on BBC radio. Back then there was no wall-to-wall music radio. Rock 'n' roll was not considered to be 'real music' by the snooty powers who controlled the Beeb and so it received very little airplay. Another problem was that the records themselves were expensive to buy and most teenagers received only limited funds. They had to save to buy them, so building a record collection of your own was a very slow (and expensive) process. The discs themselves were also quite fragile and broke easily and, as such, were a risky investment.

A popular but frustrating way to hear rock 'n' roll records was to tune into Radio Luxembourg that was beamed all the way from Europe. Luxembourg played skiffle and rock 'n' roll in the evenings, but the station signal was weak and tended to fade in and out amid a sonic swirl of burps and blips. It was like tuning in to outer space. Learning words to songs that way bordered on the impossible.

An alternative way to hear new tunes was to go into a record shop and stand inside a 'listening booth' while the shop assistant played the record you had requested because you had told them you were 'considering' buying it. This was a favoured ploy used by cash-strapped teenagers to hear a disc they liked but were not actually going to purchase. Even then it was almost impossible to catch all of the words or discern exactly what some of those words were (especially if sung by American artists) before the shop assistant twigged what you were up to and removed the record from the deck.

Consequently, lacking unlimited access to records, youngsters did not have the opportunity to play them over and over until they had learned all the words. A popular way to hear more records than you personally owned was for teens to get together in the evening at each other's homes where, armed with their own singles, they could enjoy some shared listening (although there were often other distractions on offer at such gatherings).

Paul would save his hard-earned pocket money (he also had a paper round) until he had enough to purchase his favourite singles. The very first of these was 'Be-Bop-a-Lula' that was released in 1956 and which, coincidentally, John said he performed in public for the first time that afternoon at the fete.

After getting the Quarry Men's attention with his guitar playing and knowing all the words, Paul grew in confidence sufficiently to feel encouraged to show a bit more of 'what he could do'. Spotting a piano in the hall, he sat down and accompanied himself as he ripped it up with his versions of Little Richard's 'Long Tall Sally' and Jerry Lee Lewis's 'A Whole Lot of Shaking Going On'. Paul's vocals were bang on the money and must surely have convinced John he'd happened upon a rare talent.

John: "I had a group, I was the singer and the leader; I met Paul and made a decision whether to – and he made a decision too – have him in the group: was it better to have a guy who was better than the people I had in, or not? To make the group stronger or to let me be stronger? That decision was to let Paul in and make the group stronger."[6]

John was right. Once he joined the group Paul quickly weaned John off the banjo chords his mother had taught him to get him started on the guitar. Thus Paul's entry into the group had an immediate and positive impact. He made them stronger musically by making them more competent on their instruments. His arrival in the group was also the moment the Quarry Men became something much more serious than just a bunch of school friends getting together to make some noise, have fun and attract girls.

The Quarry Men took turns to host rehearsals. When Paul joined the group these were usually held on a Saturday afternoon although later they switched to a Sunday. Paul's home, 20 Forthlin Road, Allerton, where Paul's father Jim was a welcoming host, soon became a regular place for the boys to rehearse. A pianist and former trumpet player ('Until his teeth gave out,' Paul would say) Jim McCartney would encourage the boys with their music, listen to them and make sure they all got a cup of tea when they took a break.

1, 2 & 4 Sir Paul McCartney in conversation with Bob Harris OBE and Colin Hall for the 2007 BBC Radio 2 documentary *The Day John Met Paul* written and narrated by Bob Harris, produced by Bob Harris and Trudie Myerscough-Harris for WBBC.
3 & 5 *John Lennon in My Life* by Pete Shotton & Nicholas Schaffner, Shotton and Schaffner, (Stein and Day, 1983) both quotes p.55.
6 *John Lennon in His Own Words* compiled by Miles (Omnibus Press, 1980) p.18.

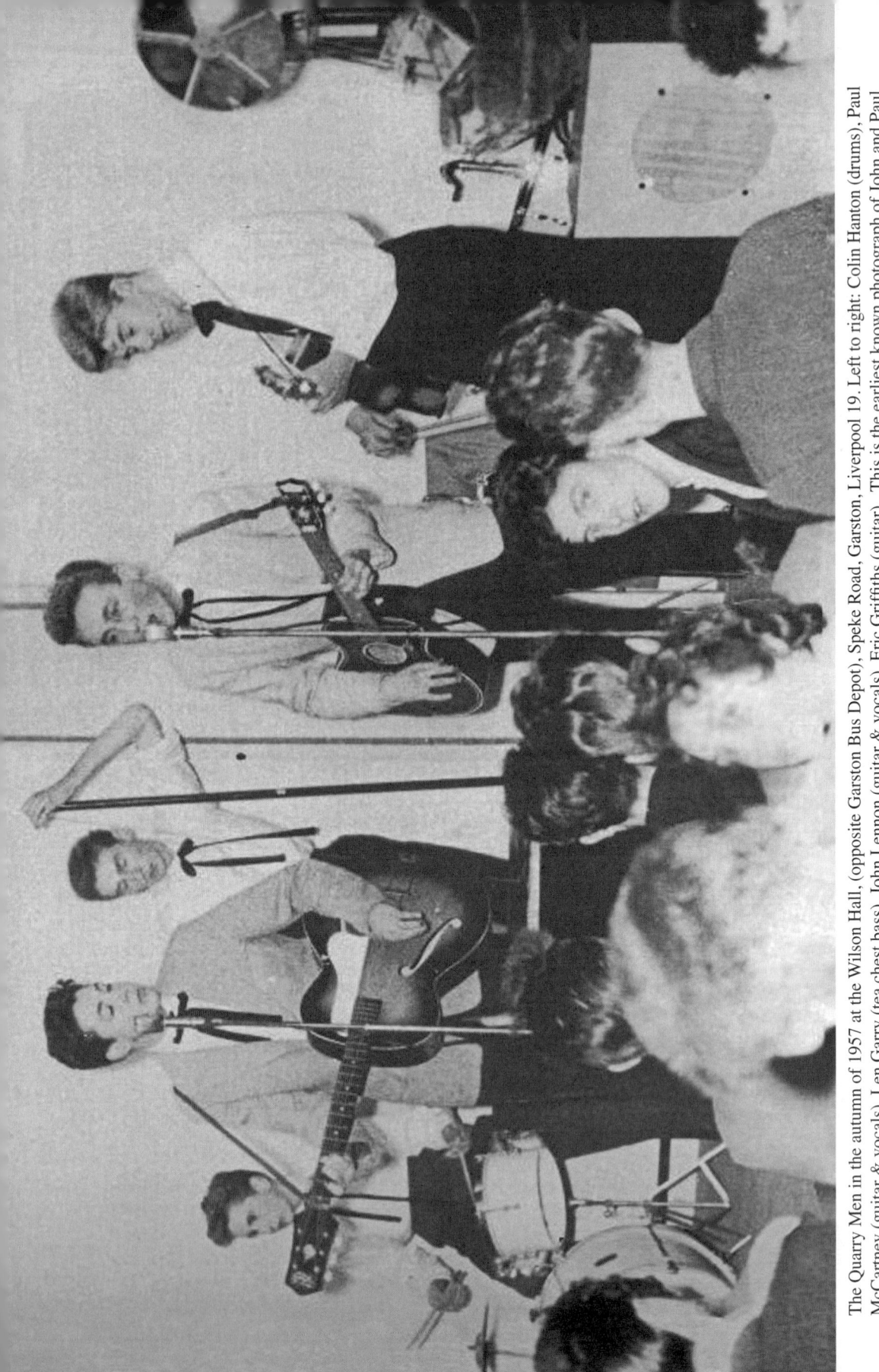

The Quarry Men in the autumn of 1957 at the Wilson Hall, (opposite Garston Bus Depot), Speke Road, Garston, Liverpool 19. Left to right: Colin Hanton (drums), Paul McCartney (guitar & vocals), Len Garry (tea chest bass), John Lennon (guitar & vocals), Eric Griffiths (guitar). This is the earliest known photograph of John and Paul performing together. (Leslie Kearney/The Quarry Men)

Chapter 7:
THE TWO OF THEM

Despite having widely different personalities, Paul and John very quickly recognised in each other a shared devotion to music and song that went far beyond the interest of the other lads in the Quarry Men. Soon they started to meet outside group rehearsals to further explore their shared passion. They visited each other's homes to talk, listen to and share records, play guitars, learn songs, eat and smoke (only if Mimi or Jim were out).

In John's house they would sometimes work on songs in his small 'box' bedroom above the front door where they would be constantly lifting the arm on his record player from the single they were playing as they tried to transcribe the lyrics and work out the chords for songs they wished to perform with the Quarry Men.

As Paul recalled in conversation with the author and Bob Harris for the BBC Radio 2 documentary feature, *The Songs the Beatles Gave Away*: "We used to go up in John's bedroom and I remember learning a Chuck Berry song and we thought we'd found like a mistake on it, some little thing, I can't think now what it was … But anyway we were taking the words down, that's basically what we'd do, go up to the bedroom to take down the words … 'Sweet little sixteen', stop! Stop the record player, write that down. 'She's got the grown up blues', stop! Write that down, stopping every little line to get it all. Once you had it, what a feeling: you know, now we've got the words to 'Sweet Little Sixteen'! It was great, it was fantastic."[1]

Another place in 'Mendips' where John and Paul loved to rehearse was the glazed front porch: "In the front vestibule, which was our echo chamber, that was where me and John used to go and I remember particularly singing 'Blue Moon' an Elvis song. On the record it had a lovely tape echo and so we always used to try and find rooms, it often used to be lavatories which had a very good acoustic, but this little front vestibule was fantastic. I remember us often learning our songs there with Aunt Mimi saying, 'John what are you doing in there with your little friend.' 'We're playing Aunty!' It was just a special place in the house to take two guitars."[2]

At Paul's house they would sit together, ensconced in the cosy front living room where Jim's piano was situated.

Together they would scrutinise each record label for the names written in brackets underneath the song's title because these were the name or names of a song's composer. In this way they quickly discovered that many of their favourite American records were not always written by the performers themselves but by teams of writers like Jerry Leiber and Mike Stoller, Felice and Boudleaux Bryant, Barry Mann and Cynthia Weil, Gerry Goffin and Carole King. These writers were literally 'hit machines', scoring hit after hit by supplying songs for artists such as Elvis Presley, the Everly Brothers and the Drifters. When Buddy Holly (as one of the Crickets) entered the UK charts for the first time in October 1957 with 'That'll Be the Day', John and Paul's respect for him soared when they realised not only did he and the Crickets perform on their records, but Buddy also wrote or co-wrote the tunes they sang. And it was the same with Eddie Cochran, another early hero, as well as the one and only Chuck Berry.

Even before they met, inspired by the songs and writers they revered, both John and Paul had composed tunes of their own.

In the living room at 20 Forthlin Road, not long after moving in, in 1956, Paul had composed two tunes on his father Jim's piano. Both were in the style of the dance band/music hall songs he'd so often heard his dad perform. One was a fragment originally titled

'I Call it Suicide' for which he struggled to find a suitable rhyme for 'suicide'. The second was a very catchy tune which he later completed as 'When I'm Sixty-Four'. For anyone – never mind a boy aged only just 14 – these are remarkably sophisticated pieces.

Paul never forgot either tune. In 1967 he revisited 'When I'm Sixty-Four' and, replete with a full set of lyrics, it appeared on *Sgt. Pepper*, while in 1970, on his eponymous first solo album *McCartney*, a fragment of 'I Call it Suicide' can be heard at the end of track 5, an instrumental medley entitled 'Hot as Sun/Glasses'.

(On the expanded special edition of *McCartney*, released as part of the 'Paul McCartney Archive Collection' in 2011, the song is simply called 'Suicide' and a fuller version of the tune opens the CD2 Bonus Audio disc, although even on this the original rhyming problem has not been resolved. Paul's enduring faith in this tune extended to him offering it to Frank Sinatra when many, many years later the latter inquired if Paul had a song especially for him.)

Up the hill in his bedroom at 'Mendips', armed with his brand new acoustic guitar, sometime in the spring of 1957, John wrote a calypso. At the time the media and record companies were touting 'calypso' as the 'next big thing' after rock 'n' roll. (In 1957 the record label RCA awarded Harry Belafonte the first ever Gold Record for 1 million sales of his long player, 'Calypso', which had been released in 1956. RCA proudly declared that this was the first album ever to sell in such quantities.)

John: "The first song I ever attempted was called 'Calypso Rock', because the big question at the time was whether calypso would take over from rock 'n' roll."[3]

Unlike Paul, John never re-visited this tune because by his own admission, he could never remember it: "The trouble was, I could never remember the song the next morning. What I had to learn was to play the same phrase over and over again until it stuck and then go onto the next bit."[4]

As their fascination and appreciation for songs, songwriters and composition intensified, it was not long before the two budding songsmiths began rendezvousing not to simply learn existing recordings to play with the Quarry Men, but to share tunes they themselves had composed. In each other they had discovered a kindred spirit.

As 1957 drew to a close, Paul played John the first song he had written on guitar, 'I Lost My Little Girl' and John reciprocated by performing 'Hello Little Girl' for Paul (or maybe it was the other way around). In doing so they had connected on a creative and artistic level that most teenage skifflers and rock 'n' rollers of that time would never have contemplated. While their contemporaries were happy to learn and play 'covers', the concept of writing songs of their own was one with which few others engaged in Liverpool. In this respect John Lennon and Paul McCartney were almost unique among their peers.

Paul: "We just talked to each other and we'd written a couple of little songs. I had one – the first one I'd ever written on guitar – called 'I Lost My Little Girl' and he had one. I can't actually remember it now, I can barely remember my own ones, but we then started sitting around and making a couple of the very early ones up that never saw the light of day. One was called 'Just Fun', another called 'Too Bad about Sorrows', I can vaguely remember them but they're not very good. And that was the start of it because once we were into the game of 'let's try and write a song' that was it and we just carried on in that vein. Then we moved on to things like 'One after 909' which is a very early one which is quite nice – that's probably one of the first ones that started to be vaguely good."[5]

John's song that slipped Paul's memory was, of course, 'Hello Little Girl'. (The presence of the words 'Little Girl' in both titles is also an interesting coincidence.) That both the boys' first solo tunes, in their original incarnations, owe a clear stylistic debt to Holly helps to pinpoint when they were both written, for Holly first appeared in the UK charts, as an uncredited member of the Crickets, in September 1957 with 'That'll Be the Day'. By the last week in October '57 this amazing song was number 1, where it stayed for a further two weeks. Both as a solo artist and then again as an uncredited member of the Crickets,

Holly released two more singles in December 1957: 'Peggy Sue' (under his own name) followed very shortly by 'Oh Boy' (again as one of the Crickets). Both songs went Top 10 in the UK in January 1958, reaching number 6 and number 3 respectively.

On 12 July 1958, the Quarry Men recorded their own version of 'That'll Be The Day' with Paul's 'In Spite of all the Danger' on the 'flip side' for which Paul credited George Harrison as the co-author.

Colin Hanton drummed with the Quarry Men from late 1956 to early 1959 and performed on the recording of 'In Spite of all the Danger'. Around the same time as that song he remembers Paul introducing another self-penned tune to the group called 'I Lost My Little Girl': "Although we worked on it, it never became part of our set. Paul just never felt happy with it."[6]

Indeed, the first commercial release of 'I Lost My Little Girl' did not come until 1991 when Paul included it in his set for an appearance on MTV's 'Unplugged' series. It was released on disc as *Paul McCartney Unplugged (The Official Bootleg)* CDP 79641 22. In his liner notes for the album, Mark Lewisohn recommended fans to listen out for Paul's *"authentic Holly hiccup"*.

Paul's teenage friend and early guitar playing partner Ian James remembers Paul singing it to him not long after he had written it. They were together in Forthlin when Paul mentioned he'd written a song and, not being one to hold back, sat right down and played 'I Lost My Little Girl' to him: "I was extremely surprised on one visit when Paul invited me up to his bedroom and began to play and sing the first song he'd ever written, 'My Little Girl' I think. I'd never considered composing my own songs."[7]

Derivative though they were in style, 'Hello Little Girl' and 'I Lost My Little Girl' by John Lennon and Paul McCartney respectively, marked the beginning of a musical collaboration that would shake the world. The natural progression from sharing their own self-composed songs was to write collaboratively. From almost the moment they did so they also made an agreement that, whoever wrote or initiated a song thereafter, it would become a shared composition, a 'Lennon-McCartney original'. Later John and Paul would say that their ambition was to become the British 'Goffin and King'. Once initiated, this musical collaboration would last the lifetime of the Beatles and was a major factor in propelling the group to the top of the charts around the world.

---

1 & 2 Sir Paul McCartney in conversation with Bob Harris OBE and Colin Hall for the 2007 BBC Radio 2 documentary *The Day John Met Paul* written and narrated by Bob Harris, produced by Bob Harris and Trudie Myerscough-Harris for WBBC.
3 John Lennon to Raoul Pantin in the *Trinidad Express*, 4 May 1971.
4 John Lennon from an interview with Mike Hennessy in the *Record Mirror*, 2 October 1971. Both John's quotations re: 'Calypso Rock' unearthed by Mark Lewisohn for *The Beatles – All These Years: Volume One: Tune In*, (Little Brown, 2013).
5 Sir Paul McCartney in conversation with Bob Harris OBE and Colin Hall, March 2009 for the BBC Radio Documentary *The Songs the Beatles Gave Away,* written and narrated by Bob Harris, produced by Bob Harris and Trudie Myerscough-Harris for WBBC.
6 Colin Hanton from his memoir *Pre:Fab!* by Colin Hanton with Colin Hall (The Book Guild, 2018) p.304.
7 Ian James as a memory for Sylvia Hall to pass on to visitors to 20 Forthlin Road in her role as custodian of the property (2019).

Chapter 8:
AND THEN THERE WERE FOUR

When the summer of 1957 ended Paul (age 15) returned to school at the Liverpool Institute High School for Boys.

Meanwhile, having failed all his O Level exams, John (age 16) could not return to grammar school. Aunt Mimi's worst nightmare had come true and she was more than anxious as to what was to become of her wayward nephew now that he faced having to find a job. She knew that John was not a practical lad and that he would struggle to hold down what she viewed as a 'dead-end job' for very long.

Fortunately, despite even failing his Art O Level exam (a subject at which every teacher believed John excelled), the Art College in Liverpool were shown some of his work and after he attended an interview John was offered a place. The only possible stumbling block was that having failed his O Levels he was not eligible for a discretionary grant towards his further education and so this meant the only proviso attached to the offer of a place was that his aunt had to agree to support him financially for the next three years, which she did.

Although she viewed a qualification in 'Art' as limiting the kind of career opportunities John could pursue and that art school was a bit of a come down from her dreams of university, Mimi was pragmatic. She agreed to fund him, no doubt hoping the extra time spent studying would at least give him time to sort his ideas out, grow up a bit and get this ridiculous skiffle and rock 'n' roll obsession out of his system. At the same time he would (all fingers crossed) gain some sort of qualification and therefore more chance of eventually finding employment more suitable to a boy of his abilities.

Not having to hold down a job nor study for A Levels (although art college would make some demands on his time) most definitely suited John Lennon down to the ground, especially as National Service (i.e., conscription) ended in 1957 for all those born on or after October 1939.

And so for the next three years, John Lennon attended Liverpool College of Art, located at 68 Hope Street on the corner with Mount Street. Effectively this meant John and Paul were studying in buildings situated right next door to each other. George Harrison was also a pupil at the Institute. He and Paul had already connected through their regular bus journeys to school in which they had discovered a shared passion for electric guitars. Could there ever have been a more convenient or providential coincidence?

Paul: "Before I moved to live in Allerton at 20 Forthlin I lived in Speke … where George lived and we both went to the same school, the Liverpool Institute, the Inny. I'd get on the bus which would go into Liverpool and the next stop George would get on … He's a year younger than me but I'd see he had the school uniform on and he had a great hairdo – big quiff – we used to call it a turban, it looks like a fuckin' turban! So he was great, I was impressed by him. It's what happened in those days: anybody who looked a bit groovy you'd think, I'll keep an eye on him. One day there was a seat next to me and no other seat available so he had to come and sit by me and we struck up a conversation and realised we both love rock 'n' roll and guitars. That was the main thing, we started talking guitars."[1]

As 1957 morphed into 1958, George Harrison became a fully fledged member of the Quarry Men. When Paul heard George play he realised what an amazing guitar player he was and made it his mission to get him to play for John. The legend is that, atop a bus one night as George and some of the Quarry Men travelled home from a gig in

Garston, George was encouraged to play the Bill Justis instrumental 'Raunchy'. John was sufficiently impressed with the youngster's prowess and joined with Paul to bring George into the group and instruct Quarry Men manager Nigel Walley to sack guitarist Eric Griffiths.

Paul: "George brought his guitar, the case almost dwarfed him, and I remember we were on the top deck of this empty double decker bus, no one there, we were all just sitting around and I said, 'Go on, play it!' ... George's big party piece was 'Raunchy' by Bill Justis ... and we were blown away ... John was like 'Wow, what? He's almost a professional!' It was great, he played it great. And it was George ... It was one of those 'oh we've got to have him in' moments."[2]

Reluctantly Nigel did as he was asked, but attempted to soften the blow by offering Eric the olive branch of switching to electric bass in order to keep his place in the group. Given the expense Eric knew he would incur to do this, he angrily declined. Eric's departure meant that by December 1957 schoolboy friends and founding members Pete Shotton, Rod Davis, Len Garry and now Eric Griffiths had all gone from the Quarry Men, leaving John, Paul, drummer Colin Hanton and new boy George as the new line-up. During 1958, pianist John Duff Lowe, a friend of Paul's at the Institute, joined for a short time.

1 & 2 Sir Paul McCartney in conversation with Bob Harris OBE and Colin Hall for the 2007 BBC Radio 2 documentary *The Day John Met Paul*, written and narrated by Bob Harris, produced by Bob Harris and Trudie Myerscough-Harris for WBBC.

Chapter 9:
LENNON AND McCARTNEY ORIGINALS

1958
Was the year of ... the Munich Air Disaster in which eight players from Manchester United died ... when work on the M1, Britain's first full-length motorway began ... BOAC's Comet 4 made its maiden flight ... parking meters were first installed in the UK ... Cliff Richard reached number 2 with his debut single, 'Move It' ... John Stephen opened his first boutique on Carnaby Street ... Ian Fleming's first novel featuring James Bond, Dr. No *was published ... Michael Bond's* A Bear Called Paddington *was published ... the first Little Chef diner was opened (in Reading, Berkshire) ... the Notting Hill race riots occurred ...*

1959
Was the year ... Fidel Castro came to power in Cuba ... the Dalai Lama and tens of thousands of Tibetans fled to India when China invaded Tibet ... the Antarctic Treaty was signed in Washington by 12 countries ... the 'Barbie Doll' was launched ... Alaska and Hawaii became the 49th and 50th States of the USA ... the St. Lawrence Seaway was opened ... NASA introduced the first USA astronauts to the world ... Buddy Holly died ... British fishing boats were fired upon by Icelandic gunboats ... Juke Box Jury began its long run on BBC TV ... Jazz and Blues singer Billie Holiday died ... Poet Allen Ginsberg wrote 'Lysergic Acid' ... Harold Macmillan was re-elected as Prime Minister in the UK ... the first Mini Cooper was built ... the first telephonic cable linking the US and Europe was inaugurated ... the first Grammy Awards were held in LA ... seven European nations signed the Stockholm Convention to form the European Free Trade Association ... Allan E. Gant of North Carolina created the prototype for what became known as 'pantyhose' ...

As the new year dawned and they were back at school and college, John, Paul and George would convene at lunch times in the basement canteen of the Art College to play their guitars. For songwriting, however, John and Paul needed privacy.

Paul's house was the most convenient place in which to find this because his dad was at work and they would have the house to themselves during the day. Ever since their mother Mary had died, Paul and his brother Michael had had their own keys to the house. Thus Paul, with John in tow, began the habit of 'sagging' school in the afternoons. They would catch the number 86 bus to return to 20 Forthlin Road where they would play their guitars, learn songs and write. Mimi, of course, would have been apoplectic to know John was not attending college after the debacle of his exam results and all the money she had since spent equipping him for college, and so this was very much a clandestine affair. Equally, Jim would not have been very pleased at all with Paul. His son's act of truancy would have confirmed Jim's original warning to Paul that John would get him into trouble.

At Forthlin, John and Paul sat in the front, south-facing living room to play and write. A three-piece suite with the sofa's back to the window encircled the fireplace. A wooden stand with a television on the top shelf and a radio below stood to the right of the fireplace and to the left against the wall stood Jim's upright piano. The boys would arrive at about two in the afternoon, knowing Jim would not be returning until around six in the evening. This gave them about three hours for their music. Before Jim returned they would clear up and ensure that no trace of their presence was left to arouse his suspicions that someone had been in the house while he was out.

When John and Paul penned tunes, the lyrics and chord changes were dutifully recorded in a school notebook of Paul's (which he still has).

"I would write down anything we came up with, starting at the top of the first page with 'A Lennon-McCartney Original'. On the next page 'Another Lennon and McCartney original'. All the pages have got that. We saw ourselves as very much the next great songwriting team. Which funnily enough is what we became!"[1]

Sometimes Paul would sit at his dad's piano, but mostly they sat facing each other, eyeball to eyeball, guitars in hand.

According to Paul their first truly collaborative song was 'Too Bad about Sorrows', followed by one called 'Just Fun'. By July 1958, Paul had written 'In Spite of all the Danger', although he credited this to 'Paul McCartney and George Harrison' because of the latter's lead guitar solos he contributed to the tune.

"We would write down the words and if we needed to we might write the name of the chords, but we wouldn't really bother too much. We had a rule that came in very early out of sheer practicality, which was, if we couldn't remember the song the next day, then it was no good. We assumed that if we, who had written it, couldn't remember it, what chance would an ordinary member of the public have of remembering it? And it was a rule we stuck to, right up until the introduction years later of Philips cassette recorders. That was a complete revolution in songwriting because you could just record it. It meant, however, you remembered some bad songs."[2]

Speaking about all the songs he and John wrote over the entire span of their partnership, Paul noted: "I was very lucky because when I was writing with John everything we sat down to write did work out. Just under 300 songs."[3]

The sessions at Forthlin were always productive, as Paul says they never came away from a writing session without something. Occasionally they wrote at 'Mendips' in John's small 'box' bedroom, but being left- (Paul) and right- (John) handed made this difficult, the necks of their guitars would bang into each other. This was because John's single bed was situated under the window, wall-to-wall across the room, which meant it just fitted, there was no space at either end, just wall.

"We'd sit down for a 2- to 3-hour session and our energy and our willpower was so strong we wouldn't go home without one, so that was a great motivating thing. But if I'm on my own and the song's not working out I can sort of let it dribble away."

One of the early songs Paul remembers John playing to him at 'Mendips' was 'I Call Your Name'. "We worked on it together, but it was John's idea. When I look back at some of these lyrics, I think, wait a minute. What did he mean? 'I call your name but you're not there.' Is it his mother? His father? I must admit I didn't really see that as we wrote it because we were just a couple of young guys writing. You didn't look behind it at the time, it was only later you started analysing things."[4]

Although John and Paul began writing together in late 1957, first as Quarry Men and then in 1960 as the Beatles, they did not include their own songs in their set lists.

Colin Hanton, the Quarry Men's drummer recalls that, "Each time we met ... the more obvious the musical bond between John and Paul became ... The more time they spent together outside of group rehearsals more often than not they'd come to practices with new songs for us to add to our repertoire, which would be covers, not Lennon and McCartney originals."[5]

This was because both the Quarry Men and later the Beatles were gigging groups whose audiences did not want to hear songs they did not already know, but wanted songs with which they were already familiar.

As the months passed, John and Paul's friendship grew ever closer as the music forged a real bond between the two. Paul's father might have been wary of John's influence on his son, but he encouraged them with their music, as did John's mother Julia. Given Aunt Mimi's strong personality and indifference to his musical interests, Julia's support must have been inspiring for her son. Sadly, Julia would never know just how much so.

On 15 July 1958, as she so often did around that time, Julia visited her sister Mimi at 'Mendips' for a cup of tea and a chat. As she left the house that evening and crossed Menlove Avenue to her bus stop on the other side she was knocked down by a motor car. The impact of the collision killed her instantly. It is impossible for anyone to know how devastating this must have been for John, his sisters Julia, Jacqueline, her partner Bobby and her sisters Mimi, Harriet, Anne and Elizabeth.

John: "It was the worst thing that ever happened to me ... I was 17. That was another big trauma for me. I lost her twice. When I was five and I moved in with my auntie, and then when she physically died. That made me more bitter; the chip I had on my shoulder I had as a youth got really big then. I was just re-establishing the relationship with her and she was killed."[6]

Just three days before Julia's tragic death, the Quarry Men (personnel: John, Paul, George, Colin Hanton, John Duff Lowe) had recorded their version of the Crickets' 'That'll Be the Day', backed by Paul's 'In Spite of all the Danger', at Percy Phillips' studio in Kensington, Liverpool. Only one copy was ever made of this disc which was essentially a 'demo'. However, it received a huge, international release in 1995 when both sides were included on *The Beatles Anthology 1* (Apple 7243 8 34445 2 6) which reached number 1 in Australia, Canada, France, Germany, Netherlands, New Zealand and the USA. In the UK it peaked at number 2.

The loss of Julia devastated John and very soon thereafter the Quarry Men fell into disarray. Gigs dried up, John Duff Lowe left the fold and, in early 1959, following a drunken row with John and Paul, Colin Hanton walked out. Reduced to a three-piece, the Quarry Men hit a hiatus. George began 'freelancing' with another group called the Les Stewart Quartet who played every Sunday night at the Pillar Club situated in the cellar of 'Lowlands', 13 Haymans Green, the headquarters of West Derby Community Association. It was a members-only club specifically for teenagers. John sometimes accompanied George to these performances, as did Paul.

By the time the Quarry Men recorded 'In Spite of all the Danger', George had acquired a Hofner President (which he later swapped with Ray Ennis of the Swinging Bluegenes for a Hofner Club 40) on which he had stuck a pick-up. In doing so he became the first out of he, John and Paul to go electric. Paul quickly followed suit and, by the time of the recording, had also put a pick-up on his Zenith and purchased an Elpico amp.

Despite the Quarry Men's lack of action, John and Paul continued to compose. 'Sagging' off school abated somewhat and any new tunes were mostly written individually. During this time Paul was the main contributor. He and John would work on these together and they were always credited as another 'Lennon-McCartney Original'. Interestingly, among these tunes were future 'giveaways': 'World Without Love', 'Like Dreamers Do' and 'Love of the Loved'.

A turning point in the group's fortunes came one Sunday night after a Les Stewart Quartet performance at 'Lowlands', a Victorian mansion situated in West Derby, Liverpool. In the early Sixties it was home to the 'Pillar Club', a music venue for teenagers. The Quartet, plus Les Stewart's girlfriend Shelagh Maguire, were greeted by a lady who said she lived just across the road from the club at 8 Haymans Green. The lady was Mona Best and she informed them that she was considering opening a similar teenagers' coffee club in the cellar of her house. Mona's 17-year-old son, Pete, had apparently told her how much he and his friends enjoyed the music nights at 'Lowlands' and this had inspired her to consider opening a similar members-only club for teenagers in her house. She invited the Quartet – Les, George, Ken Brown, Ray Skinner and Shelagh – to have a look at the cellar. They were impressed and when Mrs. Best invited them to help her convert the space into a club they readily agreed. In return she offered them a weekly residency and an invitation to perform on the opening night, Saturday 29 August 1959.

As the opening night drew near, potential disaster struck when a row among the Quartet caused them to disband. With just a few days to go, Mrs. Best was suddenly minus an opening act. George acted immediately to save the day by calling on John and Paul to combine with himself and fellow guitarist Ken Brown from the Quartet to play. Although they had rarely performed together during the last four months John and Paul were up for it. They even had time to contribute to the painting and decorating of the club in the few days leading up to its opening.

On the day before the show, with help from Aunt Mimi, John lay down the deposit on his first ever all-electric guitar, a Hofner Club 40. (He'd saved some of the money himself by working for four weeks on a building site.) Thus it was as a bass-free, all-electric guitar group, that a rejuvenated, reconstituted Quarry Men opened Mrs. Best's members-only teenage coffee club. Mrs. Best had decided to call the venue 'The Casbah Coffee Club', but it would be forever referred to as simply, 'The Casbah'.

For John, Paul and George their performance was a turning point. It galvanised them as a group once more but left them short of a player or two. Ken Brown was never going to be a part of their inner circle and would remain a Quarry Man for only five months. Drummers were always hard to find (drums cost so much) and none of them liked the name 'Quarry Men'. It had become an anachronism. John was no longer a schoolboy and the name was too redolent of skiffle music when they were now effectively a rock 'n' roll outfit.

During autumn 1959, John Lennon, aged 18 but going on 19, fell in love with fellow art student Cynthia Powell. He had also become close friends with the art college's most talented student, Stuart Sutcliffe. Earlier in the summer he had failed his Intermediate exam but had been allowed to stay on at college to re-sit his exams in May 1960. In September Paul, aged 17, entered his last year at the Institute to study for his A Level examinations. George, aged 16 and a serial truant, had left school at the end of the summer term to supposedly find employment.

Growing ever more serious about their group, the boys knew that they were overloaded with guitarists and until they found a drummer and a bass player they were really just 'half a group'. Few club owners fell for their oft repeated assertion that the 'rhythm is in the guitars'. They also needed to fix that name: 'The Quarry Men' had become oh so 'square'!

THE TOP 30 MOST POPULAR UK CHART HITS IN 1958
01 The Everly Brothers: All I Have to Do Is Dream / Claudette
02 Connie Francis: Who's Sorry Now?
03 Perry Como: Magic Moments
04 Connie Francis: Stupid Cupid / Carolina Moon
05 The Kalin Twins: When
06 Michael Holliday: The Story of My Life
07 Max Bygraves: Tulips from Amsterdam / You Need Hands
08 Marvin Rainwater: Whole Lotta Woman
09 Elvis Presley: Jailhouse Rock
10 Vic Damone: On the Street Where You Live
11 Lord Rockingham's XI: Hoots Mon
12 Tommy Edwards: It's All in the Game
13 Dean Martin: Return to Me
14 The Everly Brothers: Bird Dog
15 Pat Boone: A Wonderful Time Up There
16 Elias & His Zig-Zag Jive Flutes: Tom Hark
17 Dean Martin: Volare
18 Conway Twitty: It's Only Make Believe
19 The Four Preps: Big Man
20 Marino Marini and His Quartet: Come Prima
21 Frank Sinatra: All the Way / Chicago

22 Danny & The Juniors: At the Hop
23 Cliff Richard & The Drifters: Move it
24 Johnny Mathis: A Certain Smile
25 The Crickets: Oh Boy
26 The Platters: Twilight Time
27 Pat Boone: April Love
28 Jerry Lee Lewis: Great Balls of Fire
29 Marty Wilde: Endless Sleep
30 Ted Heath and His Music: Swingin' Shepherd Blues

THE TOP 30 MOST POPULAR UK CHART HITS IN 1959
01 Russ Conway: Side Saddle
02 Cliff Richard and The Drifters: Living Doll
03 Buddy Holly: It Doesn't Matter Anymore
04 Bobby Darin: Dream Lover
05 Elvis Presley: A Fool Such as I / I Need Your Love Tonight
06 The Platters: Smoke Gets in Your Eyes
07 Shirley Bassey: As I Love You
08 Craig Douglas: Only Sixteen
09 Cliff Richard and The Shadows: Travellin' Light
10 Russ Conway: Roulette
11 Bobby Darin: Mack the Knife
12 Chris Barber's Jazz Band: Petite Fleur
13 Lonnie Donegan: Battle of New Orleans
14 Emile Ford and The Checkmates: What Do You Want to Make Those Eyes at Me for?
15 Marty Wilde: A Teenager in Love
16 Ricky Nelson: It's Late
17 Jerry Keller: Here Comes Summer
18 Elvis Presley: One Night / I Got Stung
19 The Everly Brothers: ('Til) I Kissed You
20 Paul Anka: Lonely Boy
21 Connie Francis: Lipstick on Your Collar
22 Shirley Bassey: Kiss Me Honey Honey Kiss Me
23 Marty Wilde: Donna
24 Anthony Newley: I've Waited So Long
25 The Teddy Bears: To Know Him Is to Love Him
26 Adam Faith: What Do You Want?
27 Slim Dusty: A Pub with no Beer
28 Little Richard: Baby Face
29 Johnny and The Hurricanes: Red River Rock
30 Jane Morgan: The Day the Rains Came

1, 2 & 5 Paul McCartney *Many Years from Now*, Barry Miles (Vintage, 1998) p.36, p.37 & p.46.
3 & 4 Sir Paul McCartney in conversation with Bob Harris OBE and Colin Hall for *The Songs the Beatles Gave Away*, BBC Radio 2, 2009, written and narrated by Bob Harris, produced by Bob and Trudie Myerscough-Harris for WBBC.
6 *Pre:Fab!*, Colin Hanton with Colin Hall, (The Book Guild Limited, 2018) p.29.
7 *John Lennon in His Own Words*, compiled by Miles, (Omnibus Press, 1980) p.23.

Chapter 10:
1960: THE FUTURE STARTS HERE

1960
Was the year that ... in Greensboro, North Carolina, four black students staged a sit-in at a segregated Woolworth's lunch counter which kick-started a series of non-violent protests across the southern USA ... Elvis returned from military service in the USA ... The Flintstones was aired on American TV ... the Polaris missile was test-launched ... President Eisenhower signed the Civil Rights Act into law ...

1960 was not just a new year, it heralded a new decade, a new dawn. As such it offered the chance of a fresh start and new promise. For John, Paul and George, however, in reality little had changed.

Putting aside the absence of a drummer, the lack of a bass guitar player was a lingering concern. Logically, as the group now consisted of three guitarists (four if Ken was included, but he wasn't) one of them *could* have switched, but this was not going to happen. Bass was somehow seen as the least attractive instrument to play in a group and so they began to ask friends to buy a bass and fill the vacancy. Ken was not approached but George's guitar playing friend Arthur Kelly was. As far as Arthur was concerned it was a case of bad timing. Although he had just begun work, the price of a bass (around £60) was prohibitive and he knew his parents would not be happy with him frittering away his time and energy on being in a group when he'd finally found a steady job. John's student friend Rod Murray was asked and although he was not a rock 'n' roll aficionado he said he'd make one in the college workshop. That would have helped, but the problem was, how long would that take?

Along with everyone else, Stuart Sutcliffe was asked, but he, like Rod, was a cash-strapped and a (very serious) art student who could barely afford his rent and painting materials.

As their desperation increased, the Quarry Men's fortunes dramatically turned almost in an instant. Out of the blue Stuart came upon some extra money. He had submitted a painting entitled 'Summer Painting' for the prestigious 'John Moores Liverpool Exhibition 2' which was held at the Walker Art Gallery for two months and had opened in mid-November, 1959. Actually, Stuart's painting was only half a piece, having originally spread over two canvasses, but he only managed to deliver one of them to the exhibition. On the way back to collect the other piece he and the friend who had helped him carry the first piece to the gallery stopped off for a pint and somehow the other piece never arrived. Two thousand pieces had been submitted in 1959 for the exhibition of which only 157 were eventually exhibited, including Stuart's, testament indeed to his prodigious talent.

When the exhibition closed in January 1960, John Moore liked Stuart's work so much he offered to buy it. Before he knew it, Stuart was £90 richer. In 1960, £90 was a lot of money. Immediately John, Paul and George honed in on him and offered Stuart a place in their group on either bass or drums: his choice, of course.

Stuart was not steeped in rock music in the way that his friends were, but John was very persuasive and Stuart keen to try. He chose the bass and on Thursday 21 January 1960, using £15 from his art sale, put down the deposit on a Hofner 500/5 four-string electric bass plus carrying case. It was a big decision for a student with so much promise as an artist, but very little as a musician. His action must have caused both the college and his parents much alarm. Artistically, Stuart was on the cusp of great things, but was now committing himself to the rigours of playing in a not very good, drummer-less, manager-less rock 'n' roll band.

George Harrison remembered that, "Stu had no idea how to play it. We all showed him what we could, but he really picked it up by just coming round with us and playing on stage."[1]

As luck would have it, at the very moment Stuart stepped up as the first electric bass player for the Quarry Men, the group lost its precious residency at the Casbah. Toward the end of January, Ken Brown had turned up feeling unwell and did not perform. Instead he took the door money while the group played using his amplifier. At the end of the evening Mrs. Best insisted on giving Ken his share of their £3 fee, which angered John, Paul and George, who felt he hadn't earned it. The result was a bout of teenage petulance as, in protest, they quit their residency. They also ditched Ken. Ken wasn't too bothered because he had seen this coming and had started playing with Mona's eldest son Pete, Chas Newby and Bill Barlow in a group they called the Blackjacks.

Despite this hiccup, with the addition of Stuart on bass, the four Quarry Men were shaping up into an all-electric rock 'n' roll outfit. Admittedly Stuart had yet to learn the bass, but as George quipped, "It was better to have a bass player who couldn't play than to not have a bass player at all."[2]

Whatever the level of Stuart's technical prowess on bass, a drummer remained a necessity, as did some bookings. (To help with the latter a manager would have proven very useful.) They also desperately needed another amplifier. An unplugged electric bass guitar was a contradiction in terms. Bookings wouldn't be any good without enough amps. Despite his handsome new bass, Stuart resolutely refused to cough up even more of his precious art money for an amp. With Ken gone the Quarry Men were reduced to just Paul's tiny green Elpico AC-55.

Importantly, they had still not come up with an alternative to that old-fashioned band name.

A home-recorded tape exists from early 1960, recorded not long after Stuart had acquired his bass guitar, which appears to feature only John, Paul and Stuart. Of a low standard musically and featuring eight untitled pieces, one of which is described by Mark Lewisohn as "a tune that might be called 'Well Darling' and could be a 'Lennon-McCartney Original'."[3]

The only other original tune on the tape is a Paul instrumental called 'Cayenne'. This is, however, evidence that some compositions were still forthcoming in what was otherwise a very dry period for Lennon and McCartney.

Around the same time as this, John moved from 'Mendips' to share a flat with Rod Murray, Stu Sutcliffe, Margaret Duxbury and Margaret Morris. Crucially, Flat 3 Hillary Mansions, Gambier Terrace, allowed John to escape Mimi's relentless scrutiny (and criticism). At a time when the tension between the two was becoming more fractious every day as she desperately tried to keep him focused on his studies, the opportunity to escape to a place where no one was constantly on his back was irresistible. Out of Mimi's reach and ensconced in Flat 3, John Lennon was able to bond with Stu as well as spend more private time with his girlfriend Cynthia.

By proxy the flat became a hangout from home for all the Quarry Men. They would meet to rehearse, help Stuart learn the bass, stay over and plot their future. Compared to the many other groups emerging onto the thriving Liverpool music scene, in terms of equipment they were still only half a group. They had a long way to go to catch up with the likes of Cass and the Cassanovas and Rory Storm and the Hurricanes. Rory Storm was a charismatic frontman renowned for his on-stage acts of derring-do, while his drummer was regarded as one of the best in the city. His name was Richard Starkey, but everyone knew him as Ringo.

In 1960, such was the growing demand for live 'beat music' throughout the city, groups found themselves in demand on week nights as well as weekends. Some were even able to earn a good wage from doing so. Others, like the Quarry Men, were most definitely not in this league at all.

---

1 *The Beatles: The Authorised Biography*, Hunter Davies, (Heinemann, 1968) p. 65.
2 *The Beatles, Anthology*, TV series, ITV (1995).
3 *The Beatles – All These Years: Volume One: Tune In*, Extended Special Edition, by Mark Lewisohn (Little, Brown, 2013) p.581.

Chapter 11:
THE JACARANDA

Active on this burgeoning Liverpool scene was entrepreneur Allan Williams, a devotee of clubs. In 1958 he had opened the 'Jacaranda', or 'Jac' as it soon became known to its regulars. Situated at 23 Slater Street opposite Jackson's art shop, students of the art college soon gravitated towards the club which quickly became a student hangout because of its bohemian ambience. It was not licensed, but Williams and his wife Beryl had registered it as a private club, which allowed it to open its downstairs basement after midnight, and which in turn attracted a particular audience comprising workers who worked unsocial hours, such as entertainers and nurses.

Williams himself described the Jac's clientele with these words: "Artists, musicians, pimps, beggars, ordinary layabouts and all the rag-tag-and-bobtail of Liverpool 8..."[1]

Rod Murray and Stuart Sutcliffe had decorated the club's basement during which time Allan and Beryl had grown to like them very much. As might be expected, in turn John also became a frequent visitor and George and Paul occasionally spent time there.

Sometime in early spring 1960, when he was living in Gambier Terrace, John wrote his first tune since penning 'What Goes On' a year earlier while still living at 'Mendips'. Cynthia recalled sitting in the 'Jac' helping him with lyrics for a 'train song' he called 'One After 909'. (George Harrison's best friend Arthur Kelly says that he sat in with John, Paul and George (no Stuart) when they recorded a version of John's new tune at Percy Phillips' studio in Kensington.)[2]

Around the same time as 'One After 909', John possibly also penned an instrumental called 'Winston's Walk'. No one can be exactly sure whether he or Paul wrote this particular tune. Leading Beatles expert Mark Lewisohn is inclined to think it was more likely to have been Paul because he wrote several other instrumentals during this period, including 'Hot as Sun' and 'Catswalk' (both of which he would later re-visit).

Witness to the expanding music scene in the city, the Williams gave the Royal Caribbean Steel Band a residency in the Jac's basement and when, on Monday nights, they took a night off, Cass and the Cassanovas would play. Before he knew it, Allan became an agent for all types of musical acts in Liverpool. He took 10% from any bookings he obtained. In turn the 'Jac' became even more *the* bohemian place to be.

Williams watched with great delight as the popularity of the Royal Caribbean Steel Band transformed the Jac: "... the people liked it. The place was jam-packed every night, couples necking and dancing and drinking Coke. It was unlicensed, but people brought in liquor and spiked their soft drinks ... There was a camaraderie about the place. Everyone knew everyone else, more or less..."[3]

As Williams was soon to find out, students, nurses and entertainers were not the only ones who visited his club. Without introducing himself, a German entrepreneur had slipped in one night and, unknown to Williams, had offered his resident steel band good money to quit Liverpool to work in a club he operated in Hamburg. So tempting was the offer, some of them accepted and absconded. Understandably irked by their disloyalty, Allan was no doubt also amused by their naivety when, so thrilled with their good fortune, they sent him a postcard informing him just what a fabulous time they were enjoying in Germany.

Their postcard was persuasive enough to ignite Allan's natural curiosity. Together with Lord Woodbine (so-called because of his predilection for those famous cigarettes), the erstwhile leader of the steel band, but who had *not* absconded, he took advantage of a trade 'jolly' in Amsterdam to extend his trip and visit Hamburg to see for himself what

Allan Williams photographed in Liverpool on 11 July 2015 with the author.

all the fuss was about. Williams was on a mission. His plan was to grab a slice of the Hamburg cake for himself by striking a deal with club owners to send more Liverpool music acts to play.

Williams was convinced that the deal-clincher in any meeting he may have was the hastily recorded tape of Liverpool groups he had made before he left. Featuring Cass and the Cassanovas and one or two others, Allan was convinced that once his fellow German entrepreneurs heard his tape they'd be falling over themselves to sign Liverpool groups.

Many adventures later and still clutching the precious tape, Woodbine and Williams found themselves situated in St. Pauli in the very heart of Hamburg's notorious red-light district. Specifically, they were in a cellar bar known as the Kaiserkeller where, in front of them, stood the most unbelievably dull group of musicians Williams had ever heard. In that instant he believed he had struck gold. Within minutes he and Lord Woodbine were introducing themselves to the Kaiserkeller's owner, Bruno Koschmider. A potentially lucrative deal was tantalisingly just a handshake away when the night collapsed in tatters around their ears. The tape failed to play properly, instead it just made strange noises and left Allan with nothing whatsoever to sell and only the exit to contemplate.

1 & 3 Allan Williams from his autobiography (co-written by William Marshall), *The Man Who Gave the Beatles Away*, (Coronet Edition, 1976) pp. 14 and 15.
2 Arthur Kelly in conversation with the author, 2019.

Chapter 12:
THE SECOND 'E'

Back in Liverpool, life for one particular Quarry Man was proving tense.

17-year-old Paul should have been focusing on his forthcoming A Levels but the Quarry Men, plus the lure of the flat in Gambier Terrace and mixing with student types had become very appealing distractions. Emotionally his feelings were no doubt all over the place as he felt jealousy for the growing closeness he witnessed developing between John and Stuart while at the same time he had become romantically very close to a girl called Dot Rhone*.

(*Dot and Cynthia became good friends. When in May/June 1961 Cynthia Powell moved to live in a bedsit on Garmoyle Road, near Penny Lane, Dot joined her to keep her company and help share costs.)

Bookings for the group had stalled: agents and club owners were not flocking to book the drummer-less Quarry Men. Ever hopeful Paul and Stuart were active in writing letters to managers of prospective venues but it was all to no avail. (Whether they actually sent any is another matter.)

One opportunity to perform that had come their way at this time was to play the monthly Saturday night Art College dances which gave Stuart valuable stage time.

They also used this downtime in the Quarry Men's gigging schedule to resolve two other sources of irritation which they felt were holding them back: the search for a name and a second amplifier they could use.

In a letter Stuart wrote dated the 27 March 1960 requesting a booking for the group he can be seen to have begun writing the words 'Quarry Men' but three letters into doing so he crossed them out and replaced them with 'Beatals'. His letter is the clearest evidence we have of when the vexed issue of a new and better group name had finally (more or less) been resolved.

In so much of what they did at this time, Buddy Holly was the influence. John had been particularly taken with the word 'Crickets' as a group name. He liked it because, to a British person, the word 'Cricket' had more than one meaning. It made people think. So John began to think of other insects that maybe had a name that carried more than one meaning: "The idea of beetles came into my head. I decided to spell it BEAtles to make it look like beat music, just as a joke."[1]

It was a fascinating choice: changing the second 'E' was a simple stroke of genius. John and Paul preferred 'Beatles' from the get-go while Stuart liked to spell it 'Beatals'. Paul remembered meeting with Stuart and John outside Gambier Terrace and as they walked towards nearby Huskisson Street they told him that their new idea for a group name was 'The Beatles'. He liked it and like his fellow bandmates Paul enjoyed how that double meaning thing made people stop and think.

It was quirky and a definite (and conscious) departure from the usual format for group names popular in Liverpool at that time: Gerry and the Pacemakers, Rory Storm and the Hurricanes, Cass and the Cassanovas, Derry and the Seniors, Ian and the Zodiacs …

The second major issue they resolved was the lack of a second amplifier. The one that came their way wasn't actually something they owned either individually or had acquired as a group investment. Even so there is no doubt that in their heads they considered it to be 'their amp'. In fact it was the property of the Art College, specifically the Students' Union of Liverpool College of Arts ('Sulca'). Fellow student and member of the Student Union committee Bill Harry had been proactive in persuading Sulca to 'acquire' it for them.

Bill was a good friend of Stuart's who was becoming closer to John. Bill persuaded the committee to purchase an amp specifically for use at the monthly art school dances. The Beatles had told Bill that in return for this favour they would play those dances. It is believed that Sulca bought a 15-watt two-input Selmer Truvoice Stadium amplifier but the evidence is hearsay. It was certainly a powerful piece of kit for the day and there is no doubt the Beatles did 'loan' whatever amp it was for other functions they played elsewhere. (Eventually the amp disappeared with them to Hamburg … never to be seen by the college again.)

Appropriately John, Paul, George and Stuart made their performance debut as the all-electric, amplified 'Beatles' at one of the Art College dances. (They soon became known as 'the college band' and would be booked to play the dances along with local acts such as the Merseysippi Jazz Band.) One thing for sure is that while they might not have played too well, they would have been very loud.

It was around this time, spring 1960, that George went back to the Casbah. (Mona had no issues with him for it had been Paul and John who had kicked up the fuss over Ken Brown being paid when he hadn't played.) On his return George learned something that was to prove very important in the months to come and this was that Mona's son Pete had suddenly and mysteriously left school and split his band, the Blackjacks. Pete was a very bright pupil who had been on schedule to take his A Levels that summer. The plan had been that he would go to college to study to become a PE teacher (he was a good rugby player) but out of the blue three months ahead of his exams he quit school. No one really ever knew why. He simply stopped going and stayed quietly at home …

Meanwhile following on from their debut at the Art College dance John, Paul, George and Stuart played their first 'public' show with a name approximating 'Beatles/Beatals'. It was at the Lathom Hall in Seaforth, Liverpool where, on 14 May 1960, as the 'Silver Beats', they played an unannounced audition for Crosby-based promoter Brian Kelly. They passed the audition and on the strength of this Kelly offered them a paid booking at the same venue one week later on Saturday 21 May 1960. Unfortunately for Brian 'fate' was going to intervene in a big way and the 'Silver Beats' were not only unable to honour the engagement but in their excitement as to what had happened to them in the days between the gigs they forgot to tell him that they couldn't do so …

---

1 *The Beatles: The Authorised Biography,* by Hunter Davies (William Heinemann Ltd, 1968) p.69, as told by John Lennon to Hunter.

Chapter 13:
ALLAN AND LARRY MAKE PLANS

Since his return from Hamburg, Allan Williams had not been idle (he never was). Notably he'd visited the Empire to catch the ground-breaking Larry Parnes-promoted very first all-rock 'n' roll package tour of the UK. The tour docked in Liverpool from 14 to 19 March (12 shows). Headlining this historic (and protracted) tour were two 'real deal' first generation American rockers, Gene Vincent and Eddie Cochran. Support came from the first wave of successful British rock 'n' rollers (all of whom Parnes managed): Billy Fury, Joe Brown, Vince Eager and Tony Sheridan. (When the tour moved on for its final dates, another Larry Parnes protégé, Liverpool singer-songwriter Johnny Gentle, performed in place of Billy Fury.)

John, Cynthia, Stuart, their art school friend Tony Carricker and George Harrison all went to see the Vincent and Cochran show. Paul possibly did or possibly he didn't, he remembers both not going and going. Ringo might have. Guitarist Johnny Guitar from Rory Storm and the Hurricanes did, as did future Beatles-people Neil Aspinall and Pete Best.

The tour was very big news and although he preferred the intimacy of the 'Jac', Allan Williams' curiosity would not let him stay away. What he saw amazed him. He'd never seen anything like the show before. The energy it generated and the wild, cacophonous reaction it drew from its teenage audience was awesome. Right away Allan wanted a piece of the action. Almost without hesitation he contacted the promoter, Larry Parnes, to see if a deal could be struck.

Famous as the man who, in 1956, gave Britain its very first home-grown rock 'n' roll star, the one and only Tommy Steele, Parnes was now promoting a 'stable' of young male artists that included Billy Fury, Vince Eager, Marty Wilde, Terry Dene, Dickie Pride, Lance Fortune, Georgie Fame and Johnny Gentle. (Not their real names, of course, but names Parnes chose for them.) The idea was for them to begin as rock stars and graduate to become all-round entertainers. By 1960 Tommy Steele was well on the way to making this crossover.

(*According to* The Guinness Book of British Hit Singles, *of these artists Billy Fury and Tommy Steele were the most successful. Between 1959 and 1966, Fury had 27 Top 40 chart entries, which included 19 Top 20 entries, of which ten cracked the Top 10. Between 1956 and 1961 Steele made the Top 40 some 24 times, of which six were Top 10 hits including a number 1 with 'Singing the Blues' (for one week in January 1957, and his version of this song re-entered the charts on two further occasions). Later Georgie Fame hit the UK chart 12 times between 1964 and 1969, which included scoring three number 1s 'Yeh Yeh' (1965), 'Get Away' (1966) and 'Ballad of Bonnie and Clyde' (1967).*)

Allan Williams' idea was to link with Parnes to bring Vincent, Cochran and other Parnes-managed acts back to Liverpool and stage a huge concert with extra support coming from emerging Liverpool 'beat' groups for whom Williams was now acting as agent. It was a bold move for someone who had never done anything on this scale before, but Williams was a man on a mission and there was no stopping him.

He struck gold. Or so it seemed. Parnes told Williams that Cochran and Vincent were taking a two-week break from their UK tour immediately after a show at the Bristol Hippodrome on Saturday 16 April. Immediately after that show they would fly home to Los Angeles and return to the UK to continue the tour at the end of the month. By chance, Tuesday, 3 May 1960, was free. Williams moved quickly, secured the Liverpool Boxing

Johnny Gentle, Hal Carter and Eddie Cochran. Hal Carter (real name Harold Carter Burrows) had been hired by Larry Parnes in 1959 and was Billy Fury's friend and tour manager. (John and Gavin Askew)

Stadium, agreed with Parnes a fee of £475, signed on the dotted line and before he had time to draw breath had secured Vincent, Cochran and eight other acts from the Parnes stable to play Liverpool again. Allan was on a roll. This was the big time!

Very sadly tragedy struck on Saturday, April 16* when, just before midnight, the private taxi in which Cochran and Vincent were travelling from the Bristol Hippodrome to London Airport swerved off the road in Chippenham and hit a lamppost. While Vincent survived Cochran died as a result of the injuries he received.

(*The accident occurred just before midnight, but Eddie Cochran was not pronounced dead until the afternoon of 17 April 1960.)

On hearing this awful news, Williams fully expected the three-hour concert he had arranged for 3 May would be pulled. To his surprise, however, Parnes informed him that although Gene Vincent had been injured he would have recovered sufficiently to play the show, was Williams still interested? Williams most definitely was and confirmed his wish to press on with the event, only this time he decided he would add even more acts to the bill and that the additional acts would be more of the Liverpool groups for whom he was agent.

The event quickly took on an energy all of its own. In spirit it was a wake for Eddie that built inexorably into a big, noisy and emotional night on Merseyside. In hindsight it was also something so much more. Allan Williams' concert served notice of something new and important stirring in the clubs and dance halls of Liverpool: a sound so big and beat heavy it was destined to reverberate around the world.

The Liverpool groups, which included Rory Storm and the Hurricanes, Cass and the

Cassanovas, Gerry and the Pacemakers, Derry and the Seniors, played the first half, the professional acts the second. Alongside Gene Vincent there was another American artist called Davy Jones, a black singer from the Little Richard school of rock 'n' roll. Also on the bill were 'Italy's Fabulous' Nero and his Gladiators, an instrumental group who dressed in togas and laurel leaves but were in fact British. Most of the other professional artists were part of Larry Parnes' fabled 'stable' and included Lance Fortune, Dean Webb, Peter Wynne and Julian 'X'. (Fortune had scored a number 4 UK hit with 'Be Mine' earlier in the year.)

An interesting professional singer also highlighted on the bill was 'Mal Perry'. Born Malcolm Levy, he was from Liverpool, had attended Quarry Bank and knew John Lennon. Perry had been writing his own songs since he was 10 years old. By 1958 Mal had signed to the new Fontana label and released his debut single, 'Lollipop'. A few years later John and Paul tried to interest him in recording one of their compositions, an offer Mal declined.

By the time Vincent took the stage on that memorable night of 3 May what had started as a rowdy, raucous show had become even rowdier, noisier, wilder and impassioned. Liverpool music historian Mick O'Toole who witnessed it all recalled: "The Stadium show was a total madhouse. With its seating the stadium wasn't set out like the Empire and people were dashing about all over the place. There were no marshals or stewards and no discipline among the crowds."[1]

Stuart Sutcliffe and George Harrison definitely attended, as did one Richard Starkey because he was drumming for Rory Storm's Hurricanes as 'Ringo Starr'. Also in attendance, inquisitive as ever to know what was happening on the Liverpool pop music scene, was local record store manager Brian Epstein who used the opportunity to meet Larry Parnes.

George Harrison's memory of the event provides a fascinating insight into how the Beatles viewed their potential at that moment in time. It is especially enlightening considering that at the time the newly named Beatles couldn't get a gig to save their lives and had not been invited to play the Stadium.

"We were nothing, just out of school, and we were amateur and we were hopeless, and Rory Storm and the Hurricanes came on at the Stadium and he was big. He came on amazing (doing) 'What'd I Say' and the band rocking, all doing the steps with the suits on, and he's jumping about like a loony – and even then I just remember thinking, 'Well we're better than them!' even though we hadn't done anything. And it wasn't an ego thing, it was with no qualifications at all, but there was something about us that was cocky, that knew something was going to happen."[2]

For the beat groups of Liverpool, the concert was, as Adrian Barber of Cass and the Cassanovas neatly summed it up, 'a light bulb moment': "None of us knew of any other groups until Allan Williams' gig at the Stadium. I'm sure we were vaguely aware there was something going on, but we weren't a community by any means. At that Stadium show we became aware of all the other bands in Liverpool, about twelve in total."[3]

At the after-show party at the Jacaranda, Larry Parnes and Allan Williams hatched a mutually beneficial business plan. Larry Parnes was in constant need of backing groups for his 'stable of solo artists' who were forever touring the land. This was never easy to achieve, especially in London where such musicians did not come cheap. That night in Liverpool, Parnes realised that the local groups Allan Williams represented were not only talented but less expensive than their contemporaries in London. With Williams promising to provide such backing groups for his solo singers, Parnes believed he had solved a pressing problem of never having enough players to back his artists. Even better, it would be more economic.

In the back of Parnes's mind as he and Allan talked was the knowledge that coming up in June he had two acts signed to play two separate ballroom circuit tours of Scotland: Duffy Power and Johnny Gentle. Duffy Power (born Ray Howard) was from London and

Johnny Gentle (born John Askew) was from Liverpool. Parnes had signed them both in 1959 and got them record deals with Fontana and Philips respectively.

Parnes agreed with Williams that he would travel to Liverpool on Tuesday, 10 May to audition the groups he'd seen at the Stadium with a view to signing them to back his acts. Williams arranged for the auditions to be held at the Wyvern Social Club, Seel Street, starting at approximately 10am. Williams had acquired the lease for this particular club and planned to have it converted into a nightclub he intended to call the 'Blue Angel'.

Ahead of his arrival, Parnes alerted Williams that he also needed a group to back his current major star signing Billy Fury during his forthcoming summer season in Great Yarmouth. As a consequence, Parnes arrived in Liverpool for the auditions, accompanied by Mark Foster from his L.M.P. Entertainments company, plus teen sensation and local hero, Billy Fury.

Suddenly Allan was mixing with the big boys. In one fell swoop he had become Liverpool's impresario to go to. And go to him John Lennon did …

1 *The Perfect Storm Part 3 – 1960*, Spencer Leigh, www.spencerleigh.co.uk/2013
2 George Harrison interviewed by Alan Freeman, BBC1, 6 December 1974 from *The Beatles – All These Years: Volume One: Tune In*, Extended Special Edition, by Mark Lewisohn (Little, Brown 2013) p.612.
3 Adrian Barber, lead guitarist with Cass and the Casanovas, interviewed by Spencer Leigh, and quoted in *The Beatles – All These Years: Volume One: Tune In*, Extended Special Edition (Little, Brown, 2013), p.613.

Chapter 14:
WHAT THE HELL HAVE YOU SENT ME HERE, LARRY?

Out of the blue and just a few days before Parnes and Fury were due in town, John Lennon informed Allan that he and Stuart were in a group and asked if he could 'do something for them'. Specifically, he requested that the Beatles be included in the imminent auditions for Billy Fury. That Stuart was in a group with John Lennon came as a complete surprise to Allan, but he liked Stuart and was keen to support him. He asked John to describe the group's line up and when Lennon admitted they did not have a drummer he offered to find them one.

John's request dramatically turned the tide of inertia that had overcome the Beatles. From dreaming about being a proper rock group but having no gigs and no drummer to advance their cause, out of the blue they were on the cusp of getting a drummer and possibly going on tour to back a bona fide rock 'n' roll recording star. Allan Williams truly was *the man* on Merseyside.

Good to his word, Williams quickly recruited a drummer for them. Older than the Beatles, Tommy Moore had a day job at the Garston Bottle Company. Despite his preference for jazz, Tommy nevertheless agreed to turn up at the Wyvern Social Club on Seel Street on Tuesday, 10 May 1960 to play for the Beatles at the audition.

This was the cue for the Beatles to get their act together. Accordingly, they began to rehearse in earnest. They also bought matching stage clothes: black shirts with silver trim, black 'jean-like' trousers and white top 'bumper' shoes. The 'look' was definitely not the usual beat group style, it was much more 'art school'. On the day of the audition it definitely set them apart visually from the other groups.

John Lennon: "We looked arty compared with other groups who looked like clerks or dockers. We looked like students … so we had a bit of a classy touch straight away, which was different."[1]

Rory Storm and the Hurricanes passed on attending the audition in part because they had already accepted a summer season at Butlin's holiday camp in Pwllheli, North Wales, and in part because Rory was in no mood to risk losing his backing group should they be successful. Hence he would not allow them to attend, but he made sure he and Johnny Guitar *were* present mainly so that he could get his photograph taken alongside Billy Fury (the Storm and the Fury!).[2]

So when the day of the audition arrived Williams had lined up Cass and the Cassanovas, Derry and the Seniors and Gerry and the Pacemakers from the Stadium show for Larry to hear. To give more choice and showcase the depth of talent in Liverpool, Williams added Cliff Roberts and the Rockers, the Pressmen and … the Beatles.

On the day, Tommy Moore's prevailing work commitments caused him to be late and so, very reluctantly, Johnny Hutchinson from the Cassanovas stood in for him. Cass of the Cassanovas had also persuaded them to change their 'rubbish' name from just 'The Beatles' to a proper group name. No one is exactly sure what they used, but it was an approximation along the lines of 'Long John and the Silver Beatles'.

It was not only sartorially that the Beatles stood apart from the other groups that day. They most definitely did musically.

George Harrison did not mince his words, describing their performance as, "A bit of a shambles … it felt pretty dismal."[3]

Johnny Gustafson from Cass and the Cassanovas concurred: "They made an awful racket, a raucous row. George's guitar playing was poor, stumbling … They were

Johnny Gentle: singer, songwriter and recording star. (John and Gavin Askew)

amateurish, but they could sing. John and Paul's vocals were pretty good, enough for me to notice them."[4]

Just how good or how poor they actually were has become clouded in myth and mystery. Adding more confusion to the plot, Allan Williams said they did well enough to be offered the most coveted spot of all, that of backing Billy Fury in Great Yarmouth. This seems quite incredible, but whether it was or not, it didn't happen. Unfortunately, the offer came from Parnes with a proviso that they 'dump' the bass player. Such was his loyalty to the group and to Stuart, John Lennon resolutely refused to do so. As a result, none of the groups auditioned that day walked away with that precious contract to back Fury.

Not all left empty-handed, however, for Cass and the Cassanovas were chosen to back Power and Gentle on their June jaunts around Scotland, while Derry and the Seniors were offered a place on a Parnes summer show in Blackpool, 'Idols on Parade'.

Enthused by their experience at the audition and encouraged by Williams, the Beatles now began to perform/practise regularly at the 'Jac'. It's unlikely Tommy Moore accompanied them on these occasions, but Ringo Starr saw them for the very first time around about then when he turned up with Rory and Johnny Guitar at the club on Saturday 14 May 1960. (As has been noted at the end of Chapter 12, that same evening the Beatles played their audition for Brian Kelly at a 'jive' dance at Lathom Hall in Seaforth, north Liverpool, their first appearance in a genuine rock venue. Kelly was impressed enough to book them again for the following Saturday 21 May, at the same venue.)

Any disappointment they may have felt about declining the Fury offer quickly faded when out of the blue the Beatles found themselves back in the frame for a booking to back another Parnes' act: Liverpool-born John Askew aka 'Johnny Gentle'. Apparently Gentle was not only booked to tour Scotland in June, but had an additional and earlier nine-day Scottish jaunt scheduled to start within days on Friday 20 May. Parnes had been unable to secure a backing group for him and so, by Tuesday 17 May, he was on the phone to Allan Williams desperate for musicians to fill the hole.

All the groups Williams turned to – Cass and the Cassanovas, Rory and the Hurricanes, Gerry and the Pacemakers, Derry and the Seniors – were, because of prior engagements or individual 'day job' work commitments, unable to step in and support Gentle. And so with just two days to go, and desperate not to let Parnes down, Williams turned to the Beatles. £75 was the fee he dangled in front of them, £15 per group member, but once more there was a proviso: the contract stipulated that there had to be five of them, the group *had* to have a drummer. They *so* wanted to go, but in their experience drummers were almost extinct in Liverpool, what chance of finding one in such a short time?

Undeterred, Allan Williams embarked on the task of persuading Tommy Moore to take time off from the Bottle Company and join the Beatles in Scotland. The other boys in the group had some persuading to do themselves. Paul McCartney was a week away from sitting his A Levels and should have been revising, George had only just landed a much-prized apprenticeship as an electrician at Blackler's Department Store, Stuart was approaching his Finals at art college and John also faced exams. Despite fierce opposition from all of their parents (except for John who, because he was not living at home at this time, simply never informed Aunt Mimi) they refused to lose out on what they each saw as a golden opportunity. This must have taken real guts to do and reflects the determination and self-belief with which they were infused. Indeed, such was the overwhelming draw of going out on the road as a bona fide rock 'n' roll group, John, Paul, George and Stuart simply could not resist the call and their enthusiasm eventually swept any parental opposition aside (and there *was* opposition).

Paul McCartney: "We all thought, 'This is it! We've arrived, we're showbiz people now.'"[5]

The absolute significance of this opportunity in the minds of the Beatles is evidenced by the fact that, despite such short notice, they seized upon it and against all the odds were all aboard the train. It was a big, big deal for them: here they were within a matter of days of having virtually no gigs at all to being paid as professional musicians to go on tour with a recognised recording star. They were the first Liverpool rock group to do so.

Apparently it was at this time that the group decided, once and for all, to drop the 'Silver' from their name and become simply, 'The Beatles': "While Stu held out for Beatals just a little longer, and Allan Williams continued to call them the Silver Beatles (and advertise them this way) well into the summer, they were, clean and clear, *the* Beatles."[6]

In the spirit of the times they changed their names. George became 'Carl Harrison' after Carl Perkins, Stuart became 'Stuart de Stael' after his favourite painter Nicolas de Stael, Paul became 'Paul Ramon' telling Mark Lewisohn he did so because it sounded 'like a sexy French name' and Tommy Moore signed autographs as 'Thomas Moore'.[7]

John was adamant he did not change his name, although Paul has said he definitely did. Apparently he became 'Long John Silver' or at least 'Johnny'. Not that it matters too much, but what matters most is that for these young Liverpool rock 'n' rollers opportunity had knocked and they had not hesitated to not only open the door but to walk straight through into an unknown future.

Billed as the 'Beat Ballad Show', it was to be a full-on experience with seven shows packed into nine days:

20 May, The Town Hall, Marsh Hill, Alloa
21 May, The Northern Meeting Ballroom, Church Street, Inverness
23 May, Dalrymple Hall, Seaforth Street, Fraserburgh
25 May, St Thomas' Hall, Chapel Street, Keith
26 May, The Town Hall, High Street, Forres
27 May, The Regal Ballroom, Leopold Street, Nairn
28 May, The Rescue Hall, Prince Street, Peterhead

When advertising space allowed, in local journals venues described Gentle as 'Star of TV and Decca Recording Fame'. They may have got his record label wrong (he was signed to Philips, not Decca) but they got right the bits that really mattered: TV, Recording, Fame and Star.

When the Beatles arrived in Scotland on Friday evening 20 May, awaiting them in the ballroom of Alloa Town Hall in Clackmannanshire, was none other than the star of the show: Johnny Gentle himself. From the get-go they took to Johnny and he to them. Together they enjoyed a good working relationship.

A Scouser just like them, Johnny Gentle may not have been in the top echelon of the Larry Parnes stable yet, but he was on his way as a bona fide recording artist with a good voice. Significantly he wrote many of his own songs which, once they got to know, would surely have resonated with John and Paul in particular. His records were not songs to which the Beatles would have been instinctively drawn to perform themselves, and they certainly weren't troubling the charts, but they were being critically well received in the music papers and being played on the radio. Gentle was a 'name' and very much a 'star' who was appearing in the major fan magazines. He was filling theatres and this tour was serious stuff. In this moment of time he was the 'real deal' to which the Beatles aspired.

It should be noted that while not a chart act at the time the Beatles toured with him, Johnny Gentle was considered to be a contender … No less an authority on 'pop music' than acclaimed television producer, Jack Good had proclaimed him as such, writing that: "Johnny Gentle is one of the new school – good-looking, quiet, relaxed". Good had predicted Gentle's rise as a major member of the Larry Parnes 'stable' in his weekly column that he contributed to the UK's popular music weekly *Disc*. In the 2 January 1960 edition, in an article entitled, 'Gentle, Eager and Fury Tussle for Coveted Spot', Good had focused on "the fierce rivalry in the Parnes stable." Noting that Tommy Steele and Marty Wilde were the undisputed top two in this hierarchy, Good speculated as to who was ultimately going to join them in that upper tier. Good wrote that although Vince Eager currently held that position, "Johnny Gentle is coming up very strongly to challenge both Fury and Eager … he does very well in a noise dominated show through sheer contrast and relief." Acknowledging singer Dickie Pride as a major talent within the Parnes stable, Good discounted him as a contender because he was, apparently, "unpredictable and … self-opinionated." With Pride unlikely to change his ways, Good concluded that, "Meanwhile Gentle, Eager and Fury fight it out over his head."[8]

This was not only setting the bar high but Good was clear in his opinion that Johnny Gentle had what it took to make the top.

Two weeks later, in the same music weekly, *Disc*, singles reviewer Don Nicholl had this to say about Gentle's new release 'Darlin' Won't You Wait', describing it as "a light flowing romancer which weaves a pretty spell. A song which won't take long to make you join in … Johnny Gentle handles it with the soft touch necessary." Giving it three stars (out of five) Nicholls predicted that "given a push" Johnny's single could make the chart.[9]

Nicholls' review suggests that Johnny was not a rocker, for example, in the same vein as Billy Fury. However, this was undoubtedly more to do with Larry Parnes and how he tried to mould his artists' style/public persona to match the names he bestowed upon them than on Gentle's own personal musical preferences.

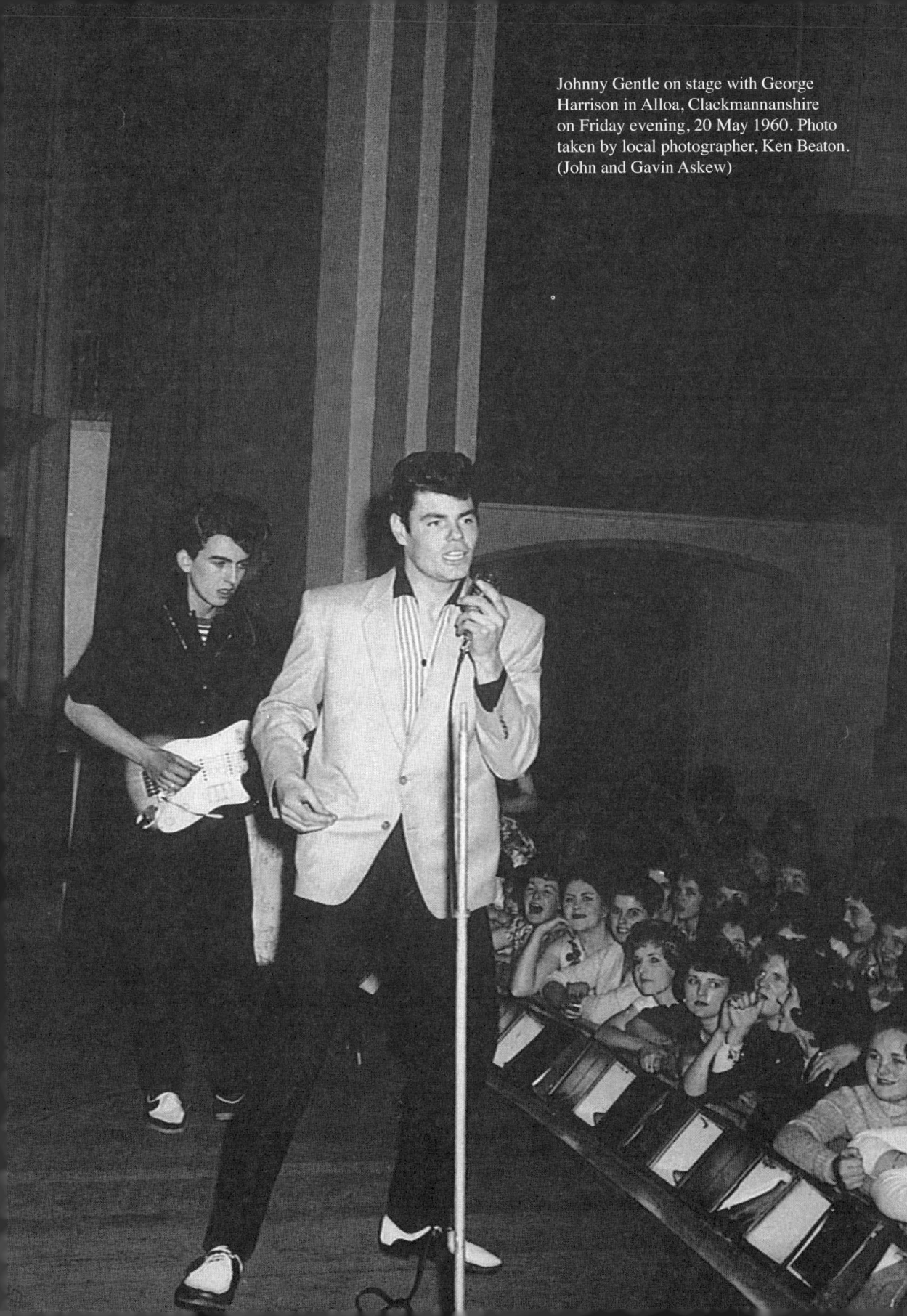

Johnny Gentle on stage with George Harrison in Alloa, Clackmannanshire on Friday evening, 20 May 1960. Photo taken by local photographer, Ken Beaton. (John and Gavin Askew)

Gentle was used to not meeting his backing group until the day of the show. This was the lot of most solo singers in those days, but the 'Silver' Beatles must have appeared more ramshackle than most. They only had one set of stage clothes, one decent amp and looked a mess. While Johnny was a genuine 'star', the Silver Beatles were mere beginners, amateurs in comparison.

Because Larry Parnes never quite knew precisely who would be backing Johnny (or any of his other stars for that matter) for live performances, to keep things simple Johnny was advertised as 'Johnny Gentle and His Group'. Once he and the Beatles had assembled north of the border, however good or bad they turned out to be, there was no going back: the tickets were selling, the shows *had* to go on.

George Harrison: "We were like orphans. Our shoes were full of holes and our trousers were a mess, while Johnny had a posh suit ... We were crummy, horrible, an embarrassment ... We didn't have amplifiers or anything."[10]

Johnny Gentle: "We met up in Scotland about half an hour before we were due on stage. Fortunately, I had sent them a repertoire of the sort of things we'd be likely to do. They did practise it. When we met up I gave them the keys and when we got together they were sort of half way there with the session."[11]

Entitled the 'Beat Ballad Show Tour' (which neatly summed up from where Gentle was coming in terms of his performance and as a recording artist) John, Paul, George, Stuart and Tommy not only backed Johnny as 'His Group', but as 'The Beatles' they also played a set of their own at each venue.

Johnny's set remained the same for each night of the tour and, surprisingly, did not include any of the songs he had released as singles. Johnny's memoir says, "His stage act consisted mostly of slow ballads and although blessed with a strong voice the nearest to rock Johnny got was when he blasted out Buddy Holly's 'It Doesn't Matter Anymore'."[12]

Gentle's memoir also lists the songs Johnny and the Beatles ran through prior to going on stage together that first evening in Alloa as being: the aforementioned Buddy Holly's 'It Doesn't Matter Anymore', plus Buddy's 'Raining in My Heart', Elvis's 'I Need Your Love Tonight' (which was released as a double A-side with 'A Fool such as I' which had topped the UK charts in May 1959), Ricky Nelson's 'Poor Little Fool', Eddie Cochran's 'C'mon Everybody', Jim Reeves' 'He'll Have to Go' and a song recorded in the Fifties by both Jim Reeves and Elvis – 'Have I Told You Lately?'. As always Johnny closed his set with a rousing version of Peggy Lee's 'Ok, You Win' (from her 1959 album *Things Are Swingin'*) during which "the band and him traded responses with the audience." (Peggy Lee was just one of many artists who liked this song. Written by Mayme Watts and Sid Wyche it was first released as a single by Ella Johnson in 1955. Count Basie, Eydie Gorme and Bobby Darin were just three of many others to record versions.)[13]

George Harrison recalled that Gentle rocked it up even more by performing versions of the Elvis songs 'Teddy Bear' and 'Wear My Ring around Your Neck' (UK chart hits for the King in 1957 and '58 respectively).

Mark Lewisohn notes that other songs in the Gentle repertoire (but not necessarily performed on the 'Beat Ballad Show' tour) included his take on 'Only Sixteen', a UK number 1 for Craig Douglas in late August and all of September 1959, 'Living Doll', a number 1 for Cliff Richard in the summer of '59, 'A Teenager in Love', another summer of '59 UK hit for three acts – Dion and the Belmonts with their original US version, Marty Wilde and Craig Douglas. Marty Wilde took the song all the way to number 2. Apparently Johnny also did a version of the popular jazz standard 'I'm Confessin' (That I Love You)' that had begun life in 1929 with the title 'Lookin' for Another Sweetie' when recorded by Thomas 'Fats' Waller and His Babies. It gained new lyrics and became 'Confessin' a year later.)[14]

The opening show in Alloa also featured performances from local Scottish acts: Alex Harvey and the Beat Band (billed as 'Scotland's own Tommy Steele') and 'Ballad Singer' Babby Rankine.

THE SONGS THE BEATLES GAVE AWAY

Tickets cost 4/- each before 10pm and 5/- after 10pm. Doors opened at 8:30pm with the show running from 9:30pm until 1:30am. Due to the late finish, buses had been laid on 'After the Dance to the HILLFOOTS DISTRICT'.[15]

Johnny, the undisputed star of the show, took the stage from 10:30 until 11pm. For the 'star' to perform for only half an hour or so was the norm back then. This was not an event to which the youngsters had come just to sit and listen to a series of acts perform, but primarily it was a 'Late Night Dance'. That's how it was advertised and so for the majority of the evening the kids expected to strut their stuff, dancing to 'live' music as well as to records. Consequently, the support acts would have been booked expressly to provide the music for the kids to dance to. According to Gentle after his performance, the Beatles played their own set until midnight before Alex Harvey took the stage from 12 to 1:30am. (In 1971, commenting on their tour with Johnny Gentle, John Lennon said they'd only perform for about 20 minutes on their own.)

During Johnny's performance, as arranged before the show, local freelance photographer Ken Beaton took some pictures. These were taken during Johnny's second song, a performance of Buddy Holly's 'It Doesn't Matter Anymore'.

One of Ken's photographs was a magnificent full-length shot of Gentle on stage with guitarist George Harrison in the background. Years later, when Johnny's son Gavin developed this picture to expose more of its background, just behind George's left shoulder John Lennon's profile could clearly be discerned.

Another of Beaton's photographs accompanied a report on the concert published in the local newspaper. Entitled 'Gentle Admirers Were Gentle', it was to be the only write-up the tour received and made no direct mention of Johnny's backing group. However, it did note that while the show was packed and there were lots of screams it was more decorous than other recent beat shows staged in the Town Hall. Some girls did try to mount the stage to get closer to Johnny and someone did throw pennies at the star. Fortunately, the police were on hand to ensure law and order was maintained: the penny-thrower was swiftly ejected and the girls failed in their attempt to reach Johnny G.[16]

N.B. *In his memoir Johnny Gentle (and Ian Forsyth) list the songs the Beatles played in their solo spot on that first night in Alloa:*
'Hello Little Girl' (a Lennon-McCartney 'original')*
The Everly's 'Bye Bye Love'
Little Richard's 'Tutti Frutti', 'Long Tall Sally' and 'Lucille'
Eddie Cochran's 'Twenty Flight Rock' and 'Hallelujah I love Her So'
Elvis's 'Stuck on You'
Buddy Holly's 'That'll Be the Day', later 'Words of Love'
Gene Vincent's 'Be-Bop-a-Lula' and 'Wild Cat'
Ray Charles's 'What'd I Say'
Chuck Berry's 'Little Queenie'
The Olympics 'Hully Gully'

(On the fourth show of the tour, Wednesday 25th May 1960, at St. Thomas' Hall, Chapel Street, Keith, apparently, the Beatles tried out some other songs in their set which were:
'One After 909' (a Lennon-McCartney 'original' recently completed by John in the Spring when he was living in Gambier Terrace)**

Buddy Holly's 'Words Of Love'
Little Richard's 'Jenny Jenny' and a medley of his tunes, 'Hey Hey Hey' and 'Kansas City' (which went down particularly well)[17]

* & ** *Johnny's memoir does not quote the source for this list of songs – which is impressive in its recall - and so cannot be verified but it is interesting given it includes two 'originals' at a time when the group was not known for including such material in their stage repertoire.*

So ramshackle were they that first night, according to Johnny Gentle, that Duncan MacKinnon the promoter in Scotland who acted for Larry Parnes, got on the phone after the first night in Alloa to complain, "What the hell have you sent me here, Larry?" Gentle himself was not fazed by McKinnon's dismay. "I was so used to having groups that I hadn't worked with before – that's how it was in those days. Unless you were Billy (Fury) or Marty (Wilde) you had a different group each time and some were good and some were bad. As it happens, I thought the Beatles were pretty good. I got a call the next day from Larry who said Duncan was upset … I told him, 'Look Larry, we'd only got together half an hour before we went on stage. I think the lads will be good because they're enthusiastic and they want to learn, they're watching me like a hawk.'"[18]

Gentle remembers that, as they had the next day off, he suggested that they all rehearse and see how it went after that: "We rehearsed all day the next day and we went out on that night and it was a different story completely. MacKinnon was knocked out, so the problem was no more. They (the Beatles) were with us from then on right until the end of the tour and they improved each show that we did. And because they were coming into their own by the end of the tour I'm getting encores and girls screaming. Afterwards I remember George saying that, on reflection, 'It was hard work, wearing black shirts, shoddy shoes and jeans – we didn't feel up to it'. But John Lennon said that he enjoyed it, that it was the start of things to come."[19]

As a more rehearsed Johnny Gentle 'and His Group' took the stage in Inverness on Saturday 21 May, back home in Seaforth, an increasingly agitated and angry Brian Kelly was waiting for that very same 'Group' to turn up at the Lathom Hall. Confronted with an empty stage and a roomful of eager teenagers all revved up to be entertained by, and 'jive' to, his headline act 'The Silver Beats' he was an unhappy man who was becoming unhappier by the minute. (Fortunately he'd also booked Kingsize Taylor and the Dominoes, and so all was not lost for poor Brian Kelly and his expectant punters.)

Life on the road in Scotland was not comfortable for the Beatles. It was thankless. They did not receive expenses and so had to pay for their own meals and on two occasions had to pay for accommodation. They travelled in a van in which there weren't enough seats. Group camaraderie was in short supply among the so-called 'friends'. The hapless Stu Sutcliffe bore the brunt of everyone's sharp tongues and rampant egos. John Lennon recalled that, "We were terrible. We'd tell Stu he couldn't sit with us, or eat with us. We'd tell him to go away, and he did … That was how he learned to be with us. It was all stupid, but that was what we were like."[20]

Poor Tommy Moore, some nine years older than Lennon, was also a prime target. For a start, Tommy liked jazz, he was much older than the others and unable to compete with their cruel jibes. Bob Wooler could see he was ripe for John's vitriol: "Tommy Moore came in for the Lennon treatment … he was not able to cope with the Lennon attitude and, taking his lead, McCartney could be similar … poor Tommy had to mind his p's and q's with them. He was so forlorn because their IQs were miles ahead of his."[21]

During a day's break in Inverness (Sunday 22 May 1960) Johnny Gentle, John Lennon and George Harrison took the opportunity to hang out together. As mentioned previously, Gentle was not just a performer, he also wrote songs and on the two singles he'd released in 1959 three of the four songs featured were his own compositions: 'Boys and Girls (Were Meant for Each Other)', 'Wendy' and 'I Like the Way'. As they sat around jamming, Gentle played a song he was working on called 'I've Just Fallen for Someone'.

Johnny Gentle: "The middle-eight was a bit unfinished and I didn't like it. But as I say, we were jamming around and I played it to John and he said, 'Yeah, that's a good song, are you going to record it?' I said, maybe one day in the future but not with that middle-eight. He started thinking for a minute and then he said, 'This could fit in'. And, from nowhere he started playing: *'We know that – we'll get by, just wait and see / Just like the – song tells us / The best things in life are free.'* And it did, it went absolutely perfect. He didn't want

John Askew aka Johnny Gentle's handwritten music and lyrics for his song 'I've Just Fallen'. Adam Faith recorded this tune as 'Ive Just Fallen for Someone', as did John Askew himself under the name of Darren Young. Written while on tour in Scotland in May 1960 John enlisted the help of his backing group's rhythm guitarist, John Lennon, with the middle-eight. (John and Gavin Askew)

any credit for it. In those days I threw things to other songwriters, anything I could think of. But I thought, blimey, a young lad of 19 – I was 22 at the time – you know, I'd written quite a few, recorded quite a few, and I thought, he's got talent."[22]

And so, without blinking an eye, John Lennon had helped Johnny Gentle complete 'I've Just Fallen for Someone'. John Lennon never referred to the tune himself but significantly his middle-eight referenced Barrett Strong's lyric from his song, 'Money', a tune that John most definitely made his own as a Beatle.

Gentle's song, replete with the uncredited John Lennon 'giveaway' middle-eight, was eventually recorded by Adam Faith and released in 1961 as track two, side one of his eponymous second album which peaked at number 20 in the UK album chart on 24 March 1962. It also featured as one of three tunes culled from the *Adam Faith* album for a second EP release of tracks from the album that bore the same cover photograph and title of the LP (the fourth track on the EP was his number 4 single from 29 November 1961, 'The Time Has Come').

In the summer of 1962, Gentle also recorded and released the song under his new stage name, Darren Young. Issued on the Parlophone label, it was the B-side of 'My Tears Will Turn to Laughter'. Gentle wrote both sides of the single and for the first time his compositions were credited under his real name, John Askew. Chart-wise the single sank without trace.

'I've Just Fallen for Someone' may not count as the first Beatle 'giveaway' because it was, in essence, Gentle/Askew's own song, but it maybe counts as the first 'donation' to a tune. As things are today, any contribution to a song would count as a collaboration and consequently a share in any royalties earned.

Back on the Scottish tour, the day after the songwriting session, just three days into the excursion, the Dormobile van in which they were all travelling (driven by Johnny Gentle himself on this occasion) collided with a car. Fortunately, they were mostly unscathed, except for poor Tommy who was hit in the face and ended up in hospital. Bruised and battered with stitches in his face and several teeth missing, valiantly he struggled on playing but received no thanks or respite whatsoever from Lennon's cruel barbs.

They returned to Liverpool on Monday 30 May. During ten days away they had played seven shows in the space of eight days. This represented seven more shows than they had played in the preceding five months. Never having played before with all electric guitars including bass and a drummer they had been inexperienced to say the least. Paul would describe it in a BBC Radio 2 documentary, *The Beatles in Scotland*, which was broadcast on 24 September 1996, as "a vital experience" during which they learned being on tour was "no breeze".[23]

Johnny Gentle and the Silver Beatles had got on well on tour and so it was not surprising that the solo star looked them up the next time he was back in Liverpool. Together with his father, Johnny turned up at the Jacaranda in the hope the boys might be there. Unfortunately they weren't, but Allan Williams directed them to the Grosvenor Ballroom in Liscard, Wallasey where they were scheduled to play that evening. The date was Saturday 2 July 1960 and Johnny decided to surprise them and turn up at the show. He was warmly received and invited on stage to perform some tunes with his former backing band. Apparently the Silver Beatles and Johnny ran through their complete Scottish tour set.

Back home from their Scottish adventure, it was time to put the lessons learned on the road into practice. For this they needed to be performing regularly, remunerated for what they did and so able to invest in some decent equipment.

It was Allan Williams who saw to it that the momentum was not lost. While they had been in Scotland he had secured them regular gigs 'over the water' (aka the River Mersey) on the Wirral peninsula. Consequently, on their return a series of shows at the Grosvenor Ballroom, Liscard, Wallasey, and the Institute in Neston, had been booked.

By now Williams had become the rock on which the Beatles depended. The group and their girlfriends were regulars at the 'Jac' and Allan was finding them gigs and generally championing their cause.

A major hitch occurred on Monday 13 June when, at a booking at the 'Jac', Tommy Moore finally quit the group. Nothing would entice him back, he had taken all he could. John's sharp tongue had done for him, "I'd had a bellyful of that Scottish tour when we got back, and I'd had a bellyful of Lennon."[24]

By pure chance a new drummer joined briefly, one Norman Chapman, but his tenure was cut short by his call up for National Service.

That John and Paul were continuing to write their own tunes as well as learn lots of covers is evidenced by a tape they made in June at 20 Forthlin Road. By then the Beatles had acquired a Selmer Truvoice amplifier and Paul borrowed a tape recorder so they (mainly John, Paul and Stuart) could record some tunes. 19 songs were cut. They were mainly covers and included tunes by Carl Perkins, Gene Vincent, Elvis Presley, Duane Eddy and others. Most interestingly the tape includes six 'originals': 'One After 909', 'I'll Follow the Sun' and 'Hello Little Girl', plus three others. The group never returned to the other three they recorded on this tape and Mark Lewisohn identifies them by the following titles: 'Some Days', 'You Must Write Everyday' and 'You'll Be Mine'. John had written 'One After 909' while living in the flat on Gambier Terrace. 'Hello Little Girl' was his from late 1957, while Paul's song 'I'll Follow the Sun' had been written earlier at 20 Forthlin Road some time during the first half of 1959.

ADAM FAITH
b. Terence Nelhams-Wright, 23 June 1940, Acton, London
d. 8 March 2003, Stoke-on-Trent, Staffordshire

Adam Faith
Parlophone LP PMC1162
Arranger, Conductor and Musical Director: John Barry
Les Reed, piano
Mike Peters, bass
14 tracks (seven each side)
Side 1, Track 2: I've Just Fallen for Someone (Askew)
Released 1961

Adam Faith
with accompaniment directed by John Barry
Parlophone EP GEP 8851
Recording first published 1961
Side 2, Track 1: 'I've Just Fallen for Someone' (Askew)

DARREN YOUNG
aka Johnny Gentle
b. John Askew, 8 December 1936, Liverpool
A-side: 'My Tears Will Turn to Laughter' (Askew)
Ardmore & Beechwood Ltd
Parlophone 45R 4919
B-side: 'I've Just Fallen for Someone' (Askew)
Lawrence Wright
Both sides recorded with John Barry and His Orchestra
Release date: 15 June 1962

Both the above mentioned versions of Johnny's song were released on Parlophone before the label released any material by the Beatles ('Love Me Do' was issued on 5 October 1962).

Johnny aka Darren did not make the chart with his single although it sold approximately 30,000 copies. He did not release any more material as Darren Young and later briefly joined the Viscounts with whom in 1964 he cut a single for Columbia entitled 'Sally' (B-side 'On Broadway').

Johnny wrote songs for Troy Dante and Jess Conrad and during the Sixties continued in his own right as a singer playing mainly clubs. By the early Seventies, John had left show business and built a successful career with his own building and carpentry business.

Addendum: *The Life and Times of singer-songwriter Johnny Gentle*
Born in a terraced house just off Scotland Road on 8 December 1936, John Askew grew up in what was always described as a 'tough' area of Liverpool, close to the docks. The Askews – Mum, Dad, John and his sisters Ann and Joan were a close family. His mum wanted John to become a singer while Dad simply wanted him to be happy and believed that gaining a trade would help his son achieve this. John would go on to achieve both his parents' ambitions for him.

It was his skill with wood that allowed John to build his own first guitar in 1957. Aged 20/21 at the time, he was working as an apprentice carpenter for shipbuilders Harland & Wolff. Spotting a plan to make your own guitar in a back issue of The Woodworker magazine, he persuaded his kindly supervisor to allow him, as part of his 'training', to use offcuts of wood to make an instrument. Not long after it was completed John began singing with his friend Bobby Crawford and the two would perform together at local social and working men's clubs. At sea during his downtime he continued to practise his guitar playing and singing. One of his favourite tunes to perform was Ricky Nelson's version of Sharon Sheeley's 'Poor Little Fool' (a recording that was graced by James Burton's wonderful guitar playing).

On returning to Liverpool in 1958 after completing his first voyage as a fully fledged ship's carpenter, John found his mother to be critically ill. Sadly, she died not long after and John, emboldened by success in a Butlin's Pwllheli Holiday Camp talent contest, made the momentous decision not to return to sea but to pursue a career as a singer. In the process John Askew became 'Rick Damone' in honour of his American rock 'n' roll heroes Ricky Nelson and Vic Damone.

As Rick Damone, he enjoyed success in another talent contest, this time one held at Liverpool's Locarno Ballroom in late 1958 (among the contestants might well have been the Quarry Men who had a penchant for entering such contests ... and losing). His prize was a paid residency at the club. This success inspired Askew to re-locate to London, the home of the UK's music industry where he survived by mixing working on a building site with playing the occasional gig at the 2i's in Soho and writing songs.

While in London he wrote – in his own name – to music impresario and manager of Billy Fury, the one and only Larry Parnes. Parnes was impressed enough by what he read to invite John to meet him at his Oxford Street office. At his audition John played his own songs 'Wendy' and 'Boys and Girls (Were Meant for Each Other)' which Parnes liked. Realising the talent Askew possessed, the impresario quickly arranged a recording test for him with Philips which, as fully expected, John passed. Next came a recording contract and a debut single comprising both songs he had sung for Larry. 'Wendy' was chosen for the A-side and it was released during the last week of March 1959.

Reviewed in the music journal Disc by Don Nicholl (28 March 1959) Johnny's first single achieved a creditable 3 stars. Nicholls described 'Boys and Girls' as a 'quiet ballad' possessed of a 'a country style' and Johnny as having "an easy, liquid voice". Significantly he compared Johnny to singer Russ Hamilton (who'd scored a number 2 UK hit in 1957 with 'We Will Make Love') and declared that Johnny struck him "as a better vocalist". Nicholls also noted that, "Both numbers on this record were written by Gentle himself."[25]

From the moment John Askew had written to Parnes he knew that if he passed his audition Larry would choose a new stage name for him. And so it came to pass: Johnny Gentle was what he came up with, believing it reflected Johnny's quiet nature. As such Johnny became the fifth recruit to Parnes's famous 'stable' of young rock 'n' rollers (Tommy Steele, Marty Wilde, Billy Fury and Vince Eager had preceded him). At first, Johnny had misgivings with 'Gentle' as his new stage name, but he grew to like it and it certainly beat Parnes's original suggestion of 'Tim McGee', which Askew had simply refused to countenance as soon as it had been suggested.

As Johnny Gentle, life took on a different hue. He had become a 'star' and was soon living in a flat in Paddington in a house which locals dubbed 'Rock and Roll House' because other tenants included Billy Fury, Gerry Dorsey (aka Engelbert Humperdinck), Joe Brown, the Viscounts, the Dallas Boys and, for a brief time, American rocker Gene Vincent.

1960 dawned with Johnny Gentle enjoying his third, critically acclaimed single release 'Darling Won't You Wait' hitting the shops and for which hopes were high. Elsewhere, TV producer Jack Good was tipping him in Disc as an artist on a par with Billy Fury, while he featured regularly in the pages of popular teen magazines Roxy, Girl and Boyfriend ... He was cresting a wave of popularity and for one night only found himself added to the Eddie Cochran-Gene Vincent tour when it rocked up in Bristol at the Hippodrome on Saturday 16 April.

Having driven himself and his girlfriend Marjorie Overall (Marj) to the gig, Johnny had promised another performer on the show, vocalist Peter Wynne, a lift back to London. After the show Eddie Cochran popped in to his dressing room to inquire if he, his girlfriend Sharon Sheeley (a songwriter who had penned 'Poor Little Fool' among others) and Gene Vincent could share a lift with Johnny back to London where they were hoping to catch a plane back to the USA to take advantage of a two-week break in their UK tour itinerary. Unfortunately Johnny's car was too small to accommodate them: with himself, Marj and Peter already aboard there was only one seat left and so reluctantly he couldn't help Eddie.

Instead Eddie, Sharon and Gene, together with tour manager Patrick Tompkins, hired a driver, one George Martin and his car to take them to the airport. On their way the car went out of control and hit a concrete lamp post. The impact threw Cochran from the vehicle. The singer endured massive head injuries from which he did not recover. Sharon, Gene and Patrick were also injured but survived. George the driver was largely unscathed. No other vehicles were involved in the accident. Ironically, on their way home that night, Johnny, Marj and Peter not only passed the scene of the accident but, as they were running short of petrol, and all-night garages few and far between, the recovery team *at the accident allowed them to siphon some fuel from the tank of the damaged vehicle which enabled them to complete their journey home ... they did so completely unaware of the circumstances surrounding the accident ... Although he knew he could have done nothing to prevent what happened that night, it was an evening that haunted Johnny for many years to come.*

1 John Lennon from an interview with Pete McCabe and Robert D. Schonfeld, September 1971, as quoted in the Extended Special Edition of *The Beatles – All These Years: Volume One: Tune In*, by Mark Lewisohn (Little, Brown, 2013) p.614.
2 The story of why the Hurricanes did not attend the Larry Parnes audition and of Rory having his photo taken with Bill Fury, told by Johnny Guitar to Dave Ravenscroft at the Beatles Convention, the Adelphi Hotel, Liverpool, 30 August 1998.
3 *The Beatles Anthology*, by The Beatles, (Cassell & Co. 2000) p.44.
4, 5, 6, 7, 14 *The Beatles – All These Years: Volume One: Tune In*, Extended Special Edition, by Mark Lewisohn, (Little, Brown, 2013), pp.616, 625, 624, 627.
8 *Disc* (The Top Record & Music Weekly) published every Thursday price 6d. Edition no. 93, 2 January 1960, From Jack Good's article on p.18 entitled 'Gentle, Eager and Fury Tussle For Coveted Spot'.
9 *Disc*, 16 January 1960, Edition no.95, From 'Disc Date', Singles Reviews by Don Nicholl, p.16.
10 *The Beatles Anthology*, the Beatles, (Cassell & Co. 2000) George Harrison comment from p.44.
11, 18, 19 & 22 Johnny Gentle interviewed by Bob Harris OBE for the BBC Radio 2 documentary, *The Songs the Beatles Gave Away*, broadcast 28 November 2009, written and narrated by Bob Harris, produced by Bob and Trudie Myerscough-Harris for WBBC.
12, 13, 15, 17 *Johnny Gentle & the Beatles First Ever Tour* by Johnny Gentle & Ian Forsyth (Merseyrock Publications, 1998) p. 40, 41.
16 *The Alloa Circular and Hillfoots Record*, 25 May 1960 and featured in *The Beatles – All These Years: Volume One: Tune In*, Extended Special Edition by Mark Lewisohn, (Little Brown, 2013) p.627/8.
20 *The Beatles: The Authorised Biography*, Hunter Davies, (Heinemann, 1968) John Lennon p.71.
21 *The Best of Fellas: the Story of Bob Wooler* by Spencer Leigh (Drivegreen Publications Limited in association with Jim Turner, 2002) p. 67.
23 *The Beatles In Scotland*, BBC Radio 2, 24 September 1996.
24 *The Man Who Gave the Beatles Away*, Allan Williams and William Marshall (Coronet Books, Hodder and Stoughton, 1976) Allan Williams recalls Tommy Moore's reaction to touring Scotland as a Silver Beatle, p.53.
25 *Disc*, 28 March 1959, Edition 60, 'Our Weekly Disc Date' with Don Nicholl, p.7.

PART 2

HAMBURG

Chapter 15:
PETE BEST TO THE RESCUE

Mid-1960 reality for the Beatles was that the dates Allan had found for them on the Wirral came to an end and drummer Norman Chapman disappeared into the army. Once again personnel issues were threatening to grind the group to a halt. Not only that but pressure from concerned parents to sort themselves out (i.e. get a job) was never far away.

It was certainly the case for Paul, whose father Jim clung to the hope his son would buckle down once and for all to his studies. George's father Harry had been mortified by his son abandoning his precious apprenticeship as an electrician at Blackler's store in Liverpool on a whim to play his guitar in Scotland for a week. (George's mum, Louise, always supported him in his musical endeavours.) Neither father had changed their views. By this time John had failed his final art school exams and made the decision to become a professional musician. Mimi knew exactly what her errant nephew had been up to and was, predictably, outraged. In 1961, only Stuart had the security of continuing at art college for a fifth year.

Cynthia Lennon: "All the ideas that everyone else had for him of making an impact on the art world faded into the back of beyond with incredible rapidity, and with almost no regret at all. John's aunt … Mimi, however, was distraught and agitated at the prospect of her charge racing headlong into an unpredictable future armed only with an old guitar, with no qualifications and virtually penniless. Her view of his future couldn't have been blacker…"[1]

To add to their woes John and Stuart were about to be evicted from Gambier Terrace.

And yet, once again, just as it truly seemed all was finally drawing to a close for the luckless Beatles, Allan Williams intervened to provide a lifeline.

His relationship with Parnes had soured to such an extent that an arrangement he'd agreed with the London-based entrepreneur for Derry and the Seniors to appear for a summer season in Blackpool, as part of the 'Idols on Parade' show, fell through. The problem here for Williams was that he had persuaded the group to give up their well-paid jobs to undertake this booking. Suddenly, and not without reason, the boys in that group were distinctly unhappy and pressurising him to find an alternative.

What happened next to save the day was an unbelievable series of coincidences.

In a moment of desperation, on July 24, Williams took Derry and the Seniors to London to the famous 2i's Club where he knew the manager, Tom Littlewood, whom he hoped could help. By the most amazing stroke of good fortune, Littlewood's regular groups were all away on tour and so Derry and the Seniors were invited to set up and play. Even more unbelievably, sitting in the corner of the 2i's, was Bruno Koschmider from the Kaiserkeller in Hamburg. He was there to recruit another English group for his club. Once the five-piece Seniors took the stage, Koschmider knew he need look no further. They blew him away. Together with Williams he signed a contract for Derry and the Seniors to be paid £100 a week (less 10% for Williams) to play 30 hours a week for two months at the Kaiserkeller. The group were delighted and a week later as July became August they were in Germany and had begun their residency in Hamburg.

This stunning piece of good fortune was to provide the lifeline the Beatles so desperately needed.

For the beleaguered Beatles, their gigs on the Wirral ended abruptly after a show at the Grosvenor on Saturday 30 July, when Wallasey Corporation finally cancelled the season of 'jive' nights after repeated complaints about violence and rowdy behaviour at the venue. After this the only work they obtained was backing a striptease artiste appearing at Williams's private members' club, The New Cabaret Artists Club. Situated in Liverpool 8, Williams operated this venture with Lord Woodbine. Despondency was in the air but the Beatles never succumbed to it as a group. For them, hope sprang eternal and their faith that "Something will happen" was a constant mantra.

And, of course, it did: Derry and the Seniors had no sooner arrived in Hamburg when something happened that changed everything for ever for the Beatles.

As August entered its second week, Koschmider informed Williams that he needed another group to appear at a second club he ran called the 'Indra' on Grosse Freiheit, an offshoot of the Reeperbahn. He was converting the Indra from a transvestite cabaret club into a rock music club which he was determined to open on Wednesday 17 August. Koschmider was adamant that, just like Derry and the Seniors, the group he wanted for his new venture had to be a five-piece replete with a drummer. In his efforts to oblige Bruno, Williams turned to his usual stalwarts Cass and the Cassanovas, Gerry and the Pacemakers and Rory and the Hurricanes.

Fortuitously for John, Paul, George and Stuart, for one reason and another, Williams's preferred choices were all unavailable at such short notice and so it was, once again, with no one else able to step into the breach, Williams fell back on the Beatles.

So that they could undertake the engagement he even told them that he would drive them to Hamburg in his own van. Without hesitation they agreed, but with Tommy permanently back at work in the bottle factory and Norman in the army they were once again reduced to being a drummer-less four-piece group and the contract was absolutely clear: they had to be a five-piece *with* a drummer. With just a handful of days to go before they had to depart for Germany, they had to act swiftly. Their determination was rock solid, this was an opportunity they simply had to grab: the lack of personnel had to be sorted.

After drawing blanks in their search, George's recent trip to see Mona at the Casbah Club now paid dividends. The boys in the Beatles turned to Pete Best, Mona's son, who they knew had played drums with Ken Brown in the Blackjacks and whom George Harrison knew had just quit the group. Even more surprisingly for such a bright grammar student, Best had also quit school in order to 'try his hand' in the entertainment business. After the way they had treated his mother Mona by quitting the Casbah in their pique over cash, the Beatles' request for Pete to link up with them was a bit of a cheek, but they were utterly determined as well as desperate. Paul made the call and Pete amazingly said yes and attended an audition at one of Williams's clubs on Saturday 13 August. By then this could have been little else than a formality rather than a serious audition because the Beatles had no alternative, whatever they thought of Pete and his drumming, time had run out: it was a case of no Pete Best/no drummer = no Hamburg. Pete was *in*.

As departure zoomed closer by the hour, one after another Beatle parent capitulated in the face of the inevitable. Jim McCartney knew Paul's mind was set and no amount of persuasion on his part would deter him. He relented and let his son have his birth certificate in order to obtain a passport. Harry Harrison had also softened, he himself had gone abroad at 17 and deep down he understood his son's motivation to try something he was desperate to do before it was too late to do so. Louise always supported her son and so George had no problem getting his passport.

Stuart hesitated the most as he contemplated what going to Hamburg really meant for him. He was about to enter his fifth year at college and had already invested so much in his studies, had been so successful and received great acclaim for his talent. During his fifth year he would be studying for his ATD (Art Teacher's Diploma) which in turn would provide him with the much coveted security of 'a job for life' should he choose to take it. He was also the least musically competent member of the group, so for him there was much more to lose by going to Hamburg. At the eleventh hour he made his decision: his desire to be a rock 'n' roller had not waned. On Saturday 13 August, Stuart attended the Passport

Office in Liverpool and obtained his passport. This really was a case of leaving it to the last minute, for the office was only open on Saturdays 'for cases of special emergency'. By Monday morning Stuart, passport in pocket, was on his way to Hamburg.

From the moment Pete Best had been asked to accompany the group abroad he had agreed. Fortunately, he already had a passport.

Of all people, it was John Lennon who nearly did not make it. Not because he did not want to go, but because Aunt Mimi was so angry with his reckless and wayward attitude towards leaving college for the precarious life as a musician, she claimed she could not find his birth certificate, thus putting at risk his ability to obtain a passport. A virtual last-minute Monday morning dash *sans* his birth certificate to the Passport Office in Liverpool was required to secure the necessary papers. Clutching them in his hand, John immediately legged it to the Jacaranda where Allan and Beryl Williams, Beryl's younger brother Barry, Lord Woodbine, Paul, George, Stuart and Pete were loading up Allan's Morris J2 Minibus for the trip to Hamburg.

Nine people, plus all their guitars, drums, amps and personal luggage, were eventually crammed together inside (and on the top of) this small vehicle as it travelled all the way to Hamburg. Allan even took a diversion to London to pick up a tenth passenger, a Herr Steiner, an interpreter from Austria to whom Allan had agreed to give a lift.

At Harwich they boarded an overnight ferry, after which they took a circuitous, tiring trek via Arnhem to Hamburg. Over 36 hours of travel elapsed from when they left the 'Jac' to when they finally drove through the Reeperbahn and stumbled out into the bright and flashing lights of Grosse Freiheit. Every sense must have been working overtime as they took in what was to be their home and place of work for the next two months. The contract to which they had all committed their signatures bound them to work every day from 17 August until 16 October with only Mondays off. When everything had been added up, taken out and paid, each Beatle earned just about £14 for 40.5 hours work per week. (As mid-October approached their contract was extended until the end of November.)

There was no going back now, although in the early days given their dismal, dirty, miserably cold living quarters, relentless work and the seediness and violence of the neighbourhood, they must have longed for the comforts of home. They lived communally, there was no privacy, they washed in sinks, their laundry piled up, they ate bad food, and smoked excessively. When they were playing, drink was plentiful, often donated by grateful customers, so performing drunk was not unusual. Drugs – Preludin – also became integral to their ability to stay awake and keep on playing for hours and hours. This was the Reeperbahn and so sex was a given. It was forever on the menu and they were young men with young men's appetites and the menu offered a lot more than the usual bangers and mash that would have been on offer back home in Liverpool.

Fairly quickly Pete found a girlfriend and spent his downtime with her which left the other four to hang out together. Being so much in each other's company bonded them even more closely, except for Paul and Stuart. The tension between the two did not abate as Paul became more jealous of Stuart's closeness to John. To add to the friction, Paul became further irritated by Stuart's lack of ability on the bass: it seemed the more they played, in Paul's opinion Stuart never really improved and Paul fancied he could play the instrument better himself. These differences simmered beneath the surface and although there were regular flashpoints as a band, John, Paul, George, Stuart and Pete grew stronger and better. Playing the Indra night in, night out changed them beyond recognition.

Originally Derry Wilkie and the Seniors had been more than disappointed when they learned that Allan Williams was about to bring the Beatles to Hamburg. Allan had written to Howie Casey of the Seniors to inform him of his intention to do so and, almost by return, received a swift, sharp response. Howie was not one to mince his words and, un-minced, they went something like this: "We've got a great fucking scene going here in Hamburg. Now you want to fuck it up by sending over that bum group, the Beatles. They're no f-in' good. We don't want them here and they will be bad for the scene ... Don't send the f-in' Beatles."[2]

Clearly the Seniors remembered them as the ramshackle unit they had been back in Liverpool when they had auditioned for Larry Parnes. Howie urged Williams to bring over a group of the calibre of Rory Storm and the Hurricanes. The Seniors desperately wanted to keep the bar set high and the good thing going that they had created for themselves and Liverpool's other 'elite' groups.

Understandably then, when the Beatles rocked up in Hamburg, Derry and his cohorts were visibly underwhelmed, but their opinion changed very quickly when Howie caught their show at the Indra: "My jaw went to the floor. There was such a difference from what I'd seen at the audition. There was something there, a spark, that extra little bit. We did a bit of harmony singing but they were marvellous at it. They were stunning. You knew they were going to go places."[3]

On 4 October 1960, after some 48 nights on stage at the Indra, complaints from residents concerning the noise forced Koschmider to move the Beatles to the Kaiserkeller which was also on Grosse Freiheit Strasse. At the Kaiserkeller they had to alternate with Rory Storm and the Hurricanes who had arrived in Hamburg just three days earlier. Still very much a 'star' attraction with the Hurricanes was their drummer Ringo.

It was at the Kaiserkeller, egged on by enthusiastic patrons to 'mach Schau', that the Beatles' stage show became even more energetic, alcohol-fuelled and (on John's part especially) much more outrageous.

Inevitably working so closely together, Rory and his Hurricanes and the Beatles grew very close. In particular John, Paul and George became enamoured with Ringo as a drummer. Like Derry and the Seniors before them, the Hurricanes also had to adjust the negative opinion they had of the Beatles. Ringo summed it up by saying: "They were *great* in Hamburg. Really good – great rock. That's when the battle started. We played twelve hours on a weekend night between two bands. That's a hell of a long time, especially when in each set we were trying to top them and they were trying to top us."[4]

George was not so impressed with Ringo's group. In a letter to Arthur Kelly he wrote: "Rory Storm and the Hurricanes came out here the other week, and they are crumby. R does a bit of dancing around but it still doesn't make up for his phoney group." However, he was not entirely damning: "The only person who is any good in the group is the drummer."[5]

The Beatles themselves were an immediate success at the club.

Rory and his group received a better review on 15 October when a long-haired art student (and classically trained pianist) by the name of Klaus Voormann saw them live at the Kaiserkeller. After falling out with his photographer girlfriend, Astrid Kirchherr, Klaus had walked off into the night to think things over. Deep in thought he'd wandered onto the Reeperbahn where Astrid says, "He heard this music coming from an underground club called the Kaiserkeller. He was so intrigued he went into the club..."[6]

Like Astrid, Klaus was an 'Exi' or 'existentialist' who were influenced, among others, by (and were followers of) Jean Paul Sartre, Jean Genet and film-maker Jean Cocteau. As such he dressed and looked different to the club's regular clientele and so to venture inside the Kaiserkeller, Klaus was taking a real risk of trouble.

The music that drew Voormann into the club was, of course, rock 'n' roll and it was being played by Rory and the Hurricanes. Klaus was certainly impressed by what he heard. Although at college he had heard rock 'n' roll records by American artists, such as Fats Domino and Chuck Berry, Rory and the Hurricanes were his first experience of a 'live' rock 'n' roll group in action. They amazed him, especially their drummer: "Ringo was on drums. They were really good – just to see the drummer was incredible. I'd seen great jazz drummers at the Elbe Philharmonic Hall, and in clubs, but hearing a rock drummer was something else!"[7]

Impressed and excited though he was by Rory Storm and the Hurricanes' performance it was the group who followed them onto the stage that truly blew Klaus's mind.

"I stayed to hear the next band. They wore funny check jackets. This guy in sunglasses came on stage first, looking stunningly good ... he plugged in the bass and then the others came on. Someone said 'Hello' in German (it was Paul) and they just started playing. It was incredible – fantastic! Five people making such an amazing noise. What got me was their feel for rhythm, just a few instruments creating such a swinging, rocking music. They weren't playing wild solos. They were just young boys who, at that time, didn't have great musical capabilities, but their playing felt good, they were having fun doing it and the audience was having fun listening. It was just a fantastic feeling to see and hear all this. I was hooked."[8]

So captivated was he by the Beatles, Klaus returned the very next night with his girlfriend Astrid: "For both of us it was most definitely a life-changing experience ... from then on we went nearly every night and whenever else we could."[9]

Astrid herself told the author: "It is difficult to explain what it was like on that first night. It was like an explosion! You must not forget our fear of going there – of going down, not into a light beautiful room but somewhere that was filthy, dirty and dark. Then we looked at the stage and saw these wonderful creatures. Once I saw the Beatles my fear just went as I gazed transfixed at the five people on stage. They looked so different, and sang so beautifully. It was absolutely absorbing. I was no longer aware of the surroundings. In that instant my life had changed completely."[10]

Klaus and Astrid quickly encouraged other art student and 'Exi' friends including photographer Jürgen Vollmer to visit the Kaiserkeller. A strong friendship developed between the Beatles, Klaus, Astrid, Jürgen and their student friends. Stuart and Astrid quickly became smitten with each other and fell head over heels in love. They became engaged and he moved into her home where she lived with her mother. Despite losing his girlfriend to Stuart, Klaus was very understanding and remained a close friend of all the boys. Six years later in 1966, he was asked by John to design the cover for *Revolver*. Photographer Jurgen Vollmer was another close friend whose photo of John standing in a doorway in Hamburg was chosen for the cover of John's *Rock 'N' Roll* album in 1975.

Klaus also noted Stuart's improvement on bass: "Stuart was the heaviest rocker of the band. He really understood rock 'n' roll, he knew what it meant, what it was about and had a genuine feel for it, more so than any other Beatle. He believed in it. It wasn't just to do with the music, he really had an affinity with what it stood for. He needed it, he loved rock. He could feel every detail in the way somebody was singing or playing. He loved it to death but he himself was not a great musician. He had two hearts in his body, one was art and the other was music, and as a musician he was clever enough to realise that he was not a great player ... I just know that for the Beatles he played great bass. He played simple stuff, no messing about. He played very straight, very much on the point, and very rocky. He was really good."[11]

Paul remembered that if the Beatles were on stage, as the night wore on Ringo would often sit at the front and request mournful numbers such as 'Moonglow' and in particular the Duane Eddy instrumental '3.30 Blues'.

Klaus also noted the growing bond between Ringo and the Beatles. He saw them talking, having fun and overheard John, Paul and George discussing the possibility of changing drummers: "It wasn't said too explicitly because you don't just go and steal someone else's drummer, but they always liked Ringo."[12]

Despite Paul's dim view of Stuart as a bass player, Stuart committed even more to the group in Hamburg by buying a 16-watt Gibson Les Paul amplifier. This was the first actual piece of much revered American kit to be owned by any of the Beatles. It cost a staggering (for the time) £120, and was a big and very loud unit.

John also invested in a Rickenbacker 325 which became his signature instrument. An American instrument, he also bought an American amplifier to go with it – an 18-watt

Fender Deluxe. Because his own Rosetti was suffering from the hammering it was taking from being played every night, Paul borrowed John's Hofner Club 40 and re-strung it for a left-hander. Despite this, Paul passed on the opportunity to buy the Club 40 outright.

The Beatles' first trip to Hamburg was a towering success but it did not end well. They upset Bruno Koschmider, who was not a man to be crossed. They managed to do this by agreeing with Peter Eckhorn, the manager of the rival 'Top Ten Club' situated on the Reeperbahn itself, to play at his club. The money was going to be better as was their accommodation. Bruno retaliated by terminating their contract on the grounds that he'd discovered George Harrison was a minor (he was 17) and so he was too young to play in nightclubs. As a consequence, George was deported from Germany on 21 November.

Minus George, the Beatles honoured their contract with Bruno at the Kaiserkeller, but ahead of playing at the Top Ten Club they decided to move to the better accommodation Peter Eckhorn had arranged for them. As Pete and Paul packed their belongings, in order to see better what they were doing they apparently lit a condom and hung it on a nail which left a burn mark on the wall. Already piqued by what he considered the Beatles' 'desertion', Koschmider immediately called in the police and the two Beatles were arrested and subsequently deported for 'arson'. They arrived back in England on 1 December 1960.

John lingered a while longer until he finally left on 7 December. Stuart decided to remain in Hamburg with Astrid which, in effect, marked the beginning of his exit from the group.

Hamburg was pivotal in the evolution of the Beatles. It would continue to be so for much of the next year, but it was that very first visit in 1960 that was the most dramatic and life-changing experience of them all. It changed them for ever, not only as a group but as individuals. John nailed the significance of their German adventure when he said of himself, "I grew up in Hamburg, not Liverpool."[13]

---

1 *A Twist of Lennon*, by Cynthia Lennon (Star, 1978) p.40.
2 Allan Williams paraphrasing Howie Casey's letter in his autobiography, *The Man Who Gave the Beatles Away*, by Allan Williams and William Marshall, (Elm Tree Books Limited, Coronet paperback edition, 1976) pp. 129–30.
3 Howie Casey interviewed by Spencer Leigh, quoted in *The Beatles – All These Years: Volume One: Tune In*, Extended Special Edition, Mark Lewisohn (Little, John 2013) p.693.
4 *The Beatles Anthology*, the Beatles, (Cassell & Co. 2000) p.49.
5 From a copy of George Harrison's 18 October 1960 letter from Hamburg to Arthur Kelly as shared with the author Colin Hall, 15 August 2019.
6 & 10 Astrid Kirchherr in conversation with the author in 2001 for *Get Rhythm* music magazine, Issue 6 published August 2001.
7, 8, 9, 11 & 12 Klaus Voormann in conversation with the author for *Get Rhythm* music magazine, 2001, Issue 7, published September 2001.
13 *The Beatles Anthology*, the Beatles, (Cassell & Co, 2000), John Lennon interviewed in 1971.

Chapter 16:
DIRECT FROM HAMBURG …
THE SENSATIONAL BEATLES!

As they dribbed and drabbed back home in early December, the 'new' Beatles gradually re-assembled to take the scene in Liverpool by surprise. By the end of the month they had certainly done that to the point they were being recognised as *the* new sensation around town.

Allan Williams had set the groundwork for their return after visiting them in Hamburg in mid-October. Like many others, he had been astounded by how much they had improved. He liked their energetic 'mach schau' stage act very much and considered that they were now the best beat group in Liverpool. So impressed was he by them and by the booming rock music club scene in Hamburg, he set about opening a 'Top Ten Club' all of his own on Liverpool's Soho Street. He envisioned the elite of Liverpool's now formidable beat group scene performing there regularly, especially the Beatles. Live rock music was burgeoning in the city and it seemed a no-brainer that he, of all people, should cash-in and make a killing.

To further his plan, he quickly hired Liverpool's beat music champion Bob Wooler to be the Top Ten's day-to-day manager, DJ and MC. It was a risky thing for Wooler to agree to do because it meant relinquishing his secure job as a railway clerk.

He may have been working for British Rail, but at heart Bob Wooler was a lyricist and his lifelong ambition always was to be a songwriter. He was fascinated to the point of obsession by words … his love of music and appreciation of what made a great lyric were astounding. As he told author Spencer Leigh, "I was influenced by the great lyricists of the pre-rock period, Cole Porter, Irving Berlin, Johnny Mercer and the like, but I could never find a collaborator, someone whose heart was in it as mine was…"[1]

The risk he took by quitting his job as a railway clerk most certainly paid off, for Bob was destined to become the resident DJ at the Cavern Club and was always a passionate advocate of the Beatles. His contribution to the music scene in Liverpool, his enthusiasm for, knowledge and championing of many of Liverpool's other groups and singers, was second to none. His wit, wisdom and way with words has become the stuff of legend. His position within the history of Mersey Beat is unique, unassailable. However, his career in music nearly went up in smoke before it had really begun.

Allan's Top Ten Club, situated in a wooden building at the end of Soho Street, opened on 1 December 1960, but lasted only six days: faulty electrics caused a fire that reduced the premises to cinders. In the mere matter of minutes it took the fire to destroy the building, Williams lost his new club and Wooler his new livelihood.

By then already back in Liverpool, Paul and George visited the site the day after it had burned down. How dismayed must they have been to discover the new Liverpool hotspot designed almost specifically to champion their group in particular was now just a heap of ashes.

Williams was absolutely devastated. He became ill as a result of the disaster and was admitted to hospital. Adding to his troubles was his deep concern that because his Top Ten venture had failed before it really started meant Bob Wooler had effectively lost two jobs within a matter of days. For which Allan felt personally responsible. Nevertheless, in his absence, he prevailed on Bob Wooler to look after the Beatles and, if possible, get them some work.

Ahead of their return home, some gigs had actually been pre-arranged for the Beatles.

To fulfil these and with Stuart unavailable the group recruited bassist Chas Newby to play two pre-arranged shows at the Casbah (17 and 31 December). Chas was a friend of Pete Best's and former member of his band, the Blackjacks. Both bookings had been arranged by Pete. A student of chemistry and home from college for Christmas, Chas eventually played a total of four gigs with them over a two-week period: the two at the Casbah, another on the 24th at their old stomping ground on the Wirral, the Grosvenor Ballroom, Liscard, and most notable of all, one at Litherland Town Hall on 27 December.

"It was Pete who asked me to play bass for the Beatles. The Blackjacks had folded in April 1960 as various members returned to their education. I was studying at St. Helen's Technical College and home for Christmas. I'd been rhythm guitarist and vocalist in the Blackjacks, so the first time I ever played bass was when I started practising at Pete's house with the Beatles ahead of the four gigs I played with them. I played it upside down, because like Paul McCartney I'm left-handed. I had to borrow the bass from my friend Tommy McGurk who was right-handed and the bassist in Gene Day and the Jango-Beats. Tommy and I had been in the Scouts together."[2]

Living in the Best household at this time was Pete's best friend Neil Aspinall, a student of accountancy. A former pupil at the Liverpool Institute, Neil was a good friend of George who also knew Paul. During the spring of 1960, Neil and Pete's mother, Mona, had fallen in love and so Neil lived in the Best house with her. Pete seems to have taken this turn of events in his stride and wrote to Neil from Hamburg enthusing about how good the Beatles had become.

When Pete arranged the bookings for them at the Casbah, Neil astutely advertised these shows as, 'The Return of the *Fabulous* Beatles'. Of course, the word 'fabulous' and 'Beatles' would soon become inextricably linked.

Neil went on to become the Beatles' most trusted cohort throughout their life as a group and beyond. He is a very serious contender, if not the front-runner, for the oft-mooted title of 'the fifth Beatle'. On the evening of the 17 December, along with the members of the Casbah Club, he crammed into its tiny cellar room and was among the first in Liverpool to witness the amazing transformation that Pete had proclaimed in his letters. Fifty-seven years later the impact of what he experienced that night still resonated strongly when, on 21 June 2007, he informed Mark Lewisohn: "Wow, they were so fuckin' good. Their music was *very* different and they were scruffier than ever in twat 'ats, cowboy boots and leather."[3]

As he'd promised Allan Williams he would, Bob Wooler found work for the Beatles. Most significantly he secured a booking for them at the Litherland Town Hall. This had certainly taken some doing because Brian Kelly, who promoted the gigs at that venue, was the very same promoter whom they had let down when, without any prior warning whatsoever, on Saturday 21 May, they had failed to turn up for a booking at the Lathom Hall in Seaforth because they were in Inverness backing Johnny Gentle. In their excitement to be going on tour the boys had completely forgotten to inform Kelly they could not make his gig. Left in the lurch back in Seaforth and surrounded by some very displeased customers, an incandescent Kelly had vowed never to book them again.

Despite Kelly's mistrust, Williams's enthusiasm for how good the Beatles had become was so impassioned and Wooler's way with words so massively persuasive, Kelly backed down and agreed to give them a second chance. How pleased he must have been to do so.

This was *the* Beatles major breakthrough in Liverpool. In the story of the group few other performances are considered as compelling or as significant as this.

The poster for the Beatles' Litherland Town Hall show proclaimed the group to be 'Direct from Hamburg', which unintentionally led most of the audience to believe they were German, to the point people were surprised at how good their English was. This belief would have been enhanced when they hit the stage dressed in the black leather gear that they had started to wear in Hamburg. It was a look that immediately distanced them from their Liverpool contemporaries who were still taking the stage in matching suits and ties. (Chas Newby had borrowed a black leather jacket especially for the show. He says he stood at the back.)

Their 'look' was the instant *visual* tell-tale sign something was afoot … but ultimately it was the incredible sound the Beatles made that set them apart from any group the audience would have heard playing in Liverpool at that time. As the curtains flew back and Paul burst into his powerhouse rendition of Little Richard's 'Long Tall Sally', the fuse was lit and the fireworks never stopped exploding until they left the stage some 30 minutes later. The immediate reaction was visceral: the place not only began to rock with wild abandon, but en masse the audience rushed to the front of the stage and roared its appreciation.

The audience response was unprecedented and unrelenting. From the stage Bob Wooler watched as the audience became transfixed: "It was an amazing night. When I did hear the Beatles, I was *fab*-ergasted. Other groups were playing what was on the charts – they felt reassured that way. The Beatles liked obscure R&B stuff. They were only on stage for 30 minutes but they put everything into their performance and rocked the joint … People went crazy for their closing number which was Ray Charles's 'What'd I Say' … the audience went mad."[4]

Chas Newby recalled that when they closed with 'What'd I Say' the audience response went up several notches, so much so, "Brian Kelly sent his heavy mob (his bouncers) in to break up what he thought was a fight but there wasn't one, it was just the crowd enjoying themselves even more vigorously and enthusiastically by jumping up and down joining in the song's call and response 'Whoa, Whoas'!"[5]

For John Lennon *this* performance was the turning point: "Suddenly we were a wow … It was that evening that we really came out of our shell and let go … This was when we began to think for the first time that we were good. Up to Hamburg we'd thought we were ok, but not good enough … it was only back in Liverpool that we realised the difference…"[6]

Pete Best was equally taken aback by the audience reaction: "The kids went mad. Afterwards we found they'd been chalking on our van, the first time it happened."[7]

Billy J. Kramer first saw the Beatles that night they performed at Litherland Town Hall: "I was only in the process of starting to put a band together and I used to go there and other local hops to watch groups such as King Size Taylor, the Searchers, everybody … One night at Litherland the deejay, Bob Wooler, said, 'Next week we have a band called the Beatles', and I immediately thought that's a cool name. So I went along and at the time we were all buying suits with a matching handkerchief and a tie from Burton and Taylor's … but they definitely weren't! When the curtains opened there was Paul McCartney singing 'Long Tall Sally' and I went 'Wow!' I'd always thought Liverpool people were very special, there was something about them. I used to say to my mother one day something great's going to happen and it will come from Liverpool. She used to take me into the city centre and I would walk around Rushworth & Dreaper's (music instrument shop) and I'd see all these guitars in glass cases and it blew me away. I'd always had this feeling Liverpudlians were such unique people that something or someone special was going to come out of the city. I'd always felt the people had never been given the recognition they deserved, I never thought Michael Holliday had or Billy Fury or comedians like Arthur Askey and Ted Ray had, but when I saw the Beatles I just thought *they* were the ones, they were going to change the world."[8]

Billy was right, of course.

From this point on there would be no stopping the Beatles. 1960 had been a mind-blowing experience. By the time they played the old year out with a New Year's Eve gig at the Casbah, against all the odds they found themselves contenders for the title of Liverpool's most popular of all its beat groups. No one would have predicted that at the beginning of the year.

Two more hard-working years of constant gigging lay ahead before they became a national 'sensation', but as 1961 dawned they were already a local phenomenon. The origins of 'Beatlemania' had sparked into life.

1 & 4 *The Best of Fellas* by Spencer Leigh, (Drivegreen Publications Ltd In association with Jim Turner, 2002) p.48 and p.70.
2 & 5 Chas Newby in conversation with the author, Tuesday 01 September 2020.
3 Neil Aspinall from *The Beatles – All These Years: Volume One: Tune In*, Extended Special Edition, by Mark Lewisohn (Little, Brown 2013) p.745.
6 & 7 *The Beatles: The Authorised Biography*, Hunter Davies, (Heinemann, 1968) p.98 and p.99.
8 Billy J. Kramer interview with the author 19 October 2020.

Chapter 17:
1961 – CHAS NEWBY AND THE ECLECTIC SONG SET

1961
Was the year when ... John Fitzgerald Kennedy became the 35th President of the USA ... Russia sent the first man, cosmonaut Yuri Gagarin, into space ... the Vietnam War began 'officially' when 400 US soldiers and US helicopters arrived in Saigon ... Russia initiated the construction of the Berlin Wall ... the 'Barbie Doll' got a boyfriend called 'Ken' ... the DNA code was broken ... in the world of fashion hemlines had reached just above the knee and were to climb even higher as, thanks to designers such as Mary Quant, the 'mini-skirt' was, by 1966, a major fashion trend of the decade ...

Two years into his degree in Chemistry and Chemical Engineering at St. Helen's Technical College, once his Christmas vacation came to an end, Chas Newby put down his bass, bid farewell to the Beatles and returned to his studies. "From the moment I started rehearsing with the Beatles I was under no illusions: it was definitely only a temporary engagement, it was never an expectation that I would join the group permanently."[1]

Pete confirmed that this was the deal: "We co-opted him into the Beatle fold on the understanding that Stu would replace him if and when he returned from Hamburg."[2]

Chas says John did invite him to return to Hamburg with the group but, "With the benefit of hindsight I do not believe John was actually asking me to join the Beatles, he wasn't trying to get Stuart out of the band. Bearing in mind his relationship with Stu, that wasn't going to happen. I believe John was just so enthused with the Hamburg experience he was almost acting like a disciple for the place and wanted me and other musicians to visit the city and experience what was happening there, to experience for myself what had happened to them."[3]

Despite John's enthusiasm, Chas politely declined: "Music was never going to be a living for me, I wanted to do chemistry. John, Paul and George just wanted to be musicians. I had no ambition to become a professional musician. They had played so much in Hamburg. It had been such an intense experience that they had become very tight, very proficient. As soon as I started rehearsing with them I could feel the power and energy in their performance. Even so I just did the four gigs and returned to college a week later."[4]

Despite the audience response and the excitement surrounding the group, Chas never wavered in his decision: "In those days there was no history around us of people making it. The music industry was based in London. There were no major studios in Liverpool, everything was focused on the capital. Plus, they were getting £1 each per show, which was no living. I was working and getting my education paid for by Pilkington Glass. There was no way I'd pack that in for the uncertainty of making it as a musician."[5]

Chas was totally unaware that John and Paul wrote songs. "When I played with the Beatles they were a covers band. They didn't play any of their own stuff as far as I was aware. It was just covers. I'd no idea that they had written any songs."[6]

Describing the set he performed at Litherland Town Hall, Chas is adamant that the Beatles opened with Paul's mind-blowing take on 'Long Tall Sally' and closed with a climatic version of Ray Charles's 'What'd I Say'. Billy J. Kramer is also certain Paul opened with 'Long Tall Sally'.

Chas clearly recalls, "We played for half an hour. Litherland was the shortest concert that we did. Give or take a song or two the set list was the same for all of the four shows I performed with them that December. All the songs were 'covers' and familiar to me. We played between ten and 12 tunes. Those that I can definitely recall being in the set are:

Little Richard's 'Long Tall Sally' was our opener and we also did his song 'Ooh My Soul'. Buddy Holly's 'That'll Be the Day'.

Chuck Berry was another favourite and we played 'Johnny B. Goode', 'Rock 'n' Roll Music' and 'Roll Over Beethoven'. I was playing the latter song for the first time as it was not part of the repertoire I had played with the Blackjacks. I can't be certain we played it at Litherland.

They liked Carl Perkins a lot and so we did both 'Match Box' and 'Honey Don't'.

'Red Sails in the Sunset' (The Platters had released a version of this as a UK single in August 1960).

Elvis Presley's 'Wooden Heart'*: this was meant to be the 'calming down song' (of the audience), but it never was for as he sang it Paul would blink at the girls which got them going again!

'Hallelujah I Love Her So' (George Harrison recalled owning a copy of Eddie Cochran's recording of this Ray Charles tune that the Beatles learned. They even made a rough demo of it in June 1960 at Paul's house.)

Ray Charles's 'What'd I Say' was a huge favourite of a lot of groups in Liverpool and the Beatles closed the show with this."[7]

(*In a letter written in November 1960 while in Hamburg Paul McCartney informed his girlfriend Dot Rhone that the Beatles were learning a new German language song by Elvis Presley entitled 'Wooden Heart'. It featured on the soundtrack album to his movie G.I.Blues which was released in Germany several months before it was issued in the UK.)

Chas's comments highlight the fact that the Beatles' first visit to Hamburg in 1960 did not change the nature of their repertoire: they remained very much a 'covers' group. (Their schedule in Hamburg had been so intense it severely limited opportunities for composing, although they would have added new covers to their set lists.) As a group they were neither ready nor confident enough to start feeding their own compositions into their performances. Indeed, only one new Beatles self-penned tune emerged from that first visit to Hamburg: it was unique for it was a *John and George* instrumental.

At the start of the Sixties in the UK, electric guitar instrumentals were very popular, in particular those by Cliff Richard's backing group the Shadows who scored a string of Top 10 hits during 1960 with tunes like 'Apache', 'Man of Mystery' and 'Frightened City'. George enjoyed the Shadows' instrumentals and also admired American guitar ace and champion of 'the Twang!', the one and only Duane Eddy. Eddy also enjoyed a string of UK hits in 1960, including 'Shazam!' which was climbing the Top 10 when the Beatles were in Scotland with Johnny Gentle.

John and George's co-composition was entitled 'Beatle Bop'. More 'Shadows' than 'Duane', it had apparently been inspired by either 'Man of Mystery' or 'Frightened City' and came into its own when the group returned to Hamburg in the summer of 1961.

There are several reasons why John and Paul's songwriting partnership stalled during 1960. First there had been the lethargy of the early months of the year, which was followed by their hectic Scottish tour, and from mid-August to the end of November their non-stop gigging schedule in Hamburg had left little or no time or private spaces in which to write. At the heart of everything, however, there was the growing distance between Paul and John which had opened up as a direct consequence of the latter's closeness to Stuart.

Astrid Kirchherr could see from where Paul was coming: "Even when he was eighteen Paul was a perfectionist. His career was music and there's a boy (Stuart) who ... plays the wrong notes and doesn't bother to practise ... no wonder Paul was angry."[8]

As far as 'new' songs coming into their repertoire, they were 'covers'. Any shared 'group time' the Beatles might have enjoyed during this period would have been devoted to learning more 'covers' to feed into their act.

These were bright lads who got bored easily. Consequently, they devoured all the new releases flowing out of the USA, but in their desire to offer something different to those around them they did not limit their choice of material to just one source. The Beatles' repertoire was seriously eclectic. It drew from a wide range of genres that included rhythm and blues, pop, country and western, instrumentals, show tunes, film tunes, standards and ballads, all of which reflected their individual musical backgrounds and preferences. They would also flip new releases over to see if there were any hidden gems to be had amongst the B-sides.

The Beatles were early UK proponents of songs being recorded by black artists from the United States and being released in the UK … Arthur Alexander, Chuck Berry, the Miracles (featuring the one and only Smokey Robinson), the Olympics, Little Richard, the Shirelles, Barrett Strong, Larry Williams, and so many more. In the Fifties and Sixties (and, regrettably, long before and well beyond) in both the USA and the UK ingrained racist attitudes prevailed which fuelled inequality and allowed and encouraged discrimination to be publicly sanctioned. Inevitably this caused major social divisions within both the USA and the UK. Draconian laws, discriminatory rules and policies of segregation were enforced against black people. Sadly, such racist attitudes and divisions were not just the province of those two countries, but extended around the world.

Racism was a given in Britain. Ignorance and habit made prejudice and prejudicial actions and comments wholly acceptable elements of everyday British life.

One place such attitudes did not surface in the UK was on your record player. When the singles being released by the record companies were played on the radio, in a record booth or at home on your record player, you could not hear the colour of a person's skin. What mattered was how good the song was.

From schooldays, John Lennon was a passionate adherent of both Elvis and Little Richard.

'Come Go with Me' by the mixed-race doo-wop group the Dell-Vikings had focused Paul's attention on John Lennon the very first time he heard him perform with the Quarry Men. The tune had not made the UK charts and so you had to be something of an aficionado to have heard it. So when Paul heard John singing it, Paul would definitely have been impressed … even if John wasn't singing exactly the right words. "He was making them up … singing 'Come, come, come go with me down to the penitentiary' – I thought they're kind of bluesy but they're not the words. But that is enterprising."[9]

In their passion for music and new 'good' songs, the Beatles did not recognise the racial barriers society was keen to enforce. Like many of their Liverpool contemporaries they embraced black music and black artists as much as they did white singers like Elvis and Buddy. They promoted the songs of Little Richard and Larry Williams by playing them. Of course they quickly became aware of the ethnicity of the artists they admired so much, but this never affected their appreciation of the artist or their work. And so Black American music became a major and readily acknowledged element in the evolution of their own musical and songwriting identities.

A main aim of the Beatles was to not only keep new songs flowing into their sets, but to ensure they chose as many songs as possible that the other groups didn't do. Plus, they also did not like to repeat themselves *ad nauseam*. They went for songs that were more obscure, which is when those B-sides came into their own. What attracted them to a song was not its particular genre or whether it was an 'A-' or a 'B-side', or if it was a 'new' song or an 'old' one, but whether it was, in their view, simply a 'good song'. This search for 'good' songs meant that they learned hundreds of covers which in practical terms was like an apprenticeship in songwriting. The wealth of material they accrued and the variety of sources from which their repertoire came is a key element in understanding what made the Beatles so different from their contemporaries. Liverpool groups were dipping into similar sources as each other, but the Beatles managed to pick up on gems others overlooked. It gave them a musical edge and a broader palette on which to draw, which ultimately made them more interesting to listen to. More crucially than anything, it kept the Beatles themselves interested.

Consequently, it is safe to say that down the clubs of Liverpool and Hamburg, audiences found the Beatles served up a different set of songs than those they may have heard previously by the groups playing on the same bill as them.

Some examples of these obscure B-sides, artists and album tracks that became part of the Beatles repertoire include:

'Bad Boy' by Larry Williams, the flip side of his 1959 single release 'Dizzy Miss Lizzy'.

'Everybody's Trying to Be My Baby' and 'Sure to Fall' by Carl Perkins, both album tracks featured on his 1959 UK long player, *Dance Album of Carl Perkins*.

'Well' by the Olympics, the B-side of this American male vocal group's 1958 UK number 12 hit 'Western Movies'.

'Nothin' Shakin'' by Eddie Fontaine. Fontaine was an American singer and this song was the A-side of a single he released in 1958 which failed to chart in the UK and went no further than number 64 in *Billboard*'s Hot 100.

'I Wonder if I Care as Much' by the Everly Brothers, the self-penned B-side of their first-ever, 1957, UK Top 10 hit, 'Bye Bye Love'.

'Clarabella' by the Jodimars (former members of Bill Haley's Comets), the A-side of a single they released in the UK in 1956 but which never made the chart.

'Red Sails in the Sunset' first published in 1935 by songwriters Hugh Williams (aka Wilhelm Grosz) who wrote the music and Jimmy Kennedy the lyrics. This was a popular tune with many singers such as Bing Crosby, Jack Jackson, Al Bowlly, Louis Armstrong, and in 1951 it was a number 24 USA hit for Nat 'King' Cole and appeared on his 1952 album *Unforgettable* (re-issued in 1954). The Beatles' rocked-up version of this tune was one of the songs included on *Live! at the Star-Club in Hamburg, Germany, 1962*.

'Up a Lazy River', a 1930 tune penned by Hoagy Carmichael (lyrics) and Sidney Arodin (music). This popular song has been recorded by too many artists to mention but, significantly, Bobby Darin scored a number 2 UK hit with his version in the spring of 1960.

In a fascinating interview for *Record Collector* magazine that Spencer Leigh conducted with Cavern DJ Bob Wooler in 1998, a list was featured that Wooler said had been given to him "by a Beatles fan, who followed them (the Beatles) around Merseyside."[10]

The list features 92 songs that the Beatles fan heard the group perform (and which he annotated with who sang each song). Of these tunes only seven are Beatles original compositions: 'Beatles Bop' (instrumental), 'Hello Little Girl' (John), 'I Call Your Name' (John), 'Like Dreamers Do' (Paul), 'Love of the Loved' (Paul), 'Pinwheel Twist' (which the fan listed as an instrumental) and 'Tip of My Tongue').[11]

The whole interview makes for interesting reading ... Leigh followed up with a biography about Wooler whom he interviewed extensively, entitled *The Best of Fellas*, in which he included a list of songs he himself compiled of 'Songs covered by Mersey Beat acts up to 1967'. It's a list he shared with Wooler, who Leigh says was excited by it because "he felt it demonstrated what he had known all along – the Cunard Yanks are not part of the Mersey Beat story."[12]

Leigh's list comprises over 350 cover songs played by Liverpool artists: "60% of the artists covered are black and 30% are white US pop or rock 'n' roll artists. There are some standards and some folk and country material", which goes to show that it wasn't just the Beatles who were tuned in to American black music. The most popular artist covered was Chuck Berry who was followed by Little Richard, the Drifters and Larry Williams.[13]

Of course, it was not only their eclectic song choice that made the Beatles so different to their rivals. Other Liverpool groups might come close but none had so much talent packed into just one group. Beyond the great music and those fabulous harmonies, everywhere you looked there was something about these boys that separated them from the rest. To start with there was that intriguing name, then came the unique clothes and hairstyles, while on stage they not only sounded great but were also very sharp and very funny, they had appealing personalities and last, but certainly not least, good looks.

THE UK'S TOP 30 MOST POPULAR HIT RECORDS OF 1960
01 The Everly Brothers: 'Cathy's Clown'
02 The Shadows: 'Apache'
03 Cliff Richard: 'Please Don't Tease'
04 Anthony Newley: 'Why'
05 Shirley Bassey: 'As Long as He Needs Me'
06 Roy Orbison: 'Only the Lonely'
07 Elvis Presley: 'It's Now or Never'
08 Jimmy Jones: 'Handy Man'
09 Elvis Presley: 'Mess of Blues'
10 Jimmy Jones: 'Good Timin''
11 Adam Faith: 'Poor Me'
12 Anthony Newley: 'Do You Mind?'
13 Johnny Preston: 'Running Bear'
14 Eddie Cochran: 'Three Steps to Heaven'
15 Ricky Valance: 'Tell Laura I Love Her'
16 Johnny Kidd and the Pirates: 'Shakin' All Over'
17 Emile Ford and the Checkmates: 'What Do You Want to Make Those Eyes at Me for?'
18 Lonnie Donegan: 'My Old Man's a Dustman'
19 Percy Faith: 'Theme from "A Summer Place"'
20 Duane Eddy: 'Because They're Young'
21 Connie Francis: 'Mama' / 'Robot Man'
22 Cliff Richard & the Shadows: 'Voice in the Wilderness'
23 Cliff Richard & the Shadows: 'Fall in Love with You'
24 Johnny Preston: 'Cradle of Love'
25 Johnny and the Hurricanes: 'Rocking Goose'
26 Freddy Cannon: 'Way Down Yonder in New Orleans'
27 The Everly Brothers: 'When Will I Be Loved'
28 Jim Reeves: 'He'll Have to Go'
29 Brenda Lee: 'Sweet Nothin's'
30 Michael Holliday: 'Starry Eyed'

1, 3, 4, 5, 6 & 7 Chas Newby in conversation with the author, Tuesday 01 September 2020.
2 Pete Best from *Beatle! The Pete Best Story*, Pete Best & Patrick Doncaster, (Plexus Publishing Limited, 1985) p.81.
8 Astrid Kirchherr in conversation with Colin Hall for *Get Rhythm* music magazine, August 2001.
9 *The Day John Met Paul*, 2007 BBC Radio 2 documentary written and narrated by Bob Harris. Sir Paul in conversation with Bob Harris and Colin Hall.
10 & 11 *Record Collector* magazine, July 1998, Bob Wooler as interviewed by Spencer Leigh.
12 & 13 *The Best of Fellas: The Story of Bob Wooler*, by Spencer Leigh (Drive Green Publications Ltd In association with Jim Turner, 2002) p.132 & p.133.

Chapter 18:
BACK TO REALITY

On his return from Hamburg, Paul came under pressure from his dad to get a job. To appease Jim, Paul took a post as a 'coil winder' at Massey Coggins Ltd, in Edge Hill. Working hard each day at something from which he gained no enjoyment and for which he had no aptitude, Paul lived for the evenings and playing with the group.

Equally, Mimi put pressure on John to find employment which he resolutely resisted. There is no doubt that Mimi could be very pointed in her observations, so life at 'Mendips' must have been undoubtedly fraught if not tetchy at times.

Despite once more not having a bass player, the Beatles were not deterred from building on the reputation their appearance at Litherland Town Hall had generated. They were booked to play all over the city with barely a break in between. Rather than search for a new bass player, Paul improvised with his broken down Rosetti which he fitted out with piano strings. It made a weird sound, so most of the time he didn't plug it in but mimed instead … and, anyway, the Beatles' sound was so loud the lack of bass generally went unnoticed.

Promoter Brian Kelly, or 'Beekay', who had booked them at the venue for their groundbreaking performance in late December, had been so impressed he had immediately booked them for a further 36 shows around north Liverpool before 11 March 1961. The venues into which he booked them included the Aintree Institute and the Lathom Hall in Seaforth, where Bob Wooler staged the dances for him. As the new year progressed, Wooler swiftly emerged as a prime mover on the Liverpool beat music scene whereas, after leaving hospital, Allan Williams became less of a player. His main focus became the Jacaranda and the Blue Angel, his new nightclub. As a result, his interest in the Beatles declined, although he did assist Paul and Pete in getting their bans overturned so that they could return to Germany. Despite his lesser-involvement, Williams's continued role in the affairs of the Beatles, which had never been formally agreed, made him as near to being their manager as was possible without the existence of a formal contract between them.

Pete and Mona Best had stepped up to take charge of bookings for the Beatles and in this venture they were supported by Bob Wooler. The Beatles stored their equipment at the Casbah and members of Pete's family provided the transport to convey said amps and drums to every booking. Significantly, Pete's best friend, Neil Aspinall, drove the Beatles to and from their shows.

Bob Wooler helped extend the Beatles' reputation beyond the Brian Kelly/Beekay venues and promotions. With Bob's kind interventions they soon found themselves performing for a growing number of other promoters who had cottoned on to the money to be made from the burgeoning new music scene in Liverpool and, in particular, to the impact of the Beatles. In 1961, new venues and new groups opened, formed and appeared almost on a daily basis. Most notable among the promoters was Sam Leach who energetically promoted gigs all over the city and who, on seeing the Beatles for the first time, told them to their faces with absolute certainty that they were going to be 'as big as Elvis'. They thought Sam was nuts: Sam knew he wasn't.

Meanwhile in that Liverpool bastion of Jazz, the Cavern, the tide was also turning. New owner Ray McFall had initiated Wednesday 'Rock Nights' and in October 1960 he started running lunchtime sessions on four days of the week which soon became five. In January 1961, McFall installed Bob Wooler as the Cavern's resident compere, DJ and talent booker. It did not take Bob long to book the Beatles for a lunchtime session. (The Cavern's Wednesday Rock Nights were a non-starter for the group at this time because they were booked to appear elsewhere by promoters Brian Kelly and Vic Anton.)

The Beatles' return to the Cavern (they had appeared there as far back as the very early days of the Quarry Men) was lunchtime on Thursday 9 February 1961. Proprietor Ray McFall was instantly blown away by what he saw and heard, insisting Bob should sign them up for as many lunchtime sessions as possible.

Ahead of all this, on 4 January 1961, Rory Storm and the Hurricanes returned from their trip to Hamburg. Less enamoured than the Beatles by their three months away, neither were they as professionally empowered by the experience as John, Paul, George, Pete and Stuart had been. On arrival home in Liverpool, Rory and the Hurricanes soon discovered that, for them, things had changed. To begin with bookings were in short supply and so several of Rory's group went on the dole while their drummer dreamt about becoming a hairdresser. Even so, together with Johnny Guitar, the Hurricanes' guitarist, and Rory himself, Ringo attended Litherland Town Hall on Thursday 5 January to catch the Beatles' performance.

What Rory, Johnny and Ringo witnessed was a sobering revelation. Dave Jamieson, a friend of theirs who accompanied them to the show, noted their reaction: "The curtains opened, Paul went into 'Good Golly Miss Molly', the crowd rushed forward and that was it, the place just took off. The Beatles were in leathers and black T-shirts – they were rebels. Richy (Ringo), Johnny and Rory never said anything about being overtaken, they didn't say anything at all."[1]

The two groups were often booked onto the same bills as each other, but despite his on-stage flamboyance Rory and his Hurricanes had been eclipsed. They remained immensely popular, but it was the Beatles' star that was now permanently in the ascendant. When the Beatles were on stage, Ringo would often go out front and watch them: "I just loved the way they played: loved the songs, the attitude was great and I knew they were a better band than the one I was in."[2]

The dilemma over the lack of a bass player was resolved when, in mid-January, Stuart returned briefly to Liverpool. Astrid joined him a few weeks later. He had come home because his temporary residence permit in Hamburg had elapsed and he wished to apply to join the fifth year of his Art Teacher's Diploma course at the art college which he had put on hold in order to join the Beatles in Hamburg. His interview was not until the end of February and so for a while he rejoined the Beatles on bass. During this time, one night in Seaforth during a Beatles show at Lathom Hall, Stuart was set upon by a gang of vicious Teds and badly beaten. This violent assault was to have consequences no one could have envisaged at the time.

From the very start of the year, the Beatles had embarked on an almost never-ending round of shows on Merseyside. As February approached, they had some 36 bookings spread over 24 days. Some nights they played a 'double shuffle' – which meant they appeared at two different venues. Paul must have been knackered for he was still working the weekdays at Massey Coggins.

Only by the skin of his teeth did he make the Beatles' first lunchtime session at the Cavern on Thursday 9 February. He had to bunk off work and got into trouble for doing so. They played a second lunchtime session on the 21st and somehow he made that one as well and survived in his job. However, he knew that if he bunked off again it would mean losing his job, something he was reluctant to do because he did not wish to upset his dad. When a third lunchtime session was booked for 28 February it became crunch time for Paul. When he began to waver, John Lennon made it clear to Paul he either had to be at the Cavern or he'd be out of the Beatles. Forced to choose between his father and the group, Paul chose the latter.

It must have been a tough decision for him to make. Paul did not like to go against his dad, but instinctively, intellectually, creatively and emotionally he knew there was really no choice at all: music and the Beatles, not coil winding, were his lifeblood.

By March, the Beatles were playing more bookings than ever: they were booked 'exclusively' to the Cavern's lunchtime sessions and had made their first night-time appearance at the club on 21 March. Elsewhere they were appearing regularly at Sam Leach-promoted extravaganzas.

Despite this seemingly endless stream of remunerated work, they were also focused on making a return to Hamburg. When they had left Germany, Peter Eckhorn had invited them to return in April for a month's residency at his Top Ten Club, St. Pauli, Reeperbahn 136 Hamburg, which was a definite step up from the Kaiserkeller.

It was thanks to the combined efforts of Astrid and Stu in Germany, Peter Eckhorn at the Top Ten Club and Allan Williams in Liverpool (who wrote to the German consul in Liverpool) that the ban barring Paul and Pete's return to Hamburg was overturned. As March became April 1961, the Beatles were back in Germany.

Allan Williams did not transport them to their destination this time: they travelled by train and boat.

Allan Williams had been instrumental in helping the boys not only to return to Hamburg, but in securing them work with Peter Eckhorn. As the group returned to Germany, Allan was actively negotiating on their behalf to get their nightly income at the Top Ten increased from DM35 each to DM40 each. Williams was also negotiating for Eckhorn to pay him DM120 each week. The idea was Eckhorn would dock this sum directly from the Beatles' wages and it would be deposited into Williams's own Hamburg bank account. This was the commission Williams felt he was due from the group for getting them the improved-rate gig at the Top Ten. The Beatles, however, saw this deal somewhat differently and despite all that Williams had done for them they were determined they would not pay him a penny. When Allan got wind of their decision not to pay him his commission, a strictly worded letter was delivered to them in Hamburg warning of dire consequences should they renege on their agreement. Of course they didn't pay him and Allan did not carry through his threats. And so it was that for all the effort, time, loans and expense he had incurred in getting them their gigs in Hamburg, Allan Williams was never reimbursed.

When, later, Brian Epstein came asking about the reliability of the Beatles as business partners, Williams was unequivocal in his advice: "Don't touch them with a fucking bargepole".[3]

Stuart's interview at the College of Art on 23 February did not go as expected. On paper it had seemed like a formality, but remarkably this wasn't the case. He was not offered a place on the teaching course. As a result, he determined to return to Hamburg to be with Astrid. Shortly after the Beatles' debut night-time booking at the Cavern, Stuart departed taking with him his bass guitar and amplifier. Not long after he left on 28 March, John and George set off for Hamburg, followed a few days later by Paul and Pete, which meant that by the evening of Saturday 1 April all five Beatles were back on stage in Hamburg.

(Back in the UK, at the same time the Beatles travelled to Hamburg, Ringo and Rory and the Hurricanes journeyed to Butlin's holiday camp to play a second summer season.)

The schedule that faced the Beatles in Hamburg was gruelling in the extreme. For just DM35 each per night, they played seven nights a week: seven hours a night on weekdays, eight at the weekends, with a 15-minute break every hour.

On stage they would be joined by Tony Sheridan (a singer-songwriter and acclaimed guitarist from England) which lessened the load somewhat and from whom they learned a lot. A feature that endeared the Top Ten club to them, especially John, was the Binson echo system that Eckhorn had installed on the microphones. This gave them the vocal quality of their favourite American records. Ever since he first sang in his aunt Mimi's porch at 'Mendips', John Lennon had always preferred his voice to be treated with echo (reverb). Paul would say of the porch (or 'vestibule' as he refers to it) that, "It had a great bathroom acoustic, we called it our echo chamber."[4]

Paul was still clinging to his broken down Rosetti guitar, but soon had to give up on it. He reverted to playing the club's terrible old upright piano. The piano playing he did during his second trip to Hamburg considerably improved and refined his keyboard skills. Ever after, among the Beatles, Paul was undoubtedly their best pianist.

The craziness of their second trip to Hamburg persuaded some of the Beatles to regularly consume small white diet pills called 'Preludin' or 'Prellies' which contained an 'upper' called phenmetrazine. These kept them wide-awake throughout each gruelling nightly session, but also made them thirsty so, at the same time, the boys consumed a lot of beer. Later the beer was replaced by Scotch whisky and coke.

Always the leader, it was John who consumed the most pills, then George and then Stu. Paul, ever the cautious one (his mum had been a nurse), would have preferred not to take them, but under coercion from John and George he succumbed, but in lesser quantities than either of them. Pete disapproved of drugs, so didn't pop the pills, but he *did* drink a lot of beer. Off stage, just as he had done during the first trip in 1960, Pete socialised separately.

Within the group, Paul's frustration with Stu's general lack of musicianship continued to fuel his jealousy of Stu's closeness to John, but along with John and George, he also became concerned by Pete. Not only didn't he fit in socially, but they began to criticise his drumming. Paul would pick him up for falling asleep on stage. Tony Sheridan, their co-performer with them, was the most scathing. *Agent provocateur* John Lennon even goaded Sheridan and Best into a fist fight which both claimed they won. On a visit to Hamburg during this time, Cynthia observed Pete as having become somewhat of a 'misfit' or 'loner' within the overall group dynamic.

At the same time, Stuart, who was already suffering from a grumbling appendix, began to complain that he was suffering from headaches although he got no sympathy from the others. With Astrid's help and encouragement Stu completed the full-on black leather look the group had begun to favour the last time they were in Hamburg. She bought him black leather trousers to go with his black leather jacket. The others soon followed suit.

Keen to remain in Hamburg with Astrid and to resume his studies, Stuart applied for a place at the Hamburg College of Fine Arts (as a sculptor, rather than a painter). Scottish-born sculptor Eduardo Paolozzi, a renowned pioneer of 'pop art', was then a visiting professor at the college where he taught ceramics and sculpture. He was impressed enough with Stuart's work to offer him a place (and a grant) which meant he would renew his studies on 1 June. Stuart's decision to return to full-time study effectively meant he would have to leave the group. As his start date was just one month before the Beatles' residency at the Top Ten ended, he was concerned not to let his friends down and so he continued to perform with them as bassist until the end of June.

In effect this meant Stuart was painting or sculpting during the day and then playing at night. This would have been a demanding schedule for any young man, but even more so for one who was now clearly physically unwell. Astrid became increasingly concerned for Stuart's well-being: there had never been much of him in the first place, but now he was painfully thin, his appendix was constantly bothering him and his sickly headaches had not abated. Unsurprisingly the physical demands of sculpting and performing on a daily basis caused him to miss some nights at the Top Ten and when he did it was Paul who picked up the bass in Stuart's place.

When Stuart finally quit the group, Klaus Voormann half-expected to be asked to take his place on bass in the group: "Stuart's decision to leave wasn't easy, but he really wanted to get on with his painting..."[5]

On the eve of the group's departure from Hamburg, the Beatles and their friends joined together in an emotional farewell. Klaus was particularly sad to see his friends about to disappear: "I remember a farewell party for the Beatles when they left Hamburg in 1961 ... I sat outside with John. I said to him, how about me playing bass for the Beatles, now

Stuart has left? And he replied, 'Sorry Klaus, Paul's already bought the bass.' When I think about it I'm still so surprised that I asked to play for them, that's so unlike me!"[6]

Eventually Klaus – himself a classically trained pianist who, as a boy, gave concerts playing Beethoven sonatas and Chopin etudes – bought Stuart's bass which marked the beginning of his own career as a bassist. It was to prove an exceptional journey. Not only did Klaus go on to play with Paddy, Klaus and Gibson, Manfred Mann ('Mighty Quinn', 'Semi-Detached Mr. James', 'Just Like a Woman', etc.) and the Plastic Ono Band ('Live Peace in Toronto') but he also played bass on several early solo albums from John, George and Ringo, which included playing on specific tracks such as 'Imagine', 'Mother', 'Cold Turkey', 'Instant Karma', 'My Sweet Lord', 'It Don't Come Easy'. As a session musician in L.A. in the Seventies, he played on the worldwide hits 'Without You' (Harry Nilsson) and 'You're So Vain' (Carly Simon) … Klaus is also a very fine artist who, in 1966, won a Grammy for his design of the cover for the Beatles' *Revolver* album.

John was right, Paul had purchased a bass guitar for himself from the Steinway shop in Hamburg. He could have bought Stuart's from him, but for some reason chose not to (and that's why Klaus did). Concerned not to go into debt, Paul chose a relatively cheap Hofner 500/1 violin bass. Once bought, however, the price did not matter: Paul fell in love with the instrument and it became his 'trademark' guitar. It was much lighter than Stuart's which was a real bonus given how long Paul spent on stage each night. A deciding factor was that living in Germany he was able to order a left-handed version. When it arrived, Paul was the proud owner of a guitar that, for once, he did not have to convert from right- to left-handed. And so it was he became bassman for the Beatles.

Stuart's demise as the group's bassist came soon after the tensions between he and Paul had come to a head. Reflecting on her visit to Hamburg during their second trip, Cynthia would later observe how Stuart had to restrain himself from reacting to Paul's continual criticisms. The rivalry that had been festering between the two for nearly a year and a half finally came to a violent head one night on stage when Stuart lost control. Paul said something to him that crossed a line and drawing on a strength which belied his diminutive stature, Stuart surprised his tormentor by picking Paul up and then throwing him onto the piano, after which the two tore into each other with flying fists. Soon the boys were rolling around the stage locked in a furious but ultimately inconclusive contest.

The rumble did little to resolve any ill-feeling between them, but it did provide conclusive proof that they could no longer co-exist within the same group. It was fortunate for all concerned that Stuart very soon after exited the Beatles.

Around the same time as the Sutcliffe-McCartney fist fight, the end of the Beatles' residency at the Top Ten Club was in sight. Not long before they left Hamburg they signed to record some songs as Sheridan's backing group.

It is often assumed that the Beatles signed directly with the German label Polydor, but this was not the case.

They recorded for Polydor at the behest of composer, orchestra conductor and record producer, Bert Kaempfert. From before the Beatles had set foot in Hamburg, Sheridan was an established rock 'n' roll star in the city and Kaempfert wanted to record him in the hope he would score some hit records in Germany. He was also impressed with the Beatles whom he'd seen performing alongside Sheridan at the Top Ten Club and thought they would be the perfect act to support Sheridan on record.

Kaempfert already had a separate deal with Polydor's parent company Deutsche Grammophon Gesellschaft (DGG) in which he had agreed to place all the recordings made by Bert Kaempfert Produktion with them.

As was the norm in such circumstances, Kaempfert signed John, Paul, George and Pete to a recording contract. Signed on 19 June 1961, the contract was between them and his own company BKP (Bert Kaempfert Produktion). For the mores of the times it was a fair deal, obviously weighted in favour of Kaempfert, but not as ruthless as many such deals could be in those days. Written in German, the individual Beatles had no idea just what they were agreeing to, but signed nevertheless. In effect it bound them as recording artists to Kaempfert for the year 1 July 1961 to 30 June 1962, thereafter it could be renewed automatically every year unless terminated by either side, a process for which they had to provide three months' notice.

The contract gave Kaempfert the right to use a different name for the group if he wished, and which he did. Thus when the songs recorded with Sheridan were released the group were known as 'The Beat Brothers'. This was an astute move on Kaempfert's part because in the future it allowed him to use other musicians to back Sheridan and call them by that same name.

The actual recording session was completed over two days, 22 and 23 June, on the stage of the Friedrich-Ebert-Halle high school (with the curtains drawn). The tunes were recorded onto a portable tape recorder. On 22 June they cut 'My Bonnie Lies over the Ocean', 'The Saints', 'Why (Can't You Love Me Again)' and the John and George instrumental 'Beatle Bop' which now became known as 'Cry for a Shadow.'* On 23 June, they recorded a version of Jimmy Reed's 'If You Love Me Baby (Take Some Insurance Out on Me, Baby)', 'Nobody's Child' and 'Ain't She Sweet'. While Sheridan sang lead on most of these songs, John took the lead vocal on 'Ain't She Sweet'. The group personnel featured Sheridan on lead guitar, John on rhythm, George on lead and rhythm, Pete on drums. Paul played bass for although Stuart was present he did not perform.

Kaempfert later culled 'My Bonnie' / 'The Saints' from the sessions and licensed these to Polydor who released them as a single in Germany on 23 October 1961. 'My Bonnie' was the A-side. The record climbed to number 32 on the German charts and to number 4 on the local Hamburg chart. Only Sheridan's name appeared on the single, but on the LP that followed the Beatles were name-checked as his backing group, but not under their official group name 'The Beatles', but as 'The Beat Brothers'. This was exactly as per his contract with the boys and so suited Kaempfert's personal purposes, but it also possibly helped avoid any unwanted confusion with the German word 'peedles' which is slang for 'penis'. The single received a UK release on 5 January 1962, but before then it was available only as an import.

(*During these sessions, 'Beatle Bop' was re-titled 'Cry for a Shadow' ahead of its release, no doubt for the very same reason that Kaempfert had doctored the group's stage name, i.e., to avoid the word 'peedles'.)

Not long after signing with Kaempfert on 28 June 1961, John Lennon and George Harrison signed a second contract. This one was a publishing deal with Tonika (a publishing company set up by Kaempfert and his friend Alfred Schacht) giving them the copyright for 'Cry for a Shadow'. Again it was written in German and so both Beatles would not have known the contents of the deal to which they were agreeing.

Kaempfert did not take any photos of Sheridan and/or the Beatles, but each Beatle was asked to pen a biography. Of note among the comments the boys made were one by John in which he said he had written 'a couple' of songs with Paul, and another by Paul in which he upped John's estimate to around '70'. Quite an exaggeration, especially when during 1961 John and Paul do not appear to have written a single song either together or alone. (In the early days Paul, by his own admission, was not averse to exaggerating the number of tunes he and John had composed.)

The Beatles' towering schedule in Hamburg no doubt contributed to this as did the fraught relationship between Paul and Stuart. They simply would have not had time to do so or maybe the inclination: Mark Lewisohn estimates that during their second visit to Hamburg they clocked up 503 hours on stage. Add this to their first visit and you have a running total of 918 hours of performance time, or as Lewisohn further equates these hours: this is equal to 612 90-minute concerts or 1836 half-hour gigs. (Half an hour was the usual time-slot for a top-of-the-bill act on the package tours that were so popular in the 1960s.) This is a truly phenomenal and exacting schedule. And while it meant they might not have been adding to their own Lennon-McCartney songbook, they were learning a lot of covers which ensured their apprenticeship in songwriting continued apace.

For Pete Best the recording sessions with Bert Kaempfert carried a worrying foretaste of what was to come. Karl Hinze, who engineered the sessions, did not consider Pete's drumming to be good enough. Apparently Pete speeded up during songs.[7]

As a consequence, Pete had to suffer the indignity of being told he could not use his bass drum or tom-tom on the sessions. He was relegated to playing just a snare, hi-hat and ride cymbal. The other Beatles who, among themselves, had already expressed concerns over Pete's drumming, took on board Hinze's concerns for future reference. Pete himself overcame the setback with aplomb and performed well throughout the sessions.

That Pete was picked out for such criticism is ironic given that he himself and (back home) his mother, Mona, were working so hard behind the scenes to set up bookings for the Beatles' imminent return to Liverpool. They were working hard not only to secure the group employment, but, in order to reflect their popularity, an increase in the performance fees they were charging promoters. At the same time, Neil Aspinall had tired of accountancy, quit his job and put down a deposit on a van. In effect he'd become the full-time driver and personal assistant for the Beatles. The term usually used for someone in Neil's capacity was road manager or 'roadie', but Neil was so much more than this. A more accurate word might be 'indispensable'.

By Monday 3 July after sad farewells to Stuart, Astrid, Klaus and their other Hamburg friends (including Tony Sheridan), the Beatles were back home in Liverpool. Now a fully leather-clad quartet and one personnel change away from being the finished article, they were more than ready to rock their hometown again.

Coincidentally, just a few days later, Ringo Starr turned 21. He was certainly enjoying his life as a Hurricane, no doubt about that: as a group they were at their most sartorially colourful and as wild as ever on stage and their diary was bursting with bookings. But at the same time Ringo was becoming aware that compared to groups like the Beatles, who seemed to be making waves and getting better all the time, Rory and the Hurricanes had possibly plateaued. For sure, Butlin's was a terrific residency, but they hadn't been invited back to Hamburg which he would have liked. For all his flamboyance and good looks, Rory had not caught the attention of the entertainment moguls of the time as might have been expected. Larry Parnes had been, seen and heard the group and had effectively passed on them. So while Ringo was in a good place as he 'came of age', his concern was that maybe his 'moment' as an entertainer had come and this was the limit of it. Such was his desire for something else to happen he had considered an invitation from Gerry Marsden and his group to join them when they returned to Hamburg at the end of July, weirdly – not on drums – but as bass guitarist! He didn't do so, but significantly, Ringo had *thought* about it. Something inside was telling him it was time to make a change, indeed: it was now or never.

---

1 *The Beatles – All These Years: Volume One: Tune In*, Extended Special Edition, Mark Lewisohn (Little, Brown, 2013) p.841.
2 *The Beatles Anthology*, the Beatles (Cassell & Co, 2000) p.57.
3 *The Man Who Gave the Beatles Away*, Allan Williams and William Marshall, (Coronet Books, 1976) p.212.
4 Sir Paul McCartney interviewed by Bob Harris and Colin Hall in 2006 for the BBC Radio 2 documentary *The Day John Met Paul* first broadcast in 2007, written and produced by Bob Harris OBE, produced by Bob Harris and Trudie Myerscough-Harris for WBBC.
5 & 6 Author's own interview with Klaus Voormann, published as 'Klaus Voormann: The Quiet Man Of Rock', *Get Rhythm* music magazine, September 2001.
7 Hinze interviewed Ulf Kruger for 'Die Beatles In Harburg' (Christians Druckerei & Verlag, Hamburg, 1996) p.99.

Chapter 19:
GUITARS, GROUPS AND GIGS

On their return from Hamburg, the Beatles found the burgeoning of the 'beat music' scene they had left behind in Liverpool had continued unabated. The city was awash with groups, guitars, gigs and venues. As each day dawned it seemed like a new group was being formed. If there weren't 300 groups out there already, there soon would be. So vibrant was the scene it was about to have its own dedicated monthly newspaper called *Mersey Beat*. Of all the groups whose names would soon be filling the pages of *Mersey Beat*, none were more exciting, more popular or more regularly featured than the Beatles.

From now on, thanks to Mona Best's best efforts, links between the Beatles and the Cavern Club strengthened considerably. Situated on Mathew Street in the heart of downtown Liverpool, Ray McFall's Cavern Club became the veritable heartbeat of the Liverpool music scene. With Bob Wooler at the helm, it went from strength to strength and for the Beatles it became home turf, it was where they enjoyed performing the most. They not only played regular lunchtime gigs, but an initial seven-week Wednesday night booking that was extended to last the whole year. From their debut lunchtime gig on 9 February 1961, until their final performance at the venue on 3 August 1963, DJ Bob Wooler put the number of times the Beatles played the Cavern at 292.

On 31 October 2020, broadcaster and author Spencer Leigh wrote a fascinating piece in his column in the *Liverpool Echo*, stating that when he had personally inquired of Bob Wooler the veracity of his figure, Bob had confessed he had rapidly determined the number over a drink in The Grapes. Spencer added that in 1985, author Mark Lewisohn's meticulous research had led him to determine Bob was only ten gigs out and that the figure was actually 282 performances. Just two years later, Spencer noted that Phil Thompson's painstaking research of the *Echo*'s own microfiches lowered the figure yet again to 276. Clearly pinning down the exact number is not a precise science. Whichever figure you choose it's still a tremendous number of gigs, and to this day the Cavern remains, for fans from around the globe, a kind of musical Mecca, and most certainly the spiritual home of the group on Merseyside.[1]

Beyond the Cavern, the Beatles played a regular Thursday night slot for Mona at the Casbah, and on the other nights of the week their availability was quickly snapped up by promoters, such as Brian Kelly, Wally Hill and Sam Leach.

Hamburg, which had been so integral to the development of the group, still featured in their itinerary, but over the next two years Liverpool was where they really wanted to be.

During the following year, 1962, the Beatles played three more residencies in Hamburg, each of them at the newly opened Star-Club.

By the second of those Star-Club residencies (during which they shared the bill with their hero Little Richard) Ringo had become their drummer. Earlier in 1962, Ringo had returned to Hamburg separately from either the Beatles or the Hurricanes to play a residency at the Top Ten Club. He had shocked everyone, none more so than Rory and the Hurricanes when, with next to no warning, he left them at the very end of 1961 to accept an invitation to return to Hamburg at the very start of January 1962 to drum in the Top Ten's newly formed house band alongside Tony Sheridan, ace pianist Roy Young and bass player Colin Crawley. He returned home a week or so early from this engagement on receiving the news that his much-loved grandmother Annie Starkey had died. Once home his plans remained vague. The Hurricanes had kept his place on drums vacant (stand-ins had been employed during his absence) but whether he would rejoin he had not yet decided.

Peter Eckhorn's place as the pre-eminent rock music club owner in Hamburg also came to an end *before* the Beatles returned in '62. It was not by choice but because a certain Manfred Weissleder had decided to become involved in that lucrative scene. Weissleder was a wealthy entrepreneur, not averse to using violence as a means of getting his own way. He opened a club called the Star-Club in a building that had once been a cinema. It was a big venue situated on Grosse Freiheit in the heart of St. Pauli. Eckhorn's rival had the money and the muscle to lure the big acts. His strong-arm helper was Horst Fascher, an ex-boxer who'd served time for killing a man in a street fight and who had taken a real shine to the English rock musicians who frequented St. Pauli.

(Inevitably when, as the then brand new manager of the Beatles, Brian Epstein, received a visit in Liverpool from Fascher asking him, on Weissleder's behalf, to send the Beatles to play a residency at the Star-Club in April, Brian did not argue. It would have undoubtedly seemed best not to. A verbal contract already agreed with Eckhorn went out of Epstein's office window as he sealed a deal that sent the Beatles to Hamburg to play seven weeks at the Star-Club from 13 April to 31 May, 1962, the first two weeks of which they were on the same bill as Gene Vincent.)

Overshadowing everything on that April '62 trip to Hamburg was the devastating news that Stuart had died.

John, Paul and Pete had flown to Hamburg (via Amsterdam) on 10 April, the very day that Stuart passed away. On their arrival in Hamburg they had been treated to a meal by Manfred Weissleder and were unaware of the tragedy. George's departure had been delayed by one day because he was recovering from German measles. The news of Stuart's death had reached Liverpool on the 10th: Astrid had sent telegrams to Millie, Stuart's mother and to Allan and Beryl Williams. Alan in turn had contacted Brian Epstein and arranged for Millie Sutcliffe to join Brian and George on their flight (again, via Amsterdam) to Hamburg on 11 April. When George was told what had happened he broke down in tears.

Oblivious to what had happened, John, Paul and Pete went to the airport to meet Brian and George. Brian had sent them a telegram asking them to be there. In that message he had mentioned Millie would be accompanying them but had not said why. No doubt Brian thought they would have already been made aware of what had happened.

On arrival at the terminal, the three Beatles were joined by Astrid and Klaus who had arrived to collect Millie. Immediately the boys wanted to know where Stuart was and it was at that point Astrid broke the news to them of his passing.

They were devastated. John Lennon literally broke down. He became hysterical, unable to contain his emotions. Pete Best wept uncontrollably. Paul felt dreadful too, but not in the same way. He put his arm around Astrid but his sadness was cut through with personal regret. He had treated Stuart badly and now there was no way back, no reconciliation or apology possible. "It was really sad for me because I hadn't liked him and it's ... too late when someone dies – you can't go back (and say) 'Hey Stu, I was only kidding...' His Mum and his sister never felt too good about me."[2]

Stuart's family, like Astrid, were utterly heartbroken. But for Astrid, Stuart's passing went to the very core of her being. She had been Stuart's soulmate, his heartbeat: his true love. Thereafter it was Stuart's photograph Astrid kept in her wallet.

In early 2001 Astrid kindly shared with me these thoughts:

Stuart: "The Beatles always knew Stuart was just a visitor, because his main passion was art ... I have never got over his death. He is still the love of my life, even though I have been married twice since. I still wear Stuart's ring. I never found a love comparable to Stuart's. John used to say, 'Either you live or you die' and I have always remembered that, and so I decided to live and be happy with my memories. When I am in trouble I talk to Stuart, so my life is not unhappy because he's not with me in flesh and blood, he's with me in spirit ... he is very special ... He was only 21 when he died, but even at that young age, he was not afraid of giving himself to another. He didn't hide or keep his thoughts to himself, he just gave it all so fully. I have never met a person like that, one who was so willing to give himself away to a person to whom he said 'I love you': that is very rare."[3]

John: "John was like Stuart's guardian angel. Stuart was very tiny, only as big as I am. He was very delicate and John always protected him. He was like a mum, always worried that something bad might happen … You must not forget the losses John had been through by then. His mother to whom he had grown very close, had been killed, his dad had just disappeared one day when he was very young, never to be seen again until John became famous. So John knew about sadness, he knew about losing people, and that was another factor that was very important. He was protecting Stuart. He didn't protect George or Paul."[4]

George: "He was the sweet one. He was just 17 and he would sit and look at things, politely asking, 'Can I please look at that book, that magazine?'"[5]

At the time I interviewed Astrid, George was experiencing ill health. He had been through very tough times: cancer, the horrific knife attack on Olivia and himself in their home, the loss of John. Despite all of which Astrid commented: "Through all these tragedies he is still the George he has always been: kind, helpful, and full of love for his friends."[6]

Paul: "Of course Paul hadn't been happy with Stuart's bass-playing. Even when he was eighteen, Paul was a perfectionist. His career was music, and there's a boy in the group who looks good – and John was always saying 'it doesn't matter if he (Stuart) can't play, he looks good!' But Stuart did play the wrong notes, and didn't bother to practise. No wonder Paul was angry sometimes! I perfectly agree with him, and Stuart wasn't stupid: he could have sat down for an hour or so each day and practised, but he didn't bother, he'd rather draw, so Paul was perfectly right!"[7]

Pete: "He is a lovely guy I am grateful to have met … I am still in contact with him … it was very difficult for him to be the one the band left behind…"[8]

After the trauma of that trip, the Beatles were to return twice more to Hamburg by which time Pete had been sacked and replaced by Ringo Starr.

From 1 to 14 November 1962, they played 14 nights at the Star-Club where they shared the bill with their long-time hero, Little Richard.

Their fifth and final residency in Hamburg was again at the Star-Club, 14 nights from 18 December until 31 December 1962. At some point during this time, several Beatles performances were recorded by fellow Liverpudlian Ted 'Kingsize' Taylor (of Kingsize Taylor and the Dominoes), assisted by Adrian Barber (formerly lead guitarist with Cass and the Cassanovas but at this point in his career working for Horst Fascher at the Star-Club): 100 minutes of priceless 'Hamburg Beatles' caught 'live on stage'. Of the 37 songs taped only two were 'originals': 'I Saw Her Standing There' and 'Ask Me Why', both John and Paul collaborations.

Even though by then they were signed to Parlophone and had released 'Love Me Do' (backed with 'PS I Love You') which was climbing the charts back home in the UK, they did not perform either of these songs on that New Year's Eve gig. There was also no 'Beatle Bop', no 'One After 909', no 'Please Please Me' …

But the narrative is getting ahead of itself …

Meanwhile, back in 1961 …

---

1 'Tribute Act Making Up Numbers' by Spencer Leigh on 31, October 2020 in his 'My City' column in the *Liverpool Echo*.
2 Paul interviewed by Mike Read, BBC Radio1, 13 October 1987 and quoted in *The Beatles – All These Years: Volume One: Tune In*, by Mark Lewisohn, Extended Special Edition (Little Brown, 2013) p.1158.
3, 4, 5, 6, 7 & 8 From 'Astrid Kirchherr' interviews with the author for *Get Rhythm* music magazine, August 2001.

Chapter 20:
BILL HARRY, 'MERSEY BEAT' AND BRIAN EPSTEIN

After failed careers in the army and as a student at RADA, Brian Samuel Epstein (b.19 September 1934) had returned to Liverpool to focus on a career as a businessman within the family firm, North-End Music Store, or NEMS as it was better known. By age 25 in 1959 he was the successful manager of the record department at NEMS, 12–14 Whitechapel situated in the very heart of Liverpool city centre. It was one of three such stores in Liverpool owned by the Epstein family. Prior to managing the Whitechapel store, in May 1961 Brian Epstein had been in charge of the record department in the family's shop in Great Charlotte Street. He dedicated himself to making a success of his role and very soon the department was flourishing. Although his artistic passions were for the theatre and classical music he was as fastidious about the presentation of popular music records on sale within NEMS as he was the store's classical recordings.

Suave, sophisticated, elegantly flamboyant, stylish and poised, Brian Epstein was very much the man about town. A successful and respected businessman for whom doors opened, to a casual observer Brian would have seemed to have it all ... but sadly he was beset with inner demons that never left him. Despite many acquaintances, he was essentially a loner living a solitary life, a bachelor for whom work and his soon-to-be utter devotion to the cause of the Beatles became his obsession to the point of absolute loneliness.

As a Jewish person, he would have encountered antisemitic prejudice that lingered within certain elements of British society, despite the recent horrors of World War II and the Holocaust. It was a prejudice that was never far from the surface. In British society, antisemitic comments were deemed fair game and, although not antisemitic in themselves, the Beatles would make them. In society at large such comments often came disguised as 'jokes'. The stereotypical view that Jewish people were good with money had persisted for centuries ... Shakespeare's character Shylock had a lot to answer for.

More worryingly and depressingly, there were those prepared to exercise their bigotry beyond making jokes. For instance, the Epsteins' local synagogue on Greenback Drive had been burned to the ground in 1959, and Brian felt more comfortable not using his middle name 'Samuel' in his business dealings, believing it identified him as being Jewish. Apparently, according to renowned Liverpool lawyer Rex Makin, a neighbour of the Epstein family, Brian was uncomfortable within his religion: "Brian disliked being a Jew. He didn't mix, he wasn't part of the community as such ... He even disliked his middle name Samuel but his father was traditional and his mother was traditional and he respected that."[1]

Later, in 1967, Epstein himself commented, "Religion doesn't appeal to me now. I can't take it. I'm respectful when I should be, no more. It doesn't worry my parents."[2]

His biographer, Ray Coleman, described Brian as 'a socialist at heart' who always voted Labour, believing socialism to be more humanitarian than the other parties. In his 1989 biography, *Brian Epstein: The Man Who Made the Beatles*, when discussing the subject of religion, Coleman described Brian as being 'decisively neutral' and quotes Epstein in 1967 as saying, "I refused to help Israel's war effort (The Six Day War, June, 1967) because I'm as sorry for a wounded Arab as I am for a wounded Israeli. People fundamentally are all the same and I can't discriminate ... I believe in, and want to help as far as I can, to understand mankind whatever colour, creed, religion or nationality."[3]

No doubt Brian's view of Judaism was, in no small part, shaped by the religion's view of homosexuality. Most orthodox ministers of those times were adamant that it ran contrary to the teachings of the Bible and so condemned it out of hand. Brian would have felt such rejection acutely, understanding that within his own community there was no place for one like him … he would be considered as an outcast.

Of course such attitudes towards homosexuality were not just the province of Judaism. In the UK it was illegal. Britain was a buttoned-down society and its aversion to those who stepped outside what was considered sexually 'normal' was reinforced by laws that could send a man to jail for indulging in a sexual liaison with another.

Thus, within his private life, as a homosexual man in 1960s Britain, Brian was forced to live half a life, unable to express his sexuality as openly and as freely as he would have wished.

His close friend at that time, Joe Flannery, recalled visiting the first gay bar on Dale Street with Brian which had opened in 1960. It was called 'The Bonaparte' and run by ex-merchant navy steward Gordon Shearer, who later opened a basement bar on Stanley Street named 'Paco's', a venue where plain clothes police would visit … intent on making arrests and of which Flannery observed, "It was known as the rent office. Brian would go there. He was more frivolous than me. He had a flat on Falkner Street for entertaining. I wasn't so open. I only went to Paco's once."[4]

And so it was that Brian Epstein walked an emotional and physical tightrope. Always at risk of being 'outed', he was a target for blackmail and the ever present threat of scandal that could have been his ruin … When he became aware of the Beatles they became not only his raison d'être but a glorious diversion from the reality of his inner demons.

It was Epstein's profile as the manager of one of the city's most successful record stores that drew him to the attention of Bill Harry, editor of the fledgling *Mersey Beat* music newspaper. (The newspaper was Harry's brainchild. Together with his partner Virginia Sowry ((the couple had met at the Jacaranda and later married)) they provided most of the copy, while his friend Dick Matthews, a professional photographer, took the pictures of the groups. It was a friend of Dick's, Jim Anderson, who loaned Bill the money to get started.)

Costing 3 pence a copy, *Mersey Beat* had been launched on 6 July 1961, just days after the Beatles returned for their second residency in Hamburg. Reporting on the thriving music scene in the city and the stars who came to Liverpool to perform, the newspaper's pages were filled with photographs of local groups, advertisements, local record charts, gig guides, TV, film and record reviews. Tapping, as it did, directly into Liverpool's burgeoning youth market, it soon became extremely popular and an absolute 'must-read' for them. That Liverpool could support such a fortnightly listings publication is evidence of just how many groups and venues there were in and around Merseyside and how active the scene was. Its pages accurately reflected the vibrancy of what was happening and kept its readers in the loop of all that was going on and coming up. Its very existence not only helped popularise the Liverpool music scene of its day, but validated its importance as a cultural phenomenon of which its young people could feel they were an integral and important part. Among the city's cognoscenti, it quickly became their 'bible'. Accurately documenting those heady times, it fittingly gave its name to a style of rock 'n' roll that was initially unique within the city, but which morphed into a national craze known as 'beat music'. Not only that, but for just 3 pence, a *Mersey Beat* reader got a lot for their money.

A former student, classmate and friend of John Lennon's at Liverpool College of Art (who had persuaded the college to purchase an amplifier that the fledgling Beatles came to consider as their personal property), Harry persuaded John to contribute to the first edition with an article entitled 'Being a Short Diversion on the Dubious Origins of the Beatles'. As time passed and the Beatles were often in Liverpool during the day and in-between bookings, John and Paul would spend lunchtimes chatting with Bill and Virginia in their spartan attic office at 81a Henshaw Street. John was very pleased Bill Harry liked his writings and so it wasn't long before John had his own zany 'Beatcomber' column in *Mersey Beat*.

Brian Epstein, circa September 1964, just turned 30. The photo was taken not long after the Beatles had just returned from their second visit and first concert tour of the USA.
(Trinity Mirror / Mirrorpix / Alamy Stock Photo)

Earlier in the year on 20 June, Harry had approached Brian Epstein to ask him if he would be prepared to invest in *Mersey Beat*. While Brian politely turned down Bill's request*, Ray McFall of the Cavern accepted. Brian did agree, however, to take a dozen copies of the newspaper for sale in NEMS, which sold so quickly he was amazed and promptly ordered a dozen more. When these also flew off the counter he was so impressed he ordered twelve dozen of the second edition. Published on 20 July 1961, the second edition carried the banner headline: 'Beatles Sign Recording Contract', which highlighted the breaking story that the Beatles had signed with producer Bert Kaempfert of German record label Polydor to make four records per year. The story was accompanied by one of Astrid Kircherr's photographs of the group, her first to be published.

The first edition of Mersey Beat sold 5,000 copies, but at its height its circulation rose to 75,000.

Epstein was so taken with Mersey Beat he asked Harry if he could review records for it. Harry agreed, knowing that to have one of the city's major record shop managers writing for Mersey Beat was a real coup.

Each succeeding edition was full of articles about the Beatles and Harry himself talked to Brian on many occasions about the group.

*(*Fast forward to 13 September 1964: Brian's NEMS Enterprises bought a controlling stake in Mersey Beat. His idea was to turn it into a national music newspaper ... with Bill Harry as editor. To this end Harry came up with the name Music Echo but was dismayed when Epstein began making appointments without consulting him and so he resigned.)*

Despite having its very own very popular newspaper, Brian was not moved by anything he read to investigate Liverpool's burgeoning popular music scene further, even when Bill Harry informed him Mersey Beat intended to publish a list of the 280 'beat' groups known to be resident within the city. With hindsight it seems incredible that Epstein remained so uninterested, but his attention was eventually drawn to what was going on when, on 28 October 1961, a young pop music fan called Raymond Jones walked into NEMS in Whitechapel and requested a copy of a record entitled 'My Bonnie'. What drew Brian's attention was that Jones said it was by a local group called 'The Beatles' ...

At this time the record was only available on import in the UK and so, not unsurprisingly, NEMS did not have any in stock, but Raymond's request had grabbed Epstein's attention sufficiently that when two further customers made the same request, Brian became determined to track the single down. Unfortunately, none of his suppliers had ever heard of a group called 'The Beatles'. Every search drew a blank. Not someone easily dissuaded, with the help of his personal assistant Alistair Taylor, Epstein discovered that a record called 'My Bonnie' had been released in Germany on the Polydor label. It was not actually by 'The Beatles', but by a group calling themselves 'Tony Sheridan and the Beat Brothers'. Convinced this was the record he was after and that possibly, just possibly, his customers had got the group's name wrong, Brian ordered a box of 25 singles. Trusting that Jones and the others had *not* got the name wrong, Epstein placed a notice in the window of NEMS stating 'Beatles Record Available'. Within a day all 25 singles had been sold, including one handed over to a very grateful Raymond Jones.

Impressed, Brian immediately ordered a further two boxes which sold out within three days. Brian was now on a mission. Convinced he had stumbled upon a potential hit record, he approached Polydor to secure a UK release for it. When his request was curtly rebuffed, Epstein became even *more* determined to prove his judgement was right and theirs wrong.

Thus, when Bill Harry arrived with the next edition of Mersey Beat, Epstein finally inquired where this much vaunted group 'The Beatles' could be seen. Harry was surprised that it had taken Epstein so long to seek out the group whose name and photograph appeared so regularly both on the cover and within the pages of Mersey Beat. He took delight in informing Epstein that they regularly performed at lunchtimes just around the corner from NEMS in the Cavern, a cellar club on Mathew Street, no more than a three-minute walk away.

And so it was, accompanied by his right-hand man, Alistair Taylor, on Thursday 9 November 1961 at approximately 12.30pm, Brian Epstein entered the doorway to the Cavern for the very first time. Together the two besuited men descended the steep steps into the cellar below where, among the much younger clientele, they sat at the back of the middle aisle, facing the stage.

"I had never seen anything like the Beatles on any stage. They smoked as they played and they ate and talked and pretended to hit each other. They turned their backs on the audience and shouted at them and laughed at private jokes. But they gave a captivating and honest show and they had very considerable magnetism. I loved their ad libs and I was fascinated by this, to me, new music with its pounding bass beat and its vast engulfing sound."[5]

Truly captivated, Brian Epstein had immediately recognised the potential of the four young men standing on stage in front of him. Diamonds in the rough they may have been, but Brian's instincts told him that they were unique, that he had stumbled upon a supremely natural, very rare, and very special talent. They had a sound Epstein believed would appeal to anyone lucky enough to hear them sing and play. Instinctively he knew from that very first moment they could be huge.

So spellbound was he, every fibre of his being told him this was a defining moment in his life and, if only they would let him in, their lives too. In that very instant Brian Epstein knew that he wanted to manage the Beatles: "Never in my life had I thought of managing an artiste or representing one, or being in any way involved in behind-the-scenes presentation, and I will never know what made me say to this eccentric group of boys that I thought a further meeting might be helpful to them and to me. But something must have sparked between us because I arranged a meeting at the Whitechapel store at 4.30pm on December 3rd,1961* 'just for a chat'."[6]

Bob Wooler was at the Cavern and saw for himself Epstein's reaction to the Beatles: "He knew straight away he wanted to manage them, but he didn't rush in as he needed a getting-to-know-you period first. He went to a couple of other venues to see what they were like and how they behaved and he found them very animalistic. They were unkempt, they didn't comb their hair, they were lithe and physically attractive."[7]

(*Sunday 3 December was actually their second meeting with Epstein, but the one at which they agreed he could manage them. Their first meeting, at which Epstein broached the prospect of him becoming their manager, was Wednesday 29 November 1961. At the behest of the Beatles, Bob Wooler accompanied them at that meeting (at which John Lennon referred to Wooler as his 'Dad'.))

The Beatles were certainly impressed that such a prestigious businessman, well known to record fans like themselves, should be showing an interest in them. Brian Epstein was a cut above. He belonged to a genuinely well-to-do Liverpool family. From the way he spoke to the way he dressed he oozed class and sophistication which very, very few people had done in the group's journey so far. For Epstein to take an interest they felt was a step in the right direction, and if nothing else, worth investigating.

John Lennon: "We had complete faith in him when he was runnin' us. To us he was the expert. I mean, originally he had a shop. Anybody who's got a shop must be all right."[8]

---

1 & 4 *The Liverpool of Brian Epstein* by Jeremy Deller & Paul Ryan (Tate Liverpool, 2007) Rex Makin as quoted on p.18, Joe Flannery on p.10.
2 & 3 *Brian Epstein: The Man Who Made the Beatles*, by Ray Coleman, (Penguin Books, 1990) p.381.
5 & 6: *A Cellarful of Noise*, Brian Epstein, (Souvenir Press, 1964) p.44.
7 *The Best of Fellas: the Story of Bob Wooler*, by Spencer Leigh (Drive Green Publications Ltd In association with Jim Turner, 2002) p.156.
8 *Apple to the Core* by Peter McCabe and Robert D. Schonfeld, (Sphere Books, 1973) John Lennon August 1971, p.31.

Chapter 21:
WITH OR WITHOUT A BARGEPOLE

At the very first meeting between the Beatles and Brian Epstein on 29 November caution was in the air, there was some inevitable sounding out on both sides, but underlying all this a sense of excitement pervaded.

The Beatles wanted to know the exact nature of Brian's interest in them and Brian wished to know more about their potential to be managed: most importantly, were they already under contract? He knew they must already have a recording deal as he was already selling copies of 'My Bonnie'.

As encounters go it was both tentative and direct. They learned Brian was very interested in managing them to the point he had already booked to go to London on Friday 1 December to sound out record companies for a possible audition for the group. That in itself really was something. He was honest and told them he'd never done anything like it before, that if they entered into an agreement it would be a learning curve as well as a partnership for all of them, but their roles as artists and manager would be clearly defined.

Brian asked about the recording of 'My Bonnie' and their contract with Bert Kaempfert and asked to see this before his forthcoming trip to London.

They told him about Allan Williams, but that they were not in any management agreement with anyone at that moment. Pete told him he and his mother, Mona, arranged all their bookings.

The meeting ultimately went well, first impressions were positive. They adjourned to 'think about it' and meet again a few days later after Brian's trip to London on Sunday 3 December 1961 at 4:30pm.

Brian Epstein made it his job to visit Allan Williams. Allan was still smarting from the callous way he felt the Beatles had dealt with his claim for commission. Despite Allan's forthright honesty (which included telling Epstein not to touch them with 'a fucking bargepole'), Brian was not deterred.[1]

Around the same time as Brian Epstein was becoming acquainted with the Beatles, the ever-ebullient Sam Leach had re-emerged on the Liverpool music scene. Sam was a serious contender for the role of Beatles manager. Never one to do things by halves he was back with (among other enterprises) Operation 'Big Beat', a series of five mega-shows staged at the Tower Ballroom, New Brighton, just across the Mersey estuary from Liverpool. Over seven months, in what was a very big auditorium, Leach featured the best of the Liverpool groups together on five bills, four of which were headlined by the Beatles. These were big ballroom shows capable of accommodating thousands of fans, many of whom were bussed in from Liverpool.

Leach's aim was to put the Beatles on in London and get the industry movers and shakers to come along. Once seen and heard he believed it was inevitable that he and the group would hit the big time. Leach was very much a part of the Beatles story at this point and always insisted that they accepted an offer he made to manage them. Unfortunately, nothing was ever put on paper and signed and as history shows, despite Sam's best efforts, they chose Brian Epstein instead.

Brian's trip to London was impulsive but not crazy. NEMS was a respected record retail store in the British music industry, Brian's name was well known and his store sold tens of thousands of pounds of records each year. He was a major and respected customer. Doors did open for him at the top-selling record companies: EMI and Decca.

Crucial to anything happening for Brian or anyone else, he needed to know how tied they were to Bert Kaempfert. On Brian's behalf, EMI took the Kaempfert contract to have it translated. Only when that information was ascertained would any of their producers have been able to make any moves (should they have wished to). At EMI, Brian Epstein left a copy of 'My Bonnie' with his contact Ron White, the company's general marketing manager. He was careful to note that it was the backing group on that record not the singer he was asking EMI personnel to focus on. White agreed that once the content of the contract was known and that, if it was positive news, he would draw the single to the attention of EMI's four label bosses/senior A&R Managers. A&R or Artists and Repertoire Manager was the title used before 'producer' became more popular.

The four musical aces at EMI were:
Wally Ridley at HMV: a veritable legend of Britain's 'Tin Pan Alley', which was the name given to Denmark Street situated on the very edge of London's West End. Once metal working had been a major trade on the street, hence its nickname, but by the 1950s it was home to several music publishers. It was they who provided the hit songs for the record companies and, as such, they were a major cog in the UK's music industry. Among Ridley's many responsibilities for EMI, was to pick American RCA Victor product for release in the UK. In 1956, despite the huge esteem in which he was held, he was subjected to much initial derision when he chose 'Heartbreak Hotel' by Elvis Presley. How wrong he proved his detractors to be.

Norman Newell, Columbia: writing for the veritable *All Music* website, Bruce Eder describes Newell as the 'Golden Boy of EMI'. From the end of the 1940s until the beginning of the 1960s Newell walked on water. EMI gave him the biggest budget and as Eder noted Newell "had the highest visibility of any music producer in England". Add to this, Newell was a renowned songwriter whose hits included 'A Portrait of My Love' and 'This Is My Life'.

Norrie Paramor, also at Columbia: Paramor was responsible for, among many others, the records by teen sensations Cliff Richard and the Shadows (who were all over the British charts at this time) and Helen Shapiro. He wrote songs, fronted an orchestra and beyond his salary as an A&R was making a lot of money from various *other* musical endeavours.

George Martin, Parlophone: Martin was best known at this point for his comedy productions for Bernard Cribbins and individual Goons, Peter Sellers, Spike Milligan and Michael Bentine, along with many others, but he had also worked with the Vipers Skiffle Group. His experience with them would come in useful when he began to work with the Beatles. Around this time Martin was also working with popular UK vocalist Matt Monro, a singer in the Sinatra style of crooners. Earlier in 1961, George Martin produced 'You're Driving Me Crazy' by the Temperance Seven which climbed all the way to the top of the UK chart to reach number 1 for a week right at the end of May.

As a first move on behalf of a group he had only just met, and with whom he had no legally binding relationship, Brian Epstein had done remarkably well to access such important players in the UK recording industry. He had shown an intent no one else the Beatles knew at that point could match. From nowhere to the desks of the top music men in Britain, there was no other agent or promoter in Liverpool who had that kind of clout, not even Sam Leach. The Beatles could not fail to be impressed.

Something even more tangible followed when Epstein called in on Decca. They more than matched EMI's cautious interest. Irrespective of the outcome of the translation of the Kaempfert contract, they promised to invite the Beatles to London for an audition.

Epstein's achievements proved very impressive for the boys waiting back in Liverpool, he'd scored a real result.

To put Epstein's achievement in some perspective: for such an important customer as Brian Epstein, it was possibly the least either of those recording companies could do as a mark of respect and, *if* this group turned out to be half as good as he was claiming, they were quids in. So, by inviting Brian Epstein to meet their A&R men made prudent business sense, for ultimately they had nothing to lose and everything to gain ... but the fact that Epstein was willing to put his reputation on the line on their behalf was not lost on the Beatles.

1 *Brian Epstein: The Man Who Made the Beatles* by Ray Coleman, (Penguin Books, 1990) p.78.

Chapter 22:
THE TWIST AND THE STORY OF HANK BALLARD

Liverpool's popular music fans may have been focused on the city's burgeoning beat music scene, but like everyone else around the world a dance called the 'Twist' was the big, big news of the entertainment world and it had captivated them too. It was a global phenomenon within the world of popular music and Liverpool kids were not immune to its appeal. The 'Twist' is what they were doing down the Cavern and everywhere else they ventured out to dance.

The Beatles recognised this and tipped their hat to the craze by weaving three twist tunes into their set. Pete Best, in a very rare excursion from behind his drum kit (Paul would sit in for him), sang 'Peppermint Twist'* and the 'Twist'.

(*'Peppermint Twist' *was an American dance record recorded and released by Joey Dee and the Starliters in late 1961. By early 1962 it was the* Billboard *Top 100 number 1 that kick-started the world's obsession with the 'Twist'. It was also a tip of the hat to the fashionable New York City nightclub called 'The Peppermint Lounge' in which Joey Dee sang.)*

Much more to the point, during the evening of 22 March 1962 and backstage at the Cavern, Paul McCartney even wrote a brand new tune called 'Pinwheel Twist'.[1] This was also given to Pete to sing during his break from drumming. The song is not Paul's finest and it enjoyed only a short-lived spell in the Beatles' repertoire, but the fact that he felt inclined to write it clearly acknowledges the group's recognition of the popularity the 'Twist' enjoyed among their audiences.

The Beatles also reinterpreted Gene Vincent's 'Dance in the Street' from 1958 as a 'Twist' tune which they dubbed 'Twist in the Street'.

The story behind the success of the dance and its major hit record helps explain the business of making a record and writing songs as it functioned in the early Sixties at the very time the Beatles so craved a 'deal'.

The 'King of the Twist' was an American singer called Chubby Checker. Musically 'The Twist' was rock 'n' roll by another name and its name perfectly describes the simple dance Checker performed when he sang it. Its simplicity was a key factor in why it really caught on. Anyone could do it and so the 'Twist' became a phenomenon.

On both sides of the Atlantic, people were frantically, if not happily, putting their backs out, spraining their ankles and buckling their knees to a dance capable of being done entirely on its own, no partner required. The 'Twist' empowered people to accompany themselves to a dance because they did not require a partner. Once inside a club or dance hall, they did not have to wait for someone to invite them onto the floor. People could do the 'Twist' wherever they wanted completely solo. Even better the 'Twist' could be performed by people possessed of two left feet and so now there was absolutely no excuse left on earth for anyone *not* to get up and dance: here was a move everyone could bust in the name of cool.

Checker's debut hit record was owned by EMI in the UK and they released it on their Columbia record 'label' at the end of September 1960, where it entered the chart at number 49 but disappointingly it dropped out after that first week. All was not lost because it came back for a further week in October when it went to number 44. (To begin with EMI must have been wondering what was going on for this was a record that had peaked at number 1 in the *Billboard* singles chart in the USA in September of that year. Not only that but the dance accompanying the record was a national craze in the States. The kids were crazy for it. If ever there was a sure-fire hit single for the UK market, here it was, but initially British teens seemed distinctly unimpressed.)

Checker's record company released a follow-up in the UK called 'Pony Time', which fared better, climbing to number 27 and staying on the chart for six weeks. Again EMI must have felt disappointed, for this was another single that had peaked at number 1 in the *Billboard* Singles chart on 27 February 1961. Chubby Checker was selling millions of records around the world but, on the face of it, it seemed UK popular music fans weren't too moved by him, his records or his simplistic dance.

But, of course, they were just proving hard to get!

When Checker came back a third time with a new opus called 'Let's Twist Again' down went the barriers and they let rip. As far as the history of 'The Twist' and the UK is concerned the release of 'Let's Twist Again' signalled the moment British fans finally got into the groove. The single was destined to become Chubby's BIG record in the UK for which he has never been forgotten.

Initially, it hit the UK chart for just three weeks from 23 August until 6 September before dropping off the ladder. However, any adult thinking the 'Twist' was just another ridiculous five-minute teenage fad from the USA was in for a very big surprise on 3 January 1962, when 'Let's Twist Again' returned to the UK singles chart where it spent the next 27 consecutive weeks, and peaked at number 2 for three of them. Clearly invested with the characteristics of a boomerang, this was not the end of 'Let's Twist Again': it kept coming back for more, re-entering the UK chart on two more occasions that year before finally slipping from view. (In 1975 with 'The Twist' on the B-side 'Let's Twist Again' returned Checker to the UK charts for another ten weeks when it climbed all the way to number 5.)

He may be forever associated with 'The Twist' but Chubby did not write nor record the first version of the song. Those honours go to American R&B singer Hank Ballard who made records as 'Hank Ballard and the Midnighters'. In May 1960 EMI had released Ballard's original version of the song in the UK on their own in-house Parlophone label as the B-side to Hank and the Midnighters' version of 'Kansas City', but it had not sold.

Ultimately it is unlikely his lack of personal success with his song caused Hank too much grief given Chubby Checker's phenomenal worldwide success with his version of 'The Twist'.

The UK release of Checker's version of 'The Twist' came in September 1960 on another EMI-owned UK label called Columbia. Not unexpectedly expectations were that Chubby's version was highly likely to repeat its Stateside success here. With this in mind, to coincide with its release and in the hope of selling a few more copies by association, Hank and the Midnighters' version of 'The Twist' was re-released by Parlophone in the UK as the A-side and 'Teardrops, On Your Letter' flipped to the B-side.

As before, Hank's version failed to trouble the UK charts. While this might have been disappointing for the Midnighters as a group, it most probably didn't cause Hank too much heartache. As the writer it didn't really matter to Hank who made his song a hit, so long as they were selling records by the truck load they were making him far wealthier than he ever was before.

However many copies they sold individually both Chubby's and the Midnighters' records earned Hank Ballard a writer's royalty. While Chubby toured and performed the song every night and danced his socks off in the process, so the records continued to sell in their millions leaving Hank to do no more than stay at home and count the dollars rolling into his bank account.

As the head of Parlophone since April 1955, George Martin would no doubt have watched with interest how Ballard's original disc failed to chart in the UK but how the singer's song was a huge success as performed by a different singer on a rival EMI label. Equally he would have recognised and no doubt been impressed by how much the writer of a song could earn if it was successful, whoever sang it. From his point of view as head of Parlophone George no doubt regretted that the revenue from physical record sales of 'The Twist' was not flowing into the EMI coffers via Parlophone instead of through Columbia, although in reality he knew the volume of record sales on 'his' label did not affect the size of his personal paypacket. He was not paid by results.

As record label boss, George Martin earned a straight, reasonably good salary (renewable after three years) plus a small annual Christmas bonus. He did *not* receive *a percentage* from the sales of recorded product. So, however big the hit, however long it spent on the chart, it did not affect his income.

As a label boss, obviously chart success was very good for Martin's reputation, for it was proof to his bosses that he was good at his job and had an ear for a potential hit which would make them a profit. It helped keep him in a job that way, but he personally did not receive a greater income based on that success. That's how it was and George and every A&R man understood that. They simply did not receive a percentage from the physical sales of records.

Even so, knowing this did not make it sit right with him: he was married to Sheena (Chisholm) at the time and they had two young children (Alexis and Gregory) and like all young parents George and Sheena would have welcomed a bigger income. Not to have a greater share of a hugely successful product that he had, in most cases, helped to create and promote was extremely galling.

---

1 As recalled by eye-witness/contemporary of the Beatles, Earl Preston (of Earl Preston's TT's and later Earl Preston's Realms), source unknown but quoted in the website 'The Paul McCartney Project' under 'Pinwheel Twist (song)' (https://www.the-paulmccartney-project.com › Home › Songs)

Chapter 23:
THE BALLAD OF GRAHAM FISHER

George Henry Martin (aka Graham Fisher), born: 3 January 1926, Highbury, London
Died: 8 March 2016, Wiltshire

George Martin's career in music came about largely because of his own compositional talents.

From as far back as he could remember, George had been very interested in music. He was never 'trained' but had taught himself piano and by the time he was 15 (1941) he was running a dance band in which his sister sang.

Despite his musical prowess and being encouraged by others to take it up professionally, like most parents and guardians elsewhere in the country, his parents were less inclined to agree, cautioning the teenage George not to "mess around with music, no one makes money out of music".[1]

Ultimately, Martin had no choice in the matter of what he did next for the war intervened and aged just 17 he joined the Fleet Air Arm of the Royal Navy as an aerial observer. Fortuitously, during his four years in the Fleet Air Arm and whilst attending a concert in Portsmouth, he met Sidney Harrison who was a Professor at the Guildhall and a member of the 'Committee for the Promotion of New Music'. One evening in Portsmouth, thinking that there was no one around, Martin took the opportunity to play the piano and was overheard by Harrison who asked what it was he was playing. George replied that, "It was something I had been doodling with, one of my own pieces."[2]

Harrison was impressed enough by what he heard to suggest that Martin send the piece to the aforesaid Committee for the Promotion of New Music. From this chance encounter Harrison and Martin became pen pals: "All the time I was in the Fleet Air Arm he urged me to try and write music down and send it to him and he would criticise it and he would give me two foolscap pages of criticism."[3]

Harrison also urged Martin to get to know his marine band, learn the instruments they played and arrange music for them. Harrison's encouragement was such that when Martin was de-mobbed he met again with him, enthused once more about his talent and urged the young pianist to make music his profession.

Martin was understandably cautious, for he was now 21 and, in his own estimation, "had never learned a thing in his life". In response Harrison provided Martin with an opportunity he knew the young pianist would not be able to resist: he arranged an interview for him with the Principal of the Guildhall School of Music and Drama (founded in 1880) at which he instructed George to play all the pieces he had previously played to him.

The Principal, Edric Cundell, was as impressed as Harrison had been. In no time at all Martin was enrolled as a compositional student (studying composition, conducting and arranging) for which, as an ex-serviceman, he received a government grant.

While at the Guildhall, George Martin took up the oboe as a second subject and received additional tutoring from Margaret Eliot who was married to the eminent doctor Richard Asher, and whose three children were named Peter, Jane and Clare.

During his three years at the Guildhall (1947 until 1950), in January 1948, Martin married Jean 'Sheena' Chisholm, whom he had met in Scotland during the war when they had sung together. At the time Sheena had been serving in the 'Wrens', but was also the leading soprano at Kings College Chapel in Aberdeen.

On graduating from the Guildhall, Martin later remarked that he "emerged with enough ability to play the oboe to join in bands in the park. I had no idea of joining EMI at that point, I was just interested in music and still wanted to be Rachmaninov."[4]

To enable himself to play gigs in the evening, he took a day job at the BBC in the music library, at which point, "Out of the blue I got a letter from EMI asking me to go for an interview to take over the production of classical records for Parlophone Records who had a limited classical repertoire ... It was 1950."[5]

Right from the start at Parlophone, George found himself in the control room. "They tossed me in at the deep end: my job was to look after the music while the engineer looked after the sound. You can't work in a studio without learning about it all. Parlophone was a tiny label compared to HMV and Columbia. My boss, Oscar Preuss did all the recording himself. His big star was Jimmy Shand. We had things like the 'Luton Girls Choir' and 'Billy Thorburn's Organ Dance Band'. Eve Boswell from South Africa was on the label."[6]

Once he had served his apprenticeship with the classical people it wasn't long before his boss began giving George pop and jazz artists to work with. Parlophone had a large jazz contingent that included Humphrey Lyttelton, Joe Daniels and Freddy Randall, and George was soon doing their recordings too.

Recognising his ability as a producer, he found himself doing all sorts of recordings. He would also be given things from other labels as well: "HMV lumbered me with children's records and I met Enid Blyton and I recorded *Little Noddy* stories and *Toy Town*, all those kind of things. It was pretty good wide-ranging experience. This was all done at Abbey Road for our offices were in Abbey Road."[7]

In April 1955, Oscar Preuss retired. He had reached the age of 65 and in those days no one was allowed to work for EMI beyond that. George attended Oscar's farewell dinner at which he remembered, "They presented him with a set of *Encyclopaedia Britannica*, which I'm sure he didn't want, and then the Chairman of EMI announced his successor."[8]

Ahead of revealing the name of the new boss, the Chairman explained how the powers that be at EMI had deliberated long and hard as to who it should be because they recognised that Parlophone needed a lot of work. Fearing that it might be someone he most probably wouldn't like, to George's utter amazement the name read out was none other than his own. At just 29, George Martin had become Head of Parlophone, the youngest person ever to have a record label.

This was an astonishing achievement, but George knew all was not as it seemed: "It was a poisoned chalice in a way because I think they were thinking of shutting down the label and they thought should we give this kid a try? After all, he's cheap and if he doesn't succeed we just shut it anyway."[9]

Of course George Martin *did* succeed. He made Parlophone work. The hits began to mount up. Among the many acts he produced was a skiffle group called the Vipers whose records (briefly) chased Lonnie Donegan's up and down the charts. Paul McCartney was a Vipers fan and in 1999 on his *Run Devil Run* album released a compelling version of their 1958 B-side 'No Other Baby'. "But," said George, "I didn't get a number 1 until 1961 when I recorded 'You're Driving Me Crazy' by this weird Trad Jazz band called the Temperance Seven. They were called the Temperance Seven because there were *nine* of them and they all drank like fishes!"[10]

By 1961, at the same time George Martin was recording the Temperance Seven, he was also recording the *Beyond the Fringe* satirical ensemble at Cambridge (Alan Bennett, Peter Cook, Jonathan Miller and Dudley Moore). Recording satire and comedy artists had become a particular forte of Martin's and he would score popular hits with 'novelty' records like 'The Hole in the Ground' with Bernard Cribbins (1962) and (the less than politically correct) 'My Boomerang Won't Come Back' with Charlie Drake (1961). Famously, Martin recorded three members of 'The Goons' – Peter Sellers, Spike Milligan and Michael Bentine – but not the Goons themselves. *The Goon Show* was a favourite radio programme of all the Beatles. John Lennon owned a copy of their 1956 number 3 hit single 'The Ying Tong Song' / 'Bloodnok's Rock 'n' Roll Call', although this was released on the Decca label and therefore had not been produced by Martin.

By the time he came to work with the Beatles as head of Parlophone, George Martin was already renowned as a multi-talented, inventive, full of ideas, well respected, experienced and successful record producer. His expertise and unfazed open-minded way of working would prove crucial to capturing the Beatles' magic on record and helped further their future creative development.

As head of the label, the challenge of turning Parlophone into a receptive and creative environment for making records beyond just the narrow remit of purely classical music, held great appeal for George. "This is what attracted me to Abbey Road. When I went there I did not intend to stay, it was a stop-gap to give me a bit of money … not much! I soon found out I was in a wonderful musical toy shop. It was exciting and you got hooked – you couldn't help it in an environment like that."[11]

Aside from the joy of making music, George was also acutely aware that Parlophone was a business and in order to survive it needed to make money. Understanding the importance of record sales to EMI was one thing, but achieving these was another. Fortunately for all concerned George Martin proved not only highly proficient in the nuts and bolts of making good records but was also extremely skilled at spotting and producing hit records.

Importantly, he knew (as all A&R personnel did) the value of being able to find those someones who could pen decent tunes to provide the raw material from which 'hits' could be fashioned. Following on from that, Martin fully appreciated the importance of music publishing and the sales of sheet music. Consequently, in his search for songs suitable to record with Parlophone artists, George Martin was constantly listening to new songs and became a regular visitor to the offices of music publishers not far away in Denmark Street.

As a married man, a father, and with a mortgage to pay, George was financially stretched. He couldn't live on job satisfaction alone. Knowing Parlophone would only pay him his agreed salary and not a penny more, George recognised the importance of finding other additional sources of income. One such source to which he felt immediately drawn was to write songs of his own and get them published. He needed to pen a hit for someone!

And so it was, by the time he encountered the Beatles, George Martin himself had composed tunes for several artists at Parlophone.

How a songwriter earns money from his tunes is crucial to understanding not only what happened next in the story of George Martin, but in the story of the songs the Beatles gave away.

Here's how it works: Artists sign with record companies (aka the 'label') so they can 'record' a record for that company/label. The aim is for that record to have enough commercial appeal to become a hit on the national charts. Securing a 'record contract or deal' was the holy grail for every group on Merseyside. Signing to a label turned a group into 'a recording artiste'. As such they would have greater national exposure, especially if they scored a 'hit' and if they did, so their performance fees would exponentially increase as would their bank balances.

Part of the record label's job was to supply their artistes with tunes to record, from which they hoped the artists would score as many hits as possible.

Once they were signed, an artiste usually received an 'advance' from the 'label' in order to record or 'cut' a record. The 'advance' was not a gift, it was more like a loan that they used to make a record: the artist was expected to repay this money. The hope was that the amount could be recouped at source from the sales of a record. The record company simply deducted the amount of the 'advance' from the artist's percentage of a record's sales.

The 'label' chose the songs, produced, arranged, manufactured, promoted and sold the artist's finished product. In a typical record 'contract' or 'deal', the artist assigns the copyright in the sounds they have recorded onto disc to the record label. The record company now own that sound and will usually do so for 50 years.

A royalty rate will have been agreed with the artist as part of the recording contract or deal. This is paid to the artist (group or solo) for each record/copy (or CD, or as a download, etc) *sold* of the particular tune they have recorded. It is from this pool of money earned by the artist that the initial advance will eventually be paid back.

Whenever the record they have made is played publicly an artist will also receive a performance royalty.

From each record a royalty is also paid to the composer or publisher of each song on the disc. The composer/composers of the songs on either side of the record receive an equal royalty, however many discs are sold. So if Elsie Wilson writes a hit song (the A-side) that tops the charts, Dash Riprock who wrote the B-side, which is not the hit, will receive the same money as Elsie for every physical copy of the disc that is sold. (N.B. Beside the fact he was a good writer it is no wonder then that Cilla Black's husband Bobby Willis wrote most of her B-sides!)

Sheet music was the province of music publishers. A music publisher was/is someone whom a composer or 'original copyright owner' of a song employs to help get their songs recorded and to further promote their tunes wherever they can by persuading people to play them on the radio, as records, use them in a film on the soundtrack or to be sung/recorded as a 'cover' by other artists. This is how it worked back then, but nowadays, as well as the former outlets, a music publisher will also target downloads, films, TV, advertisements, theatre, Spotify, etc, as additional outlets for a composer's work. This multitude of potential outlets for a song did, and still does, mean a songwriter earns money from way beyond just the physical sale of records/CDs on which their tune or tunes appear.

So much has the music industry changed that these days an artist who writes their own tunes may make much more money from one of their songs being used in a film or on an advertisement than from getting it into the charts.

Crucially, once a songwriter agrees a deal with a music publisher, the songwriter in effect assigns the ownership or copyright of his or her song to the publisher. Together they will have agreed that in return for his or her efforts the publisher will receive a percentage of the income generated by the song (usually 50%).[12]

In the first half of the twentieth century, the sale of sheet music was the source from which the original music charts were compiled and a major source of income for composers and music publishers, much more so than the sales of records.

This was because very few people owned record players and so very few records were sold. Both items were expensive luxury items for anyone but the wealthy. Until record players became affordable and record buying more commonplace, making music at home was how most people enjoyed hearing music. Many people played instruments and sang either by themselves or with their families. This was how 'live' music was generally enjoyed beyond listening to the radio (aka the wireless, and everyone owned a wireless) or visiting the theatre or music hall (which was a very popular and reasonably cheap form of entertainment).

In the first part of the twentieth century, many, many people/families owned and learned to play instruments: pianos, violins, ukuleles, accordions, trumpets, banjos … all were very popular.

One way for the music industry to be able to judge how popular was a song sung on the radio or in a variety theatre or on a film soundtrack, was by people choosing to perform it for themselves or by listening to members of their family doing so at home. This is where 'sheet music' came in.

To be able to learn to play the songs they liked that they had heard on the radio, at the theatre, etc., people bought 'sheet music', which was a manuscript copy of the music and words for a song. Armed with this they could take the song home to learn and play it for themselves.

Thus, charts showing the sales of sheet music were published in music journals which further helped popularise and promote tunes.

Even in the early 1960s, sheet music was still an important source of income for the music industry.

Record sales of singles, extended player records and long player records were a relatively new phenomenon in the early to mid-1950s and 'record charts' were not even ten years old by 1960.

A music publisher was/is as integral to the process of success in the popular music industry as the artist themselves and the record company. Their work as 'pluggers' of a song could/can make or break a composer's work or an artist's career.

From this it can be seen that a writer of a song (and its publisher) could make more money than the artist who performed it (unless the artists and writer were one and the same person) because they got a writer's royalty when a record was sold and further royalties from sheet music sales and other uses or 'exploitation' of their songs. Whenever the record was played they got a royalty irrespective of who was singing it. Music publishing was big business and remains so to this day. Hence Hank Ballard was quite happy to let Chubby Checker do all the hard work of performing.

George Martin was not just an excellent, inventive record producer with an uncanny ear for a potential hit tune, he was also a classically trained musician who liked to write music of his own. Indeed, by the time the Beatles arrived at Parlophone some of Martin's compositions had been performed and recorded by artists on the Parlophone roster. It was a way he had chosen to make some much-needed extra money beyond his salary as a producer. Initially, Martin did not publish his tunes in his own name, but under pseudonyms. By 1960 he had not enjoyed any big hits, but his music was out there, it gave him the chance of doing so and *that* is what mattered … for once a tune is out there then there is always the potential that someone will pick up on it and then, who knows what may happen…?

But to return to the central narrative … Despite the almost all-consuming phenomenon of 'The Twist' up and down the land, in his job as head of Parlophone, Martin was enjoying considerable success with a series of records he had personally produced and which had become big hits in the UK: 'You're Driving Me Crazy' by the Temperance Seven and 'My Boomerang Won't Come Back' by comedian Charlie Drake.

Something else that irked Martin as head of Parlophone was that although EMI owned major American label Capitol, neither 'Crazy' nor 'Boomerang' were released on the Capitol label in the States. In the USA, Parlophone product was being farmed out to smaller, less well-known US labels, like Vee-Jay, which seriously limited their chances of success because those lesser labels did not receive the substantial promotion budgets of Capitol product … *more of which later.*

During the early part of 1957, George fell in love with his secretary at Parlophone, Judy Lockhart-Smith. Given the moral climate of the time, theirs was forced to be a clandestine relationship, but the situation became intolerable for everyone concerned and so George left Sheena and their two children to move into a flat of his own (not too far from Judy's apartment that she shared with two other girls). Once they were able to spend more time together, Judy wanted to help George achieve his full potential as a musician and to enjoy greater success. As has been noted, ever since he had been at Parlophone he had enjoyed writing or co-writing tunes and some of these had been recorded by artists for the label. When he had done this, George had created a pseudonym for himself. The name he settled upon was 'Graham Fisher'. Fortuitously, Judy had a good grand piano in her rooms and encouraged George in this endeavour.

In 1961, 'Graham Fisher' (music) co-wrote the tune 'Can This Be Love', while Herbert Kretzmer wrote the lyrics. By May, top British vocalist Matt Monro had recorded this song for Parlophone (George Martin producing, of course) and along with its B-side 'Why Not Now' it had climbed as high as number 24 in the UK chart: in effect, George aka 'Graham Fisher' had written his first 'hit'.

With the bit now firmly between his teeth and encouraged by Judy, George was inspired to write more. It wasn't long before he came up with 'Double Scotch' and 'The Niagara Theme', but this time Martin ditched Graham Fisher and copyrighted these under his own name. His choice of publisher proved highly significant. It was his good friend Dick James who had started out as a singer. (Any kid growing up in the mid- to late-1950s would sing along to Dick's version of 'Robin Hood' that played over the closing credits of the popular children's TV series, *The Adventures of Robin Hood*, starring Richard Greene in the title role. Dick also sang the theme tune for another popular children's TV series, *The Buccaneers*).

As his hair fell out and his singing career drew to a close, James had joined Sydney Bron Music as a music 'plugger', but by 1961 had decided to set up on his own as 'Dick James Music'. By then George Martin and Dick James had been good friends for ten years. George recognised Dick was ambitious, an enthusiastic and successful plugger, keen for success in his own right, and so he copyrighted both of his new songs to Dick James Music. 'Double Scotch' was Dick's first such copyright.

Right from the start, James enjoyed a good reputation, he was trusted and respected, in a sea of sharks he was considered to be an honest broker. His ear for a good tune was sound, people would take time to listen to a song Dick James chose to recommend or 'back' or 'plug'. And so, on 21 September 1961, Dick James Music opened up for business on the first floor of 132 Charing Cross Road, bang on the corner of Denmark Street, London. The address was all important, for Denmark Street was already famously nicknamed 'Tin Pan Alley' and as such was the home of British music publishing, the very hub of the music industry. It was to the music publishers whose offices filled the buildings along this small London street that A&R (Artist and Repertoire) men (nearly always men in those days) from EMI and Decca would head in search of songs for their artists to record. This is where the hits of tomorrow could be found. Writers and record companies also knew that publishers could be relied upon to rigorously 'plug' records once a song had been duly recorded, in order to further increase the income they could make from publishing a tune.

Dick James had also done his background work. He didn't want to be just another plugger and publisher. He wanted to offer something different. He knew the world of Tin Pan Alley well and was fully aware that American companies had Tin Pan Alley's pluggers and publishers in their sights and so he set out to be different to the rest. From the outset, James decided he was going to promote home-grown talent. Rather than American writers, Dick James Music would focus on 'securing and exploiting works by British writers'. He didn't rule out publishing works of 'foreign origin', but most definitely, whenever it could, for Dick James Music 'the accent will be on British works'. So read the words of a handwritten note James lodged with PRS (the Performing Right Society) as he set up shop. How prophetic could he possibly have been?

And so George Martin's 'Double Scotch' had its publisher and one week after Dick James was resident in Tin Pan Alley, Parlophone released 'Double Scotch' as recorded by the Ron Goodwin Orchestra. It was copyright 001 for Dick James Music. Wheels within wheels were beginning to turn. Little did Mr. George Martin and Mr. Dick James realise that, at that very moment, they had established a working relationship that was to set both men on the most fabulous (and lucrative) journey they could have ever imagined.

Notes 1 to11 inclusive: Sir George Martin in conversation with Bob Harris OBE and Colin Hall for the 2009 BBC Radio 2 documentary *The Songs the Beatles Gave Away*, written and narrated by Bob Harris, produced by Bob Harris and Trudie Myerscough-Harris for WBBC.
12 Lee Ann Obringer, 'How Music Royalties Work', 24 May 2003: HowStuffWorks.com. <https://entertainment.howstuffworks.com/music-royalties.htm> 11 January 2019.

Chapter 24:
RIGHT THEN, BRIAN – MANAGE US
(Passing the Decca Audition)

When Brian Epstein returned from London and met with the Beatles for the second time, at the appointed time of 4:30pm on Sunday 3 December 1961, he was faced with just three of them: John, George and Pete. Paul, for reasons best known to himself, chose to be late. Well, and truly, late. Brian must have been unnerved by this blatant show of disrespect, for he looked upon punctuality as a virtue and tardiness as a personal insult. The situation no doubt put everyone on edge. On phoning Paul's home and being told Paul had only just got up and was in the bath but would be along after that, Epstein finally erupted. Rightly so, Paul's behaviour was impolite. George Harrison managed to calm the situation down when he responded to Brian's outrage at Paul's unforgivable tardiness with a typical off-the-cuff remark that, "Well he may be late but he's very clean."[1]

Paul's eventual arrival allowed Epstein to pour forth the results of his visit to London on their behalf. He made it clear that much hinged on the details of their contract with Kaempfert, but everything Brian had achieved in London must have sounded very good indeed to the four Beatles. He had proven his interest was genuine and that doors opened for him. Not only did he make promises ... he kept them.

Paul was more guarded than John, George and Pete. He was particularly keen to know the details of any potential contract between them and Epstein, especially Brian's percentage.

Despite Paul's caution they all appreciated the fact that *should* they sign with him their energies would become more focused on simply making music and less burdened by the business side of being in a group. For one thing, Brian Epstein was set on ensuring they received higher fees for the shows they played. Pete was relieved that if they signed, Brian Epstein would become responsible for securing bookings for the Beatles which would remove a major weight from his shoulders. Epstein would also supervise and be responsible for their accounts and tax situation. His business know-how was very persuasive in suggesting he was the ideal person for the job.

It was a Sunday evening and at seven o'clock the pubs opened and so the meeting reconvened to a nearby pub. Nothing was agreed or signed at this point, but they were edging very close. As the evening moved beyond contractual discussions, Mark Lewisohn suggests that it was then that Brian Epstein discovered that John and Paul had written some songs together.[2]

This would have been a major discovery and would have further convinced Epstein of the Beatles' artistic potential. True, it had been a while since they had come up with any new tunes, but significantly they *had* composed in the past, and so there was nothing to stop them doing so again in the future. More to the point they still remembered their early attempts, although on stage, as a rule, the Beatles did not perform these tunes regularly.*

(*How well the Beatles kept John and Paul's songwriting under wraps at this time is evidenced by this comment by Astrid Kircherr in 2001: "In Hamburg the only original song I remember them playing was 'One After 909'. They were amazingly talented beyond the other bands that played, but when they released 'Love Me Do' it was a revelation.)[3]

Confirming how this accomplishment had impressed Brian Epstein, Lewisohn says five days after this meeting Brian wrote a letter in which he mentions it and spoke highly of the quality of one tune in particular which possibly Epstein had, by then, heard them perform. (Lewisohn posits the Beatles show at the Cavern on 6 December for when Brian would have done so.)[4]

That this was the case is further supported by the fact that it was in December 1961 that John and Paul's professional confidence was such they started to perform some of those old 'Lennon-McCartney originals' regularly on stage at the Cavern. The three tunes that entered the Beatles repertoire at this time were Paul's 'Like Dreamers Do' (1959), followed by John's 'Hello Little Girl' (1957) and then Paul's 'Love of the Loved' (1959). Initially, elsewhere than the Cavern, they kept to their 'all-covers' sets, but a crucial sea change had occurred. (All three 'original' tunes would be among the songs the Beatles eventually 'gave away'.)

Brian had no doubts about their collective appeal as a group, but this hitherto unknown creative element of their talent added an extra dimension and made his conviction even greater. His reasoning was that this would be a feature of their work that would resonate with those A&R men in London. It utterly confirmed his opinion that the Beatles were destined to be 'bigger than Elvis'.

It is most likely that, before they parted company on the 3 December, the decision had been made to invite Epstein to manage them. And even if it was not on that exact occasion, it was certainly close to this date. As the accepted leader of the group, the others looked to John to voice their decision, for even at this point in time it was a 'given' that the Beatles were still John Lennon's group. The others may raise concerns (and Paul, more than most, *did*) but they would not oppose John. He himself always maintained that the decision was mutual between the Beatles and Brian Epstein, that the Beatles 'allowed' Brian Epstein to manage them, that they weren't picked up off the street, they allowed him to take them …

That it was John, who made the invitation, left no room for doubt in Brian's mind as to who called the shots within the Beatles. Brian never forgot John's words: "Right then, Brian – manage us."[5]

Brian's assessment of the hierarchy within the group meant it was to John he would always turn when there was something he needed to achieve within 'the boys', as he affectionately dubbed them. He would outline his ideas to John first. John himself admitted he was closest to their manager: "In the group I was closest to him, and I did like him. He had great qualities and he was good fun. He had flair. He was a theatrical man rather than a business man, so in that way I liked him … We'd never have made it without him and vice versa. Brian contributed as much as us in the early days and he was the hustler."[6]

Passing the Decca Audition

Soon after their Sunday meeting, the results of Brian's trip to London took practical shape when, towards the end of the week, EMI replied with a translation of the Kaempfert contract. It was good news. Epstein learned that only three months' notice needed to be served to free the group from their commitments to their German producer. As this was the case, EMI kept their promise to pass on copies of 'My Bonnie' to Messrs. Martin, Newell, Paramor and Ridley.

Likewise, Decca did not take long to keep their word to Brian about a possible audition. They didn't wait to invite the Beatles to London, but instead, on 13 December, they sent newly promoted A&R man Mike Smith to Liverpool to hear the Beatles play the Cavern.

It was the night John first sang his then favourite new song to the audience at the club: 'Please Mister Postman' by the Marvelettes which had only just been released in the UK. (Billy Hatton of the Four Jays, soon to become the Fourmost, was mightily impressed that the Beatles had nailed this song so quickly and in doing so made it their own, commenting it would have taken his group a month before they could have played it as well as John, Paul, George and Pete.)

On the same bill were Gerry and the Pacemakers and the Four Jays.

The knowledge that Smith was in the audience with Brian Epstein was electrifying. It was not usual for an A&R person to travel beyond London to check out an artist or artistes, but Decca had just announced a change of policy to become more focused on discovering British talent. Smith had just been promoted from being assistant to Decca's chief A&R man Dick Rowe to a fully fledged A&R man in his own right.

That night at the Cavern, Mike Smith was there in his new capacity. It *was* an audition and Smith was duly impressed: the Beatles passed their 'audition' and so Smith invited Epstein to bring them to London for a commercial/recording test. (It was from such 'tests' that not only would an artist's suitability to make records be judged but, if successful, their first single would be usually chosen from what they had recorded.)

Confusingly the Beatles referred to their commercial 'test' as their 'audition'.

The date set for this prestigious event was: 1 January 1962. (It was not until 1 January 1974 that New Year's Day became a Bank Holiday in the UK.)

Smith's invitation absolutely vindicated John's faith in Epstein: being the best in Liverpool was one thing, but making records in your own right was another. Their fingertips were now surely touching the 'toppermost of the poppermost' and it was Brian who had made that happen!

Just as Christmas 1961 was building towards being a very happy one indeed for the Beatles, EMI went and spoiled the party. A few days before their trip to Decca's London studio for their commercial/recording test, EMI (in a letter from Ron White) informed Brian that having listened to 'My Bonnie' all four A&R managers had made the decision not to offer the group a recording contract. (It has since been suggested that only two – Ridley and Newell – of the four A&R men had actually played the single, and that, for whatever reasons, Paramor and Martin had not.)

For sure this would have been a significant blow, but with Decca interested and the Beatles having passed their audition with Mike Smith in Liverpool, Epstein could let EMI's decision ride.

THE UK'S TOP 30 MOST POPULAR HIT RECORDS OF 1961
01 Elvis Presley: Wooden Heart
02 Del Shannon: Runaway
03 Helen Shapiro: You Don't Know
04 John Leyton: Johnny Remember Me
05 Helen Shapiro: Walking Back to Happiness
06 Eden Kane: Well I Ask You
07 The Everly Brothers: Walk Right Back / Ebony Eyes
08 The Allisons: Are You Sure?
09 Billy Fury: Halfway to Paradise
10 Elvis Presley: Are You Lonesome Tonight?
11 Elvis Presley: Surrender
12 Ricky Nelson: Hello Mary Lou / Travellin' Man
13 Shirley Bassey: Reach for the Stars / Climb Ev'ry Mountain
14 The Everly Brothers: Temptation
15 Elvis Presley: His Latest Flame / Little Sister
16 Petula Clark: Sailor
17 The Shadows: Frightened City
18 The Temperance Seven: You're Driving Me Crazy
19 The Marcels: Blue Moon
20: Johnny Tillotson: Poetry in Motion
21: Frankie Vaughan: Tower of Strength
22 Andy Stewart: A Scottish Soldier
23 The Shadows: FBI
24 Clarence 'Frogman' Henry: (I Don't Know Why) But I Do
25 The Temperance Seven: Pasadena
26 The Highwaymen: Michael
27 Cliff Richard: Theme for a Dream
28 Helen Shapiro: Don't Treat Me Like a Child
29 Bobby Vee: More Than I Can Say / Staying In
30 The Shadows: Kon-Tiki

1 *A Cellarful of Noise*, Brian Epstein, p.49.
2 & 4 *The Beatles – All These Years: Volume One: Tune In*, Extended Special Edition, by Mark Lewisohn, (Little, Brown, 2013) p.1018.
3 Astrid Kircherr in conversation with the author in Hamburg, 2001 from 'Astrid Kircherr: In My Life', *Get Rhythm*, Issue 6, August 2001.
5 *A Cellarful of Noise*, Brian Epstein, p.51.
6 *Apple to the Core* by Peter McCabe and Robert D, Schonfeld, (Sphere Books, 1973) Chapter 2, pp.31/2, John Lennon quotation dated August 1971.

Chapter 25:
THE DECCA TAPES

1962
Was the year when Nazi war criminal Adolf Eichmann was hanged in Israel ... Dr.No, the film, was premiered in the UK ... on 14 October the Cuban Missile Crisis began and for a very tense two weeks the world held its breath as it stood on the edge of the nuclear precipice ... pull-tab drink cans were introduced ... The Rolling Stones played their debut gig at The Marquee Club in London ... Hollywood star, Marilyn Monroe died ...

The Beatles finished 1961 on 27 December with a special occasion at the Cavern. Called 'The Beatles Christmas Party', the bill also featured Gerry and the Pacemakers and Kingsize Taylor and the Dominoes. It turned out to be more special than expected. Pete Best became ill and George asked Ringo Starr to sit in for him. The Hurricanes weren't playing that night and so he obliged.

The paths of the Beatles and the Hurricanes had been crossing ever since they played at the Kaiserkeller in the autumn of 1960 and during 1961 they'd seen a lot of each other in Liverpool. George was closest to Ringo, but John and Paul also enjoyed it when Ringo sat in with them. Ringo's presence just felt right: as a quartet they bonded. George would remark many years later that with Ringo in the group they felt 'complete'. He elaborated by saying they would hang out together after a gig and have fun, whereas Pete didn't do that, he was very much a loner and just disappeared once a gig was over.

Any chance of Ringo joining the Beatles at this point went west when he quit the Hurricanes to go to Hamburg to play in a Top Ten house band fronted by Tony Sheridan. His quitting floored the Hurricanes, who did not seek a replacement and decided to use stand-ins instead, just hoping for his eventual return. Quite simply, Ringo had become restless, keen for greater success and fully aware that as a group Rory Storm and the Hurricanes were beginning to slide. From being the biggest in 1960, they'd slipped throughout 1961 and when a *Mersey Beat* popularity poll was published in early 1962, the Hurricanes were in fourth place behind the Beatles as winners, Gerry and the Pacemakers as runners-up and the Remo Four in third place. During 1962 they slipped even further behind.

Like Ringo, the Beatles would also be returning to Hamburg, but overriding any thoughts of that or of replacing Pete with Ringo took a back seat as the new year loomed, for right then and there they had much more pressing matters on their mind.

The Beatles' Decca 'Audition'
At 11am on New Year's Eve 1961 (a Sunday), driven by Neil, the Beatles travelled south to London in a van especially hired for the trip. Brian Epstein went by train. It was a hellish 11-hour journey as Neil battled his way through snowstorms, dense fog, ice, and all that a ferocious British winter's day could throw at them, before he could safely deliver the boys at their destination.

Arriving at the Royal Hotel on Woburn Place, at about 10pm they rendezvoused with Brian and spent a late evening of dining, drinking, and window shopping. They also took in the obligatory visitors' trip to Trafalgar Square to catch the annual 'New Year' celebrations before falling into their beds just hours ahead of their precious 'test'.

By travelling to Liverpool and hearing the Beatles at the Cavern, Mike Smith had actually already 'auditioned' the group and they'd passed. What they were in London for was not an audition as such, but a 'commercial test'. Based on how they sounded in this recorded 'test', the decision would be made as to whether they would or would not be offered a recording contract. A 'commercial test' allowed a record company to hear just how well an artist took to recording, how commercial an artist sounded and ultimately, if they were worth taking a punt on. Usually if they were deemed good enough to be offered a contract it was from the material they had recorded at their 'commercial test' that songs were chosen for release as the A- and B-sides of an artist's debut single.

Monday 1 January 1962 was a bitterly cold day with temperatures dropping as low as -16 C (as recorded at Northolt Airport, Greater London). As they braved that deep freeze, the Beatles were taking their first real step towards becoming the British Elvis Presleys. They were always ambitious and had huge confidence in their abilities, but they also knew nothing came easy. Progression came in small steps. Passing their audition had been one thing, but it was the 'commercial test' that would secure them a record contract: *this* was the major first step on the slippery ladder of national success and 'pop stardom'! After that came releasing a record, then came promoting it and hopefully taking it into the charts, and only after that might come the possibility of challenging for a number 1 hit …

A recording studio is a place of work and for young musicians in 1962 they were, in many ways, quite forbidding places. A uniformed commissionaire would have been on duty at the front door. Inside, the staff dressed formally: producers wore suits, technical engineers wore white lab coats and maintenance workers wore brown. There were set working hours. Everyone was on the payroll. The atmosphere and environment within the Decca Studios was that of a workplace where a serious job was being done, which, of course, it was.

When the Beatles entered the doors of Decca Studios, 165 Broadhurst Gardens, West Hampstead, London, the building would have felt as sombre and formal as it had been for decades. A serious atmosphere would have prevailed with little to identify it as one of the hearts of the UK 'entertainment' industry. There may have been a smidgen of excitement that morning because of a rumour that Decca and EMI, both global corporations, were about to merge. But maybe not, as this was a frequent rumour, so most probably everything and everyone was carrying on as normal: decorously.

Arriving at the front door at 10am as requested, the Beatles were immediately directed by the commissionaire to the back door because they turned up lugging their equipment with them. Once inside, as they proceeded to set up in the studio, they quickly encountered problems with their amplifiers that they had hauled all the way down from Liverpool. As a constantly gigging group, the gear was constantly in use, it was always turned up loud, but now they discovered that when turned low for the purposes of recording it emitted a hum. This was not acceptable and so the studio engineers insisted they plug into studio amps which meant that *they* would control the sound balance, not the band. Unnervingly, Pete had to set up behind isolation screens which meant the others couldn't see him. To further compound a stressful situation, Mike Smith arrived an hour late, which upset Brian (that well-known stickler for punctuality). Also, for a New Year's Day, it was a very early start for 'the Boys'.

It was not the best of beginnings but, when 11am came round, the Beatles finally found themselves standing inside one of London's most prestigious recording studios raring to record. It was almost four and a half years since John and Paul had first been introduced to each other in Woolton, Liverpool. In front of them, ensconced inside a glass booth, were a bevy of engineers and producer Mike Smith with his finger hovering above the 'record' button. How nervous and excited must they have been?

The 'test' ran from 11am to noon approximately, during which time the Beatles cut 15 tracks, i.e., one song every four minutes. They did run-throughs but the recordings were all first takes with no 'over-dubs'.

The 15 taped songs reflected very much the range of their 'live' repertoire of the time and included three self-penned tunes, the inclusion of which may well have been encouraged by Brian Epstein in order to highlight John and Paul's budding compositional gifts. Certainly the set accurately reflected the eclecticism and versatility of the Beatles and highlighted the fact that three of the boys could handle lead vocals.

Strangely, given how much a highlight of their act that they were, their three-part harmonies were not too much in evidence. Listening to the recordings at nearly 60 years removed, it's clearer than ever that the Beatles never really got going that morning. It was as if the freezing conditions outside had followed them into the studios.

In an interview with Paul Drew on American radio in 1975, John Lennon commented that they recorded more or less their Cavern stage set of the time. Unfortunately, the Cavern audience weren't there with them in the studio for the group to feed off their enthusiasm, for their performance is generally stilted and nerves creep in as energy leaks out.

The performances captured aren't those of the mesmerising Beatles that their audiences would have so much enjoyed during most of their 349 'live' performances in 1961. The tape as a whole is a pale shadow of what they could do. Although Lennon is not always at his peak vocally and neither is Paul, it is still clear they are both very good vocalists. George is most probably the most confident. Most unfortunate of all, once again Pete Best did not shine. Unlike in Hamburg, he was allowed to use his full kit, but like the other occasion nerves crept in and he held back, occasionally struggled with the tempo and showed little variety in his style. He isn't the engine powering the group on that a band really needs their drummer to be. Many years later Mike Savage, the balance engineer for the session, told writer Mark Lewisohn he thought, "Pete Best was very average and didn't keep good time … If Decca was going to sign the Beatles, we wouldn't have used Pete Best on the records."[1]

With Ringo's recent, warmly appreciated stand-in performance at 'The Beatles Christmas Party' still fresh in their minds, the commercial test did not bode well for Pete.

In Michael Braun's brilliant fly-on-the-wall, John-Lennon-endorsed, 'Love Me Do', John says of their Decca experience: "We didn't sound natural."[2]

John's candour expresses a good reason why their trip to London on that occasion did not produce the offer of a contract.

Despite these reservations, the Decca tape *is* a fascinating historical aural document. Certain elements of the Beatles' magic *do* shine through, such as their harmonies (on 'Hello Little Girl') while 'Three Cool Cats' catches the Beatles' sense of humour, and George delivers some good guitar playing on tracks such as 'Crying, Waiting, Hoping'.

For the purposes of this publication, the Decca Tapes are also a brilliant insight into the musical melting pot of the Beatles' influences and the compositional sources on which John and Paul (and later George) were drawing at this time.

So, for what lay ahead, a brief examination of those 15 tracks is hugely instructive.

The Decca Tapes
Date: Monday 1 January 1962.
Artistes: The Beatles: John Lennon, Paul McCartney, George Harrison, Pete Best.
Recordings made by: Decca's A&R assistant and producer Mike Smith, and balance engineer Mike Savage.

The songs were recorded in mono. Prior to recording a song, they had performed a run-through in preparation.

The list below is not the order in which the songs were recorded that morning for that is unknown.

My list begins with the three 'originals' written by John and Paul. After that the list features the 12 'covers' they recorded. For those songs the title of each is followed by its composer/composers, its year of release in the UK, the name of the artists who recorded it or whose version the Beatles favoured, on which label it received its UK issue, plus its UK chart placing (if any) in brackets. Accompanying each song is other relevant information.

1 'Hello Little Girl' by John Lennon and Paul McCartney
Written by John Lennon towards the end of 1957, it was the first tune he felt confident enough to play and sing to Paul. It is also the first to be credited to the 'Lennon-McCartney' partnership. The inspiration for this song apparently came from a song John's mother Julia used to sing around her home at 1 Blomfield Road, entitled 'Scatterbrain'. 'Scatterbrain' was a 1939 dance-band and film number written by Khan Keene, Carl Bean, Frankie Masters and Johnny Burke. Frankie Masters and His Orchestra had originally recorded it with Frankie on vocals. What captivated/intrigued John about the tune was the "rhythmic flow" of lines such as:
'When you smile it's so delightful
When you talk it's so insane
Still it's charming chatter, scatterbrain'

At the time John composed (on guitar) 'Hello Little Girl', he was a devotee of Buddy Holly and the tune materialised as he experimented with chords and phrases he was playing in the style of Holly. What emerged was a tune that sounds nothing like 'Scatterbrain' but whose lyrics do have a similar "rhythmic flow".[3] Written in the first person, the song is very 'catchy and direct' which is, again, very much in the style of Buddy Holly. (A home demo of the song from 1960 exists.)

2 'Like Dreamers Do' by John Lennon and Paul McCartney
Another very early 'Lennon, McCartney original', mainly written by Paul in 1959, who also sang it on stage. Followed swiftly by John's 'Hello Little Girl', this was the first Lennon-McCartney song that the Beatles began to sing regularly at the Cavern.[4]

3 'Love of the Loved' by John Lennon and Paul McCartney
In reality this was another early Paul McCartney tune, but another credited to the 'Lennon, McCartney' partnership. It was most likely composed in 1959. Paul's girlfriend of the time (later fiancée) Dorothy Rhone, says it was written for her, although Paul has never publicly acknowledged this.

4 'Money (That's What I Want)' written by Tamla Motown founder Berry Gordy Jr, Janie Bradford – Barrett Strong (London HLU 9088) April 1960
In 1959 it became the first US Motown hit when Barrett Strong recorded it.
On stage this driving rhythm and blues tune was a song John had very quickly made his own.

5 'Till There Was You' written by Meredith Wilson, recorded and released by Peggy Lee (Capitol CL 15 184) for whom it was a minor hit in March 1961 (number 40) and again in April (number 30).
The song came from Wilson's musical, *The Music Man* (1957) which was made into a film in 1962. It's a song with which Paul regularly wooed the girls down the Cavern. Hearts would flutter and dreams take flight when, with eyes turned upward, he crooned the tune.

6 'The Sheik of Araby' written by Harry B. Smith, and Francis Wheeler (lyrics), Ted Snyder (music), written in 1921 and first performed by Eddie Cantor in the 1922 stage musical *Make It Snappy* and then in the 1940 film *Tin Pan Alley* starring Alice Faye and Betty Grable.
The Beatles based their version on a TV performance by Joe Brown in 1961 (seen most probably by George if not the others). George was a great fan of Joe's, especially enjoying Joe's prowess on the guitar. The two men went on to become close friends. However, if ever there was a track the Beatles should have left at home in Liverpool on this cold and frosty day in London it was this one.

7 'To Know Her Is to Love Her' written by Phil Spector and released in the UK in October 1958 by the Teddy Bears (London HL 8733) for whom it became a UK number 2 hit.

8 'Take Good Care of My Baby' written by Carole King, Gerry Goffin and released in the UK by Bobby Vee (London HLG 9438) in October 1961, and with which he scored a number 3 hit. Included no doubt because John and Paul admired songwriters Goffin and King and as evidence that the Beatles were in tune with the charts and could quickly incorporate new or current hits into their act.

9 'Memphis Tennessee' written, recorded and released by Chuck Berry (London HLM 8921) in July 1959. (It did not chart in 1959 but reached number 6 in the UK in 1963.) Like Buddy Holly, Chuck Berry was most definitely on the Beatles' radar, as he was for most British groups of that era (especially the Rolling Stones). In the Beatles' eyes, Holly and Berry rocked and rolled most persuasively, but equally as importantly, they both wrote great lyrics. They would have admired how, with just a few well chosen words, they both painted vivid aural pictures and like few others authentically got beneath the skin of how it felt to be young, restless and in love.
   For a week in February 1972, John and Yoko Ono co-hosted *The Mike Douglas Show* in the USA. Among their guests that week was Chuck Berry, of whom John said, "If you had to give rock 'n' roll another name, you might call it Chuck Berry." He also performed 'Memphis Tennessee' live with Chuck on the show. (They also performed 'Johnny B. Goode'.)

10 'Sure to Fall (In Love with You)' written by Carl Perkins, Quentin Claunch, Bill Cantrell. As sung by Carl Perkins on his 1957 LP *The Carl Perkins Dance Album* (Sun SLP 1225) which was released in the USA and re-released there in 1961.
   When Carl's album was released in the UK in 1959, John Lennon (who had previously purchased the singles 'Blue Suede Shoes' and 'Matchbox') bought himself a copy and liked every track on it. No doubt this is where and when the Beatles first heard 'Sure to Fall'. (Remarkably, six of the album's songs were later recorded by the Beatles, either as a group or as solo artists.)
   In 1961, Carl's album received a second release in the UK, this time it was re-titled *Teen Beat: The Best of Carl Perkins* (London HA - S 2202).

11 'Three Cool Cats' written by Jerry Leiber (lyrics), Mike Stoller (music) and recorded and released in the UK by the Coasters (London HLE 8819) in 1959 as the B-side to 'Charlie Brown', which was a number 6 UK hit.
   As writers for Elvis, Leiber and Stoller would definitely have been on the Beatles' radar. This song gave rein to the Beatles' on-stage sense of humour, but somehow this Decca performance never quite engaged the listener in the same way it would have done 'down the Cavern'.

12 'Crying, Waiting, Hoping' written by Buddy Holly and released as the B-side of Buddy's 1959 number 13 UK single 'Peggy Sue Got Married' (Vogue Coral Q 72376).

13 'September in the Rain' written by Harry Warren, Al Dubin – Dinah Washington (Mercury AMT 1162) December 1961, Dinah Washington's sole UK single hit which charted twice between November 1961 and January 1962, spending just four weeks in total in the UK Top 50, peaking at number 35 during its first run in '61.
(In 1966 Liverpool group Paul and Ritchie and the Crying Shames released their version of the song on the Decca label. The production credit on the label read 'Meeksville Sound', i.e., Joe Meek.)

14 'Besame Mucho (Kiss Me a Lot)' written by Consuelo Velazquez (music, lyrics): Velazquez was a Mexican singer, pianist and songwriter, who, in 1940, wrote the song, a bolero. Sunny Skylar wrote the English lyrics for it in 1944 when it was a hit for the Jimmy Dorsey Orchestra.

The Beatles took their version from the Coasters who, in 1960, released a double-sided version Parts I & 2 (London HLK 9111) in the UK, but it did not chart here. Earlier in April in the USA, it had reached number 70 in *Billboard*'s Pop Chart.

15 'Searchin' written by Jerry Leiber (lyrics), Mike Stoller (music) and recorded by the Coasters (London HLE 8450). Released in the UK in 1957 when it enjoyed a single week on the charts at number 30.

N.B. *An aside re: Musical notes and the influence of other songs/genres on the Lennon-McCartney original compositions 'Love of the Loved' and 'Like Dreamers Do'*
'To Know Her Is to Love Her'
This early Phil Spector composition was mightily enjoyed by the Beatles and according to Paul McCartney the first three-part the group ever did when they learned it one afternoon at 20 Forthlin Road. In his excellent CD booklet notes for 'Beatles Beginnings Volume 3: Silver Beatles' (Rhythm and Blues Records RAND8007) Nick Duckett comments that, "It's likely that Paul was thinking of the unusual harmonies of the Teddy Bears bridge section when constructing the equally improbable chord structures of his 'Love of the Loved'."[5]
'Darktown Strutters Ball'
Written by Shelton Brooks in 1917 and recorded by many artists since. Joe Brown and The Bruvvers released their version in the UK in the spring of 1960 on the Decca label and enjoyed a number 34 hit with it.

Joe Brown was a contender for the Beatles' favourite British rock 'n' roller. Under Brian Epstein's NEMS banner, in July 1962, they performed two gigs with him at Southport and New Brighton.

This song is a jazz standard often performed by New Orleans Dixieland bands and features an interesting harmonic device (chords moving through I-II-IV) that the Beatles would use in some of their own songs, such as 'You Won't See Me' and 'Like Dreamers Do'. Both songs are in the key of A major as is Joe Brown's 'Darktown Strutters Ball'.
'I'll Build a Stairway to Paradise'
Written by George Gershwin, and Jim Mac's favourite tune. George Harrison was of the mind that Paul's 'Like Dreamers Do' exuded the influence of Jim's musical tastes on his son. So it is that the weird intro to the Beatles' version of 'Like Dreamers Do' references 'I'll Build a Stairway to Paradise' by speeding up the chord sequence of the verse (although the Beatles use different chords which bounce in and out of key to give the intro a rising sound). Paul: "We were listening … to 'Like Dreamers Do', one of my early songs … and George and I looked at each other and said, 'That's your old man, that's 'Stairway to Paradise'. So a lot of my musicality came from my Dad."[6]

Decca: What happened next?

The Beatles *did* hear the tape before they left the studio that day. They were savvy enough to have known it wasn't great. Mike Smith did not commit there and then to signing them. He couldn't. Instead he simply told them he'd be in touch. He may have been an A&R man but he was newly appointed and it was too early in his tenure for him to sign the Beatles on the spot. Smith was under instructions to run such decisions by his head of department, a chap called Dick Rowe. That was why, despite being called for a commercial test, the Beatles were left hanging in the balance as to whether Decca was actually going to sign them. Rowe was busy at the time with a Billy Fury film called *Play It Cool!*, after which he was America-bound for several weeks. The portents were still in their favour, however, because of Decca's much publicly lauded intention to focus on gaining more single record successes with British artists.

With that very remit in mind, Smith had another group booked for a test at Decca. They came from Dagenham and called themselves 'Brian Poole and the Tremeloes'.

On their return to Liverpool, the headline news in that week's *Mersey Beat* proclaimed

'Beatles Top Poll!' which would no doubt have helped quell any sinking feelings the group may have had about events in London. Not only this, but Brian had secured a British release for 'My Bonnie' which came out on Friday 5 January 1962 to encouraging reviews. Despite early acclaim, the record was not 'plugged' sufficiently well and it did not make the charts, although, surprisingly, it was a hit in 'Mendips' where, apparently, John's Aunt Mimi liked it and proudly played it to her student lodgers.

Mersey Beat's Poll, announced on Thursday 4 January 1962

1. The Beatles
2. Gerry and the Pacemakers
3. The Remo Four
4. Rory Storm and the Hurricanes
5. Johnny Sandon and the Searchers
6. Kingsize Taylor and the Dominoes
7. The Big Three
8. The Strangers
9. Faron and the Flamingos
10. The Four Jays
11. Ian and the Zodiacs
12. The Undertakers
13. Earl Preston and the TTs
14. Mark Peters and the Cyclones
15. Karl Terry and the Cruisers
16. Derry and the Seniors
17. Steve and the Syndicate
18. Dee Fenton and the Silhouettes
19. Billy Kramer and the Coasters
20 Dale Roberts and the Jaywalkers

Of course, by the time of the trip to London to record for Decca and the Mersey Beat poll, Brian Epstein had visited the Beatles' parents. He knew it was important to do so as soon as possible (and of course Paul, Pete and George were still underage and would need their parents to countersign any contract he was proposing for them). Brian was keen that they knew who he was and what he hoped to achieve for their sons. He was a good man and wished their parents to understand he had their best interests at heart. He also knew his job would be much easier if he had them on board.

Visiting John's Aunt Mimi would no doubt have been a challenging experience, but of much more significance was his meeting with Pete's mother Mona at their home in Hayman's Green. After Allan Williams, of all the folk in Liverpool who had helped the Beatles both before and after their visits to Hamburg, Mona had done more than most to further their careers (Sam Leach included). Her efforts to secure bookings and give them bookings herself at the Casbah was as close as to becoming their manager as anyone else had come since Allan Williams' early efforts on their behalf. Few could have argued against Mona or have been surprised if she already considered herself to *be* their manager!

Within the Best home, Brian found that things had changed quite dramatically. Amid the excitement that Pete's music career was going from strength to strength there was the unexpected news that Mona was pregnant. She and Neil were expecting a baby. Irrespective of Brian Epstein's arrival on the scene, this effectively heralded the end of Mona's work on behalf of the group. Mona was canny and could see that Epstein was exactly what the Beatles needed at this moment in time to take their careers even further. She also wanted the best for her son. She did not contest Brian's right to become their manager. "He was so keen and full of enthusiasm. He was also young and certainly seemed to be the type of person who could do something for the Beatles."[7]

It was on Wednesday 24 January 1962 that the Beatles finally signed a contract in which they agreed Brian Epstein was to be their manager. It was the third draft of the document Brian had had drawn up. John, Paul, George and Pete signed and Brian's personal assistant Alistair Taylor also signed, but Brian never did. Significantly Brian had had the parents written out of the third draft. The omission of James McCartney, Harold Harrison and John Best was quite something for, in the eyes of the law, it actually rendered the contract null and void. 'The boys' never noticed (or if they did they kept very quiet about it).

As far as they were concerned they *had* signed a legal document with Brian in which they agreed he could be their manager for the next five years … although there was a clause that said after a year, either side to the agreement could terminate it by giving the other side three months' notice of their intention to do so.

Obviously Brian's lawyers had strongly advised against omitting the parents, but he was adamant. He knew exactly what he was doing. He himself said he did so to give the Beatles an easy way out should he not achieve what he'd promised to do for them. He wanted no rancour or ill-feeling should things not go the way they all hoped they would.

Even more generously, Epstein agreed to perform all his duties for them for just a 10% commission rate which, should the Beatles earn more than £1500 per annum would rise to 15%. This was exceptionally benevolent when you add in the fact that Epstein was acting not only as their manager but also as their agent. Agents usually charged a separate fee to that of a manager, but Brian was performing both roles for one fee. More than this the group and the manager were partners, Brian would always consult 'the boys' (as he referred to them) on important issues. This kind of business relationship in the music industry was practically unheard of. For Brian the whole adventure had given his life focus. He'd begun to grow tired of managing the family record store, he was an ambitious, creative, intelligent and talented man and now in the Beatles he had found a challenge in life that he considered worthy of his talents.

Signing a management deal with Brian Epstein changed everything for the Beatles. His assertion that the Beatles would become 'bigger than Elvis' equally surprised, impressed and charmed the group, just as it had when Sam Leach had used almost the same words to express his faith in their potential.

As 1962 progressed, Brian encouraged the Beatles to become more 'professional'. This included not eating, swearing and smoking on stage, playing for a set time (usually an hour) and dressing more acceptably. Accordingly, they quit the leather for superbly crafted mohair suits which were especially designed for them. The epitome of cool, 'the boys' looked sharp decked out in their new gear! They all agreed to do this because they knew Brian was right. Their appearance had to open doors not keep them closed. Brian paid them regularly (on Fridays) and their pay packets included details of their forthcoming bookings.

When Brian had learned that John and Paul wrote songs together he knew this was special. As far as he knew none of the other Mersey groups were doing this and so he encouraged Lennon and McCartney to start feeding their own tunes into the Beatles' 'live' repertoire.

Just as everything was going so swimmingly, there came an unexpected bombshell.

EMI had already rejected the Beatles, but then … so did Decca.

All details in this book that appertain to the very early songs written by Lennon and McCartney come from a variety of sources, including Bob Harris's and my interviews with Sir Paul McCartney and artists such as Billy Hatton and Cilla Black. Beyond these the most helpful/informative sources are pages 516 to 517 of *The Beatles – All These Years: Volume One: Tune In*, Extended Special Edition, by Mark Lewisohn, (Little, Brown, 2013). Other specific references are:

1 *The Beatles – All These Years: Volume One: Tune In*, Extended Special Edition, by Mark Lewisohn, (Little, Brown, 2013) p.1059.
2 *Love Me Do! The Beatles Progress*, published by Penguin in 1964, on p.49.
3, 4 *The Beatles – All These Years: Volume One: Tune In*, Extended Special Edition, by Mark Lewisohn, (Little, Brown, 2013) p.399.
5 Nick Duckett from his booklet notes (p.27) for 'Beatles Beginnings Volume 3: Silver Beatles' CD
(Rhythm and Blues Records RAND8007).
6 *The Beatles Anthology*, by The Beatles (Cassell & Co, 2000) p.18.
7 *Beatle! The Pete Best Story* by Pete Best and Patrick Doncaster (Plexus Publishing Limited, 1989) p.127.

Chapter 26:
THE CAVERN CLUB: THE LUNCHTIME SESSIONS

'The venue with the menu with the mostest' (Bob Wooler, DJ at The Cavern)

Freda Kelly counts herself fortunate to have seen the Beatles at the Cavern before they became nationally famous. Through her frequent visits to the club she quickly became their friend. Here she kindly shares her memories of those special times …

"I'm an Irish girl, Dublin born, but in 1958 when I was 13 my family moved to Liverpool. By the very early Sixties I had begun work for Simpson Roberts & Co (Princes Foods) whose office was situated on the corner of Stanley Street (at no. 46) and Mathew Street. The plan was that a short while later I would go to Oxford to complete a course in banking and then go to work for the Midland Bank.

"The area around Stanley Street and Mathew Street was much different back then than it is today when it has become a tourist hub (with all that entails) and retail centre. In the 1950s and '60s shops were few and far between, it was mainly a commercial area with lots of offices and functioning warehouses.

"I hadn't been long at Simpson Roberts when one day in late 1961/early 1962 two of my co-workers, Bernie and Mike, invited me to join them on their dinner break when they were planning on nipping round the corner for the lunchtime session in a subterranean music club suitably called 'The Cavern'. It was good fun they said, something a bit different to do and they thought I would enjoy it, would I like to join them?

"It sounded good to me and so not long after I found myself standing in the dimly lit basement of a small, three-aisled space staring at a tiny raised platform that passed for a stage and on which a rock and roll group were in full swing. The name on the bass drum was most unusual and told me the four boys in front of me were 'The Beatles'. That struck me as different and from that moment on I was transfixed. I absolutely loved what I heard. It was a life-changing moment.

"Those now-famous Cavern Club lunchtime sessions were held each weekday from 12 noon until 2.15pm. A different group were booked each day to play two sets at each session. I lived and died in that club and soon became what they called 'a Cavernite'.

"I've estimated that I saw the Beatles on at least 200 occasions. Not just at the lunchtime sessions, I would attend evening shows as well and occasionally go to other clubs like the Iron Door, but I wasn't as keen on those places. I was a Beatles fan, I wasn't any other group's fan, so wherever the Beatles played I would try and get to that venue. That said, nothing compared with seeing them at the Cavern and while I always enjoyed the evening shows nothing compared, nothing was ever as good as seeing the Beatles in my lunch break.

"When the doors opened at noon the group booked for that day would play twice, once from 12.15 until 1pm and then again from 1.15 until 2.15pm. Two sets. I had an hour for lunch and to me the second session was always the best so I would schedule my dinner for between 1 and 2pm. However, I would always try to stretch my work in the morning to last until about 1.10/15pm, which meant I was always a tad late going to lunch, but as a result I could stay right to the end of that second session at the Cavern. Working in Stanley Street helped me to do this, for if I ran I was literally two to three minutes away from the club. That closeness to the Cavern was crucial for it meant I could stay right until the very end of a performance before legging it back to work!

"Shopworkers only got 45 minutes for dinner, and as there weren't very many shops in

The central Arch of the Cavern Club, Liverpool. (Ursula Wildling)

that part of the city in those days not many shopworkers attended the lunchtime sessions, it was mainly office workers like me who got an hour for dinner. As an office worker I was given luncheon vouchers which were worth 3 shillings each. It was thanks to my vouchers that I could afford to go each day to the Cavern, for I would sell mine for 2 shillings and out of that two bob I could afford the 1 shilling entry and spend the other shilling on a cheese and onion cob (bread roll) and a cup of tea. Thelma was the name of the lady who worked in the club's cafe.

"My preference was always for the second session because sometimes musicians would be late or took time setting up and you could miss part of their set if you went for that first set. By the time I arrived just after 1pm everything was already set up and I would hear the full second session. You knew it was the end when Bob Wooler, the Cavern's DJ would play either 'Love Letters' by Ketty Lester or 'I'll Be There' by Bobby Darin. That was the signal for me to leg it back to work! (The Cavern did not close although the sessions ended and sometimes groups would hang around to rehearse after the punters had all gone. You would often be able to hear them if you were outside in the street.)

"There was no cloakroom open at lunchtime and in all my time attending gigs at the Cavern I never saw Cilla Black working there, although I knew Cilla and saw her at the club because I palled around with her friend Pat Davies.

"What I loved so much about those lunchtime shows was they were so informal. The club was never chocker (full), you could always sit down if you wanted to (although I rarely did) because it was never full, there'd be about 30 to 40 people at most. Not many people knew about it and you had to be working in the area to attend at such a time. It would be different at the evening shows when the club would draw a much bigger audience.

"When I arrived my 'spec' was the first aisle on the left from the stage. I stood there, leaning on the wall, I couldn't be seen from the back and could look directly onto the stage. There were three aisles – the stage (which was not very high because the arched ceiling above was low) was at the end of the middle one. It was a small space with just enough room for two microphone stands, three wouldn't fit. Everyone could talk with the

Beatles or whichever group was on stage because the club was so small and we were all so close to that space. The band room was at the end of the third aisle, just one step down and the door always seemed to be open, it was only very seldom closed.

"I never danced when the Beatles were on stage because I wanted to watch them. You could go into the band room before they were due on stage and chat with them. You might mention to them that it was someone in the audience's birthday and ask could they say hello, or request a song. I might ask George if he could sing 'Three Cool Cats' and he might reply, 'We did that in the first half', so I might ask John if he could sing 'Anna'. If they were on stage you could do the same. I loved to hear John sing 'Anna' and sometimes when I asked he wouldn't go straight into it, but later he would. Depending what mood John was in he might say something to someone in the audience like, 'You're late' or 'I like your hair', but he was as blind as a bat without his glasses and so generally couldn't see too much!

"Paul was always polite, I never really saw him moody, John you knew to tread carefully around to try and judge his mood first before speaking to him, George was delightful and Pete was the quiet one. I liked him but he was a different personality to the others. When Pete left I already knew Ringo from his being the drummer in the Hurricanes, Rory Storm's group. Ringo, or Ritchie as we called him, always seemed to be happy, he was a fun person to be around.

"I never knew who wrote the songs they sang. Obviously for most of the time they played the Cavern they weren't performing their own tunes, they were singing other people's songs. When they introduced a song they didn't usually say very much about it at all, more often than not they just went straight into a number without any introduction, although if they were playing a request they would say who it was for. Comments about who had written a particular song were not usual. None of the groups did that.

"The Beatles' performances at the Cavern lunchtime sessions were different to how they'd be in the evenings. They were much more informal, there didn't seem to be a set running order, but in the evenings there would be. The lunchtime performances felt more like rehearsals. You could easily chat to them on stage. They didn't play two days on the trot at the lunchtime sessions. One week they'd do Monday, Wednesday, Friday and the next they'd only play Tuesday and Thursday. Other groups played the other days, Gerry and the Pacemakers would alternate with them as did the Four Jays (aka the Fourmost), Pete MacLaine and the Dakotas, Billy Kramer and the Coasters, I also saw Tommy Quickly and his sister Pat perform at the lunchtime sessions.

"Later, after the Beatles had signed with Brian Epstein and had scored hit records, if acts such as the Stones, Yardbirds and Stevie Wonder were in Liverpool, they would play the lunchtime sessions and so I got to see them there as well.

"The Beatles played so many times and knew so many songs it was incredible. The tunes I particularly remember liking and requesting apart from 'Anna' and 'Three Cool Cats' were 'The Sheikh of Araby', 'Besame Mucho', 'A Taste of Honey' … I liked them doing 'Love of the Loved', but I didn't know John and Paul had written it. It was just a new song they had started to sing at lunchtime and I remember requesting that one.

"I also liked 'PS I Love You'. In fact, I preferred 'PS I Love You' to 'Love Me Do'. I was working for Brian Epstein when they released them as their first single and so by then I knew John and Paul had written them, it was a case of 'oh yeah, they sing them down the Cavern!' But it was only then that I realised they actually wrote them.

"Later I thought it was good that others recorded their songs, but I always preferred the Beatles' own versions to other artists' covers of their tunes. I did like the way Cilla did 'Love of the Loved', although that wasn't strictly a 'cover' because they didn't release their own version, they did give it to her.

"As time passed and I saw them so many times, I got to know each of the Beatles well and as a consequence I also got to know Brian Epstein … so much so that when I was just 17, he asked me to work for him at NEMS Enterprises (not to be confused with NEMS Limited which was his father's company). At first there were only three of us in the office: Brian, Beryl Adams and myself. Beryl and I would address him as 'Mr. Brian' and his brother as 'Mr. Clive'. Brian employed me first as a secretary, but in late 1962 when Bobby Brown decided not to run the Fan Club anymore, in addition to my secretarial duties, Brian asked me to also run the Fan Club. And so it was that in the end I didn't go to Oxford or work for the Midland Bank. Instead, from 1962 until 1972, I worked for Brian and the Beatles. I just happened to be in the right place at the right time and was *so* pleased I was! What a life it turned out to be! It was so exciting. I was in the very eye of the hurricane. So much was happening all of the time. I feel so lucky to have been a teenager in the Sixties: I loved that period of my life.

"Although the Beatles started to have serious hits in 1963, it wasn't until 1964 that, for me, the penny dropped as to just how popular and famous they had become. In '63 they could still walk around Liverpool without being bothered. There was none of the hysterics that was later associated with them. A fan might nudge you and say, 'Oh, there's Paul', but it was no great deal, they wouldn't run up and bother him.

"Where I worked at number 12–14 Whitechapel in the NEMS office, Brian's other artists as well the Beatles would drop in all the time. Groups like the Fourmost, Gerry and the Pacemakers, the Big Three, Billy J. … their girlfriends would also drop in. As they worked at nights the group members would usually have the afternoons free and quite often came downtown to hang out and so the office became a popular gathering spot. One of my jobs for Brian was to type out the individualised wage slips that all his artists received.

"And then in '64, on the same day in July, Friday the 10th, both the northern premiere of *A Hard Day's Night* and the civic reception at Liverpool Town Hall were scheduled and from the airport right the way into the city centre the streets were thronged. All of a sudden it was a case of, 'Where did all these people come from?' For me personally, that's the moment when the full force of how popular they had become really struck home. That, for me, was the moment Beatlemania registered.

"The Beatles have been a part of my life ever since the moment I first set eyes upon them at that first lunchtime session I attended. I stopped working for them in 1972 because it felt right to do so. Things were changing in their lives and mine. I left Liverpool, but I didn't disappear, I just stepped into another life. I was married, I became a mum. I lived a new and wonderful life which I loved. I'm currently back on Merseyside and some 27 years into a different job which I love. In recent years I have engaged again with those fabulous years of my youth and it has been fun to do so. I have not written a book, but in 2013 I did make a documentary for my grandson so he will know what his grandma got up to when she was a teenager. It's called *Good Ol' Freda* and people seem to enjoy it. The Beatles and their families endorsed it which made me very proud and happy.

"I am pleased Colin Hall has written this book about the songs the Beatles did not record or release themselves. It shines a light on a different, often overlooked, aspect of their story which deserves to be remembered. It is good to know that the stories of Cilla, the Fourmost, Billy J., Tommy Quickly, Jackie Lomax and all the others included here have been captured and brought together in one place. What happened to them is important. They were integral to all that happened to the Beatles and Liverpool back then and so it is good to know their stories can be enjoyed once more by all those who love the Sixties as much as I do."

Freda Kelly
June 2020

Freda. (Trinity Mirror / Mirrorpix / Alamy Stock Photo)

I am forever indebted to Freda Kelly for contributing this chapter.

I am equally indebted to Ursula Wildling for the use of her marvellous photo of inside The Cavern circa 1965 which is very much as Freda remembers it.

For those wishing to learn more about the history of The Cavern Club, which goes from strength to strength in Liverpool, they may like to check out *The Best Of Cellars, The Story Of The Cavern Club* by Phil Thompson (Tempus Publishing, 2007), The Cavern Club: *The Rise of The Beatles and Merseybeat* by Spencer Leigh (McNidder & Grace, 2016) and *Cavern Club, The Inside Story* by Debbie Greenberg (Jorvik Press, 2016), Good Ol' Freda, (2013 Documentary film, directed by Ryan White.)

Chapter 27:
THE BALLAD OF DICK ROWE

Brian Epstein's entry into the lives of the Beatles had been dramatic, hugely positive and immediately productive. The visit of Mike Smith to the Cavern and the subsequent commercial test recording at Decca had been impressive major achievements. So when Decca invited him to lunch in London on Tuesday 6 February 1962 in their sixth-floor Albert Embankment executive club, Brian must have expected the company was about to offer him a contract for the Beatles to sign. Instead, Decca followed in EMI's footsteps and turned the Beatles down. Brian was devastated. It was a crushing and unexpected blow.

The traditional tale has Dick Rowe, chief A&R man at Decca, telling Epstein they didn't like the Beatles' sound and that groups of guitarists were on the way out. Short, sharp and to the point. That is how Epstein told it in his autobiography, *A Cellarful of Noise*. This is maybe all we need to know, but as ever in life things were maybe not this simple. As time has elapsed, so this straightforward version of events has been contested and added to.

As might be expected, Dick Rowe certainly and consistently denied saying anything of the sort. (It does sound like a rash and ill-considered thing for one of Rowe's stature to have said.) Mike Smith has said he thought he would be allowed to sign both the Beatles and Brian Poole and the Tremeloes. (He'd even singled out 'Like Dreamers Do' as a potential first A-side.) But when he ran his idea past Rowe, as he was obliged to do at the time, he was told he couldn't sign them both, he had to choose just one. Hence the Beatles were rejected. Smith says that on the basis of the studio 'commercial tests' both groups had recorded, Poole and the Tremeloes sounded better and so he chose them. As John commented, "We didn't sound natural."

The fact that Poole and the Tremeloes lived nearer to London (in Barking) no doubt helped Smith's decision-making, for he also intended to use whichever group he signed as backing singers and musicians for other Decca artists. For such purposes, Poole and the Tremeloes' proximity to London would have been easier and more economic to organise. Tony Meehan (the ex-Shadows drummer, age just 18 at the time) was, by then, an A&R man at Decca and also came into the story at this point, when Rowe apparently suggested to an irate Epstein that maybe Meehan could, as a private arrangement (costing £100), record the Beatles and Decca would release the resulting single. John, Paul and George said Meehan had actually been in the recording booth the day they recorded their tape and they felt very strongly that he had been influential in Decca's rejection of the Beatles.

Whatever the machinations truly were, in the end a very miffed Brian Epstein returned to Liverpool where he penned a brief letter that informed Dick at Decca that the Beatles would *not* be accepting his 'kind offer' to cut a disc with Tony Meehan because, "the Group has received an offer of a recording Contract from another Company."[1]

They hadn't received any such offer, but his letter summed up Brian's extreme pique and ultimate faith in the Beatles.

George: "Prior to going to Decca, we had that feeling that we'd do well if only somebody big in the record industry would give us a chance. Now we'd actually had a chance and we'd come unstuck. We began to wonder, all over again, whether there was much point in trying to get away on a national level. Maybe we reckoned, it was only Liverpudlians and Germans who could see anything in our sound. Silly way of thinking, sure – but we'd been batting our heads against a brick wall for a long time, remember."[2]

Picking themselves up from this double-rejection was a considerable challenge for the group but that is exactly what they did, for on 8 February they played an audition in

Manchester to appear on BBC Radio. They duly passed and on 7 March performed for the Beeb in front of an audience on a show that was broadcast the very next day on the 'Light Programme' to an audience approximating 2 million.

In the face of the rejection from EMI and Decca, Epstein was even more determined to procure the Beatles a recording contract. Having gone in through the front door as a VIP, but ultimately achieving nothing tangible, he began to pursue less direct avenues.

Thus, clutching 'The Beatles Decca Commercial Test Tape', he returned to London and made his way to one Robert Boast, the manager of HMV, the huge and famous record shop on Oxford Street. Boast could not help Brian directly, but he did suggest that instead of using tape to push the Beatles, Brian should use 78rpm demonstration discs ('demos'). His reasoning was simple: recording managers would always have an office record player, but not all would have a tape player. To further assist Brian, Robert Boast took him to HMV's small recording studio on the first floor where, from the precious Decca tape, disc cutter Jim Foy made 78rpm acetate discs of the songs for Epstein.

As this process was being carried out, Brian commented that three of the songs had been written by two of the group. On hearing this Boast asked if the songs had been published, which of course they hadn't. Epstein knew virtually nothing about music publishing or its essential role within the music machine and so, as a further favour to Epstein, Boast told him that the offices of Ardmore and Beechwood, one of EMI's publishing companies, were situated on the top floor of HMV. Within minutes, Brian Epstein was sitting in the offices of Ardmore and Beechwood talking to their general manager, Sid Colman, who expressed interest in Ardmore and Beechwood possibly publishing the songs.

Inadvertently Brian Epstein had struck gold thanks to the three 'old' Lennon-McCartney 'originals' they had recorded. The interest in the Beatles he so passionately wanted someone to take had finally occurred. Sid Colman was a bigger player in the whole razzamatazz of the recording industry than Epstein possibly realised at the time. The fact that Sid was making him an offer was a big deal and Brian should have been more interested than he maybe was.

There is no doubt Epstein *was* pleased, but his overriding goal at that moment in time was to secure the Beatles a recording contract. That was the holy grail of his management deal with 'the boys' and in his mind achieving this overshadowed anything else.

Epstein understood that Colman could place John and Paul's songs with other artists to possibly turn into hits, but that was not what he wanted. Brian wanted, and the Beatles themselves most definitely wanted, *the Beatles* to personally record those hits, not someone else. And so a compromise was achieved: Colman would help the Beatles obtain a recording contract and in return Brian promised Ardmore and Beechwood would get the publishing.

A second assault on the closed doors of the mighty EMI had begun. Brian wasn't exactly going in through the back door this time, it was more a case of slipping in through a side entrance.

A date for Brian to meet with Parlophone's head man, George Martin, was made for 13 February. Brian was taken aback when George said he had not heard of the Beatles because it ran contrary to what the letter of rejection from EMI had suggested.

Brian 'bigged-up' the Beatles to Martin (it was easy to do, they were very big in Liverpool and getting bigger all the time). Time was short, however, and Epstein says he only got to play two songs to Martin, 'Hello Little Girl' and 'Till There Was You'.

George Martin was not impressed by either: "I thought the songs were very grotty, the sound they were making was unusual but it wasn't very clear."[3]

On his return to Liverpool, Brian's office phone stayed silent. George Martin did not get back in touch.

Seemingly, Brian's quest had ended in another dead end.

Or so it seemed.

But, as history tells us … this was not the case.

The Beatles had caught the interest of a key player within London's music industry.

Sid Colman's right-hand man at Ardmore and Beechwood was music plugger Kim Bennett (real name Thomas Whippey). He'd missed Epstein when the latter had met Colman, but on his return to the office Colman had been quick to play him one of the 78s he'd been given. The song he chose was 'Like Dreamers Do'. Immediately Bennett's ears pricked up. He liked what he heard and encouraged Colman to pursue his contacts at EMI, which he dutifully did, but came back deflated. No one Colman had tried (presumably Ridley, Newell, Paramor and Martin) wanted to know.

Bennett was not easily rebuffed, he'd liked what he'd heard and did not want to give up. His instincts told him he was on to something. His concern was that if he pursued A&R beyond EMI they would immediately suss that he'd met with rejection on his home turf, so would be unlikely to help. So the ingenious Bennett proposed to Colman that Ardmore and Beechwood should put it to EMI's managing director Len Wood that they gave *them* a record deal and they would pay for the Beatles to record the song. Colman was taken with the idea and made the suggestion, but Wood rejected the idea out of hand.

And so, once again, EMI had proven impervious to persuasion and the Beatles remained without a recording contract.

---

1 *Brian Epstein*, Ray Coleman, (Penguin Books, 1990) p. 99.
2 George Harrison quoted in *The True Story of the Beatles* by Billy Shepherd (Beat Publications Ltd, 1964) pp.130/1.
3 Sir George Martin in conversation with Bob Harris OBE and Colin Hall for the 2009 BBC Radio 2 documentary *The Songs the Beatles Gave Away*, written and narrated by Bob Harris, produced by Bob Harris and Trudie Myerscough-Harris for WBBC.

Chapter 28:
A SIMPLE TWIST OF FATE

Life in Liverpool continued as normal for the Cavern's very own, homegrown rock 'n' roll stars, the Beatles: more bookings, more fans, more accolades, another visit to Hamburg, but most frustratingly there was no record contract in the pipeline.

Back in London, for George Martin, life had become more challenging than ever. His marriage was over and he missed his children, but Sheena would not grant him a divorce. He was paying the mortgage on the house he'd been living in with her and their children while he himself was back living in his 'bachelor' flat. He and his secretary Judy Lockhart Smith had become closer than ever, but could not disclose their relationship and certainly could not co-habit. Financially, this situation stretched George to the limit for he was on a fixed income at Parlophone. He had pressed for a producer's royalty, but to absolutely no avail. He was earning some extra cash from songwriting, writing TV theme tunes and film scores, but not at a level that would allow him to quit his post at EMI …

(One such tune that *did* earn George a steady income was 'The Niagara Theme'. Published by his friend Dick James, it had been picked up by Dick Rowe at Decca who recorded it with an ensemble he called the Cambridge Strings. It was the A-side of Decca 11429 with 'Death March' (from the film *The Sleepwalkers*) on the B-side. It did not become a hit, but did catch the ear of producers of programmes for the BBC's Light Programme and, as such, earned him a steady amount of extra income over 1962 and '63. Ironically, Dick Rowe released the recording on Friday 2 February 1962, a few days before he informed Brian Epstein that Decca didn't want the Beatles. Dick James had been the driving force behind the project and not only does his name appear on the label, so does George's as composer, while the record's producers are named as Dick Rowe and Mike Smith.)[1]

The story of 'The Niagara Theme' chalks up an interesting coincidence and at the same time reveals how small and tight-knit the UK's recording industry was at the time the Beatles came to town.

Of particular irritation to George Martin at EMI, was the success his fellow A&R colleague Norrie Paramor at Columbia was achieving. The two men's salaries were very much the same, but compared to Martin, Paramor was living the life, seemingly rolling in money, and worse: he made no attempt to hide it.

Paramor's wealth reflected that he had several income sources: band leader, pianist, arranger. In addition, he was amassing considerable songwriting royalties from the singles Columbia released in a way that George Martin wasn't. Paramor achieved this by ensuring his artists recorded B-sides that he had penned. Paramor wrote under a variety of pseudonyms (36 according to Mark Lewisohn). In particular, top-selling Columbia stars Cliff Richard and the Shadows were regular recipients of Paramor compositions. Martin bridled at what he saw as Paramor's exploitation of his position.

In purely professional terms, George was proving very successful in his role as A&R man for Parlophone. Martin's assistant Ron Richards looked after the label's 'pop' releases, while George had gained a reputation as a producer of more diverse material, especially comedy.

Indeed, during the heyday of the 'Twist', Martin produced a major UK Top 10 hit with Bernard Cribbins called 'The Hole in the Ground'. A wry and funny satire on the class system, this very popular record had taken a long time for Martin to put together, but the result was a comedy classic. It spent 13 weeks on the chart, including two weeks at number 9 in April 1962. Sir Joseph Lockwood, the chairman of EMI, was a particular fan and suggested that Cribbins should make an LP of similar material. Accordingly, EMI managing director Len Wood put this idea to Martin, hoping that Martin would agree and by doing so Wood would, in turn, please Sir Joseph. George, however, was not compliant, saying that to make an album of the same quality would take much time and patience, and so he did not pursue the idea for Wood, although Cribbins returned to the UK Top 10 in August that year with another Martin-produced comedy classic, entitled 'Right Said Fred'.

In declining Wood's request, George Martin was not being purposefully difficult, but simply realistic. Making such an album was not as straightforward as making an album of 'ordinary' songs. "I got labelled as a comedy producer but you couldn't find a formula that worked for everything. If Cliff Richard had a big hit, all his producer Norrie had to do was find a reasonable song and he could go on making hit after hit. If you made a song which was a hit with someone like Bernard Cribbins you had to find a song that suited him or get someone to write something and that was really hard. You couldn't just go to Tin Pan Alley and find something, it was very specialised."[2]

At the same time as George was enjoying single success with Cribbins, his three-year contract review came up. Previous requests by Martin that EMI should consider paying producers a royalty based on the success of their work had fallen on deaf ears, but despite these previous rebuttals it was an issue Martin was not prepared to drop given his desperate need for extra income. Consequently, when he met with Wood in the spring of 1962 to agree a renewal of his contract, the understandably frustrated George Martin once again placed the idea on the agenda. Once again Wood was resistant, even when Martin suggested if it was not agreed he would resign. Wood knew how much Martin enjoyed his work at EMI and simply called his bluff. In reality, such were the financial demands on him, Martin knew he could not leave and so, reluctantly, he once again signed on the dotted line and committed himself to a further three years as Head of Parlophone *sans* a record sales royalty.

If George Martin had set out to deliberately irritate Len Wood during the early months of 1962, he couldn't have done better than he did (albeit inadvertently). First had been his reluctance to pursue the Bernard Cribbins comedy album idea, which had truly irked Wood, and then George had followed up with his continued and (from Wood's perspective) irritating demands for a producer's royalty. And then came another incident to upset the applecart. Yet again, from George's perspective, it was utterly inadvertent, but for a third time he managed to upset the highly moral and religious Wood. The difference being was that this time, Martin added a dash of spice to the pot: he upset his boss on 'moral grounds'.

It happened when George asked Judy to accompany him to Blackpool to a festival of live and recorded music to which he'd been invited as a representative of EMI. As it was well away from London, George took the chance to invite Judy along in her capacity as his secretary. This was all well and good, but it meant their guard was down and unfortunately they were less careful to hide the closeness between them which was duly noted and reported back to Wood in London. In an era when adultery was seriously frowned upon, a man of Wood's moral and religious outlook was bound to be outraged. And he was. That EMI employees Martin and Lockhart Smith had, for clearly quite some time, been conducting their clandestine and shameful affair right under his very nose and he had not noticed, only added to his ire.

In the midst of all this tumult, Wood met with Sid Colman who inquired yet again why he had turned down what he thought was Kim Bennett's excellent idea that publishers Ardmore and Beechwood be allowed to cut a disc by the boys from Liverpool called the Beatles, the ones who wrote their own tunes. Wood remained adamant: he was not prepared to change his mind about that particular venture, but he was prepared to provide Ardmore and Beechwood the opportunity to acquire the copyright on 'Like Dreamers Do' that they so desired. Recognising Bennett and Colman's absolute conviction that the song had hit potential, so Wood decided that EMI *were* going to sign the Beatles after all. They *would* be offered a contract with Parlophone which meant George Martin would become responsible for them. Wood knew Martin had already passed on this group, but he felt EMI had nothing to lose: they would not be paying the Beatles an advance, recording costs were low, and if it was a hit then EMI would make money, on top of which there could be publishing royalties for Ardmore and Beechwood to reap. In one fell swoop he could keep Sid Colman sweet and embarrass George Martin by going over his head.

As Kim Bennett put it: "The Beatles record was going to be made as a gesture to Sid, to give Sid Colman a sop. Len was going to bow to our wishes at last."[3]

Wood no doubt believed that by ordering Martin to sign the Beatles, despite his earlier lack of interest in them, it would clip his rebellious producer's wings and in the process remind him who was boss. George Martin would have known exactly what was going on, that Wood was pulling rank, but it's doubtful he lost any sleep over it and he was too professional to allow this to faze him and so he did not oppose Wood's directive. Anyway, in practical terms, he would simply let Ron Richards handle the recording session.

This remarkable series of events that led to the Beatles eventually being offered a recording contract with Parlophone/EMI was unearthed by author Mark Lewisohn. For his remarkable tome *Tune In* of 2013, Lewisohn interviewed Norman Smith who was EMI's balance engineer at Abbey Road at the time, and who confirmed the tension between Wood and his errant A&R manager George Martin: "Len G. Wood didn't approve of people having affairs, and he certainly did not approve of George going off with his secretary. Not at all. I think it offended his moral standards, L.G. virtually ordered George to record the Beatles."[4]

Coincidental to the time the Beatles began to feature in George Martin's life, he was actively looking for (and had been doing so for a while) a singing star with whom he could make a string of hit records to match that of his rival Norrie Paramor at Columbia: "I was looking for something like this, I didn't think it was the Beatles, I didn't know it was a group like the Beatles. I was thinking of Cliff Richard, my big opposition so to speak. I thought it was so easy once you get a big star to make hit records, so I was looking for something."[5]

Despite auditioning several artists, Martin had not found what or 'whom' he was looking for. What he wished was to personally discover and choose the artist rather than have Len Wood foist an act upon him, especially one he did not believe fitted the profile for what he was searching. That grated on him. But George Martin was nothing if not open-minded and intuitive. Once he got to know the Beatles it didn't take him long to realise his pursuit of the goose that would lay the golden eggs was over.

Meanwhile, Brian Epstein's dogged determination to get the Beatles a record contract had finally paid dividends. His decision to track down every contact he had, had turned up trumps. His afternoon at HMV record store as the guest of Robert Boast had been an inadvertent master stroke, although he most probably never knew quite how or why.

He and the Beatles would not have cared much anyway about the behind-the-scenes machinations that led to the offer from Parlophone. It may have been EMI's comedy label, but it was a record deal and they and George Martin were about to enjoy the last laugh.

The Beatles were in Hamburg on their third visit (by which time they were growing weary of the place) when, out of the blue, Brian Epstein was invited by EMI to attend a meeting at Abbey Road at 11:30am on Wednesday 9 May 1962 with George Martin of Parlophone Records Company Limited. It was the second piece of good news he'd received around that time because the BBC had invited the Beatles to Manchester again to record another show for broadcast on national radio.

As far as Epstein was concerned, an invitation to Abbey Road to meet with George Martin could surely only mean one thing … couldn't it …?

---

1 *The Beatles – All These Years: Volume One: Tune In*, Extended Special Edition, by Mark Lewisohn, (Little, Brown, 2013) p.1087 + The author's personal copy of 'The Niagara Theme' by The Cambridge Strings.
3 & 4 *The Beatles – All These Years: Volume One: Tune In*, Extended Special Edition, by Mark Lewisohn, (Little, Brown, 2013) p.1179 and p.1180.
2 & 5 Sir George Martin in conversation with Bob Harris OBE and Colin Hall for the 2009 BBC Radio 2 documentary *The Songs the Beatles Gave Away*, written and narrated by Bob Harris, produced by Bob Harris and Trudie Myerscough-Harris for WBBC.

Chapter 29:
THE CLOSED DOOR OPENS

And it certainly did!

Epstein was elated. George Martin was also feeling good, for prior to the Beatles' arrival he was enjoying Top 20 success in his own right as a composer (albeit of a B-side). Johnnie Spence and His Orchestra were midway through a 13-week stint in the UK singles chart with the 'Theme from Dr. Kildare'. *Dr. Kildare* was a very popular American TV series that was enjoying great success in the UK, thanks in large part to the dashing good looks of its star, Richard Chamberlain. Released on Parlophone and produced by George Martin, the B-side of Johnnie Spence's hit was 'The Midnight Theme' composed by none other than Graham Fisher. On the very day Martin met Epstein, Spence's record was at number 20 completing a six-week run in the UK Top 20. Martin was no doubt looking forward to the royalty payment he would receive from this success.

His meeting with Epstein was very much to the point and lasted less than an hour.

Martin and Epstein took to each other and the meeting got off to the best of starts when Epstein heard the words he wanted to hear: Martin was going to sign the Beatles to record for Parlophone.

The contract offered was EMI's standard deal. Big acts like Cliff Richard, Adam Faith and Helen Shapiro were all signed to EMI on the same contract. It was for four years, but after the first year EMI could choose whether to renew or not. It stipulated that the Beatles would record a minimum of six 'sides' (songs/tunes) which in effect was three singles of which EMI owned the sole right of production and reproduction. EMI would bear the costs of recording and of studio time. There would be no 'advance' on royalties. Royalties were paid at a rate of one penny per single (a 45rpm double-sided disc). Royalties were paid quarterly and on only 85% of sales (the missing 15% was to cover the cost to the company of returned discs, broken discs and promotional copies). The contract was for the world, for sales outside the UK the group would receive half the prevailing royalty rate.

Of course Brian knew before Martin even went over the details of the contract that record sales rarely made artists rich. He was the owner of a record shop and knew the way it worked. A penny a single split five ways (Brian's percentage and the rest split equally between John, Paul, George and Pete) would not go far. A million-seller would only net the boys just £750 each. Where some immediate real money rolled in for an artist on the back of a hit record was from personal appearances, which would considerably increase on the back of a hit and for which they could increase the fees they charged accordingly.

As part of the meeting, Martin and Epstein agreed that the Beatles would attend Abbey Road on Wednesday 6 June 1962 for their first recording session. It would be between 7 and 10pm and they would have to arrive early to set up and prepare. George had only heard John and Paul sing and wanted to determine who would be the singer. Brian wrote a different lead singer's name on the 78rpm acetates he played to Martin: 'Hullo Little Girl' (Brian wrote the title 'Hello' as 'Hullo') was by 'John Lennon & The Beatles', 'Till There Was You' was by 'Paul McCartney & The Beatles', which led Martin to assume the group would, in the tradition of 'Cliff and the Shadows', be billed in the same way. His job was to decide exactly just 'Who' and the Beatles it would be. Apparently George asked that at the forthcoming session the Beatles perform other songs from their repertoire because he had not been overly impressed by the two he had already heard.

And so the meeting concluded with Martin assuring Brian Epstein that he would receive a contract ready for signing from EMI within two weeks.

The Brian Epstein who walked out of Abbey Road that morning was totally ecstatic. He was a man fulfilled. From seeing and hearing the Beatles for the first time ever at the Cavern on 9 December 1961, exactly six months later on 9 May 1962, he had achieved what he described as "the ultimate – this, to us, was the greatest thing that could happen."[1]

From Abbey Road he went directly to the Post Office in St John's Wood, phoned his parents (who had feared that the Beatles would be a folly of Brian's he would long regret) and sent two telegrams: one to the Beatles in Hamburg care of the Star-Club, and one to Bill Harry at *Mersey Beat*, for there was no doubt whatsoever in Brian's mind that this would be headline news in Liverpool!

The Beatles were elated. They responded individually to Brian with messages asking, 'When will we be millionaires' (John), 'Please wire ten thousand pounds advance royalties' (Paul), and 'Please order four new guitars' (George).

The actual telegram sent to the Beatles in Hamburg was soon lost, but Pete Best remembered it as saying: 'Congratulations Boys EMI Request Recording Session Please Rehearse New Material'.

There is no doubt they were surprised by this change in their fortunes, especially as they knew EMI had originally rejected them, but they were not overly concerned as to what had caused this sudden change of mind. What they were most concerned about was that phrase 'Please Rehearse New Material'. What exactly did that mean?

From what they had learned about record companies at this point was that most artists who signed a record deal would be expected to record songs provided for them *by* the label. The record company made the choice, not the artist. This was because record labels were considered to be best placed to know what songs would fare best in the market place and so dictated and controlled the recorded output of their artists. It could be a song from the artist's own repertoire that the group played well, or possibly a tune written by themselves if it was deemed good enough, or very possibly one written for them by the record label's A&R man himself, but most likely it would be a song obtained specifically for them from 'Tin Pan Alley', the UK's very own hit-making community. As such, it was almost a given that it would be a song with in-built 'hit' potential, composed by a professional and proven 'songwriter'.

This did not sit right with the Beatles. From forming the Quarry Men in 1957, John had decided the songs his group sang, not someone from outside of the group. As the Beatles, they were their own bosses not somebody else, they collectively chose what songs they performed. The songs the Beatles sang defined them. Fearing a crucial loss of creative control, John and Paul decided that what Brian meant by his phrase 'Please Rehearse New Material' was that *they* themselves should *'write'* new material to rehearse and not just choose a new 'cover' to perform. What other interpretation could there possibly be?

It was a logical conclusion for the group to draw, especially by John and Paul, who knew that ever since Brian had learned they wrote their own tunes had actively encouraged them to include more of these in the Beatles' 'live' repertoire. It was how it had been when they recorded for Decca, Brian had encouraged them to include three of their own compositions for that session. And so it was that from the very start the Beatles bucked the tradition of the record company always choosing the material an artist would record. Even more remarkably, the Beatles went one step further and insisted on recording their own, self-penned songs. As recording artists, the Beatles would never be a 'covers' band again. (Although on early albums they did include their versions of other artists' tunes, most notably 'Twist and Shout', 'Till There Was You' and 'Money'.)

After an almost two-year hiatus, Brian's telegram was the green light for the 'Lennon-McCartney' songwriting partnership to once more draw breath. From now on there would be no learning of new 'covers' to divert them.

Of course, John and Paul most definitely *did* write the group's singles, it was never a task consigned to someone else. The songs they composed became the crucial difference between them and other artists. They were fresh, new tunes that no one had ever heard before. As such, their singles could never be compared to someone else's version of an existing song. Their artistic vision would not be dictated by or compared to someone else's pre-existing material or style.

Equally importantly, there would be no competition: another artist in another studio somewhere would not be recording the very same song that their particular A&R had also heard and thought had hit potential. So often at that time in the history of pop music an artist would record the same song as another and thus they would be in direct competition with one another on the charts. This often meant some songs/artists did not climb the charts as high as they might have done had sales not been split by there being more than one version available. (For example, in the summer of 1959, 'A Teenager in Love' was on the charts by three different acts.) This never happened to the Beatles, for the tunes they recorded were always unique to them.

The 'Lennon, McCartney songbook' became the keystone of the group's success and gave them their sonic individuality. Seizing creative control for themselves from the outset became a game changer, not only for the Beatles, but within the music industry itself. They blazed a trail and established a blueprint that artists in the future could and would follow, an innovation that more or less became the 'norm' as major artists would more frequently eschew 'Tin Pan Alley' to write and perform their own material.

1 *A Cellarful of Noise* by Brian Epstein (New English Library, 1964), p.12.

Chapter 30:
EYEBALL TO EYEBALL: SONGWRITING

"...the songs of Lennon and McCartney are distinctly indigenous in character, the most imaginative and inventive examples of a style that has been developing on Merseyside during the past few years..."
from 'What Songs the Beatles Sang' by *The Times* music critic, William S. Mann, published 27 December 1963.

The Beatles' recording career in their own name began in 1962 with the release of 'Love Me Do' on Parlophone Records. It was one of the very first Lennon-McCartney 'originals' ever written some four years earlier in 1958 when Paul was just 16. He described it as a 50-50 effort, but John disagreed, remembering it as mainly a Paul song to which he'd contributed 'something to the middle eight'. In its original incarnation it was quite poppy, certainly more Buddy Holly than Muddy Waters.

From the start of the Beatles' recording career, Paul and John would 'big up' their repertoire of already composed songs to impress journalists, and whoever else was asking.

Paul has said that they would try and persuade people that he and John had about a hundred songs before 'Love Me Do' was released, which he readily admits was a "slight exaggeration", putting the actual figure at less than 20 (which, as this chapter hopes to show, is a modest calculation).

In November 2020, in an interview published by *Rolling Stone* magazine, he commented on this subject to Taylor Swift: "Let's face it, you crave fame and attention when you're young. And I just remembered the other day, I was the guy in the Beatles that would write to journalists and say [speaks in a formal voice]: ‚We are a semiprofessional rock combo, and I'd think you'd like [us] … We've written over 100 songs (which was a lie), my friend John and I. If you mention us in your newspaper…' You know, I was always, like, craving the attention."[1]

Given Paul's admission of exaggeration as to the number of songs they actually composed in Liverpool ahead of signing to Parlophone, and to track the phenomenal acceleration in the Lennon-McCartney rate of composition from June 1962 onwards, it seems appropriate to list just how many songs (and approximately when) they had actually written by the time 'Love Me Do' was released.

In addition to this I have included a section detailing the tunes they composed during 1963 up to the point they moved from Liverpool to live in London. These are songs that were not necessarily written at either John's home 'Mendips' or Paul's at 20 Forthlin Road, several were written 'on the road', but in some cases completed/ polished back in Liverpool.

All songs marked in the following list with a single asterisk * denote those that were not released commercially by the Beatles during their life as an active unit, but which were gifted to other artists.

Songs Written or 'Polished' by Paul McCartney at 20 Forthlin Road 1956–1962

1956

'Suicide' aka 'I Call It Suicide' aka 'Call It Suicide' (a fragment). "My Dad had a piano so I would play around … on the piano, I would always try and write and I had this song which started off alright but it was really laboured rhymes, so it was starting off like a nice little Sinatra thing but then, when it gets into 'ruin-ied' and 'sui-inied' it tripped up, so I could never finish it…"[2]

'When I'm Sixty-Four' (tune only at the piano): late spring 1956.

(Which of these piano songs came first is unclear)

'I Lost My Little Girl' is the first song Paul wrote on guitar and which he describes as, "a very direct response to the death of my mother." Mary had died on 31 October 1956 not long after the family had moved into number 20. "I wrote this song later that same year. I was 14 at the time."[3]

1957/58

'Too Bad About Sorrows', again written late 1957/possibly early 1958, Paul has been quoted as saying this was the very first co-write, written at Forthlin and the first to go into Paul's school exercise book as 'A Lennon-McCartney Original'.

'Just Fun' late '57/early '58, another one written at Forthlin when he and John were playing truant from school and art college respectively and another remembered by Paul as one of the first 'Lennon-McCartney' originals.

'Thinking of Linking' is a Paul song written after attending the cinema around about the time George joined the Quarry Men i.e., circa late '57 early '58. George remembered accompanying Paul to the local Gaumont one evening: "I remember once sitting in the cinema on the corner of Rose Lane, not far from where he lived, near Penny Lane. They showed an ad for Link Furniture: 'Are you thinking of Linking?' Paul said, 'Oh that would make a good song,' and he wrote one that went 'thinking of linking my life with you.'"[4]

While he had the germ of an idea at the cinema Paul specifically recalled writing it in the front room at Forthlin and in an interview with Mark Lewisohn from 1987 even came up with some of its lyrics … 'Well I've been thinking of linking my life with you, etc.' How long Paul persevered with the tune before moving on to something new is not known. It seems he never got much beyond one verse but, like most things he has ever written he never forgot the tune (and some words).

Subsequent renditions many years later suggest it had a life beyond his front room. During the 'Get Back - Let It Be Sessions' he returned to it twice on the 3rd and 29th of January 1969. On the 3rd he sang a brief fragment in which he did not remember the words too well, making some of them up as he went along. A phrase he used on that occasion was 'I've been thinking that you love me' after which, for a while (on some bootlegs), 'Thinking of Linking' was erroneously titled 'I've Been Thinking That You Love Me' or more simply, 'Thinking That You Loved Me' thus inventing a 'new' song. The 'Get Back' version on the 29th featured John singing which further suggests that originally the song had been part of, or at least considered for, the Quarry Men's repertoire … It was not until the 'Threetles' sessions for *The Anthology* that Paul, George and Ringo delivered the best version fans are ever likely to have. During this version Paul comments that there wasn't a second verse and from the words we hear it is obvious that 'Thinking of Linking' and 'I've Been Thinking That You Love Me' are one and the same song and that in the past the latter had simply been confused with the former.

1958

'In Spite of All the Danger' was penned between spring and early July 1958. It was recorded by the Quarry Men on Saturday 12 July 1958 at Percy Phillips' studio, 38 Kensington Road, Liverpool. On the handwritten record label the song is co-credited to 'McCartney, Harrison'. Paul gave a writing credit to George for the guitar break he contributed. An edit of the Quarry Men recording appears on the first CD release of *The Anthology* trilogy.

'Because I Know You Love Me So': early January, maybe June 1958, ('A Lennon-McCartney original') This was another song the Beatles revisited (as a 1 minute 32 second countrified version) during the 'Let It Be/Get Back jam sessions' and which officially surfaced for the first time in 2003 on the *Fly On The Wall* bonus disc issued as part of the *Let It Be … Naked* two CD set.

'Love Me Do': sometime in (early?) 1958. Paul describes this as a 50-50 co-write with John, although the latter said it was a Paul song to which he made only a small contribution.

'Catswalk'* (later re-titled 'Catcall') a Paul instrumental from 1958.

'Fancy Me Chances with You' a John and Paul co-write from 1958. This early Lennon-McCartney collaboration received its first official airing in 2003 with the release of *Let It Be … Naked* when, towards the end of the *Fly On The Wall* additional disc that accompanied the main album, a 22-second version of 'Maggie Mae' segues into a 27-second snatch of the song. Similarly on the *Let It Be* 6-Disc Special Edition released in October 2021 the same coupling turns up on CD 2 (*Get Back - Apple Sessions*) as Track 2. In the excellent 100-page hardback book accompanying the 2021 package, on p.82 Paul is quoted from 3 January 1969 talking to Michael Lindsay-Hogg explaining that it was a song from when he and John would sag off school and art college to go, "Back to my house and the two of us would just sort of sit there and write 'Love Me Do' and 'Too Bad About Sorrows' … there's a lot from back then … that we never reckoned cos they were all very unsophisticated songs."[5]

'I'll Wait 'Til Tomorrow': a Paul song from this period, of which he was reminded by Pete Shotton in 1969, which prompted him to sing some of it (accompanied by John) during the *Get Back* rehearsal sessions).

'You're in My Little Book' … no details, but it was mentioned by Paul in a 2001 interview for *Reader's Digest*.

1959

'Michelle' an instrumental to begin with which Paul composed in the style/same vein as 'Trambone' by Chet Atkins who released that tune in 1957. As John's guest Paul would attend parties at the home of John's art school teacher Austin Mitchell where he would play his tune. Several years later Paul decided to add some lyrics, some of which he sang in French having asked Ivan Vaughan's wife Jan, a teacher of French, to write these specifically for him.

'Hot As Sun', an instrumental, most probably originated by Paul in early 1959. Paul released a version of this on his first solo album *McCartney* (1970) on which a very brief fragment of 'Suicide' can be heard right at the very end of the track.

'Cayenne', an instrumental, most probably originated by Paul in early 1959.

'Winston's Walk': an instrumental possibly written in early '59, maybe by John (his middle name *was* Winston) but it could just have easily been a Paul tune.

'I'll Follow the Sun' was written sometime between January and July 1959
'Love of the Loved'*   "   "   "   "
'A World without Love'*   "   "   "   "
'I'll Be on My Way'*   "   "   "   "
'Like Dreamers Do'*   "   "   "   "

This tranche of songs shows that by the end of 1959 Paul McCartney had already written

enough songs to be legitimately described as a tunesmith, and a very good one at that!
N.B. *A very early version of 'I'll Follow the Sun' was taped around this time, featuring John, Paul, George and someone on drums (quite possibly it was Mike McCartney).*

Late 1950s or early 1960s: *'Tell Me Who He Is'*, an unrecorded song, the lyrics for which Paul unearthed while researching his 2021 publication *The Lyrics*.

1960
1 *'Somedays'*
2 *'Well Darling'*
3 *'You Must Write Every Day'*
4 *'You'll Be Mine'* a Lennon-McCartney co-write
1, 2, 3, and 4 are among songs heard on home tape-recordings made at Forthlin during two sessions recorded circa 1960. On these tracks the 'band' comprised John, Paul and George.
Eight instrumental tunes were recorded at the same time as these songs. None were given specific names by the group although, later on, to identify the tunes, compilers of bootleg tapes and Beatles writers/scholars gave the tunes titles of their own, such as 'Come On People' and 'I'll Be Leaving', but the group never named these tunes. (Stu Sutcliffe played bass on some of these rambling instrumental tracks.)
'Keep Looking That Way' and *'Years Roll Along'* are songs for which no home tapes exist, but which Paul mentions in a letter he composed sometime during the spring of 1960 intending to send it to promoters in an attempt to gain some much-needed gigs for the Beatles. In the letter he states that he and John had written over 50 songs, including the two aforementioned, plus 'One After 909' and 'Thinking of Linking'.

1962
'Tip of My Tongue*: written just before 3 September 1962, composed specifically for consideration as a follow-up to 'Love Me Do' and introduced to the Beatles on the afternoon of 3 September when the group gathered at the Cavern to rehearse numbers they were going to take to a session with George Martin at Abbey Road the very next day. It lost out to John's 'Please Please Me'.
'Hold Me Tight' was a Lennon-McCartney collaboration composed at 20 Forthlin in October, again as a possible follow-up to 'Love Me Do'.
'I Saw Her Standing There' was originally written by Paul on Monday 22 October 1962 and 'polished' by John and Paul at 20 Forthlin Road during the second half of November 1962.

Paul Songs written elsewhere during 1961 and '62
'Tell Me if You Can': written in Hamburg in June 1961, a co-write with Tony Sheridan.
'Pinwheel Twist': written by Paul backstage at the Cavern sometime in March/April 1962 and premiered the very same evening.
'PS I Love You': written in Hamburg, May 1962, this is a Paul song that John described as Paul trying to write a song in the vein of 'Soldier Boy' by the Shirelles. Paul himself has described it as his attempt at a generic 'letter song' that was not based in reality and has denied it was written for his then girlfriend Dot Rhone back home in Liverpool.

Songs written or 'polished' by John Lennon at 'Mendips' 1957–1962 – All dates approximate!

1957
'Calypso Rock', early 1957.
'My Love Is Like a Bird', early '57 (a fragment only).
*'Hello Little Girl'**, towards the end of 1957 (most probably December). A John tune but credited to 'Lennon-McCartney'.
1957/58
'What Goes On', late 1957/early '58 (mainly the melody and chorus). It's a song John later developed for Ringo to sing on *Rubber Soul* which Ringo further adapted for himself and for which he received a credit as co-writer.
1958
'That's My Woman', early 1958. In an interview in 1964, John said this was the second song he wrote after 'Hello Little Girl'.
'I Call Your Name', early 1958, and then developed with Paul in John's bedroom at 'Mendips', but Paul credits this as John's song and in conversation with the author suggested the lyric was possibly a reference to Julia who died on 15 July that year in a road accident close to 'Mendips'. John himself had this to say of his song: "That was my song when there was no Beatles and no group, I just had it around. It was my effort as a kind of blues, originally, and then I wrote the middle eight when it came out years later. The first part had been written before Hamburg, even."
1959
'Winston's Walk': an instrumental possibly written in early '59, maybe by John (his middle name *was* Winston) but it could just have easily been a Paul tune.
1962
'Won't You Please Say Goodbye', summer 1962 (mentioned by John during the *Get Back* rehearsals).
'Please Please Me', written in his bedroom as a potential follow-up to 'Love Me Do' within two days of returning from the Beatles' recording session with George Martin at Abbey Road on Wednesday 6 June 1962. It was John's song, but 'polished' late on the night of Saturday 9 June at Paul's house as they sat together at Jim's piano.

John songs written elsewhere during 1960–1962

1960
'One After 909': as a student at art college, John briefly shared Flat 3 Hillary Mansions, Gambier Terrace, with fellow students Stuart Sutcliffe, Rod Murray, Margaret Morris and Margaret Duxbury where, in spring 1960, he wrote, 'One After 909'. Cynthia says he also worked on this tune at the Jacaranda.
'I've Just Fallen for Someone': a song written in May by Johnny Gentle. The singer was on tour and the Beatles were backing him. It was while enjoying a day off in Inverness, Scotland, that John contributed the 'middle eight' to Gentle's tune but was not credited. It was later recorded and released by Adam Faith and Johnny Gentle himself as Darren Young.
1961
John and George Harrison co-wrote **'Beatle Bop' (aka/re-titled 'Cry for a Shadow')** in 1961 while they were in Hamburg.
1962
Sometime around March/April 1962, just ahead of Paul composing **'Pinwheel Twist'**, John composed **'Ask Me Why'**. In part it was inspired by the Miracles' song 'What's So

Good about Goodbye'. 'Ask Me Why' is significant, not only because it was John's first composition (with some input from Paul) since 'One After 909', but because it reflects the Beatles' huge enjoyment of, and the growing inspiration they were deriving from, singles being released in the UK by black American artists. These artists included the Marvelettes ('Please Mr. Postman'), Etta James ('Something's Got a Hold on Me'), the Chantels ('Soldier Boy' and a B-side, 'Summertime'), the Shirelles (another B-side, 'Boys') and others including Smokey Robinson and the Miracles. 'Money' was a great favourite of John's and this had originally been released in 1959 by Barrett Strong on Tamla Motown (indeed it was the label's first hit in June 1960).

'Do You Want to Know a Secret?': written in autumn (October) 1962 at 36 Falkner Street where John and Cynthia were living after their marriage in August.

1963: Beyond Liverpool

In 1963 'Beatlemania' kicked off in the UK. The Beatles were hugely popular and hugely successful. From then on the demand for product was constant and insistent. John and Paul were not fazed. Rather, they were energised and engaged. They were well into their stride as composers and even amid the hurly-burly of touring and playing live were able to find quiet places in which to hide themselves away and write. As they were so much in demand, and away from home on tour most of the time, only a few songs were actually written at either 20 Forthlin Road or 'Mendips' during this year. Indeed during the summer the group temporarily resided in the President Hotel near Russell Square in Bloomsbury.*
A famous series of photographs were taken of the group by Norman Parkinson while they were living at the hotel, on Thursday 12 September. Two days previously on the 10th they had given the Rolling Stones first go at 'I Wanna Be Your Man' (which they always intended for Ringo) before recording it themselves at Abbey Road on 11 and 12 September.

So, the majority of their new songs were either written or started on the road, away from home, maybe at the President with a few later 'polished' on rare days off at home in Liverpool.

(*The Beatles finally left their Liverpool homes to reside somewhere more permanent in London when they moved to live together (at least for a short while) in Mayfair in Flat L, 57 Green Street during the autumn of 1963.)

The following songs were all credited as co-writes despite whoever initiated them.

John and Paul co-writes/collaborations written *on the road* in 1963 or elsewhere

'All My Loving': very much a Paul song that he began on a tour bus when, beginning on 18 May 1963, the Beatles were on the road with Roy Orbison. It was an unusual song for Paul, if not almost unique, for he came up with the lyrics first, which he had not done before. Once they arrived at the venue he wrote the music on a piano he found backstage.

'From Me to You' is a definite co-write, written on 28 February 1963, as John and Paul travelled from York to Shrewsbury on the Helen Shapiro tour bus. The title was inspired by *NME*'s letter page which was entitled 'From You to Us'.

'This Boy': a Lennon-McCartney original emanating from John's liking of Smokey Robinson and the three-part harmony tunes he wrote, in this case 'I've Been Good to You'. The tune also references Bobby Freeman's 'You Don't Understand Me, and the Teddy Bears' 'To Know Him Is to Love Him'. It is a three-part close harmony song Paul said they wrote while on tour with Helen Shapiro. Apparently they'd arrived early at the next venue (about one o'clock in the afternoon) and decided to try and do some writing, so they went up to their hotel bedroom where they sat on their twin beds, and facing each other, 'eyeball to eyeball', wrote 'This Boy'.

'Thank You Girl': a John and Paul co-write composed in February 1963 while they were

on the Helen Shapiro tour.

'Not a Second Time' was written by John Lennon in early September 1963 when once again Smokey Robinson was his inspiration. It was written just ahead of the Beatles recording it on 11 September, when John introduced it to the group for the first time.

'I Wanna Be Your Man': a song Paul had begun and which was completed on the hoof on Tuesday 10 September 1963, when he and John visited the Rolling Stones who were in rehearsal in London. The Stones needed a follow-up to their debut single, 'Come On' and not being ones to miss an opportunity, John and Paul suggested 'I Wanna Be Your Man', a song they already had in mind for Ringo to sing on what would become the *With the Beatles* long player. When the Stones expressed interest, the two Beatles spent a few minutes putting the finishing touches to 'I Wanna Be Your Man'. The Stones recorded it in early October and It became the Stones' first UK Top 20 single when it reached number 12 in November 1963.

'All I've Got to Do' is most definitely a John song in origin and one of several he wrote in the style of Smokey Robinson whom he admired very much as a writer. Indeed this was inspired by Smokey's 'You Can Depend on Me'. Looking to the future and the next market to conquer during 1963, Brian encouraged John and Paul to write songs with American teens in mind. In interviews John said the song was written with the American market in mind, noting that few British teenage boys would have a phone in their home on which to call anyone, whereas American teens most probably would have done. The other Beatles were not aware of the song until he played the song to McCartney moments before the group began recording it (11 September 1963). This means it could have been written while temporarily residing at the President hotel. The Beatles never played it live.

Three collaborative tunes completed/polished at Forthlin but begun elsewhere in 1963:

'Misery' (January) a co-written song begun backstage at the King's Hall in Stoke-on-Trent on 26 January 1963 and then completed at 20 Forthlin Road. A week later they joined Helen Shapiro for her nationwide UK tour and had ideas that the song might be suitable for her.

'She Loves You': written on 26 June 1963 while the Beatles were on tour in Newcastle. A totally collaborative song composed in their hotel bedroom and 'polished' the next day back home in Liverpool at Paul's home (in the dining room at the back of the house).

'It Won't Be Long' (July) began with the chorus which was written by John and together with Paul, it was completed at 20 Forthlin Road in July 1963.

John and Paul collaborative songs written at their respective homes in Liverpool in 1963

'There's a Place': a co-write which John described as his attempt at a "Motown, black thing." It was written together *at Forthlin* in early February 1963 just ahead of recording it on the 11th.

'I'll Get You': a rare collaboration at John's home, it was co-written in the early summer of 1963 in his bedroom at Mendips, possibly as a follow-up to 'From Me to You'.

And in the meantime, let's not forget...

George Harrison

'Don't Bother Me': the first song to be written by George Harrison (in his own right). George had very quickly realised how songwriting was earning John and Paul a lot more than he and Ringo were from the phenomenal success of the Beatles. This galvanised him into composing songs of his own that could be recorded by the group. 'Don't Bother Me' was written as an exercise to see if he actually could compose. Clearly he could! It was written in Bournemouth when the Beatles were playing six nights at the Gaumont Cinema. George took ill while the group were staying in Bournemouth and wrote his first song while he was sick in bed at the Palace Court Hotel. The website *The in-depth story behind…* suggests that 19 August 1963 as the most likely date on which he began to compose the tune.

Ringo Starr

'Don't Pass Me By'. This well-known Ringo tune was one he sang on the *White Album*. It had been a work in progress since 1962 which is when he first played it to John and Paul who were not impressed. But, good chap that he is, Ringo stuck with it and its quirky fiddle and funky country arrangement graces the album perfectly.

1 'Paul McCartney & Taylor Swift' Musicians On Musicians by Patrick Doyle, *Rolling Stone* magazine, 13 November, 2020.
2 Sir Paul McCartney in conversation with Bob Harris OBE and Colin Hall for *The Songs the Beatles Gave Away*, BBC Radio 2 (2009).
3 *The Lyrics: 1956 to the Present*, by Paul McCartney (Edited by Paul Muldoon) (Published by Allen Lane, 2021) a self-portrait in 154 songs split into two volumes.
4 George Harrison recalls a night at the cinema with Paul McCartney in *The Beatles Anthology*, by The Beatles (Cassell & Co, 2000) p.97.
5 *The Beatles: Let It Be*, 100-page hardback book issued as part of the 6-disc special edition of the *Let It Be* album (Apple, 2021). Paul's comments to Michael Lindsay-Hogg from the Chapter entitled 'Rehearsals and Apple Jams' by Kevin Howlett p.82.

Elsewhere my research for the correct dates and other details for this chapter has drawn on the following sources:
Sir Paul McCartney from interviews with Bob Harris and myself, 2006 and 2009.
The Beatles – All These Years: Volume One: Tune In, Extended Special Edition, by Mark Lewisohn, (Little, Brown, 2013).
The Complete Beatles Recording Sessions, Mark Lewisohn, (The Hamlyn Publishing Group Limited, 1988) p. 12.
The Beatles As Musicians: The Quarry Men through Rubber Soul by Walter Everett, (Oxford University Press, USA, 2001).
Early Beatles Songs https://earlybeatlessongs.weebly.com (This excellent website also leans heavily on Lewisohn and Everett as invaluable sources.)
'The in-depth story behind …' www.beatlesbooks.com
Paul McCartney: Many Years from Now, Barry Miles, (Vintage, 1998).

Chapter 31:
IN A DIFFERENT KEY, THE RETURN OF 'LOVE ME DO'

John and Paul's response to Brian's request for 'new' material was to go back almost to the beginning and re-visit a composition from 1958: Paul's (with some help from John) 'Love Me Do' was reworked to be less of a 'pop' song and into something altogether more bluesy. Integral to this was a change in its key from A to G and crucial to its new 'blues' feel was the introduction of a harmonica into the arrangement (played by John). Such innovations effectively turned 'Love Me Do' into another song altogether.

The inspiration for the harmonica came from Bruce Channel's massive UK number 2 hit (April/May 1962) 'Hey! Baby' which predominately featured the harmonica-playing of Delbert McClinton. John Lennon: "It was just after 'Hey! Baby' came out – we were hoping to be the first British group to use the harmonica on record."[1]

Shortly after the re-working of 'Love Me Do', the Beatles were in Hamburg where Paul composed a brand new song called 'PS I Love You', and so when the Beatles returned home from Germany to attend that all-important recording session they did so with three 'new' original tunes in the bag: 'Love Me Do', John's slightly earlier 'Ask Me Why' and now Paul's 'PS I Love You'.

By mid-May, Epstein had received the recording contract from EMI. Witnessed by Bob Wooler, he promptly signed and returned it to EMI, dated 4 June 1962. The contract itself started on 6 June.

When they arrived at Manchester Airport on Saturday 2 June they were collected by Neil Aspinall who handed each Beatle an envelope. Inside were copies of *Mersey Beat* music paper featuring the news of their contract with EMI, and in addition lists Brian had compiled of their forthcoming bookings for the next 40 days and nights. Brian was nothing if not attentive and business-like. Despite being on the verge of becoming recording artists, there was to be no break in their performance schedule.

As they were now officially EMI recording artists, Epstein's memo underlined the fact that from now on they were true professionals, most definitely the real deal. John Lennon: "Brian put all the instructions down neatly on paper and made it all seem real. We were in a daydream till he came along. We'd no idea what we were doing, or where we'd agreed to be. Seeing our marching orders on paper made it all official."[2]

First on Brian's list were two days designated to private rehearsals at the Cavern. This time Brian intended that the Beatles would be going to London and Parlophone properly rehearsed, unlike their earlier foray to Decca.

They spent this time well and it enabled Brian to send George Martin a list of 33 songs they had rehearsed. At the top of the list was an 'opening medley' which comprised three songs they believed showcased the group's singing/performance at its best: 'Besame Mucho' (Paul), 'Will You Love Me Tomorrow' (John) and 'Open (Your Lovin' Arms) (George). They had done this in response to a request from Martin who wanted to assess the individual singing of each of the group's vocalists and so the medley had been devised to allow him to do so. Unknown to the Beatles, in his mind George Martin was still deliberating whether to market the group as 'Paul McCartney and the Beatles' or 'John Lennon and the Beatles', etc. That's the way it was currently being done in the industry and, of course, Martin's thinking in this matter would be very much dictated by the chart-topping, Norrie-Paramor-produced, mega-successful 'Cliff Richard and the Shadows'. The Beatles, of course, would *not* have known this was at the back of Martin's mind and had they done so would have soon put him right. They were the Beatles, no more, no less.

After the 'opening medley', the songs most rehearsed at the Cavern were the resuscitated 'Love Me Do' and the new-writes: 'Ask Me Why' and 'PS I Love You'.

They travelled to London on 5 June and stayed at the Royal Court Hotel on Sloane Square. Neil drove them there in the van together with all their equipment. As ever Brian travelled by train and met them at the hotel. At 7pm Wednesday 6 June they entered EMI's famous Abbey Road Studios for the very first time. They no doubt struggled a bit because they had their equipment with them and had to lug this themselves into the building via the back door.

Nevertheless, back door or bathroom window … the Beatles had arrived.

1 *The Beatles – All These Years: Volume One: Tune In*, Extended Special Edition, by Mark Lewisohn, (Little, Brown, 2013) p.1194, this is a John Lennon quotation from an interview with Chris Roberts for *Melody Maker*, 21 December 1963.
2 *The Beatles: The Authorised Biography*, Hunter Davies, (Heinemann, 1968) p.132.

Chapter 32:
GEORGE MARTIN'S TIE

Martin designated the Beatles' first session to Ron Richards, who was assisted by Norman Smith (balance engineer), Ken Townsend (technical engineer) and Chris Neal (tape operator). All three wore white laboratory coats as per the industry norm. George had told Richards he would call in sometime during the recording to see how things were progressing. That Martin was not there in person to meet them would have been noted by Brian Epstein and, with some justification, interpreted as a slight.

A first studio session such as this was never a random affair, but intended not only for a producer to assess how an artist responded to being in the studio, but also to prepare some tunes for release as a first single. In those days, song selection was not usually the artist's prerogative, but the record company's. The industry 'norm' would have been for George Martin, as producer, to send the Beatles songs in advance to learn. The A&R in charge generally trusted their own judgement as to what was a potential 'hit' over that of a new artist's. In most cases the A-side would be a newly minted tune that the A&R would have sourced from a songwriter on 'Tin Pan Alley' (Denmark Street) that was being pushed by a particular music publisher they favoured or with whom they had enjoyed success previously.

Of course, in the case of the Beatles, Martin knew Len Wood had promised Ardmore and Beechwood the publishing on one of the group's own compositions and so George most probably felt any choice in the matter had effectively been taken from his hands and that the Beatles would have known which song this was.

Martin had never heard the Beatles 'live' in person before this session and, not only had he not sent them material to learn, but he had not taken the precaution to have any studio musicians on standby should any of the group not be up to it as an instrumentalist. This was unusual behaviour for any A&R, not least George Martin.

Of course, Brian Epstein had sent Martin a list of songs that he thought the producer might consider hearing them perform. At the session, George Martin apparently did not specifically request that the Beatles perform 'Like Dreamers Do' which was the very song that (unknown to either them or Brian Epstein) had placed the group inside Studio 2, Abbey Road for the very first time. It was a strange omission given the persistence of Colman and Bennett at Ardmore and Beechwood, who were determined to secure the publishing for that very song which they had identified as a potential 'hit'. Why this was the case has been lost in the fog of time.

Thankfully for Colman, the self-penned songs 'Love Me Do', 'Ask Me Why' and 'PS I Love You' were in the Beatles' armoury that evening. Consequently, Len Wood's promise to Ardmore and Beechwood that they would receive the publishing for a Lennon, McCartney song that would be released as a single could still be met, albeit not with the tune they had already identified as having 'hit' potential.

Something was going on here and it feels very much like George was responding very casually to Len Wood's apparent 'coercion' that he record the group.

For a brand new artist and mere freshers in the recording environment of a major label, in this particular matter the Beatles were being given amazing free rein. The reason for this is most likely because up to this point no one, George Martin included, at EMI itself had actually 'discovered' the Beatles for themselves, they were no one individual's 'baby' and, as such, they were not being championed by any one of the company's principal A&R men. Thus, no one within EMI had 'invested' any of themselves in the group and so had nothing to prove. They were simply a name on a document, an obligation to be filled.

It has long been forgotten whether the Beatles played the 'opening medley' that evening or what other songs they rehearsed in the studio before they moved to record. However, by the time it came to wind up the session, Ron Richards had chosen four songs to be put onto tape: 'Besame Mucho', 'Love Me Do', 'PS I Love You' and 'Ask Me Why'.

From these, two would be chosen as the A- and B-sides of their first Parlophone release. It seems Ron Richards favoured 'Besame Mucho' and 'Love Me Do' to be the chosen ones. It was during the recording of 'Love Me Do' that Norman Smith and Chris Neal began to take a closer listen, for here, to their ears, was something different, something more earthy, more bluesy, more 'original' than they had expected to hear. Chris was despatched to fetch George Martin.

In this instant George Martin's personal 'road to Damascus' moment had arrived.

A fan of the harmonica, George Martin had issued records by acclaimed blues duo Sonny Terry and Brownie McGhee and so, as he entered the sound booth/control room, his interest was immediately seized by the sound of John Lennon's harmonica.

From that moment onwards Martin became 'engaged'. The group did *have* something to offer and finally he had heard it. This bunch were not yet another version of 'Cliff Richard and the Shadows'. The Beatles were something much tougher, less clean sounding and smooth, their sound, judged by the standards prevailing on the charts at the time, was neither 'pop' nor particularly 'commercial'. But it had something: in essence the Beatles' sound was different, original and authentic.

As he took control of the session, Martin's attention was taken by what he described as a 'glitch' in the Beatles' arrangement of 'Love Me Do'. Lennon was not only singing the lead vocal but playing harmonica as well, and so whenever the tune demanded Lennon switch immediately from one to the other there was no time for him to do so.

When Martin entered the recording studio below the control booth to discuss this 'glitch' with the Beatles it was the first time he had met the boys in person. And so, not only had he finally deigned to introduce himself, but was doing so to re-arrange a tune on which they had already so carefully worked. But he was the boss and so they listened closely and then they did as he told them to do. He wanted Paul to sing the line 'Love Me Do' to free John to focus on harmonica. For Paul this was a potentially massively nerve-wrecking moment. Already nervous and focused on the group's big moment in the studio, suddenly, without any warning, he was being asked to assume the lead vocal at crucial points in 'Love Me Do'. This was something for which he was *not* prepared: the version Martin was asking them to perform was not how the group had rehearsed the song. To this day Paul says he can still hear the wobble in his voice whenever he listens to the original acetate from that first recording.

Finally, when recording that evening was complete, the Beatles climbed the 20 steps inside Studio 2 to the control room to join George, Ron, Ken, Norman, Chris, Brian and Neil for a playback and a brief talk by George on technical aspects of studio recording and their responsibilities as 'Parlophone artists'. According to Norman Smith, the Beatles were totally unresponsive. Sensing the tension in the air, George spoke a second time to invite comments, encouraging the boys to speak out if there had been anything they didn't like. At first an embarrassed silence reigned until, finally, George Harrison thought of something he wished to say. George Martin never forgot the young Beatle's reply. Looking directly at the producer, a deadpan George Harrison simply commented, "Yeah, I don't like your tie…"[1]

For a split second, silence hung in the room … then came the laughter. From being taken aback by Harrison's cheek George Martin got the joke. George had broken the ice and so the Beatles opened up and everyone left the session feeling good. The impression left on Martin was that if he wasn't in awe of their talent or music – and he wasn't particularly – as individuals he recognised the Beatles' charisma and ability to move an audience.

"I thought it (George's comment) was so funny. They had this irreverent look at life, particularly at me and I loved them for it. I immediately gravitated to them as personalities. They charmed the pants off me and I thought, if they can do that to me I reckon they can do that to an audience."[2]

And so it was that the group who, unwittingly, had arrived at Parlophone unloved and unwanted as a chore for someone to do something with, had finally been 'discovered'. Within EMI they had found someone who was beginning to realise how special they were and who would become their champion and mentor.

In that same instant, just as George Martin discovered the Beatles, so the Beatles discovered George Martin.

---

1 & 2 Sir George Martin in conversation with Bob Harris OBE and Colin Hall for the 2009 BBC Radio 2 documentary *The Songs the Beatles Gave Away,* written and narrated by Bob Harris, produced by Bob Harris and Trudie Myerscough-Harris for WBBC.

Chapter 33:
THE BALLAD OF PETE BEST

After they had gone, George Martin listened again to the Beatles' tape. What he heard he still did not particularly like. While not as stilted and under par as the Decca tapes, what they had laid down at Abbey Road was still not the Beatles firing on all cylinders.

Brian Epstein had informed *Mersey Beat* that a single would be released in July. John Lennon was hoping the A-side would be 'Love Me Do'. From the perspective of 2020, to think the overblown 'Besame Mucho' was in the running to be their first A-side beggars belief. Thankfully it didn't make the final cut.

Meeting and hearing the Beatles cured George Martin of his self-inflicted Norrie Paramor-induced 'Cliff Richard and the Shadows' obsession. The more he deliberated, the more he realised he had happened on something rather different, here was a group that broke the mould. This lot were unlike anything already out there. This was a strength that could be exploited. They played their own instruments, had three lead singers, who also sang great harmonies and two of them wrote their own material. Plus, they dressed differently and looked different. No pop star wore their hair like the Beatles in 1962. This unconventionality drew him even closer to them.

Having finally engaged with the four young men, George Martin realised he had chanced upon something quite … unique. The Beatles were a real discovery.

The only problem was their music. What they had left at Abbey Road was not good enough for release. He knew he would have to bring them back into the studio to try again. Not only that but he did not think any of their own songs were strong enough to be the A-side. Therein lay his problem, for he also knew that one of the three would have to be on the first single because of Len Wood's promise to Ardmore and Beechwood. That part of the deal Martin knew he *had* to honour.

Ron Richards was duly despatched to Denmark Street to find a suitable ditty for the Beatles to record as their first A-side. Martin was prepared to let 'Love Me Do' be the B-side to keep the publishers happy, but before it could grace even the B-side they would have to re-record it. Once Ron had found a 'special' song, George would send it up to the group in Liverpool for them to rehearse. It might take time but there was no pressure, George Martin was prepared to wait. One thing was for sure, however, there would be no debut single by the Beatles in July.

Having got Paul to sing lead when John stepped up to play harmonica, George Martin knew what it would take to further fix 'Love Me Do'. One Beatle and one element in particular had caught both his attention and that of Ron Richards, but not in a good way. Unfortunately, it was Pete and his drums.

Ron Richards: "Pete Best wasn't very good. It was me who (later) said to George Martin, 'We've got to change this drummer'."[1]

George Martin concurred and indeed, at the end of the session, while Pete was out of the room, had voiced his opinion to Brian, John, Paul and George. He also told them that the next time the Beatles came to record he would hire a session drummer. Martin's intention was not for the Beatles to replace Pete completely, only in the studio: for the purposes of recording, Martin had decided he would employ a tried and tested session drummer.

Like others before them, George and Norman Smith also noticed that Pete kept himself to himself, saying nothing in the control room while the others were in full flow. Pete himself said, in his autobiography, *Beatle!*, that he never spoke to George Martin during that evening while George Martin described Pete to Mark Lewisohn as being "very much the background boy."[2]

All of which had resonated with John, Paul and George.

The session at Abbey Road had also resonated with John in other ways. He knew full well that 'Love Me Do', 'Ask Me Why' and 'PS I Love You' had not blown anyone's socks off at EMI. John himself had not been impressed by what he heard in the control room. He knew they needed stronger material of their own. Within days, sitting upstairs at 'Mendips', he was inspired to write, 'Please Please Me'. The song and its words arrived together as one: "I wrote it in the bedroom in my house at Menlove Avenue, which was my auntie's place … I remember the day and the pink eiderdown on the bed."[3]

John's inspiration came from two sources. One was the style and sound of Roy Orbison. Orbison's records were dramatic and epic, his singing impassioned, bordering on operatic. He would begin quietly and build to a crescendo. His records were brief and to the point, emotional boleros, powerful and tender wrapped into one utterly compelling whole. The second source was a tune made popular by Bing Crosby in 1932 called 'Please'. John most probably heard it from his mother Julia. It wasn't the tune so much as its words that fascinated him. John had a fascination for words that had two meanings and so the clever opening line of 'Please' had grabbed his attention and stayed with him from the moment he heard them: 'Please, lend your little ear to my pleas'.

John may have taken inspiration for the title from Bing's song, but 'Please Please Me' was, in his original working of the tune, *all* Roy Orbison in style. It is also different from most love songs of its day in its earthy directness. This is no sweet cajoling of a lover, but a very much to-the-point pleading for his girl to do right by him as he does for her.

'Please Please Me' was pure John, but after he composed it at 'Mendips', he and Paul worked on it together at the piano in Paul's house on Saturday 9 June, observed by trusted super fans from the Cavern: Lindy and Lou. The song would take a back seat for a while, but it was in the bag, another 'Lennon-McCartney original' that they could play next time they went down to Abbey Road. It is a strong, melodic song that reveals just how quickly John Lennon was learning the game.

Meanwhile, the Beatles' career continued its upward trend with another fine performance on the BBC radio programme, *Here We Go*. Broadcast on 15 June, they performed 'Ask Me Why'. The producer Peter Pilbream was sufficiently impressed to keep them on his list of artists to call back for more appearances. Previously, immediately after recording their performance for this show in Manchester on 11 June, as they left the Playhouse Theatre, fans mobbed Pete Best.

Despite (maybe partly because of?) Pete's popularity with the girls, his place within the Beatles was no longer certain. The other boys' concerns about his drumming had been confirmed by the session at EMI and George Martin's subsequent decision to hire a session drummer the next time they attended Abbey Road to record.

John, Paul and George did not savour future recording sessions with drummers they did not know. They wanted someone who would already know the songs, was from Liverpool and with whom they had a bond. That drummer had to be someone with whom they both performed *and* recorded. He had to be one 'of them'! There could be no occasional interlopers, no break in the camaraderie.

Paul McCartney: "It had got to the stage that Pete was holding us back. What were we gonna do – try and pretend he was a wonderful drummer? We knew he wasn't as good as we wanted."[4]

Ousting Pete from the Beatles was a very unpleasant thing to have to do, but even so John, Paul and George were united and adamant that he had to go. They were equally adamant as to who they wanted as his replacement: Ringo Starr.

Despite the strength of their convictions and all they had been through together over the last two years, they lacked the bottle to tell Pete to his face.

They decided this difficult task came within their manager's remit. In this situation there were echoes of 1957 when John and Paul decided they could not face telling founder member Eric Griffiths that he was no longer a Quarry Man. Instead, back then, they had delegated the job to their manager Nigel Walley.

And so it fell to the hapless Brian Epstein to wield the axe. He had no desire to do so. He had known the boys were unhappy with Pete, but had hoped they could find a way to keep him in the group. Initially Brian was not enamoured with the thought of Ringo as Pete's replacement, but knew that his views on the matter would not be countenanced. The boys wanted Ringo and so Ringo it would be.

Despite losing Pete, the boys did not want to lose Neil Aspinall at the same stroke, but they knew that as Neil and Pete were such good friends and Neil was Mona's partner, his allegiance to the Beatles was likely to be sorely tested by such a move.

A big chap by the name of Mal Evans, a Cavern regular, had become a friend of the Beatles by now and through them he acquired the job as doorman or 'bouncer' at the club. Brian had also started to offer him work at some of the Beatles' shows beyond the Cavern, so their road crew had recently gained a second member.

Brian's uncomfortable predicament was made more tortuous by the fact that Pete was under contract to Brian as one of the Beatles. This obliged Brian to provide Pete with paid work even if he was no longer a member of the group. Even if the Beatles had broken up and reformed immediately without Pete and then, as a newly configured Beatles, had signed a new contract with Brian, Brian would have still been contractually bound to Pete by the original agreement.

So despite the uncomfortable task of telling Pete he was 'out', this was the additional convoluted legal mess that Brian had to negotiate if he was to avoid Pete being able to go to law over loss of earnings (at the very least). There would be nothing 'cut and dried' about it. Consequently, the situation dragged on for over a month.

During all this time, Ringo was well aware of what was going on. He'd been approached by John, Paul and George and had agreed he would join the group. In the meantime he continued to work the summer season at Butlin's with Rory Storm and the Hurricanes while secretly awaiting the 'call' so that he could hand in his notice and join the Beatles.

It was a fraught time, especially for Brian Epstein. Pete carried on as normal, although on one occasion a confidante of Brian's *did* let slip something was afoot but when Pete confronted Epstein the latter denied it to be true.

Also during the period leading up to Pete's dismissal several interesting events occurred. The Beatles played the Casbah for the last time on 24 June, not long after which it closed. By then Mona was in the last stages of her pregnancy and her beloved mother had succumbed to cancer. On 21 July, Mona Best gave birth to her and Neil's baby. The little boy was named Vincent Rogue Best, although as he grew up he called himself 'Roag' (he still does).

Good friends Dot Rhone and Cynthia Powell were by then living in bedsit accommodation at 93 Garmoyle Road near Penny Lane, which was just a short bus ride away from the homes of their boyfriends Paul and John. It was here that Cyn broke the news to John that she was pregnant … John was left speechless, but after a protracted silence told her that, "there's only one thing for it Cyn, we'll have to get married."[5]

Cynthia's mother Lillian, who was briefly back from Canada where she now lived, took the news well despite having little affection for John. Having little affection for Cynthia, Aunt Mimi was distinctly unhappy and would refuse to attend the wedding and, initially, would not allow the couple to live with her at 'Mendips' (despite her opposition to the couple's union she gave John the money to buy the rings). Brian Epstein was brilliant and arranged the wedding for them, which was scheduled for 23 August. He also allowed them to live at a small flat he owned on Falkner Street.

Not long after this, Paul's relationship with Dot broke up and she moved back home to live with her parents.

Meanwhile, Brian continued to juggle with the problem of what to do with Pete. He became increasingly concerned, knowing that the dirty deed had to be done in advance of a visit from a film crew from Granada TV to the Cavern on 22 August. Brian had agreed they could film the Beatles 'live', but of course now he did not want Pete to be part of the shoot.

A sense of desperation kicked in. Brian began to be concerned that once Pete was dismissed there would not be enough time for Ringo to fulfil his holiday camp commitment with Rory Storm and the Hurricanes in time to join the Beatles on stage at the Cavern on 22 August. Epstein even asked Joe Brown and the Bruvvers' drummer Bobby Graham to join the Beatles on a short-term basis to cover this eventuality. (The Beatles performed with Joe and his band at two consecutive gigs on Merseyside on 26 and 27 July.) When Graham declined, Epstein turned to Johnny 'Hutch' Hutchinson of Liverpool's hugely acclaimed Big Three. John Lennon was just one of many musicians on Merseyside who considered Hutchinson to be the city's best drummer (even better than Ringo). Hutchinson, however, bore a deep-rooted loathing of the Beatles and consequently he also declined.

Brian's link to the Big Three was more than passing. They were a hugely popular band on the Liverpool beat scene and Epstein had started to manage them. They were one of Brian's early signings after Gerry and the Pacemakers and Billy J. Kramer. John Lennon had recommended them and from 1 July 1962 they came under contract to Brian and NEMS Enterprises Ltd.

Epstein had made the decision to represent other Liverpool artists in order to build a roster of acts (or 'stable' as Larry Parnes would have described them) in order to empower his position as manager of the Beatles. Brian's initial thinking was to continue to operate from Liverpool and not to move to London. Moving to London made sense because it was the capital of the UK entertainment business and it was what people did when they became successful. Epstein was less inclined to do this because he could see Liverpool was bursting with young talent and he reasoned that he could help these artists while at the same time they could help him. He realised that having a bevy of acts under contract would strengthen his hand when dealing with the music industry, aka record companies, agents, etc, who were based in London. For one thing, it would allow him to put shows together comprising most or even all his own acts. Furthermore, when promoters came calling for the Beatles and they were unavailable, Brian could offer an alternative. It all made eminent good sense and Brian was in a privileged position for, in the main, the best of Liverpool wanted to be managed by him. At first-hand, the Beatles' Scouse contemporaries had witnessed the great job he had done for them, and was continuing to do, and were more than eager for a piece of that particular cake.

Unfortunately for Brian, the Big Three proved to be difficult, if not awkward, customers to deal with. Before the Big Three, the second act Brian had signed to NEMS Enterprises Ltd were Gerry and the Pacemakers who were more than happy to go along with what Brian insisted had to be done to become successful.

One thing Epstein made clear to everyone who joined him was that the Beatles would always be his priority.

While NEMS Enterprises Ltd was expanding its power base in Liverpool, down in London, George Martin had become aware of a song composed by a young writer called Mitch Murray (born Lionel Stitcher). It was entitled 'How Do You Do It'. Martin recognised it as a very catchy, commercial tune. It had been turned down by Adam Faith and Brian Poole and the Tremeloes, but Parlophone's Ron Richards recognised the song's hit potential, so much so he wanted to record it and so he played Murray's demo acetate to music publisher (and ex-Parlophone recording artist) Dick James. Mitch Murray, however, would not sign a publishing deal with James until he knew just who would be recording his tune. By Friday 27 July, George Martin had heard 'How Do You Do It' and considered it a very likely number 1 for someone and that *that* someone would be the Beatles. In his head, Martin was convinced he had found the A-side of their debut single. Dick James happened to be at EMI that day and let Murray know his song had been picked up for release by a group called the Beatles, all the way from Liverpool.

Martin lost no time in sending an acetate of the song to Brian Epstein, along with a note inviting the Beatles back down to EMI on Tuesday 4 September to record 'How Do You Do It' as the A-side for their first single.

The Beatles' reaction was unanimous. They did not like the song one little bit. To their way of thinking this was the kind of song someone like Cliff Richard might record, which immediately alienated it from the Beatles. "We hated it and didn't want to do it," said Paul McCartney in conversation with BBC Radio 1's Nicky Campbell on 19 November 1991. "We felt we were getting a style, the Beatles' style, which we were known for in Hamburg and Liverpool, and we didn't want to blow it all by suddenly changing our style and becoming run of the mill."[6]

The Beatles had no choice in the matter. Record companies ruled the roost. Whether they liked it or not, the Beatles would have to record their version of 'How Do You Do It' when they returned to EMI in early September and so, with the greatest of reluctance, they set about re-arranging it to be more in keeping with their own style. (The original acetate had been recorded in a light, poppy vein with Adam Faith in mind.) Re-working it was not a labour of love for the Beatles. Pete was not included in this task because, whether Ringo had replaced him or not within the group, by then the others were determined Pete would not be the drummer in the studio on 4 September.

Brian Epstein could no longer put off the dirty deed of dismissing Pete. Too many deadlines were approaching in which the Beatles did not want him involved. And so on Thursday 16 August 1962, Brian invited Pete (and Neil) to his office on Whitechapel, Liverpool, where, after some hedging, he delivered the hammer blow: Pete was out, he was no longer drummer for the Beatles, Ringo was in.

Ahead of the meeting, Epstein had circumvented the tricky obstacle of providing Pete with paid work by suggesting to a young, upcoming Liverpool group called the Mersey Beats that Pete could join on drums. They already had a drummer, but he was set to leave when they went out on tour with a singer called Mike Berry. Although he didn't manage the Mersey Beats, Brian had been mentoring them with a view towards management. Big fans of the Beatles, they were happy to accept Brian's offer of Pete joining their group.

According to Pete, after telling him he was out and Ringo was in, in response to Pete's inquiry as what was to become of him now, Epstein replied that as long as Pete remained under contract to him Brian would pay him the wage he was earning at that time and hopefully put him into another group of which Pete would become the leader.

After two very tense hours, Pete Best left Brian's office and, accompanied by Neil Aspinall who had been waiting downstairs, retired to a nearby pub. Pete was, of course, devastated. Brian had told him that not only did John, Paul and George not think he was a good enough drummer, neither did George Martin at Parlophone. Pete found this hard to accept. After all the long hours and hard work he had put into their cause, he was convinced that there was some other reason, something they were not telling him. How could they do this to him? "My mind was in turmoil. How could this happen to me? Why had it taken two years for John Lennon, Paul McCartney and George Harrison to decide that my drumming was not of a high enough standard for them?"[7]

During their time in the pub, despite being angry on his friend's behalf, Neil Aspinall resolved that he would not be resigning his post with the group and informed Pete of his decision. This could not have been easy for either party to contemplate, but miraculously it did *not* bring about the end of their friendship.

Later that afternoon, Brian Epstein wrote to his lawyer, David Harris, requesting him to draw up another contract between himself and the Beatles, in which Ringo Starr's name should replace that of Pete Best. At the same time, Brian's fee was increased from 10%

to 20% when each member of the group was earning over £100 per week and that this would rise to 25% should they each earn over £200 per week.

Having done the deed, Epstein could now welcome Richard Starkey, aka 'Ringo Starr', as the new fourth Beatle. As per John Lennon's advice, Ringo shaved off his beard and combed his hair forward to look as much the part as possible. On 18 August, he played his first booking with them at Hulme Hall, Port Sunlight on the Wirral across the River Mersey, away from Liverpool. Neil drove them there and back.

How Pete Best must have been hurting. Only he will ever know exactly what demons had been released inside his head.

It is a measure of Pete that he has carried that weight of rejection for so long with dignity. In his home city he has become a legend for whom the spotlight is never far away. All who meet and know him speak of him warmly and with respect.

---

1 *The Beatles – All These Years: Volume One: Tune In*, Extended Special Edition, by Mark Lewisohn, (Little, Brown, 2013) p.1226. Ron Richard's quotation came from Mark's own interview with him 18 January 1987.
2 *The Beatles – All These Years: Volume One: Tune In*, Extended Special Edition, by Mark Lewisohn, (Little, Brown, 2013)p.1230.
3 *All We Are Saying: The Last Major Interview with John Lennon and Yoko Ono*, interviews conducted by David Sheff for *Playboy*, 24 September 1980, edited by G. Barry Golson (Sidgwick & Jackson,2000) p.168.
4 *The Beatles – All These Years: Volume One: Tune In*, Extended Special Edition, by Mark Lewisohn, (Little, Brown, 2013), Paul interviewed by Tony Fletcher for *Jamming*, Issue 14, 1983. Quoted in *Tune In* on p.1238.
5 *A Twist of Lennon* by Cynthia Lennon (Star, 1978) p.73.
6 *The Beatles – All These Years: Volume One: Tune In*, Extended Special Edition, by Mark Lewisohn, (Little, Brown, 2013), p. 1281.
7 *Beatle!*, by Pete Best & Patrick Doncaster, (Plexus, 1985) p.166.

Chapter 34:
INJECTING VIGOUR

Immediately prior to their second session at Abbey Road, Paul McCartney had penned a new song especially for the occasion called 'Tip of My Tongue'. It was catchy and upbeat, but much later Paul would admit it was not his finest piece of work. Nevertheless, along with 'Please Please Me', it was added to the songs they had chosen to perform in the studio on Tuesday 4 September.

When they returned to EMI and Abbey Road on that date, they flew to London from Speke Airport on the outskirts of Liverpool. Their mode of transport reflected the continued upswing in their fortunes. Brian was with them while Neil had driven down with their equipment in the van. As before, they stayed in the Royal Court Hotel, Sloane Square.

They had been asked to arrive by 2pm and were booked-in for two sessions, a three-hour rehearsal in Studio 3 (not recorded) from 2 to 5pm and an evening session from 7 to 10pm (which would be recorded). It was from the second session that two sides were going to be chosen for their first single which was now scheduled to be released one month later on Friday 5 October.

George Martin and Ron Richards listened closely to the afternoon rehearsal. As the 6 June session was not going to be used, this was a new beginning. The two producers wanted to assess the group afresh with a special eye on the new drummer. To this end, Martin had not engaged a session drummer as he had previously said he was going to do.

Brian Epstein said that six songs were rehearsed. Unfortunately, no list exists to confirm exactly what those songs were, but it is highly likely they were: the compulsory 'How Do You Do It', plus 'Please Please Me', 'PS I Love You', 'Ask Me Why', 'Tip of My Tongue' and 'Love Me Do'.

In George Martin's judgement, 'Please Please Me' dragged. He suggested they double the speed to inject the tune with some vigour. John and Paul duly took note of his advice. As for 'Tip of My Tongue', Richards and Martin felt it needed more work.

As for the new drummer, George and Ron thought him an improvement on Pete, but they were not particularly impressed. Apparently, Ringo let the nerves of being in a studio for the first time overwhelm him: during the rehearsal for 'Please Please Me' he lost the plot and attempted to play bass drum, hit-hat, maracas, tambourine and cymbals all at once. George determined from this display that the next time he *would* employ a session drummer.

Martin and Richards liked John and Paul's new arrangement for 'How Do You Do It' and so it was one of the two chosen to record in the evening. They were certain this would be the A-side. The other tune chosen was 'Love Me Do'. George was still not enamoured by 'Love Me Do'. He liked the harmonica, but otherwise thought it was poor. As it was to be the B-side, however, it did not matter much, it would just fade away, for who listened to or played B-sides? The answer, in George's mind was, nobody.

The session ran way over time, but by the end Martin felt he had what he needed for a debut single. The Beatles felt very different. There was no way they wanted to release 'How Do You Do It'. They were adamant and upset. With John leading the way, they argued their case for 'Love Me Do' as the A-side. They pleaded but Martin stood firm. This was amazing stuff: artists contesting the word of the producer, the absolute expert in such matters. He was the man after all *paid* to make *the* decisions.

When they left the studio that night, the Beatles would have felt dejected rather than elated. Their worst fear had been realised: 'How Do You Do It' was to be their first single.

At this point, fate intervened and George Martin changed his mind. He did so *not* because he'd seen the light and now agreed with the Beatles that their tunes were better, rather he remembered EMI's obligation to Sid Colman and Kim Bennett at Ardmore and Beechwood. They were the first to protest at the choice of 'How Do You Do It'. They had been responsible for the Beatles getting a recording contract expressly so that Ardmore and Beechwood could obtain Lennon-McCartney song copyrights. They had expected one of John and Paul's songs to be the A-side ('Like Dreamers Do') but now believed that by giving them the B-side (which wasn't even the song that had prompted their interest in the group) EMI was merely paying lip service to their agreement which, in their book, simply was not good enough.

Next, Martin visited Dick James and when he played him the Beatles version of 'How Do You Do It' the music publisher was not enthused: he simply did not like their version. When Martin played James 'Love Me Do' and suggested he would make 'How Do You Do It' the B-side, James refused. He knew that Mitch Murray's song was too good to be hidden away on a B-side and he was certain Murray would agree with his prognosis, (which he did). Murray didn't like what had been done to his tune, and remained convinced of its hit potential: it simply had to be an A-side for someone. And so Murray refused, the Beatles' version was not released even as a B-side. This meant it was back to the drawing board for George Martin in his quest to discover that first Beatles' A-side.

Consequently, a third session was booked at Abbey Road for Tuesday 11 September. It was to be just a half session (4:45 to 6:30pm) because the Beatles would only be required to record a B-side for 'Love Me Do'. Martin had become weary of the episode and delegated Ron Richards to run the session. However, this time, to make sure things ran smoothly, he would hire a session drummer!

And so, for the second time in a week, the Beatles and Brian flew down to London while Neil drove down the day before with all the group's equipment. Once again they stayed at the Royal Court.

On entering Number 2 Studio, the Beatles were shocked to see a drum kit already set up and a drummer waiting to play. His name was Andy White, an experienced and professional drummer. After Ringo's madcap moment the previous Tuesday, George Martin was taking no chances: White was reliable to a 'T'.

Ringo was torn apart. He blamed George Martin completely: "I was devastated ... I hated the bugger for years."[1]

The song that had been chosen as the B-side for 'Love Me Do' was Paul's 'PS I Love You'. This time the Beatles were ready and in the right frame of mind. Within ten takes, 'PS I Love You' was in the bag. Ringo even got to play tambourine on the session. Recorded live and Paul in fine voice, it sounded very good.

With time to spare they decided to record 'Please Please Me'. John and Paul had worked on the arrangement and, as per George Martin's request, had quickened the tempo. John, Paul and George were now well into their stride and produced such a good recording it was earmarked for the next session for more tweaking before it would be ready to be considered for release.

Things were going very well indeed. They had breezed through the session so swiftly there was even time for one more try with 'Love Me Do'. This time Andy White was recorded on drums and Ringo played tambourine. The end result was not much different to the one recorded with Ringo on drums, except this version had tambourine on it. In the end it was the version with Ringo on drums that was chosen for release.

A protracted affair was finally at an end. George Martin had both an A- and a B-side by the Beatles good enough to be pressed. It was much to his chagrin that 'Love Me Do' was to be their debut release, for he had never rated the song and still didn't: he felt he had been coerced into its release. However, he had grown to like the Beatles and believed they could achieve a 'hit' given the 'right' song, but for now they would have to wait, for he was convinced 'Love Me Do' wasn't that song. As a consequence of his indifference towards their debut single, Martin was not moved to promote it very much, believing the group would be better served by him and EMI as a whole with their follow-up.

Of course, what the Beatles and Epstein may not have realised as they exited the studio that evening, was that over the three sessions they had played for EMI, George Martin had secured the six 'sides' or recordings which was all the company's contract with the Beatles committed them to do. All the more reason then for 'Love Me Do' to be a hit in order to ensure that there would be a next time.

From here on in, it was over to the fans and pluggers. The Beatles already had a very strong following in Liverpool and the North West of England, and so, with a little help from their friends in the local media, hopefully 'Love Me Do' would do the job and make the charts ...

History tells us that everything went more or less to plan. While George Martin did not engage in the promotion of the single, Brian Epstein *did*. His astute attention to detail, his determination, his belief in the group and his unrelenting efforts to promote the Beatles, helped make their debut a 'hit'. This was no small feat given the great indifference with which the Beatles were met in the capital where people in general took a very condescending view of anything from 'up North', especially something bearing such a ridiculous name ...

1 *The Beatles Anthology*, by The Beatles, (Cassell & C0, 2000) p.76.

Chapter 35:
LOVE ME DO: A UK Chart History

'Love Me Do' was released in Britain on 5 October 1962 and from then on made steady progress up the UK charts. It entered the Top 50 at number 49 on 17 October and peaked at number 17 on 2 January 1963 (according to the 'Official' Charts). Of course a record's placings in individual charts published by newspapers such as *New Musical Express* and *Melody Maker* did not always coincide with the Official Chart and so it was with this record: *NME* and *MM* had 'Love Me Do' at number 17 a week earlier, in late December 1962.

Unfortunately, many years later the Official Charts data, collected from a wider source, placed 'Please Please Me' as only reaching number 2, whereas *NME* and *MM* had placed it at number 1.

Despite this incontrovertible evidence to the contrary, such is the power of memory over facts that like so many of that Sixties generation I still count 'Please Please Me' as the first ever Beatles number 1 because it reached that position in the *NME* chart. Likewise, for me and other countless *NME* readers, 'Love Me Do' was at number 17 by late December 1962.

Despite all George Martin's misgivings, 'Love Me Do' spent 18 weeks in the UK Top 50, reaching number 17 twice: 2 January (Elvis was at number 1 with 'Return to Sender') and 16 January 1963 (by then Cliff was at number 1 with a double-sider, 'The Next Time' / 'Bachelor Boy'). It didn't matter to anyone in Liverpool who was at number 1, what mattered was that 'Love Me Do' was a *bona fide* UK Top 20 hit record. Not bad for a debut single record written by a couple of unknowns. It was a proven success and more than worthy of a follow-up.

Freda Kelly was just one die-hard Cavern fan and Beatles Fan Club member who went straight out and purchased a copy of the group's debut: "All the Cavernites bought 'Love Me Do'. I bought it and didn't even have a record player. People bought it to get it into the charts."[1]

Soon to become a secretary for Brian Epstein at NEMs, as we know, Freda would later become the Beatles Fan Club secretary. Maureen O'Shea and Jennifer Dawes had originally run the Club (set up in 1961) but when they relinquished their posts Roberta 'Bobby' Brown shouldered the responsibility. Bobby attended the 26 November recording session at Abbey Road when she was implored by John to play piano on 'Please Please Me' (which she declined). As the pressure of work built up, at Brian Epstein's suggestion, Bobby would be joined in her task by Freda. By the end of 1962, a Southern branch of the Club was opened, headed by Richmond-based Bettina Rose. One record out and already two Fan Clubs. In itself the necessity for two Fan Clubs says much about how ecstatically and in such numbers 'Love Me Do' was being received by fans up and down the land.

The Beatles' debut single spent its last week in the Top 50 at number 44 on 13 February, after which it spent a further 36 weeks in the bottom half of the Top 100. Not bad for a record the experts at EMI did not rate very highly.

At this time, a budget UK record label called Cannon had begun issuing six-track compilation EPs of current chart songs. Each tune was recorded by musicians specifically for the label. It was a cheap way for fans to purchase a whole bunch of hits. Towards the end of 1962, one of Cannon's EPs carried a version of 'Love Me Do' as recorded by the Sparrows. As such, it was the first recorded 'cover' of a Beatles, Lennon-McCartney song.

As 'Love Me Do' dropped down the charts, 'Please Please Me' was already climbing.

Things were moving fast and from here on in the only way for the Beatles and Brian Epstein was 'up'.

THE UK'S TOP 30 MOST POPULAR HIT RECORDS OF 1962
01 Frank Ifield: I Remember You
02 Mr Acker Bilk: Stranger on the Shore
03 The Shadows: Wonderful Land
04 Cliff Richard: The Young Ones
05 Elvis Presley: Can't Help Falling in Love / Rock-a-Hula Baby
06 The Tornados: Telstar
07 Elvis Presley: Good Luck Charm
08 Chubby Checker: Let's Twist Again
09 Frank Ifield: Lovesick Blues
10 Mike Sarne with Wendy Richard: Come Outside
11 Ray Charles: I Can't Stop Loving You
12 Joe Brown: A Picture of You
13 Pat Boone: Speedy Gonzales
14 Cliff Richard: Do You Want to Dance / I'm Looking Out the Window
15 Elvis Presley: She's Not You
16 Helen Shapiro: Tell Me What He Said
17 B Bumble and the Stingers: Nut Rocker
18 Chris Montez: Let's Dance
19 Little Eva: The Loco-Motion
20 Bobby Darin: Things
21 Roy Orbison: Dream Baby
22 Del Shannon: Swiss Maid
23 Karl Denver: Wimoweh
24 Ronnie Carroll: Roses Are Red (My Love)
25 Neil Sedaka: Happy Birthday Sweet Sixteen
26 Del Shannon: Hey Little Girl
27 Elvis Presley: Return to Sender
28 Eden Kane: Forget Me Not
29 Brian Hyland: Ginny Come Lately
30 Susan Maughan: Bobby's Girl

1 *The Beatles – All These Years: Volume One: Tune In*, Extended Special Edition, by Mark Lewisohn, (Little, Brown, 2013) p.1376. Freda Kelly interviewed by author Mark Lewisohn 28/03/2003.

Chapter 36:
PLEASE PLEASE ME

The Beatles re-visited Abbey Road on the evening of Monday 26 November 1962 and very swiftly recorded a new version of 'Please Please Me' replete with all the improvements George Martin had suggested, including the addition of harmonica. Only George Martin, Norman Smith and a tape operator were present, there was no drummer on standby and Ringo gave his best. 'Please Please Me' proved to be a breeze to record and so they also recorded 'Ask Me Why' one more time. The new take sounded very much like earlier attempts, but crucially it was now Ringo pounding the skins on the version that would be released. It took just six takes to nail it.

The session was more relaxed and convivial than previous visits. The Beatles were getting the hang of the recording process and George Martin was getting the hang of the Beatles. A mutual appreciation was growing between them. George was now convinced the Beatles had more to offer than most groups and wanted to help them achieve the success he now believed they deserved. All in all, it was a confidence-raising, feel-good session for all of them and an important ego boosting experience for Ringo.

George Martin was so upbeat and impressed that at the end of recording 'Please Please Me' he famously congratulated the Beatles with the words, "Gentlemen, you have just made your first number 1 record."[1]

Martin knew, as they did, there was no popular recording artist in Britain who was making a sound like this. They were unique. When fans got to buy this record and take it home to play it on their own gramophones, the song leapt out of the speakers with a vitality and power that felt like the Beatles were actually playing live in their own living room. There was none of the polite and careful airy pop of Cliff Richard and the Shadows, this was something much more raw-boned, direct and loud. Earthy and irrepressible, the Beatles' sound was all-encompassing, it enveloped you and pulled you close. No other UK pop star was making records as sonically dynamic and as irresistible as this. By comparison, Cliff's sound was tepid.

From being a non-believer, George Martin had become an absolute convert.

Martin was so enthused he was convinced the record had the potential to be big not only in the UK but in America as well. Furthermore, he was contemplating making a long player record with the Beatles. From such a man as Martin, this was a real accolade and proof positive of how quickly and firmly he had come round to their cause.

For the moment, however, enthusiasm generated by this session had to be put on hold as the Beatles returned to Liverpool and their endless succession of bookings. There were also two weeks in Hamburg to endure right at the very end of the year. No one wanted to go, but they were contractually bound and Brian would not countenance the Beatles breaking their promise. For Epstein it was not just a matter of legality, it was a matter of professionalism, morality and loyalty to the fans.

Released on 11 January, 'Please Please Me' entered the UK Top 50 at number 45 on 23 January 1963. 'Love Me Do' was still at number 28. From there, 'Please Please Me' climbed rapidly to reach number 3 by 13 February and by the 27th of that month it was at number 2, a position it held for two weeks, (27 February and 3 March) before slipping to number 3 on 13 March. On 20 March it climbed back to number 2 for one more week after which it began its descent down the Top 50, spending its last week at number 42 on 22 May, by which time the Number 1 selling record in the UK for three weeks on the trot was a tune called 'From Me to You'.

All three Beatles chart A-sides and B-sides were John Lennon and Paul McCartney compositions.

After just three singles, the Beatles had reached the pinnacle of UK popdom. From that point on, there would be no stopping them.

'Beatlemania' literally took the UK by storm and Brian Epstein's long-held contention that the Beatles were destined to become 'bigger than Elvis' would no longer be met by those within the music industry with either incredulity or scorn …

1 *All You Need Is Ears*, George Martin and Jeremy Hornsby, (Macmillan,1979) p.30.

PART 3

NORTHERN SONGS

Chapter 37:
PUBLISHING

"The outstanding English composers of 1963 must seem to have been John Lennon and Paul McCartney, the talented young musicians from Liverpool whose songs have been sweeping the country since last Christmas , whether performed by their own group, the Beatles, or by the numerous other teams of English troubadours that they also supply with songs."
from 'What Songs the Beatles Sang' by The Times *Music Critic, William S. Mann, published 27 December 1963*

The rise of songwriters 'Lennon and McCartney' or 'McCartney and Lennon' – take your pick – was as meteoric as that of the Beatles themselves. From having composed a mere handful of songs between 1957 and 1962, as 1963 dawned, John and Paul became prolific.

In the excitement of recording 'Love Me Do', Ardmore and Beechwood's claim for its copyright was not overlooked, especially by them. Not long after the 11 September visit to Abbey Road, Ardmore and Beechwood sent Brian Epstein a simple publishing agreement for both songs on the single. It was the usual kind of agreement that most songwriters would sign. Brian received it 'for and on behalf of Lennon/McCartney'. Its contents gave EMI's music company (Ardmore and Beechwood) in perpetuity the 'full copyright for all countries'. This was standard procedure.

Under the contract, John and Paul would receive 10% from retail sales of sheet music (after the first 500 copies had been sold), 50% of the publisher's receipts/royalties from record sales containing either song ('mechanical rights') in the UK and abroad, and a further 50% of royalties received from any sub-publishing contracts outside the UK. They would also receive 50% of money brought in by the PRS (Performing Right Society) a body which collects royalties for its members whenever their songs are performed in public, broadcast or transmitted. The PRS divides the money it collects equally between the artist and their publisher. Of course they have to be members of PRS for this to happen, of which the Beatles already were. This was the body of the deal and for the time it was the standard format of all such publishing deals. There were ten clauses to which Brian added an eleventh: 'That were (sic) sheet music, records, publicity etc is concerned credit will be given to "LENNON/McCARTNEY".'

The agreement was backdated to 7 September 1962. Brian shared it with Paul, John and Cynthia in his Falkner Street flat where he had invited John and Cynthia to stay after they had married and Aunt Mimi would not allow them to live with her at 'Mendips'.

The meeting was informal but of mighty significance because it was here that John and Paul made legal and binding their old teenage pact to credit their songs as 'joint' collaborations. From that point onwards it was legally agreed that whoever originated a tune it would be presented as a 'Lennon and McCartney original'. The massive difference now was that whether a tune was co-written or penned individually they would all be treated as 50-50 collaborations. In effect, John and Paul were agreeing to share the money equally whoever wrote a song. It kept things simple. Halves. In doing so, they remained true to their original youthful vision of what making music together was all about. It kept faith with that incredible musical bond forged in the bedroom and living rooms of their respective homes in Liverpool: 'Mendips' and 20 Forthlin Road.

It is also testament to how close both men were as friends.

This monumental decision would impact not just on the lives of John and Paul, but on the Beatles as a group. It also opened a divide within the Beatles that would become more significant as time passed. Where previously all things within the group had been shared equally, from now on they would not. Whenever a Beatles record was released, John and Paul would automatically earn a lot more than George and Ringo. Whatever contribution the latter two might make to a song during its evolution either on stage or in the studio (and both George and Ringo's contributions should never be underestimated) they would not receive a compositional credit. The 'original' songs on Beatles records were John and Paul's and they got the money for writing them.

This is a problem faced by all bands for whom only one or two of its personnel write the songs, and it often becomes a recipe for unrest and jealousy that can cause groups to break up. However much a group member may feel that they have contributed to the style and recognisable 'sound', if they aren't credited as a co-writer they receive no financial recompense other than from the physical sales of the records. When the spoils aren't equally divided, you can't blame those who have given all they can to make things happen and are part of the group's identity not to feel some resentment. It's only human nature and the Beatles were all too human.

Fortunately, for the world and their fans, the Beatles earned a lot of money and all four would become wealthy beyond their wildest dreams, but this agreement sowed a seed of separation that did not go unnoticed. Certainly not by George Harrison who commented to broadcaster Alan Freeman in 1974: "An attitude came over John and Paul of 'We're the grooves and you two just watch it'. They never said that, or did anything, but over a period of time…"[1]

As to the publishing agreement with Ardmore and Beechwood, John and Paul made one amendment of their own and that was to that eleventh clause that Brian had added. Once rewritten, this clause now stated that when Paul was the main writer the credit should reflect that and be written 'McCartney-Lennon' and when it was John who was the main writer it would be written 'Lennon-McCartney'. As for 50-50 collaborations, that would be decided when those tunes occurred. Dutifully, Brian changed his own addition and re-wrote 'LENNON/McCARTNEY' as 'McCARTNEY/LENNON' because both sides of 'Love Me Do' were mainly Paul songs. (Ironically 'Love Me Do' was eventually issued with 'Lennon-McCartney' credited as the songwriters while 'Please Please Me' was credited 'McCartney-Lennon'.)

At that same meeting held to agree to allow Ardmore and Beechwood to have the copyright for 'Love Me Do' and 'PS I Love You', it was agreed that, in their capacity as songwriters, John and Paul would sign a separate management contract with Brian Epstein.

Brian's lawyer David Harris was duly informed of the need for a second 'songwriters' contract for just John, Paul and Brian.

At the time he received this instruction from Brian Epstein, Harris had just finished drafting a new contract for Brian to sign with John, Paul, George and Ringo as Beatles, it would last for five years from 1 October 1962 until 30 September 1967. The new Beatles contract not only included Ringo, but this time Brian *would* sign it. (This new Beatles contract was carefully worded to avoid the tricky situation Epstein had encountered when dismissing Pete Best.)

In their separate songwriters' contract, John and Paul ('The Composers') appointed NEMS Enterprises Ltd (Brian) as their sole representative manager and agent for the next five years. Brian's commission was 20%. This agreement did not include any mention of the order of compositional credits, but the document they signed named 'the composers' in the order of Lennon and McCartney. This was never changed.

It is not known if George and Ringo ever knew about the second, songwriters' contract between Brian and John and Paul. They never mentioned it publicly. Of the decision to exclude George in particular from the songwriting team, Paul has been quite candid, allowing a quotation from himself to appear in *The Beatles Anthology*, in which he commented, "It was an option to include George in the songwriting team. John and I had really talked about it. I remember walking up past Woolton Church one morning and going over the question: 'Without wanting to be too mean to George, should three of us write or would it be better to keep it simple?' We decided we'd just keep it to two of us."[2]

From 1957 onwards, when John and Paul tentatively began sharing songs, they declared a shared ambition to become the 'British Goffin and King': now they were *en route* to become exactly that, if not more.

The signing of a songwriting agreement with Brian and a publishing agreement with Ardmore and Beechwood opened the door for many more Lennon-McCartney songs to be included in the Beatles' repertoire.

It was a brilliant move. Singing more original songs further distanced the Beatles from other UK groups and helped establish their unique musical appeal and identity. One of these 'new originals' that started to appear in their set was actually an 'oldie' from 1959, Paul's 'I'll Be on My Way'. Another was a brand new McCartney tune called 'Hold Me Tight'. Sitting in the front room at 20 Forthlin Road, John helped Paul with the song's arrangement which Paul had written with the view to it being a possible single. Its structure and style reflects the Beatles' then-current admiration and love for those beloved singles they were devouring and covering by black groups from the USA, in this case particularly the Shirelles.

As the manager and agent of songwriters 'Lennon and McCartney', despite the difficulties of accessing exposure in the media of the day, Brian Epstein was diligent in his duties. Equally so, Ardmore and Beechwood were no sloths in plugging their new songwriters and their group, the Beatles. Despite working relentlessly to break the Beatles in the UK on radio and TV via appearances on shows like ITV's brand new and mightily important *Thank Your Lucky Stars*, Kim Bennett's work on their behalf somehow failed to impress Brian Epstein. This was unfortunate and unfair, but it was Brian's perception.

The truth was that opening the doors of national newspapers and music rags like *NME* was certainly an uphill task, especially for a group from 'the North' that journalists had not seen or heard of (because such scribes were, in the main, too idle and arrogant to journey beyond London). The prevailing attitude was 'what has the North got to offer that we don't already have in the South?' Plus, the Beatles' name was too easy to mock, more often than not it induced derogatory sniggers and 'what kind of name is that?' kind of comments. Not all reporters were like this, but many were and so major media outlets proved initially resistant to the Beatles' charms.

Bennett had not let himself be deterred and was just turning things around when Brian's impatience got the better of him. He decided Ardmore and Beechwood had been complacent and had not done enough to promote 'Love Me Do' and so they could not be trusted with 'Please Please Me'. They would not be getting the publishing for that song.

George Martin had done little to promote 'Love Me Do' and, ultimately, did little to promote the cause of Ardmore and Beechwood. At least, not in the mind of Brian Epstein. While recording 'Please Please Me', however, somewhat belatedly and rather like Sid Coleman and Brian Bennett of Ardmore and Beechwood before him, he had very much come round to the Beatles' cause and in the process had recognised that in John and Paul the group possessed two very promising songsmiths. As a result of his revised opinion, he was fast becoming their champion and inclined to distance himself from the tortuous route by which the Beatles had obtained their record contract with Parlophone. Ardmore and Beechwood had undoubtedly been the Beatles' (thus John & Paul as songwriters) original champions and it was their persistence, not George's, that had secured the group a record deal with Parlophone.

So, possibly it was no wonder that when Brian wanted away from Ardmore & Beechwood, Martin did little to intervene on their behalf as, working for EMI, he no doubt should have done. Like so many who were to become such crucial players in the Beatles' story, it had taken a moment or two of catch up but by then, George Martin was ahead of the pack. For him, the situation around the Beatles had changed dramatically.

From being an obligation, the group had become an inspiration. He was now tuned in and turned on to the point he was already planning to cut a long playing record with them early in 1963, despite the fact that at that time the Beatles had only released one single (of which he had not thought very much). This is the rate by which George Martin's admiration for the Beatles had soared. A date had even been set for this very purpose: 11 February 1963. Moreover, Martin was contemplating recording it 'live' at the Cavern in Liverpool.

Amid all this excitement and change of attitude, George Martin would have known instinctively that a new start at EMI was in order for the Beatles, with himself leading the charge. Ardmore and Beechwood (apparently) did not fit with his plan. With this in mind (and a whole lot more besides), he directed Brian towards a publisher whom he believed was just the man for Lennon and McCartney ...

And in the process apparently nearly cut himself out of the Beatles story altogether ...

---

1 *The Beatles – All These Years: Volume One: Tune In*, Extended Special Edition, by Mark Lewisohn, (Little, Brown, 2013). George Harrison in conversation with Alan Freeman on BBC Radio 1, 6 December 1974 and quoted in *Tune In* on p.1343.
2 *The Beatles Anthology*, by The Beatles, (Cassell & Co, 2000) p.96.

Chapter 38:
DICK JAMES HAS A GREAT NOTION

Dick James was an East End boy, the son of Polish Jewish immigrants. Born Reginald Leon Isaac Vapnick in 1920, as a young man he had enjoyed a career as a singer (interrupted only by his time in the army during WW2). After the war he changed his name to the more 'commercial' sounding Dick James.

In 1956, George Martin signed Dick James to Parlophone and produced James's biggest hit, 'The Ballad of Davy Crockett', backed by 'Robin Hood', which spent eight weeks in the UK singles chart from 26 January to 15 March 1956, all of them in the Top 20. 'Robin Hood' was the official B-side and was the theme tune to the very popular children's TV series, *The Adventures of Robin Hood*, starring Richard Greene in the title role. *The Guinness Book of British Hit Singles* has the B-side 'Robin Hood' being the song that was credited with making that eight-week chart run. However, it also credits the record making the chart again in May 1956 as a re-entry for just one week, peaking at number 29, but this time *both* sides are credited as reaching that position.

The artist credit for 'Robin Hood' as it appeared on the Parlophone record label was 'DICK JAMES with Stephen James and his Chums and Ron Goodwin's Orchestra'. Stephen was James's son.

When, in 1958, Dick's singing career began to ebb, he changed to work as a music plugger for Sydney Bron Music. Able to call on the contacts he had made in the music industry as a singer, he was successful in this new role. So much so, he decided to switch to become a music publisher in his own right and on 19 July 1961 established Dick James Music. (In 1963, he was joined by his son Stephen and in 1969 the pair created a record label of their own entitled DJM, which issued the first records by Elton John, having earlier, in 1967, signed Elton and lyricist Bernie Taupin to Dick James Music as their publishers. There is no doubt Dick James knew a hit song when he heard one.)

After what he perceived as Ardmore and Beechwood's failure, Epstein originally had it in mind to approach Hill & Page, an American publishing house with an office in London. They published most of Elvis's hits, so in Epstein's mind, who better to publish 'Please Please Me'?

George Martin listened and did not deter Epstein from this train of thought. No doubt, however, especially as Brian was so opposed to Beechwood and Ardmore, he felt it would have been remiss not to suggest Dick James as well. After all, Dick was not only a colleague and friend, but had published some of George's own compositions. Significantly, Martin also knew James had a policy of pushing UK writers and UK talent over Americans. This fact was very much in James's favour, for it would place John and Paul at the front of a small pack and not as just two of the many writers already signed to Hill & Page. With Dick James they would not be two of many, but would have their publisher's full attention as he strived to make a name for himself. All these factors would have impressed George Martin.

The logic of Martin's reasoning was as persuasive as it was sound.

But in promoting James he was sailing particularly close to the wind as far as his own career at EMI was concerned. As a personal appointee of the company's charismatic head, Chairman Sir Joseph Lockwood ('Sir Joe' as he was popularly known), he would have known loyalty to the company was held by his boss as a supreme virtue. For Sir Joe it was a line to be crossed only at an employee's extreme peril.

Equally George would have known that the very idea to install Ardmore and Beechwood as EMI's own in-house publishing company within the HMV store, had been Sir Joe's very own. The very aim of which had been to facilitate the making of demos from tapes brought in by unknown artists – exactly as Brian Epstein had done with the Beatles. The group's signatures on an EMI contract owed their presence on the document thanks, therefore, to an innovation of their esteemed Chairman Joe …

In his biography of Sir Joseph Lockwood, his personal assistant William Cavendish, comments, "As a consequence Sid Coleman … published the first two L&McC songs. It was an act of disloyalty for George Martin, as an EMI manager, to take the Beatles' future publishing away from the company."[1]

It would have been deemed George's duty to do all he could to persuade Brian to stay with Ardmore and Co. Despite the ascendancy of Ardmore and Beechwood within EMI and the possibly dire consequences leading from his actions, not only did George suggest Dick James to Brian, he introduced the pair over the telephone, during which conversation James invited Brian to a meeting in his office on 27 November 1962, the day after the euphoric 'Please Please Me' session.

Whether George Martin was being foolhardy, inspired, simply taking a risk or a man on a mission to surround the Beatles and equip Brian and the boys with whom he perceived to be the best in the business, it's not easy to say. Possibly he was still miffed by the impasse he had come up against when discussing his new contract with Len Wood and looking to score one back. Whatever his motivation he resolutely pressed on. There again he had listened to Brian and believed that whatever he said Brian was not for turning.

But he did not escape unscathed. As he would surely have known … Sir Joe did get to learn what he'd done …

And he was most definitely not happy with Martin for giving "the Beatles' music publishing to a little man with an office around the corner".[2a]

As a result, neither was Managing Director, Len Wood (aka LG). Already unhappy and shocked by George's behaviour and insistent salary demands, Wood was incensed by George Martin's latest antics and moved to sack him. According to William Cavendish, Sir Joe's biographer, although the latter was immediately very angry and knew how Wood was leaning, Lockwood stepped back from pushing Martin over the precipice and spared him. Instead, "By docking GM's Christmas bonus as a punishment, LG/Wood created a permanent rift between the two of them. Fortunately, losing the Beatles' publishing failed to damage EMI, as Martin and the Beatles were firmly committed by contract to record for the company. Also, Brian Epstein was not really responsible for the situation."[2b]

There's no doubt Wood would have known, particularly after George's recent requests, how the loss of his bonus would have stung him financially.

Prior to Epstein's arrival, James had done some background research on the Beatles. He had made a phone call to Peter Pilbeam, the BBC's producer for the radio show *Here We Go*, on which they had appeared twice. Pilbeam had a very good opinion of the group and gave a positive response. Meanwhile, his own son Stephen was already a fan of 'Love Me Do' as was Dick's own receptionist, Lee Perry. When Dick James put these enthusiastic responses together with George Martin's obvious belief in the group, he was already of a mind to publish 'Please Please Me' before even meeting their manager. When Epstein played James the acetate from the previous evening's session, James was immediately convinced that the Beatles had a potential number 1 hit on their hands and desperately wanted a piece of that action. He also knew that the song would only achieve the success it deserved *if* it received the right exposure and he believed himself to be *the* man to achieve this for them.

In 1962, the most prestigious, powerful and persuasive means of gaining nationwide exposure would be for the group to appear on ITV's new and hugely popular flagship 'pop programme', *Thank Your Lucky Stars*. In the UK, TV was still in its infancy as a source of mass entertainment. Its audience was huge, but there were only two channels and so limited chances for exposure for artists. Every pop star wanted to appear on *Thank Your*

Lucky Stars, but as Kim Bennett could testify, making this a reality for an artist was no easy task.

With Epstein sitting right in front of him, James decided to put the ball into play immediately. He picked up his telephone and called Philip Jones, the producer of *Thank Your Lucky Stars*. Jones knew Dick James very well, for he had produced James's 1950 shows for Radio Luxembourg. With Epstein listening and watching on incredulously, over the phone, Dick James played the Beatles' acetate to his former producer. Jones never hesitated. What he'd heard was enough. On the spot he offered the Beatles a place on *Thank Your Lucky Stars*. There and then he agreed to film them on Sunday 13 January 1963, just two days after 'Please Please Me' was to be released.

Within minutes of meeting Brian Epstein, Dick James had performed the miracle that Ardmore and Beechwood had singularly failed to do. A single phone call was all it had taken. Epstein needed no more proof as to the genius of Dick James. Here was a man who made things happen: he was the man for the Beatles and most definitely he was the man to be trusted with John and Paul's publishing.

Epstein knew instantly that James had the show business nous he personally lacked at this stage: "To handle the sheet music and publishing side of the business, John, Paul and I linked with Dick James, an honourable and well-regarded publisher who had been a well-known band singer ... When I met him he had a small publishing office, but huge integrity."[3]

One of the decisions made with James was that Brian Epstein emphatically did not want anyone else to record a John and Paul song, unless he, John and Paul agreed. It was made clear that Dick James would *control* the copyrights. Brian did not want the competition of other versions of a new Beatles' song being available at the same time the Beatles' own version was on the charts. Brian and Dick knew that the prevailing practice on Tin Pan Alley was for a publisher to promote the song *over* a particular performer and so, consequently, many times several versions of the same song sung by different artists would be vying with each other for a place on the charts. This would mean a song that was selling really well would not get to the top because its sales were split between the various versions on sale. By making this arrangement with Dick James, the pair were subverting what had become the standard practice of the all-powerful Tin Pan Alley for many, many years.

James proved to be so much more than just John and Paul's publisher, he became Brian's man in the capital looking after the interests of not only the Beatles but of all the artists Brian would eventually sign to his newly formed (May 1962) NEMS Enterprise Ltd. This was an entirely separate company to NEMS Ltd. The latter was his father's business in Liverpool where Brian had been working as the manager of its Whitechapel branch when he discovered the Beatles. NEMS Enterprises gave Brian autonomy and financial independence from his parents' business.

Events were happening so rapidly it was hard for the Beatles to keep track. Importantly, on Sunday 2 December 1962, they travelled to Peterborough to support headliner Frank Ifield. This booking had been arranged by Brian after he met Ifield backstage at the Empire in Liverpool, where the chart-topping Australian had been performing. At the meeting, Brian had been interested to learn just how the touring circuit worked, to which end Ifield directed Epstein to Arthur Howes, who promoted most of the package tours doing the rounds in Britain in the 1960s. When Epstein contacted Howes, the latter was already aware of 'Love Me Do's' presence on the chart and offered the Beatles an expenses-only slot supporting Ifield when he played Peterborough on 2 December. Ahead of the Peterborough show, Epstein met Howes in person and on the basis of the success of 'Love Me Do', Howes offered them the opening slot on a forthcoming Helen Shapiro package tour scheduled for February and March 1963.

Added to this, Howes mentioned the possibility of a place for the group on a March 1963

UK tour starring American singing sensations Chris Montez and Tommy Roe. However, while the Shapiro tour dates were signed and sealed, Howes wanted to assess the group for anything beyond that. Where he made his assessment was in Peterborough.

Although the Beatles were personally disappointed with their performance in Peterborough, Arthur Howes heard enough to sign them to an exclusive deal in which he would be their promoter until the end of 1965. Furthermore, they were added to the Montez-Roe tour. And so the Beatles' upward spiral of success continued. The result of signing with Howes was that they would be gigging throughout February and March 1963. They were used to constant gigging, but the difference now was that they would be performing across the nation, not just buzzing around Liverpool and the North West.

A day after meeting Arthur Howes, the Beatles met Dick James in his office at 132 Charing Cross Road. It was an eventful trip because on that occasion John and Paul signed publishing agreements with James. What they signed was typical of the times: the publisher took the copyright. This was the way it had been ever since music publishing began. James took 10% expenses from the royalties earned and the rest was split 50-50 between James on the one side and John, Paul and NEMS Enterprises Ltd (Brian) on the other. It was James's job to plug 'Please Please Me' and 'Ask Me Why', both songs for which he now 'owned the copyright'.

Ironically, James's job as publisher and plugger of 'Please Please Me' was given a kick start by all the unrecognised work Kim Bennett had done on their behalf for 'Love Me Do', for there was by then an awareness of the Beatles within the industry thanks to its presence on the charts.

'Please Please Me' was a stronger product and so the reluctance that Bennett faced melted away. Bennett had got them their first BBC radio play (to an estimated audience of approximately 5 million) when 'Love Me Do' was featured on *Twelve O'Clock Spin* on 31 October 1962. He topped this with a play on *Two-Way Family Favourites*, which boasted an audience of over 17 million. Bennett had laid the groundwork for what came next. His achievements cannot be over-estimated.

Admirable though Bennett's efforts were, the clincher was that James secured that all-important *Thank Your Lucky Stars* television appearance. He followed up with a 'live' performance slot for them on the legendary BBC 'pop' music radio show, *Saturday Club*. Scheduled for 22 January, just like *Thank Your Lucky Stars*, it was a perfect springboard for the launch of 'Please Please Me'.

From now on, the Beatles' star was not only in the ascendant, it was sky-rocketing faster than they could ever have hoped for.

At the same time Dick James came on board, Brian Epstein recruited fellow Liverpudlian Tony Barrow as NEMS Enterprises Ltd press officer. How they needed one!

As 1963 began, the Beatles were running at full pelt just to keep up with themselves. A potential number 1 record was just weeks from release. A national tour was soon to begin. TV appearances, radio slots, requests for interviews … offers were piling in and Brian did everything he possibly could to maintain this stunning momentum.

The team he built around the Beatles – Aspinall, Martin, James, Howes, Barrow and himself – were all first-rate individuals and professionals absolutely dedicated to the cause of the Beatles. Added to this, mighty man mountain Mal Evans, the bouncer at the Cavern, was establishing himself as their 'protector' and soon joined Neil as a roadie for the group. A man of hidden talents (as will be seen) he was a great addition to the team. And then there were the stalwarts of the Beatles Fan Clubs Bobby Brown and Freda Kelly in the North and Bettina Rose in the South.

Despite how time-consuming caring for the Beatles had become, at the same time Brian Epstein was in the process of establishing his own 'stable of stars'. The acts he signed initially were all from Liverpool. A city rich in untapped talent, Epstein was keen for them all to enjoy success: "After the Beatles, I had signed Gerry and his Pacemakers, Billy J.

Kramer and the Dakotas, and a group called the Big Three. I was taking a close interest in ... Priscilla White, and I had half an eye on the star potential of the freckled lad named Quigley. It was, in fact, all happening."[4]

On a visit to Liverpool to hear the Beatles perform in the Cavern where he was contemplating recording them 'live' for their first album, George Martin had been amazed at what he heard beyond the Beatles.

One singer in particular had caught his attention just as it had Brian's. His name was Gerry Marsden, lead singer and frontman of Gerry and the Pacemakers. Brian took Martin to hear Gerry and his group perform in Birkenhead before taking him to the Cavern to hear the Beatles. Martin was moved enough by what he heard to offer Marsden and the Pacemakers a 'commercial test' at Abbey Road, from which they all hoped a single could be chosen and a record deal secured. Of course, Martin had an excellent song in mind for Gerry to record for his debut single. He had recently recorded it with another group from Liverpool who had ultimately turned against it in favour of another tune for their debut release. Martin, however, remained convinced that that group had walked away from a certain number 1.

He was right.

The song was, of course, Mitch Murray's 'How Do You Do It'. Published by Dick James, Gerry and the Pacemakers were to prove Martin, Murray and James 100% right about its hit potential.

Martin also heard the Fourmost (formerly the Four Jays) and liked them enough to offer them a commercial test. Epstein had already offered to manage this group, but they declined because they had good jobs and apprenticeships with excellent prospects and were not prepared to take the risk of giving all that up for the perils of a life in show business. When Epstein informed them of Martin's interest he again offered to manage them. Again they turned his offer down and declined Martin's offer to record at Abbey Road. Jobs for life were hard to come by in those days and so, for the Fourmost to relinquish jobs that would provide them with a secure future (and a pension) was both a big ask and a big risk. Show business and the world of 'pop' stardom was notoriously fickle and short-lived. It was littered with artists who'd been here today and gone tomorrow, so initially Fourmost's Brian, Mike, Billy and Dave were not tempted to relinquish their day jobs.

Epstein's management of Liverpool's powerhouse trio, the Big Three, would be short-lived but he did make things happen for them by signing them to Decca. Their debut single, 'Some Other Guy', was released in early 1963.

Brian also signed a handsome young singer called Billy Kramer, "Because John Lennon of the Beatles thought a lot of his voice."[5]

As 1963 advanced, Epstein rapidly became the man to be signed to in a management deal. Possessed of the Midas touch, he also had direct access to the most exciting new hit songwriters on the block ... John Lennon and Paul McCartney, to whom he could turn to provide his other artists with hit songs.

1, 2a & 2b *His Master's Voice: Sir Joseph Lockwood and Me*, William Cavendish (Unicorn, 2017) Kindle edition, chapter 19 'Sir Joe Becomes Intoxicated with Beatlemania', all quotations from Loc 1513.
3, 4 & 5 *A Cellarful of Noise*, Brian Epstein (New English Library, 1964) p.96, p.65 & p.70.

Chapter 39:
CATSWALK

Within only a very short time, Dick James became very excited by his new relationships with Brian Epstein and the Beatles. He was convinced of the potential of John and Paul's songwriting talent. So great was his conviction, he foresaw a publishing future that was likely to generate huge financial rewards to whoever owned their future copyrights. Naturally, after what he'd already achieved for the Beatles, he wanted to be *that* person. He knew he could also be making a big mistake, but he didn't think so and he certainly did not want others to profit from any hesitancy on his part.

As the saying goes … a person must make his/her move before their move is made for them.

However much he could conjure dreams about this fabulous scenario, James knew only too well that just as simply and unceremoniously as had happened with Ardmore and Beechwood, Brian Epstein, John and Paul could quit Dick James Music for someone else. Changing publishers was a routine occurrence within the music industry. Nothing was set in stone. He was currently flavour of the month with Brian Epstein and 'the boys' mainly for working the miracle of *Thank Your Lucky Stars* and *Saturday Club*, but it was early days and much could happen and many big promises could be made by others to entice them away …

With this in mind, Dick James became determined to secure John Lennon and Paul McCartney into a binding longer-term publishing deal. To this end he came up with the idea of establishing a new music publishing company. The new company would be jointly owned by himself and the partnership of Lennon, McCartney and NEMS Enterprises Ltd (Epstein). There would be a 50-50 split of the profits. In this way John and Paul would not be signing away the ownership of their copyrights, they would have secured joint ownership of them. Each new tune would have to be individually assigned to the new company, but in addition to the usual royalties earned from sheet music sales, broadcast and mechanical fees, unlike other publishing contracts they would also receive 50% of the company's profits.

This was a good deal for Lennon and McCartney. It was virtually unique in the world of publishing and was further proof that they were breaking free of convention and establishing a new order. They would earn more than royalties. For Dick James it meant he gave away half his claim on copyrights and half his earnings, but crucially he did not lose John and Paul's songs. In the long term (which was the view James was taking) James stood to earn a lot of money should his belief in their songwriting potential be proven right.

Brian Epstein was taken with James's idea and so Epstein's lawyer David Harris drew up the contract. The way it worked was that a new company was established in the joint ownership of Dick James Music as half owner and John, Paul and NEMS Enterprises (Brian Epstein) as the other half owners. What the actual split was is unclear, but it wasn't quite 50-50. Dick James and his partner Charles Silver always seemed to own a crucial 1% more, making it a 49-51% split in their favour. Just how John, Paul and NEMS Enterprises Ltd (Brian) split their 49% is unclear. Paul seems to have got 20%, but then it is not clear if John got 19% and Brian 10% or if John got 20% and Brian 9%.

Whatever the actual percentage splits between them, Lennon and McCartney agreed that for the next three years they would assign all their new song copyrights to the new company and that the number of new songs assigned during that period should be no less than 18. James took 10% of the company's gross earnings in payment for administrating

Dick James in 1966 pictured sitting at his desk in the offices of DJM music publishing company. (Pictorial Press Ltd / Alamy Stock Photo)

and managing the company's business.

There is no doubt that James was taking a huge risk with this venture. At this point, Lennon and McCartney had only delivered one Top 20 song and the Beatles were on the charts for only the first time. Nothing was a given. However, James had heard 'Please Please Me' and that was the clincher. He was long in the business and knew a hit when he heard one. If Lennon and McCartney could write a tune this good then they could write others … James trusted his ears and believed he was on to a winner.

How right he was!

The contract that created this new limited company was signed in 1963 (the Beatles had very reluctantly been in Hamburg for the last two weeks of 1962) by which time it had been decided to call it 'Northern Songs Limited' after Dick James had suggested it as a name to reflect the fact that John and Paul were both northerners.

Before signing to Ardmore and Beechwood and then Dick James Music and the formation of Northern Songs Limited, John Lennon and Paul McCartney had struggled with the concept of 'owning' a song. Paul has since explained that although he and John fully understood the concept of owning a car or a guitar because they were physical, tangible items, they struggled a bit with 'owning' a song, which was something more nebulous and, as such, having a 'copyright' of or owning a song took a bit longer for them to get their heads around. Ruefully, Paul has also commented that no doubt the publishers of Tin Pan Alley would have been rubbing their hands in glee as they saw them coming.

Of the Northern Songs deal with Dick James, Paul has also said he and John believed they owned the company outright, that it was their company, that they owned it 100%. Initially they did not realise they (a 'they' which included Brian Epstein) owned only 49% while the larger 51% belonged to Dick James and Charles Silver.

Herein lay a massive problem for the future. At the time, it was not only John and Paul who were in the dark about the 'ins and outs' of publishing deals, so was Brian Epstein. This tiny detail carried massive implications for who actually owned Northern Songs. In retrospect, Paul has suggested Brian was not astute enough, while John believed Dick James "carved Brian up a bit".[1]

At the time that all the contract-writing and signing was going on, John, Paul, George and Ringo were on a roller-coaster journey that was thrilling and sensational. Every day brought a myriad of new demands upon them and their time. As a result, their attention was elsewhere, business was 'boring' and as a result they signed contracts without properly examining them in great detail. Everything was all happening so fast they did not have time (or the inclination) to stop and read the small print, they left that for others to do on their behalf. These 'others' were people whom they trusted and believed possessed the knowledge and experience they personally lacked. Unfortunately, it seems those 'others' either did not understand the small print or failed to read it carefully enough. In essence, all four Beatles were just happy to be signed, making records and on the charts. They had faith in the people around them, as evidenced by Paul's comment at the time that, "We've got people we trust – our manager, our recording manager, our publisher, our accountant – they're all trustworthy people, I think. So we leave it to them and I don't have to worry."[2]

The pressure on John and Paul right from the very start of their recording career was to provide fresh 'original' Beatles product. With an album due to be recorded on 11 February 1963, songwriting had become a priority for them. As 1962 drew to a close, Paul was suitably inspired to compose one of the all-time great Beatles songs which also stands as one of the all-time great opening tracks ever on a debut album: 'I Saw Her Standing There'. It was composed between very late Monday 22/early 23 Tuesday October 1962, as Paul was travelling back from a booking in Widnes to Rory Storm's home. The tune simply came into his head during the car journey and arriving at Rory's home he picked up a guitar and played what he had in his head. Soon he had the first two lines: 'She was just seventeen, She'd never been a beauty queen'. Paul and his then girlfriend Celia Mortimer hitch-hiked to London the next day (Tuesday) to stay with Paul's old schoolfriend Ivan Vaughan and, while they wandered around the capital and took in the sights, Paul was making up more lines for the song with Celia helping out. She provided a line to rhyme with 'We danced through the night', which is, of course, 'And we held each other tight'. (No doubt in the modern world of songwriting Celia would have been given a co-writing credit for her contribution.)

A month later, Paul finished the song with John when they got together in Paul's front room at 20 Forthlin Road. It is a moment caught on camera. Mike McCartney, Paul's brother, was there with his camera and captured the two at work in a sequence of brilliant photographs. Huddled in the corner of the living room, leaning over their guitars, John and Paul are focused on the old exercise book of Paul's from the Inny which lies in front of them on the floor and in which he has written the lyrics. This can be seen (upside down) as can Paul's various crossings out and corrections.

These wonderful images now hang in the corner of that old living room inside Forthlin Road, exactly where the boys were sitting, and are part of the marvellous collection of Mike McCartney 'photies' (his word) displayed inside the house that is now owned by the National Trust (and therefore open to the public). Paul has commented to Mike that this is his favourite of all the photographs taken of the Beatles because it captures exactly what 'they were about'.

That, from the very outset of their relationship with Dick James, Paul and John recognised the value of someone else – not just the Beatles – recording their songs, was evidenced not long after 'I Saw Her Standing There' slipped into the Beatles' live repertoire. One afternoon in (possibly) early December, (author Mark Lewisohn postulates either the 5th or 7th) 1962 at the Cavern, the group made a rough demo tape of four Lennon-McCartney tunes with a view towards possibly including some of them on their debut album and also for Dick James's benefit. It included tunes of theirs he had not heard. It was very much a private tape and featured takes of 'I Saw Her Standing There', 'Catswalk' and 'One After 909'. The idea being that Dick James might be able to place these with other artists to record (providing they were happy with his choice of artist).

In particular, it seems Paul had it in mind that 'Catswalk', an old instrumental of his from 1959, might suit British guitar legend Bert Weedon. Weedon was famous among many aspiring British guitarists for his popular tutor, *Play in a Day*. He had enjoyed a UK number 10 hit single in 1959 with his version of 'Guitar Boogie', after which he'd had seven other hits, but although he had come close none of these seven had made the Top 20 again and only one had snuck into the Top 30.

With 'Catswalk', Bert could have become the first artist to record 'a Lennon and McCartney original' and the first recipient of a Beatles 'giveaway', but it never happened. Apparently, Bert did not even hear it, never mind think about recording it. As was the way in those days, in the first instance, Dick James offered 'Catswalk' to Bert's producer/A&R at HMV, Wally Ridley. It would have been Ridley's job to listen to it and make the decision whether or not to pass it on to Bert for his consideration. Ridley must not have felt that Paul's tune was right for Bert for he never passed it on ...

The version of 'I Saw Her Standing There' on this tape was unusual in that on this particular take the group gave it in an R&B arrangement on which John played harmonica. Possibly they played it this way because John and Paul thought it might suit being covered by an R&B artist ... as a consequence, James gave it to Duffy Power, more of whom later ...

Addendum: JAEP MUSIC LTD.
Brian Epstein very quickly learned the value of publishing. Impressed by Dick James and his idea to form Northern Songs he was equally taken with James's suggestion that the two of them form 'Jaep Music Limited' to look after the publishing for the rest of Brian's NEMS' artists ... the name for their company being a combination of James and Epstein. And so it was that on 17 May 1963 the publishing company Jaep Music Limited was incorporated with Dick James and Brian Epstein as directors. It was a wise and lucrative move.

Jaep published George Harrison's very first solo composition to be recorded and released by the Beatles which was called 'Don't Bother Me' and featured on their 1963 long player, With The Beatles. *Another significant signing to Jaep was Bobby Willis. Bobby was Cilla Black's partner and future husband. A talented tunesmith he wrote all the B-sides for Cilla's many hit singles.*

1, 2 *The Beatles Anthology*, by The Beatles, (Cassell & Co, 2000) p.98.

Chapter 40:
SHAKE IT UP BABY

"The time is bound to come of course, when everything in the Top 20 will be sung by, written by, sponsored by or inspired by Messrs. Lennon and McCartney!"
Don Nicholl, *Disc* music newspaper, 10 November 1963

1963
Was the year when ... President Kennedy was assassinated in Dallas, Texas on Friday 22 November ... two days later his assassin Lee Harvey Oswald was gunned down by Jack Ruby ... Vice President Lyndon John was immediately sworn in as Kennedy's successor ... in the USA, Congress enacted 'equal pay for equal work' laws for women ... the first episode of the science fiction series, Dr.Who, *was broadcast by the BBC ... the World's first disco, the Whisky a Go Go was opened in Los Angeles in California, USA ...*

Volcanoes erupt suddenly and often without warning. That the Beatles erupted onto the British music scene in just such a manner is no exaggeration. Whatever or whoever lay in their way would be unceremoniously swept aside as the Beatles rapidly became a national sensation during 1963.

During this tumultuous year their records began to be played regularly on the radio, they frequently appeared on TV and all their records – singles, extended play and long play – sold in vast, mind-boggling quantities.

Their second single 'Please Please Me' was released on 11 January and kicked the new year off in fine style by rising to number 2 by 27 February. In total it spent a total of 15 weeks in the Top 40. After 'Please Please Me' came three straight number 1 singles: 'From Me to You', 'She Loves You' and 'I Want to Hold Your Hand'. Their debut album *Please Please Me*, recorded in just one day on 11 February 1963, was rush released on 22 March and by 6 April it had entered the charts. By 11 May it was at number 1 where it remained for an incredible 30 unbroken weeks. This was unheard of success. The album finally dropped to number 2 on 7 December 1963 but kept that place for another 16 weeks. *Please Please Me*'s run in the Top 20 album chart came to an end on 11 July 1964.

The long player record that finally knocked *Please Please Me* off that top spot was their very own follow-up album, *With the Beatles*. This was rapid, vast, incredible, dazzling and unprecedented success.

The Beatles' debut extended player record was issued on 12 July 1963. All four tracks were culled from their debut long player, *Please Please Me*. It was called *Twist and Shout* after one of the LP's most popular tracks. It entered the UK's EP chart on 20 July 1963 and stayed on the chart for 64 weeks, 21 of which were spent at number 1. It sold over 800,000 copies and was the fourth biggest selling record of 1963 after 'She Loves You' (1–1.5 million sales), 'I Want to Hold Your Hand' (1–1.25 million sales) and the Dave Clark Five's 'Glad All Over' (1 million sales approximately).

To this day, *Twist and Shout* remains the best-selling EP in the UK. The iconic black and white cover picture showing the Beatles leaping in the air above what appears to be a broken-down wall was taken by Fiona Adams. She shot the picture on a bomb site just behind Euston Station. Tony Barrow provided the sleeve notes. Interestingly, the two John and Paul songs that featured on the EP, 'Do You Want to Know a Secret' and 'There's a

Place' are credited to 'McCartney-Lennon', not 'Lennon-McCartney' as later became the norm … Indeed, *all* the original John and Paul songs on the *Please Please Me* album are credited as 'McCartney-Lennon' compositions.

The EP sold enough to be quoted in the UK's singles chart where it reached number 2, thus topping Brian Poole and the Tremeloes' single version of 'Twist and Shout's' success which had peaked at number 4.

During the first six months of 1963 in Britain, over 2.5 million records were sold by artists from Liverpool. These sales came from just seven records, all of which were produced by George Martin. If ever a year belonged to one pop artist and one producer it was 1963: and, of course, they were the Beatles and George Martin.

As that mind-boggling year drew to a close, the word 'Beatlemania' had been coined by the UK's popular press to describe the teenage frenzy the Beatles excited wherever they went. As 'I Want to Hold Your Hand' topped the UK singles chart over Christmas 1963 into the new year, the mayhem and the success was set to continue unabated. Indeed, it would rise to yet another level during 1964 when the single topped *Billboard*'s Hot 100 singles charts in the USA. This was the last major territorial breakthrough for the Beatles. The USA was the biggest selling record market in the world. The advent of 'I Want to Hold Your Hand' to the top of the Hot 100 is now defined as the day the 'British Invasion' of rock groups began. It is most certainly the day 'Beatlemania' hit America. The Beatles were now poised to conquer the world and in the process 'I Want to Hold Your Hand' eventually sold over 12 million copies worldwide.

It is difficult to imagine just how the Beatles as a group must have felt. From being relative unknowns at the start of 1962, they were at the centre of an unprecedented whirlwind, the most famous people on the planet. Their lives would never be the same again. Going to the shops on their own was no longer possible. As they surveyed the welter of Beatles' records and cover versions of 'Lennon-McCartney' tunes riding the charts around the globe, John, Paul, George and Ringo, and Brian Epstein, must have found it almost impossible to take it all in. The faces on the TV did not belong to someone else, they were theirs. They were headline news wherever they went.

Over at number 32 Charing Cross Road, London, there is no doubt whatsoever that Dick James and Charles Silver would be reading the papers and watching the television, all the while rubbing their hands in absolute glee … their business gamble had been bang on the money!

An invaluable source of information re: 'Twist And Shout' was/is the www.jpgr.co.uk website.

Chapter 41:
THE HIT MACHINE TURNS ON

Conscious of the publishing deals they had signed and the establishment of Northern Songs Ltd, John Lennon and Paul McCartney were absolutely clear how important it was to have as many of their own songs on their first long player record. It was also usual to build a long player record around an artist's current or most recent hit single. As the date for recording drew closer, they therefore knew they already had four songs that would be included: 'Love Me Do', 'PS I Love You', 'Please Please Me' and 'Ask Me Why', which comprised both sides of their first two singles. George Martin was going to follow the established format of including 14 tracks on their debut long album, seven each side. The recording for the record was scheduled for just one day, 11 February 1963, which coincided with a break in their schedule as members of the Helen Shapiro tour.

To save some of that precious studio time from having to rehearse new songs, George Martin suggested the Beatles record songs that were 'current' staples in their repertoire and therefore already well rehearsed. Although they were rapidly drafting John and Paul songs into their live set, the Beatles were still very much a 'covers' band and so their non-Lennon-McCartney choices for *Please Please Me* reflected the then current listening habits of the Beatles and their predilection for melodic R&B from the USA. As close friend and music writer Ray Coleman commented: "The bulk of the material on the Beatles debut album encapsulated their influences to date … Instead of going for the obvious versions of Elvis or Pat Boone hits, the Beatles chose obscure songs which they admired, the Shirelles and the Cookies were not names English audiences were too familiar with."[1]

Not surprisingly, the songs and the artists who had originally recorded these covers directly influenced the style of John and Paul's own compositions that they composed for the album. As such, the covers were all American in origin:

'Anna (Go to Him)' written and originally performed by Arthur Alexander.

'Chains' written by Gerry Goffin and Carole King and originally recorded by the Cookies (Little Eva's backing group).

'Boys' written by Luther Dixon and Wes Farrell and originally performed by the Shirelles.

'Baby It's You' written by Mack David (lyrics), Barney Williams (aka Luther Dixon) and Burt Bacharach (music) and originally performed by the Shirelles.

'A Taste of Honey' written by Bobby Scott and Ric Marlow (written first as an instrumental, but in 1962 a version with lyrics was recorded by American singer Lenny Welch and it was his version that the Beatles adapted for themselves).

'Twist and Shout' by Phil Medley and Bert Berns, who later was credited as Bert Russell (the song was originally recorded by the Top Notes, but first became a hit in the USA in 1962 by the Isley Brothers).

Even without composing new songs, Lennon and McCartney already had enough 'old' songs upon which to draw for *Please Please Me* if they had so wanted to use them. For a start there was Paul's 'Like Dreamers Do', the *very* song from the Decca tape that had caught the ears of Kim Bennett and Sid Colman at Ardmore and Beechwood. More recently Paul had come up with a couple of new tunes called 'Hold Me Tight' and 'Tip of My Tongue', both composed as possible follow-up singles to 'Love Me Do'.

He himself never felt that either of those quite worked as he'd have liked them to in the studio, but this was no problem, for Lennon and McCartney were on a roll, the songs were beginning to flow and so they simply wrote some more. Thus, apart from 'Love Me Do', 'PS I Love You', 'Please Please Me' and 'Ask Me Why', all the other original songs on the album were (relatively) brand new compositions: 'I Saw Her Standing There', 'Misery', 'Do You Want to Know a Secret' and 'There's a Place'.

'I Saw Her Standing There' was a Paul song written originally over several days in Liverpool and London in late October 1962. A month or so later, it was completed in Paul's home when John agreed with Paul that the line 'Never been a beauty queen' did not sit right and needed fixing. Sitting with Paul in the living room of 20 Forthlin Road, John came up with the line 'You know what I mean' which was perfect 'Liverpool' vernacular and ideal for 'I Saw Her Standing There'…

For Paul, 'I Saw Her Standing There' set a marker: "I think that was where the collaboration really started to take shape because basically it was my song. When John and I wrote it was basically one of our songs we'd done off campus and we'd meet up and he'd go, 'I've got a bit of an idea for one', and then we'd finish it together." Paul believes that changing the 'beauty queen' line was a stylistic innovation: "That suddenly started to be very kind of 'Beatley' and even now it is a good little Beatle line, 'She was just seventeen, You know what I mean', and everyone *does* 'know what you mean' … especially when young guys (himself and John) were singing it. And that's how it started to develop – toing and froing."[2]

'Do You Want to Know a Secret' was a John song written not long after he and Cynthia had married (23 August 1962) and were living as guests in Brian Epstein's apartment on Falkner Street in Liverpool 8. Epstein had let them borrow this flat because immediately after their marriage, John's Aunt Mimi had not allowed them to move in with her. It was not played 'live' by the Beatles. John had decided it suited George's voice better and gave it to him to sing on the album. The secret John was sharing was that he was in love with Cynthia. Brian Epstein was encouraging John and Cyn to keep their marriage secret because the prevailing belief in those days was that girl fans did not like their favourite pop star to have a girlfriend, never mind be married. Pop stars were viewed as objects of desire. The fantasy was they were 'available' and so their popularity was better served if they were not in a binding relationship.

'Misery' was a joint collaboration written just before the Beatles' participation on the Helen Shapiro tour. John and Paul started it backstage in Stoke-on-Trent on 26 January 1963 and completed it at 20 Forthlin Road.

'There's a Place' was a co-write. The inspiration for the song's title came from 'Somewhere', a very popular tune from Leonard Bernstein's musical *West Side Story* with lyrics by Stephen Sondheim ('There's a place for us, Somewhere a place for us'). Paul had the soundtrack album. Lyrically it sounds like John, but it was co-written. Another 20 Forthlin collaboration and for its time something different: an upbeat song of contemplation, the other side of John Lennon and Paul McCartney, an early example of how what they were writing was a bit different, or as Paul describes it, it was "a bit more cerebral."[3]

'There's a Place' was not a straightforward love song, it was more about escaping from the blues: the place to which the singer refers is somewhere he/she can go 'When I feel low, When I feel blue, And it's my mind…'. It was a live staple of the Beatles' 1963 set. John called it his attempt at 'a sort of Motown black thing'. Indeed it was. Motown was in its infancy in 1963, almost unknown in Britain, but the Beatles had been fans from the start. They loved the Motown sound, its exuberance, rhythmic drive and soaring harmonies and were early exponents of acts on the label like the Miracles, Marvelettes and Barrett Strong. They would mention Motown acts and records in interviews and, maybe the greatest compliment of all, they recorded versions of Motown tunes such as 'Please Mr. Postman', 'You've Really Got a Hold on Me' and 'Money' long before Tamla was a popular, household label in the UK.

As 1963 zipped along, so John and Paul were 'in the zone'. Within the Beatles camp, the demand for Lennon-McCartney songs was unrelenting. The next single was always due and a second album was to be recorded before the end of the year, its release to coincide with the lucrative Christmas market … Record companies were businesses, not patrons of the arts, and making a profit was paramount. Pop music was a vibrant but unpredictable market. If an artist was popular and selling, a record company would adhere mightily to the dictum of 'making hay while the sun shines'.

As a consequence of this demand and the productivity of Lennon and McCartney, the two accumulated a small surplus of material that were possibly not going to be released by the group themselves. The early 'surplus' material comprised mainly older 'original Lennon and McCartney songs' from the Fifties. The group preferred to record the new tunes they were writing, but the older songs were not left forgotten, unloved and unsung: they retained a currency between Paul and John.

Brian's other artists were, mostly, *not* writers and he quickly recognised that the gift of a John and Paul song would go a long way to secure them a much-needed debut hit. To link a new artist with a new Lennon-McCartney song that the Beatles themselves had not recorded gave that new artist kudos and the likelihood of greater media attention than other competing, debut artists. Equally importantly, it kept the Lennon and McCartney imprint in the public domain, especially when new Beatles product was not.

John and Paul were also fully attuned to the financial benefits of other artists recording songs they had written.

Songs that had been composed before the advent of 'Beatlemania' and which were still looking for a home included: 'Like Dreamers Do', 'Tip of My Tongue', 'Love of the Loved', 'Hello Little Girl' and a string of instrumentals including the aforementioned 'Catswalk'.

1 *Lennon: The Definitive Biography, Anniversary Edition*, by Ray Coleman (Pan Books, 2000) p.393.
2 Sir Paul McCartney in conversation with Bob Harris OBE and Colin Hall, copyright WBBC, for *The Songs the Beatles Gave Away*, BBC Radio 2, 2009, produced for WBBC by Bob Harris and Trudie Myerscough-Harris.
3 *Paul McCartney, Many Years from Now*, Barry Miles (Vintage, 1998) p.95.

Private letter from Mark Lewisohn to the author dated 14 May 2012 (used here with kind permission) and *Tune In*.

Chapter 42:
WRITING A SWIMMING POOL

In her 2005 autobiography, *John*, Cynthia Lennon brilliantly nailed the relationship between John Lennon and Paul McCartney: "They had a strong sense that their success depended on the connection between them. Paul's organised, conscientious way of going about things, he wrote down all the lyrics in a notebook he carried with him, was in sharp contrast to John's 'anything goes' style ... But they complemented each other. John needed Paul's attention to detail and persistence; Paul needed John's anarchic, lateral thinking."[1]

Talking to Bob Harris in 2007 for the Radio 2 documentary, *The Day John Met Paul*, Cynthia provided a further insight into Lennon and McCartney's relationship: "With John and Paul there was competition. They really wanted to improve on or beat each other to a certain extent at their talent, singing and everything else ... which never changed, they were always competing. In many ways, they were like chalk and cheese, but on another level they were just joined together at the hip in terms of music. The way that they combined their talents was just meant to be, it was magic."[2]

This element of John and Paul's creative relationship was something recognised and commented on by George Martin: "The guy who was the lead vocalist was generally the guy who initiated the song, with a little help from his friends. A lot of the songs were written purely by either John or purely by Paul, but in the very early days their songs were complete collaborations because their ideas were so limited. They'd say, 'I'm stuck for a line, what have you got?' They really did work with each other very closely. But as they got more successful they each wanted to be the kingpin and so they would listen to the other guy's song and then say, 'Oh god that's great, I've got to do better,' and their collaboration was more of a competition than a collaboration. They would climb on each other's shoulders eventually to get where they wanted."[3]

There is no doubt whatsoever that all of the Beatles revelled in the fact that for the first time in their lives they were beginning to make some 'real' money. One of the first manifestations of this was that during 1963 they moved out of their Liverpool homes to relocate to London, where they lived first in various apartments and from there to 'posh' homes in the suburbs, except for Paul who stayed in London. Paul was the last to move to London, where he lived first in an apartment with the other three Beatles and then with the Asher family before buying a house in St. John's Wood.

Paul McCartney has always been quite candid that from the moment he and John realised they could 'own' a song they had written, and which the Beatles recorded, they would earn more than George and Ringo. They luxuriated in the potential a publishing deal had to help them become rich: "John and I literally used to sit down and say, 'Now let's write a swimming pool'. We said it out of innocence. Out of normal fucking working-class glee that we were able to write, 'a swimming pool'. For the first time in our lives we could actually do something and earn money."[4]

1 *John*, Cynthia Lennon, (Hodder & Stoughton, 2005) p.205.
2 Cynthia Lennon in conversation with Bob Harris for *The Day John Met Paul*, 2007 BBC Radio 2 documentary written and narrated by Bob Harris and produced by Bob Harris and Trudie Myerscough-Harris for WBBC.
3 Sir George Martin in conversation with Bob Harris OBE and Colin Hall for the 2009 BBC Radio 2 documentary, *The Songs the Beatles Gave Away*, written and narrated by Bob Harris, produced by Bob Harris and Trudie Myerscough-Harris for WBBC.
4 Interview with David Fricke for *Rolling Stone* magazine published 8 February, 1990.

Chapter 43:
A SONG THEY WERE SINGING

From Saturday 2 February until Sunday 3 March 1963, the Beatles were mostly on the road in the UK, undertaking their first major UK package tour. They were fourth on an 11-act bill and as such were limited to performing just four songs. Top of the bill was teen singing sensation Helen Shapiro. At only 16 years of age by the end of 1962, Helen had already scored five Top 20 UK hits, including two number 1s: 'You Don't Know' (July 1961) and 'Walkin' Back to Happiness' (September 1961).

Other artists on the tour included popular UK singers Kenny Lynch and Danny Williams (who had scored a number 1 hit in 1961 with 'Moon River'), Irish comedian Dave Allen and a vocal harmony group from Bristol called the Kestrels, among whom were future songwriting duo Roger Cook and Roger Greenaway. (In collaboration with Bill Backer and Billy Davis, Cook and Greenaway went on to write, among many others, 'I'd Love to Teach the World to Sing (In Perfect Harmony)', a UK hugely popular number 1 hit in 1971 for the New Seekers.)

The tour commenced on Saturday 2 February at the Gaumont in Bradford, and on 10 and 11 February the Beatles took time out to travel to London to record their debut long player record. Between 12 and 22 February they played their own shows before linking up again with the Shapiro package on 23 February.

John and Paul used the time between the dates on the Shapiro tour to write. During the second leg of the tour, travelling on the tour bus, they composed 'From Me to You', which became their third UK single and first number 1.

Prior to her tour, Helen Shapiro's A&R at Columbia, Norrie Paramor (George Martin's *bête noire*) had been looking for material to record with her for her next long player which he was considering recording in Nashville (which he and Helen eventually did: *Helen in Nashville* was released in 1963). John and Paul were approached for a song for this project and came up with 'Misery'. It was very much a joint collaboration. John described it as "kind of a John song more than a Paul song, but written together."[1]

Paul concurred: "It was our first stab at a ballad and had a little spoken preface. It was co-written … you could have called us hacks, hacking out a song for someone."[2]

And so it was that Norrie Paramor was the first recipient of a Lennon-McCartney song written specifically for an artist other than their own group. Paul told Alan Smith, the Liverpool-born editor of *NME*: "We were asked by Norrie Paramor to write a song for Helen Shapiro … We've called it 'Misery', but it isn't as slow as it sounds. It moves along at quite a pace and we think Helen will make a pretty good job of it." Interestingly, Paul added, "We've also done a number for Duffy Power which he isn't going to record."[3] *(This statement begs the question, was the word 'isn't' in Paul's comment a typo that was not picked up on before* NME *went to press?)*

Ultimately, Paramor felt that 'Misery' was not suitable for Helen and passed on it.

Helen and the Beatles hit it off from the moment they met: "We travelled together on the coach and we got on great. They were all very new and shiny then, but they were friendly and I loved them, I watched every one of their performances … they were respectful and really quite protective of me, especially John."[4]

She had no idea that they had written a song for her that Norrie Paramor had turned down: "When I first met them, at the beginning of the tour, when I was introduced to them and Paul was the spokesman, that was when Paul told me they had written this song 'Misery' and they had submitted it for me for my Nashville album … that apparently (it) got turned down by my record producer before I even knew about it, let alone heard it."[5]

The Beatles recorded their own version of the song for their debut album, but John and Paul had not given up on finding a home for it with another artist. Having failed with Helen Shapiro, undeterred, the two songsmiths found a willing taker in Kenny Lynch who was also on the tour.

In her autobiography *Walking Back to Happiness*, Helen Shapiro commented, "I could kick myself when I think I could have been the first artiste to record a Beatles' song*, but I don't begrudge good old Ken having that honour."[6]

And so it was that Lynch has the distinction of being the first well-known artist to record and release a cover version of a Lennon-McCartney/Beatles song as the A-side of a single. He was also the first black artist to record a song written by Lennon and McCartney.

(*Had Helen cut 'Misery' as a single, neither she nor Kenny Lynch would actually have been the first to record and release a 'cover' of a Beatles' song. As noted earlier that honour goes to a little known group called the Sparrows, who cut a version of 'Love Me Do' in 1962 (circa November) which was released as one of six tracks by different artists on a 'Various Artists' extended player compilation issued on the budget Cannon label and entitled Cannon Hits of Today (Cannon EP 005).)[7]

Lynch's version was lighter, less bluesy, more poppy than the Beatles' own. Not long after recording it, he met John and Paul in Dick James's office. After playing them his version, Lynch was taken aback when John commented, "Your singing's OK, but who's that playing the telephone?" John was no more impressed when Lynch informed him the guitar player was the one and only Bert Weedon. (The very Bert Weedon whom earlier Paul had hoped would record 'Catswalk'.) Lynch said Lennon continued by describing Weedon as "last" (as in 'awful') which, at the time, was probably the most damning word in a Scouser's vocabulary.[8]

John was no doubt reacting to Weedon's clean, smooth sound which carried distinct echoes of the Shadows. John considered Weedon's playing to be 'old style' and at odds with the tougher edge he thought the song should have had. He was right, but in truth there are very few guitarists of Lennon's generation who do not acknowledge Weedon's influence on learning how to play guitar, for he was the author of every budding guitarist's teaching manual. Entitled *Play in a Day*, Weedon's tutor went on to sell 2 million copies to an audience eager to master the instrument. Its acolytes included Paul and George of the Beatles, Keith Richards, Pete Townsend, Brian May, Sting and Eric Clapton. The latter was in no doubt of its significance: "I wouldn't have felt the urge to press on without the tips and encouragement Bert's book gives you. I've never met a player of any consequence who doesn't say the same thing."[9]

Ultimately, 'Misery' does not count as a Beatles 'giveaway' because the group recorded and released it themselves. There is no doubt, however, that they had a good go at giving it to Shapiro. Norrie Paramor's decision *did* mean it went up for grabs and that Kenny Lynch has the honour to be the first well-known artiste to recognise the hit-writing potential of John and Paul and the first to release a 'cover' of a Beatles tune.

What the story of 'Misery' demonstrates is that John and Paul were willing and active participants in encouraging other artists to record their material. The duo were not only considerably engaged in the process of songwriting for the Beatles, but clearly understood the value of other artists recording their tunes. Financial considerations apart, the endorsement and kudos of someone else recording their material was a significant step in the direction of achieving their joint ambition to be recognised as songwriters in the class of Goffin and King.

Kenny Lynch's recording of 'Misery' (despite John's put down) is worthy of further investigation because not only was Lynch a very popular entertainer and contributor to the Sixties music scene in Britain, his version is better than John's comment might otherwise indicate. The story also offers a snapshot of how the music industry operated at the time when Lennon and McCartney were virtual unknowns.

KENNY LYNCH

Kenny Lynch in 1963, the year he toured with Helen Shapiro and the Beatles and recorded 'Misery', the first ever commercial recording of a Beatles song aimed at making the UK singles chart.
(Pictorial Press Ltd / Alamy Stock Photo)

b. 18 March 1938, Stepney, London
d. 18 December 2019 in the UK

MISERY (2:04)
(Lennon-McCartney*)
Dick James Music Ltd**
HMV Pop 1136
*On test pressings Paul's surname was misspelt 'McCarthney'.
**By the time the sheet music was printed the publishing credit read 'Northern Songs Ltd.'
B-side: Shut the Door (Lynch).
Both sides with orchestra conducted by Harry Robinson.
Bert Weedon played guitar on 'Misery'.
Released: Friday 15 March 1963, the day after *Record Retailer* reviewed it.

Chapter 43: A SONG THEY WERE SINGING

A week later the Beatles issued their debut album, *Please Please Me*, which featured their version.

Reviewing Kenny's new single in its 16 March 1963 edition, the *NME* declared, "The song is very attractive with a medium-paced beat."

Over at *Disc*, reviewer Don Nicholl rated it highly enough to receive a 'DNT' (i.e., a 'Don Nicholl Tip', which highlighted 'a disc that looks like spinning right to the top'), commenting that, "it was not so doleful as you might think" and "catchy enough to send Kenny up on the roof of sales once more."[10]

Paul described 'Misery' as one of Kenny's 'minor' hits, but the truth is it never troubled the charts. Lynch himself has said it only sold 7000 copies. However, either side of releasing 'Misery', Kenny enjoyed two UK number 10 hits with his version of 'Up on the Roof' at the end of 1962 going into early 1963, and 'You Can Never Stop Me Loving You', a hit in June 1963.

When he recorded 'Misery', Lynch was already a songwriter in his own right (he wrote its B-side) and among many others he later co-wrote three storming songs for the Small Faces. The first (written in collaboration with Mort Shuman) was their single 'Sha-La-La-La-Lee' which peaked at number 3 in March 1966. Lynch sang the high harmonies on the single and (with Jerry Ragovoy) also penned 'You Better Believe It' and 'Sorry She's Mine', both of which featured on their debut album. Indeed, both had been considered as possible follow-up singles to 'Sha-La-La-La-Lee' until Stevie Marriott and Ronnie Lane came up with 'Hey Girl'.

Kenny Lynch also co-authored (again with Mort Shuman) 'Love's Just a Broken Heart' which Cilla Black took to number 5 in the UK singles chart in February 1966.

In 1973, Kenny appeared on the cover of the Paul McCartney and Wings LP, *Band on the Run*. He is the escaping prisoner standing immediately behind Paul, his head just above Paul's shoulder.

Aged 80 in 2018, Kenny Lynch was still performing and during that year he enjoyed a successful UK tour in which he co-headlined alongside Jimmy Tarbuck and Anita Harris before starring in ITV's five week series entitled *Last Laugh in Vegas*. Very sadly, as this book was being written, it was announced that, aged 81, on 18 December 2019, Kenny had passed away.

---

1 *All We Are Saying: The Last Major Interview with John Lennon and Yoko Ono*, conducted by David Sheff (Sidgwick & Jackson, 2000) p.169.
2 *Paul McCartney, Many Years from Now*, Barry Miles (Vintage,1997) p.94.
3 *The Beatles off the Record*, Keith Badman, (Omnibus Press, 2007) p.51.
4 *The Liverpool Echo*, 20 April 2012 from 'The Beatles, Helen Shapiro … and God' an interview with Helen by Dawn Collinson.
5 Gary James' Interview With Helen Shapiro – ClassicBands.com
6 *Walking Back to Happiness*, Helen Shapiro, (Harper Collins, 1993) p.103.
7 Dave Ravenscroft, details of The Sparrows version of 'Love Me Do' sourced from:
   https://www.discogs.com/Various-Cannon-Hits-Of-Today/release/5137342
   https://dannyfriar.wordpress.com/2015/06/11/0889-love-me-do-the-sparrows-1962/
8 *John Lennon*, Ray Coleman (Futura, 1984) p.162.
9 Eric Clapton quoted in a eulogy by Neil McCormick that began with the words, 'Farewell Bert Weedon' published in the *Daily Telegraph*, 21 April 2012.
10 *Disc*, UK music weekly, Edition 260, 16 March 1963, p.8, from 'Disc Date' by Don Nicholl and his review entitled, "Misery' Lynch Is Not So Sad' on p.8.

Chapter 44:
THE POWER OF SONG

As Kenny Lynch was taking his chances with 'Misery', another 'cover' of a Lennon-McCartney was taking shape. Duffy Power, late of the Larry Parnes 'stable of stars' (which he'd left in 1961) had heard 'I Saw Her Standing There' and just eight days later cut his own version for Parlophone. It was produced by Ron Richards, George Martin's right-hand man. Ironically, Power, of course, had been one of two Larry Parnes' stars that the Silver Beatles had unsuccessfully auditioned to back in May 1960.

By now Power had tired of his early Sixties 'teen idol' image and of cutting 'pop' style records that were more 'Bobby' (in the vein of Messrs Rydell and Darin) than full on rock 'n' roll. Now he wanted to flex his musical muscle and produce material of greater substance that would also more accurately showcase his true abilities as a singer. By early 1963, noted music biographer Colin Harper says Power had become 'consumed by the blues' and was enamoured with London's emerging rhythm and blues scene. In order to achieve the emotive sound he wanted on record, Power invited leading lights of that new scene, the Graham Bond Quartet, to back him in the studio.

When Dick James offered Power 'I Saw Her Standing There', what Power heard on the Beatles' demo, as an emerging purveyor of R&B, would have strongly recommended the song to him, for it featured some John Lennon harmonica. (The demo came from the same 'Dick James tape' as 'Catswalk' which the publisher had tried to guide Bert Weedon's way.)

It was the second cover of a Lennon-McCartney song by a well-known artist, and like Kenny Lynch's version of 'Misery' it inexplicably failed to make the charts in the UK. Maybe it was because the Beatles' spirited version had become available (it was the lead track on their debut album) at the same time as Power's version was released as a single.

DUFFY POWER
b. Raymond Leslie Howard, 9 September 1941, in Fulham, South West London
d. 19 February 2014 in London
With the Graham Bond Quartet
Graham Bond, Hammond organ
John McLaughlin, guitar
Jack Bruce, bass,
Ginger Baker, drums

***I SAW HER STANDING THERE* (2:25)**
(McCartney-Lennon)
Northern Songs Ltd.
B-side: Farewell Baby (Bond)
Recorded: 20 February 1963
Producer: Ron Richards
Released: 26 April 1963

Duffy Power, one of Larry Parnes' most talented discoveries who hoped to re-launch his career and musical identity when he cut a cover of 'I Saw Her Standing There' in 1963.
(Pictorial Press Ltd / Alamy Stock Photo)

The Graham Bond Quartet were a prodigiously talented group who all became major stars of the Sixties in their own right. Together with Power, the GBQ stripped 'I Saw Her Standing There' down and slowed the tempo to invest it with a bluesier feel much more in keeping with their own style.

Apparently, Paul and John were not so keen on Power's interpretation, believing it to be 'too jazzy' and suggested he re-recorded it. Power duly obliged, but paid little attention to their advice: his second version differed very little from his first. The result was a fine record that still sounds good today. It did not make the charts, but it did help Power navigate his move from teen idol to a singer of more serious intent.

Don Nicholl at *Disc* seemed to share John and Paul's lack of enthusiasm for Duffy's version. Awarding it just two stars, he described it as a "Medium beater with the Graham Bond Quartet backing beefily". He also noted that it was a McCartney-Lennon number that Duffy 'chanted'. Hearing it now, this author feels Duffy was short-changed by these opinions.[1]

Power went on to make many fine recordings and work with musicians of the highest calibre, but his career never fulfilled the potential he possessed. He remains an artist truly worthy of 'discovering' and his cover of 'I Saw Her Standing There' is surely one of the most accomplished Beatles covers ever.

This important departure in style for Power later saw him, in 1964, front Alexis Korner's Blues Incorporated on the album *Sky High*. He formed a true but short-lived 'supergroup' comprising himself, Terry Cox (drums), Danny Thompson (bass) and John McLaughlin (guitar), called Duffy's Nucleus. Sadly, they only released one single, a version of 'Hound Dog' that was released in 1966 on the Decca label.

Another early recipient of a Lennon-McCartney original were the Rolling Stones. Like Kenny Lynch and Duffy Power, the Stones were given first dibs on a Lennon-McCartney tune that ultimately the Beatles *did* record and release themselves, which immediately makes the Lynch, Power and Stones records strictly 'cover versions' and not 'giveaways'.

However, the importance of these songs and the stories of how the artists received them clearly demonstrate John and Paul's active participation in encouraging others to record their tunes. As such, they are well worth telling.

Sir Paul McCartney: "It seemed like – wow – you know, what a great lark, coming down to London, writing songs for a living … 'wow'. So we were very happy to do that. What happened then was you'd be trying to sell them…"[2]

And so it was with the Stones …

From the moment the Beatles heard the Stones they were fans and very quickly became friends. The Beatles even played their part in encouraging Decca to sign them. As Paul remembered: "George Harrison mentioned them to a guy called Dick Rowe who had been famously the guy who turned the Beatles down and was never going to live it down … So, he was chatting with George at a party and asked, 'Do you know of any other good groups? I've got to sign something good for Decca', and George said, 'Well there is this band called the Rolling Stones down the Crawdaddy Club at the Station Hotel in Richmond, you can see them down there'."[3]

THE ROLLING STONES
Mick Jagger – vocals, harmonica
b. Michael Philip Jagger on 26 July 1943 in Dartford, Kent
Keith Richards – guitar, backing vocals
b. Keith Richards on 18 December 1943 in Dartford, Kent
Brian Jones – guitar, harmonica
b. Lewis Brian Hopkin Jones on 28 February 1942 in Cheltenham, Gloucestershire
d. 3 July 1969 in Hatfield, Sussex
Bill Wyman – bass guitar
b. William George Perks on 24 October 1936 in Lewisham, London
Charlie Watts – drums
b. Charles Robert Watts on 2 June 1941 in London
d. 24 August 2021 in London

Dick Rowe clearly listened to George's advice and very quickly signed the Stones to Decca. At that point in their history, the Stones did not write their own songs, their reputation had been built on their prowess as interpreters of Chicago Blues with a penchant for the music of Chuck Berry and Bo Diddley. Their very first disc was a cover of Berry's 'Come On' which peaked at number 21 in the UK, late September '63.

By the time the Beatles got to know the Stones, the latter's manager was none other than teenage whizz-kid Andrew Loog Oldham, former publicist for Brian Epstein at NEMS. Oldham was keen for the Stones to emulate John and Paul and start writing their own songs, but before Jagger and Richards did so they urgently needed a follow-up single to 'Come On'.

The Rolling Stones as they were in 1963. Still very much a blues and R&B band and only just learning the game as writers of their own material. Standing, left to right: Mick Jagger, Brian Jones, Keith Richards. Sitting: Bill Wyman and Charlie Watts. (Pictorial Press Ltd / Alamy Stock Photo)

Luckily for Oldham, his friends and former clients, John and Paul were on hand to lend a hand.

When, for the 2009 BBC Radio 2 documentary *The Songs the Beatles Gave Away*, Sir Paul reminisced with broadcaster Bob Harris about being 'John and Paul, songwriters', in 1963 he provided a marvellous insight into how the pair would actively 'share' their material with others: "One day John and I were walking along Charing Cross Road, the main reason being that it was 'Guitar Centre'; there must have been about 5 or 6 guitar shops, so this was like Valhalla for us. We would just go along and drool at the windows, you know – 'wow!' look at that Hofner, Gretsch, Gibson. It was our idea of an afternoon out. We would literally do that all the time *and* Dick James our publisher was there."[4]

Paul recalled that this was exactly what John and Paul were doing when they were spotted by Mick Jagger and Keith Richards. "We went in to see Dick and when we came out, just me and John, all dressed in black, were walking down Charing Cross Road when we saw some people go by in a taxi who shouted at us. It was Mick and Keith, so we thumbed a lift with them…"

Ensconced together inside the taxi, Mick explained that the Stones were in need of a follow-up single, but didn't have one. Paul listened attentively and, not one to hold back, leapt to their rescue. "They were 'Blues' guys, they did mainly 'Little Red Rooster' and things like that, so now into this songwriting game I said, 'We've got one'. I explained 'Ringo traditionally gets a song … and he's just got this one on our album (*With the Beatles*) that we've just recorded called 'I Wanna Be Your Man', it's kind of Bo Diddley (I knew they did a lot of Bo Diddley stuff). We'll send you it if you want. So we knocked up another little acetate and that became their next A-side."[5]

It's not quite how Mick Jagger or Andrew Loog Oldham remember the story, but give or take the location and exactly how it was presented to the Stones, Paul's story nevertheless captures the essence of how he and John would gift a song to others.

(In 1968, Jagger recalled that the Stones were actually already rehearsing in the studios on Tuesday 10 September '63, when Oldham brought Lennon and McCartney to the session to hear them and it was at that point John and Paul offered them 'I Wanna Be Your Man'. Significantly, Jagger noted, "They were really hustlers then. I mean the way they used to hustle tunes was great: 'Hey Mick, we've got this great song.' … So they played it and we thought it sounded pretty commercial, which is what we were looking for, so we did it like Elmore James…")[6]

Bill Wyman also recalled the session and explained how, when Brian Jones applied his slide guitar to the mix, the Stones turned 'I Wanna Be Your Man' from a beat style tune into more of an Elmore James/Stones-style R&B number. That they certainly did can be heard by just playing the two versions back to back: the Beatles' and Stones' versions of the song provide very different interpretations of 'I Wanna Be Your Man'.

THE ROLLING STONES
I WANNA BE YOUR MAN (1:44)
(Lennon, McCartney)
Northern Songs Ltd
Decca F.11764
B-SIDE: Stones* / Stoned
(Nanker, Phelge) **

*Early pressings misspelt 'Stoned' as 'Stones' making those original copies much prized by collectors.
** 'Nanker, Phelge' is a collective name applied to whole-group collaborations on early Stones records, i.e., Mick Jagger, Brian Jones, Keith Richards, Charlie Watts and Bill Wyman, also included was manager Andrew Oldham and original founder member pianist Ian Stewart.
Recorded on 7 October 1963 at Kingsway Sound, London.
Production, both sides: Impact Sound
'Impact Sound' was the Stones' manager Andrew Loog Oldham and Eric Easton.
Released in the UK: 1 November 1963. It was the Rolling Stones' follow-up to their debut single 'Come On'.
'I Wanna Be Your Man' first charted on 20 November at number 41 and eventually peaked at number 12 on 15 January 1964. It remained on the chart for 16 weeks.
Released in the USA on London 9641 on 17 February 1964, where it failed to chart. It was later re-released in March as the B-side to 'Not Fade Away' which peaked at number 48

in the *Billboard* chart.

'I Wanna Be Your Man' is one of the few Rolling Stones records to feature only Brian Jones on backing vocals.

It gained a coveted top 'DNT' rating from *Disc*'s singles reviewer Don Nicholl, whose review was preceded by the headline "Lennon, McCartney + The Rolling Stones = a big hit". He himself described it as "a raucous, belting beater which is chanted at flat-out pace. The guitar sound is good and earthy and the whole production has an exciting on-the-spot quality."[7]

Addendum: *Duffy Power*

After recording just one single with his group Nucleus in 1966, Duffy Power was briefly without a record label, but cut publishing demos for Marquis Music on which he was backed by Bruce, Baker, McLaughlin, Cox and other luminaries. These were collected for an album release in 1971 entitled Innovations. *A critic for* Gramophone *magazine was mightily impressed by the record and compared Power's vocals to those of Billie Holliday, by writing: "At his finest he communicates the same sense of emotional involvement, the same distraught lyricism." High praise to say the least.*[8]

For more information about this often overlooked UK singer, the best place to start is undoubtedly music journalist Colin Harper's excellent website: colin-harper.com

As for Power's music itself, the following are highly recommended:

Leapers and Sleepers *(RPM Records UK, 2010)*, a double CD compilation of Power's Sixties Parlophone releases.

Innovations, *(Transatlantic, 1971)*, re-released on CD at the start of the 2000s.

1 *Disc* music weekly, Edition 268 published 11 May 1963, 'Disc Date' with Don Nicholl, p.10.
2, 3, 4 & 5: Sir Paul McCartney in conversation with Bob Harris OBE and Colin Hall for the BBC 2009 Radio 2 documentary *The Songs the Beatles Gave Away*, written and narrated by Bob Harris, produced by Bob Harris and Trudie Myerscough-Harris for WBBC.
6 "I Wanna Be Your Man by the Rolling Stones Songfacts". *www.songfacts.com*
7 *Disc* music weekly, Edition 294 published 9 November 1963, 'Disc Date' with Don Nicholl, p.10.
8 The critic from *Gramophone* is quoted in 'Duffy Power Obituary", by Colin Harper, published in the *Guardian* newspaper on 27 February 2014.

Chapter 45:
A GIVEAWAY SPURNED …

1963 was undoubtedly the year of Beatlemania and Mersey Beat. The city of Liverpool was rapidly becoming perceived as a Mecca for emerging musical talent. Hundreds of groups were already playing the circuit while others were breaking up, making up, forming and re-forming almost on a daily basis. Liverpudlians couldn't walk down Lime Street without tripping over agents, managers and A&R men (sadly, it appears, no women back then) rushing from the station towards the Cavern, Iron Door, Downbeat, Mardi Gras, Blue Angel and other assorted music clubs in search of groups and singers to sign. Provided they had a Scouse accent and could fart in tune, fame and fortune were theirs for the taking.

Daily newspapers, not just the music press, vied for the latest on the Beatles. The search for the next big thing soon became a national sport … anywhere in the country where a youth had been spotted carrying a guitar, reporters would be despatched *post haste* in search of 'Bury's answer to the Beatles', 'Walsall's answer to the Beatles', 'Peterborough's answer to the Beatles', 'Leamington Spa's answer to the Beatles' … but few of them ever were. Tottenham's Dave Clark Five mounted a mighty challenge towards the end of the year, and the Rolling Stones would run them neck and neck for most of the Sixties, but in terms of record sales the Beatles were untouchable, the true leaders of the pack.

As for Liverpool, Brian Epstein had a head start on his rivals and was dutifully hoovering up those acts he considered possessed of the talent and star quality to 'make it'. The Beatles had helped Epstein find his *raison d'être* and now he was living it: he had become a 'star maker'.

As a consequence of his success with the Beatles (followed by Gerry and the Pacemakers, Billy J. Kramer and Cilla Black) for a while among the groups in Liverpool getting signed by Epstein became their goal, to the extent that poet Roger McGough sagely notes in in his 2005 autobiography, *Said and Done*: "Outside Epstein's empire there was a growing sense that if the Nemsmobile didn't stop to pick you up you'd be doomed to a life on the hard shoulder, and it wasn't endearing to watch butch guitarists and tattooed drummers flirting with Eppy."[1]

As a star maker, Epstein had a vision of how an artist should present him or herself to the public. A modern, well-cut suit (or dress in the case of Cilla Black) was *de rigueur*, as was a fresh, clean shirt and tie. Artists might have long(ish) hair, but this should always be clean and tidy. Good manners (no swearing) were important, punctuality was crucial and on stage strictly no eating, drinking or smoking were allowed. Mostly his acts were happy to go along with this smoothing of their rougher edges because on a daily basis they were witnessing what he was achieving with the Beatles. They believed him to have the Midas touch, the consensus was 'what worked for them can work for us, Epstein knows what he is doing'. And, early on, he did (mostly).

The first of these to sign to Epstein's roster were Gerry and the Pacemakers. They were an immediate success. Bright and breezy, Gerry and his group were happy to listen to Eppy's advice. They had already taken advantage of the Beatles dissing on the Mitch Murray-penned, George Martin/Dick James-championed 'How Do You Do It' by recording it for themselves. Signed to Columbia, urged on by Martin and Epstein, Gerry and the Pacemakers took the tune (and the Beatles' re-arrangement of it) to the very top of the UK chart. It hit number 1 on 17 April 1963 and remained on top of the pile for the next three weeks. Scoring a number 1 with your very first single was, and remains, a mighty achievement for any artist. In doing so, Gerry and the Pacemakers became the first of Epstein's protégés and the first 'Mersey Beat' group to reach number 1 in all the UK charts. Not even the Beatles had achieved this.

In Gerry Marsden, Brian Epstein believed he had discovered a star in the style of former British rocker Tommy Steele, who by then was in the process of morphing from rock 'n' roller into a popular 'all-round entertainer' and in doing so building a show-biz career for life. Not exactly a matinee idol, Gerry had a wonderful, strong and distinctive singing voice and, like Steele, a cheerful, ebullient personality. Instantly likeable and irrepressible, Gerry was a natural.

In 1963, he and his group, alongside the Beatles, rode the cusp of a wave called the 'Mersey Sound' and so first and foremost it was teenagers to whom they appealed. A peek at the other side of their big number 1 hit reveals that Gerry Marsden and Les Chadwick (the Pacemaker's bassist) had written the B-side, 'Away from You': John and Paul weren't the only songwriters on Merseyside! Already Gerry and Les had realised the value of not merely performing on a record but of writing a tune that would also be on that disc. The group stuck with this winning formula for their follow-up release, 'I Like It'. This was another Mitch Murray-penned A-side which gave the group their second number 1 and, as before, Marsden and Chadwick contributed the B-side, 'It's Happened to Me'.

With their third single came their third straight number 1, 'You'll Never Walk Alone', which was written by Richard Rodgers and Oscar Hammerstein II (from their 1945 musical *Carousel*). As the B-side, Gerry and the Pacemakers recorded a Gerry solo composition, 'It's Alright'.

With the release of this single Gerry and the Pacemakers unwittingly ensured Scouse immortality, for their version of 'You'll Never Walk Alone' has become so much more than just another hit record. To the supporters of Liverpool Football Club it is an anthem, a prayer, a code for life and as such Gerry and the Pacemakers' star will forever shine on Merseyside.

Gerry then began to write the group's A-sides himself, including 'I'm the One', which peaked at number 2, and 'Ferry Cross the Mersey' which was a number 8 hit in January 1965. The entire group – Gerry Marsden, Freddie Marsden (drums) Les Chadwick (bass) and Les Maguire (piano) – were credited as co-composers of 'Don't Let the Sun Catch You Crying', which peaked at number 6 on 13 May 1964. It was their fifth consecutive Top 10 single and a tune that has been much covered by other artists ever since. (Duly noting Gerry's songwriting talent, Dick James formed a publishing company with him called 'Pacermusic'.)

No wonder then that Gerry and the Pacemakers did not turn to John and Paul for a song to help them on their way. They did have a stab at recording John's 'Hello Little Girl', but were not happy with it and it remained unreleased until 1991 when their version appeared on *The Best of Gerry and the Pacemakers: The Definitive Collection* (United Artists). Rather like the Beatles' version of 'How Do You Do It', the Pacemakers' version of 'Hello Little Girl' lacks verve and sounds like a song they were performing 'by numbers' with little real intent of doing much with it. As one of Liverpool's main rivals to the Beatles, it's clear from the lacklustre performance that Gerry and the Pacemakers did not want to make it to the top riding on the coat tails of the Fab Four … which, of course, they didn't.

Very sadly Gerry Marsden passed away on 3 January 2021.

---

1 From *Said and Done* by Roger McGough (Arrow Books, 2006) p.177, from the chapter entitled 'Macca's Twenty-First' in which the poet recalls scenes missed at Paul's birthday party held at Aunty Jin's house in Huyton on 18 June 1963.

Chapter 46:
EPPY GETS IT WRONG

Epstein's third signing, the Big Three, did not fare as well under his management. He never quite came to terms with what and who they were as a group. What they were was 'wild' and certainly not easy to manage. They were never going to accept the level of control he attempted to exert as a manager.

As a group, they had evolved from Cass and the Cassanovas and comprised Adrian Barber on guitar, Johnny Gustafson on bass and Johnny Hutchinson on drums. Three very strong individuals whom Gustafson described as "down to earth, working-class, tough, scruffy." When it came to rock 'n' roll, the Big Three regarded the Beatles as 'college' boys, believing themselves to be much more the 'real thing'. No wonder that, from the start, Epstein found them challenging.

Revered on Merseyside for their powerhouse rock 'n' roll, there was an edge to the Big Three's music few others in Liverpool possessed. Plus, they were very, very loud. Their unruly manner could sometimes erupt into trouble both on and offstage. Founder member, guitarist Adrian Barber (who designed the Big Three's famous huge 'coffin' amplifiers), was so unhappy with Epstein's attempts to 'tame' the group by improving their appearance, amending their act to include more 'poppy' or 'soft' songs and then adding a fourth player to their line-up, he quit the group.

As they had requested of him in late 1963, Epstein got the Big Three a residency at the Star-Club in Hamburg, but before they went he insisted they expand to include a fourth member, namely guitarist Brian Griffiths. This was the final indignity for Barber. He fulfilled the group's contractual agreement in Hamburg, but did not accompany the group when they returned to Liverpool. He was done with them. Griffiths stayed with the group.

Good to his word, Epstein did get the Big Three a recording contract with Decca. They attended Decca's studio the very day they returned from another trip to Hamburg going straight into Decca's studio to cut a version of 'Some Other Guy' (Leiber, Stoller, Barrett). This was a hugely popular song with Mersey groups, including the Beatles. Paul called it a "muso's song". John took the lead vocal on the Beatles' version, and film exists of the Beatles performing it at the Cavern.

Among the Liverpool groups, however, it was the Big Three who were considered to deliver the definitive version. Unfortunately, when they arrived at Decca they were tired from travelling and bass player/singer Johnny Gustafson's voice was not at its best: "This was actually a demo tape (we made) for Decca. My voice was completely gone. We'd come back from Hamburg that very morning and were thrown into Decca's studio number 2 in the basement. It was horrible. We were croaking like old frogs … The bass sound was non-existent and the drum sound was awful."[1]

Considering the session at Decca to be just a run-through, the Big Three believed their version of 'Some Other Guy' as no more than a 'demo' and were certain that before its release they would be allowed to re-record it. After all, it was their signature song, their debut release and they wanted to do it and themselves justice. When Epstein informed them that Decca were going to release the 'demo' and that there would be absolutely no opportunity to re-record it, Gustafson says the group went 'berserk'. The Big Three in berserk mode would have been a difficult place to be, but for all the anger they expressed the group's rage cut no ice, Epstein refused to confront Decca and secure a second take.

By now, Epstein was starting to become distracted. Trying to keep a handle on the Beatles' runaway success, while at the same time trying to manage a growing and demanding 'stable' of stars, some of whom were beginning to enjoy national success themselves, was proving a bridge too far.

As far as Epstein was concerned, Decca had made their decision and that was it, they were the record company and they knew what they were doing. He resolutely stuck to his guns, however misguided the Big Three felt this decision was, and however utterly misguided the decision actually *was*.

'Some Other Guy' was released in March and it charted for the first time at number 45 on 17 April 1963 on the very same day fellow Scousers Gerry and the Pacemakers hit number 1 with 'How Do You Do It?' The week after, 24 April, 'Some Other Guy' climbed to number 37, but there it stalled. Elsewhere on the chart, Gerry was still at number 1, 'Please Please Me' was on its way down at number 22, but more significantly, right behind it and straight in at number 23, was 'From Me to You'. The week following, Gerry was enjoying his third week at the top, when 'From Me to You' had raced to number 3, but 'Some Other Guy' had dropped to number 40. Five weeks later it had dropped out of the Top 50 completely.

For such a popular Liverpool group who believed implicitly that they were the best in the city, such a low level of success with their debut, compared to the records of rivals the Beatles and Gerry and the Pacemakers, would have been a bitter pill to swallow.

Undeterred by the lukewarm reaction to 'Some Other Guy', and possibly feeling it proved his point that the Big Three needed to record more commercial tunes, and ignoring their point that it was not what they considered to be the 'finished product', Epstein continued to try and 'mould' the trio into a more media/chart-friendly act. Their second release was a Mitch Murray tune called 'By the Way', a catchy, upbeat but ultimately tame pop song for a group such as the Big Three. For them it was lightweight, and a long, long way away from the music of Ray Charles that the trio loved and had introduced into the music scene on Merseyside when they began to feature 'What I'd Say' in their set. Predictably, the group did not like the song one little bit, but it did garner them their one and only Top 30 hit. Released in June, by 14 August it climbed to number 22, but there it stopped. Stalled on the very edge of the Top 20, it went no higher and within six weeks it had dropped out of the Top 40. True, it had done better than 'Some Other Guy', but its success was still not worthy of such a great group.

The group also released a 'live' EP called *The Big Three at the Cavern*. This pumped and exciting record was much more like it and featured their version of 'What I'd Say'. Recorded by their Decca producer Noel Walker, it was released in November 1963 and peaked at number 6 in the EP chart in 1964. The success of this EP suggests that, *had* Epstein and Decca listened to the group, things might have turned out much differently and much more successfully than they did …

Significantly, Brian did not suggest a Beatles tune for the Big Three to record …

It's not that Brian Epstein didn't *try* to garner the Big Three success. He most certainly did. Beginning on 7 March in Nottingham and concluding in Romford on 16 June, Epstein staged a series of concerts around the UK featuring only his artists. Entitled the 'Mersey Beat Showcase', the Beatles headlined with Gerry and the Pacemakers, Billy Kramer and the Coasters, and the Big Three, as support acts.

For the Big Three, however, as far as Epstein was concerned, it was a last throw of the dice. He had grown tired of their confrontational attitude and when it appeared they were on the verge of splitting he withdrew from managing them. The date he informed them of his decision was Saturday 20 July 1963, three days after 'By the Way' (published by Jaep Music Limited) had entered the charts. The Big Three went on to sign a new deal with Danny Betesh of Kennedy Street Enterprises, but the group's best, legend-in-the-making days were behind them.

For 1963, the Big Three were unique, a powerhouse trio ahead of their time (Cream, the Jimi Hendrix Experience were several years away). Maybe, given their rambunctious internal dynamic, it was inevitable that they would fracture at the very point it all should have been kicking off for them.

It's a mark of how potent their reputation was that to this day within the Liverpool cognoscenti their legend still rides high.

---

1 Johnny Gustafson, in conversation with Spencer Leigh and quoted by Bill Harry in 'The Big Three Story', Mersey Beat, www.triumphpc.com/mersey-beat/a-z/bigthree

Chapter 47:
1963, BILLY J. GETS ON HIS WAY ...

"Handsome Billy J., with his horde of admirers, portrays the sincerity and humility of a great pop artist..." Dick James (The Big Beat Album, *1963)*

BILLY J. KRAMER
b. William Howard Ashton on 19 August 1943 in Bootle, Lancashire

The next of Brian Epstein's Liverpool signings, Billy J. Kramer, has the accolade of being the first to score hits with songs John and Paul wrote and which the Beatles never released or recorded during their active lifetime as a band. These are tunes that can be accurately described as 'giveaways'.

And, of all the artists to whom John and Paul gave songs away, Billy was the king.

Kramer's recording career was undoubtedly helped by his close association with the Beatles, but Billy J. had the looks, style and talent to be a star in his own right. The Beatles recognised this themselves and not only recommended him to Brian Epstein as an act to sign, but also wrote several tunes specifically for him to record and shared others that they also cut themselves. Either John or Paul or both attended his recording sessions for the songs they gave him, and during the Beatles' relentless touring schedule of 1963, Kramer with his backing group, the Dakotas, was often support.

Between them for 21 weeks of 1963, the Beatles and Billy J. Kramer occupied the number 1 spot on the UK official singles chart with songs written by John Lennon and Paul McCartney. (This total would be even more if 'Please Please Me' and 'Do You Want to Know a Secret?' were to be included in the totals, for both records reached number 1 in the *NME* and *MM* charts.) This was a phenomenal achievement and so it was that, for a brief period of time, in terms of creative input, writers Lennon and McCartney were sustaining both theirs and Billy J's recording careers.

(In addition, during 1963, John and Paul provided 'giveaways' to two other Liverpool acts managed by Brian Epstein, namely the Fourmost and Cilla Black, and at the same time gave a nudge to the Rolling Stones' fledgling recording career with a song they shared with them called 'I Want to Be Your Man'.)

Like the Beatles, William Howard Ashton was a war baby. Born in 1943, he came from a working-class family and was the youngest of seven. He grew up in Bootle which is to the north of Liverpool, close to the docks. Its close proximity to the docks meant that it had been mightily bombed during the war: some 80% of its houses had been hit or set on fire.

Billy's family lived on Hankey Drive in a two-up, two-down house with an outside toilet. "Dad was a docker, but when I was growing up he worked in a timber yard. Mum worked in Jacob's biscuit factory and she scrubbed bar floors as well."[1]

As a small boy, he was soon enjoying music and his talent as a singer was quickly noted: "I went to Orrell Primary and sang in the choir there. One day when we were all singing our teacher Mr. Burke ran round the class saying, 'You're in, you're in...' (the choir). He wanted me to sing solo but as a kid I was self-conscious and overweight and I just didn't want to do it."[2]

A *Liverpool Echo* 'Pop Special' edition from 1963 carried an interview with Billy J. in which he commented that he was 8 when his teacher selected him from 40 other 'suitable pupils' to make up a 15-strong school choir 'for local singing festivals'. Two years later, the choir were finalists in a choral competition held at the Winter Gardens, Blackpool.[3]

Billy J. Kramer in 1963. Just 20 years old and, by the end of the year, a regular at the top of the UK hit singles charts. (Pictorial Press Ltd / Alamy Stock Photo)

Billy's secondary school, St. George of England High in Bootle, was one of the brand new secondary modern schools that had been (and were still being) built up and down the land at the end of World War II. At St. George, Billy was noted for his sporting prowess (cricket, swimming, football) *and* his musical talent.

Although it was brand new, Billy was disappointed St. George didn't have a choir. However, there was one musical treat that the school provided each year that really fired his imagination: "I used to love the Philharmonic Orchestra coming to visit that school. They'd perform pieces like 'Peter and the Wolf' in the school hall which I really enjoyed."[4]

Despite this annual treat, Billy found the music lessons at St. George's to be dull and dry because they focused purely on theory. Even so, he still managed to impress his teacher: "I just didn't take it in, but when I was 13 I'd bought this cheap acoustic guitar and had sat on the stairs at home and taught myself to play. My music teacher at St. George was quite taken aback that I could play anything on my guitar and not only that but, without the music, I could transpose things mentally into different keys."[5]

In that 1963 'Pop Special' edition of the *Liverpool Echo*, Billy recounted how, as a 13-year-old rock 'n' roll fan, on Saturday afternoons he'd catch the Corporation bus from Linacre Lane into Liverpool city centre to window-shop around the musical instrument stores. His attention was drawn "to the gleaming guitars they had on show, but I couldn't afford one on a schoolboy's pocket money but, eventually, I talked my mother into adding a couple of quid to my savings so that I could get my first cheap, unpolished guitar for Christmas. That was in 1955."[6]

At the same time as Billy had begun to play guitar, so did his good friend Ray Dougherty, and it wasn't long before they began playing together. Like so many Liverpool musicians of their generation, the two boys were inspired by Lonnie Donegan and skiffle music, but with the advent of Elvis they graduated to rock 'n' roll.

In the summer of 1958, aged just 15, Billy left school and took a job with British Rail as an apprentice engineer. In those days such a position would have been highly sought after and considered to be 'a job for life'.

However, at the same time, music had become more than just a hobby for Billy. He and Ray had formed a group called the Phantoms. Billy says they began by playing in the street: he played rhythm guitar while Ray played lead.

With the advent of skiffle and rock 'n' roll, forming a group in Liverpool with your friends became a popular thing to do (especially for young men). As a result, Billy and Ray didn't have to go far to find other lads to join them: "The bass player, George Braithwaite, his back gate was opposite mine and Ray's gate was opposite our drummer's Tony Sanders…"[7]

Almost from the moment he left school, despite holding down an apprenticeship, the more he played with the Phantoms the more he knew he had found his true calling in life. At first, Billy did not sing, he played rhythm guitar. Another boy from Bootle, Joe Leary, became their singer.

Looking back to those very early days of playing in a group, Billy says: "You have to give that era so much credit because it was after World War II, it was tough growing up, there wasn't much around, we all grew up on ration books, there was a lot of bands around, but there wasn't a lot of money in it. I left school at 15, was doing this heavy job at BR during the day, going home and in the evening loading a van to go to a gig, unloading it, loading it back up again, getting home late and going back to work early the next morning. The other guys in the group were doing the same, working by day, playing at night. We put in the work."[8]

Like most groups, finding a space to rehearse was always a problem. Even with the amps turned down, groups make a noise (and drums aren't made to be played quietly). Fortunately, Billy and his friends found somewhere local where they could rehearse regularly without having to worry about the noise: "We used to rehearse in an ex-serviceman's club on Fernhill Road in Bootle (known as 'ODVA' or 'the Orwell and District

Veterans' Association'). In return for using the space, and because we were also using electricity, Charlie Phillips, the chairman, said we had to play a show on a Saturday night to pay for it, although we did also get a pint of beer each for doing so."[9]

The Phantoms' show proved so popular they were asked back and were soon playing regular bookings at ODVA. "From nothing, from just being a hall where some people played darts and dominos, people started to form a line every Saturday night to hear us play."[10]

The Phantoms' first change in personnel occurred when one summer, out of the blue, singer Joe Leary left to go and work at Butlin's. A replacement singer called Bruce was recruited, but he failed to appreciate Billy dating his girlfriend and almost immediately quit. It was at this point Billy gravitated towards the position of frontman. "We had a lot of singers and they'd leave … I remember going on the 61 bus with all our equipment to perform an audition at the Aintree Institute for a promoter called Brian Kelly ('Bee Kay') and that was the start for me as singer for our group. (It was also the first time I met the Beatles in person, although I had first *seen* them when they played the Town Hall Ballroom in Litherland in late December 1960.) We got six gigs from that audition. To be honest, I had no intention of being a frontman when I started, I just thought it's a novelty, and did it for the guys' sake."[11]

By now Billy had become the proud owner of a Hofner Club 60 guitar, having loaned the money to do so from his brother Ronnie. A guitar like that cost 40 guineas and would have been a big outlay for a young lad like Billy who was only on "50 bob a week" (£38/39 at today's value), so Ronnie's help was mightily appreciated. To go with it, Billy bought a Vox amplifier. Unfortunately, disaster struck not long after: "The first gig we did with me as the designated singer (at the Conservative Club, Green Lane) I had my guitar stolen! I couldn't afford another and so that was *it*."[12]

Becoming singer had been a big ask for Billy, a real challenge. Although he had enjoyed singing as part of a choir at primary school, he never sang solo, the very idea of being out front made him feel very uncomfortable. Billy declined all requests by his teacher to do so because he was physically self-conscious and lacking in self-confidence. All the reasons why he had not wanted to sing in the school choir now came crashing back when he stepped up to front the Phantoms: "I was a very shy, self-conscious kid with a big hang-up about my appearance. People talk about this sort of thing quite openly today, but you didn't in those days. I suffered from low self-esteem and it hadn't gone away. I learned to deal with it, but it was very difficult. I would have a few drinks and unfortunately one drink leads to another and before you know it you're drinking too much."[13]

Thinking back to those days and his struggle to feel comfortable as the frontman, Billy says, "Even today I still get that same nervousness before I go on stage … I think there's a side of me that was always looking for beyond perfection … now I wonder what exactly did I expect? Did I want the audience to jump up and down and tear their hair out every time I sang? Even if a gig could not have gone any better, I always felt unsatisfied. It's an awful feeling inside, but I recognise that it was there in me, even when we had our first skiffle group."[14]

Of course, Billy did bite the bullet, became vocalist for the Phantoms and around the same time chose a stage name for himself. After a brief period as 'Billy Forde' he became Billy Kramer, and the Phantoms became the 'Coasters': "One day all the guys in the band said I had to have a stage name and I said I wasn't interested. Looking back 'William Howard Ashton' wasn't a bad name, but even so I just said whatever it is it's got to be Billy 'something'. They drew up a list of names and phoned up the operator and asked her which she liked the best, and she chose Billy Kramer, and so that's what it was until a while later John Lennon came up with the unique idea of calling myself 'Billy *J.* Kramer'."

From the moment Kramer encountered the Beatles at the Aintree Institute, they proved to be mentors, especially John. It was the beginning of a personal and professional relationship between Billy and the Beatles that served all concerned exceedingly well. At their first meeting, John had let Billy play his prized Rickenbacker ("I was intrigued, I'd never seen one before").[15]

Later on, when the Beatles and Billy J. (who was by then 'with' the Dakotas) toured together, the Beatles would watch him and suggest things to improve his performance. "It might be John and George or Paul and Ringo but they always watched from the side of the stage and when I came off they'd make critiques. John's thing was all about 'the show'. To begin with I just went out there and sang songs. People don't realise you can learn songs, you can become a good singer, but how you portray yourself and portray songs to an audience, well, some people have a natural gift for it but it was something that I felt I had to learn: stagecraft. The Beatles' advice was always given in a good spirit, never in a knocking way, it was always in a helping way."[16]

One of the early comments John made after watching Billy perform was that although he'd enjoyed their performance he wanted to know, "Where was the show?"

Lennon's words had a profound effect on the way Billy Kramer perceived himself and the art of performance. "The message John was trying to deliver to me was that when I go on stage, I should be as different as possible from the guy in the street. I'm naturally an introvert, but once I started singing, whenever I got on stage I became an extrovert. So I realised I should stop walking through the crowd to get to the stage, which allowed all the people to see me before we started to play. I felt that when you appear on stage it is like an illusion, so from then on, I always found a back way onto the stage to create the sense of a 'show' that John was talking about."[17]

He certainly did. Soon after, Billy Kramer not only took the stage with the Coasters via the back door, he also began to dress flamboyantly. He purchased a gold lamé suit and matching golden boots. As a consequence, some promoters began billing him as the 'Golden Boy' which put Rory Storm's nose out of joint, but garnered Kramer and his group prestigious bookings at the Cavern and the Iron Door.

By now they had also gained a manager called Ted Knibbs. Because Billy and all the members of his group (which now included his cousin Arthur Ashton on guitar) were working boys, Ted could only accept evening bookings on their behalf. The combination of late nights and early starts was always tough for all of the boys to sustain.

As for their repertoire, like all the groups in Liverpool, including the Beatles, Billy Kramer and the Coasters were a 'covers' group. Even in this respect, Billy recalls the Beatles were different because they "covered tunes by people I'd never heard of." He has memories of them down the Cavern singing songs like 'Money', 'Slow Down', 'Chains', 'Boys', 'A Taste of Honey', 'Your Feet's Too Big', 'Some Other Guy' and 'Besame Mucho'. "I thought they were very smart in the covers that they did. Most of the bands around were doing the same covers, the same chart songs, but the Beatles weren't. Things like 'Slow Down' and 'Money' I'd never heard them. The way Paul used to do 'A Taste of Honey' was unique and I used to love the way they'd do 'Three Cool Cats' together."[18]

Like most of his contemporaries on the Liverpool beat music scene, Billy J. was unaware that the Beatles wrote their own tunes (let's face it at that point in their history the Beatles were doing a good job of keeping these well hidden) and he vividly remembers the night he discovered that they did. It was Monday 10 September 1962 and he and the Coasters were supporting the Beatles at the Queen's Hall in Widnes. "I wasn't aware of their songwriting ability until that gig we did with them at the Queen's Hall. The Beatles were the closing act and were in their dressing room rehearsing 'Twist and Shout' when I went in to talk with them. I mentioned that I'd heard that after the show they were going down to London to record. They said they were and so I asked them what they were going to do? They replied, 'a couple of things we've written ourselves', which took me by surprise and with barely a moment's hesitation I responded by asking, 'Why don't you get some top American writers to write something for you?'"[19]

In 2020, and with the benefit of much hindsight, the humour of that exchange is not lost on Billy J.: "When I think about it now I can't believe I really said that!"[20]

His response to hearing the first single taken from the Beatles' 11 September recording session, 'Love Me Do', was typical of many fans in Liverpool who'd heard them down the Cavern: "My first thought was, it's okay but what happened to 'Money' and 'Twist and Shout'? I was expecting something like that and frankly 'Love Me Do' was a bit laid back, which came as something of a disappointment, but when I heard them do 'Please Please Me' at the Poll Winners concert at the Majestic Ballroom in Birkenhead (15 December 1962) I was amazed: the improvement over 'Love Me Do' was tremendous, my instant response was: 'Wow! That *is* going to go!'"[21]

By the time of the Poll Winners concert, Brian Epstein was not only aware of Kramer and the Coasters (having seen them several times when they had played on the same bills as the Beatles) but had been sufficiently impressed to be considering managing Kramer.

It was around the time of the Poll Winners concert that Billy's apprenticeship suddenly became problematic. He had learned he was to be transferred to Crewe to continue his training, which would have meant having to move there as well, leaving him no alternative but to quit the Coasters. By coincidence, not long after receiving this news, he met Brian Epstein in the Grapes pub on Mathew Street to whom he explained his dilemma.

Things moved quickly from this point on, for just a few days later Ted Knibbs contacted Billy: "Ted called me and asked, did I fancy taking a ride into Liverpool and so we went into the city to a restaurant (at the time I wasn't used to going into restaurants because back then we didn't have the money). Brian Epstein was already there and when I took a seat Ted, who was a very honest man, turned to me and said, 'You know, Billy, I've done as much as I can for you and Brian is interested in handling your career.'"[22]

As far as his career prospects were concerned, this offer seriously upped the ante for Billy: either sign with Brian and become a professional singer and benefit from all he could do for him or quit and concentrate on his career on the railway.

It was a big ask, but ultimately an offer Kramer could not refuse. Despite the huge value set on apprenticeships back then, Kramer knew this kind of offer only came along once in a lifetime. When he broke the news to his parents, despite the value placed on apprenticeships, they were immediately supportive, his father told him he had to accept Brian's offer or face a lifetime of regret for not doing so.

Despite the huge risk it involved, Billy broke his indentures (of which he'd completed four of six years), quit British Rail, signed with Brian Epstein and became a full-time musician. "I wouldn't have done it for anybody else, but I'd seen the moves Brian was making with the Beatles. Let's face it, back then to be a year or two away from being a qualified engineer, a guaranteed future, a job for life with a pension, to take a chance of success in show business was a bit scary, but I really thought that if anybody could do it for me, it was going to be Brian."[23]

Billy was just 19.

A key moment in Epstein's decision to make his offer to manage Billy had occurred on 15 December 1962 at the annual *Mersey Beat* newspaper poll results evening at the Majestic Ballroom in Birkenhead, when he witnessed Kramer and the Coasters' performance. They had come third after Lee Curtis and the All-Stars (featuring Pete Best) who were second to the Beatles. All three groups performed that evening. Estimates of just how many beat groups there were in Liverpool at that time vary between 300 and 400 and so to come third in such a prestigious poll was a great marker of any group's popularity. Kramer and the Coasters were pulling in the crowds because they put on a good show. As the frontman, Kramer was a major factor in their success: he was a good looking guy who particularly attracted the girl fans. No wonder Epstein's attention had been drawn to them for it was clear they had everything going for them to make it.

Kramer and the Coasters had not only come third in the main poll, but had also won a prize for being 'the best known non-professional group in Liverpool'. It was another significant marker of their prowess. Epstein himself presented them with this prize: "It was partly because I was impressed with this achievement that I signed him, and also because John Lennon of the Beatles thought a lot of Kramer's voice. He was, I thought, an outstanding artiste for his age and experience."[24]

Make no mistake, for John Lennon to comment on another artist's singing was high praise indeed. His championing of Billy was duly noted by their manager and undoubtedly contributed to Epstein's decision to sign him (even though George Martin later expressed some reservations).

Despite his growing admiration of Billy, Brian Epstein had no wish to sign a singer or a group just because they looked good but whom, when they located to Abbey Road to record, George Martin would not find good enough. Such caution meant that prior to signing Billy Kramer and the Coasters, Epstein arranged for them to be recorded playing for a whole evening. What he heard of the Coasters did not impress. Epstein knew that if he was not impressed then neither would George Martin be. And so when it came, his offer of management extended only to Kramer. He was not prepared to sign the Coasters.

This left Billy with a second, even bigger decision to make, not only whether he should give up his apprenticeship and sign with Epstein, but whether to do so *without* the Coasters.

When Billy explained his dilemma to British Rail, they showed no sympathy: "I'd done four years and had two to go, so I went to talk to the boss and tried to talk him into letting me stay in Liverpool because my parents were getting old and I didn't want to leave them at home. He told me 'to grow up and face the world, you either go or you know the alternative.' Also they said they couldn't guarantee me a job when the two years in Crewe ended and so they let me go."[25]

Leaving the Coasters was an even tougher decision for Billy J. to make because he was so close to them as individuals. They had literally grown up together. However, the reality of the situation was that, in terms of a career, they did not take the music as seriously as Billy, and had Epstein wanted to sign them as well it was very likely some of them would have declined the offer because, like Billy, they also had good jobs that promised secure futures which may, ultimately, have been too much for them to risk sacrificing.

"It was very difficult. I said to them that I'd had this offer from Brian, but if they wanted to just carry on the way we were doing I wouldn't take it. I wouldn't go with it, I'd work something out. I'd go to Crewe and come home at the weekends to play with the band, but they said no: 'Billy you've got to take this chance, you've got to go for it.' And so it was, to succeed they knew and I knew I was going to have to go it alone."[26]

---

3 & 6 *Liverpool Echo* 'Pop Special' edition 'Salute To The Beatles' (Price 1/-) published in 1964, from a Billy J. Kramer interview feature entitled 'Busy Billy J.' by Tony Barrow.
1, 2, 4, 5, 7, 8, 9, 10, 11, 12, 13, 15, 16, 18, 19, 20, 21, 22, 23, 25 & 26: Billy J. Kramer interview with the author 19 October 2020.
14 & 17 *Do You Want to Know a Secret?: The Autobiography of Billy J. Kramer*, by Billy J Kramer with Alyn Shipton (Equinox Publishing, 2016).
24 *A Cellarful of Noise* by Brian Epstein (New English Library, 1965) p.70.

Chapter 48:
WITH THE DAKOTAS

The Dakotas
Founded in September 1960 by:
Robin MacDonald (rhythm guitar)
Bryn Jones (lead guitar)*
Tony Bookbinder aka Tony Mansfield (drums) (Tony is the elder brother of Elkie Brooks)
Ian Fraser (bass guitar)**
This personnel later changed when:
* Mike Maxfield replaced Bryn Jones on lead guitar in February 1962
** Ray Jones replaced Ian Fraser on bass

Having split Kramer from his established group, Epstein's immediate task was to replace the Coasters with a first-rate backing group. With this in mind, Brian Epstein approached the highly regarded Mersey beat combo, the Remo Four. Two of them, Colin Manley and Don Andrew, had been at school with Paul McCartney. Billy was a fan of the Remo Four and well up for this collaboration, they suited his style, but unfortunately as they had just enlisted vocalist Johnny Sandon they turned down Epstein's offer.

Epstein's search for the right group led him away from Liverpool to Manchester to a professional Mancunian group called the Dakotas, who were fronted by a vocalist called Pete MacLaine and who occasionally played the Cavern. (Freda Kelly, who later worked for Brian and the Beatles, remembers seeing Pete MacLaine and the Dakotas play at the Cavern, so it is reasonable to think that is where Brian had encountered them.)

Brian was also aware that when a travelling solo singer or instrumentalist was touring 'up North' and in need of a first-class backing band, the Dakotas could be hired separately *sans* Pete and so he now sought to prise them away from him permanently because of their excellent reputation as top drawer musicians. His reasoning told him they would be ideal to back Billy J. Indeed, the Dakotas were ambitious and despite their professional relationship with MacLaine they were not prepared to let the opportunity of being managed by Brian Epstein pass them by. Although it meant they effectively became another singer's backing band, both in the studio and on the road, they left Pete and hooked up with Billy. In an ideal world they would have preferred not to be signed as a backing band, but as stars in their own right …

In recognition of the Dakotas' pride in their own musical ability and already established group identity, Epstein promised that whenever they backed Billy they would be afforded the opportunity to play a set on their own before Billy joined them on stage. Despite this, from the very start it irked the Dakotas that primarily they had been signed to back Billy and that he *was* the main man.

To ensure this combination *could* work together, Brian organised a rehearsal at the Cavern on Sunday 6 January 1963 to see how/if they gelled. From the moment they plugged in, Kramer could hear how good the Dakotas were. Unexpectedly – as far as Billy was concerned – John and Paul dropped in at the rehearsal. It was more than likely that Brian had asked them to do so in order to check out the new combination for him. When they arrived, Kramer and the Dakotas were playing some Ricky Nelson tunes and the two Beatles very much liked what they heard. Their good first impression registered with both Epstein and Billy who, once the rehearsal was over, made the decision to work with the Dakotas.

Unfortunately, it did not prove to be a comfortable working relationship. According to Billy, the existing close bond between the individual Dakotas was never extended to include him. From the outset, he says he was made to feel like an inferior musician and an outsider.

Flexing their muscle, the Dakotas persuaded Epstein to get the singer to stop wearing his colourful suits (to the gold lamé, Billy had added a pink version). This came as a blow to the young singer who felt good on stage wearing these, the guise they provided helped settle his nerves and he believed they contributed a great deal to his popularity. Certainly, when Epstein was making his decision to sign Kramer, he had seen him many times on stage dressed in his trademark suits and would have witnessed the positive reaction Kramer received from audiences. He had not commented on them before. Nevertheless, Brian sided with the Dakotas and somewhat unkindly told his new singing sensation that it was time "to put away the Christmas tree".[1]

Kramer recognised this as a case of the tail wagging the dog, against which he should have held out. "I think, in retrospect, they saw this kid from Liverpool wearing extrovert clothes with all the girls going crazy, and they were jealous. This was long before my first number 1 hit, but the underlying jealousy was there from the start. I ought to have pushed back and not accepted it from them, but it was still early days."[2]

One Epstein instruction Kramer *did* resist was his new manager's persistent requests to grow his hair to look more like the Beatles. Whenever Brian suggested this, Kramer would respond with words to the effect that he was *not* a Beatle clone, but an artist in his own right.

All the while the Beatles continued to take a keen interest in Kramer's progress and it was not long after Kramer signed with Epstein that John suggested he should add a middle initial to his stage name. Apparently, Lennon believed 'Billy Kramer' did not have the right ring to it, whereas 'Billy *J.* Kramer' did. Billy agreed and thereafter adopted the additional initial. When he asked John what he should say if someone asked what the 'J' stood for, John replied 'Julian'. Julian was the name of John's baby son, although Kramer was personally unaware of this at the time. Like many others he did not even know John was married, never mind already a father. He was soon brought up to speed.

The mismatch between Billy and his backing group became more apparent when, at the behest of Brian Epstein, he spent time rehearsing with the Dakotas in Manchester. During this brief excursion, music apart, another underlying problem emerged, that of social division. Billy J. was blue-collar, Liverpool working-class, they were white-collar, Manchester middle-class.

All the boys in the Dakotas enjoyed middle class/professional family backgrounds. Having made no secret of the fact that they felt superior to him as musicians, once he visited them in their homes, Billy believed they maybe felt the same way towards him as people. It was an attitude echoed by their parents, the mother of one who, during a visit to the family home, pressed Kramer as to why it was *he* who got all the media attention and not her boy. The exchange made Kramer feel very uncomfortable indeed.

The more he learned about their backgrounds, so Kramer's qualms about the social and musical divisions between himself and the members of the Dakotas grew. Rhythm guitarist Robin MacDonald had studied guitar at Manchester College of Music, his mother was a headmistress, his father head of Oldham School of Art. Drummer Tony Bookbinder, aka 'Tony Mansfield', had been given a drum kit by his parents when he was just 13 and had played with a show band and a trio before joining the Dakotas. His parents owned a couple of bakeries and his sister Elaine was also a very good singer who later became better known as Elkie Brooks.

The tension in their professional relationships did nothing to ease Billy's feelings of insecurity. However, despite such privileged backgrounds, Kramer never lost sight of the fact that he *was* the Dakotas equal, if not their superior, when it came to his passion for

Billy J. Kramer with the Dakotas photographed in 1963. Within the space of a year Billy J. together with the Dakotas had hit the UK Top 5 on three occasions, including a number 1 with 'Bad to Me'. As a unit in their own right the Dakotas had climbed to number 18 with their instrumental hit 'The Cruel Sea'. (Pictorial Press Ltd / Alamy Stock Photo)

the music itself: he loved to perform rock 'n' roll, it was a passion.

Although Brian Epstein's intention had been that Kramer and the Dakotas should rehearse together in Manchester, they didn't. The Dakotas simply wouldn't do it. As a consequence, while they themselves were always tight and well-rehearsed as a group, Kramer would often step on stage unrehearsed.

This situation was deeply unnerving for a young man for whom a lack of self-confidence was already an underlying issue. On reflection, and with the benefit of a lot of hindsight, Kramer now realises he should have returned from Manchester and refused to work with the Dakotas again. Billy readily acknowledges the Dakotas' superb musical ability. For him that was never an issue. The Dakotas worked quickly in the studio, there was never a need to bring in session musicians and they were very professional on stage. However, despite all this, or maybe because of it, the working relationship established in Manchester never changed.

At first, Billy kept his growing reservations to himself and it was only after he and the Dakotas returned from a trip to London to audition for the BBC, Pye and Decca (which Kramer candidly acknowledges the group passed but he didn't) that he told Epstein there was a problem: he felt the Dakotas were cold-shouldering him.

Epstein was in no mood to accommodate either Kramer or the Dakotas. He believed he knew best. His solution was not to listen to Billy and his concerns about the bickering between them, but to pack the lot of them off to Hamburg. This was Brian's blueprint for success, his theory being that it had worked for the Beatles so it was bound to work for others. As far as he was concerned, putting them together to face the rigours of a residency at the Star-Club would remedy any in-house problems and force them to bond as a unit.

Kramer was less convinced by such reasoning.

The Dakotas departed for Hamburg a week ahead of Billy, during which time his anxieties about their relationship mounted. It was January 1963 and the UK was enduring its coldest, bleakest winter on record: "They'd gone off without me while I spent a week alone in a hotel in London waiting for my passport to come through. I'd saved enough money to catch a cab to the airport, but I was so depressed the night before I left I ended up spending most of it at the pub and so had to take the bus to the terminal. I was skint when I arrived in Hamburg. Even though I had no cash I took a cab to the Star-Club, but on arrival I quickly jumped out and ran inside with an irate cab driver running and screaming after me. Fortunately, John McNally of the Searchers came out and paid my fare."[3]

Now joined by Billy, the Dakotas continued to snub their lead singer: "I always felt alone ... At the Star-Club I spent most of my time hanging out with Tony Jackson of the Searchers and became friendly with Gene Vincent."[4]

The long, exacting hours on stage in Hamburg would cause Billy to fall asleep on his feet. As a result, he took the advice of Adrian Barber (formerly of the Big Three, but by then in charge of the sound system at the Star-Club) to try the Captagon tablets that the bathroom attendant sold. Captagon was an amphetamine and it certainly kept Kramer awake through the long nights at the Star-Club, but when he returned from Hamburg he found he had become addicted. From then on, when on tour, Billy always travelled with his own personal supply of (legally prescribed) pills: "I just thought I could party around the clock, an attitude that was to later cause me a lot of pain."[5]

Isolated and turning regularly to medication to keep him going, unknown to him or the Dakotas, Kramer was about to enjoy the kind of international success and consequent full-on attention few people ever do. But now, very sadly for him, accompanying the fanfares and bright lights there would always be a dark side.

As his concerns about his professional relationship with the Dakotas deepened, Billy once more related his misgivings to Brian Epstein: "Home from Hamburg I told him not to expect anything amazing because the guys just wouldn't put the time in. To see for himself

Brian came to our first gig at Northwich Memorial Hall and it wasn't good. After that I think Brian must have had words with them."[6]

All these years later, Billy still regrets that he and the Dakotas failed to gel: "I don't like what happened. At the time I thought we're a team and if we work together we can come up with something great, but whenever we did anything everyone just dispersed, they didn't hang around, the next time we'd get together was when there was a gig. If we'd been asked to play a prolonged show beyond our usual half hour, I don't think we could have done it."[7]

What he witnessed in Northwich certainly disappointed Brian. The apparent lack of progress Billy J. Kramer and the Dakotas had achieved in Hamburg did not bode well at all. Epstein recognised that Billy's concerns were very real and that the discord between the singer and his backing band was not something that could be easily disguised or repaired.

Cold-shouldered and made to feel not good enough, Billy found himself in an incredibly uncomfortable situation, his ingrained sense of insecurity was under constant siege.

Epstein ended up having to contractually enforce the unhappy alliance he had unwittingly forged. His solution to the problem was to ensure that from that point on they were only booked to play short sets. In the future there would be just one set during which Kramer would be on stage the entire time. Often Epstein booked them to open for the Beatles, which meant they only played for 20/25 minutes. In a practical sense the strategy worked, but despite all the success Kramer never felt the Dakotas respected him as a musician or singer.

The distance between the group and Billy was reflected in their nomenclature: professionally they were never 'Billy J. Kramer *and* the Dakotas' but always 'Billy J. Kramer *with* the Dakotas'.

It was only one little word, but it was crucial: it sent a clear message that as artists they were separate entities.

Another future cause for discord and jealousy that soon manifested itself was money. When Epstein signed the Dakotas, he gave them the option to be paid either session fees or royalties for the records they cut with Billy. They opted for session fees. Kramer, given the same choice, had chosen royalties. At first this caused no friction. The Dakotas were experienced session musicians and so once a recording was made they happily took their fees and the subsequent success or not of a record was of no interest to them financially, whereas Kramer depended on a record selling before he made any money at all.

"The deal I had with Brian was that the Dakotas would make records with me, but they wanted (and were given) a separate recording contract of their own. Brian got us together and said to them on Billy's records do you want royalties or do you want session fees and they said they'd take the session fees. To me it was another light bulb moment, for if these guys had any confidence in me they would have gone for the royalties."[8]

And so it was the Dakotas got paid upfront and didn't have to worry whether the record was a hit or not because they'd already banked their fee. As time passed, however, and Billy J. Kramer with the Dakotas' first five singles were huge Top 10 hits that sold in their millions, their decision must have irked the Mancunians no end. They may have received their fee, but would have been fully aware that even though he wasn't earning a writer's royalty, Kramer's performance royalty from record sales alone meant he was earning substantially way more than them.

A mitigating factor, financially, for Robin MacDonald and Mike Maxfield of the Dakotas, was that they wrote tunes: sometimes individually and sometimes collaboratively. Consequently, they did earn writers' royalties from penning some of the B-sides to some of Billy's hits. So, for example, together they penned 'They Remind Me of You', the B-side of Billy's best-selling record 'Little Children'. MacDonald wrote 'Second to None' which was the B-side of 'From a Window', while Mike Maxfield penned the Dakotas' only Top 20 hit, 'The Cruel Sea'.

(When later Mick Green (formerly of Johnny Kidd and the Pirates) replaced Ray Jones in the Dakotas' line-up, he and Robin MacDonald proved to be a formidable writing partnership and provided some fine tunes for Billy to record, such as 'I Live to Love You', 'That Ain't Good for Me', 'Forgive Me' and 'Take My Hand', but by then ('65, '66) Billy's singles had stopped charting. Nevertheless, they beg the question of what might have been had they gelled as a quintet from the very start.)

One positive that *had* emerged from their forced exile to Hamburg was 'Do You Want to Know a Secret?' It was a song Billy *with* the Dakotas actually managed to learn and rehearse together. So much so, they featured it regularly in their sets at the Star-Club, although Kramer never sensed a great audience response towards it. It was, he also recalls, the same when they played it on their return to the UK.

That they *had* rehearsed this song together was down to the fact that for both Billy and the Dakotas it was a brand new song that none of them had heard before. As Billy was the only one with a demo, they had no alternative but to learn it together from scratch. Billy J. had received the tape from Brian Epstein before he left for Hamburg in early 1963. John himself had taped his version in Hamburg during the Beatles' final trip to the port in December 1962. Billy J. remembers that it was a simple demo of John singing the song and accompanying himself on an acoustic guitar. "John later apologised for the tape quality, but said he'd done the demo in the toilet as it was the quietest place he could find…"[9]

Apparently to prove the location of his recording John included the sound of a flushing toilet on the demo tape he provided for Billy J. …

1, 2 & 5 *Do You Want to Know a Secret?: The Autobiography of Billy J. Kramer*, by Billy J Kramer with Alyn Skipton (Equinox Publishing, 2016): p.32 & p.38.
3, 4, 6, 7 & 8 Billy J. Kramer interview with the author 19 October 2020.
9 *John Lennon*, Ray Coleman (Futura, 1985) p.174.

Chapter 49:
PAUL THROUGH AND THROUGH

John came up with the idea for 'Do You Want to Know a Secret?' some time between 23 August and 18 December 1962, when he and his new wife Cynthia were living at 36 Falkner Street, Liverpool. This was a flat owned by Brian Epstein. The couple lived there immediately after their marriage, of which John's Aunt Mimi had not approved, going so far as to not attend the wedding (although she apparently gave John the money to buy a wedding ring for Cynthia). To further make her point, Mimi would not let the couple live with her. Very kindly, and fortuitously for John and Cynthia, Brian Epstein stepped in and saved the day by letting them use his apartment until they had found somewhere of their own. The situation was urgent because Cynthia was pregnant. (However, by December 18, when the Beatles flew to Hamburg, Aunt Mimi had relented in her opposition to the couple's union and they were living alongside her in 'Mendips'.)

It was whilst living in Brian's apartment that John said he composed 'Do You Want to Know a Secret?' His inspiration came from a childhood memory of his mother Julia reciting or singing to him the spoken, introductory words to a song called 'I'm Wishing', from the 1937 Disney animated movie, *Snow White and the Seven Dwarves*.

Paul described the song as a collaboration or 'hack song' based on John's original idea.

'Do You Want to Know a Secret?' was eventually recorded by both Billy J. Kramer *and* George Harrison, who took the lead vocal on the Beatles' version. Like 'Misery' and 'I Saw Her Standing There', it was a John and Paul tune written specifically for their debut long player and, like those tunes, was also offered to others to record.

Brian Epstein not only gave it to Billy J. to learn, but he also offered it to UK singer Shane Fenton (who later metamorphosed into Alvin Stardust). Epstein did so because he was interested in managing Fenton and sweetened his offer to do so with an invitation for Fenton to record 'Do You Want to Know a Secret?'.

Fenton had been born Bernard William Jewry on 24 September 1942 in Muswell Hill, North London (although at an early age his family moved to Mansfield, Nottinghamshire) but it was as lead singer with Shane Fenton and the Fentones that he had signed to Parlophone Records. Fenton and the Fentones enjoyed four Top 40 hits in 1961/62, but only one of these reached the Top 20, 'Cindy's Birthday', which peaked at number 19 in July 1962. This meant that by 1963 Fenton was already looking to re-energise his career and it was at this point Brian Epstein tried to entice him into a management contract by offering him 'Do You Want to Know a Secret?'. Jewry was not swayed, however, and politely declined Brian's offer.

Although not written specifically for George, not long after he had written 'Do You Want to Know a Secret?', John realised it was best suited to Harrison's vocal range. (Paul recalled this differently, saying that it was always intended for George.)

George Martin thought it was also suitable for Billy J. and would make a good debut single for him. At the recording session in Abbey Road, the Dakotas laid down a more full-bodied accompaniment than the Beatles had done for George Harrison's version, and to further flesh out the song's sound Martin double-tracked Kramer's vocals to give them greater depth. Billy himself thought the first recording he made of 'Do You Want to Know a Secret' was just a guide vocal and that he would be asked to go back in and record his parts again.

"Brian had given me a tape of John singing 'Do You Want to Know a Secret?' prior to Hamburg. I took it to the Dakotas and I told them this is how I want to do it and we made up an arrangement. We did that song every night of the week in Germany and a load of times when we came back. When we recorded it with George Martin I just thought it was a recording test and we did it exactly the same as how we did it live. When George called me later and said he was going to release it, I was shocked because at the time of recording I'd felt uncomfortable because George had been somewhat remote towards me when I was introduced to him. I felt like I'd met the Duke of Edinburgh. I was away from Liverpool and overwhelmed by it all. I wasn't very pleased with my performance, I thought it could have been better."[1]

Fortunately, the negative assessment Kramer had formed of the audience's response towards the song in Hamburg and back home in Liverpool proved incorrect and in June 1963 it climbed to number 1 in the *NME* chart (crucially it stalled at number 2 in *Record Retailer*). This gave Kramer the distinction of being the first artist other than the Beatles themselves (with 'Please Please Me' in February and March) to take a Lennon-McCartney song to the top of the *NME* chart, which in its day, given the importance and popularity of *NME*, was a mighty achievement, especially with his first ever single.

Significantly, Kramer's debut carried a second Lennon-McCartney song as its B-side. This particular nugget is the one that genuinely counts as their first 'giveaway'. 'I'll Be on My Way' by Billy J. was not a song destined to be released by the Beatles during the group's lifetime, beyond taping it as part of a performance for the BBC radio series *Side by Side* on 4 April 1963. Kramer said it did not take many tries to get a version good enough for release, while other sources say it took 38 takes.

In 1980, John Lennon acknowledged 'I'll Be on My Way' to be "Paul, through and through", further describing it as "Paul on the voids of driving through the country."[2]

It was indeed a Paul original from 1959 that he'd composed on his Zenith guitar at home in 20 Forthlin Road. The song's upbeat tune and sweet style suggests that at the time he was zoned into Buddy Holly which, of course, was no bad thing.

John was never overly impressed with the song. When they started to introduce songs of their own into the Beatles' set in 1962, and 'I'll Be on May Way' was included, Lennon would apparently pull faces when he and Paul harmonised on the lead vocal. When Billy J. recorded it, George Martin double-tracked his vocal to keep it in the vein of John and Paul's original duet.

Despite John's reaction, the song is undeniably catchy. However, there is no denying the twee factor of couplets, such as, 'As the June light turns to moonlight'. Paul later concurred, admitting the song was "a little bit too June-moon for me, but these were very early songs and they worked out quite well".[3]

More to the point the tune captures from where McCartney – and Lennon – were coming in 1959, rather than to where they were headed in 1963, and although only slight the song made for a memorable debut flip-side for Billy J. Kramer.

From the remove of 2020, Billy J. recalled that, "When we recorded 'I'll Be on My Way' it came together very quickly. When people say it was just 'Moon in June' I think what the hell does that matter? It was a good pop song."[4]

Exactly!

Despite being a song the Beatles had introduced into their Cavern set to swell the number of original songs they performed, they chose not to record 'I'll Be on My Way' either as part of the Decca tape or as a studio track for EMI. As previously mentioned, however, on 4 April 1963 they did perform it for the BBC Radio Light Programme series *Side by Side*. Broadcast on 24 June that year, to date it has become the group's only known recording of the song to have surfaced and in this form it finally received a commercial release by the Beatles in 1994 as part of their *Live at the BBC* collection. (A demo is said to exist of this song which was probably given to Billy J., so that he would have had something to work from as he cut his first version prior to the Beatles' taped performance for the BBC.)

BILLY J. KRAMER with THE DAKOTAS
A-side: *DO YOU WANT TO KNOW A SECRET?* **(1:59)**
(McCartney-Lennon)
Northern Songs Ltd
Parlophone 5023
B-side: *I'LL BE ON MY WAY* (1:38)
(McCartney-Lennon)
Northern Songs Ltd
Both sides produced by George Martin
Engineers: Norman Smith and Geoff Emerick
Initially, both songs were taped in Studio 2, Abbey Road, on 21 March 1963, but the versions that were issued as the single were second attempts recorded on 14 April 1963, again in Studio 2.
John Lennon attended the recording session for 'Do You Want to Know a Secret?'
Released: Friday 26 April 1963

Entered the UK chart on 2 May 1963 at number 43, peaking at number 2 for two weeks (in both the *NME* chart and *Disc* it reached number 1, it was also placed at number 1 in the BBC's 'Pick of the Pops' chart).

This was Billy J. Kramer with the Dakotas' debut single and it remained on the charts for 15 weeks.

Kramer with the Dakotas' debut single was also released in the USA: Monday 10 June 1963, Liberty 55586. It did not chart.

It was re-released in the USA: 29 January 1964, Liberty 55667, with 'Bad to Me' on the B-side. This single also failed to chart, although 'Bad to Me' was to do much better in the USA when, in 1964, it was coupled for release with Billy J's UK number 1 'Little Children'.

In the UK, *Disc*'s singles reviewer Don Nicholl seemed to be hedging his bets by only giving Billy and the Dakotas 3 stars for their debut release. He called it a "pleasant light beater" that Billy sang "attractively and distinctively to the guitars." This, Nicholl said, achieved "a soothing effect that ought to sell."[5]

As for the B-side – the first genuine 'giveaway' – Nicholl sounds even more impressed: "'I'll Be on My Way' quickens things up slightly and there's a touch of Latin in the tempo as Kramer sings in a relaxed fashion that could bring him plenty of fans."[6]

Looking back on 'Do You Want to Know a Secret?', and his initial misgivings about it and his performance, Billy says: "It kicked. It caught the public imagination and I'm proud of it."[7]

1, 4 & 7 Billy J. Kramer interview with the author 19 October 2020.
2 *All We Are Saying: The Last Major Interview with John Lennon and Yoko Ono*, conducted by David Sheff (Sidgwick & Jackson, 2000) p.170.
3 *Paul McCartney, Many Years from Now* by Barry Miles (Vintage, 1998) p.180.
5 & 6 *Disc* music weekly, Edition 266, 27 April 1963, 'Disc Date' with Don Nicholl, p.9.

Chapter 50:
BILLY J. IN THE USA

It's interesting to note that unlike the Beatles, who made their major breakthrough in the USA in 1964 with 'I Want to Hold Your Hand', which went to number 1 when released on the USA's prestigious Capitol label, Billy J's singles were not released on Capitol.

As far as the US markets went, Kramer, like so many British artists, entered the orbit of a certain Dave Dexter Jr. who worked for Capitol in America. He had joined the company in 1943 and held the position of A&R Representative. American-based Capitol was not American-owned: since 1955, the British-owned, London-based EMI had owned it. Dexter's job was to approve or not approve records made by EMI's British artists for release in the USA on the Capitol label with all the whistles and bells that came with that honour.

There's no doubt he had a good ear, one that was particularly attuned to jazz. Among the great artists he signed to Capitol were Frank Sinatra, Kay Starr, Nat King Cole, Peggy Lee, Duke Ellington and Woody Herman. By anyone's standards that's a formidable track record. A mark of the esteem in which he was held is that in 1941 Count Basie wrote and recorded 'Diggin' for Dexter' and Jay McShann wrote and recorded 'Dex's Blues' in his honour.

However, Dave was not at all enamoured with rock 'n' roll when it broke big in the USA. Certainly, he was not a fan of Elvis Presley. It's likely he felt Frank Sinatra had a point when he described Presley's music as "deplorable, a rancid-smelling aphrodisiac."[1]

To contextualise, lest Dexter be viewed as unhip, it should be remembered that throughout the Fifties, jazz was considered the premier form of popular music and, as such, the music of an intelligent, ultra-hip, adult audience, whereas rock 'n' roll was something quite basic that juveniles might like until they grew up and gained a more sophisticated ear.

In the same way that Dexter was hip to jazz in the Fifties, so were many, many UK music fans, and they too also cocked a snook at rock 'n' roll. Alan Sytner, the first owner of Liverpool's Cavern Club, opened it in 1957 originally as an all-jazz establishment modelled on the legendary underground Parisian jazz haunt Le Caveau de la Huchette. Skiffle was allowed on 'open mic' nights, but in the early days of the Cavern, rock 'n' roll was most certainly 'persona non grata'.

Given his musical preferences, it's obvious Dexter was going to take a lot of persuading to promote any popular music artists who emanated from the UK, especially any purveyors of rock 'n' roll music. To be fair, up to this point, British artists in the main had not been particularly successful in the USA. Even so, Dexter did not help their cause and refused to have records released on Capitol even by substantial-selling UK artists, such as Cliff Richard, the Shadows, Adam Faith, Helen Shapiro and Matt Monro. (To refuse ace balladeer Matt a release on Capitol must have caused George Martin to feel particularly peeved, for his Parlophone label had been assigned the task of handling the marketing of Capitol releases in the UK, but he himself had no choice in selecting which records these would be.)

True to form, Dexter rejected Beatles product for Capitol and instead a licensing agreement was entered into with Vee-Jay, giving it the right (for five years) of first refusal on Beatles records in the USA. In doing so, Capitol did not so much turn down 'Please Please Me' and its follow-up 'From Me to You', as per the terms of the agreement, they were not actually offered to them. Thus, despite the amazing success of the Beatles in the UK throughout 1963, in the States Beatles product went out on what was considered a 'lesser' label. 'From Me to You' was released by Vee-jay on 27 May 1963, but did not sell. Even so, thanks largely to local radio play in Los Angeles by KRLA dee-jay Dick Biondi, 'From Me to You' made that station's chart at number 32 in August, after which it snuck into the 'Bubbling Under' chart of *Billboard*'s Hot 100, peaking at 116 in the same month before fading away.

Del Shannon, who had toured with the Beatles in the UK and had become enamoured by both the group and their music, released a cover of 'From Me to You' on Bigtop Records in early June 1963. Del's version entered the Hot 100 on 29 June and peaked at number 77, spending just four weeks in total on the chart and in doing so he became the first artist to have a hit in the USA with a Lennon-McCartney song.

The Beatles' fortunes in the USA took a massive turn for the better when Dexter says he heard 'I Want to Hold Your Hand' and immediately recognised how good that song was. Without hesitation, he says he ordered its Capitol release, which was accompanied by a full-on marketing campaign. Others contest Dexter's claim and say what changed things for the Beatles in the USA was not a 'eureka' moment on his behalf but that, in desperation, Brian Epstein made a personal call to Alan W. Livingston (President and later Chairman of the board at Capitol) to request 'I Want to Hold Your Hand' receive a major-label US release and that it was Livingston who personally ordered Dexter to release it on Capitol.

Whatever the machinations behind the scenes, the important thing was it *got* the major release it deserved and this certainly worked to make it a massive hit. On 1 February 1964, it became the Beatles' first chart-topping single in the USA, a position it held for seven weeks. This date not only marks the beginning of the Beatles' conquest of the USA, but also the beginning of what became known as the 'British Invasion'.

Despite the stunning success of the Beatles, Dexter still considered he knew best when it came to what Americans liked to hear, even to the extent of remixing Beatles recordings for US release, notoriously adding reverb and creating (from monaural tapes) a 'duophonic'* form of stereo. (To be fair to Dexter, by adding reverb he was just following what was regular practice for most British artist releases in the USA, not just those of the Beatles.)

(*Duophonic: a single monaural track would be split into two channels: they boosted the bass on the right and boosted the treble on the left. A split second delay was added between the channels which created a 'stereo' release.)

In his mind, Dexter made these alterations to make the Beatles' records more palatable to American audiences and there is no doubt that it was with this sonic identity that the group's albums sold by the truckload. At the time, American fans were blissfully unaware that the sound they heard had been compromised and so no one complained.

These days, Dexter's handiwork is often criticised, as was his habit of issuing Beatles albums to conform with the way *all* foreign releases in the USA were issued. In other words, they were released with different track listings to their British counterparts which was, again, the norm when a British album got a release in the USA. This was done largely because albums in the USA traditionally had fewer tracks. As a result, right up until *Sgt. Pepper*, Beatles albums released in the USA had fewer tracks and adhered strictly to the US marketing strategy of always including a few hits into the mix to make them even more marketable. (The titles of albums would be different as well, e.g., *Beatles '65* was *Beatles for Sale*. *A Hard Day's Night*, *Help!* and *Rubber Soul* retained their UK titles. *Revolver* also retained its UK title, but had three fewer tracks than its UK counterpart.) Albums, such as 1964's *Something New* and the aforementioned *Beatles '65*, would also carry the credit 'Produced by George Martin *and* Dave Dexter'. The UK version of *Help!* had one side of songs by the Beatles as featured in the film and the other of songs recorded by the Beatles, but which were not from the film. In the USA, the album was an OST release and included the songs from the film by the Beatles together with instrumental cuts performed by 'George Martin and Orchestra'. It also was credited as 'Produced by George Martin and Dave Dexter'.

The Beatles didn't like these habits, but Dexter considered he was just doing his job as he always had, adhering to company policy by compiling and releasing product in a way he believed was best suited to the American market.

It was not until *Sgt. Pepper* in 1967 that a Beatles' US album carried the exact same track listings as its UK counterpart. Apparently, Dexter's refusal to adhere to the UK's track listing caused him to be demoted, after which he claimed he had a job 'with no title'. By the mid-Seventies he left Capitol and became a writer for *Billboard*.

Unfortunately, Dexter's judgement and control affected other British artists who broke big in the US alongside the Beatles in 1963 and '64 during the 'British Invasion'. Consequently, he also rejected Parlophone stars the Hollies and Billy J. Kramer, Columbia's Gerry and the Pacemakers, Animals, Yardbirds and Dave Clark Five, HMV's Manfred Mann and the Swinging Blue Jeans. All of them were not considered suitable for major release on Capitol and received releases on labels such as Liberty and Imperial. He did, however, recommend Freddie and the Dreamers for Capitol, believing that they had what it took to be big in the USA, which pretty much says all we need to know …

There is no doubt that David Dexter Jr was a major player in the history of the Sixties British Invasion of the USA, but it is interesting to ponder how his negative view of UK popular music stars of that era impacted on Billy J's eventual Stateside career. Given Billy was the first of Epstein's 'stable' of artists to enjoy considerable UK success with Lennon-McCartney songs that fans could *not* get anywhere else, it seems likely, had someone else been listening, Billy would have enjoyed the status of having his records released on the Capitol label and consequently would have received greater promotion, which in turn would surely have led to even more hits and a higher profile. Significantly that *is* what happened to Peter and Gordon: their first three singles were released on Capitol in the USA and all three carried A-sides that were Lennon-McCartney originals the Beatles did not record and all three were big Stateside hits for them.

Dexter died aged 74 at home in Sherman Oaks, California, on 19 April 1990.

---

1 *Now Dig This*, a UK music magazine, November 2010 edition: the Frank Sinatra quotation appears in an article entitled 'I Hate Rock 'N' Roll' by Spencer Leigh pages 6–11.

Chapter 51:
GOOD TO ME

The euphoria of scoring a hit record, especially one that had reached number 1 in the *NME* chart (the bible for all music fans in the early Sixties and the chart Radio Luxembourg adhered to), must have been like scoring the winning goal in a Cup Final. For one incandescent moment, Billy J. found himself full square in the spotlight with everyone calling his name. It also set the challenge to find a follow-up that would not only return him to the chart but emulate the success of 'Do You Want to Know a Secret?'.

There would have been no shortage of offers. An artist with a number 1 record always attracts a lot of attention. At the time, Billy J. did not write his own songs and so, given how record labels operated back then, it would have been his producer George Martin's job to come up with the goods. Denmark Street would have been on red alert, its songwriters ready with songs for Billy J. and George Martin's consideration.

But Billy J. had no need to go knocking on the doors of Tin Pan Alley. The search for that tricky second hit single had already been taken care of: John Lennon had not only written a brand new Lennon-McCartney original especially for him, but its B-side was going to be a very early Lennon song (from 1958). Kramer was on a roll. He was truly blessed, although his good fortune had to first survive a difficult social encounter with John.

When, in mid-June, 'Do You Want to Know a Secret?' was still riding high in the UK Top 5, just behind 'From Me to You' which was the current number 1, an incident occurred that put Billy J. and John Lennon's friendship in jeopardy.

Earlier in the year, in the early hours of Monday 8 April, John and Cynthia's son John Charles Julian Lennon had been born in Liverpool. By then Cynthia and John were living with John's Aunt Mimi in 'Mendips', her house in Woolton. During the rest of April, while Cynthia was at home with Julian and Mimi, John and his fellow Beatles were committed to a gruelling schedule of live performances around the UK, but on Thursday 28 April suddenly they had a break. Paul, George and Ringo immediately flew off to Tenerife for a 12-day holiday, while John and Brian flew together to Torremolinos in Spain, leaving Cynthia and Julian at home with Aunt Mimi.

Returning home from their respective holidays in the sun, it was immediately back on the treadmill: wall-to-wall bookings for the Beatles and a bevy of acts for Brian to manage, each competing for his attention. Through May and June, the Beatles toured the UK with Roy Orbison.

Unfortunately, while they had been in Torremolinos, back in Liverpool speculation had been rife as to just what fun in the sun Brian and John had been enjoying. Brian's homosexuality was a thinly guarded secret in his home town and now he and John had provided the gossipmongers all they needed to fuel the ever-voracious rumour machine. As has been noted at this time, homosexuality was not just *'infra dig'*, it was illegal: men could go to prison for being gay. Rumours such as those generated by Brian and John's Spanish sojourn bordered on the scandalous. For anyone in the public eye they could prove ruinous, especially if they got into the newspapers.

The very first time after their holidays that the Beatles had a moment to stand still was on 18 June. The occasion was Paul's 21st birthday party. His Aunt Jin had kindly agreed to host this at her house in Huyton. A marquee had been erected in the back garden and there was a big cake for Paul to cut. How special it must have been for Paul to be 21 and at the same time number 1 in the UK charts ('From Me to You') and able to celebrate his success surrounded by his family and close friends.

Even more than that, Paul's new 17-year-old girlfriend, actress Jane Asher, was by his side to join in the celebrations. Bright, auburn-haired, good-looking and fashionable, she was very much at the heart of the burgeoning London scene. As Cynthia Lennon observed, Paul's family and friends could not help but be impressed: "Jane was different from the girls Paul had been out with previously. The daughter of a psychiatrist father and a music-teacher mother, she was highly intelligent and cultured. She had strong inner confidence, with a maturity and grace way beyond her years. Paul, whose working-class background couldn't have been more different, was bowled over, and from the day they met they became an item."[1]

As well as Paul's family and friends, many colleagues from the music scene in Liverpool attended, such as Billy J., the Fourmost, Gerry and the Pacemakers and the Beatles' champion from the Cavern, Bob Wooler. From beyond the Liverpool scene, hitmakers the Shadows turned up (they'd been playing a show in Blackpool).

Unknown to Bob Wooler, John Lennon had arrived at the event tired, in a sour mood and having not eaten much, added to which very soon he had had too much to drink. At the best of times John and alcohol were not good news. As Bob, John and Brian Epstein were walking from the back door of the house into the garden, Wooler unwisely made a comment to John about his Spanish holiday with Brian, which caused the Beatle to immediately kick off. He snapped and attacked Bob. They were the only three people to actually witness the attack and none of them *ever* revealed what was actually said, although in her autobiography of 2003, Cynthia Lennon said John accused Wooler of calling him 'a queer'. Whatever *was* said, John's response was swift and sharp: he gave poor Bob a battering that put him in hospital with a black eye, bruised ribs and torn knuckles … although he was not kept in overnight.

While Brian drove the bleeding DJ to the hospital, back at Paul's party the rogue Beatle was not finished.

His hackles raised, John went into the marquee where Billy J. was standing with Rose Leech, a girl he had invited to the party, and Billy Hatton from the Fourmost. Unfortunately, John made a grab at Rose who responded by hitting him. Billy Hatton leapt to Rose's defence and when Kramer intervened, John threw a punch in his direction. Billy J. held back from retaliating, but John was still not done. He began berating Kramer by telling him he was 'nothing' and that the Beatles were 'the top'.[2]

Billy J. tells it this way: "John was with Cynthia and went to touch my girlfriend, but she resisted him and so he tried to smack me, but Billy (Hatton) and I pushed him away. John then said some unpleasant things to me, but we told him he was drunk, which he was. Billy (Hatton) and I then went out and got a taxi, put him and Cynthia in it, and sent him home."[3]

The new Beatles press officer, Tony Barrow, who was already doing his best to keep the secret of John and Cynthia's marriage from leaking out to the press, now had a brand-new, potentially scandalous secret to keep. If it – and the background to it – got out, it could have potentially ruined the Beatles' burgeoning career. When the press eventually picked up on the scent of Wooler's beating, for a short while Tony managed to fend off the national press. This was fortunate because John was initially unrepentant. Thankfully, Brian Epstein's very wise counsel prevailed and by the time Don Short of the *Daily Mirror* spoke to him, the Beatle was in conciliatory mood. Three days after the incident, on Friday 21 June 1963, the *Mirror*'s back page carried a fulsome apology from John to Bob beneath the headline "Beatle in Brawl Says 'Sorry I Socked You'". (The article said that John had sent a telegram of apology to Wooler and quoted John as saying at the time he was too inebriated to know what he was doing.) Fortunately, no reference was made to *why* John had acted in this way. In the article, Bob Wooler merely commented, 'I don't know why he did it.'

It was a horrible incident, after which Cynthia said John felt very ashamed, as so he should have done. She also said to her knowledge he never behaved like that again.

In the aftermath, Bob Wooler and Brian took the counsel of the same Liverpool solicitor Rex Makin, the result of which was that Bob agreed to an out-of-court settlement for which he received £200.

Wooler and Lennon did become reconciled, Bob accepted John's apology, although he believed the telegram to have been Brian's work, not John's.

In later years, Wooler would rail against published accounts of the incident that he read. He was particularly scathing about Albert Goldman's gorily embellished account that appeared in his 1988 biography *The Lives of John Lennon*. In conversations with Spencer Leigh for the latter's excellent biography, *The Best of Fellas*, Wooler described Goldman's version of events as 'preposterous' and 'absolute nonsense'.[4]

To his credit, Wooler never sought to exploit the incident and never revealed to anyone exactly what happened that night.

Billy J. was upset with the manner in which John had behaved towards his girlfriend and himself and was in no mood to accept the second-hand apology conveyed to him by Brian Epstein on behalf of the remorseful Beatle. Billy insisted that, for it to mean anything, John's apology had to be given in person. And this is what John finally did, after which normal service resumed between the two musicians.

Billy and John's reconciliation was beneficial to them both, as John later commented, "'Bad to Me' I wrote … specifically for Billy J. Kramer. I was on holiday with Brian Epstein in Spain, where the rumours went around that he and I were having a love affair. Well, it was almost a love affair, but not quite. It was never consummated. But it was a pretty intense relationship … I remember playing him the song 'Bad to Me'. That was a commissioned song, done for Billy J. Kramer, who was another of Brian's singers. From Liverpool."[5]

'Bad to Me' was a great pop song and in *NME* it became Billy J's second consecutive UK number 1 and, significantly, his first in *Record Retailer*.

Just where and when John told Billy J. he had written a new song for him is a moot point. It might well have been *before* Paul's 21st party, when Billy J. was part of a series of 'Mersey Beat Showcase' evenings featuring the Beatles, Gerry and the Pacemakers, and Billy J. Kramer with the Dakotas, as headliners. The last one of these shows had taken place on Sunday 16 June at the Odeon Cinema in Romford, Essex, when all three of the headline acts were at numbers 1, 2 and 3, respectively, in the UK singles chart, with 'From Me to You', 'I Like It' and 'Do You Want to Know a Secret?', which was not a bad night's entertainment for the fans!

Another likely date on which John could have informed Billy J. that he had a new song for him was shortly after Paul's birthday bash on Sunday 23 June. On this date, the Beatles, Billy J. with the Dakotas and an all-Liverpool cast had gathered in the Alpha TV Studios, Aston, Birmingham, for a special edition of ABC TV's *Thank Your Lucky Stars*. Filmed during the afternoon of the 23rd, the show was screened on Saturday evening 29 June with the modified title of *Lucky Stars Summer Spin* to indicate that it was a special edition featuring an all-Mersey cast. That such a show was put together was testament to the massive impact the Beatles and other Liverpool artists were making on the UK music scene in 1963.

"John told me he'd written a song for me, but he didn't play it to me, he just told me about it. He didn't give me a demo. He said the next time I was at Abbey Road he would come along and play it for me. I didn't hear it until he turned up at my next session at Abbey Road and sat at the piano and played 'Bad to Me'. I was blown away."[6]

John was true to his word. When Billy J. turned up at Abbey Road studios for a recording session, John joined them. Billy recalls that as John sat at the piano to sing 'Bad to Me' it was the very first time he had heard the new song John had previously told him he'd written especially for him. Not only did John play the song through for Billy while sitting at the piano, he showed the Dakotas the chords.

Having delivered 'Bad to Me', John was not done. Billy J. says he remained with them in the studio and ran through a second song he had brought for them called 'I Call Your Name'. This was, of course, one of the first songs John had ever written and was now destined to be the B-side of Billy J's next single. As with 'Bad to Me', John stayed in the studio and helped steer Billy J. and the Dakotas through the music and lyrics as they recorded it.

This recording session was hugely memorable for Billy J.: "I thought 'Bad to Me' was a good song, although it didn't seem earth-shattering at the time. When he played it on piano he did it in a very simplistic way, but there was something special about the whole package of John singing to me. I can't describe what it was like to spend time with John Lennon in a room together. It was just like magic."[7]

The magic wasn't quite over for Billy J. that day, for John then asked (and Mike Maxfield of the Dakotas remembers this very clearly as well) if he could run another song by them for their opinion. The song John played to Billy J. and Mike was 'I Want to Hold Your Hand'. Billy J. was mightily impressed, so much so he asked if he could have that one too! John simply laughed and said no, he couldn't because it was going to be the Beatles' next single.

"I learned 'Bad to Me' there and then. Within three hours I'd learned and recorded it. At first it wasn't working out because I had a discrepancy with George Martin about the key. He wanted me to do it in E and I wanted to do it in D. I'd found it a little too high for me, but George disagreed. In the end I said can we move on to the next song and we knocked off 'I Call Your Name' in 20 minutes. We recorded that song before the Beatles did. I liked it because it was a rocker. I said let's put that out and put 'Bad to Me' out as another single, but George said no because I sounded too much like the Beatles on 'I Call Your Name'. We broke for lunch and when we came back I said to George, 'Come on, give me a break, let me do 'Bad to Me' in D', which we then did, he relented, and we had it within just a few takes."[8]

When George Martin used the fact that Billy sounded too much like the Beatles on 'I Call Your Name' to refuse releasing it as a single in its own right, Billy said he had been quite taken aback, commenting to the producer: "I sound like the Beatles? How bad is that?!"[9]

Billy's memories of his recording sessions were that, while George Martin kept his distance, he found he did have an ally within the production team: "I don't think George was convinced by me. I was overwhelmed at the time. I took advice mostly from Norman Smith, the engineer. He was the one who encouraged me to stand up for myself. As I became more experienced he would say, 'You tell them if you don't like it, Billy.'"[10]

Ever critical of his own work since being a choirboy, Billy J. had always doubted himself and his abilities. He worried every record he cut wasn't going to make it. As his singles climbed the charts he would worry that they would stall and start to slip. Tony Barrow, NEMS press officer, commented, "Billy J. Kramer was his own worst critic … He reckoned that each new record was going to be a loser … It was a good thing in a way, but he would have had an easier time had he built up to a No.1 record, instead of having No.1s thrust upon him at an early stage. Each success gave him more to live up to. He found this very difficult."[11]

As we know, by his own admission back then, Billy's sense of insecurity was something he was battling on a daily basis. Each single was a personal challenge, a search for perfection. From the moment a single was released he would regard its success or otherwise as a reflection on himself. If a record did not do as well as others before it, he blamed himself: "It was me as a young guy thinking, 'What have I done wrong here?' Unfortunately, that makes you chase to try and top what you've already done and it's the worst thing in the world to do. It took me a long time to get to a point where I could say to myself so long as I do something really well it's out of my control what happens to it."[12]

There is no doubt that Billy found the sudden fame and popularity that came with the hit records difficult to reconcile with his personal view of himself: "It's a very hard thing when you are this self-conscious chubby kid: you do a thing on TV in Manchester and you go back to Liverpool and you find girls outside your house and you're thinking what the hell's going on? It was quite a lot to take in. You ask yourself, 'How did I become so sexy overnight? They weren't doing that before!' It was disorientating, it was embarrassing, though I think home helped keep me grounded. I look at it now and think what a thing to have experienced, but somehow I *did*, I did get through it."[13]

In balancing the considerable rewards of fame and success with the formidable stresses that accompanied them, Billy J. was more or less on his own. Brian Epstein was having to do the same for himself. He might have been older, better educated and from a different social background, but the success of the Beatles, Billy J. and his other protégés was a steep learning curve for their manager as well. Then, as well for Brian, there were his concerns about his sexuality and his inherent sense of loneliness. To the outside world, Brian may have exuded charm, sophistication and a sense of unflappability, but inwardly he was plagued by demons of his own. Like Billy, Brian Epstein would seek refuge from his anxieties in alcohol and medication. And so, while he might suggest a week in a health farm if he thought Billy needed to lose some weight, there was no counselling as such on offer for his charges. In those days, people were less likely to talk about their anxieties and for males you were expected to keep things to yourself, to laugh things off, to internalise your concerns … to do otherwise was regarded as a sign of weakness or as unmanly.

Billy's relationship with the Dakotas only added to his sense of isolation. He was not part of a group with whom he could confide or who would share with him what was happening to them. He had no one to turn to. Everything was internalised. Groups like the Beatles had that strength of being four people in it together, but Billy was on his own. The banter between friends and colleagues, which is so often a way of releasing and dealing with stress, was not a regular or daily part of Billy's working life. "I was on my own and it was crazy."[14]

Many years later, Billy's cousin Arthur Ashton, who had been with him in the Phantoms, hit the nail on the head when he commented to him: "You got yourself in some hot water at times with your drinking and that, but I'm sure if you'd been with us that wouldn't have happened, we'd have given you a lot more support than what the Dakotas did."[15]

'Bad to Me' was an immediate hit. It is a wonderfully focused recording with a very appealing double-tracked vocal from Billy J. Over 50 years later, it still sounds fresh, supremely concise and packed with hooks, the very definition of an automatic hit, a wonderful slice of pop perfection. In an article entitled *George Martin: 20 Great Non-Beatles productions* published in *Rolling Stone* magazine on 9 March 2016, it came in at number 3 and received fulsome praise: "from the skipping beat and the lilting guitar hook Martin gave the song an uncannily Beatles-esque air: lovelorn, wistful and gently jangly … it was another feather in the producer's burgeoning cap."[16]

It was released on Friday 26 July 1963.

Not long after (19–24 August) Billy J. Kramer with the Dakotas supported the Beatles for six nights in Bournemouth, where they were headlining at the Gaumont Cinema on Westover Road. Both groups played two shows each evening and stayed at the Palace Court Hotel. (It was here during this week that photographer Robert Freeman shot the cover portrait for the Beatles' next album, *With the Beatles*, the famous 'half shadow' photograph that was very much in the style of Astrid Kircherr's wonderful photographs of the group she had taken in Hamburg.)

During this residency, Brian Epstein, the Beatles and the Dakotas helped Billy J. celebrate his 20th birthday. The Beatles acknowledged the close relationship that had developed between themselves and Billy J. when they sent him a telegram that read 'Happy Birthday from your proud parents, the Beatles'.[17]

What a birthday it must have been: not only was he having fun with the Fab Four, but 'Bad to Me' was racing up the chart. It was number 3 on 21 August and by the 28th had hit number 1, where it stayed for three weeks. (It lost the top spot to the Beatles themselves with 'She Loves You'.) No wonder the Beatles signed their telegram 'your parents' for Billy J. was almost like a professional offspring keeping it in the family for them with two massive hits, both of which John and Paul had written (as well as providing the B-sides). Not only that but Billy J. had already recorded a third Lennon-McCartney song written especially for him in readiness for release as his third single. There is no denying his success was hugely enhanced by his relationship with the Beatles. Equally, he was doing a great job on their tunes, of which they were equally proud.

John and Paul would not have kept writing songs for him if they had not thought he was the real deal.

Billy remembers that birthday celebration in Bournemouth well: "Everybody was on the stage, we set the gear up and jammed. Most of the time Paul would play drums. Later I was backstage with John and he was reading the *Melody Maker* and he told me the Beatles had just got into the charts in the States and he showed me the article." (This was a reference to the brief success of 'From Me to You' as it bubbled under *Billboard*'s Hot 100.)[18]

The front page of the 24 August edition of *Disc* music weekly not only carried the news that Billy J. was already at number 1 in its chart with 'Bad to Me', but also featured a photograph of the Dakotas and the Beatles helping Billy to celebrate his birthday while he was busy cutting the cake *Disc* had thoughtfully provided for the occasion.

It was a truly momentous week for both Billy J. *and* the Dakotas, for not only was Billy riding high in the UK charts with them with 'Bad to Me', but the Dakotas themselves were enjoying their one and only time on the charts in their own right with an instrumental tune called 'The Cruel Sea'. It moved between number 19 and 22 during their week in Bournemouth before rising again to eventually peak at number 18 on 11 September.

For Billy J. Kramer, the success of 'Bad to Me' provided proof with which he could reassure himself that he was not just a one-hit wonder. Further proof of the Beatles' personal and professional appreciation of his achievements came when, after a Granada TV show on which he had sung several Lennon-McCartney songs, Brian Epstein presented him with a 'substantial' cheque from the group for "believing in their songs before anyone else."[19]

Of course, despite such gestures, Billy J. Kramer remained super-critical, fearful that the next release was not going to be as successful as his last.

BILLY J. KRAMER with THE DAKOTAS
BAD TO ME **(2:18)**
(Lennon-McCartney)
Northern Songs Ltd
Parlophone R 5049
B-side: ***I CALL YOUR NAME*** **(2:00)**
(Lennon-McCartney)
Northern Songs Ltd
Producer: George Martin
Main engineers: Norman Smith and Geoff Emerick

Billy J. says John Lennon was present in the studio when both songs were recorded.

The only date I have been able to trace for the recording of 'Bad to Me' is Wednesday 26 June 1963, but as John was in the studio with Billy, this is unlikely for on this date the Beatles performed in Newcastle-upon-Tyne at the Majestic Ballroom after which, in their

Newcastle hotel room, John and Paul penned 'She Loves You'. It is unlikely, therefore, John would have been present earlier in the day down in London at Abbey Road with Billy and the Dakotas.

On Monday 1 July, the Beatles did attend Abbey Road to record 'She Loves You' and 'I'll Get You'. Originally a session had been booked for them between 14:30 to 17:30, but this did not happen because both songs were recorded later in the day between 17:00 until 20:45. Could it be, therefore, 'Bad to Me' was recorded in that earlier time slot, with John in attendance ahead of his evening session with the Beatles?

Released: Friday 26 July 1963.

'Bad to Me' entered the UK charts on 1 August 1963 at number 34. It reached number 3 on 21 August and peaked at number 1 on 28 August where it remained for a total of three weeks. Altogether it spent 14 weeks on the charts, ten of which were in the Top 20. It was dislodged from number 1 by the Beatles with 'She Loves You' on 18 September 1963.

The single, featuring the same A- and B-sides as in the UK, was released in the USA on Liberty 55626 on 23 September 1963, but did not chart.

It was re-released in the USA on Imperial 66027 on 30 March 1964, with 'Little Children' as the B-side. It had the distinction of being the only debut single by an artist on the *Billboard* Hot 100 for which both sides made the Top 10. 'Little Children' spent 15 weeks on the Hot 100 and peaked at number 7 on 13 June. 'Bad to Me' peaked at number 9 on 27 June 1964 and spent 10 weeks on the Hot 100.

In the UK, on 2 November, *Disc* music weekly's singles reviewer, Don Nicholl, got it right by giving the record a coveted 'DNT' review ('a disc that looks like spinning right to the top'). He considered Lennon and McCartney had served Billy "commercially" with both songs on his new single, especially 'Bad to Me', which he described as "very easy on the ear with a catchy top line that moves pleasantly and with familiarity," one that Billy J. sang "affably to a good dancing accompaniment in which the rough sound of piano is going to pull a lot of attention and assist sales considerably." Nicholl couldn't see it missing, calling it "a powerful hit parade follow-up" (to 'Do You Want to Know a Secret?') for Billy. And, of course, Don was bang on the money this time.[20a]

As for the B-side, 'I Call Your Name', Nicholl said it followed a "steady middle path with the singer sounding a little more edgy", although he considered the lyrics to be "weak".[20b]

The success of 'Bad to Me' made Billy J. Kramer with the Dakotas one of the hottest properties on the UK pop scene. As autumn approached, with just his first two releases, Billy J. had already been present on the UK singles chart for a total of 29 weeks.

The haunting 'I Call Your Name' was one of the very first songs John Lennon had ever written, composed in his tiny 'box' bedroom at 'Mendips' during the second half of 1958/ early '59. Paul remembers this as a tune they worked on together but which had been John's original idea. In 1980, in one of his last interviews, John described it to *Playboy* journalist David Sheff as "my effort at a kind of early blues". Paul pondered that the lyric 'I call your name, but you're not there' could have been, albeit subconsciously, a reference to John's mother Julia who had only recently passed away when he wrote them.

'I Call Your Name' was subsequently recorded by the Beatles themselves on 1 March 1964. It featured John on lead vocal and George Harrison playing his recently acquired 12-string Rickenbacker 360/12 guitar that he had used for the first time on 'You Can't Do That' (recorded Tuesday 25 February 1964). Their version was in the mix for the soundtrack of 'Hard Day's Night', but director Dick Lester considered that it sounded too similar to 'You Can't Do That' and so it was not used. Instead it was released on 19 June 1964 as track 2, side 1 of the Beatles' *Long Tall Sally* EP.

Addendum: *Thank Your Lucky Stars*
Lucky Stars Summer Spin
Saturday evening 29 June 1963
'TV's top pop music show begins the summer season with a tribute to the Liverpool beat scene.' The all-star 'Scouse' bill presents
THE BEATLES
GERRY and the Pacemakers
THE VERNON GIRLS
KENNETH COPE*
with the Breakaways
BILLY J. KRAMER
THE BIG THREE
LEE CURTIS
THE SEARCHERS
A panel of teenagers
and disc jockey
KENNETH COPE
comment on the latest
American releases in
Spin-a-Disc

On this occasion the show was compered by Pete Murray, not Brian Matthew who many remember was its usual presenter.

*Kenneth Cope (or Ken Cope as his name appeared on his one and only single, the truly dreadful 'Hands off, Stop Mucking About') went on to become famous as an actor, making his name playing 'Marty' from the popular TV series *Randall and Hopkirk (Deceased)*. Liverpool-born Cope was appearing in *Coronation Street* when his single was released in May 1963 on the Pye record label. The Breakaways were a Liverpool trio who are one of British popular music's best-kept secrets. One of the girls, Vicki Haseman married Joe Brown and their daughter is singer Sam Brown. After an amazingly successful career as a backing and session singer, sadly Vicki died in 1995. The Breakaways were renowned session singers and among the many recordings on which they appear are 'Hey Joe' by Jimi Hendrix, 'Trains and Boats and Planes' by Burt Bacharach and 'You're My World' by Cilla Black.

On this edition of *Lucky Stars*, the Beatles performed 'From Me to You' and 'I Saw Her Standing There', Gerry and the Pacemakers 'I Like It', Kenneth Cope 'Hands off, Stop Mucking About', the Vernons Girls 'He'll Never Come Back', Billy J. Kramer with the Dakotas 'Do You Want to Know a Secret?', the Big Three 'By the Way', Lee Curtis 'Let's Stomp', the Searchers 'Sugar and Spice'.

Such was the success of this special edition of *Thank Your Lucky Stars* (it drew an estimated audience of more than 6 million) it was followed by a second all-Merseyside edition broadcast on 21 December 1963. This second show featured the Beatles (singing four songs), Gerry and the Pacemakers, Billy J. Kramer with the Dakotas (singing 'I'll Keep You Satisfied'), the Searchers, Cilla Black (singing 'Love of the Loved'), the Breakaways and Tommy Quickly. Bob Wooler appeared as 'Spin-a-Disc's' guest compere and one of the teenage jury members was a mop-topped Liverpudlian lad named Billy Butler (later to become a legendary broadcaster on Radio Merseyside). At the end of the programme, George Martin presented the Beatles with gold discs for 'She Loves You' and 'I Want to Hold Your Hand'.

1 *John* by Cynthia Lennon, (Hodder & Stoughton, 2005) p.156.
2 *John Lennon: The Definitive Biography: The Anniversary Edition*, Ray Coleman (Pan, 2000) p.317.

3, 6, 8, 9, 10, 12, 13, 14, 15 & 18 Billy J. Kramer interview with the author 19 October 2020.
4 *The Best of Fellas* by Spencer Leigh (Drivegreen Publications Limited in association with Jim Turner, 2002) pp. 182–186.
5 *All We Are Saying: The Last Major Interview with John Lennon and Yoko Ono*, conducted by David Sheff (Sidgwick & Jackson, 2000) p.170.
7 *Do You Want to Know a Secret?: The Autobiography of Billy J. Kramer*, by Billy J Kramer with Alyn Shipton (Equinox Publishing, 2016): p.49.
11 *Billy J. Kramer with The Dakotas EP Collection*, Spencer Leigh liner notes, (I Can See For Miles Records Ltd. SEECD 422, 1995).
16 *George Martin: 20 Great Non-Beatles productions*, by Jason Heller, Al Shipley, Keith Harris, Richard Gehr & Patrick Doyle, published in *Rolling Stone* magazine, 9 March 2016.
17 *Yeah Yeah Yeah*, by Nick Churchill, (Natula Publications, 2011) p.26–27.
19 *Do You Want to Know a Secret?: The Autobiography of Billy J. Kramer*, by Billy J Kramer with Alyn Shipton (Equinox Publishing, 2016): p.68.
20a & 20b *Disc* music weekly, 20 July 1963, Edition 278, 'Disc Date' with Don Nicholl, p.8.

Chapter 52:
KEEPING BILLY J. SATISFIED

Two singles into his career, both of which had reached number 1 in *NME* (and thus number 1 on Radio Luxembourg), the second had also reached the summit of the *Record Retailer* sales chart and therefore was an undisputed *national* number 1. This was an amazing start to Billy J's career. Whatever happened next, 1963 was already a massive year for him during which he had most definitely become a 'star'.

Like Brian Epstein's other artists, the Beatles and Gerry and the Pacemakers, Billy J. had started at the very top. Of those three artists, however, Billy J. was most probably the one least well-equipped psychologically to deal with success. He was a young man who, as has already been mentioned, from an early age had always been highly self-critical and lacking in self-confidence. His relationship 'with' the Dakotas was doing little to strengthen his self-belief. By his own admission, the relentless pressure of fame and the need to stay at the top caused him to take refuge in drink and drugs.

Brian Epstein's intransigence regarding the unsatisfactory relationship between Billy and the Dakotas did not help the situation in which they all found themselves. To outsiders it would have seemed there was little to complain about. Billy was enjoying runaway success and alongside him the Dakotas were also sharing the limelight. But hindsight clearly shows *none* of the parties were as happy as they should have been: Brian, Billy and the group were caught in what we might call a 'Catch-22' situation. "Brian was very good to me. I was a working-class kid from Liverpool and thanks to him I'd enjoyed incredible success: my name was all over the place. I was number 1 and didn't want to rock the boat. Maybe if I'd been older, say 25 and not 20, and had had some experience, maybe I'd have stood toe to toe with him and said, 'I'm not dealing with this', but I couldn't. He'd made it happen for me."[1]

Despite his concerns, Billy always understood that Brian had his best interests at heart and this was reflected in late September 1963 when Brian set up a new production company entitled 'Billy J. Kramer Limited', of which he was a director.

These were fast-moving times for Billy and his success placed huge demands on him. Accordingly, while sitting on top of the world with 'Bad to Me' was a very good place to be, with it came the *increased* pressure of whether Billy 'could make number 1 for a third time?' With Paul providing his third A-side there seemed every chance that he could. It was a strong tune, very much in the style of 'Bad to Me': upbeat and packed with melodic hooks, 'I'll Keep You Satisfied' was immediately catchy.

Produced by George Martin and recorded with the reassuring presence of both John and Paul in the studio on the day, artistically, Billy was in sparkling form.

In his official biography (and with typical McCartney understatement) Paul considers 'I'll Keep You Satisfied' as, "A good one."[2]

He further explained the reasoning behind composing 'giveaways': "Billy J. was having a bit of success and because he was out of the same stable as us, it made sense for us, if we weren't having to write a lot of stuff for ourselves, to knock off a couple for friends. It was pretty much co-written: John and I sat down and purposely wrote it for Billy J. in a couple of hours."[3]

Significantly Paul also revealed an abiding (and much justified) personal affection for this particular 'giveaway': "This one is one I still like. I find myself whistling it in the garden."[4]

As with its predecessors, 'I'll Keep You Satisfied' was hot out of the blocks, released on Friday 1 November, within five weeks (4 December) it had climbed to number 4 in the Top 10. Unfortunately, that is where it stopped: it did not progress to become Billy J. Kramer's third number 1 as was expected. The next edition of the chart found the record had slipped to number 6.

It might not have made the top, but by anybody's standards the fact that 'I'll Keep You Satisfied' had nevertheless made the Top 5 was certainly no mean achievement ... except maybe for Billy.

Even to this day Billy J. blames himself for the record not making that coveted number 1 position and pinpoints the decline of 'I'll Keep You Satisfied' to one specific live TV performance.

Brian Epstein was on a roll and secured a place for Billy J. with the Dakotas on the UK's most popular and prestigious TV variety show: *Val Parnell's Sunday Night at the London Palladium*. They were booked to appear on 27 October. The show was 1960s prime time television with a huge audience (sometimes numbering 15 million). Its reputation was second to none: most artists would have given their right arm to appear on it, but for Billy J. it was a daunting prospect that went right to the core of his personal insecurities. "It stopped me in my tracks and I asked Brian if we could decline the offer since I was very nervous and I didn't feel that I had earned the right to walk the same stage as Judy Garland, Frank Sinatra and artists of that calibre."[5]

Of course Epstein would have none of this. From his managerial perspective he understood only that a performance on this show could increase Kramer's popularity and help establish him as a nationally recognised star for years to come. To convince Kramer he was right, all Brian would have felt he had to do was direct Billy J. to the impact the Beatles made on their first appearance on the show just two weeks before Billy's, on 13 October. It had catapulted them from teen sensation into a national sensation and in the process brought the mainstream media on board. Footage of the Beatles' performance, unfortunately, no longer exists, but a backstage interview and further scenes after the show as they were leaving appeared on ITN news the next evening (Monday 14 October 1963) and can still be seen. Also, the next day's newspapers were full of stories about their performance and the reaction it had produced on audiences both inside and outside the theatre. From that moment on, the word 'Beatlemania' became imbedded within the national consciousness. The professionally cynical UK press had found a phenomenon that took even their 'seen-it-all-before' breath away.

No wonder Epstein was convinced that an appearance by Billy J. on the *Palladium* would be a hugely positive career move.

In the UK entertainment world, a headline appearance on *Sunday Night at the Palladium* was very big news indeed, a pinnacle of achievement, especially for an act that appealed mainly to teenagers. It was a sure sign just how popular that particular star had become and therefore destined to receive much pre-publicity.

Typical of the reaction to Kramer's pending appearance was the edition of *Disc* published immediately ahead of Billy J. with the Dakotas' performance. It carried a four-page special supplement in which there were exclusive features on Cliff Richard, Billy Fury and two written especially for the readers by Brian Poole and Billy J. themselves. Entitled 'I'm So Excited, and Nervous, over that Palladium TV Show', Kramer wrote that his feelings about appearing on such a prestigious show "were still in a whirl" and that he was "wildly excited and dead nervous all at the same time." Explaining that he had always hoped he would one day appear on the *Palladium*, Billy said he just didn't think it would be so soon into his career. In the article, Billy J. said he had told Brian Epstein he was nervous but his manager had quickly allayed his fears by saying: "Billy, if I didn't think you were up to it, I would never have accepted the booking. I am sure it will be a great success", and that he took Epstein's confidence in him as a great compliment. In the wake of Epstein's confidence, he had made his mind up immediately "to do everything humanly possible to live up to Brian's expectations." In order to do so, Kramer noted that he and the Dakotas had been "rehearsing like mad" and that, "Having them with me means a tremendous amount."[6a]

Kramer took the opportunity to add, "It looks as if I shall be singing my new disc on the night. The title is 'I'll Keep You Satisfied' and it's written, you know, by John Lennon and Paul McCartney."[6b]

Beyond his forthcoming performance at the Palladium, Billy J's article reflected just how well his career was progressing as he mentioned his excitement at being part of the forthcoming Beatles Xmas Show along with the Fourmost, Cilla Black and Tommy Quickly, how thrilled he was at the possibility he'd be making a film in 1964 and how excited he was to be going to the States to help promote the release of 'Bad to Me'. Billy made sure to thank all his fans who had sent messages of good luck for his Palladium show before concluding, "Tell you something special … Mum and Dad are coming to London for the day. They'll be in the audience. So I've got to do my best for them, too!"[6c]

Clearly the Palladium was a very big deal for Billy (and no doubt the Dakotas). Expectations were running high, yet reading between the lines it's obvious Billy was anxious. He knew a lot was expected of him and in the build up to the show he just kept piling the pressure on himself to do well.

The very thought of stepping out on that world-famous stage prompted his old self-doubts to resurface and during the weeks preceding the show he barely slept and his anxieties caused him to drink too much and take amphetamines. To try and overcome his nerves he had a special suit made for his appearance. Just as he had 'disguised' himself in the early days with the Coasters by dressing in the gold lamé suit he had had especially made, ahead of the Palladium he felt a new stage suit could help him once more hide behind a stage persona of his own making. However, Epstein did not like Billy J's new suit and immediately had a different one made for him which he insisted Billy J. wore instead. Although Billy J. would later say Epstein was right about the suit (as he was about so many things "that my immaturity did not allow me to see"), at the time of the show Epstein's reaction to it had made him feel "very controlled" which "did nothing to help my confidence".[7]

Adding greatly to his anxiety was that he had been asked to sing edited versions of his songs: "They (the Dakotas) wanted me to take 24 bars out of that and 8 bars out of this, and I went to pieces."[8]

No wonder then that as Kramer took the stage of the London Palladium he did so beset with self-doubt.

To compound matters, in Billy J's mind, although the sound in the theatre itself was okay, he believed the TV sound was poor and that he had done a poor show. Despite Brian Epstein enthusing that he had been "wonderful", Billy J. believed differently: "The show had damaged the potential sales of the record. I believed that the record was actually better than the two previous ones, but the week after the Palladium show, sales just fell off, and it only ever reached number 4 on the charts."[9]

Billy J. was clearly upset by his performance and it has stuck in his mind ever after as the reason why 'I'll Keep You Satisfied' stalled at number 4.

The evidence of the progress of 'I'll Keep You Satisfied' up the charts suggests his performance on *Sunday Night at the London Palladium* did not impact as negatively on the sales of the record as he believes. Rather it was possibly the reverse.

Released just days *after* the show on 1 November 1963, 'I'll Keep You Satisfied' fairly rocketed up the UK singles chart and by 30 November was at number 4 just behind the Beatles, Gerry and the Pacemakers and Cliff Richard. In this respect, 'I'll Keep You Satisfied' followed that pattern set by previous hits: on its way up the charts, 'Do You Want to Know a Secret?' had taken three weeks to reach number 10, and 'Bad to Me' just two to reach number 11. 'I'll Keep You Satisfied' matched these: released on 1 November, by the end of the month it was at number 9 and by 4 December it was into the Top 5 at number

4. This rate of progress would suggest that his performance at the Palladium did nothing to hinder its success.

From then on, however, the seemingly irresistible progress of 'I'll Keep You Satisfied' towards number 1 *did* stall and the record *did* change direction. The following week (11 December) it had slipped two places to number 6 and thus began a gradual eight-week journey down the Top 50. There is no doubt, however, that this was a lot more to do with the Christmas singles market than Billy J. not doing a good job with either the record or on the TV. Rather than allowing him to give himself a hard time about his single's success, maybe those around him should have reminded him that Beatlemania was at its height and 'I'll Keep You Satisfied' was competing with not one but *two* Beatles mega-selling singles: 'She Loves You' and 'I Want to Hold Your Hand'. Not only that, but into that heady Top 20/Top 10 mix of the time, have to be factored Gerry and the Pacemakers with 'You'll Never Walk Alone' (number 1 for all of November), the Dave Clark Five and 'Glad All Over' while sitting pretty on the horizon were the Swinging Blue Jeans with a newly released sure-fire hit called 'Hippy Hippy Shake.'

Pull 'I'll Keep You Satisfied' into that frame and it makes for a formidable array of 45s with which to be rubbing shoulders.

In this context, 'I'll Keep You Satisfied' *not* making number 1 was undoubtedly a very close run thing. All these records were selling in incredible numbers. By anybody's standards, reaching number 4 amidst such contenders counts as a seriously impressive achievement.

For Billy, however, there was no consolation. He convinced himself that by not reaching number 1 he had failed and let those around him down … His response was indicative of his lack of self-confidence at the time as he struggled to come to terms with not only the effects of finding himself so suddenly famous, but of the expectations he believed others had of him. As noted earlier, with the benefit of hindsight, Billy now acknowledges: "It was me as a young guy myself thinking 'what have I done wrong here?'"[10]

BILLY J. KRAMER with THE DAKOTAS
I'LL KEEP YOU SATISFIED (2.04)
(Lennon-McCartney)
Northern Songs Ltd)
Parlophone R 5073
Recorded: 14 October 1963 in Studio 2, Abbey Road
John Lennon and Paul McCartney were present in the studio when Billy J. recorded this song.
Billy was proud of the recording: "I was very pleased with 'I'll Keep You Satisfied'. I thought it was a very well put together record. I thought it was better than what I'd done previously."[11]
B-side: I Know* (2.05)
(George Martin and Bob Wooler)

(**I Know'* is unique: a co-write between Beatles producer George Martin and the Cavern's legendary DJ Bob Wooler, although the credit on the record mis-spelt Bob's surname with two 'l's. The song was published by 'Jaep Music Ltd' and on the sheet music Bob's surname was set correctly as 'Wooler'. In an interview with Record Collector's Spencer Leigh in July 1998, Wooler said he was "hoping that George Martin and I were going to have a partnership like Lerner and Loewe or Kander and Ebb, but that was the only song we wrote together. Maybe he didn't think too much of my lyric but he was involved in so many other things.")[12]

Recorded: 22 July 1963 in Studio 2, Abbey Road
Both sides produced: George Martin
Engineers: Norman Smith and Geoff Emerick
Released: 1 November 1963

'I'll Keep You Satisfied' entered the UK chart on 13 November 1963 at 34 and between 28 November and 4 December it had peaked at number 4 (*Record Mirror* had it as high as number 3). It spent 13 weeks on the chart, only one week less than 'Bad to Me'.

Released twice in the USA: Firstly on 11 November 1963 on Liberty 55643 when it did not chart and then again on 10 July 1964 on Imperial 66048 when it peaked at number 30 on the *Billboard* Hot 100 Chart on 22 August 1964 and was on the charts for 7 weeks.

Billy's third single earned a second successive top-rated 'DNT' review from *Disc* music weekly's singles reviewer Don Nicholl, who described it as "a pleasant ballad in recognisable John Lennon-Paul McCartney style" that was "almost bound to go into the Parade." Together, Nicholl noted "Kramer and the Dakotas make it a simple romantic side with Billy double-tracking affably." (He was less impressed by George Martin and Bob Wooler's one and only co-write, 'I Know', which was on the B-side. Noting that it wasn't as catchy as the A-side, he described the tune as "harmless and lightweight," one that Billy J. sang "as if it were fragile."[13]

1, 5, 10 & 11 Billy J. Kramer interview with the author 19 October 2020.
2, 3 & 4 *Paul McCartney: Many Years from Now*, Barry Miles, (Vintage, 1998) p.180.
6a, b, & c *Disc* music weekly, Edition 292, 26 October 1963, 4 page supplement, 'I'm So Excited And Nervous, Over That Palladium TV Show' by Billy J. Kramer.
7 & 9 *Do You Want to Know a Secret?: The Autobiography of Billy J. Kramer*, by Billy J. Kramer with Alyn Shipton (Equinox Publishing, 2016): both p.63 and p.68.
8 *Billy J. Kramer with The Dakotas EP Collection*, Spencer Leigh CD booklet notes, (I Can See For Miles Records Ltd. SEECD 422, 1995).
12 Bob Wooler interviewed by Spencer Leigh for the British magazine *Record Collector*, July 1998 edition.
13 *Disc* music weekly, edition 293, 2 November 1963, single review in 'Disc Date' with Don Nicholl, p.8.

Chapter 53:
BILLY J. BOUNCES BACK

1964
Was the year when ... plans to build the World Trade Centre were announced ... in the UK Harold Wilson became Prime Minister in October when the Labour Party toppled the Conservatives from power ... in the USA, Malcolm X announced he was forming a black nationalist party ... American boxer, Cassius Clay, age 22, defeated Sonny Liston to lift the World Heavyweight Championship title for the first time ... later in the year Clay renounced his 'slave name' to become formally known as Muhammad Ali ... Studebaker-Packard began to install seatbelts as standard equipment ... the growth of the Mod subculture made itself known to the general public when Mods clashed with Rockers on several occasions in seaside towns such as Margate, Clacton and most notably Brighton and Hastings ...

Whatever doubts plagued Billy J. Kramer after what he perceived as the failure of 'I'll Keep You Satisfied' to 'only' make number 4, he was to return to the top of the UK charts in March 1964 with his fourth single release.

As 1964 dawned, he was determined to succeed in his own right and felt the need to establish some independence from the Beatles to prove he was not totally reliant on them for his success. Consequently, Billy J. resolutely resisted Brian Epstein's entreaties to record another Lennon-McCartney song for his fourth A-side.

Epstein offered him three new John and Paul tunes, including 'One and One Is Two' which they had written specifically for him (see Chapter 69). Instead, Kramer had found a song he was convinced was a sure-fire hit and well suited to his voice and style. Determined not to miss out on this tune he stood firm against Epstein's pressure.

The song Billy J. so resolutely believed would be a big hit was 'Little Children'. Written by J. Leslie McFarland and Mort Shuman, Shuman is famous for his songwriting partnership with Doc Pomus with whom he wrote such classics as 'Viva Las Vegas' (Elvis Presley), 'A Teenager in Love' (Dion and the Belmonts), 'Save the Last Dance for Me' (the Drifters) and 'Sweets for My Sweet' (the Searchers). In 1966, together with Kenny Lynch, Mort penned 'Love's Just a Broken Heart', a number 5 hit for Cilla Black.

"My feelings were I'd made a poor show on the *Palladium* and had to come up with something really special to follow 'I'll Keep You Satisfied', but at the same time I couldn't rely on the Beatles forever. So, as 1964 dawned, I began to visit music publishers to listen to demos of new songs. One time at Auerbach Music they played me an acetate of a guy called Mort Shuman singing a song he'd written called 'Little Children'. By then I'd become friendly with a guy called Jeremy Banks who owned this beautiful thatched cottage down in Rye in Sussex, and we went to stay there for a weekend and with me I took a bunch of acetates I'd collected, including the one of Mort Shuman accompanying himself on piano singing 'Little Children'. When I played it again in that cottage in Rye I knew I had to record it."[1]

Billy also knew that persuading Brian to his point of view was going to be the difficult part. On his return from Rye, he got Franklin Boyd at Auerbach to send a copy of the acetate to Brian ... when Brian presented it to him Billy feigned knowledge of it and asked "to take it home and give it a proper listen".[2]

When he and Brian met again just a few days later, Epstein offered Billy three new Lennon-McCartney tunes for consideration as his next single. But by then Billy's mind was already made up in favour of 'Little Children' and when he told Brian, his manager became visibly annoyed and told him "you do know you've turned down songs by the best songwriters in the world?"[3]

The John and Paul songs Brian offered to Billy J. Kramer were eventually recorded by other artists, but none of them made it into the charts.

Billy knew that there was a lot riding on his decision to *not* record another John and Paul tune. He was acutely aware that Brian Epstein and George Martin in particular would be watching 'Little Children's' progress on the charts with eagle eyes: "Apart from 'Do You Want to Know a Secret?', 'Little Children' was the only song that I rehearsed. Those Lennon and McCartney songs, 'Bad to Me', 'I'll Keep You Satisfied', I'd never heard them until the day of the session, but with 'Little Children' I'd thought the whole thing out, the arrangement, the rhythm guitar, the drum pattern, the overdubs. When I went into Abbey Road, Dick James was there with Brian and George Martin and they told me they felt it was lyrically a 'bit near the mark', but I said I disagreed (hadn't 'Please Please Me' also been 'near the mark'?) I told them that I thought it was the best song out of all the ones I'd had. When I recorded it I don't think anyone had any confidence in it. *Melody Maker* called it a 'slow ponderous bore'! To support the record's release, I made a short film to accompany it on TV featuring myself and a group of kids in a playground. During the making of this, huge snowflakes began to fall. The day after it was screened, apparently the record sold 78,000 copies in one day alone…"[4]

Despite Brian's pique and George Martin's doubts 'Little Children' proved Billy J's judgement to be sound: it toppled Epstein's only female protégée Cilla Black and her first number 1, 'Anyone Who Had a Heart', from the top spot in mid-March 1964. Indeed, Billy J. remained at number 1 for two weeks and in the process held off the challenges of strong singles by the Dave Clark Five ('Bits and Pieces'), the Rolling Stones ('Not Fade Away') and the Hollies ('Just One Look') before being replaced at the top by, (who else) the Beatles, with 'Can't Buy Me Love'.

And so it was. Their behind-the-scenes difference of opinion over 'Little Children' was laid to rest by the record's stunning success. It truly seemed that artists like Billy J. signed to Brian Epstein's NEMS Enterprises were on a roll to the point where it seemed that all aboard were bound for the top of the charts …

Brian Epstein's initial umbrage at Billy J's rejection of tunes John and Paul had written for him, especially one entitled 'One and One Is Two', was considerably appeased when Billy agreed that his follow-up to 'Little Children' would be another new Lennon-McCartney original.

Brian never lost faith in Billy J. Kramer. In 1964, the incredible success of the Beatles in the USA took things to another level for Brian and absorbed even more of his time, but he remained committed to doing all he could for Billy. Equally, Billy always valued Brian's support and friendship.

1, 2, 3 & 4 Billy J. Kramer interview with the author, 19 October 2020.

Chapter 54:
TOMMY QUIGLEY

b. Thomas Quigley 7 July 1945, Norris Green, Liverpool

As 1963 began, Brian Epstein was relishing his role as the man with the 'Midas' touch. He had honed in on several of Liverpool's brightest rising stars, eagerly launching them into what he believed would be the stratosphere of musical and show business success. As the year progressed, the chart successes of not only the Beatles but those of Billy J. and Gerry and the Pacemakers were proving him right.

One young artist Epstein was convinced would follow in their footsteps to become 'the next Tommy Steele' was a young Liverpool man by the name of Tommy Quigley. He'd first encountered Tommy in the autumn of 1962, but it was not until June 1963 that he joined the Epstein 'stable of stars'.

The Beatles manager originally 'discovered' the young freckle-faced Quigley singing with his group the Challengers when they opened for John, Paul, George and Ringo during one of the three consecutive evening presentations Epstein staged at the Queen's Hall, Widnes, on 3, 10 and 17 September 1962: "I was running Monday night concerts there, with Gerry and the Beatles ... and the eight to eight-thirty spot was occupied by 'unknowns' who used the opportunity for a form of audition. I paid them nothing but they got themselves a hearing."[1]

Tommy's 'discovery' had elements of 'A Star Is Born' about it. Epstein was talking business with the theatre's manager in his office, when he heard "a very fascinating voice over the amplification system. I ran from the office into the hall and saw a youth in a depressing green suit, singing his heart out to the great delight of a young, mostly female audience. I thought he was excellent, with a lot of mischief in his presence and much voice in his lungs."[2]

The chirpy boy in the 'depressing green suit' was one Tommy Quigley, a former pupil at the Croxteth Secondary Modern School, but by then a trainee fitter with the Automatic Telephone Company by day and by night a singer with a band.

Epstein met with Quigley immediately after his performance and discovered that the young singer was not under any management deal. Surprisingly, despite his obvious enthusiasm for Tommy, Epstein initially declined to manage him, offering instead to simply 'assist' his career. One of the first 'assists' Brian provided was to book Tommy and the Challengers for a debut appearance at the Cavern on Saturday 20 October 1962, when they were on the same bill as B. Bumble and the Stingers all the way from the USA and who had, earlier in the year (May 1962), scored a UK number 1 with their instrumental tune 'Nutrocker'.

Bob Wooler, who witnessed Brian's first encounter with Tommy, sagely noted: "Tommy Quickly and the Challengers were on stage at the Queen's Hall, Widnes, and there was Brian in one of his transfixed states. He said, 'Isn't he marvellous?', but I couldn't see that ingredient, although I dutifully said yes."[3]

The evening Brian first encountered the Challengers, they comprised Tommy on vocals, John Bedson or Ian Bailey on drums, Robin Gilmore on lead guitar, Ray Dawson (Anderson) on bass guitar and Pete Wilson on rhythm guitar.

A month later, in an article published in the 18 October to 1 November edition of *Mersey Beat*, entitled 'Mersey Roundabout' and written by 'Virginia', it was announced that "Vocalist Tommy Quigley of the Challengers will soon have company on stage – his twin sister (Patricia Quigley) is to sing with the group…"

And so it was the Challengers added a second vocalist.

Although Epstein claimed that on the night he first met and spoke to Tommy Quigley, Quigley had told him "he was not managed", this was not strictly true for at the Queen's Hall, Tommy and the Challengers were accompanied by David Bramwell who was fulfilling the role of manager. In fact, immediately prior to their performance at the Queen's Hall, the Challengers had appeared in an advert for the 20 September to 4 October edition of *Mersey Beat*, in which they were described as 'a group from Maghull, Manager: Mr. D Bramwell, 14 Norton Grove, Maghull; MAG 3923'.

In fact, it was David who had persuaded Bob Wooler to let the group perform during the half-hour period Brian designated as 'audition time' for up-and-coming hopefuls. His recall of that evening is that, from the get-go, Brian was mightily taken by Tommy and commented to Bob Wooler that "he thought he had the same sort of 'impish personality as Gerry Marsden', but right from the start he considered the Challengers to be 'ugly' and wanted to minimise their influence. He even asked them to change the name of the group to Tommy Quickly and the Stops. It was Brian who came up with the name 'Tommy Quickly'…"[4]

The delay in Epstein signing Quigley right away was apparently not because of David's presence as manager, but due to Brian's existing 'stable' of artists (aka NEMS Enterprises) having expanded so rapidly he felt he needed time to 'consolidate' rather than add to his list of charges. Consequently, it was not until June 1963 that Epstein succumbed to Quigley's pleas (relayed to him via Bob Wooler) and signed him to a management deal.

The very moment Epstein *did* sign Quickly, Brian's now apparently infallible star-making machine kicked into over drive: having already persuaded Tommy to change his name from 'Quigley' to 'Quickly', he secured him a recording contract with Pye Records, but sacked the Challengers. Apparently (as David Bramwell had noted) Brian did not think they looked the part. Tommy also received the now familiar Epstein personal 'makeover': a new hairstyle and a stylish new suit replete with instructions to smarten up his appearance.

Within a month (18 July) *Mersey Beat* carried a brief note informing its readers that the Challengers had lost lead singer Tommy Quickly and replaced him with Steve Aldo.

With George Martin in great demand, and Brian also eager to 'spread his wings' and place artists with other record labels, he asked Dick James to help him secure Tommy a record deal with a label outside the EMI family. Using his many contacts, James was able to link Epstein with Ray Horricks who had recently switched as A&R from Decca to Pye.

By then, such was Epstein's reputation within the music industry that the opportunity to produce one of his Liverpool protégés was an offer too good to refuse. Horricks had no trouble in persuading Louis Benjamin, the head of Pye, to sign Quickly especially as the singer came with an almost sure-fire ticket to immediate chart success: the gift of an original song for his first A-side courtesy of Lennon and McCartney…

---

1 & 2 *A Cellarful of Noise*, Brian Epstein, (New English Library, 1964), p.72.
3 *Record Collector* magazine, July 1998, Bob Wooler interviewed by Spencer Leigh.
4 David Bramwell MBE, MSc, PhD, FLS from *Mersey Beat*/Bill Harry/Mersey Beat Ltd TRIUMPH PC.

Chapter 55:
TOMMY QUICKLY, SOLO STAR

And so it was that on the day after his 18th birthday, Monday 8 July 1963, Tommy Quickly found himself in a studio recording his debut single. Rising star Les Reed was in the producer's seat and it was he who also arranged both 'Tip of My Tongue' and its B-side 'Heaven Only Knows'.

Tommy's A-side was, in the main, a Paul composition. Many years later, with typical Lennon acerbity, John described 'Tip of My Tongue' as "another piece of Paul's garbage, not my garbage."[1]

Paul had written it sometime towards the end of August/the very beginning of September 1962, in anticipation of the Beatles' pending recording session at Abbey Road on Tuesday 4 September. Ahead of their trip to London, the Beatles convened for a rehearsal at the Cavern on the afternoon of Monday 3 September. It was there that Paul introduced 'Tip of My Tongue' to the group to learn for consideration as a possible A-side. John had written 'Please Please Me' for the same 4 September recording session. Compared to how John's tune turned out, Paul's 'Tip of My Tongue' did not stand up. Upbeat and catchy it certainly was, but it lacked the punch and drive of 'Please Please Me'. Even so, it wasn't discarded, for not only was it rehearsed prior to the Abbey Road session, but for several weeks after, 'Tip of My Tongue' became an early Lennon-McCartney tune performed by the Beatles as part of their live set.

When 4 September arrived, more than anything, EMI (i.e., George Martin) were focused on the Beatles recording 'How Do You Do It' for their first A-side. This they did during the evening session when 'Love Me Do' was also taped as the B-side. Earlier, during the two to five-thirty afternoon session, 'Tip of My Tongue' was very likely to have been among the five original songs they rehearsed. (There is no documentation detailing exactly which songs were practised, but the other four were most probably 'Ask Me Why', 'PS I Love You', 'Please Please Me' and 'Love Me Do'.) It is clear from this probable list of songs the Beatles presented for George Martin's consideration, that from the very start they were intent on recording original material rather than 'covers' of other writers' songs. Most certainly they had taken against 'How Do You Do It', but equally certainly George Martin and his production team were not impressed by any of John and Paul's originals. Martin thought 'Please Please Me' dragged and needed to be speeded up. As for 'Tip of My Tongue', George and his team felt the arrangement required further work.

Despite this original lukewarm reception for the tune from George Martin, when Brian asked Paul for a song for Tommy Quickly, it was 'Tip of My Tongue' that McCartney offered. In 2009, Paul McCartney made the following observation about it: "The truth is, some of the songs (the Beatles gave away) you'd (as in himself) not been able to make it work for you but it was still a song. 'Tip of My Tongue' was not a bad title. It was memorable, but how do you get it to work as a song? I never really thought I'd got this one to work, but then Brian came up and said that Tommy would love a song and I said I have this one, but I'm not sure about it, but if he likes it he can have it, so he took that one."[2]

When Tommy Quickly stepped up to the microphone inside Pye Records London studio, Brian was there to lend his support. On this occasion, session musicians would have provided the accompaniment. Dick James's part in helping secure Brian with the link to Pye was rewarded not only by his having a cut of the publishing (via Northern Songs) for the A-side, but also the B-side. The B-side, 'Heaven Only Knows' was penned by none other than Mitch Murray in collaboration with Barry Rapport and was yet another tune

Tommy Quickly from Norris Green in Liverpool. Singing star, photographed in 1964. (Pictorial Press Ltd / Alamy Stock Photo)

published by Jaep Music Ltd.

(In 1963, Dick James wrote of Tommy that he was "a very young artist of great ability and charm", whom he believed "will prove an undoubted top-of-the-bill success in months to come.")[3]

TOMMY QUICKLY
TIP OF MY TONGUE (2:02)
(Lennon, McCartney)
Northern Songs Ltd
Piccadilly 7N.35137
Tommy Quickly
Recorded: 8 July 1963
B-side: Heaven Only Knows
(Mitch Murray, Barry Rapaport)
Arranger/accompaniment directed by (on both sides): Les Reed

Les Reed was a very talented songwriter who penned the Applejacks' Top 10 hit 'Tell Me When' and, with Gordon Mills, Tom Jones's first number 1, 'It's Not Unusual'. In the mid-Sixties, Reed formed a formidable writing partnership with Barry Mason and among the many hits they penned were 'Delilah' and 'The Last Waltz'.

On 30 July 1963, to much fanfare, 'Tip of My Tongue' was released in the UK. Among the fanfare was a full-page advertisement on the cover of the 2 August 1963 edition of *NME*, proclaiming Tommy's debut single as 'Another Smash Hit from the Sensational Songwriting Team of John Lennon and Paul McCartney'.

That same week, the 3 August edition of the UK's *Disc* music monthly carried a smaller advert for Tommy's debut single while, on page 8 in his 'Disc Date' singles reviews, Don Nicholl gave 'Tip of My Tongue' a 3-star recommendation. "Tommy Quickly has a vocal style which is somewhat deceptive. There's a pungency about it which grows on you and I think the teenager will grow into quite a seller." However, that Don was not totally convinced by what he had heard was apparent when he added, "I don't think the ballad is one of the composers' better efforts, but it's catchy – and with publicity pressure behind it, could do nicely."[4]

Unfortunately for Tommy and Brian Epstein, the 'publicity pressure' alluded to in Nicholl's review did not deliver and inexplicably Quickly's debut single failed to chart. For once, the kudos of having an exclusive Lennon-McCartney song to sing failed to work the usual magic for its recipient.

Brian Epstein was undeterred. Convinced of Tommy's innate 'star potential' and that the public would soon be won over to Tommy's cause, he pulled out all the stops to promote him, lavishing time and money on the young man's initial career. In Tommy he sincerely believed he had discovered the real deal. So much so that in his autobiography of 1964 Brian Epstein confidently and proudly proclaimed: "He is going to be a star."

George Martin was never quite as convinced. "Brian Epstein was building his stable and each artist that he got he would bring to me because he thought I was the wizard who could turn them into hit-makers. And so he brought me Cilla, and Gerry, and Billy J. Kramer, the Fourmost and even a bloke called Tommy Quickly, but the degrees of success these people had was gradually diminishing with each one he got."[5]

---

1 *All We Are Saying: The Last Major Interview with John Lennon and Yoko Ono*, conducted by David Sheff (Sidgwick & Jackson, 2000) p.194.
2 & 5 Sir Paul McCartney and Sir George Martin in conversation with Bob Harris OBE and Colin Hall for the 2009 BBC Radio 2 documentary, *The Songs the Beatles Gave Away*, written and narrated by Bob Harris, produced by Bob Harris and Trudie Myerscough-Harris for WBBC.
3 *The Big Beat Album* (Dick James, 1963).
4 *Disc* music weekly, edition 280, 3 August 1963, single review in 'Disc Date' with Don Nicholl, p.8.

Chapter 56:
LETTING TOMMY GO

Epstein's faith in Quickly's star potential almost knew no bounds. As subsequent singles also flopped, Epstein became relentless in his efforts to make the magic work. He included Tommy on three Beatles tours, a Beatles Christmas show (on which he performed 'Winter Wonderland' and 'Kiss Me Now'), a Gerry and the Pacemakers Christmas Show, a Gerry and the Pacemakers tour and a Billy J. Kramer tour. By the time he was finished, among the very many expenses Epstein had paid out to advance Tommy Quickly's cause was $30,000 on a 1964 promotional tour of America. Unfortunately, it seemed the more he tried and the more he spent the more the public resisted.

'Tip of My Tongue' was issued as a solo release, but after this Epstein installed one of Liverpool's finest groups, the Remo Four, as his backing group. He'd initially thought of them to back Billy J. Further singles were issued under the name Tommy Quickly and the Remo Four. This was a wise move on Epstein's part, for the Remo Four were a first-class Liverpool group who had a real instrumental edge and provided Tommy with great support both on stage and in the studio.

Despite their huge musical talent, the Remo Four could not coax a chart hit out of Tommy. No wonder for his follow-up to 'Tip of My Tongue' was 'Kiss Me Now' / 'No Other Love' (1963, Piccadilly 7N 35151). It failed to impress the record-buying public because it was banal. (It received a lacklustre 3-star review in *Disc* in which all Don Nicholl could find to say about it was that "it should do well" and was "a bright uptempo love song". Nicholl seemed more impressed that Tommy was backed by the Remo Four and that the B-side 'No Other Love' took its melody from Dvorak's Humoresques.)[1]

During 1964, amidst much activity, including lots of live appearances, Tommy and the Remo Four recorded and released four more singles: 'Prove It' / 'Haven't You Noticed' (1964, Piccadilly 7N 35167), 'You Might As Well Forget Him' / 'It's As Simple As That' (1964, Piccadilly 7N 35183), 'Wild Side of Life' / 'Forget the Other Guy' (October 1964, Pye 7N 15708) and right at the very end of the year 'Humpty Dumpty' / 'I'll Go Crazy' (December 1964, Pye 7N 15748).

Only one of these came close to giving Quickly the major breakthrough he needed: Hank Thompson's big country music hit from 1952, 'The Wild Side of Life' (written by Arlie Carter and William Warren). Tommy's version spent eight weeks on the UK chart from late October through November 1964, but never went beyond number 33. (It did better in the *NME* chart and in the edition published Friday 6 November 1964 it had cracked the Top 30 and made number 27.)

For Epstein, this was something, and at this encouraging sign of chart activity he was swift to respond. On 25 November, with Tommy in tow and accompanied by Derek Taylor, Brian flew to Los Angeles to promote 'The Wild Side of Life' which by then had been released in the USA on Liberty F-5575.

All his efforts were in vain, however, for the record sank like a stone in the USA.

As a young 14-year-old at the Liverpool Empire on Sunday 8 November 1964 to catch the Beatles show, I saw Tommy perform. Mary Wells closed the first half of the evening and Tommy was one of the other support acts. He was backed by the Remo Four who had earlier performed a set of their own. Against a barrage of unrelenting screams intended almost entirely for the Beatles, undeterred he bounced on stage and throughout remained focused and cheerful. Amazingly, through the cacophony of high-pitched wailing, Tommy managed to tell us that his set was being recorded for release as an EP, an announcement that unleashed another round of frenzied wailing.

Unfortunately, the minor UK success of 'The Wild Side of Life' was not enough to save Tommy's recording career. Only one of the tracks recorded at the Empire ('Humpty Dumpty') was ever released: despite Tommy and the Remo Four's best efforts and the single being promoted as having been recorded 'Live at the Liverpool Empire', nothing could disguise the fact that beneath the razzamatazz it was what it was: a dire song. A waste of everybody's time: Tommy deserved far better. It was a last, desperate throw of the dice.

The EP he had mentioned never materialised and neither did anything else. His recording career was over. Even so, it was not until 23 April 1966 that it was announced in *Disc and Music Echo* that NEMS Enterprises had let him go.

When it came to Tommy Quickly, Brian Epstein's Midas touch very sadly deserted him. While his failure wounded Brian, more crucially Tommy's career in show business never really materialised. Author Ray Coleman commented in his biography of Epstein, *The Man Who Made the Beatles*: "Quickly had released five lively singles – and all had flopped. Brian was horrified and dumbfounded. For the first time his innate commercial judgement had been rejected by the public.

In his office Quickly's name became taboo. Staff asking questions, or sympathising, were ignored … and an Epstein silence spoke volumes for his feelings."[2]

Many years later, reflecting on Tommy's professional relationship with Brian, Bob Wooler ruefully commented that, "Brian put him on Beatles tours backed by the Remo Four. Tommy got into the charts with a country and western number, "The Wild Side of Life", and how prophetic that turned out to be as he went on the wild side of life. Tommy got marvellous exposure but all to no avail. Eventually Brian dropped him because he hated failure."[3]

Epstein's feelings apart, more importantly one can only imagine how this impacted on Tommy's confidence and ego. Tommy was a very young man, his self-belief had been given a real hammering and he had to bear his lack of success in the full glare of the spotlight. Coleman noted that Quickly himself was obviously hurt by his lack of single success, but tried to hide this. Typical was this comment from an interview between Coleman and Quickly in 1965: "I want to be in this business for ever. I don't want to be a pop star for today and then get forgotten. That's what hit records are all about."[4]

Despite the bravado of his words, for Tommy and the way he had been promoted as a 'pop star', a 'hit record' was a core requirement of such a role and was exactly what he needed to kick-start his career. To be forgotten you have to have been known in the first place.

---

1 *Disc* music weekly, edition 293, 2 November 1963, single review in 'Disc Date' with Don Nicholl, p.8.
2 & 4 *Brian Epstein: The Man Who Made the Beatles*, Ray Coleman, (Penguin Books, 1990) p.197.
3 *Record Collector* magazine, July 1998, Bob Wooler interviewed by Spencer Leigh.

Chapter 57:
SUCCESS LIKE FAILURE

Of all Brian Epstein's protégés, the story of Tommy Quickly is the most distressing. He was not alone but he was the most noticeable. Others who did not lift off at all included the Rustiks, a group from Devon, and solo singer Michael Haslam. Despite signing to NEMS Enterprises in 1964, they quickly faded (almost) into oblivion. Neither were recipients of a John and Paul 'giveaway' but, along with Tommy, to their credit they filled prized support slots on the Beatles' and Mary Wells' 26-date UK tour of that year.

The trouble was they were unknowns and, in theory, to be on a Beatles tour should have given them maximum exposure, but quite simply no one was interested. Certainly not the fans and not the music press. The Beatles had not toured the UK for almost a year and so fans had become desperate. Starved of contact with the group for so long, from the moment they entered each venue the fan focus was entirely on the Beatles and no one else (except maybe Mary Wells). Throughout every show, screaming for the Beatles drowned out all the other acts. None of the support acts, apart from Mary Wells, had any familiar songs for the fans to latch onto or recognise and so they were just a hindrance to be endured before they could get to John, Paul, George and Ringo. In such an environment it was impossible for any of them to be heard or make any significant impact. I saw the show in Liverpool (note: I use the word 'saw' very carefully, I didn't hear more than a few words sung/spoken by any of the acts) and none of the other acts made any impression at all. How could they have done given the barrage of noise that continually swept over them on stage? It simply did not abate. Putting unknown acts into that mêlée was almost cruel.

Very early on in his stable-building, Brian had misjudged what it would take to manage the Big Three. The careful, manicured and smart appearance that worked for others was not what they were about. Neither was the lightweight, anonymous pop of 'By the Way'. Brian had a formula for success to which he expected his acts to adhere, but woe betide them if they didn't!

By the time of the Rustiks and Michael Haslam, Brian Epstein was also over-stretched. A manager who liked to devote himself personally to his acts, he simply no longer had the time to do so. Maybe he had become over-confident and his judgement of artists not as sure as it once had been. Given the explosion of British musical talent that was rocking the UK charts at this time, the Rustiks and Michael Haslam were up against some very tough competition and possibly did not receive the support or telling exposure they needed to survive. And they didn't.

Neither were the recipients of a John and Paul song which might well have helped them kick-start their careers as recording artists.

Bolton-born Haslam had been rescued from working in a leather tannery by Epstein. Described as a 'balladeer', his first single was released on Parlophone. Entitled 'Gotta Get a Hold of Myself', it was described in the 1964 Beatles tour programme as 'a dramatic orchestra-backed number which is both tuneful and exciting'. Unfortunately, neither tuneful nor exciting enough to put it into the charts.

The Rustiks from Paignton in Devon had won a beat music competition held on Westward Television. Broadcast 'live' on 9 July 1964, Brian had been a judge, as was Dick Rowe from Decca. Suitably impressed, Brian signed them to a management deal. The group's debut single was called 'What a Memory Can Do' and released on the Decca label. Writing in the 4 September 1964 edition of *NME*, reviewer Derek Johnson described it as an "attractively lilting rockaballad". Commenting that it was mainly sung in unison and benefitted from "a well-constructed lyric", Johnson told you all you needed to know when he added, "but not a particularly distinctive melody".

On 23 April 1966, in the first edition of the merged music newspapers, *Disc and Music Echo*, an advert for NEMS announced that Brian had not renewed the management contracts of either act.

Tommy Quickly was much more Epstein's kind of act and so his lack of success was as puzzling then as it is now.

Maybe not the best singer in the world, Quickly had an appealing stage presence and could hold an audience. In himself he was a personable young man much in the style of Gerry Marsden and Peter Noone, aka 'Herman' of Herman's Hermits. Of course, Marsden and Noone had the talent to match their personalities and it was this (plus their ability to write some good songs of their own) that ultimately took them to the top and kept them there. Thrust into the spotlight before he was really ready, the weight of expectation placed upon Tommy's shoulders proved too much for him to realise. Too young, no doubt misunderstood, and lacking the support he needed, Tommy Quickly never got the chance to prove himself.

Brian had immediately picked up on Tommy's bubbly stage personality and believed he could see a star in the making.

Tommy's Pye Record producer Roy Horricks described Quickly as "very hard working" and "very self confident". He believed Quickly had what it took to make it: "Tommy had an ingrained professionalism but he knew his place with Brian."[1]

The answer to the question, 'What went wrong for Tommy?' is therefore open to interpretation.

One thing that Epstein and his team definitely did not get right were the songs. When he signed Quickly to a record deal, he fed the singer a diet of 'pop', not the more R&B type of material with which he was more familiar and used to singing. Unfortunately, none of the 'pop' songs he recorded were distinctive enough in themselves, not even 'Tip of My Tongue'. It may have carried the Lennon-McCartney imprimatur, but it was undeniably one of their weaker efforts and Paul himself has recognised that it was not fully formed.

(Of course, hindsight is a great thing, and back in 1963 to have suggested to Brian Epstein that a Paul and John song was a bit of a clinker would have been sacrilege.)

Former manager Dave Bramwell believes Tommy's story could have turned out so much better. "Tommy ... is a much maligned person ... considered to be one of NEMS failures, but it needn't have been that way ... Tommy was great at 'Buddy Holly' songs and at some of the so-called R&B that made up the classic Mersey sound..."

What Tommy should have been singing appears to have been a bone of contention from the start. Dave Bramwell recalled, "A quite heated discussion with Brian over coffee in the Kardomah Cafe basement, with Paul and George present, about what Tommy should record, my suggestion being two of the classics as nobody had yet done this. Brian however insisted on Lennon & McCartney originals and, of course, had his way..."[2]

More than the music, Bramwell believes the most significant factor in Tommy's inability to make the most of his opportunities was Tommy himself. "The principal one ... boils down to the fragility of his character. He was immature for his age ... and something of a rabbit. One of our main problems was keeping him out of the hands of irate fathers!"[3]

Prizing Tommy Quickly away from the Challengers was another mistake. (Epstein's decision had nothing to do with the Challengers' musical ability, it was about their looks and appearance.) Epstein had not got to know his charge well enough when he made this error of judgement. As we have seen, splitting Billy J. from the Coasters had repercussions for Kramer.

According to Bramwell, a university student himself, "Tommy had a domineering father ... who was something of a bully ... Tommy was, in fact, quite physically frightened of him.

In the Challengers … he found a refuge amongst a group of better educated people: Ron Gilmour was at Liverpool University, Ray Dawson and Pete Wilson were both grammar school boys and all three (unusual for groups of the time) could read and write music."[4]

Reading between the lines, it seems likely that Epstein saw the Challengers as a possible threat to his authority (just as he was intimidated by the collective academic success of the Fourmost) but by sacking them/not offering them a contract he effectively removed the rock on which Tommy depended more than anyone – especially Epstein himself – realised at the time. At the very point, under Brian's management, he began to move beyond the familiar world of the clubs in Liverpool and further afield would have been when Tommy needed that support the most. Instead, in one fell swoop, the familiar camaraderie with which Tommy Quickly had so far benefitted and thrived was removed. He was cast adrift.

Billy J. Kramer says at the time he wasn't quite sure why Brian signed Tommy, but in an effort to try and help the latter Brian would put them both on the same tours and ask Billy to double-up with Tommy to keep an eye on him. While Billy says, "Tommy was the nicest of guys", unfortunately Billy's advice, such as it was, went largely unheeded.

And then there was the major disappointment of the 'No Reply' session.

John Lennon had written 'No Reply' in May 1964 while in Tahiti where he and his wife Cynthia had been on holiday with George Harrison and Pattie Boyd. Once back in London, Lennon finished writing the song with a little help from his friend Paul, who said: "We wrote 'No Reply' together but from a strong original idea of his." Paul described 'No Reply' as John's version of 'Silhouettes' by the Rays.[5]

On 3 June, after having spent several days previously at Abbey Road recording songs for the non-soundtrack side of 'A Hard Day's Night', the Beatles, with stand-in drummer Jimmie Nicol, spent the morning rehearsing material that they would be performing on their forthcoming tour of the Netherlands, Australia and New Zealand. Ringo had fallen suddenly ill that very same morning and was in hospital. As the tour kicked off the very next day when the Beatles were scheduled to fly to Copenhagen for two shows, the rehearsal with Nicol was more than imperative.

Once the rehearsal was over, however, the Beatles remained at Abbey Road to record demos of some new songs which included 'No Reply'. Although it had been written primarily for the Beatles, John donated 'first use' to Tommy Quickly.

Dutifully, and no doubt very gratefully at the time, Tommy attempted a recording of the song. Here was a tune so much better than 'Tip of My Tongue'. Of all the singles he had been offered or released it should have been the song that became the making of Tommy Quickly, 'pop star'. Certainly the Remo Four thought 'No Reply' would propel them all into the charts.

Recording took place one July night in Pye's London studio. Backing Tommy were Colin Manley (lead and rhythm guitar), Roy Dyke (drums), Don Andrew (bass guitar), Paul McCartney (tambourine) and John Lennon (percussion).

Colin Manley noted that the 'percussion' for which John was credited was simply the clinking of a couple of Coca-Cola bottles. Brian Epstein was in attendance to lend support and to coach Tommy who was struggling with his vocals. Producing the session was Tony Hatch. Manley remembered that once the backing tracks were recorded, John Lennon relaxed and sent his chauffeur Alf Bicknell out to buy a bottle of whiskey for them to enjoy while Tommy got on with the singing. As might be expected, everyone imbibed and Manley's memory was that they all got "pretty stewed."

It was the point at which things became difficult.

Before he had even set foot in the studio that night, Tommy must have been extremely nervous. As far as the charts were concerned, he was still a stranger and so tantamount in his mind would surely have been the pressure to secure that elusive hit single. For all his on-stage personality, the yardstick for success for a young singer like himself was to

Brian Epstein with three of his singing stars from Liverpool: Tommy Quickly, Cilla Black and Billy J. Kramer. (Trinity Mirror / Mirrorpix / Alamy Stock Photo)

become known for at least one big 'hit' tune.

Tommy so needed this recording to work for him.

The presence of Brian Epstein, John Lennon and Paul McCartney would have surely intensified the pressure inside his head to the point that even before he began to sing his nerves must have been jangling, his throat seizing up …

Unfortunately, on this occasion, it seems from all that has been written and said, alcohol also played a part. Tommy had a good voice but drink made him struggle to stay in tune. No amount of coaching was going to help that situation. After a noggin (or more) of Lennon's whiskey it seems Tommy did not become relaxed, in fact the more he tried to hit the notes the more elusive they became. Several vocals were attempted but Tommy never quite nailed it. Reportedly, the session was abandoned after 17 takes.

Set for release on 7 August 1964, Tommy's version was never completed and consequently never released. By late September the Beatles reclaimed 'No Reply' for themselves. John delivered a stunning vocal and it was issued as track one, side one of *Beatles for Sale*. It was one of the highlights of the album, a tune most other groups – had they been given it – would have released as a single. No wonder the Remo Four were so disappointed. Here was true Beatles gold and Tommy had let it slip through his fingers.

Many years later, original drummer with the Remo Four, Harry Prytherch, ruefully observed, "The biggest mistake the Remo Four made was to become a backing group for other singers such as Johnny Sandon, Cilla Black and Tommy Quickly … They were a great instrumental group with good harmonies and a smart stage show. They should have made the charts in their own right without becoming someone's backing band."[6] The opportunity missed here underlines several reasons why Tommy's career stalled. His fragile nature and immaturity were one thing, but as his career progressed he apparently developed a problem with drink (and other drugs) and became difficult to handle when under the influence. He became increasingly unreliable and when he began to turn up late for some shows this was the last straw for Epstein. Tommy had crossed the line.

Tommy's exit from show business was swift and final. He quit the music industry in 1965 and joined the cast of *Five O'Clock Club*, a UK twice-weekly children's TV programme for under-12s. He appeared in 16 episodes between 25 January 1965 and 7 January 1966, hosting six of them. But that was to be it. Aged just 20, his career in show business was over. Tommy must have felt devastated and alone. Behind 'the personality' Tommy was a sensitive individual who cared about what was happening to him. Not long after he left the show he suffered a nervous breakdown and spent time in Walton Hospital, Liverpool.

At the point in his career when he needed support the most, unfortunately poor Tommy found himself yesterday's man, alone and unwanted.

One can only feel sadness for a young man who in later life, I am told, suffered brain damage following a fall from a ladder.

N.B. *Tommy Quickly and the Remo Four appeared in the 1965 music revue style film* Pop Gear *(entitled* Go Go Mania *in the USA) performing 'Humpty Dumpty'. It had been filmed in December 1964. As the despicable Jimmy Savile was the film's host, it is unlikely to be revived in its original form.*

---

1 Ray Horricks as quoted in *Brian Epstein: The Man Who Made the Beatles*, Ray Coleman, (Penguin Books, 1990) p.197.
2, 3, 4 David Bramwell, 'Tommy Quickly: A Manager Recalls': triumphpc.com > mersey-beat > tommy quickly / David Bramwell MBE as featured on Bill Harry's MERSEY BEAT Ltd website.
5 *Paul McCartney, Many Years from Now*, Barry Miles (Vintage, 1998) p.176.
6 Harry Prytherch, *www.triumphpc.com/mersey-beat/a-z/remo-four.shtml*

Chapter 58:
1963, A BEATLEBUDDY SPARES A TUNE

In '63, Brian Epstein was on a roll. From being told in 1962 that 'guitar groups are on the way out', within a year his oddly named (as in laughter inducing) guitar group from Liverpool – the Beatles – was blowing every other UK recording artist out of the water. Guitar groups were not only on the way back but were dominating the UK singles chart. The Beatles were enjoying the last laugh on their doubters while Brian was directing the careers of the biggest selling groups of them all: the Beatles, Gerry and the Pacemakers and Billy J. Kramer with the Dakotas. Together these 'guitar groups' had accounted for seven number 1 hit singles which had spent a total of 32 weeks at the top of the chart. (Plus a possible further five weeks with two singles that many fans still regard as being these artists' first number 1 hits: the Beatles' 'Please Please Me' and Billy J. Kramer with the Dakotas' 'Do You Want to Know a Secret?', which only made number 2 in *Record Retailer*.)

Epstein also guided a fourth Liverpool 'group' – the Big Three – to modest chart success during 1963 and during the summer he signed a fifth Merseyside group who, with their first two single releases, also made the UK Top 10 and Top 20 respectively. They were the Fourmost, good friends of the Beatles and the fortunate recipients of two more Lennon-McCartney 'giveaways'.

THE FOURMOST
Brian O'Hara (nickname 'Owie'): lead guitar, vocals
b. 12 March 1942, Dingle, Liverpool
d. 27 June 1999 (suicide) Wavertree, Liverpool
Billy Hatton: bass, vocals
b. William Hatton 9 June 1941, Dingle, Liverpool
d. 19 September, 2017, Liverpool
Mike Millward: rhythm guitar, vocals
b. Michael Millward 9 May 1942, Bromborough, Cheshire
d. 7 March, 1966, from leukaemia in Clatterbridge Hospital, Bebington, Cheshire
Dave Lovelady: drums, vocals
b. David Lovelady 16 October 1942, Litherland, Liverpool

The Fourmost began life in 1957 as the Two Jays when best friends Brian O'Hara and Joey Bower got together to make some noise. Born in the Dingle, Liverpool, both boys played guitars and sang. In September 1959 they became the Four Jays when bassist and singer Billy Hatton and drummer Brian Redman joined the fold. When they discovered that they shared their original name with another group, they changed their name to the Fourmost and by the time they signed with Brian Epstein the group had become the Fourmost. Along the way they had lost Bower and Redman who had been replaced by Mike Millward on rhythm guitar and Dave Lovelady on drums.

Brian Epstein wasn't the first to try and entice the boys to turn professional. In their early days, Billy Hatton had been invited to join his friend Billy Fury while 'Owie' (Brian O'Hara) had been offered a position with a television band. Offers which they had both declined. Dave Lovelady said that they were the second group Epstein had tried to sign ahead of Gerry and the Pacemakers.

The Fourmost were very popular on the Mersey beat music scene and had first played the Cavern on 1 March 1961, just a few weeks after the Beatles debuted there. Their popularity came in part from their infectious personalities as well as their musical prowess. They were a very individual act and their sense of humour both on and off the stage was something that bonded them with the Beatles. They also did great impressions of singers such as Elvis, Gracie Fields and Dean Martin – and later, of their friends, the Beatles.

Their musical talent went hand in hand with sharp intelligence. They were bright lads who all had good jobs and the prospect of professional careers (and good pensions) ahead of them, so being semi-professional musicians suited them. In the early Sixties, to walk away from the prospects these boys had ahead of them was not something most parents or individuals would countenance.

And so it took Brian Epstein three attempts before, on 30 June 1963, he finally persuaded them to sign a contract: "They, more than any of the others, were the most difficult to secure for a contract, for although they were old hands at the Cavern and enjoyed playing, they were firmly involved in apprenticeships or at college and they didn't want to know about management or full-time professionalism. Between them they have twenty-seven G.C.E. passes, I remember being impressed by this since I had none and they had promising careers ahead of them."[1]

Billy Hatton concurred: "What actually happened was that Dave Lovelady, our drummer, was studying to be an architect at the college of building, Brian O'Hara was studying to be an accountant and both had final examinations due in about six months from when Brian Epstein first asked us. He asked us three times altogether," adding that if they had told their parents that they were "giving everything up, I'm gonna get my guitar, jump into a van and travel the country and make my living in a group", the answer would have been a very definite "NO YOU ARE NOT! You couldn't turn round to your families and say, 'I'm giving it all up.'"[2]

When, at the third attempt, they did agree, it was some seven months down the road from Epstein's initial approach and their parents' opposition had wilted as they witnessed the amazing success enjoyed by Brian's other signings, the Beatles, Gerry and the Pacemakers and Billy J. Kramer. Suddenly it seemed less of a risk to give up their steady jobs, pick up their guitars and play.

In 2009, Billy said he still pondered about not taking the plunge at the first time of being asked, posing the question to himself that if the Fourmost had "signed earlier would we have been the number 1 artists? What would have happened?" Could it have been the Fourmost who were offered first dibs on 'Do You Want to Know a Secret?' or 'How Do You Do It' to help them on their way…?[3]

They were certainly close to the Beatles. Indeed, the Fourmost's professional relationship and friendship with John, Paul, George, Ringo and Pete went back to before they were both regulars at the Cavern. "The first time we met them … was Joe's Café (139 Duke Street). It was one of these places where, after midnight when the bands had finished playing, we'd all assemble … we found out we all had the same sense of humour, the same wit going on. We'd all sit together, they would come over to us or if we walked in and they were sitting down, they'd invite us over, so we were friends." As time passed and both groups played the same circuit in Liverpool the relationship between the two groups grew closer. "When we all became 'Cavern Groups' as such, that's when we did loads and loads of shows with them … You just got to know them by being backstage at the Cavern generally and then socially after that. You had to earn their respect, especially John to a degree. Paul was always a little bit, slightly aloof, Ringo was Ringo but the one people got on with, more than anyone else was George. We were actually invited to Paul McCartney's 21st birthday party, so that meant something."[4]

Evidence of just how popular the Fourmost were came at the Cavern on Thursday 5 April 1962, on a specially organised Beatles Fan Club Night. Billy Hatton recalled the Beatles' fan club secretary had polled all the fans, and the Beatles themselves, asking them, "There would be two bands on, the Beatles and somebody else – who do you want it to be? We were still called the Four Jays, and the Beatles and all the fans said they wanted the Four Jays on with the Beatles."[5]

This was a huge compliment to the Fourmost and underlines the bond between the two groups and their fans. The Beatles played the first half of the show in their old leather gear, but came out for the second half in their new 'Beno Dorn' designer suits and ties. "The Beatles used to have a lot of fun. It was not very often that they invited another band to play with them on the Cavern, that was very rare. When we did the Beatles Fan Club Show, Paul was on banjo, John was on the piano … To be invited onto the stage with them on this show was very special."[6]

The Four Jays were also support on Saturday 18 August 1962, the night Ringo Starr made his professional debut with the Beatles at the Port Sunlight Horticultural Society 'After Show Dance' held in Hulme Hall, Port Sunlight, Birkenhead.

N.B. *This was just one of many the Fourmost played as a support act to the Beatles. Famously, at the height of 'Beatlemania' they appeared on* The Beatles' Christmas Show *held at over 16 nights at the Astoria Cinema, Finsbury Park, London during December 1963 and January 1964 (by which time they had officially become the Fourmost). Billy J. Kramer topped the first half of this extravaganza. Other Brian Epstein NEMS Enterprises-managed artists who appeared on this show were Cilla Black and Tommy Quickly, for whom John and Paul had also provided the A-sides for their debut singles. Most nights there were 'two houses' for the show. One hundred thousand tickets were available. They went on sale on 21 October and by 16 November they had sold out.*

Like Billy J., the Fourmost crested the wave of Mersey Beat, with Cilla Black not far behind as the 'hit-making' combination of Lennon, McCartney, Epstein and Martin worked its magic once again to provide them all with hit singles.

Despite the endorsement of the Beatles, it was George Martin who convinced Epstein that the Fourmost were "ripe for development".[7]

Martin had heard them on a visit to the Cavern and suggested to Epstein he should bring them to London "to see if we can make a hit or two."[8]

The Fourmost's first visit to Abbey Road left an indelible impression on Billy Hatton's mind. "We set off the day before, a Monday, we're four boys from Liverpool, it was our first London hotel which had to be celebrated by going to the pub that night, obviously! We arrived at the studios the next morning and were overawed just by the size of it, the recording equipment and the whole aura. You think, this is it, this audition is gonna make or break you."[9]

Billy remembered the group's nerves were steadied by the thoughtful way George Martin and Norman Smith conducted the session. They had recognised that, for all their outer jokey confidence, the Fourmost were just four lads who once inside the studio had begun to feel out of their depth: "George was always a gentleman and Norman was as well, they didn't rush us. They gave us time and put us at ease by taking us on a tour of the recording facilities and showing us how everything worked. We did the recording test in Studio 2 and completed three songs between 2.30pm and 5.45pm: 'So Fine', 'Happy Talk' and 'Girls'. The combination of George's thoughtfulness and Norman's experience took a lot of the apprehension out of the equation. George didn't pressurise us and waited until we were ready to have a try for the most important thing we had ever attempted in our new lives as musicians: recording."[10]

The inclusion of a song like 'Happy Talk' (from the Rodgers and Hammerstein musical *South Pacific*) came from the Fourmost's penchant for injecting well received humour into their act. They could tap into all the rock 'n' roll classics, but they also leavened the mix with some comedy which gave their group its individual personality within the greater body of Mersey groups. It was a facet of their act that appealed to George Martin, something that Billy says George picked up on when they were taking a break in the canteen. "George Martin said, 'I quite like your version of 'Happy Talk' but you do realise you were playing some of the wrong chords?' … I said, 'Does it sound different, George?'

and with adrenaline-fuelled cheek put forward the theory that the chords weren't really wrong but 'inventive'. George smiled at me and replied, 'You'll do!' He realised that we were prepared to be inventive and 'have a go' at things like that … but the actual initial recording session was something that was gonna change your life, and, in the end it was fun, but it was very, very frightening too."[11]

Exhausted but happy, the Fourmost left the studios, and "We were so broke we put our money together to go to a Chinese restaurant to celebrate and spent the night in our converted bus that was parked at a discreet distance from the studio."[12]

A few days later back home in Liverpool, Brian Epstein called the boys into his office to confirm that George Martin had liked what he heard and they were now EMI Parlophone recording artists.

1, 7 & 8 *A Cellar Full of Noise*, Brian Epstein, (New English Library, 1965) p.71.
2, 3, 4 and 9, 10, 11, 12 Billy Hatton in conversation with Colin Hall in 2009 for the BBC Radio 2 documentary *The Songs the Beatles Gave Away*, written and narrated by Bob Harris OBE and produced by Bob Harris and Trudie Myerscough-Harris for WBBC.

Chapter 59:
ONLY SO MANY BEATLES SONGS TO GO ROUND

Having been given the go-ahead by George Martin and signed to Parlophone, the next job was to find the Fourmost their first A-side. Normally it would have been their producer, George Martin's job to find this. (B-sides weren't too problematic and usually came from a group's stage repertoire, which they knew well and which would not take too long to rehearse and record in the studio. There were exceptions to this rule of thumb, as with the Big Three and 'Some Other Guy' which was a tune from the group's stage set chosen specifically as an A-side because their version was rated the best in Liverpool.) The norm in the early Sixties was for whichever A&R person was in charge to visit Denmark Street to search out a suitable tune. Equally the accepted studio code of practice was that an artiste sang what they were given, like it or not.

Fortunately for them, the Fourmost were not in this situation simply because their manager was Brian Epstein and they were good mates of the Beatles. The choice of A-side would still not be theirs, but they would know the song they would be given would be well suited to them. "The Beatles liked us … because we used to do a lot of comedy songs and some weird jazz songs. But when you started recording you were recording for the pop world, not yourselves. Luckily for the people who signed with Brian Epstein was that, usually, they had first crack at Lennon-McCartney songs. It wasn't dyed in the wool that when you signed to Brian Epstein you would get a song from John and Paul. You had a far better chance of doing one, but if John and Paul thought you weren't capable of doing it, you didn't get it, simple as that! However, just the fact that they had written one of those songs, you were half way up the ladder and … John and Paul always needed to approve it anyway. I don't think there was one song that we did that they did not want to listen to and then the message would come back from Brian Epstein, yes the lads like it, it's going to go out…"[1]

With a recording date just two days away at which they expected to be recording their first single, the Fourmost had plenty of B-sides (such as 'Happy Talk') from which to choose, but still had not been given anything from John and Paul to learn for the A-side.

Being kept on tenterhooks was worth it, for when it did arrive the Fourmost's all-important first A-side was delivered in person by John Lennon, with a little help from his friend George Harrison.

"It was Sunday 4 August 1963* and we were playing at the Queen's Theatre in Blackpool with the Beatles topping the bill. We were beginning to panic because we were due to record our first A-side with George Martin in Abbey Road on the following Tuesday afternoon. In between shows (6:00pm and 8:15pm) when Brian Epstein came into our dressing room we said, 'We're very, very worried Brian, we've got this session and we haven't got an A-side. We've got the B-side – loads of those, but no A-side.' So he came down later and said, 'John and George said they'll see you after the show.' So, after the show, things are getting sorted and John Lennon said, 'Come down to me Aunt Mimi's. Me and George will be there – Paul can't be there – but we've got a song for you.'"[2]

(*The Beatles appeared in Blackpool on three consecutive Sundays during July 1963: 7th, 14th and 21st. For the first two dates they played the ABC Theatre, but on the 21st there was a change of venue and they performed at the Queen's Theatre. On the 7th and 21st, the Fourmost were support. Two weeks later and the Beatles were back in Blackpool for another show at the Queen's Theatre on Sunday 4 August with the Fourmost once again as support.)

Billy Hatton and Brian O'Hara had been to Mimi's before and so, as John requested, it was there that they rendezvoused late that night with John and George. "Brian O'Hara and myself drove down to Aunt Mimi's house, 'Mendips', and sat in the front room. In those days there were no tapes with little batteries in, they were all mains charged and so we plugged one of these in. Everybody was virtually falling asleep they're that tired. And then John and George sang, in little croaky voices, very, very sore, but enough for us to get the melody and work out the chords. So he gave it us. It was 'Hello Little Girl'*, a John Lennon composition that we took away with us from the house."[3]

(*Of course 'Hello Little Girl' had been the very song Brian Epstein had tried to persuade Gerry and the Pacemakers to record earlier in the year as their third single.)

Now proud possessors of an 'original' Lennon and McCartney song for their debut A-side the daunting task facing Billy, Brian, Mike and Dave was that they had less than one day to learn and arrange John's tune before recording it at Abbey Road on the Tuesday morning. Billy recalled that on leaving 'Mendips', "Brian O'Hara went home to have a sleep, I went home to work out what key we were going to do it in, work out all the lyrics, all the chords and everything before I got to sleep, because we were leaving that same Monday afternoon to drive down to London, find the hotel (celebrate) and do our first recording session on the Tuesday morning. As a group we had to learn our first A-side on the way down in the van."[4]

Despite the tiredness, the nerves and the never-before-heard song they had been given to record, it was the sheer excitement of what they were doing that provided the Fourmost with the energy to carry them through: "It was a brand new song for us. When we actually did 'Hello Little Girl' in the studio, it was the first time we'd ever played it through amplifiers and with microphones in front of our faces. Now, you would not get that today! But in those days, between 2:30 and 6:45pm we had the A-side done, the B-side ('Just In Case') done and one other possible B-side ('Little Egypt') done. They don't write them like that anymore!"[5]

Billy acknowledges the part played by George and Norman in making that session work so well. "You could not wish for two better people … I think George Martin knew that with some of the Liverpool bands that there was something you *could* sell, because everything was so new in those days. Brian Epstein used to come into Studio 2 now and again. He was just pleased to see his boys in the studio, so he would sit there with a permanent grin on his face."[6]

Billy Hatton (and George Martin) recognised that coming from Liverpool played a major part in the success of Epstein's artists: 'One thing that did help was that Liverpool character, it was not over confidence but a willingness to try something new. That mattered an awful lot. Even though they were a bit scared about being in the studio, it didn't defeat them, it encouraged them to sing a bit better and to play a bit better … It does matter, you must have a go – if you make a mistake, you laugh it off. George Martin said to us one time, 'It's amazing the amount of material you guys from Liverpool can get through, some people come down and they're totally overawed in the studio: they make a mistake and they fall to pieces. You guys make a mistake and say we've got to do it better … and you normally do."[7]

Of 'Hello Little Girl' and the Fourmost's version, Bill commented: "It was such a simple song and sometimes they're the hardest to make something of. 'Hello Little Girl' was written by a young boy, but to make it into a 'pop song' was left to the Fourmost, which we did. We kept it simple: the lyrics were sung very, very brightly and maybe that gave it a bit of an edge, I don't know. When the Beatles (who always wanted to know who was covering their songs) heard it they said it was fine. The next one we recorded was a more difficult song, but the first one was simple, just do what you can … you know."[8]

George Martin commented, "The Fourmost were a good lot, they were a good band and they did actually give the song their own identity, it wasn't just a copy of a demo."[9]

John Lennon had not written 'Hello Little Girl' especially for the Fourmost, although he eventually gifted it to them. Written in late 1957 it was not the first tune he had composed but one of the very first and the one that he felt confident enough to play to someone else. That someone was, of course, Paul McCartney. Even back in 1957, when John was just 17 and Paul only 15, and they had only just met, John Lennon thought enough of Paul McCartney as both a friend and a musician to trust, respect and to care about his opinion. Paul reciprocated by playing his own 'I Lost My Little Girl'. In their first roughly taped incarnations, both songs reflected the influence of Buddy Holly on the two budding composers.

Having begun in a good place they would never look back.

In his 1980 interview with David Sheff for *Playboy* magazine, John had this to say about 'Hello Little Girl': "That was me. That was actually my first song. I remembered some Thirties or Forties song which was … 'You're delightful, you're delicious and da da da. Isn't it a pity that you are such a scatterbrain.' That always fascinated me for some reason or another. It's also connected to my mother. It's all very Freudian. She used to sing that one. So I made 'Hello Little Girl' out of it."[10]

As it evolved, the song's tight doo-wop harmonies and warm, hum-a-long mmmm's, made it eminently catchy and so it's surprising the Beatles abandoned it.

Interestingly, two of the first songs composed by John and Paul that were recorded by other artists had been inspired by John's memories of his mother: 'Do You Want to Know a Secret?' came from memories of Julia singing 'I'm Wishing' from Disney's 1937 animated feature film *Snow White and the Seven Dwarves*, while 'Hello Little Girl' from Julia singing 'Scatterbrain' (composed in 1939).

John was not a prolific writer, especially in the very early days when his energies were distracted and split by having to learn covers, rehearse and perform. With such activities taking up most of his time, when it came to provide three original songs for the 'Decca Tapes', John did not pen a new tune but placed his confidence in what for him was already the tried and trusted 'Hello Little Girl', while Paul provided 'Like Dreamers Do' and 'Love of the Loved'. All three became hits for other artists.

THE FOURMOST
HELLO LITTLE GIRL **(1:50)**
(McCartney-Lennon)
Northern Songs Ltd
Parlophone R5056
Recorded at Abbey Road on Tuesday 23 July 1963
Producer: George Martin
B-side: Just in Case
(Boudleaux-Bryant)
Producer: George Martin

The songwriter for the B-side was Boudleaux Bryant. His name is mistakenly written on the label to include a hyphen between 'Boudleaux' and 'Bryant' making it seem as if he was two people (which he wasn't).

Boudleaux famously co-wrote songs with his wife Felice but they also wrote individually. Together they wrote many tunes for the Everly Brothers including 'Bye Bye Love', 'Wake Up Little Susie' and 'Take a Message to Mary'. The Everly Brothers were very popular with many Liverpool artists including the Beatles. 'Just in Case' was a Boudleaux solo tune originally written for the Everly Brothers for their 1960 album *It's Everly Time*.

Released: Friday, August 30, 1963.

Entered the UK chart on 12 September 1963 and by 30 October was peaking at number 9. On the charts for 17 weeks.

'Hello Little Girl' was released in the USA on 15 November 1963 on ATCO 6280. It failed to chart.

Disc singles reviewer Don Nicholl, typical of many within the music business, made it clear he thought highly of the Fourmost from the outset. In his 4-star review of 'Hello Little Girl' he took time to individually name each member of the group, describe their line-up, that they were from Liverpool and that their debut was "a Beatles item". He also clearly rated

The Fourmost in 1963. Let to right: Mike Milward (rhythm guitar, vocals), Brian O'Hara (lead guitar, vocals), Dave Lovelady (drums, vocals) and Billy Hatton (bass, vocals). (Pictorial Press Ltd / Alamy Stock Photo)

'Hello Little Girl' itself, writing that it "should bring them quick success with three of the group singing the happy beater and working in some falsetto for effect." He also very much liked their take on 'Just in Case', an American number which he says "the team rattles off smartly, the guitars providing a spry crisp noise indeed." Closing his lengthy review, he commented, "Could well be that this group will line up alongside the other Mersey winners."[11]

Addendum 1: *The Story of Brian Epstein's Original Acetate of 'Hello Little Girl'*
As explained in an earlier chapter, during 1962, Brian Epstein had four of the songs from the Decca Tapes converted into two-sided 10" acetates at the HMV store on Oxford Street, London to use as demonstration discs (or 'demos') for easier use by A&R men. One of these was 'Hello Little Girl' which was coupled with 'Till There Was You' on the other side. 'Hello Little Girl' ('Hello' misspelt by Brian as 'Hullo') is labelled as being by 'John Lennon & The Beatles' and 'Till There Was You' by 'Paul McCartney & The Beatles', which reflects that this is how the group was possibly expected to be named – either John or Paul being chosen as the lead name on the label, as per the fashion of the day. Although the Beatles would not have countenanced such labelling, just which Beatle was to be identified as the frontman on record labels remained unresolved at that time by prospective A&Rs.

In 2016, the only known copy of the 'Hello Little Girl' demo was re-discovered wrapped in paper in his loft by its owner, Les Maguire. Former keyboard player with Gerry and the Pacemakers, Les had stored it a long time ago after having been given it by Brian Epstein.

Epstein (whose handwriting is on the label) gave the original demo to George Martin when he was trying to bend Martin's ear to the Beatles' cause. Unmoved, Martin had passed it back to Epstein who in turn later passed it on to Gerry and the Pacemakers to learn and record, which (somewhat half-heartedly) they did. Epstein had suggested it as their third single, but the group did not want to release it for they already had their hearts and minds set on recording 'You'll Never Walk Alone'. As a result, they recorded a tepid version (by their standards) of John's song, after which Epstein gave the Beatles demo to Les. (No wonder John and George had to drive from a gig in Blackpool to meet with the Fourmost in Mimi's front room to wearily play the song to them, taping it as they did so: Brian no longer had the original Decca demo.)

Gerry and the Pacemakers' instincts were proved absolutely right. They most certainly made the right choice of song for their third single. Their version of 'You'll Never Walk Alone' became their third straight number 1 and hogged the top spot for four consecutive weeks. With the passage of time the Pacemakers' version has become iconic within the city of Liverpool. Not only is it part of the very fabric of Liverpool FC, who adopted it as their club song, but also of the city itself where it is a regularly sung hymn of hope and unity.

After all these years, and as he felt it was no longer of any use to him, Les decided to give what (amongst record and Beatles collectors) had become a 'Holy Grail' to his granddaughter to help her purchase a house of her own once she completed her accountancy exams. As a result, on 22 March 2016, it was auctioned at Omega Auctions, Warrington with a reserve of £10,000 ($14,207). Outbidding collectors from China, Europe and North America, a collector living in the North West of England acquired it for £77,550 ($110,226).

Addendum 2: *A Snapshot of the Fourmost and the UK Top 50, 30 October 1963*
In the week 'Hello Little Girl' made the Top 10, Brian Poole and the Tremeloes were number 1 with 'Do You Love Me', Gerry and the Pacemakers were at number 2 (and just one week from the top) with 'You'll Never Walk Alone', while the Beatles and 'She Loves You' were still bobbing around the top three.

Straight in at number 29 and rocketing towards the very top were the Searchers with 'Needles and Pins', Cilla Black had climbed ten places from number 50 to number 40 with her debut release, 'Love of the Loved' and at number 47 Billy J. Kramer was coming to the end of 13 weeks on the chart with 'Bad to Me'. A few places below at number 42 and coming to the end of a 14-week run on the chart, having peaked at number 21, were the Rolling Stones with their debut single 'Come On'.

Significantly, in that same UK chart at number 28 (having climbed 18 places) was a trio of folk singers from the USA called Peter, Paul and Mary and a song called 'Blowin' in the Wind', which had been written by a 22-year-old folksinger from Minnesota called Bob Dylan. Just prior to their UK success, Peter, Paul and Mary had taken Dylan's song to the very top of the Billboard *Hot 100* in the US.

Also accompanying the Fourmost in the Top 50 that week were, among others, Elvis ('Bossa Nova Baby'), Chuck Berry ('Let It Rock' / 'Memphis Tennessee'), Bo Diddley ('Pretty Thing'), Ray Charles ('No One'), the Drifters ('I'll Take You Home'), the Ronettes ('Be My Baby'), the Crystals ('Then He Kissed Me'), Buddy Holly ('Wishing'), Rick Nelson ('Fools Rush In') and Cliff Richard ('It's All in the Game') and so the list went on ... Brian, Billy, Mike and Dave of the Fourmost were in excellent company.

1, 2, 3, 4, 5, 6, 7 & 8 Billy Hatton in conversation with Colin Hall, 2009, for the BBC Radio 2 documentary *The Songs the Beatles Gave Away*, written and narrated by Bob Harris OBE and produced by Bob Harris and Trudie Myerscough-Harris for WBBC.
9 Sir George Martin in conversation with Bob Harris OBE and Colin Hall for the 2009 BBC Radio 2 documentary *The Songs the Beatles Gave Away*, written and narrated by Bob Harris, produced for WBBC by Bob Harris and Trudie Myerscough-Harris.
10 *All We Are Saying: The Last Major Interview with John Lennon and Yoko Ono*, conducted by David Sheff (Sidgwick & Jackson, 2000) p.172.
11 *Disc* music weekly, edition 284, 31 August 1963, 'Disc Date' with Don Nicholl, p.8.

Chapter 60:
A LIVER BIRD SINGS

CILLA BLACK
b. Priscilla Maria Veronica White in Vauxhall, Liverpool on 27 May 1943
Married Bobby Willis on 25 January 1969, at the Marylebone Registry Office, London. The couple repeated the ceremony for their families at St. Mary's Church, Woolton, Liverpool on 25 March 1969.
d. Estepona, Spain on 1 August 2015, age 72
"Liverpool's First Lady of Song" Dick James, 1963

On Sunday night 9 December 1962, George Martin first visited the Cavern to hear the Beatles perform on their home territory. In his autobiography, *A Cellarful of Noise*, Brian Epstein recalled that as they entered the club Martin drew his attention to "the chirpy cloak room attendant with bright orange hair".[1]

The young girl was 'Swinging' Priscilla White aka 'Cilla Black' and along with Beryl Marsden she was already a well-known female face on the Liverpool music scene. Both girls knew their way around a song and kept critical Liverpool audiences well entertained and asking for more.

In the mazy mythology of Mersey Beat, Cilla Black is always cast as the hat-check girl at the Cavern who occasionally sang with the Beatles. It is more likely that the truth is she never was employed as the official 'hat-check girl', but very occasionally when she was short of cash would persuade the doorman to let her in for free if she helped with the coats. At one stage she was juggling three jobs: as a secretary, as a waitress at the Zodiac Club and as an occasional hat girl at the Cavern.

Cilla was born in 1943 and home for the White family was number 380 Scotland Road, or 'Scottie' Road as all Scousers called it. It was a rough, tough area where the Irish Catholics ('Left Footers') would live while the 'Proddy Dogs' (Protestants) lived on Netherfield Road. The divisions between the two communities were strong and sectarianism in the Fifties was as rife in Liverpool as it had ever been.

Scottie Road is about a mile long. Constructed in the last quarter of the 18th century it was originally part of a road that, if you followed it to its end, would take you to Scotland, hence its name. As the 19th century began, so the road was widened and housing for working people grew up along its sides. The area's population increased greatly during Victorian times when, especially between 1845 and 1849 – during the 'Great Hunger' in Ireland – many thousands of Irish people were forced to flee their homeland to settle there.

At one time the area was home to some 200 public houses and until 1929 was represented in Parliament by an Irish Nationalist MP.

In her autobiography, *What's It All About?*, while Cilla Black acknowledged that Scottie Road was always a tough place to grow up, she also recalled that as both a child and then later as a teenager, walking home after dark she always felt totally safe.

By the 1960s, Scotland Road, as an area in which to live, was in decline. Many houses from the 1930s had already been demolished and in their place new corporation flats were being erected. After World War II, alongside these changes many former residents were rehoused in new council houses on new council estates being built across the city, in such places as Croxteth, Kirkby, Huyton, Norris Green and Stockbridge Village.

Amidst all the hurly-burly, change and economic difficulties of post-war Liverpool, Cilla enjoyed a happy childhood growing up in a spacious flat above George Murray's barbers shop (who rented the rooms to the Whites) behind a branch of the Midland Bank (who were the landlords of the White's apartment). Living with her in number 380 was Mum (Priscilla), Dad (John) and older brothers George and John. When Cilla was about five, the family were joined by 'little Allan' who was Auntie Ann's baby whom Cilla's mum and dad adopted when he was about nine months old. Auntie Ann would always visit at weekends. A close-knit unit, the children were raised in a home in which church and family were the cornerstones of everyday life. Cilla noted that, "We all grew up aware of what it meant to be good neighbours, good Samaritans, and a help to other people."[2]

Music was integral to family life. All her family loved to listen to music and to play it and so from the moment she was born music filled Cilla's ears. The White's living room housed a 'great big radiogram' and the family piano Dad had bought from NEMS' Everton store. Dad played the harmonica and Mum, who loved opera and country and western, loved to sing. On Saturday nights after the pubs had closed, family, friends and neighbours would convene in the White's kitchen-cum-living-room where the men would drink Guinness and the women shandies to the accompaniment of much singing and dancing. From age 5, Cilla was allowed to join in. She would stand on the kitchen table and entertain everyone with a song.

Cilla was only 11 going on 12 when Bill Haley and his Comets broke big in the UK with 'Rock Around the Clock'. Haley's record was a turning point for her: "I couldn't believe my ears. From then on I'd spend every penny I could on rock 'n' roll."[3]

As she entered her teens (1956), Cilla became besotted with American teenage singing sensation Frankie Lymon and his group, the Teenagers. Lymon was just a year older than Cilla. Standing in the family bathroom and utilising that room's in-built echo to capture the reverb of those early American rock 'n' roll records, she would sing Lymon's big hit song 'Why Do Fools Fall in Love'. Lymon's voice had not broken, which meant Cilla could sing in his key and imitate his voice. She recalled that from the moment she obtained a copy of the single she drove her family 'around the bend' as she played it over and over again.

When Cilla left school in 1958, despite singing whenever she could and dreaming of a life as a singing star, Cilla was disgruntled to read that her final report did not recommend her to be 'suitable for stardom', but that 'Priscilla is suitable for office work'.

Undeterred, Ms. White informed her career's advisor that she didn't need a career because she was going to be a star. Equally undeterred, the advisor told her that before that happened Cilla still needed to get a job and so, bowing to the reality of having to earn money in order to survive, she attended Anfield Commercial College on a year's secretarial and shorthand course.

She may have knuckled down, but she had not given up on her dream and so it was that Cilla White continued to burst into song whenever the opportunity arose. It wasn't long before during lunchtimes at Anfield Commercial College she was entertaining her friends by singing to them.

Along with close college friends, Pauline Behan and Pat Davies, Cilla just wanted to have fun and the trio did so by constantly doing the rounds of the popular Merseyside clubs.

Cilla's love of music and hearing it played 'live' meant that she was aware of the Beatles from as early as their performances at the Jacaranda: "When I was 14 I was aware of a band called the Silver Beatles and they used to play in the basement of a club called the Jacaranda. Quite frankly I didn't think they were much cop, so I wasn't really a big fan … they were just a band in Liverpool."[4]

In those early, pre-Hamburg days, Cilla thought more of Rory Storm and the Hurricanes (with Ringo on drums) and Gerry and the Pacemakers, who were both, to use her phrase, 'big bands'.

One morning at College, Pauline (who later married Gerry Marsden) suggested that they should all go to the Iron Door club on Duke Street to hear Rory Storm and the Hurricanes perform. The girls needed no second invitation.

From the moment they arrived at the Iron Door, Cilla sensed Pauline was up to something as she positioned Cilla and her other friends from college right at the front of the stage immediately in front of the group. During a break in the Hurricanes' performances, Cilla saw Pauline eagerly and persuasively talking to the group. Only slowly did she realise that her friend was asking if Cilla could sing a number with them.

Pauline was determined and the Hurricanes unable to resist. Before Cilla knew it, Wally the bassist had put a mic in front of her face and she was on stage belting out her version of 'Fever'. Her performance went down so exceedingly well that after her debut she frequently sang on stage with the Hurricanes.

One of the songs she particularly recalled singing with them was the Shirelles number, 'Boys', which was the very same song drummer Ringo Starr liked to sing during his 'Ringo Starrtime' solo spot with the Hurricanes. Cilla said it took some negotiating before Ringo agreed she could sing the song, but on the strict condition that she could *only* do so as a duet with him. Even after he agreed he didn't make it easy for Cilla to sing it: he would not move his microphone to accommodate her, she had to bend over his drums to sing into his mic that was positioned over his drum kit. Despite this, her relationship with the Hurricanes flourished and it meant that from very early on in her singing career Cilla was a good friend of Ringo.

Word soon spread beyond the Iron Door that Cilla was a good singer and audiences would shout at whatever group was on stage to let Cilla join them to 'have a go'. In most cases they willingly did and as a consequence Cilla sang with several groups besides Rory Storm and the Hurricanes, including Kingsize Taylor and the Dominoes, the Fourmost and maybe, most impressively of all, with the Big Three.

The Big Three were her favourite band. She would sing with them at the Zodiac Club on Duke Street. "The Big Three was a really big band with whom I occasionally sang: I was called 'Swinging Priscilla' and was with the best band in Liverpool."[5]

That, of course, would have immediately impressed the Beatles who mightily admired the Big Three.

Working, as she also did, as a waitress at the Zodiac coffee lounge, it was not only where she built her reputation for singing with the Big Three but was where she met her future husband Bobby Willis (a good singer and songwriter himself).

Local promoter Sam Leach was the first to encourage Cilla in her own right by booking her for her first gig which was at the Casanova Club where she was billed as 'Swinging Cilla'. Gigs such as this and her performances with some of the most popular groups in the city helped her to build a considerable reputation as a singer.

Her opinion of the Beatles changed when they came back from their first trip to Hamburg: "That's when I got into the Beatles and the only way I noticed them was they looked great. They were all in black leathers, all looking like bikers. They had the shocking pink cheese cutter hats and we all thought, 'WOW!'. We all thought they were sex symbols. Pete Best was with them at the time. It was in a ballroom and I looked around and all the kids were just dancing and the music was just so exciting! When you got over the sexiness/the look of the Beatles, then you concentrated on the sound and that was when I became a fan."[6]

The new sounding, new look 'Hamburg' Beatles left such an indelible impression on Cilla's mind that many years later she provided a detailed description of Lennon's appearance to Ray Coleman: "John's hair was much longer then than Brian Epstein ever let him wear it later on. It was brushed forward instead of back and had an enormous pink leather hat over it. He had black leather pants on, lined with red satin, black T-shirt, black leather jacket and high black boots with Cuban heels. I took one look and thought: 'Oh, my God!'"[7]

As with the Hurricanes it was Pauline Behan who wore the Beatles down to allow Cilla to sing on stage with them. This event occurred post-Hamburg and Cilla was convinced they were too popular to let anyone join them on stage. Her friend Pauline was unmoved by Cilla's point of view and was able to persuade her to join her at the Iron Door again: "I was 15 and at Anfield Commercial College and Pauline said, 'Let's go down to … the Iron Door', where there was an early session. I asked her, 'What do we want to go down there for?' And she said, 'Well I want you to see my boyfriend.' So, we went to the Iron Door where the Beatles were playing."⁸

Once at the Iron Door, Cilla asked Pauline to point out which boy was her boyfriend and she pointed out George Harrison. Cilla was duly impressed, telling Pauline, "He's alright."⁹

Cilla said Pauline then had to tell her the names of the other boys in the group because at this time she did not know them: "I said who's that over there … it was Paul. AND Paul was so pretty…!"¹⁰

In between songs Pauline and her friends began to pester the Beatles to let Cilla sing a song with them. As with Rory and the Hurricanes the tactic worked. "John Lennon got a bit fed up and said, 'OK Cyril! Come up and have a go!'"¹¹

For a while after that John would always refer to Cilla as 'Cyril'.

The next thing Cilla knew she was on stage with the Beatles and John Lennon was asking her what did she want to sing. "I asked if they knew Sam Cook's version of 'Summertime'? And they played 'Summertime' and I sang and that was the first time I realised that a girl singer sings in a completely different key to a guy. I sounded a bit like Yma Sumac!* But that was my first introduction to the Beatles. I hung out with them. I was already appearing with the Big Three by then and they thought the Big Three were fantastic. That was the beginning of a friendship."¹² (Cilla confirmed that the Big Three were John Lennon's favourite Liverpool group.)

(*Yma Sumac (b. 10 September 1923 – d. 1 November 2008), was a Peruvian coloratura soprano who, in the 1950s, became internationally famous as an exponent of exotica and mambo music. She had a range of four and a half octaves (a trained singer's range would usually be three octaves). Sumac could sing notes in the low baritone register and notes above the range of a normal soprano and was also able to hit notes in the whistle register. For an example of her incredible vocal range listen to 'Chuncho (The Forest Creatures)' from 1953.)

Cilla's stage name Cilla 'Black' came from an article that appeared in the very first edition of *Mersey Beat* (6 July 1961) in which editor Bill Harry got her surname wrong, calling her 'Black' instead of 'White'. When Brian Epstein signed Cilla to NEMS he did so as 'Cilla Black', preferring this to her actual surname.

Cilla's contract was signed on 6 September 1963 at 380 Scottie Road because Epstein needed Cilla's father Mr. John White to sign on behalf of Priscilla because she was under the age of 21. On presenting the contract, which was in the name of 'Cilla Black', Cilla's father very carefully read the document before declaring that there was a 'glaring' error: Epstein had got Cilla's surname wrong. John White was not happy.

It took over 20 minutes before Dad would concede that, for reasons purely to do with show business, 'Black' was better than 'White'. The change apparently made him feel as if he was giving his daughter away. As Cilla would recall, "Not all the changes in my life met with the approval of me dad. Although he was generally happy for me, he didn't approve of the change of name from White to Black, which began as a misprint in *Mersey Beat*."¹³ According to Cilla, John Lennon first introduced her to Brian Epstein. In some accounts she says it was at the Tower Ballroom, New Brighton, where she was appearing with Kingsize Taylor and the Dominoes and the Beatles were top of the bill. "I noticed a very smart man deep in conversation with John. John told me it was their new manager, but I just laughed because I thought this was another of John's jokes. Then he took me over and introduced me. It was Brian Epstein and he'd just signed the Beatles. Even then John was still doing his 'Cyril' thing with me: 'Come over here, Cyril, I want you to meet Brian Epstein.'"¹⁴

On which night at the Tower Ballroom this introduction took place cannot be an exact science because just what Cilla (or John) meant by 'signed the Beatles' is also not an exact science. Most commentators agree that the verbal contract was most probably agreed on Sunday 3 December 1961, but it could have been a day or more after that. (They didn't actually sign a contract with Epstein until Wednesday 24 January 1962 and even then it wasn't legally binding.)

It is unlikely to be the 3 December agreement with Epstein to which John referred in his conversation with Cilla, for she was most probably not at the Tower Ballroom in New Brighton because on the next three occasions the Beatles appeared there (8, 15 and

Boxing Day 1961) Kingsize Taylor and the Dominoes, with whom she was singing at the time, were not on the bill.

The introduction could have been made on an earlier date. It had been on Wednesday 29 November 1961 that the Beatles (with Bob Wooler in tow) *had* attended a meeting with Epstein in his offices at NEMS on Whitechapel. It was at that meeting that Brian first floated the idea of managing them. Just a few days later on Friday 1 December 1961, Kingsize Taylor and the Dominoes *did* support the Beatles at the Tower Ballroom. This date ties in better with Cilla's memory that John first introduced her to Brian at the Tower Ballroom.

To confuse matters further, in her 2003 autobiography (on p.64) Cilla says it was *at* the Cavern where Lennon introduced her to Epstein, as 'Cyril', and with the recommendation that he should sign her.

Whatever the exact location and timing was, it is apparent that from the moment the Beatles engaged with Epstein he had been made aware of Cilla's presence as an artiste on the Liverpool beat music scene. That Cilla had been personally recommended and introduced to him by the Beatle he most admired would not have been lost on Brian Epstein.

Cilla herself was surprised that it was John who recommended her and not Ringo. "I was much closer to Ringo … I thought it was Ringo who told Brian … to take me on as a singer. I bumped into Ringo and I remember thanking him and he said, what are you thanking me for? And I said for putting in a good word for me. He said, it wasn't me, it was John … Out of all the people I wouldn't have thought John would have been the one … John had a shy side, he was very shy of women actually. That's why he had this abrupt, aggressive sense of humour."[15]

Despite the impressive introduction from Lennon, for Brian Epstein to sign Cilla there were some hiccups along the way to be overcome, such as a failed audition at the Majestic Ballroom in Birkenhead when, at Brian Epstein's request, she sang a song with the Beatles. Previously in Birkenhead with the Big Three, Cilla had sung 'Summertime'. Whereas she had rehearsed this song with them and they played it in the right key for her, she hadn't rehearsed it with the Beatles and they didn't. "The music was not in my key and any adjustments that the boys were now trying to make were too late to save me. My voice sounded awful … As the last notes of the music faded away, I risked a peep over towards Brian. He was clearly not impressed … 'Thank you, Cilla', he called politely as he stood up and left."[16]

As she approached her twentieth birthday (May '63) Priscilla was still singing in the clubs, waiting tables at the Zodiac and occasionally hanging hats elsewhere. Not much else in fact had changed except that professionally she had become known as 'Cilla Black'.

From the moment 1963 began, the Beatles stormed the charts with 'Please Please Me', followed by 'From Me to You' and 'She Loves You', Gerry and the Pacemakers scored two number ones with 'How Do You Do It' and 'I Like It', while Billy J. Kramer with his reluctant Dakotas enjoyed two massive singles with 'Do You Want to Know a Secret?' and 'Bad to Me' … but for Priscilla White it must have seemed that it was all happening for everyone else in Liverpool except 'Cilla Black'.

And then suddenly, it was …

---

1 *A Cellarful of Noise*, by Brian Epstein (New English Library, 1964) p.67.
2 & 3 *What's It All About*, Cilla Black, (Ebury Press, 2003), p.3 and p.25.
4, 5, 6, 8, 9, 10, 11, 12 Cilla Black in conversation with Bob Harris OBE for the BBC Radio 2 documentary *The Songs the Beatles Gave Away* (2009), written and narrated by Bob Harris, produced by Bob Harris and Trudie Myerscough-Harris for WBBC.
7 & 14 *Lennon: The Definitive Biography, Anniversary Edition*, by Ray Coleman (Pan Books, 2000) p.251.
13 *Step Inside*, by Cilla Black, (J.M. Dent & Sons, 1985).
15, 16 *What's It All About*, Cilla Black, (Ebury Press, 2003), p.6.

Chapter 61:
THE SOUND OF SCOUSE

Everything changed during the space of one night for Cilla Black when she decided to accompany her good friend Pat Davies to the Blue Angel Club.

Coincidentally, on this particular night, *Mersey Beat*'s amazing editor Bill Harry and his wife Virginia were also there, as were Brian Epstein and Andrew Loog Oldham. As Harry later recalled, when he and Virginia arrived the pair were deep in conversation. Just 19 years old, very savvy and already flying, Oldham had joined Brian Epstein's NEMS as publicist for the Beatles. Previously, among his many jobs, Oldham had been assistant to John Stephens on Carnaby Street and then Mary Quant. So fast was he moving, Loog Oldham's feet were barely touching the ground: by June he would be producing the Rolling Stones' first single.

Bill Harry was a big fan of Cilla and had written an article about her in the first edition of his marvellous *Mersey Beat* music paper in which he famously got his 'White' mixed up with his 'Black'. He had also asked her to write an article about fashion for the paper and viewed her primarily as a girl with a passion to become a jazz singer in the style of her idol, Peggy Lee.

His memory of that all-important night at the Blue Angel is crystal clear. Seeing Cilla and her friend Pat Davies at the bottom of the stairs, Bill approached her and, "Took Cilla over to Epstein, introduced her and asked him if he would listen to her sing." Having gained Epstein's attention, Bill quickly "arranged for Cilla to join the group on stage and sing the number 'Boys'", after which he "brought her back to introduce her to Epstein and left her to it. She then told me that Epstein had arranged a meeting for her at his office the next day and she became the first female artist in his stable."[1]

The group who happily allowed Cilla to sing with them that evening was not a jazz group but a beat combo called the Masterminds.

In her second autobiography, Cilla writes a slightly different version of this story. In her version, Cilla says she was on the floor with John Reuben's modern jazz group and singing mainly non-rock 'n' roll (because the Blue Angel's clientele were posher and more sophisticated). In particular, she says she was singing her version of Della Reece's 'Bye Bye Blackbird'. Brian Epstein was captivated, asked why Cilla had not sung like that at the Majestic and offered to manage her on the spot. A meeting was arranged for the next day in his office from which Cilla Black never looked back.

Bill Harry was bemused as to why Cilla changed the story in this way. So much so he contacted one of the Masterminds who not only remembered backing Cilla on 'Boys' but also meeting Andrew Loog Oldham. Harry also contacted Loog Oldham who also confirmed that he remembered Bill approaching Brian and arranging for Cilla to sing that night. (Oldham was so impressed by the Masterminds he signed them and got them to record Bob Dylan's 'She Belongs to Me'.)

In his autobiography, Brian Epstein acknowledged that before he signed her he was aware of Cilla as one of the girls who was always around the Cavern and that he even knew she sang, but there again, as he points out, nearly every one who frequented the Cavern was either a guitarist or singer: "Though I liked Cilla … I had no ideas of management until midway 1963. I first heard her sing with the Beatles but had not been generally impressed … but the next occasion was early one morning in the Blue Angel Club in Liverpool. She looked, as always, magnificent, a slender graceful creature with the ability to shed her mood of dignified repose if she were singing a fast number. I watched her move and I watched her stand and I half closed my eyes and imagined her on a vast stage with the right lighting. I was convinced she could become a wonderful artiste."[2]

Cilla Black photographed in 1964 as pop fans of the Sixties will remember seeing her singing her heart out in front of the cameras on TV. (Pictorial Press Ltd / Alamy Stock Photo)

Cilla Black was the last Liverpool artist Brian Epstein signed and the *only* girl. As he commented, "This is not accidental; for I was finding it difficult … to select talent from so much in the beat city … and I didn't care to dilute the special attention I wanted to give Cilla by managing a girl-competitor."[3]

Once Cilla was signed with Brian, like those before her, there followed 'commercial tests' with George Martin at Abbey Road and in late August she was back in the studio to record her first single. As with Billy J. and the Fourmost before her, Brian had arranged for her to record a John Lennon and Paul McCartney 'original'. The theory being, why change a winning formula?

Cilla: "Once I was signed up with Brian and we all came to London we were all one big happy family then. When Paul said, 'I've got a song for you,' I replied, 'You used to sing that in the Cavern! 'Love of the Loved' is not a new song!' He said, 'I know but I think it will be good for you. If I used to sing it at the Cavern it meant that I liked that song, I wouldn't perform the song if I didn't like it.' I said, 'OK, I'll do the song.'"[4]

On being first introduced to Cilla, George Martin recalled, "Cilla was still a teenager and she had this kind of very strident voice … a corncrake voice … you could hear her at the end of the street."[5]

And so it was that the unknown artist and the already acclaimed producer entered the studio to cut Cilla's debut 45 … history was in the making.

CILLA BLACK
LOVE OF THE LOVED (2:00)
(Lennon-McCartney)
Northern Songs Ltd
Parlophone R 5065
Recorded at EMI Studios, London (Abbey Road) on 28 August 1963
Producer: George Martin
B-side: Shy of Love (Willis)

Cilla had learned very early on that not only was Bobby Willis the love of her life, but that he was a very talented singer and songwriter who could have possibly carved out a solo career of his own. Proof of this was 'Shy of Love', which was not only a song of Bobby's that Cilla loved, but so did George Martin. He was more than happy for it to be the B-side. From then on, while Bobby agreed with Cilla not to pursue his own singing career, he supplied many songs for Cilla to record including most of her B-sides.
Released: Friday 27 September 1963.

Entered the UK singles chart on Thursday 17 October 1963 at number 50.

Cilla's debut release was a modest hit that peaked at number 35 on 6 November 1963 and spent a total of six weeks on the chart (50, 40, 35, 50, 39, 50).

Released in the familiar green Parlophone sleeve, very early copies of the single were printed with Cilla's name misspelt as 'Cilia' on both sides.

In a compendium of sheet music published in 1963 entitled *The Big Beat Album*, that included 'Love of the Loved', Dick James described Cilla as 'Liverpool's First Lady of Song', before adding, "she has the talent, charm and sincerity to make a tremendous contribution to the entertainment industry." He was certainly on the money with that prediction![6]

Her debut number was never a personal favourite of Cilla's, or at least the arrangement wasn't. "I got to the studios and I was expecting a rock and roll band – and they were proper musicians and I thought, oh no, oh gosh! There was a seven-piece, maybe ten-piece and they had a brass section. So I wasn't quite happy with 'Love of the Loved' but I was so thirsty and hungry for fame that I agreed to do it and to promote it. I couldn't moan at George Martin because I didn't know him that well and I was just so thrilled I had a recording contract, but actually to this day I don't like the arrangement of 'Love of the Loved'. I loved the way Paul did it at the Cavern."[7]

In her second autobiography, Cilla says she did not enjoy a single moment of the 'Love of the Loved' session. She felt nervous and somewhat embarrassed because George Martin kept pulling her up over her Scouse accent. "Every time I sang 'thurr' instead of 'there', George kept pulling me up, 'That word sounds much too Liverpudlian...'"[8]

The perfectionist in George Martin was not easily satisfied. Equally, Cilla was not a quitter, and so, respectfully, she tried again and again to get it right for him. Instead of the usual four or five takes it took a total of 15 before she nailed it to his satisfaction.

By the time of her second autobiography, Cilla had come to appreciate from where George Martin was coming: "Now, when I listen to my early records, I can see what he was on about. 'Where' and 'there' were the two words I had not lost my Scouse pronunciation on. I might have thought I had total accent control of 'Love of the Loved', but I hadn't. I still said, 'thurr'."[9]

Despite the tension during the recording session and dreading the results, Cilla was relieved when she heard the playback. "When I sat listening with George they sounded absolutely smashing. OK 'Love of the Loved' didn't have the group sound that I'd wanted, but it didn't half sound professional. Nobody could have been more surprised than I was."[10]

Disc music weekly's singles reviewer, Don Nicholl, gave 'Love of the Loved' a cautious 3-star review. He described Cilla as, "A young woman with a hard trumpeting vocal manner that's not unlike the sound of Shirley Bassey at times," although, he was quick to point out, "Miss Black is not the same sort of ballad singer." Noting Cilla came from Liverpool and that 'Love of the Loved' had been written for her by "Messrs. Lennon and McCartney," he called it "a song with an urgent strut to it ... as if it's in a hurry to reach the best sellers. Which it may." As for Bobby's 'Shy of Love', he was abrupt and to the point: "A double tracker. All shout and no soul."[11]

Significantly, it impressed the Cavernites, the Beatles' number 1 fans in Liverpool, who were not easily won over to other acts doing Beatles covers. One of whom was Freda Kelly for whom the song was a particular favourite: "I used to request 'Love of the Loved' at the lunchtime sessions, this was before the Beatles gave it to Cilla. I don't like people doing Beatles songs, I prefer their own versions, but I liked the way Cilla did 'Love of the Loved'."[12]

Despite the tension she endured during the recording of this Lennon-McCartney 'giveaway', and although it was only a modest hit, it nevertheless launched Cilla's singing career as a chart artist in the UK.

The potential suggested by her debut release was more than realised when she followed-up with two successive massive UK number ones:

'Anyone Who Had a Heart' (Bacharach/David) Released 31 January 1964.
'You're My World (Il Mio Mondo)'* (Bindi/Sigman/Paoli) Released 1 May 1964.

Both of these chart-toppers were produced by George Martin and the B-sides for both singles were penned by Bobby Willis ('Just for You' and 'Suffer Now I Must').

(*'You're My World' was Cilla's first US release. It peaked at number 26 on 1 August 1964 and was to be her only Top 40 hit in the USA, although it reached number 4 in Billboard's Easy Listening Chart. Despite its modest US chart success, Cilla was elated when she learned, via Ringo Starr, that Elvis had a copy of her single on his personal jukebox in Graceland.)

Cilla's success was well earned and confounded some early doubters including Sir George Martin: "Cilla became a much bigger star than we first thought because when I first met her she was still a teenager and she had this very strident voice you could hear at the end of the street. She was a kind of equivalent of Lulu and we all expected her to be a 'Shout'** kind of person. 'Love of the Loved' showed that it was what I call 'the corncrake voice'. So when Brian brought me 'Anyone Who Had a Heart' which he'd heard in America, I said, 'That would be great for Shirley Bassey' who I was recording at the time. And he was quite cross and said, 'It's not for Shirley, it's for Cilla!' I said, 'Do you think Cilla can do it?' And he was convinced she could and of course she could, she did a great job on it."¹³

(i.e., **raucous, bluesy, powerhouse vocals.)

Addendum: *Cilla and Burt*
That George Martin's guidance helped Cilla develop her vocal talent (and that she was a willing and able student eager to progress her craft) was clear a few years later when Burt Bacharach came calling …

Cilla's success with 'Anyone Who Had a Heart' did *cause bad feelings with Dionne Warwick who considered it to be her song and, indeed, Burt Bacharach had written it especially for her but, as George Martin noted,* "That didn't stop Burt from coming to me in 1966 and saying, 'I'd like to have Cilla for my next song' which surprised me. It was 'Alfie' and that really tossed Cilla in the deep end for we did it live in number 1 studio at Abbey Road with a large 48-piece orchestra with Burt sitting at the piano waving his hands around. Cilla, with just screens to afford some separation, sang live with the orchestra. There was no question of over-dubbing. She was terrified, it was a lot of pressure. She has often said in retrospect that she really loved me after that because I really rescued her because Burt would listen to something and say, 'Right let's do another one' and was driving her, knocking her into the ground. We had a great take and so after we did an unsuccessful take I said to Burt, 'What are you looking for?' He replied, 'That little bit of magic' to which I replied, 'Burt I think if you listen again I think you'll find that little bit of magic is on Take 3'. And Take 3 is the one you hear."¹⁴

Cilla and Bobby: inseparable, soulmates.
(Pictorial Press Ltd / Alamy Stock Photo)

---

1 Bill Harry, *Mersey Beat*, Triumph PC, www.triumphpc.com › mersey-beat › archives ›
2 & 3 Brian Epstein, *A Cellarful of Noise* (New English Library, 1965) p.68 and p.70.
4 & 7 Cilla Black in conversation with Bob Harris OBE for the BBC Radio 2 documentary *The Songs the Beatles Gave Away*, narrated by Bob Harris and produced by Bob Harris and Trudie Myerscough-Harris for WBBC.
5, 13 & 14 Sir George Martin in conversation with Bob Harris OBE and Colin Hall for the 2009 BBC Radio 2 documentary *The Songs the Beatles Gave Away,* written and narrated by Bob Harris, produced by Bob Harris and Trudie Myerscough-Harris for WBBC.
6 *The Big Beat Album* (Dick James, 1963), a compendium of sheet music, Dick James quoted from his preface.
8, 9 & 10 *What's It All About,* Cilla Black, (Ebury Press, 2003), p.79.
11 *Disc* music weekly, edition 288, 28 September 1963, 'Disc Date' with Don Nicholl, p.9.
12 Freda Kelly in conversation with the author, June 2020.

Chapter 62:
1963, ONE OF THE IN-CROWD

Just like Billy J. before them, courtesy of a song written by John Lennon, the Fourmost had enjoyed Top 10 success with their very first single. And just like Billy J., the success was sudden and exciting, but once 'Hello Little Girl' began to slip down the chart, in order to build on its success, it became necessary for the Fourmost to follow up with a second release while the group's name remained fresh in the fans' minds.

Again, like Billy J. Kramer and Cilla Black, the Fourmost were members of an exclusive club. They were part of manager Brian Epstein's NEMS Enterprises 'stable of artistes' and good friends with the Beatles. Having had a little help from those friends with their first single, John and Paul were on hand again to offer another song for them to record as its follow-up. It was a tune that John had composed (no doubt with input from Paul) called 'I'm in Love'.

In 1971, John claimed ownership, saying, "Me – I wrote it for the Fourmost", but by 1980 John seemed less sure, "That sounds like me. I don't remember a hell of a thing about it."[1]

The Fourmost were of the same opinion of John (in his 1971 interview) that it was written especially for them and that they were gifted the song as a direct result of the success of 'Hello Little Girl'.

Billy Hatton: "They (John and Paul) virtually said to us they were happy that our first record had been a hit, but 'You are better than that, so that's your start up the ladder'. They said, 'We've got this song and when we've finished it, this is for you. So you can show people you can play your guitars, you can do your harmonies, and how well you can sing but with a better song'. It was only years later when people reminded me that Lennon and McCartney had written a song especially for our band. You only realise after the huge success they'd had what a great honour it was … not many people can say that."[2]

While 'I'm in Love' was most probably written with the Fourmost in mind, there is no doubt that before it was gifted to them John Lennon *did* help Billy J. Kramer record a version. Kramer recalls, "In the autumn of 1963 I was doing a session, recording a B-side or something when John and Paul came in and said, 'You've got to do this'. It was 'I'm in Love'. We had about 20 minutes and we knocked it together and I don't know why but we never got round to finishing it. The Beatles thought it would be a great song for me. I should have gone back and finished it, it would have been a hit – as it was for the Fourmost."[3]

It was on 14 October 1963 that George Martin produced the session with Billy J. and the Dakotas, accompanied by John and Paul in the studio. Billy and the Dakotas very quickly learned and recorded the song although they never finished it. It was not long after this, however, that the Fourmost made their recording which *was* released. Maybe the reason why Billy J's version wasn't completed was because very soon after John and Paul (mainly Paul) came up with 'I'll Keep You Satisfied' for him it was selected as his next A-side. It was the right decision. 'I'll Keep You Satisfied' was certainly a very strong song and perfectly suited to Kramer. It was the bigger hit as well.

A bootleg tape has emerged of the Kramer-Lennon 'I'm in Love' session, on which John can be heard shouting to Billy J. words to the effect, "Adam Faith, you fool!" Billy's response was "I can't get it, John". George Martin then responded by commenting to Billy J. that, "I give you full permission to come to one of the Beatles sessions on Thursday and shout at John whenever you like."[4]

What that exchange was all about apparently is that John was trying to teach Billy how to sing the opening line. Prior to Lennon's 'Adam Faith' comment someone in the studio – most likely Mike Maxfield – suggests they start the song 'in Bm' rather than Cm in which they had previously been playing it. This suggested change of key possibly hints that as they were attempting it, it was a little too high for Billy J. Just why Adam Faith came into the conversation is open to conjecture, maybe John wanted Billy to sing more like Adam or was berating him for singing too much in Adam's style. Whatever, at the time, unfortunately for Billy J., the session ended and he didn't complete his recording.

However, EMI did include a remastered version from the session (complete with the comments from John Lennon and George Martin) on the 1991 compilation release *The Best of Billy J. Kramer: The Definitive Collection* (Imperial, CDP-7-96055-2-) and it was there again on another compilation entitled *Do You Want to Know a Secret? The EMI Recordings 1963–1983, Billy J. Kramer with the Dakotas* (EMI, 2009).

The song received a third outing in Billy's name in 2014 when he recorded a brand new version for his new, well received studio album *I Won the Fight* (2014) that he dedicated to Brian Epstein. At the time of this album's release, Kramer had begun writing his own songs and was campaigning to have Brian Epstein inducted in to the Rock 'N' Roll Hall of Fame. By the time 'I Won the Fight' was released, Billy J. had succeeded: Epstein had been inducted.

Meanwhile, back in 1964, the Fourmost agreed with John and Paul, believing this new tune would better represent their musical attributes than 'Hello Little Girl' had.

They cut two versions in October and it was released in mid-November 1963. This time there was no cliff-hanging early morning wait at 'Mendips' for the tune to arrive or desperate dash to the studio having to learn the song as they went along and, unlike Billy J.'s attempt to record the song, John Lennon did not attend either recording of the Fourmost's sessions.

The song was originally delivered to them in the form of a tape recording. Billy Hatton: "This time it was just John Lennon on his own tape recorder. But this time John was gracious enough to give us a piece of paper with some chords written on it, that's all we had. What we wanted to do with the song was left up to us. Because we were the happy-go-lucky, zany Fourmost we thought we should keep that (vibe) going (on the recording)."[5]

Billy Hatton's comment is interesting, for clearly (unlike Billy J. before them) they had had no guidance from John on how to perform the song and kept to their own vision of themselves as a group. The result was the Fourmost's original recorded attempt and was performed in a jaunty mode. An acetate was made and handed to Brian to play to John and Paul who didn't like it.

A week or so later the group were back in London where Brian Hatton says Epstein, in diplomatic mode, delivered the verdict. "The lads like what you did, but do you think you can do it better? Two reasons, it's too bright and chirpy, and too quick. If you could slow the tempo down and give it a bit more punch in the arrangement."[6]

From this it would seem that John Lennon and Paul McCartney were confident that the Fourmost could still deliver the tune to their satisfaction, provided they re-arranged it to their exact specifications.

Dutifully, the Fourmost returned to Studio 2 where under the tutelage of George Martin and Norman Smith they cut a second version. "This time," Billy Hatton recalls, "they (John and Paul) liked it and it was released."[7]

THE FOURMOST
I'M IN LOVE **(2:07)**
(Lennon-McCartney)
Northern Songs Ltd
Parlophone R 5078
Producer: George Martin
Recorded: October 1963
Released: Friday 15 November 1963

Entered the UK chart on 26 December 1963, peaking at number 17 by 12 February 1964. In *Disc* it climbed to number 15 on the chart published for the week ending 8 February and in the *Record Mirror* chart it reached number 8 on 29 February despite having been on the way down for the two weeks prior to that higher listing.

B-side: Respectable

(O. Isley, R. Isley, R. Isley)

This song was written by the Isley Brothers: O'Kelly, Rudolph and Ronald. It appeared on their debut solo album *Shout!* released in the USA in 1959. The title track of this album had been a hit for the Isleys in the USA and later, in May 1964, became a debut hit for Lulu and the Luvvers in the UK.

'I'm in Love' was also released in the USA: ATCO 6285 on 10 February 1964 where it failed to chart.

The new Fourmost single received good reviews. "Some of the major DJs at the time like David Jacobs … all backed the song because they loved it … and it had the support of writers."[8]

It certainly did. *Disc*'s Don Nicholl, already a fan of the Fourmost, gave it the equivalent of a 5-star review by bestowing it with one of his much sought after 'DNT' accolades ('a disc that looks like spinning right to the top'). Describing it as, "A friendly (and oddly quiet) romancer," he also called it 'pert' and topped his review with a headline announcing: "This Beatles composition could send the Fourmost into the 30."[9]

(Several months later in his review of the group's debut EP, *The Fourmost Sound*, *Disc*'s Nigel Hunter also waxed lyrical about 'I'm in Love', saying: "The boys do a splendid job on 'I'm in Love' which is a typical example of the melodic simplicity and appeal of the two Beatle beat-ballad writers.")[10]

Surprisingly it appeared that the fans weren't quite so keen: it only climbed as high as number 17 on the singles chart. Why 'I'm in Love', which what was a patently better song than their first release and given great treatment by the group, did not at least match the commercial success of 'Hello Little Girl' is baffling. Billy Hatton's theory is that, "It was so different from 'Hello Little Girl' that the punters went, 'Are you sure this *is* the Fourmost?' So instead of climbing up the charts it crept up them. It was a better song … we, Brian Epstein and the Beatles all decided that although it was a good record, it did not suit our happy go lucky image."[11]

Whether this is a correct analysis or not, according to Billy Hatton, John Lennon was convinced he knew the real reason: "John actually said to me, 'It's because you used them other chords at the start.' I replied, 'Well we just thought they sounded a bit more harmonious.'" Apparently John reflected for a moment before replying, 'I liked them'.[12]

Most probably that said it all. Whenever John or Paul gave an artist a song they believed that artist would be best served by sticking as closely as possible to what they were given and not deviating from the chords and/or arrangement provided …

(It's a point Paul would make several years later to Badfinger when they cut 'Come and Get It'.)

---

1 *All We Are Saying: The Last Major Interview with John Lennon and Yoko Ono*, conducted by David Sheff (Sidwick & Jackson, 2000) p.172 (Originally published in *Playboy*, 1981).
2, 5, 6, 7, 8 & 10 Billy Hatton in conversation with Colin Hall for the 2009 BBC Radio 2 documentary *The Songs the Beatles Gave Away*, narrated by Bob Harris and produced by Bob Harris and Trudie Myerscough-Harris for WBBC.
3 Billy J. Kramer interview with the author, 19 October 2020.
4 CD: *Do You Want to Know a Secret? The EMI Recordings 1963–1983*, Billy J.Kramer with the Dakotas' (EMI, 2009).
9 *Disc* music weekly, edition 295, 10 November 1963, 'Disc Date' with Don Nicholl, p.10.
11 *Disc*, edition, edition 310, 29 February 1964, 'EPs with Nigel Hunter', p.11.
12 John Lennon's comments as reported to the author, Colin Hall by Billy Hatton in conversation at 'Mendips', 2009.

Chapter 63:
A HORRIBLE, MOURNFUL DIRGE

The relative poor chart showing of 'I'm in Love' was immediately addressed by the Fourmost in early 1964 when they opted not to turn to John and Paul for a third song. Billy Hatton: "There were only so many Beatles songs to go around, then you had to stand on your own two feet."[1]

From this observation it seems most likely that they were not actually offered a third tune.

Undeterred, the Fourmost took matters into their own hands (no doubt with guidance from Brian Epstein) and paid a visit to Denmark Street, specifically to the offices of Dick James. Already an admirer of the group, James had noted their "great musicianship, sense of humour, intelligence, all adding up to a very talented quartet."[2]

And so it was, James played them several songs, none of which struck a chord until he remembered a demo that had only just arrived in the morning's post. The song he played them was called 'A Little Loving'. Written by Russ Alquist (the husband of actress Juliet Mills), the Fourmost were immediately taken with it. Well, three of them were. Owie wasn't, but was voted down, and it became the Fourmost's new single. More in the upbeat vein of 'Hello Little Girl', and therefore maybe more suited to their image and style, this song restored the Fourmost to the Top 10 (number 6 in May 1964) and was their biggest hit.

Ironically it was during 'A Little Loving's' excellent run on the chart that relationships soured between Brian Epstein and the Fourmost. He had booked the group into a variety show at the London Palladium, headlined by established Liverpool singer Frankie Vaughan, comedian Tommy Cooper and Cilla Black who by then had scored two huge number 1 hits.

Epstein's idea for casting the Fourmost in this variety setting revealed his awareness of the extra dimension to their talent: comedy. He thought the run at the Palladium would establish them in a more 'show business' context beyond just relying on making records and scoring hits. In essence Epstein *was* looking to the group's future. Unfortunately, the show's success stalled their progress. It proved so popular it ran way beyond the predicted few weeks and lasted for more than six months from May until December.

The success of the show was credit to all the artists concerned, but for the Fourmost it came to feel like a trap. This upset them because just at the very moment they were enjoying their biggest hit to date they could not capitalise on its success because they were effectively confined inside the Palladium by the contract Brian Epstein had agreed on their behalf. By reaching the Top 10 during their residency at the Palladium their fee *had* increased but as Billy Hatton said, "We were getting £600 a week at the Palladium when if we could have toured we could have been getting £600 a night!"[3]

Hatton and his fellow group members believed Epstein should have ensured that there was a 'get-out' clause in their contract with the promoter at the Palladium, so that if such a situation arose they could be replaced by another act, but Brian had not negotiated any such clause.

The result was four very frustrated young men who felt Epstein had let them down badly. Consequently, when Epstein visited them backstage at the Palladium the group raged at him. They were adamant that their predicament was his fault for getting them to sign a poor contract. While they recognised the 'prestige of playing the Palladium' they also understood the small fortune in concert fees on which they were missing out.

Owie, Billy, Dave and Mike were intelligent men and eager for success (and that included charging the appropriate fees). The more Brian insisted the Palladium was a 'career builder' the more they railed. Epstein was mortified and hurt by one of his favourite acts challenging him in this way.

Inevitably this confrontation spoiled the relationship between Epstein and the Fourmost. From then on he delegated contact with them. Billy Hatton says on a later occasion when Epstein sent them a copy of *The Fiddler on the Roof* soundtrack with directions to record a tune from the show (that the Fourmost considered to be a "horrible, mournful dirge") the group smashed the record to pieces and returned it to Epstein with a message on the sleeve that read: 'No thanks, the Fourmost'.

Looking back on these episodes Billy Hatton reflected, "We were reasonably distant after that."

Billy also added, "Even though we'd never have made it without him, I think Brian was far too sensitive to be a good business manager. He was very upset that one of his acts should have a go at him as we did, questioning his ability. And really, if you weren't Brian's friend, he couldn't function as your manager."[4]

After the success of 'A Little Loving', the Fourmost never made the Top 20 again. They came close with their version of 'Baby I Need Your Loving' (number 24 on 20 January 1965 and on the charts for 12 weeks which was as long as their previous hits had charted) but their other singles were less successful: 'How Can I Tell Her' (number 33 on 26 August 1964) and 'Girls, Girls, Girls' number 33 on 19 January 1966).

During 1964 guitarist Mike Millward was diagnosed with throat cancer from which he recovered and in 1965 he took the lead vocal on the Fourmost's excellent cover of the Four Tops' 'Baby I Need Your Loving'. The group made a memorable appearance on TV's *Ready Steady Go!* to promote the song. Besuited and looking good, Mike wore his best Buddy Holly black-rimmed specs. Introduced by Cathy McGowan, the Fourmost performed/mimed the song whilst standing aboard a mobile rostrum and admirably keeping their balance as a couple of stagehands pushed it across the studio floor and through a crowd of dancing fans.

RSG! was by then the best pop music programme on television. Even though they would mime, the groups were nevertheless 'live in person' in the studio and closely surrounded by the audience. For teenagers in the Sixties *RSG!* was unmissable. Broadcast on Friday nights the show's big boast was that, *'The weekend starts here!'* It certainly did. It felt like the best teen party ever. Sharp, fast, packed and perpetually in motion, to mime their songs the musicians appeared to emerge as if by magic from within the audience itself. *RSG!* was possessed of a vibrancy that caught the zeitgeist of the times much more so than its closest rival *Thank Your Lucky Stars*, which felt stilted by comparison.

During 1965, ill health struck Mike again. He was diagnosed with leukaemia from which, very sadly, he did not recover. Aged just 23 he passed away on 7 March 1966.

This was an unbearably tragic blow for Mike's family and friends. The Fourmost were rocked to the core, but with the support of Liverpool musicians including George Peckham they were able to continue. (In 1969 Peckham left the Fourmost to run a recording studio and founding member Joey Bower rejoined the group.)

Addendum: *The Continuing Saga of the Fourmost and Paul McCartney*
In his official biography Paul made this assessment of 'Hello Little Girl', 'I'm in Love' and the Fourmost: "Unfortunately the words aren't too wonderful. They're a bit average, but the Fourmost were eager to have a hit and they were very good friends of ours. They were more of a comedy group, a really very funny cabaret act, and when it came to making a record and being serious on a TV show, they always laughed and giggled. They were always having such a laugh, it was very difficult for them. They just weren't the kind of guys who were going to get a major hit. I tried a few times."[5]

This is an interesting assessment from Paul and is backed up by many others who recognised the Fourmost's flair for comedy, especially their impressions of other music stars. They were spontaneous, sharp, great impersonators and maybe, given greater guidance than they received, could well have become an act very much in the vein of the Barron Knights* (whom they preceded and ironically who appeared with the Fourmost on the Beatles Christmas Show of 1964).

(*The Barron Knights achieved success in the Sixties when they released a series of popular comic hit singles on which they parodied artists and hits of the day, three of which made the Top 10. They enjoyed enduring success and a further 13 Top 50 hits. The Fourmost had all that it would have taken – and more – to emulate them.)

Unfortunately, the Fourmost suffered the same fate as many of Brian's stable of stars as the demands on his time managing the Beatles increased. Inevitably Epstein was drawn away from spending time on and with his other acts such as themselves. He would have been only too aware of this neglect and it undoubtedly caused him anxiety. As a result, acts such as the Fourmost felt neglected and ultimately became victims of Brian's loss of interest.

The sad reality was Epstein did sign too many acts and quickly discovered he did not have the time he needed to spend with them individually. With the exception of Cilla Black, this situation was exasperated when his personal problems overcame him and he became ever more distant and unable to help his protégés develop their careers and sustain the early successes they had gained.

The Fourmost, who were undoubtedly a talented group of individuals, more or less disappeared from the national consciousness and quickly became unfashionable. They did not adapt and their image was at odds with the eras of R&B and then psychedelia. As has been suggested, good management would have directed them into becoming 'all round entertainers' where the pressure for the next hit single would have been less demanding and they could have turned their attentions to developing those other sides of their considerable talent.

Through it all, however, the Fourmost were not forsaken by Paul McCartney. He maintained an interest in his friends' success. One of his songs they tried to fashion into a hit was 'Here, There and Everywhere'. Unfortunately for them this is one of Paul's most tender and enduring Beatles songs and his rendition on Revolver is most probably the definitive of all that have ever been attempted. The Fourmost's version did not carry the same emotive tenderness as its composer's, being a tad too Mersey Beat/workmanlike in its production and performance values.

Released on 5 August 1966, 'Here, There and Everywhere' failed to make the UK chart, although it became a very brief, minor hit on the USA's Cashbox 100 when it got to number 97 on 24 September 1966. That was during its second week on the chart after which it disappeared. The same week 'Here, There and Everywhere' made the Billboard Bubbling Under Chart when it went in at number 120 but, sadly, after that it bubbled no more.

Undaunted, in 1969 Paul McCartney suggested a song called 'Rosetta'. Composed by Earl Hines with lyrics written by William Henri Woode (the arranger for Hines' orchestra) it had been first recorded in 1933 by Hines and his Orchestra from which point it became both a pop and jazz standard recorded by many artists, sometimes with and sometimes without lyrics. No doubt this was a tune Paul's father Jim would have played at Forthlin, hence Paul's familiarity with it and belief that it was suitable for the Fourmost. His conviction was such he produced and arranged it for them. Dave Lovelady remembered that, "Paul liked the way we could mimic instruments with our voices, our 'mouth music' if you like. Brian O'Hara was a trumpet and we were the trombones. We used it on 'Rosetta' and the Beatles did the same thing on 'Lady Madonna'. There were proper instruments on our record as well. I was playing piano at the session, but Brian O' Hara told me to play it badly. I soon found out why, when Paul said, 'Look, I'll do the piano bit,' and so he ended up playing on our record."[16]

Paul also produced the single's B-side, 'Just Like Before', a song actually written by

Billy Hatton pictured with the author in 2009 outside the front porch of 'Mendips', the house in which he and Brian O'Hara sat in the front room while John Lennon and George Harrison ran through and recorded a rough demo of 'Hello Little Girl' for the Fourmost to take to London to record as their debut single.

Brian O'Hara, although on the label it was credited to 'A. Benny'. O'Hara apparently gave the publishing to Apple Publishing as thanks for Paul's support for the Fourmost.

Unfortunately, despite Paul's interest and close involvement, 'Rosetta' was released in the UK on Friday 21 February 1969 on CBS but failed to chart.

Later that year on 24 October 1969, the Fourmost continued their Beatles connection when they recorded a version of Paul's 'Maxwell's Silver Hammer' (released on Abbey Road, 26 September 1969). They recorded it in the newly named Strawberry Studios (formerly Inner City Studios) in Manchester. (Members of Hotlegs, aka 10cc, had purchased the premises and given it its new name.)

For some reason the Fourmost chose to release 'Maxwell's Silver Hammer' under the name 'Format'. The new name did not improve their fortunes for again they failed to make the chart, after which as obscurity beckoned they very quickly ditched the new name and returned to calling themselves 'The Fourmost'.

1, 3 & 4 Billy Hatton in conversation with Colin Hall for the 2009 BBC Radio 2 documentary *The Songs the Beatles Gave Away*, narrated by Bob Harris and produced by Bob Harris and Trudie Myerscough-Harris for WBBC.
2 *The Big Beat Album* (Dick James, 1963).
5 *Paul McCartney, Many Years From Now*, Barry Miles, (Vantage, 1998) p.181.
6 Dave Lovelady quote from 'The Fourmost' by Bill Harry, *Mersey Beat*, www.triumphpc.com/mersey-beat/a-z

Chapter 64: 1964 AND THE BEAT GOES ON

One look at the UK charts throughout 1963 and it is abundantly clear that Epstein really did possess the 'Midas touch'. The outstanding commercial success of his artists achieved had, by the end of the year, made Liverpool the very hub of British popular music.

THE UK'S TOP 30 MOST POPULAR RECORDS OF 1963
01 The Beatles: She Loves You
02 The Beatles: From Me to You
03 Gerry & the Pacemakers: How Do You Do It?
04 Gerry & the Pacemakers: I Like It
05 Frank Ifield: Confessin'
06 Gerry & the Pacemakers: You'll Never Walk Alone
07 Cliff Richard: Summer Holiday
08 Ned Miller: From a Jack to a King
09 Cliff Richard: The Next Time / Bachelor Boy
10 Brian Poole & the Tremeloes: Do You Love Me?
11 The Searchers: Sweets for My Sweet
12 The Beatles: Please Please Me
13 Billy J. Kramer & the Dakotas: Bad to Me
14 Frank Ifield: Wayward Wind
15 Jet Harris & Tony Meehan: Diamonds
16 The Shadows: Atlantis
17 Roy Orbison: In Dreams
18 The Shadows: Foot Tapper
19 Billy J. Kramer & the Dakotas: Do You Want to Know a Secret?
20 The Springfields: Island of Dreams
21 Roy Orbison: Blue Bayou / Mean Woman Blues
22 Ray Charles: Take These Chains from My Heart
23 The Crystals: Then He Kissed Me
24 Andy Williams: Can't Get Used to Losing You
25 Wink Martindale: Deck of Cards
26 Cliff Richard: It's All in the Game
27 Jet Harris & Tony Meehan: Scarlett O'Hara
28 Elvis Presley: Devil in Disguise
29 The Shadows: Dance On!
30 Billy Fury: Like I've Never Been Gone

As 1964 dawned, the Beatles were at number 1 and number 2 respectively with 'I Want to Hold Your Hand' and 'She Loves You', while a further four records in the Top 50 were John Lennon and Paul McCartney compositions ('I'll Keep You Satisfied' by Billy J. Kramer with the Dakotas, 'Hello Little Girl' and 'I'm in Love', both by the Fourmost, and 'I Wanna Be Your Man' by the Rolling Stones). Six of the acts on the chart were Liverpool groups (the Beatles, the Fourmost, the Searchers, the Swinging Blue Jeans, Gerry and the Pacemakers, and Billy J. Kramer).

From this perspective the 'Mersey Sound' was alive and kicking and Lennon and McCartney were coining it in.

During '64, Billy J. Kramer with the Dakotas and Gerry and the Pacemakers continued to score hits, but both were eclipsed by Cilla Black as she emerged as a major artist on the UK pop scene.

The Merseybeats* became the last major beat group from Liverpool to bother the charts during the Sixties. They seemed destined for great things – and certainly had the talent to do so – but despite three Top 20 hits during 1964 were unable to sustain significant chart success beyond that. The Mojos (more of whom later) enjoyed a Top 10 hit with 'Everything's Alright' but faded quickly thereafter.

(*When success stalled for the Merseybeats in 1966, Tony Crane and Billy Kinsley from the group emerged as a duo and scored a magnificent number 4 UK hit with a cover of the McCoys' 'Sorrow' from which George Harrison 'borrowed' the lines 'with your long blonde hair and eyes of blue' for his song 'It's All Too Much' which featured on the Yellow Submarine *original soundtrack. In October 1973 David Bowie took his version of the song from his number 1* Pin Ups *album to number 3 in the UK singles chart. Later Billy Kinsley became a member of the very successful Liverpool Express who scored three UK single hits in 1976. When the 2000s arrived so did a reformed Merseybeats with Crane and Kinsley still out front and to this day they continue to pack in audiences wherever they perform.)*

And so, as ever in life and popular music, things were not going to remain the same: 1964 was the year of change, for while the Beatles went from strength to strength 'Mersey Beat' yielded fewer chart acts and by the end of the year it had had its day.

The phenomenal success of Mersey Beat had caused an earthquake in the UK's London-centric music industry. Suddenly record companies were forced to ponder the likelihood that there was life beyond the capital. The almost unthinkable had occurred: A&R men were having to contemplate venturing 'up North' in their search for 'the next big thing'. And when they did they quickly discovered a wealth of talent: the Searchers (Liverpool), the Animals (Newcastle), the Hollies (Manchester), the Applejacks (Birmingham), the Moody Blues (Birmingham), the Zombies (St. Albans), Them (Belfast) and so the list went on.

And so it was that during 1964 the UK saw the rise of major groups and artists who went on to enjoy a lasting impact on the charts and popular music history both in the Sixties and beyond. Most significantly the Rolling Stones became regulars in the Top 10 and the main rivals to the Beatles in terms of chart success and popularity. Other UK legends of the Sixties who enjoyed their first chart successes during 1964 included Manfred Mann, the Animals, the Hollies, the Dave Clark Five, the Zombies, Peter and Gordon, Lulu, the Moody Blues, and significantly the Kinks, who announced their presence during September with the stunning 'You Really Got Me' which was number 1 for two weeks.

Importantly the Beatles were already living in London by mid-1963. They had decamped en masse from Liverpool. First, during the summer, they all resided at the Hotel President, Russell Square, Bloomsbury and by the autumn they each had their own room in a flat (Apartment L) on the fourth floor of 57 Green Street, near Hyde Park. It was a very brief co-habitation with John and Paul soon to move out.

The move to London was significant for, as the prime movers and shakers on the music scene, the Beatles immediately became the toast of London's 'hip' society. Life would never be the same.

As 1964 broke, Beatlemania continued to be rampant. Everything that happened to them that year was to crank it up to yet another level.

Nothing did more to move the Beatles to another level than the stateside success of 'I Want to Hold Your Hand'. In January the single made number 1 on the *Billboard* Hot 100 and was followed in February by the group's first-ever visit to the USA where, on the 7th, approximately 73 million Americans tuned into their performance on the *Ed Sullivan Show*. From this moment on the popularity of the Beatles became a phenomenon that shook the world and made them the most famous people on the planet. Entertainers before them had enjoyed massive worldwide fame and popularity but none, not even Elvis, had experienced the fanatical intensity and power of what overtook the Fab Four.

It was unprecedented and astonishing: at its most extreme it was also *very* scary.

Throughout 1964 everything they did was eagerly anticipated and acclaimed. In March they began filming their first feature film, *A Hard Day's Night* (title courtesy of Ringo) and John Lennon's first book, *In His Own Write* was published by Jonathan Cape. On 4 April the Top Five places on the *Billboard* Hot 100 were occupied by Beatles records. On 6 July the world premiere of *A Hard Day's Night* was held in London and four days later Liverpool honoured the Beatles with a civic reception at which over 100,00 Scousers turned out to celebrate their heroes' return.

On the same day as the civic reception, the Beatles third album, *A Hard Day's Night* was released. It was their first album release on which *all* the songs were written by John and Paul. It was an instant number 1 on the UK album chart. In August the Beatles returned to the USA for their first full concert tour. During the tour, whilst in New York, the group met Bob Dylan for the first time. Following their autumn tour of the UK on 4 December the group released their fourth long player: *Beatles for Sale*. By 19 December it was number 1 on the UK's album chart having displaced their own *A Hard Day's Night*.

This was clearly a huge, adrenalin-fuelled year for John Lennon, Paul McCartney, George Harrison and Ringo Starr. The intensity and unrelenting work schedule under which they operated was incredible and mind-blowing. In 1995 in an interview for *The Beatles Anthology*, George would say of Beatlemania, "They (the fans) gave their money and they gave their screams but the Beatles kind of gave their nervous systems. They used us as an excuse to go mad, the world did, and then blamed it on us." In the same publication Neil Aspinall recalled John Lennon commenting that, "We gave the whole of our youth to the Beatles."[1]

Beatles for Sale reflected the impact on the relentless and accelerating journey on which the group had been. Its mood reflected a step back from the euphoria, the lyrics of John and Paul's songs were darker, more ruminative, the beat and musical style had broadened to encompass country and the influence of Bob Dylan. In effect the 'Moptop' days were coming to a close, they were already looking for the escape hatch and a move away from the mania towards the next challenge.

The demands on the Beatles' time and creativity had become immense and while it did not mean they stopped 'giving' songs away, the acts to whom they gave them diversified and hailed from further afield than Liverpool. Only Cilla and Billy J. from Brian Epstein's Liverpool stable of stars received songs during 1964, the other four lucky recipients reflected the wider musical community in which they were now mixing. Another major shift in the songs that they 'gave away' was that they became mainly Paul songs. At this point, as Lennon-McCartney tunes by the Beatles seemed to be almost permanent fixtures on the charts, or tracks they released on albums were being covered by so many other artists as singles, John was less inclined to compose 'new' material for others. The need to 'write a swimming pool' was no longer as pressing as it once had seemed.

For Paul, however, the drive to write did not dim, it was always irresistible. "What was very exciting was that music publishing was a different game then, it was the hangover of Rodgers and Hammerstein and all the great writers, the idea of Broadway and EMI Records … it was a very glamorous thing. I remember in *101 Dalmatians*, the guy is a writer, so this idea of a guy on a piano in an attic was a very romantic thing. We loved that idea."[2]

As 1964 began, that romantic idea of being 'the guy in an attic writing songs on a piano' had *already* become a reality for Paul thanks to his girlfriend, Jane Asher and her marvellous family.

---

1 George Harrison quoted on p.354 and John Lennon on p.161 in *The Beatles Anthology* (Cassell & Co, 2000).
2 Sir Paul McCartney in conversation with Bob Harris OBE and Colin Hall for the BBC Radio 2 Documentary *The Songs the Beatles Gave Away*, 2009, written and narrated by Bob Harris, produced by Bob Harris and Trudie Myerscough-Harris for WBBC.

Chapter 65:
THE SONGWRITER OF WIMPOLE STREET

On 18 April 1963, the BBC broadcast live, in front of an audience, one of three radio concerts they had scheduled to be performed at the Royal Albert Hall in London, England, during the first half of that year. The Beatles appeared on one of these (of which only the second half was broadcast). It was their first appearance at the famous concert hall and the show was called 'Swinging Sound '63'. Appearing with the Beatles were an array of artists who included Del Shannon, the Springfields, Kenny Lynch, Shane Fenton and the Fentones, and George Melly who introduced the Beatles.

It was something of an extravaganza and meant that the Beatles were present at the venue for most of the day and into the evening rehearsing twice and performing twice.

Also present was 17-year-old 'up-and-coming' actress, Jane Asher.

As Mark Lewisohn notes, Jane was already a 'teen' TV personality who had been a panellist on *Juke Box Jury*. As a child actress she had appeared in films such as *Mandy* (1952), *The Quatermass Experiment* (1955) and in 1961 she co-starred in *The Greengage Summer*. (With older brother Peter, when she was younger she had also appeared in the very popular UK TV series *Robin Hood*). Earlier in the evening at the Royal Albert Hall for the BBC's weekly listings paper, the *Radio Times*, Jane had posed 'screaming' for the Beatles. After the broadcast was over she interviewed the group. Paul was entranced and soon the pair were a couple and began a five-year relationship. As Cynthia Lennon commented: "Paul fell like a ton of bricks for Jane."[1]

Soon the young couple were the talk of the town and equally quickly, the darlings of the media ...

At the same time Jane soon introduced Paul to her amazing family:

Margaret, Jane's remarkable mother who had a full-time career as a music teacher, as well as looking after three children and running the large family town house in Marylebone in the West End of London, 57 Wimpole Street. She was an oboist who had been a full-time professor at the Royal Academy of Music and a guest professor at the Guildhall School of Music where one of her students had been George Martin ...

Jane's father, Richard, like her mother, was also a remarkable person, highly regarded as 'one of the foremost medical thinkers of our times'. In 1951 in his post as senior physician at the Central Middlesex Hospital, he wrote an article for *The Lancet* in which he described and named 'Munchausen Syndrome'.

Paul was suitably bowled over by Jane's family, describing her mother Margaret as "a very warm person, a very nice mumsy-type woman, great cook, nothing was too much for her, a really nice person." He also took to the other members of her family: "Richard the dad was a wacky medic, very intelligent, very eccentric. But terrific and a great person to know. Then there was Jane's older brother Peter, who was an interesting, bright guy, also very interested in music and very musical. There was a lot of connection there. Clare was a very nice younger sister, a lot of fun."[2]

Not happy at all in the small back bedroom in the Green Street flat he shared with John, George and Ringo, if it got late Paul would be invited to stay the night at Wimpole Street rather than return home. One time, realising how much Paul hated Green Street, Jane suggested that he should move in with her family at Wimpole Street, informing him her mother would let him have the attic room.

Paul took next to no persuading: 'It was everything Green Street was missing ... people ... food and a homey atmosphere, and Jane being my girlfriend, it was ... perfect!"[3]

Cynthia Lennon astutely observed how much Paul enjoyed his new life with the Ashers in their family home: "Jane came from a very intelligent and talented family and Paul was thrilled to be part of it. Jane's mother was a fascinating lady, a classical musician, a real individual who took Paul into her home and made him one of the family … Paul was in his element…"4

And so it was that in November 1963 McCartney moved to live with the Ashers in their wonderful, rambling family home, a Georgian terrace house with six floors. 57 Wimpole Street began in the basement in which there was a piano and on the top floor, in what had formerly been servants' quarters, next to Peter's bedroom, Paul was given a room of his own.

Paul loved his life there. Margaret spoiled him and he was soon being treated like one of the family. The basement housed the music room in which Margaret taught her students, Paul loved this room and described it as his 'base', the equivalent of the front room of his family home on Forthlin Road. It had a piano and was now somewhere he and John could get away from it all to write. John Lennon particularly remembered writing 'I Want to Hold Your Hand' in that basement music room with Paul and himself sitting side by side, 'eyeball to eyeball', playing the piano.

It was not the only Beatles song composed there. It was first and foremost a working space, there were no armchairs, no other distractions, and in this little room cluttered with music stands Paul McCartney wrote (among others) 'And I Love Her', 'You Won't See Me', 'I'm Looking Through You', 'Eleanor Rigby', 'Every Little Thing', 'I've Just Seen a Face', 'We Can Work It Out', and 'Here, There and Everywhere'. Several of which were no doubt inspired by Jane.

Paul's bedroom, like Peter's, was at the top of the house in one of the attic rooms. There was no lift and climbing up and down those six flights of stairs must have kept Paul very fit! He continued living there until March 1966 when he and Jane moved to live in McCartney's own home in St John's Wood.

In his small attic bedroom, next to the bathroom, there was one window that overlooked Browning Mews, a wardrobe, single bed, a wall shelf, and his Hofner bass stood in its case in a corner of the room. Too small to accommodate his record collection, these precious artefacts were to be found outside his room on the landing on a wire rack situated on top of a low wooden trunk, next to which was an old black telephone. Later, somehow, a piano found its way into the top garret, Peter's larger room. Paul was to comment that it was on that piano that one morning he fell out of bed and immediately sat down to play the chords to a song he had 'dreamed' … and which he would call, 'Yesterday'.

1 & 4 *A Twist of Lennon* by Cynthia Lennon (Star, 1978) p.121.
2 & 3 *Paul McCartney: Many Years from Now* by Barry Miles (Vintage, 1998) p.104.

Chapter 66:
PETER ASHER AND THE ELVIS MANIAC

Peter Asher, who is two years older than his sister Jane, had also been a successful child actor. A very serious young man and member of MENSA he had previously attended Westminster School, a public school attached to Westminster Abbey, and he later read philosophy at King's College London. He was also very musical. He liked to sing and could play piano, guitar, oboe and double bass, although he would modestly comment that he never played anything well. His mother (and his father, who liked to play classical music on his out-of-tune grand piano in his parlour) undoubtedly influenced Peter's love of music, but his career as a musician was very much down to his own ambition.

From playing guitar in a school skiffle group and bass in a traditional Dixieland jazz band he gravitated to rock 'n' roll when his school friend Gordon Waller got him into Elvis, Buddy Holly and the Everly Brothers. By 1962, he and Gordon were performing together as an 'Everlys-inspired' duo. "We had met at school and started singing together. By the time Paul was living in my parents' house we were already playing parties, little gigs, coffee houses and whatever we could get."[1]

Paul described Gordon Waller to his biographer Barry Miles as 'an Elvis maniac' who did a very good impression of the King. Paul further described him as being very good company and less focused on his studies than Peter. Consequently, it was he who persuaded Peter to play truant (echoes of Paul himself and John here) so that the pair of them could play lunchtime gigs.

When Paul moved to live with the Ashers he quickly bonded with Peter, music being something with which they connected right away. Paul was soon aware that Peter and Gordon were performing as a duo and actively seeking to be signed: "Paul moved into our house and stayed there about two years. It was during that time Gordon and I were specifically talent scouted when we were playing at the Pickwick Club."[2]

The duo had been given their two-week, late-night booking at the Pickwick (15–18 Great Newport Street) courtesy of its owner, Harry Secombe, the very well-known, popular Welsh singer, actor, comedian and ex-Goon (Neddie Seagoon). (*The Goons* was a very popular anarchic radio show that lampooned the British 'Establishment' and was the brainchild of madcap comedic genius Spike Milligan. All the Beatles were devotees of the show.)

Secombe was impressed enough to recommend Peter and Gordon to Norman Newell*, A&R manager/head of EMI's Columbia label and so it was that Newell visited the Pickwick to hear them perform: "Norman came in one night and liked the way we sounded and signed us up."[3]

(*Newell was not only a highly respected and successful record producer, he was also an acclaimed lyricist. Together with Cyril Ornadel he had written 'Portrait of My Love', a number 3 UK hit in 1960 for Matt Monro which was also an international hit for Steve Lawrence. By 1999 'Portrait of My Love' had received 2 million radio plays.)

Newell recognised the influence of the Everly Brothers on Peter and Gordon and was particularly taken with their version of the folk song 'Five Hundred Miles' which they performed on the night he had attended the Pickwick. The song had become very popular in the USA and Europe during 1963 when American singer Bobby Bare's version had made the US *Billboard* Hot 100 Top 10. On hearing Peter and Gordon sing this song, Newell decided to offer the duo a deal fully intending that their version of 'Five Hundred Miles' would be their debut A-side and on the B-side would be their own self-penned 'If I Were You'[1] which Newell liked.

Peter Asher: "Out of commercial consideration you made sure you put one of your own

Peter Asher and Gordon Waller in 1964 at the time of the release of their debut single, 'A World Without Love'. Paul had originally composed this song one evening in 1958, aged 16, as he walked home from John's across Allerton Manor golf course. (Pictorial Press Ltd / Alamy Stock Photo)

songs on the B-side. When Norman signed us there were some songs we were doing in our show he already liked, one of them might have been a song we wrote, I'm not sure, I didn't think it was but he wanted to record us, thinking we'd be somewhere in the folky direction."[4]

Peter and Gordon were excited about being signed but had ideas of their own about what song should be their debut A-side … they knew they performed 'Five Hundred Miles' well but were not convinced it should be the A-side of their debut release. And by the time it was up for consideration they knew exactly who to ask for a possible alternative.

Peter Asher: "Norman Newell liked our version of '500 Miles' and things like that but he also said if you know any other good songs feel free to suggest them as well. That was when I remembered this song, 'A World without Love' I had heard Paul sing and which Paul had explained to me was an unfinished song that the Beatles were *not* going to record. I asked Paul, 'Is that song still an orphan, is anyone doing it?' He told me the Beatles were not going to record it and they hadn't given it to anybody, he hadn't even finished it. I said, 'We now have a record deal, what are the chances we could give that song a try?' And he said, 'Fine!'"[5]

'A World without Love' was one of the first tunes Paul had ever composed. It began life in 1959 when he was just 16/17 and living at 20 Forthlin Road. Apparently the tune first came into his head one evening as he walked home after visiting John at 'Mendips'. As he often did, Paul had taken the short-cut over the golf course that lay between 'Mendips' and his home. On such occasions, if it was dark, he was in the habit of strumming his Zenith for all he was worth. At the same time, he would sing at the top of his voice in order to allay his fears as to what or whom may be lurking out there in the shadows and gloom. And so it was that during one of these scary late-night walks home 'A World without Love' came to be.

In March 2009, Sir Paul explained to Bob Harris and the author what lay behind offering Peter and Gordon 'A World without Love': "There were loads of songs. When I was living in Liverpool I had this little room and I had my guitar and my dad had a piano so I would play around on those things … I would always try and write … I'd been writing quite a bit before I met John and the songs weren't quite formed, but they weren't bad ideas. Until I got with John I didn't get used to the idea of 'right, finish it off, here it is, make it proper'. So I had a few songs hanging around … and I had this idea for this song called 'A World without Love' but I hadn't done anything with it. Then … my girlfriend Jane Asher's brother Peter was joining up with Gordon Waller to make Peter and Gordon who were going to be a pop act and they said, 'Have you got a song?' This was the question everyone asked. And being me, I said, 'yeah' and … would try to find something. But I thought that one, 'A World without Love' would fit very well because of the nature of their voices and the kind of songs that they did. It worked very well and they made a good little record of it. And it was their first number 1. So I was pleased to be able to do that for them and for Jane, so there were loads of little connections which all worked out well."[6]

Asked if, at the time, he and Gordon were aware of the enormity of Paul's gesture, Peter Asher was very honest: "Did I realise what a big deal that was? No! In retrospect yes because it's the song that changed my life. At the time it was like, 'Oh good, I like that song, it will be nice to get to record it'. It was very nice of Paul to let us do it. We knew it was great, we loved the song but hey, the Beatles were not going to record it. It was sitting there but we didn't go, 'Oh this is incredible, this is amazing!'"

Peter and Gordon's treatment of 'A World without Love' was a definite step away from the 'beat' group sound and style that was so popular at the time. As Peter has noted, they liked the Everly Brothers and so the American duo were their blueprint and their version of Paul's tune had a more acoustic arrangement than the Beatles' own singles of that time. Indeed, in retrospect it can be recognised that the duo's soaring harmonies and more acoustic sound in some ways predated 'folk-rock'.

In general terms the way they worked together on songs was that Gordon sang the melody and Peter the harmony. And so, as a duo specialising in two-part harmonies, 'A World without Love' suited them perfectly.

Peter: "In the case of 'A World without Love', 90% was just thirds. There wasn't much of an arrangement to it. Geoff Love, who worked on the recording, was a very nice guy and an arranger in England and the arrangement was very much one I figured out with him. I pretty much knew how I thought we could do it. Some of our later records Geoff wrote for strings and horns and other stuff, but in this case it was just a rhythm section which we figured out between the musicians, ourselves and Geoff on the actual session."

Peter remembers having to 'nag' Paul to complete the bridge which he did just in time for the recording session. To those listening closely to what is after all a song of Scouse origin, the lyrics of the bridge are interesting, especially the phrase 'I know not when'. Such a phrase is maybe not typical of a lad from Liverpool and reveals a possible indication of the growing influence of Paul's living with the Ashers …

In his now legendary interview with David Sheff, John Lennon concurred with Paul's memory, although as ever he had something to add of his own. "He was already more of a songwriter than me when we met. So I think that was also resurrected from the past … I think he had the whole song *before* the Beatles and gave it to Peter and Gordon … Paul never sang it. Not on record anyway. That has the line 'Please lock me away' – which we always used to crack up at…"[7]

PETER AND GORDON

Peter Asher
b. Peter Asher on 22 June 1944 in London, England
Gordon Waller
b. Gordon Trueman Riviere Waller on 4 June 1945 in Braemar, Aberdeenshire, Scotland
d. 17 July 2009 in Norwich, Connecticut, USA

A WORLD WITHOUT LOVE (2:38)
(Lennon- McCartney)
Northern Songs Music NCB
Columbia DB 7225
Recorded: 21 January 1964 in Studio 2 at EMI Studios, 3 Abbey Road, St. John's Wood, London
Paul McCartney did not attend the recording.
Producer: Norman Newell
Accompaniment directed by: Geoff Love
Recorded: 21 January 1964
B-SIDE: If I Were You (Asher-Waller)
Accompaniment directed by: Geoff Love

Guitar legend Vic Flick played the distinctive 12-string guitar part on the track.
Flick (b. Victor Harold Flick in Worcester Park, Surrey) had, in 1962, as a member of the John Barry Seven, played lead guitar on the track 'The James Bond Theme' for the *Dr. No* film soundtrack album. He contributed to the James Bond soundtracks throughout the 1960s and all the way through to the late 1980s. He played this famous riff on a 1939 English Clifford Essex Paragon Deluxe acoustic/electric guitar that he plugged into a Fender Vibrolux amplifier. For his work he was paid a one-off fee of £6.

Vic was also a session musician and member of the George Martin Orchestra. His guitar playing can be heard on the soundtrack to *A Hard Day's Night*, most notably on the instrumental track 'Ringo's Theme (This Boy)' on which he played his Olympic white 1961 Fender Stratocaster. Later Vic, along with most of the original *Goldfinger* soundtrack musicians, played on the soundtrack to the Beatles' second feature film *Help!* to provide some 'James Bond sounding' music. He was honoured at the Academy of Motion Picture Arts and Sciences (who also dole out the Academy Awards or 'Oscars') in 2012 for *The Music of Bond: The First 50 Years*. In 2013 he became the fourth recipient of the National Guitar Museum's 'Lifetime Achievement Award' for his 'contribution to the history of the guitar'.

Released in the UK on 28 February 1964, 'A World without Love' entered the UK singles chart at number 39 on 18 March 1964. It remained on the charts for 14 weeks, reaching number 1 for two weeks from 29 April 1964 to 6 May 1964. Its last week on the chart was spent at number 37 (17 June 1964).

Released in the USA on Capitol 5175, it spent 12 weeks on the *Billboard* Chart, reaching number 1 on 27 June 1964.

Surprisingly the review that appeared in *Disc* was tucked away in the 'In Short' review column where Don Nicholl only awarded 'A World without Love' 3 stars, calling the song "an impressive ballad" that the duo sang "simply" and of which "some moments are very Beatlish."[8]

Not too many artists make number 1 on both sides of the Atlantic with their first single. 'A World without Love' became a veritable 'worldwide smash hit' for Peter and Gordon. Its other international chart positions are very impressive:

Australia: number 2
Canada: number 1
Ireland: number 1
New Zealand: number 1
Norway: number 8

John Lennon's dismissive attitude towards 'A World without Love' was, as he himself was happy to admit, because he found the first line of the song, 'Please lock me away' amusing. This meant the Beatles never *did* record the song. The solo demo of the tune Paul recorded in the attic of 57 Wimpole Street (without the then unwritten bridge) remains in the possession of Peter. Apparently on the same tape Paul sings a lively version of 'I'll Follow the Sun', another very early 20 Forthlin Road composition. A 30-second excerpt from Paul's demo of 'A World without Love' was leaked to YouTube in 2013. (And, at the time of writing, it's still there…)

By the end of 1964, 'A World without Love' was one of seven songs written by Lennon and McCartney to make *Billboard* magazine's Hot 100 number 1 slot during that year. The other six were 'I Want to Hold Your Hand', 'She Loves You', 'Can't Buy Me Love', 'Love Me Do', 'A Hard Day's Night', and 'I Feel Fine', all of which were performed by the Beatles. This remains an all-time songwriting record.

The massive worldwide commercial and popular success of 'A World without Love' is testament to Paul's faith in his song. People absolutely loved Peter and Gordon's performance of it. Along with Elton John's 1974 version of 'Lucy in the Sky with Diamonds', it is one of only two Lennon-McCartney songs recorded by artists other than the Beatles themselves to reach number 1 in the *Billboard* Hot 100 Chart.

And, if any more accolades are required to prove its worth: 'A World without Love' was included in the Rock and Roll Hall of Fame's '500 Songs That Shaped Rock 'N' Roll'.

(*Peter and Gordon's haunting version of '500 Miles' was eventually released on 5 June 1964 as track 2, side 1 of their eponymous debt album.)

1, 2, 3, 4 & 5 Peter Asher in conversation with the author in 2019.
6 Sir Paul McCartney in conversation with Bob Harris OBE and Colin Hall for the BBC Radio 2 Documentary *The Songs the Beatles Gave Away*, 2009, produced by Bob Harris and Trudie Myerscough-Harris for WBBC.
7 *All We Are Saying: The Last Major Interview with John Lennon and Yoko Ono*, conducted by David Sheff (Sidwick & Jackson, 2000) p.172 (Originally published in *Playboy*, 1981) p.173.
8 *Disc* music weekly, edition 310, 29 February 1963, 'In Short' reviews by Don Nicholl, p.10.

Chapter 67:
MAGIC IS STILL THERE

The sudden and worldwide success of their debut single meant that in an instant Peter and Gordon became not just national UK pop stars but internationally famous as well. With such breathtaking success came all the rewards, demands and pressures that fame and popularity on this scale inevitably brings. One of the most pressing of all the pressures they faced was to strike again while the iron was hot and produce a follow-up to their debut single. This was a mighty challenge. Having started at the very top, whatever they produced next would have to be something very special to match the stunning success of 'A World without Love'. As a consequence, expectations ran high.

Such pressure did not faze Paul McCartney. Not long after the duo returned from their first trip to the USA he delivered a newly minted tune written especially for them: 'Nobody I Know'. Pure 100% McCartney but, as ever, co-credited to John and Paul, of which John later simply commented, "Paul again. That was his Jane Asher period, I believe."[1]

In this instant Paul was following the well-worn path for songwriters in that, if they have penned a hit for someone they usually expected to be called upon to provide the follow-up. And that is exactly what happened here. (As it had with composer Mitch Murray and his hit songs for Gerry and the Pacemakers.) That Paul McCartney had no one but Peter and Gordon in mind when he composed 'Nobody I Know' was confirmed when he told his biographer Barry Miles that he wrote it specifically for the duo.

In similar vein, he was to specifically compose 'I Don't Want to See You Again' for the duo. Peter Asher: "At that age you kind of take things for granted, so we knew it was great, things were fantastic, as in, 'Our record's ('A World without Love') doing really well – my god it's number 1 – this is so cool!' Indeed, our first record was a number 1 pretty much everywhere, so we lucked out in that regard. At the time, however, we didn't truly realise that was a one in a billion chance: now it is very clear. But back then you kind of went, 'Oh great, we made a good record, it's a hit, this is great.' We were very busy. Nothing had prepared us for what happened but at that age you take life as it comes and it was all good."[2]

Unlike other artists who face the challenge of finding and selecting a follow-up to a hit record, in Peter and Gordon's case the challenge of finding a follow-up to such a massively successful international hit was even greater than for most others. Fortunately for them this pressure was reduced when they found themselves once more gifted with a second 'Lennon-McCartney original': "Paul wrote 'Nobody I Know' for us. He may have started writing it for the Beatles but half way through thought this would be good for Peter and Gordon, one way or another he gave it to us specifically."[3]

PETER AND GORDON
NOBODY I KNOW **(2:27)**
(Lennon-McCartney)
Northern Songs Music NCB
Columbia DB 7292
Producer: Norman Newell
Arrangement: Geoff Love
12-string Guitar (both sides): Eddie King Recorded: April 1964 at Abbey Road, London
As with 'A World without Love' Paul did not attend the recording.
B-SIDE: You Don't Have to Tell Me (Asher-Waller)

Released on 29 May 1964 it remained on the charts for 11 weeks peaking at number 10 on 8 July 1964. Its last week on the chart was spent at number 47 on 19 August.

Released in the USA on 15 June 1964 on Capitol 5211, it spent 9 weeks on the Billboard 100, peaking at number 12 on 1 August 1964.

The chart success of 'Nobody I Know' in both the UK and the USA was more 'moderate' than its predecessor, which was surprising given it was another brand new 'original Paul McCartney song' that the Beatles themselves had not recorded. In truth, Paul himself was not entirely satisfied with it: "I wrote that, custom built for Peter and Gordon. That little bit of melody always irritated me. It wasn't a very big hit but it was okay."[4]

Even so the crystal-clear, two-part harmonies and distinctive 12-string guitar were another step away from the prevailing beat music and another step towards what would soon become known as 'folk-rock'.

Music critic Derek Johnson in *NME*'s 29 May edition certainly enjoyed 'Nobody I Know' enough to make it his top pick of that week's singles with the page headline, 'Magic Is Still There for Peter and Gordon', before going on to describe it as, "Slightly faster than 'World without Love' it's a rhythmic rockaballad with an infectious beat – and the appealing lyric is handled most convincingly by the boys." After admitting that Peter and Gordon's debut disc ('A World without Love') took a little time to register with him, Johnson declared, "I found myself singing along with this new one from the start – possibly because it's a more simply constructed melody."[5a]

Johnson described Peter and Gordon's self-penned B-side 'You Don't Have to Tell Me' as a "wistful medium twister" that showcased the boys' "distinctive vocal blend".[5b]

Similarly, a week earlier (23 May) *Disc* music weekly's Don Nicholl had given P&G's new single a longer, more fulsome (if somewhat reserved) review than he did its predecessor, calling it, "A very simple tune and a pleasing set of lyrics with a happy little romantic approach." (Little?) However, despite awarding it a coveted 'DNT' rating, Nicholl somehow still managed to sound less than enthused when he commented: "Nothing to tax anyone's memory or imagination ... it's bound to pop into the Top Twenty without any trouble at all." Of Peter and Gordon's performance he noted, "The boys duet to a clean rhythm noise from guitar and drums." (Noise?) Musical director Geoff Love received a credit for his work on both A- and B-sides of the record of which Nicholl seemed more enamoured by Peter and Gordon's own composition, 'You Don't Have to Tell me'. After saying Love "keeps things moving effortlessly", he adds, approvingly, that Love's "Delayed echo gimmick and double-tracking is attractive and used briefly here."[6a]

In an article published in the same edition as his review, *Disc*'s Don Nicholl contributed a piece to his regular 'Behind the Singles Scene', entitled 'Peter and Gordon Owe a Lot to Guitarist Eddie', in which he said, "Peter and Gordon ought really to add an 'Eddie' to their credits for the new single which rates a 'DNT' this week. For Eddie King, of their backing group, supplies some very pretty guitar noise on their new disc." Nicholl continued his piece by explaining how on the night before recording 'Nobody I Know', Peter, Gordon and Eddie were working on the song as they travelled back to London on the M1 from a show: "In the minivan King and the boys tried out the guitar figures for the runs and bridge which Eddie was to supply for the disc. Result is a big help to the record's charm." On the session itself King played 12-string guitar.[6b]

For Peter and Gordon it must have seemed like a case of 'another day, another hit', but once a hit is a hit an artist's mind inevitably turns to what comes next. While Peter and Gordon in no way assumed that Paul would keep on writing hits for them, they were fully aware that without the hits a pop star's career was as like to disappear out of sight as it was to continue. This was especially the case in those heady days of the Sixties when a pop star's success was measured in how many hit singles they could amass, but which had a tendency to dry up as quickly as they had arrived.

So ephemeral was 'pop' success, Peter Asher recalled, "The one question in every interview you could be certain you would be asked – and the Beatles were equally susceptible to this – was, 'What are you going to do when it's all over?' You always got that question because it was an assumption that a career in popular music would be a couple of years."[7]

Peter Asher, however, was unlike many pop stars for whom a world beyond being a star was already beckoning, he had known from the moment he stepped into a recording studio exactly what he would do in the event of their career ending: "I had decided I wanted to be a record producer from the first time I was in the studio. I loved it that you could hire great musicians and tell them what to do, I loved the technological aspects of it. I found every aspect of it exciting. I knew it was a longer-term ambition but I did decide in my own head that record production was something I thought I could do, and that I wanted to do. A little while after that, probably a year or so later, I did make my first record as a producer."[8]

But in 1964 those days were some time and several hit records away. After 'Nobody I Know', Paul stepped up with yet another custom-written tune for the duo's third single: 'I Don't Want to See You Again'. An upbeat, gossamer kind of song replete with a lush string accompaniment that was most probably a bit too sweet for Paul's liking, again, he did not attend the recording session so had had no say in the matter.

On receiving three straight McCartney originals, Peter Asher is both philosophical and honest, and could be speaking about either record 'Nobody I Know' or the third song Paul gave the duo when he says: "We were grateful, delighted, but everything changes when you have a number 1 record: all the songwriters in town are writing songs for you and so all of a sudden we were getting lots of songs, but the one we got from Paul was, not surprisingly, the best one. 'I Don't Want to See You Again' was a really good song and we were happy to record it."[9]

PETER AND GORDON
I DON'T WANT TO SEE YOU AGAIN (1:59)
(Lennon-McCartney)
Northern Songs Ltd
Columbia DB. 7356
Producer: Norman Newell
Accompaniment directed by: Geoff Love
As with both 'A World without Love' and 'Nobody I Know' Paul was not present at the recording of this song.
B-SIDE: I Would Buy
(Asher-Waller)
Accompaniment directed by: Geoff Love
Recorded early August 1964

Released in the UK on 11 September 1964 where, surprisingly, it failed to chart.

This really was quite surprising. Paul, Peter and Gordon must have been taken aback by the new single's lack of impact in the UK. After all, the duo were one of the year's biggest-selling UK artists and to miss out on the chart altogether (especially with another McCartney song written specifically for them) was almost unthinkable, but it is exactly what happened. What they would do if it did fail had actually been commented on in *Disc* in its edition for the week ending 12 September. Given a 'Very Good' 4-star rating by Don Nicholl, he opened his assessment by noting, "Peter and Gordon are said to be worried about this, their third disc. If it doesn't hit, they'll start thinking about quitting the business." This was a very dramatic opening indeed to a review of a single. However, Nicholl was quick to allay any fan alarm when he continued by saying, "Well, I think it stands a good chance of keeping them in the game." Of the song he described it as a "Brisk Lennon-McCartney composition that paces along fairly urgently, and with a rather better lyric than tune." Of P&G's performance he wrote: "The boys duet it competently to an interesting Geoff Love accompaniment." As for their own tune 'I Would Buy', Nicholl noted that it "ventured close to the folk song boundaries."[10]

Talk about tempting fate!

Fortunately, all was not lost, for when it was released in the USA it did achieve a favourable chart placing.

Issued in the USA on Capitol 5272 on 21 September 1964, 'I Don't Want to See You Again' spent 9 weeks on the *Billboard* Hot 100, peaking at number 16 on 7 November 1964.

The close harmonies and 12-string guitar of Peter and Gordon were making a definite impact. They certainly caught the ear of folk singer and Beatles fan Gene Clark. During 1964 at the Troubadour Club in Los Angeles, Clark met fellow folk musician and Beatles admirer Jim (later Roger) McGuinn and suggested they team up as a 'Peter and Gordon' type act that eventually morphed into the Byrds.

As 1964 ended, Peter and Gordon were an international act. The lack of success of their third single in the UK was unexpected but no more than a hiccup. After all it was a Top 20 hit in the USA, the world's biggest-selling record market ... nevertheless their career demanded hit singles in order to flourish and so, for their fourth single release, the duo changed the format. This time they stepped out of Paul's compositional orbit to cut their version of a song Del Shannon had originally written for US R&B singer Lloyd Brown.

They became aware of Del's song during the second half of 1964 when they were on tour in Australia where 'A World without Love' had been a number 1 hit. On the bill with them were the Searchers and Del Shannon. One night, sitting in their dressing room, Peter and Gordon overheard Shannon next door singing 'I Go to Pieces' to the Searchers in the hope that they would be interested in recording it. The Searchers passed on Del's song but Peter and Gordon believed it could be the song to return them to the upper reaches of the UK singles chart. Shannon was more than happy for them to record it. (He himself recorded a superb version of 'A World without Love' on his 1964 album, *Handy Man*.)

And so it was that on their return to the UK, Peter and Gordon went into Abbey Road where they recorded a fine, lonesome version of Del's song. John Burgess produced, Geoff Love arranged it, Peter and Gordon played guitars and once again Eddie King contributed distinctive 12-string to a great recording. But, when it was released (Columbia, DB 7407) on 21 November 1964, just like 'I Don't Want to See You Again' it failed to make an impact on the UK Top 50 although, as with 'I Don't Want to See You Again' it was a big hit in the USA. Released in December in the States it peaked at number 9 on the Billboard Hot 100 on 20 February 1965, while in the Cashbox Top 100 it climbed three places higher to number 6.

British music fans definitely missed out, for Peter and Gordon's version of 'I Go to Pieces' is a real gem. Why it did not take off in the UK is hard to fathom, especially as it became an international hit reaching number 11 in Sweden, number 21 in Canada, while in Australia the track was a double A-side hit reaching number 26 in tandem with its B-side 'Love Me Baby'.

'Love Me Baby' was a cracking rocker written by the duo themselves. Its sound was distinctly more Rolling Stones than Beatles or folk rock, maybe because the distinctive harmonica on the recording was played by Rolling Stone Brian Jones.

Peter and Gordon and Paul McCartney did re-unite for one last throw of the dice in 1966, but throughout 1965 the duo, very successfully, turned for A-sides to older songs that they liked and had already been hits for other artists. They issued three 'cover' singles that year, two of which went Top Five in the UK: Buddy Holly's 'True Love Ways' (number 2 in April) and the Teddy Bears' (Phil Spector-written) 'To Know You Is to Love You' (number 5 in June). The third, their version of Barbara Lewis's 'Baby I'm Yours', peaked at number 19 in October 1965.

'Baby I'm Yours' was a song written by Van McCoy especially for Barbara Lewis and that Peter Asher particularly liked. It had been released by Barbara on the Capitol label and in June it had peaked at number 11 on the 21 August Billboard Hot 100 Chart. In deference to this, Peter and Gordon's American record label, which was also Capitol, did not issue their version as a single in the States.

Addendum: *Eddie King and the Kytes*

By the time Peter and Gordon recorded 'Nobody I Know', ace guitar player Eddie King was the guitarist who performed on the song (not to be confused with renowned Alabama-born Chicago blues guitarist/singer-songwriter). As reviewer Don Nicholl had noted in his 'Behind the Singles Scene' piece quoted earlier in this chapter, Eddie also played in the duo's backing and touring band, a three-piece from Bristol comprising Eddie himself on guitar, Freddie Allen on bass and Julian Bailey on drums. How they got the gig to back Peter and Gordon was that they had been booked onto the same show as the duo at a large variety club in the North East of England. As Eddie recalled, "They (Peter and Gordon) had a record, 'World Without Love' which had just hit number 1, but they didn't have a backing band and were basically two guys sitting on stools with guitars. They asked us to back them so we told them, 'OK, if you stand on stage!' The upshot of this was that we became their backing band from then on. I travelled all over the world with them for the next two years and played on all their records as well as recording with many other mainly 'Abbey Road' artists. The other two guys played in the backing band in the UK and Europe. During this time, I released a couple of singles under my own name, not UK hits but one was a number 5 in Japan! So, in 1966 when the work with P&G was slowing, so the three of us (in the backing band) tried a record together as the Kytes, which was 'Blessed' backed by 'Call Me Darling' which featured Dave 'Dobie' Gillis on bass. I can't remember how we signed to Pye but I think it was down to knowing some people there in A&R and just taking the record in."[11]

A second Kytes single was released on the Island label, 'Running in the Water' backed by 'End of the Day'. Both singles were highly acclaimed and are now equally highly sought-after collectors' items.

---

1 *All We Are Saying: The Last Major Interview with John Lennon and Yoko Ono*, conducted by David Sheff (Sidwick & Jackson, 2000) p.172 (Originally published in *Playboy*, 1981) p.194.
2, 3, 7, 8 & 9 Peter Asher in conversation with the author, 2019.
4 *Paul McCartney: Many Years from Now* by Barry Miles (Vintage, 1998) p.112.
5a, 5b *New Musical Express*, 29 May 1964, single review by Derek Johnson.
6a *Disc* music weekly, edition 322, 23 May 1964, Singles review by Don Nicholl, p.5.
6b *Disc* music weekly, edition 322, 23 May 1964, 'Behind The Singles Scene' by Don Nicholl, p.10.
10 *Disc* music weekly, edition 338, 12 September 1964, 'Singles with Don Nicholl, p.10.
11 Eddie King in correspondence with the author and 'The Kytes and Eddie King' – Posted 8 April 2014 by 23 Daves – Left and to the Back website, left-and-to-the-back.blogspot.com

CHAPTER 68:
1964 ELSEWHERE AND AT OTHER TIMES

The Beatles' diary for 1964 is awash with dates that included two major visits to the USA (the second of which incorporated their first real 'tour'). The first of their USA excursions was preceded by a three-week 'marathon' season at the Olympia Theatre in Paris. In addition to these visits there were European tours which took in Denmark, the Netherlands and Sweden, not to mention tours much further afield in Australia and New Zealand (taking in Hong Kong on the way). In between touring they made their first film, *A Hard Day's Night*, and wrote and recorded all the songs for its soundtrack album. This is not to mention various and numerous radio and TV appearances. And then there were other recording sessions which yielded three number 1 singles: 'Can't Buy Me Love' (April), 'A Hard Day's Night' (July), 'I Feel Fine' (December) and their second number 1 long player for that year, *Beatles for Sale* (which, in December, displaced their own *A Hard Day's Night* from the top spot on the UK long player chart).

This tumultuous year concluded with a major autumn UK tour followed in late December by 'Another Beatles Christmas Show' which extended into mid-January 1965 (two performances a day, give or take a day, and only four full days off in total, one being Christmas Day).

Its predecessor, 'The Beatles Christmas Show' had run from 24 December 1963 until 11 January 1964. Just three days after they had completed that initial 'Christmas Show' series of shows, the Beatles found themselves in Paris from Tuesday 14 January until the afternoon of Wednesday 5 February 1964 where they played a three-week season at the Paris Olympia.

'Home' for them during that period was the prestigious George V Hotel, just off the Avenue des Champs-Élysées in the heart of the city's 'Golden Triangle' (very posh). While ensconced in the George V they heard the stupendous news that they had made number 1 in the USA single chart: 'I Want to Hold Your Hand' was sitting right at the very top of the *Cashbox* Record Chart.

This was the pinnacle they had always dreamed of reaching. They had made it to the very top in the home of their beloved rock 'n' roll.

Despite the euphoria of this success, while they were in Paris there was no resting on their laurels for any of the Beatles, especially Paul and John. A piano was moved into one of their suites to enable them to compose and practise and it was on this instrument that, one night after returning from performing at the Olympia, John and Paul (with some input from George) completed a song they had already begun that they intended to be for Billy J. Kramer. Most likely Brian Epstein had asked them to do so as a follow-up to 'I'll Keep You Satisfied'. The tune they completed in Paris was called 'One and One Is Two', the backstory of which is superbly reported in Michael Braun's excellent 1964 fly-on-the-wall' Beatles memoir *Love Me Do: The Beatles' Progress*, more of which later ...

'One and One Is Two' was one of three new John and Paul compositions Brian Epstein presented to Billy J. Kramer for consideration as the A-side for his follow-up single to 'I'll Keep You Satisfied'. By then, however, and unknown to Epstein, Billy had discovered a new song he really liked called 'Little Children' which he desperately wanted to record for his next single. So intent was he on recording 'Little Children', Billy J. turned down the new songs John and Paul had written. Epstein was so seriously miffed by Billy J's independent stance he informed Kramer that by turning down Paul and John's songs they had written *especially* for him he was in effect insulting the greatest songwriters in the world.

A weaker person would have been quelled by such a comment, but not Billy J,. who knew there was absolutely no way in which he was trying to insult John and Paul. He was simply convinced of 'Little Children's' hit potential and prepared to stand his ground rather than pass on the opportunity it offered. (Some time after the event John Lennon confided in Billy J. that he thought that if he had recorded *any* of the three tunes by himself and Paul that Brian Epstein offered him then Billy would not have done his career 'any favours'.)

Nevertheless, the strength of Epstein's reaction to Kramer's rejection of the Lennon-McCartney songs clearly registered with Billy. A compromise had been reached: "By the time we went into the studio we had already decided that the follow-up to 'Little Children' would be 'From a Window' which *was* another Lennon-McCartney song."[1]

Epstein, no doubt with help from Dick James, now embarked on a quest to place 'One and One Is Two' with another singer or group. As with 'I'm in Love', which had apparently been offered to both the Fourmost *and* Billy J., so 'One and One Is Two' was offered to the Fourmost after being spurned by the latter.

Unlike Kramer, the Fourmost actually went into the studio with Paul McCartney on bass to have a crack at the song. It was not to be for even with the tune's co-author on board they were unable to fashion a version they felt was strong enough to be released as a single. According to lead guitarist and singer Brian O'Hara, "There just wasn't any meat in the song and we couldn't get anywhere with it."[2]

With the Fourmost unable to make something of 'One and One Is Two', Epstein and James were faced with a very unusual situation: a brand new Lennon-McCartney song that admittedly the Beatles themselves had not recorded, but which was nevertheless up for grabs but so far had been rejected … how could this possibly be? To whom should they turn to next?

Enter, the Rhodesians … from Salisbury: Salisbury, Rhodesia that is. (Now known as Zimbabwe.)

---

1 *Do You Want to Know a Secret?* by Billy J. Kramer, (Equinox, 2016) p. 72.
2 *Beatles Undercover*, Kristofer Engelhardt (Collector's Guide Publishing Inc. 1998) p.171.

Chapter 69:
1964, DIAMONDS, RHODESIANS AND STRANGERS ...

Of all the artists who were the recipients of a John and Paul 'giveaway', none proved more elusive than the Strangers with Mike Shannon. My sincere thanks for kick starting my research for this chapter go to Dave Ravenscroft who sent me an article he had unearthed about the Strangers and who also helped me source a rare copy of 'One and One Is Two'.

The Rhodesians began life as the Diamonds in Salisbury, Rhodesia (now Zimbabwe). They were Peter Dene (lead guitar, born in Cape Town, South Africa), Tony Hulley (rhythm guitar, born in Marandellas, Southern Rhodesia), Hugh 'Sandy' Miller (bass guitar, born in Floof, Natal), Maurice Fresco (drums, born Salisbury, Southern Rhodesia) and Harry Hayden (singer), a group of friends who enjoyed music and decided to make some sounds of their own.

At this time, Mike Shannon was not a member of the group, their original lead singer was Harry Hayden. From the very start with gigs at venues in Salisbury, such as the Meikles Hotel and the Coq d'Or, the Diamonds' reputation grew and soon gigs in the north of the country in places such as Kite and Ndola were forthcoming.

They were a self-contained group who utilised their own individual skills to support themselves as a band: rhythm guitarist Tony was an electrician by trade and took responsibility for all things electrical, bassist Hugh was a good artist and took care of posters and bookings, drummer Maurice had a head for numbers and looked after their finances, while lead guitarist Peter and singer Harry (later Mike) were responsible for the group's repertoire. These additional practical skills (on top of their excellent musicianship) enhanced the Diamonds' reputation as a great band to book. So much so that they were asked to perform 'live' on the very night television was launched in Rhodesia: 14 November 1960.

Their appearance on TV was the moment that things really began to happen for the Diamonds. Legendary South African jazz musician, clarinetist and band leader Dan Hill spotted them that evening and signed them to a five-year contract with CBS.

The boys were obviously delighted but as their career started to lift-off, the prospect of the Diamonds travelling, or possibly even living abroad, to further advance their career caused singer Harry Hayden to let it be known the prospect of re-locating abroad did not sit right with him. And so it was that Constable 6066 Mike Stapleton from the British South Africa Police Force (who had sat in with the Diamonds on some appearances) took over on vocals. (Stapleton had been born in England and, aged 5, had moved to South Africa with his family. Apart from working as a police officer apparently Mike had also been a long distance swimmer and an insurance salesman.) He not only left the police to sing for his supper with the Diamonds, but he also adopted a different stage surname and became known thereafter as 'Mike Shannon'.

The sequence of and exactly how and why such events occurred is not easy to piece together, but Shannon must have been considered the full-time frontman of the Diamonds by the time they recorded their debut album for CBS, for on its cover the group's personnel lists him, not Harry Hayden, as vocalist. Shannon even composed a song for the record, 'Thundering Smoke'. Indeed, the Strangers were no slouches when it came to providing original material for themselves and individually they contributed a further six tunes to the record's 16 tracks: lead guitarist Peter Dene wrote four, while rhythm guitarist Tony Hulley and drummer Maurice Fresco composed one apiece.

Released in 1961, the album, entitled *Cool Rock* (CBS-ALD 6546), included both sides

The Strangers with Mike Shannon from Rhodesia (now Zimbabwe) photographed in 1964 by which time they had re-located to London. (Pictorial Press Ltd / Alamy Stock Photo)

of their debut single which comprised their version of 'Midnight Special' backed by the Pete Dene original, 'Echo'.

In 1962 they released their second album *Dancing for Diamonds* (6572). They also spread their wings by recording a collaborative album with Dan Hill who persuaded the Diamonds to include female vocalist, Dana Valery in their ranks. Dana was Italian-born but her family had emigrated to South Africa in 1947 where, aged just sixteen, she had begun her singing career in Johannesburg. Her elder brother was the singer and actor Sergio Franchi.

The collaborative album with the Diamonds was released under the title of *Dan, Dana Valery and the Diamonds* (CBS-ALD 6597). It comprised tracks performed by a variety of combinations of the artists credited on the album's cover: 'Dana Valery, Dan Hill and the Diamonds', 'Dan Hill and Dana Valery', 'The Diamonds with Dan Hill', 'Mike Shannon and the Diamonds', 'Dana Vallery and the Diamonds', 'Dan Hill', 'Dan Hill and His Orchestra', 'Dana Valery and Dan Hill and Orchestra', 'The Diamonds'.

It proved to be a one-off idea. Dana went on to enjoy a successful solo career and relocated to the UK and then the USA where she released records and appeared on TV programmes (including an appearance on the *Ed Sullivan Show* in 1968). Among her many achievements as a singer was to star in all three productions of the South African musical revue *Wait a Minim!*: the original in South Africa in 1962, the London production in 1964 and the Broadway production which ran from 7 March 1966 to 15 April 1967. For all three productions Dana recorded 'original cast' albums.

Back in Rhodesia, the Diamonds continued as a unit in their own name and cut a series of records: *The Diamonds on Tour*; *The Diamonds Do the Shadows* (cut after they opened for the Shadows in Salisbury); *Diamonds Instrumental*; *Dancing for Diamonds*; *The Diamonds at the Fresco Terrace*.

Mike and the Diamonds were nothing if not prolific.

They were an in-demand live act and as well as the Shadows they supported Chet Atkins and Jim Reeves. Chet, who at the time endorsed Gretsch guitars, of which the Diamonds then owned two, joined them on stage for a few numbers. At a later gig when one of the Diamonds' Gretsch guitars had to be replaced, a call was made to Atkins who by then was in Pretoria, but he made sure a new Gretsch was delivered, by taxi, to the Diamonds in Johannesburg. The band and Atkins remained friends thereafter.

Jim Reeves was another international singing star who was hugely popular in South Africa where, in the early Sixties, he was considered to be 'more popular than Elvis'. Jim was impressed by the Diamonds when they supported him on tour, so much so he apparently recorded a couple of their original songs including 'Pink and Blue Cadillac' written by their bassist Sandy Miller. Jim Reeves toured the country in 1963 and while in South Africa he made a film entitled *Kimberley Jim* which was released after his death. One of the first things Reeves bought for himself when he became successful was a 1960 Cadillac Eldorado Seville. It was much treasured by the singer. Unfortunately, I have not been able to track down Reeves's recording of 'Pink and Blue Cadillac'.

Ironically the group enjoyed their only Rhodesian chart hit almost by proxy when a single, 'I Talk to the Trees', was released under the name Mike Shannon, but on the label the words 'vocalist with THE DIAMONDS' featured alongside his name. The B-side was Mike's version of 'Let's Twist Again' and again the label noted he was 'vocalist with the Diamonds'. It charted in Southern Rhodesia where it peaked at number 4 on 15 September 1962. It was the group's only hit single anywhere.

Records in South Africa and Rhodesia were pressed in very small quantities because even if they were hits they did not sell in large numbers because they sold mainly to the minority white populations. Hence simply having a hit record did not make Rhodesian artists a lot of money. To achieve sales that would make them rich an African artist would have to sell records in Europe or the USA.

In 1963 came another LP release, this time entitled *Mike Shannon and the Diamonds* while Mike also released an album with Dana Valery entitled *Two Diamonds*.

Clearly by the time these albums were released Mike Shannon and the Diamonds were an established, highly respected and successful band in both South Africa and their native Rhodesia. The desire to capitalise on their talent and become even more successful and earn a lot more money must have been strong. To achieve this, they knew it really meant becoming known to a much wider audience. They needed to establish themselves on the international stage and to acquire some big hit singles elsewhere in the world. Logically, where better for them to do so than the United Kingdom which at that very moment in time was rapidly becoming the centre of the popular music world?

Mentor Dan Hill knew singing star Eve Boswell (he had made records with her) a hugely successful South African artist who was by then herself based in the UK. To this end Dan helped link the Diamonds with Eve.

A mightily gifted singer, pianist and dancer, Eve enjoyed huge popularity in Britain in the Fifties. She appeared regularly on TV, radio and in concert. She enjoyed a minor hit with 'Sugar Bush' in August 1952 but strangely enjoyed only one Top 10 hit in the UK with a song called 'Pickin' a Chicken' which was produced by George Martin and released on the Parlophone label. It peaked at number 9 on 9 February 1956. A look at this chart finds several links to the story of the Beatles. Perched one place higher than Eve was Lonnie Donegan with 'Rock Island Line'. Bill Haley and 'Rock Around the Clock' had just slipped out of the Top 10 from number 8 to number 14 and was in its 19th week on the chart. Just below Bill Haley at number 16 was a certain Dick James with Stephen James and His

Chums and the double A-sided hit (an uncredited George Martin production) 'Robin Hood / The Ballad of Davy Crockett. (Number 1 was Tennessee Ernie Ford with 'Sixteen Tons'.)

The shift in music tastes brought on by the advent of the Sixties and the advent of 'Beat' music caused Eve's popularity to wane a little, but in 1963 she apparently agreed to help Mike and the Diamonds when they decided to try their luck in Britain. In re-locating to London they became the first band from South Africa to move abroad in search of fame and fortune.

Almost as soon as they arrived in the UK they discovered that they shared their group name with an already established British band. They then decided upon calling themselves 'The Strangers' but found there was already a British band of that name. To make life easy they settled on 'The Rhodesians' which did not produce problems with anybody's copyright.

There are two candidates for the UK group who were already calling themselves the Strangers in 1963 when the Rhodesians first attempted to call themselves by that name.

It may have been the Strangers from Liverpool. In his occasional column for Mersey Beat, *called 'The Roving I' published in October 1961, the Cavern's DJ, Bob Wooler published a list he had compiled of those he considered to be the ten most popular beat groups on Merseyside ... he later told author Spencer Leigh that the rankings "were decided more by the audience reaction I witnessed at dances than by my own opinion."*[1]

Occupying the first four places in Wooler's list were the Beatles, Gerry and the Pacemakers, Rory Storm and the Hurricanes, the Remo Four, while at number 5 were the Strangers. Wooler told Leigh: "The Strangers were a very good band who could communicate and it was always fun when they appeared at Aintree Institute, Hambleton Hall or the Cavern."[2]

Frontman for the Strangers was singer Joe Fagin who later enjoyed a solo Top 10 UK hit when he reached number 3 for two weeks in early 1984 with 'Breakin' Away' / 'That's Livin' Alright'. (Both songs were from the hugely popular UK comedy-drama series Auf Wiedersehen Pet.*)*

Alternatively it could have been a group from Dudley in the West Midlands who also called themselves the Strangers. Formed in late 1959 by pupils attending Dudley Grammar School, original member Tony Dalloway said, "The lifespan of the Strangers was from 1960 to 1965."[3]

They recorded four tracks for Decca in 1964 which featured on a compilation long player entitled Brum Beat. *Norrie Paramor had, apparently, coined the name 'Brum Beat' to identify beat groups from the Birmingham area, but it was Les Reed from Decca who used it first as the title of a showcase 'various artists' album entitled* Brum Beat *released in 1964 (Decca LK 4598). It featured bands who were active on Joe and Mary Regan's famous 'Regan Circuit', which included the Plazas at Old Hill and Wandsworth, the Adelphi in West Bromwich and the Ritz at King's Heath. None of the bands featured on the 16-track compilation actually came from Birmingham itself, but no one was complaining. The bands were: the Blue Stars (Cannock), the Mountain Kings (Walsall), Dave Lacey and the Corvettes (Stourbridge), the Kavern Four (Cannock) and the Strangers (Dudley).*

In 1965, the Strangers originally from Dudley morphed into a very popular drumbeat group they called Finders Keepers.

(It was clearly a popular name at that time for in 1963 another beat group, this time from Balbriggan, Dublin, in the Republic of Ireland, got together and called themselves the Strangers. Famous for their vocal harmonies they were very soon being described as 'Ireland's Beatles'. The group's popularity endured and in 1967 they were voted 'Best Irish Beat Group' in New Spotlight *which was, from 1963 until 1979, 'Ireland's No.1 Young Entertainment Weekly'. In the same year, they scored their first Irish Top 10 hit (number 6) with their debut single released on the Pye label which featured their versions of two songs taken from the Monkees' album* More of the Monkees, *namely Neil Diamond's 'Look Out (Here Comes Tomorrow)' and Mike Nesmith's 'Mary Mary'. The Irish Strangers folded in 1972 before briefly reforming in 1977/78.)*[4]

Meanwhile …

Not long after they arrived in England, the Rhodesians parted company with Eve Boswell to be represented by Foster's Agency. They quickly became regulars at London's 'Astra Club' although they also performed widely around the UK and joined tours of Europe alongside bands who were soon to become very popular in the UK and beyond. As bassist Sandy Miller recalled: "This was before anybody had made it in the true sense of the word. We were all on the road chasing the same dreams. Everyone got on pretty well and there was almost a community spirit amongst the musicians. Little did we know at the time just how big some of our contemporaries were to become." Indeed they were, for among their fellow companions on the road were the Rolling Stones, the Dave Clark Five, Lulu, Millie Small, and the Bachelors.

It was whilst on tour in Europe that the Rhodesians encountered an act from Liverpool who, by then, were already making a massive impact on the UK charts. Returning from a gig at a club in Frankfurt the Rhodesians encountered a group and their broken down vehicle stranded at the side of the road. They stopped to lend a hand and before they knew it the Rhodesians were giving a lift to and towing Billy J. Kramer, the Dakotas and their broken down vehicle all the way back to the UK.

Not too long after this chance roadside encounter and rescue, the Rhodesians were introduced by their agent to the Beatles' 'management'. Just who comprised the Beatles' 'management' is not known. Was it just Brian Epstein, or Brian and Dick James … or maybe another combination? Here the story becomes patchy and just how, or who did help the Rhodesians gain access to a song written by John Lennon and Paul McCartney, is not on record.

The Beatles were completing the filming of *A Hard Day's Night* and John and Paul were very busy penning new songs, one of which was 'One and One Is Two', a tune penned not for the film but specifically for Billy J. Kramer. Ultimately Billy J. turned it down but told me that he had not played a part in securing the song for the Rhodesians.

Described as a 'spare song' that had not made it onto the film's soundtrack, nevertheless the Rhodesians must have been astounded by their good fortune: relative unknowns in the UK, they had become recipients of a brand new, previously unheard and unrecorded Lennon-McCartney original. Surely, they must have dared to believe, that here – at last! – *was* that big break they had worked so hard for so many years to achieve – their passport to a sure-fire big hit record from which their star would soar. Without hesitation they accepted the offer.

Of course the song that the Rhodesians were 'given' was the tune Paul, with some help from John, had specifically penned for Billy J. Kramer, but which he *and* the Fourmost had both already rejected: 'One and One Is Two'.

The completion of which, as noted in the previous chapter, was witnessed by writer Michael Braun and described in his marvellous 1964 memoir, *Love Me Do: The Beatles' Progress*, which was written directly from the inside looking out.

Sitting next to them in the privacy of their own company, Braun watched and listened to the Beatles reacting and interacting to everything and everyone that they were experiencing. His economic prose, sense of humour and attention to detail catches the heartbeat of every moment. And the Beatles did not hold back. They provided pure writer's gold: spontaneous and unguarded copy, that captures John, Paul, George and Ringo as they were still learning the game.

Given access all areas to the Beatles by manager Brian Epstein, the author had accompanied the group to Paris in January 1964 and was present one evening when John and Paul finished the song in their suite at the George V Hotel after a performance at the Olympia Theatre. Of that evening, Braun recalls that Paul was still wearing his stage make-up and John was wearing a polo-neck sweater and sunglasses. The two songwriters took it in turns to sit at the piano or at the table with a guitar. At one point John played some harmonica. "A microphone leading from a tape-recorder was strapped to a floor lamp."[5]

Braun observed the two Beatles as first Paul sang what they had written so far before the two of them began experimenting with additional words and lines … at various points George stuck his head in the door and at one point Ringo wandered around complaining he was bored and asked if George would like to accompany him to a nightclub to listen to some jazz. George suggested that John and Paul drop one of the 'one and one is two's' out and John agreed that that bit did 'get on me nerves' and started to experiment with different rhyming words 'true', 'blue', 'point of view'.[6]

At some stage while playing the chords to the song on his guitar, John donned a leather cap, informing Braun that Paul had bought a Bob Dylan record on the cover of which there was a photo of Dylan wearing a cap just like his. John commented that he now thought that everyone would think he had copied it from Dylan.

John and Paul taped 'One and One Is Two' three times, after which John was happy with it but Paul felt they had not succeeded in getting a good take. Braun notes that the words for the song were written on George V notepaper and lay spread around the suite alongside hundreds of fan letters. As John chatted to Braun, the author says Paul made some final revisions to the lyric before the two Beatles taped the song one more time. On completion of this final take, Braun comments that Paul prefaced the tape "with a message for Dick James, who is expecting the tape in London the next morning, 'I guess this is okay'."[7]

Tellingly, Braun concluded his story with a final remark from John: "Billy J. is finished when he gets this song."[8]

THE STRANGERS with MIKE SHANNON
ONE AND ONE IS TWO **(2:10)**
(John Lennon/Paul McCartney)
Northern Songs Ltd
Philips BF 1335
Mike Shannon: lead vocals
Peter Dene: lead guitar (and band leader)
Tony Hulley: rhythm guitar
Hugh 'Sandy' Miller: bass and clarinet
Maurice Fresco: drums
B-side: Time and the River
(Aaron Schroeder/Wally Gold)
Released: 8 May 1964

Unfortunately, only minimal details have survived of this recording.

One thing that is clear is that the group changed their name for the single's release.

Philips Records were based at Stanhope House near Marble Arch and had their own recording studio in the basement, which was managed by Tom Stephenson who had joined Philips in 1956 from EMI where he had worked as tape editor. Chief recording engineer around this time was Peter Olliff, ably assisted by Roger Wake and Gary Moore. Philips' A&R man was John Franz. Franz's right-hand man was Paddy Fleming whose job it was to promote 'finished product' with the BBC (radio and television) and elsewhere.

From this it is fairly certain to say John or 'Johnny' Franz produced 'One and One Is Two' and that the session was engineered by Peter Olliff with the assistance of Roger Wake and/or Gary Moore. When it came to promoting the single Paddy Fleming no doubt gave the record his best shot, but even so it did not chart anywhere.

To all intents and purposes, the Strangers were in good hands for this was a proven winning combination – Johnny Frantz was one of the most successful UK producers of the 1960s and only a few months before recording the Rhodesians, aka 'The Strangers with Mike Shannon', he had produced 'Juliet' by the Four Pennies. At the time 'One and One

Extract from the singles review page of *NME* dated Friday 8 May, 1964 and featuring critic Derek Johnson's review of the Strangers with Mike Shannon's debut single, 'One and One Is Two'.

Is Two' was released (8 May) the Four Pennies and 'Juliet' were at number 12 in the UK charts and well on their way to becoming number 1 on 25 May.

On the very day of its release, the Strangers received a very favourable review from Derek Johnson in *NME*'s 8 May 1964 edition where, under the title 'Mike Shannon', he opined: "A thumping, walloping beat sets the scene for the latest John Lennon-Paul McCartney composition 'One and One Is Two' (Philips). Opening as a unison vocal by the Strangers, it develops into a solo voice showcase for Mike Shannon with Liverpool-style oh-yeah chanting in the background." Johnson continued by saying that, "On first playing, it didn't strike me as one of the Beatle boys' greatest numbers. But after three spins I found it was growing on me. The catchy simplicity of the lyric allows you to join in."[9]

Johnson was possibly more impressed by the B-side, "A clean-cut beat-ballad treatment of the oldie 'Time and the River' is well handled by Mike. One or two words jarred in his delivery, but clearly he has distinct promise."[10]

Just a day later, *Disc* music weekly weighed in with another positive review, noting that, "A John Lennon and Paul McCartney song, 'One and One Is Two' makes a nice capture for this South African group's British disc debut." Giving the single a 3-star rating in its 'In Short' reviews column it predicted, "Probably not a wild hit, but a brisk beginning."[11]

The portents must have looked and felt very good.

The change of name from the Rhodesians was a sound move given that at the time the British and Rhodesian governments were locked in stalemate over the future of Rhodesian independence. British prime minister Harold Wilson and Rhodesian prime minister Ian Smith had reached an impasse. Before Britain would agree independence it insisted that Ian Smith had to agree that in the future there would be majority rule. At the time Smith and the incumbent Rhodesian government comprised members mostly from the country's white minority population which represented just 5% of the Rhodesian population. Tensions were running very high and by the autumn of 1965 Smith and his government would issue a Unilateral Declaration of Independence which the British declared was treasonous. By 1970 the Smith administration declared Rhodesia to be a republic which failed to gain the foreign recognition Smith had hoped for. Not long after, guerrilla warfare broke out (the Rhodesian Bush War) and it was not until 1980 that an internationally recognised independence was finally achieved and the country became formally known as Zimbabwe.

As far as the Rhodesians and their change of name goes, what is odd is *not* that they changed their name but that they were able to do so to a name they had previously been prevented from using because there was an existing UK outfit performing under that name. While the Strangers from Liverpool had no doubt disbanded by then, the Strangers from Dudley were flying high … maybe the 'with Mike Shannon' is what made the difference.

As for the absolute lack of chart action encountered by the Strangers with Mike Shannon and 'One and One Is Two' there are several possible reasons why it died the death. The group made a good fist of the recording, there is no doubt about that. They rock it up and Mike Shannon does the best he can with a lyric that is very tame and never really gets anywhere. They were far too good a group and seasoned recording artists by the time they cut 'One and One Is Two' not to make something out of what, in truth, was very little. They did. But despite their best efforts they could not gild this particular lily. (The B-side was typical beat ballad fare for the time, but at the time of writing it is over-sung and sounds insincere.)

What is certain is that like Tommy Quickly and 'Tip of My Tongue' they had been gifted one of the weakest of all Beatles' 'giveaways'. Despite Quickly's and the Strangers' best efforts, it's clear why the Beatles passed on recording either of these songs for themselves. Compared to what else John and Paul were writing and the Beatles were recording at that time, both songs sound like production-line efforts, a criticism it is almost otherwise impossible to level at the work of Lennon and McCartney. As the Fourmost had already discovered there was simply no substance to 'One and One Is Two'.

In his extensive 1980 interview for *Playboy*, John Lennon, even though he had worked on the song with Paul in Paris, declared it "another of Paul's bad attempts at writing a song." Harsh words that echoed his observation from 1964.

Sir George Martin recognised that not all the songs the Beatles gave away were their best. He, more than most people, observed that John and Paul knew that *not* everything they wrote was top drawer: "There were a lot songs John and Paul gave to people that weren't terrific. You get a great songwriter and it's just as possible for them to write an inadequate song as they are a hit song. He or she won't believe it, for within him/herself they will believe everything they do is top class. As a callous observer I know this is not true. John and Paul *did* write inferior songs which they knew about and would put them to one side and concentrate on the others. By the time they got really successful they knew what a hit song was going to do. I remember when I was doing the music for the *Yellow Submarine* film the Beatles hated it, they wouldn't have anything to do with it at all. It had been lumbered upon them by Brian in fulfilment of a contract with United Artists to be their third film. When they heard who was doing it, (it was the same people who had done a series of cartoon films in the States featuring the Beatles which stylistically were very simplistic) the Beatles said we're having nothing to do with it. They didn't realise until it was completed that the artistry that went into *Yellow Submarine* was superb. So they took no notice at all but they were contractually committed to give it four new songs. Around that time we might be in the studios working on something and hear John and Paul say, 'Well I don't know, let's give it to *Yellow Submarine* shall we?' And if you listen to the four new songs in that film you know what they are, they are not exactly the greatest."[12]

Even so a Beatles song was a Beatles song and in 1964 that was something special. On its own it was usually more than enough to garner a lot of attention and all the attendant promotion. With this in mind, for 'One and One Is Two' to not even skim the chart is surprising.

Although little can be traced about most of their time in the UK, around the time of the release of 'One and One Is Two' the profile of the Strangers with Mike Shannon was raised.

Significantly they did receive some prominent TV exposure to promote the single.

Just a week after its release, at 5.10pm on Thursday 14 May 1964, they appeared on an established young person's pop music TV show entitled *A Swingin' Time* to perform (mime) the song.

The inaugural series of *A Swingin' Time* had aired in 1963 and proved popular enough for a second series of eight programmes to be commissioned in 1964. Both series featured Rolf Harris as presenter. The Diamonds had met Harris in Johannesburg when he was there to perform. Now as 'The Strangers with Mike Shannon' he was instrumental in getting them to appear on the show, beginning with the very first programme of the new series, the format of which was described as: 'The boys and girls in the studio and guest stars: Adam Faith, Kathy Kirby, the Roulettes and introducing the Strangers with Mike Shannon.'

The group appeared twice more during the second series. On Episode 5 screened on 11 June they performed alongside their road trip friends Billy J. Kramer with the Dakotas while Petula Clark and Lulu were also on the bill.

Their third and final appearance on *A Swingin' Time* was on the show's penultimate episode that went out on 25 June. This time the stars of the show were the Bachelors and Dee Ervin (aka Big Dee Irwin). The latter had enjoyed a 1963 hit in the UK entitled 'Swinging on a Star'. It was a duet with Little Eva singer of 'The Locomotion'. When Irwin appeared on *A Swingin' Time* with the Strangers and Mike Shannon, it was to promote his new single 'Heigh Ho' on which he was backed by the Breakaways.

The incidental music for *A Swingin' Time* was credited to Les Reed. Reed was, of course, already a successful songwriter and an accomplished arranger, musician and light orchestra leader. Along with Geoff Stephens he had written the Applejacks' big hit 'Tell Me When' which had peaked at number 7 in April '64.

Maybe even more significantly the Strangers with Mike Shannon appeared on *Thank Your Lucky Stars* to promote their debut UK single. *Lucky Stars* was, of course, as already noted, one of *the* major music shows of the time. Up to 6 million would tune in to this show when it was at its peak, which it was at precisely that point in time. For a new act in the UK this was excellent prime-time exposure.

And so, on Saturday 30 May, on a bill hosted by Brian Matthew and featuring the Rolling Stones, Adam Faith and the Roulettes, and Dionne Warwick, the Strangers with Mike Shannon appeared to sing (mime to) 'One and One Is Two'.

At this point in their career there is no doubt the Strangers with Mike Shannon were mixing in the right company, getting good exposure, good reviews and making a success of their decision to relocate to the UK. Why it all did not result in chart success is a mystery. Maybe it was to do with the marketing of their records, but whatever it was they were dropped after just two singles.

Possibly their physical appearance did not chime with the times. They don't look dangerous enough. On the photograph of the band that appears on the sheet music for 'One and One Is Two' they look a tad older than their contemporaries and appear very 'straight' compared to, say, members of the Animals, Kinks and Pretty Things. Singer Mike Shannon looks particularly suave. He could have doubled for actor Roger Moore, while on the same photo another member of the group resembles Dean Martin. Ultimately they don't have an edge about them that would have immediately connected with the teenage audience of the day. Whatever, they only issued two singles and both sank without trace.

Ironically their follow-up to 'One and One Is Two' was a better sounding record by far, and written by two of the band themselves.

Released on Philips in December 1964, 'Do You or Don't You' was a Mike Shannon and Peter Dene co-write. It is a significantly more muscular and distinctive sounding record than 'One and One Is Two' and certainly more in tune with the emerging sound of new R&B acts like the Animals and the Rolling Stones. The A-side with its angry lead guitar and Mike Shannon's snarling vocals could not have been more different in mood and feel to 'One and One Is Two', but unfortunately its scornful lyric is not particularly pleasant towards its female subject and possibly limited the amount of radio plays or TV slots it received ('Please don't tease me baby, Don't say you're one of those…'). What is in no doubt is that it made no impression on the record-buying public (if they ever actually got to hear it) and consequently once again chart success resolutely eluded them. Interestingly the B-side, 'What Can I Do' was another in-house composition, this time a solo effort by Peter Dene and derivative in style of the Beatles/Beat group mode still popular in 1964.

For all the hard work and effort they had put into their time in the UK (they were never out of work) the Strangers and chart success did not coincide.

They did, however, make a significant contribution to one of the most enduring and popular hit records of the Sixties, for it is their gear that was used (apparently) by the Animals to record 'The House of the Rising Sun'.

The link between the Rhodesians from Rhodesia and the Animals from Newcastle was

English record producer, Mickie Most. He was a friend of the Strangers with Mike Shannon from before they had ventured to Britain. In 1964 in London, Most was at the beginning of what would become an amazingly successful career as a record producer.

Born Michael Peter Hayes in Aldershot in 1938, by 1964 he was making the transition from a successful career as a singer to record producing and at the same time was managing the Animals. On 18 May 1964, between stops on a UK tour, Most had booked the group into a small London recording studio on Kingsway to cut 'House of the Rising Sun' as the follow-up to their debut single 'Baby Let Me Take You Home' which had climbed as far as number 21 in April 1964. Most had produced the session for their debut hit, although by his own admission it hadn't taken much production for it was cut in just one take.

Apparently when the Animals turned up at the studio to record 'House of the Rising Sun', they did so with equipment that was in such a poor state it could not be used for recording. Most immediately thought of the Rhodesians whom he already knew and whom he also knew were now based in London (at Salisbury House in Earl's Court). A plea went out and, without a second thought, the group duly loaned Most and the Animals their immaculately cared-for equipment for the session. The resulting single went to number 1 and remains one of the defining and groundbreaking records of the Sixties. For both the Animals and Mickie Most the record was the moment that both their careers entered another dimension.

Although they would later be thrilled to know it was down to their generosity that such a groundbreaking and classic hit single had been able to be recorded when it was, at the time the Rhodesians were distinctly unhappy with the state of their equipment when it was returned. They took great pride in the care they invested in their kit. Immaculate when they sent it over, it came back replete with stains and cigarette burns that had not been there before. The group were also peeved that neither Most nor the Animals apparently ever thanked them for their generosity.

Just why Mickie Most reached out to the Rhodesians was not simply down to coincidence. He had encountered them, or the Diamonds as they would have been known at the time, when, with his wife Christina, he had relocated to South Africa in 1959. By then he had changed his name from Michael Hayes to Mickie Most and while in South Africa he had almost immediately formed a pop group: Mickie Most and the Playboys, who scored 11 consecutive number 1 singles, most of which were covers of songs by artists such as Gene Vincent, Buddy Holly and Eddie Cochran. Returning to London in 1962, Most continued working as a pop singer and had a modest UK hit in 1963 when his single 'Mister Porter' reached number 45 for a week in July. (In the same year he cut another single called 'The Feminine Look' which featured Jimmy Page on lead guitar.)

Consequently, when Mickie Most reached out to the Rhodesians, as they were then known, he and they were not strangers. It's a shame that he did not offer to manage and record them. They would surely have benefitted from the Midas touch he most certainly possessed.

What happened next to the Strangers with Mike Shannon marks the beginning of their demise as a group. No doubt feeling deflated by their lack of chart action in Britain, they accepted an invitation to audition for work in Australia which they won and were soon relocated 'down under' playing the circuit in and around Brisbane and making regular appearances on Aussie television. In Australia they initially went out as 'The Strangers' but soon returned to calling themselves 'The Rhodesians' and in 1967 cut an album entitled *The Rhodesians at Chevron Skyline Cabaret*. On the record both Shannon and Dene, apart from their usual roles as singer and lead guitarist, were each credited with also playing tenor sax. Although Pete Dene played on this record he left the group whilst in Australia and was replaced by an Australian guitarist called Graham Spedding. Singer Mike Shannon became tangled up in personal issues which impacted on the group and at some point in 1968, minus Pete Dene, they returned to South Africa where they promptly folded.

Maybe they had just been together too long and had had so many 'nearly' moments as a group that the inevitable cracks had begun to appear. Success on the scale they had wanted and tried so hard to achieve simply eluded them. Ironically, at the moment they split, a song, 'When Strangers Meet', that they had cut for the *Chevron Skyline* album, had been selected as the title song for a Frank Sinatra film. This had come about when Joe Kentridge, the former owner of Ciro's (a club in Johannesburg where the group had played), had settled in the USA after suffering a heart attack whilst visiting the country. He had passed some of the Rhodesians' songs around the American music and film industries. One of which was 'When Strangers Meet'. The film company were considering asking the Rhodesians to travel to the USA to re-record the song for the film's soundtrack. The interest came too late, for by then the original band had split, never to reform.

Individually once back on home turf 'The Strangers', aka 'Rhodesians', simply moved on.

Moved on and more or less disappeared … it has proven very difficult to trace exactly what happened next to each individual Stranger. Maybe someone somewhere will read this chapter and be able to enlighten/correct/update/satisfactorily conclude the story of the Strangers. I'd be happy to hear from them via the publisher.

What information is available about what happened next, on the limited sources I have been able to trace, is provided below:

Bassist and clarinet player Sandy Miller apparently returned to the UK and put together an all-new version of the Rhodesians. They found plenty of work in the UK, Israel and (as they were known then) the countries of Yugoslavia and Czechoslovakia, but eventually Sandy quit music full-time and went on to enjoy a successful career in commerce and industry. Apparently he continued to play solo spots on a part-time basis.

What happened to Pete Dene and Tony Hulley after the demise of the Rhodesians has not been possible for me to trace except, sadly, to learn that they have both since passed on.

As for drummer Maurice Fresco, I have failed to discover what became of him once the Rhodesians left Australia.

The further adventures of Mike Shannon are yet another mystery. All that my research has discovered is that, 'he is thought to be somewhere in South Africa', which narrows it down considerably…!

Wherever Mike, Maurice and Sandy are, my best wishes to them! Do get in touch.

My main sources of information for this chapter have been :

http://www.rhodiemusic.com/bands/bands-d.htm

Dave Ravenscroft, Beatles scholar.

Love Me Do: The Beatles' Progress (Penguin, 1964) by Michael Braun, chapter 8: Paris.

The precise birthplaces of the Strangers courtesy of research passed on to me by Mark Lewisohn.

1 & 2 *The Best of Fellas* by Spencer Leigh (Drivegreen Publications Ltd in association with Jim Turner, 2002) Bob Wooler in conversation with Spencer Leigh, pp. 97 & 98.
3 *The Strangers* a group biography by Brian Nicholls www.brumbeat.net (As updated in February 2019).
4 'The Strangers – Irish Rock Discography' Irish Rock of the 60s & 70s www.irishrock.org
5, 6, 7 & 8 *Love Me Do: The Beatles' Progress* by Michael Braun (Penguin, 1964) pages 82 and 83.
9 & 10 *NME*, 8 May 1964, Derek Johnson review, 1960smusicmagazines.com/2018/11/07/nme-may-8-1964/
10 *Disc* music weekly, edition 320, 9 May 1964, 'In Short' single review by Don Nicholl, p.9.
11 Sir George Martin in conversation with Bob Harris OBE and Colin Hall for the 2009 BBC Radio 2 documentary *The Songs the Beatles Gave Away*, written and narrated by Bob Harris, produced for WBBC by Bob Harris and Trudie Myerscough-Harris, devised by Colin Hall with Bob Harris and Trudie Myerscough-Harris.

Chapter 70:
1964, BRUM BEAT AND THE SOUND OF SOLIHULL

If 1963 was the year of Mersey Beat, then 1964 was the year the rest of the country got a look in. For record companies the search to find the 'new Beatles' had begun and it was not confined to scouring Merseyside. It went nationwide.

As the tsunami of beat music swept the country, leading the pack of hopefuls from Birmingham (Solihull to be exact) were the Applejacks.

Only three members of this six-piece band were actually born in Birmingham, two others were born in nearby Solihull, a town some seven miles from Britain's second city. The sixth member of the Applejacks had the audacity to have been born in Sheffield, Yorkshire. What mattered was that collectively, by the time they hit the chart big-time, they were all living in Solihull and had been doing so for many years. (Early in their career the Applejacks had been described as representatives of the 'Solihull Sound'.)

It was the Sheffield-born member of the group, the bass player, who, in the print and photographic media of the day, garnered a *lot* of early interest in the Applejacks for she was one Megan Davies, and in those days girls in groups were almost unknown.

Girls who played bass were even rarer … so much so Megan's presence in the group was considered groundbreaking

That's not to say that in those long-gone days '*girl* groups' did not exist, they did but that specific label was usually applied to groups of two or three girl vocalists who would stand clustered around a microphone in front of a band or orchestra and sing and dance a little. They were out front and most definitely the star attraction. As such they had a set of carefully choreographed steps, nothing too energetic, more arm and hand movement than leg, but they would not be seen playing instruments. They would each wear a matching (often sparkly) dress and, as we say in Liverpool, 'big hair' was the order of the day. In most cases this comprised a carefully coiffured wig. On stage and on record they did the same: sing and no more. They would not be just 'one of the group' but *the* featured artists out front singing. Check out the Shangri-Las or Ronettes: both classic Sixties girl groups.

The avid press reaction to a girl in a group who was not the featured lead singer but an instrumentalist says a lot about how *un*-liberated the Sixties actually were. Groups were what boys did, *not* girls. Girls were meant to be the audience, designated to do the screaming, the adoring, not the nuts and bolts stuff like playing. (The USA was one-step ahead of the UK for they could boast Goldie and the Gingerbreads, an all-female beat group comprising drums, guitar, bass, keyboards and vocalist who scored a UK hit in February 1965 with 'Can't You Hear My Heartbeat'.)

As a source of media interest in the UK, Megan was quickly joined by Honey Lantree from the Honeycombs, a group who reached number 1 in the summer of 1964 with 'Have I the Right?'. They hailed from North London and Honey was their drummer: she was an immediate sensation.

A girl in a group was a sign of the times and that those times were undoubtedly a-changing. The whole furore surrounding the 'beat music' scene was not something with which our parents in general felt totally comfortable. The majority viewed groups as long-haired boys/scruffs ('layabouts' was often used in conjunction with the words 'longhaired'), defying the rules of convention. And then along came the Applejacks and Honeycombs setting new precedents which could lead to who knew what. Since its outset in the Fifties our parents had been informed that rock 'n' roll was the 'music of the Devil'. Decadent and depraved it could lead their children astray. Here was more evidence that it most probably could — and would! First Megan, now Honey … what would girls be up to next? Before we knew it they would want to be driving trains and aeroplanes, standing for Parliament … even reading the news on television: surely, it seemed, the end of the world was nigh.

A telling insight into the mindset of the times can be gleaned from an outrageous front-page article that appeared on the cover of a 1964 edition of the *MM* which boldly declared "Honeycombs 'gimmick' charge denied." The charge (if there ever actually was one) that had apparently been laid was aimed directly at Honey Lantree: *"The Honeycombs topped the hit parade this week – and immediately slammed critics who accuse them of featuring a girl drummer as a 'gimmick'."* The article continued with the clearly outraged leader of the Honeycombs, *"guitarist Martin Murray"* fervently defending the group: *"It's just a load of rubbish – I believe we would have made it even without any so-called gimmick … Honey Lantree is a good drummer and that's the reason she's with us…"* If Murray was to be believed, the Honeycombs had resorted to violence to persuade Lantree to join the group for he told the *MM* she *"had to be bludgeoned into accepting the job".* Bludgeoned? Well into his stride by that point Murray then stressed, *"she got the job on her music – not her sex"* … and to see off any detractors still standing Murray gave it to them straight: *"She's a natural drummer and excellent at recording studios. In fact Honey's the only one of us who doesn't make mistakes at recording sessions".*[1]

That such an outrageous piece was given the prominence of a front page speaks volumes for where we were at as a nation in those days in terms of gender equality.

Meanwhile back in Birmingham, the Applejacks hadn't been the only group to attract attention from major London-based labels. In June 1963 Norrie Paramor (who apparently coined the name 'Brum Beat' to describe the sounds emanating from Birmingham) and his assistant Bill Barratt, both from EMI, visited the Moat House Club* on Bradford Street. Situated in the Digbeth area of Birmingham they were there to hold auditions with a view to signing some new groups. Thirteen acts turned up from which Paramor and Barratt emerged with five acts signed to Columbia Records, most notable of these were Mike Sheridan and the Night Riders (future members of the Night Riders included Roy Wood and Jeff Lynne), Keith Powell and the Valets, and Carl Barron and the Cheetahs. Although they all released critically well-received debut singles, none of them sold enough to break into the UK charts, neither did they with their follow-up records.

(*The Moat House was where Ray Thomas and Mike Pinder first met and decided to form a group that became the Moody Blues. Denny Laine and the Diplomats were also regulars at the club.) The Rockin' Berries were another Brum Beat group signed to Decca in 1963. They did not have any hits until they switched labels in 1964 to Piccadilly (a subsidiary of Pye) when they scored a number 3 in October with the haunting 'He's in Town'.

The story of the Applejacks was, however, something else, for not only did they have Megan on bass, they were also very young. When, in late 1963, they were signed by talent scouts from the prestigious Decca Records company, three of them were still attending school. This was yet another factor the press could not resist: a typical storyline would involve Martin, Don and Phil and the choice they faced to either stay on at school and continue with their studies or to leave and chance it all on a shot at fortune and fame. Away from the press interest this was a genuinely tough decision, but life as an Applejack won out and unlike their Brummie contemporaries, the Applejacks *did* hit the UK charts with their records. They *did* become genuine pop stars.

As such, they hold a very important place in UK popular music history as the first representatives of 'Brum Beat' to have a Top 10 record.

The core of the group, Martin Baggott, Phil Cash and Gerry Freeman had originally formed a group with Megan because they were members of the 1st Olton Scout group where her dad was scout leader. As Megan recalls, "At the age of fifteen, I moved from Girl Guides to assist with Wolf Cubs. In 1960, the 1st Olton Scout Group were preparing a 'Gang Show' and when asked 'Can anyone play an instrument?' a few of us took up the challenge. Martin Baggott, Phil Cash and I possessed guitars and Gerry Freeman was the obvious choice as the drummer because he was lead drummer in the Scout band. We all got together to perform a couple of skiffle numbers: 'Hang Down Your Head Tom Dooley' and 'John Henry'."[2]

Having enjoyed performing together for the 'Gang Show' the youngsters did not disband once it was over. And, like most skifflers, the future Applejacks progressed to playing electric instruments. As this transition occurred so Megan took up the bass: "The Shadows was the way to go … we had no Cliff Richard! It was obvious then, that one of us would have to change to bass guitar. 'Well, you're the worst guitarist Megan. You can play bass!' I'm not sure that it was actually said in so many words, but that's the gist of how I got the job."[3]

Rhythm guitarist Phil Cash remembers Megan's transition to bass slightly differently: "We had already started playing together – three guitarists, a drummer and pianist but no one knew how to play the bass – so Megan volunteered and learned to play from scratch."[4]

By the end of 1961, keyboard player Don Gould had joined the group. As they had no lead singer initially the group played instrumentals in the mode of chart toppers the Shadows and the Tornados. Along the way they changed the group name from the Crestas (as they had been known as a skiffle group) to the Jaguars. A defining moment in their history came in 1962 when they recruited lead singer Al Jackson and became known as Al Jackson and the Applejacks. Megan: "We arrived at the name 'Applejacks' by thinking around Al's name 'Al Jackson'. We had heard about 'applejack' (a drink made from fermented cider and popular in the USA) but it was only later that we found out that there was an American group called Dave Appell and the Applejacks*."[5]

(*Dave Appell was born in Philadelphia in 1922. He went on to become a well-known and highly regarded musician, arranger, music publisher and record producer. During the 1950s he fronted a group called the Dave Appell Four but was persuaded to change the name to the Applejacks. Billed as Dave Appell and the Applejacks they appeared in the 1956 film Don't Knock the Rock alongside Alan Dale, Alan Freed, Little Richard, Bill Haley and His Comets, and the Treniers. After a spell in Las Vegas, Appell and his Applejacks returned to their hometown Philadelphia to work for Cameo Records, a label founded by Karl Mann and Bernie Lowe. It was in 1958 for Cameo that Dave Appell and the Applejacks recorded two singles that became hits: the instrumental 'The Mexican Hat Dance' (number 16) followed by 'Rocka-Conga' (number 38). Later Appell became the leader of the Cameo-Parkway label's house band and backed artists such as Chubby Checker, Bobby Rydell, Dee Dee Sharp, etc. In addition to this he would often produce as well as arrange their records and with Karl Mann he co-wrote 'Let's Twist Again' for Chubby Checker. He left Cameo in 1964. Later he co-produced hits for Tony Orlando and Dawn such as 'Knock Three Times' (1970) and 'Tie a Yellow Ribbon Round the Old Oak Tree' (1973). He died aged 92 in November 2014.)

The Applejacks' reputation in Solihull had grown and grown until during 1963 they were playing a Monday night residency at Solihull's Civic Hall. At the time they got this prestigious gig, three of the group were still at school: Martin Baggott and Don Gould at Tudor Grange and Phil Cash at Lyndon School. Megan was a trainee EEG recordist, Al a hairdresser, Gerry an insurance clerk. However, wheels were turning and as Megan Davies remembers life for the Applejacks was about to change dramatically and big decisions loomed regarding their futures: "The manager of the Civic Hall, Les Holmes, was the brother-in-law of Joe Brannelly, who played banjo in the Ambrose Band in the 1940s. Joe knew someone already established in the music business who knew Mike Smith at Decca Records who in turn invited us down to London to make a demo. He liked what he heard and signed us to a deal".[6]

The Applejacks' story made good copy and very soon the national papers had picked up on them. They also made an appearance on local TV: Midlands at Six.

Almost before their feet touched the ground they recorded their first single. It was early January 1964 when they attended Decca's London studios to cut 'Baby Jane', but during a return to the studio on 12 January they cut another song, which was the irresistibly catchy 'Tell Me When'. Written by Les Reed and Geoff Stephens (a former school teacher) it became the preferred A-side of their debut single. Released in February 1964 it entered the UK Top 10 at number 9 in mid-April 1964 and climbed to number 7, a place they held for two weeks before dropping to number 14.[7]

'Tell Me When' chimed perfectly with the times – upbeat and catchy it was classic power pop and remained on the charts for 13 weeks.

Megan recalls that despite this the Applejacks themselves never lost their affection for 'Baby Jane': "At the time most of the band preferred 'Baby Jane' and considered the record to be a double 'A' side."[8]

Success and fame came instantly. What the press love to call 'overnight success' is a formidable beast. Of course it's a misleading title for there's usually nothing 'overnight' about such stories. And, as can be seen, this was the case with the Applejacks, for as young as they were, they had worked and practised hard over several years to get where they were.

When it came the attention they received was indeed challenging and swept them all along in its irresistible wake. Phil Cash remembers being woken one night by his father who had heard 'Tell Me When' playing on the radio and couldn't wait to tell him.

Next came the big decision that the press had already spotted: Decca wanted to know were they going to go further with their career in music or remain at school? The Applejacks chose music.

The tumult of it all was perfectly captured in Phil's memory of the day he left Lyndon school: "I couldn't get out because there were hundreds of fans/girls outside the front gates. So I had to turn my scooter around and get away via the back fields. It was quite scary. Someone nicked the mirror off my scooter and I never saw my satchel again".[9]

Once 'Tell Me When' began to happen, life inevitably changed for the Applejacks. Offers of tours, television and radio poured in. They were moving fast and learning every inch of the way. On 25 March 1964 they made their *Top of the Pops* debut when 'Tell Me When' was still climbing the charts having reached number 12 that week. Popular DJ Alan Freeman and the heinous Jimmy Savile were the hosts that night. Megan herself is convinced that was actually their second appearance: "It's strange, I'm sure that this was our second appearance because it was my 20th birthday and I was presented with a birthday cake."[10]

On the same show, the Beatles, who were straight in at number 8, were featured performing 'Can't Buy Me Love' *and* its B-side 'You Can't Do That'. The Beatles had been filmed especially for the show and did not appear 'live' in person.*

(*The Beatles' only 'live' appearance on *TOTP* was on 16 June 1966 when they performed 'Paperback Writer' and 'Rain'. Even so, while the group were physically present in the studio for the very first time on that occasion, it was not a genuine 'live' performance because like the other acts on the show they just 'mimed' when it came time for their record to be aired.)

The week the Applejacks appeared on *Top of the Pops*, Billy J. Kramer held the top spot with 'Little Children' and Peter and Gordon had entered the Top 20 at number 16 with 'A World without Love'. These were heady times indeed.

To be seen on TV in those days was the ultimate accolade, and to be seen on *Top of the Pops* was truly something else, literally *millions* tuned in to see the show: it was every singer's or group's goal, the irrefutable proof that they had 'made it'. They were 'STARS'!

For the record companies it was extremely important exposure for it usually meant a considerable hike in sales and helped keep a record on the chart.

And in this way the show was good to the Applejacks who appeared twice more as 'Tell Me When' continued to climb the Top 10.

On 1 April the Applejacks had reached number 9 and the same Beatles film clips that had been screened on the night they had made their first *TOTP* appearance were played once more, but by the 1st, the Fab Four were at number 1 having knocked Billy J. down to number 2 while Peter and Gordon had only climbed three places to number 13. The Applejacks' third appearance was on 15 April by when they had climbed a further two places to number 7. The Beatles were still at number 1 but Peter and Gordon had rocketed up the chart and were now just one place behind at number 2. The Applejacks remained at number 7 for another week, but did not appear on *TOTP* that second week when they were at number 7, by which time Peter and Gordon had replaced the Beatles at the top.

(N.B. In the *New Musical Express* chart 'Tell Me When' had climbed to number 5.)

On 10 April the Applejacks (a day after appearing on the popular children's TV programme, *Crackerjack*) appeared for the first time on the most 'happening' TV show of the time, *Ready Steady Go!*, to perform 'Tell Me When'. On the show with them were the Searchers with their current (soon to be number 1) single 'Don't Throw Your Love Away'. They were very much 'in-demand'. For teenagers everywhere *Ready Steady Go!* was *the* music show to catch. Not tied to the charts it gave teens a heads-up as to what was happening and what or who was on the horizon. Watching it was like having an instant party in your own living room.

When recalling the Applejacks' performances on *Top of the Pops*, Megan was convinced 'Tell Me When' had climbed higher than number 7. She was right because *they had* but then again, *they hadn't*. The confusing thing for all artists who charted in the Sixties – and their fans – is that in those days there was no national chart as such to which we could all refer as the definitive source. Footage of some editions of *TOTP* were erased and so for some shows on which the Applejacks appeared the charts as displayed on the show itself cannot be verified. Mostly artists and fans relied on the charts in *NME* and *MM*. (And of these *NME* was very much the kids' fave and which boasted on its cover of having the 'World's largest circulation of any music paper'.) These publications were teenage 'bibles': the fonts of all knowledge as far as what was happening in pop music. Their word was indeed 'gospel': their veracity never challenged.

And this is exactly what Megan and the Applejacks did, they read *NME* and in *NME* 'Tell Me When' did go Top 5, while a week earlier in the *MM* chart published on 11 April that year (the Top 10 of which appeared on the front cover of all April editions in 1964) the Applejacks were already at number 6, a rise of two places on the preceding week.

And so, by the following week on 17 April in the *NME* chart, the Applejacks were clearly at number 5, Billy J. was at number 4 with 'Little Children', the Bachelors at number 3 with 'I Believe', Peter and Gordon at number 2 with 'A World without Love' and the Beatles at number 1 with 'Can't Buy Me Love'. I could not find a copy of the 18 April edition of *MM* but it is most likely the Applejacks would have climbed a rung or two on that chart as well.

So, despite what the 'Official' chart tells us today, there is no doubt that most with-it-music-newspaper-reading kids in the Sixties would have considered 'Tell Me When' to be a Top 5 record because *NME* said it was.

The excitement surrounding groups and their records was thrilling to experience. These were undeniably exciting times for such a young group. Their rise to the top included not only *Top of the Pops* and *Ready Steady Go*, but also an appearance on the legendary BBC Radio Show *Saturday Club* when the equally legendary DJ Brian Matthew introduced them to perform 'Tell Me When'. The Dave Clark Five ('Bits and Pieces') and Peter and Gordon ('A World Without Love') were on the same show. The kids from Solihull were rubbing shoulders with the top acts of the day.

Like all artists, the rush and acclaim of a big hit mostly means your feet don't touch the ground, but as we have seen with Billy J. and the Fourmost, it also 'ups the ante' to be able to repeat the trick with the next, follow-up single. For the Applejacks that troubling concern was lifted from their shoulders when, out of the blue, they were offered a Beatles 'giveaway'. Totally unexpectedly they were invited to join what was, and remains, a select club.

---

1 *Melody Maker*, 29 August 1964, front cover feature.
2, 3 & 4 www.brumbeat.net/applejks.htm
5, 6, 8 & 10 Megan Davies in conversation with the author.
7 www.45cat.com/biography/the-applejacks-uk for details re: recording of 'Tell Me When'.
9 https://www.swanpublishing.org › Dorridge

Chapter 71:
1964, FIVE O'CLOCK CLUB

THE APPLEJACKS:
Martin Baggott, lead guitar (from early 1961).
b. Martin Thomas Baggott, 20 October 1947, Birmingham, Warwickshire
Phil Cash, rhythm guitar (from early 1961)
b. Philip Peter Cash, 9 October 1947, Birmingham, Warwickshire
Megan Davies, bass guitar (from early 1961)
b. Megan Kelso Davies, 25 March 1944, Sheffield, West Riding of Yorkshire
Don Gould, piano and organ (from December 1961)
b. Donald Peter Gould, 23 March 1947, Solihull, Warwickshire
Gerry Freeman, drums (from early 1961)
b. Gerald Ernest Freeman, 24 May 1943, Solihull, Warwickshire
Al Jackson, lead vocals (from July 1962)
b. Harry Llewellyn Jackson, 21 April 1945, Birmingham, Warwickshire

Despite all the Applejacks' TV and radio performances, and despite the fact that the Beatles were riding high on the charts at the very same time as 'Tell Me When' was climbing the Top 20, somehow the Applejacks' and the Beatles' paths had not actually crossed. Even though they had appeared on three editions of *Top of the Pops* when the Beatles had also been featured, because John, Paul, George and Ringo's performance had been pre-recorded, the two groups had not been together in the same studio at the same time.

The first time their paths did cross and the Applejacks actually got to meet and speak with the Beatles was when they were both in the same building at the same time but in different studios recording and rehearsing different television programmes.

On Tuesday 28 April 1964, the Beatles spent most of the day and evening attending final rehearsals for, and final taping of, a TV special entitled *Around the Beatles*. Filming for their first feature film, *A Hard Day's Night*, had only just been completed on Friday 24 April, but during the making of the motion picture the group (on 18 April) had also started to rehearse for an Associated-Rediffusion (aka Rediffusion London by 1964) 'one-off' TV special, *Around the Beatles*. Produced by Jack Good it featured the Beatles and guest performers, including Cilla Black, Sounds Incorporated, Long John Baldry, P.J. Proby, the Vernons Girls, Millie Small, the Jets and Murray the K (an American DJ). The Beatles pre-recorded their music and mimed to it during the show. At the start of the show they also performed a spoof rendition of the Interlude section of William Shakespeare's *A Midsummer Night's Dream* (Act V, Scene 1).

While the Beatles spent most of 28 April 1964 holed up in Studio 5A/B of Associated-Rediffusion's London Studio, aka Wembley Film Studio at Wembley Park in north-west London, the Applejacks were elsewhere in the Wembley Film Studio complex rehearsing and performing 'Tell Me When' for a very popular Associated-Rediffusion children's television show called *The Five O'Clock Club* which aired twice a week on Tuesdays and Fridays. (Each episode just 25 minutes long, the series ran for 120 episodes between 1963 until 1966.) Presented by popular children's television personality Muriel Young, the show became famous for a pair of glove puppets that appeared on every show: Ollie Beak (described as 'an opinionated' Liverpool owl) and Fred Barker, a dog. So popular did the glove puppets become that by 1965 the show would be re-named *Ollie and Fred's Five O'Clock Club*.

The Applejacks, early proponents of 'Brumbeat' and the first to take the UK chart by storm. Photographed here in 1964 at the peak of their success.
(PA Images / Alamy Stock Photo)

Finally the Beatles and the Applejacks were in the same building at the same time. And so it was that lightning struck. Not only did the Applejacks meet Ollie and Fred but they also befriended John, Paul, George and Ringo.

It was in the ATV canteen that the groups' paths finally crossed. Megan: "It seems that we all recall the moment in a different way. Two of us recall that it was while we were all in the canteen that John asked whether we had a follow-up (to 'Tell Me When') and after that we were invited to the Beatles' dressing room. We were thrilled to bits to meet them. We were very young and still sufficiently star struck to ask for their autographs. Don't forget we were fresh in the business and so to meet them was one thing, to be offered a song was beyond our wildest dreams. Paul and John had obviously talked about it and decided they had a song that would suit our style. So when we arrived in the dressing room they suggested 'Like Dreamers Do'. Two of us (Don and Al) are sure that when we were in the dressing room with them it was *Paul* who specifically offered us 'Like Dreamers Do'. Don remembers Paul sang it to us."[1]

Not that it matters too much, but Don Gould recalls it was the Applejacks dressing room rather than the Beatles' own: " Martin our guitarist was walking back to our dressing room along a corridor and he came across Paul McCartney who said, 'Hello, Applejack'. They started chatting like old mates and they came into our dressing room. Paul said, ' think we've got a song for your second single.' He told us he would get Dick James to send it to us, which he did. It was 'Like Dreamers Do' and you can see that it does have that same shuffle beat as 'Tell Me When'."[2]

The encounter at ATV wasn't the only time they met the Beatles. "After that we bumped into them on several occasions in London at the Bag O' Nails and Ad Lib, which were the clubs where all the groups hung out."[3]

For Paul McCartney the meeting in the Wembley studios meant that finally he had found a home for his much-admired 'Like Dreamers Do', the song he had written at 20 Forthlin Road in 1959 aged just 16 during his and John's initial pre-Hamburg burst of composing.

Later, as they talked together about their encounter with the Beatles and their amazement at being offered a Lennon-McCartney original, Megan says the Applejacks "wondered whether it had anything to do with the fact that Decca had initially turned them down. We were on Decca and 'Like Dreamers Do' was one of the songs they had recorded for the label during their commercial test." That could well have been a trigger but just as likely it was, as Megan also notes, because, "The Beatles made it clear to us that they thought the song was suited to our style."[4]

'Like Dreamers Do' looms large not only in the story of the Applejacks but also in the story of the Beatles. Significantly it was one of the very first Lennon-McCartney tunes that the Beatles ever performed down the Cavern. As Paul recalled: "We did a weak version arrangement but certain of the kids liked it because it was unique, none of the other groups did that … It was actually a bit of a joke to dare to try to do your own songs. They (original compositions) didn't go down well with Gerry and the Pacemakers and other groups. If they told us what they liked it would be 'What'd I Say' or 'Some Other Guy' or Little Richard stuff that I did. It was the more genuine shit, not stuff that you wrote yourself. For you to write it yourself was a bit plinky, and the songs obviously weren't that great, but I felt we really had to break through that barrier because if we never tried our own songs we'd just never have the confidence to continue writing."[5]

Author Mark Lewisohn says that it was in December 1961 that John and Paul finally took the plunge and began to believe more in the worth of their own songs and include some in their sets at the Cavern. They chose that venue to try them out because they considered it to be 'home ground' where they would receive a more open-minded and sympathetic reception. Apparently Paul sang 'Like Dreamers Do' "with his face turned up and angled, big eyes fixed on the far end of the tunnel, above the heads of the crowd."[6]

Clearly Paul already knew how to make the girls' hearts skip a beat!

It wasn't long before John added the catchy 'Hello Little Girl' to their set and then came another Paul tune, 'Love of the Loved', the big beat ballad he would eventually gift to Cilla. And, of course, Brian Epstein had been quick to recognise that having songwriters in their midst was a further unique element of the Beatles' appeal that had the potential to set them even further apart from their contemporaries and rivals.

Ultimately it could be argued, quite strongly, that 'Like Dreamers Do' was the most important song of John and Paul's early self-composed repertoire because it was the one that caught the attention of music publishers Ardmore and Beechwood, which in turn opened the door for them at Parlophone.

Included on the 'Decca Tapes', 'Like Dreamers Do' did indeed garner the attention of Kim Bennett and Sid Coleman at Ardmore and Beechwood when, courtesy of Brian Epstein, they heard an acetate of the tune. The two men very much wanted to secure the publishing on the song and were enthused to the point that, even in the face of seemingly stonewall indifference from the A&R at EMI, they had attempted to persuade Len Wood to let them finance a session themselves in which the Beatles would record it. This was a highly unusual move for a publisher to make and a clear indication of their belief in the song and its composers (if not the group) and its potential to become a hit.

EMI boss Len Wood turned down their offer but took note of Coleman and Bennett's enthusiasm. What they had suggested was an unusual move for publishers, and so trusting their instinct Wood decided EMI *would* sign the Beatles expressly so they could record the song and in turn he would be in a position to give Ardmore and Beechwood what they so keenly wanted: the copyright on 'Like Dreamers Do'.

Wood's generosity towards Coleman and Bennett was not pure benevolence. If it was a hit so EMI would benefit, but as has been noted it also gave the EMI boss a chance to make the pesky George Martin understand his place in the pecking order by landing him with something to do that he had already passed on, i.e., record and produce the Beatles. A little muscle flexing was undoubtedly going on here as well.

And so, what with the benefit of hindsight, has to be considered one of the most important songs Paul McCartney ever penned, 'Like Dreamers Do' now came into the hands of Birmingham's first group to have made the Top 10. These were most certainly amazing and exciting times for the Applejacks. One big hit to the good they now had, nestled in their pocket, what was surely set to be the next: a previously unreleased Beatles gem.

As they returned home from Wembley to Solihull that evening, how Al, Don, Martin, Megan, Phil and Gerry must have been pinching themselves at their good fortune.

Harbouring no second thoughts in accepting Paul's offer, a demo of Paul performing the song duly arrived, and before they knew it they were back in the studio to record their version of 'Like Dreamers Do'.

THE APPLEJACKS
LIKE DREAMERS DO (2:30)
(Lennon, McCartney)
Northern Songs Ltd
Decca F.11916
B-SIDE: (Boom, Boom, Boom, Boom) Everybody Fall Down
(Dello, Cane)
Musical Director: Mike Leander
Production, (both sides): Mike Smith
Recorded: 30 April 1964 at Decca Studios, West Hampstead, London
Released: Friday 5 June 1964

Mike Leander was later asked by Paul (much to George Martin's chagrin) to arrange 'She's Leaving Home' for the *Sgt. Pepper* album.

The Applejacks worked hard on 'Like Dreamers Do'. Megan Davies says they stuck closely to the demo they had received, although "Don Gould and Mike Leander arranged the piano to suit our style and provide it with our signature sound."[7]

The result was a dynamic, upbeat version of the song that seemed destined to take them straight back into the Top 10. Their version supports the faith that Kim Bennett in particular had always had in the song's potential to be a hit, for that is exactly what it became.

The producer of 'Like Dreamers Do' was *the* very same Mike Smith who had recorded the Beatles' own version of the song, but had ultimately chosen Brian Poole and the Tremeloes over the Beatles. Nevertheless, in the meantime Smith had gone on to become a very successful record producer indeed. To be fair he *had* wanted to sign both groups but was made to choose between the two by the more senior Dick Rowe.

'Like Dreamers Do' entered the UK chart on 14 June 1964, peaking at number 20 on Wednesday 5 July 1964. It spent 11 weeks on the chart, entering at number 46 and from there progressed to number 20 at its peak. This is the single's chart journey: 46, 32, 22, 20, 21, 21, 22, 26, 30, 37, 41.

Again, the *Melody Maker* chart placed 'Like Dreamers Do' higher: at its peak in the *MM* chart it broke into the Top 20 rising to number 17.

'Like Dreamers Do' was released in the USA on London 9681 on Monday 6 July 1964 where it did not trouble the chart.

In the UK the Applejacks' popularity was on a high. Their debut single had been very well received and their follow-up was much anticipated. And so in the week it was released the music newspapers were immediately on the case. In its 6 June edition *Disc* reviewer Don Nicholl rated it highly enough to be given a 'DNT' (the equivalent to 5 stars), exclaiming, "The Birmingham group should have no difficulty in reaching the Twenty once again. They're still riding a high popularity wave and they've come up with a John Lennon-Paul McCartney song to help them stay on the crest." Describing 'Like Dreamers Do' as "enjoyable" he called it a, "Happy tune" that "trots repetitively and is very easy to hold." As for the Applejacks' performance he enthused, "Sung and played without strain by the group under Mike Leander's musical direction." ('Without strain'?) [8a]

Nicholl was also taken with the B-side, declaring it to be "more excitable yet not quite so exciting. If you know what I mean." Not pausing to elaborate or enlighten his readers he concluded by saying, 'Everybody Fall Down' was, "A brash mover put over with plenty of drum rattle."[8b]

What was surprising was that the record was not as big a hit as everyone connected with it had expected. An appearance on *Ready Steady Go!* on the very same day of its release helped propel 'Like Dreamers Do' to number 20 within four weeks of its issue, but even an appearance on *Top of the Pops* on 8 July failed to lift it any higher, it simply stalled. For a further four weeks it hovered at the very edge of the Top 20, but never quite mustered enough sales to make that all-important breakthrough into the upper echelons of the UK chart.

Ironically Bennett, Colman and therefore Ardmore and Beechwood never did secure the copyright for 'Like Dreamers Do'. When it was finally released the publishing went to Northern Songs and so it was Dick Rowe who benefitted from Kim and Sid's original and unflagging belief in, and promotion of, the tune, to the point EMI actually signed the Beatles.

The Applejacks continued to tour and attract media attention during 1964 – especially when, in September, around the same time that the group released their third single, Megan Davies married Gerry Freeman at Saint Alphege's church in Solihull.

The other members of the group attended as groomsmen (also present were current boy scouts from the 1st Olton) and amidst much publicity the couple tied the knot to the sound of hundreds of screaming teenagers outside the church whom the police kept at bay behind barriers. As the happy couple left the church grounds they did so through a triumphal arch of guitars and drumsticks formed by members of friendly rivals the Conchords and the Phantoms. Such was the continuing media attention the Applejacks were attracting that not only was the wedding filmed by Pathé News (and screened nationally for the first time in their regular cinema bulletins on 28 September 1964) but immediately after the wedding ceremony, still dressed in their wedding clothes, the bride and groom were airlifted by helicopter to appear on that evening's edition of *Juke Box Jury*. [9]

Unfortunately, neither the major publicity garnered by Megan and Gerry's wedding nor the group's TV appearance on the 24 September edition of *Top of the Pops* made any discernible impact on the progress or success of the *third* Applejacks single: 'Three Little Words'.

THREE LITTLE WORDS (I LOVE YOU)
Written by Gordon Mills, 'Three Little Words (I Love You)' spent only five weeks on the UK singles chart. At the time, Gordon Mills was a hot new singer-songwriter who, in 1963, had written two big hits for Johnny Kidd and the Pirates: 'I'll Never Get Over You' and

'Hungry for Love'. (In 1965 together with Les Reed he would pen 'It's Not Unusual' for Tom Jones.)

Once again the Applejacks were blessed with material from one of the Sixties' great songwriters and supported again in the studio by the winning team of Leander and Smith who arranged and produced the new single. Once again hopes were high but, according to the 'official' chart, they failed to break into the Top 20: after a promising jump of nine places to number 23 on 4 November 1964, like its predecessor, 'Three Little Words' stalled. Within three weeks it had disappeared from the Top 50, its run on the charts over and with it, sadly, so was the Applejacks' chart history.

The October 1964 release of the group's critically well-received, eponymously titled debut album *The Applejacks* (Decca LK 4635), did not alter the picture. It sold well but did not enter the UK album chart.

Disagreements with Decca over their next single found the group left out in the cold. The label wanted them to record 'Chim Chim Cher-ee' for a January release, but the Applejacks resolutely resisted the pressure put on them to do so. Megan says the group were insulted: "There was no way we wanted to record any of that 'mamby-pamby nicey-nicey' stuff: we considered it to be an affront to us and our style of music."[10]

It was to be six months before a follow-up to 'Three Little Words' was eventually released, by which time the momentum garnered during 1964 had faltered. 'Bye Bye Girl' was released on 19 March 1965 but sank without trace. Decca released two more Applejacks singles during 1965, including on 27 August a fine version (and the first ever to be released) of Ray Davies' 'I Go to Sleep'. The final Decca single was the somewhat presciently titled 'I'm Through' which was released in December of that year. As all three singles had failed to enter the chart, so it was that Decca let the band go.

After the dizzying heights of 1964 the disappointments of 1965 must have been as extremely disheartening for the group to bare as they were mystifying.

A major result of this downturn in their chart fortunes was that the well-paid bookings the Applejacks had enjoyed as 'a chart act' dried up and they returned once more to playing local shows. Consequently, when the chance to earn better money – and have a lot of fun into the bargain – came their way, the group snapped it up. Megan has very fond memories of what came next: "We were offered a good contract to perform on the luxury cruise-liners R.M.S. *Queen Mary* and *Queen Elizabeth I* and *II* as they crisscrossed the North Atlantic bound for Bermuda and the Bahamas." And so it was the Applejacks ditched the choppy and uncertain waters of the UK charts for a life on the ocean wave. Megan is in no doubt as to what clinched the deal for them all: "The major attraction was it meant each year we got to enjoy five months of Caribbean cruises!"[11]

Significantly, in 1966, singer Al Jackson quit the Applejacks and was replaced by John Washington.

The move to work on the liners helped financially but crucially it took the Applejacks out of the game in the UK. By setting sail they effectively disappeared from the scene and even if they had *had* product to promote they simply would not have been around to do so.

Megan summed up very succinctly the impact of this decision on their career: "The downside to this is that we became pretty much isolated as pop artists and out of touch with the local and national music scene. Nevertheless, those three years at sea were great fun." [12]

During 1967 drummer Gerry Freeman left to become an in-demand session drummer and was replaced by Paul Willetts. Don Gould also left in 1967 for a successful career in music production.

Despite signing to CBS and releasing a cover of an Impressions song entitled 'You've Been Cheating', this single became the Applejack's last hurrah.

Martin Baggott quit the group and his career in music to emigrate to California. Thereafter the Applejacks disbanded.

For Megan Davies there was life after the Applejacks: she joined 'Mongrel', a Brum group that, after leaving Electric Light Orchestra, Roy Wood later re-formed as 'Wizzard'. She continued as a musician for several years and even spent some time in the Ivy Benson Band before returning to neurophysiology and to work in hospitals for many years. In 2020 Megan reflected on her life as a musician by commenting: "Early on I had married another musician and so one of us had to get a proper job! At one time I worked for the NHS at the National Hospital for Neurology and Neurosurgery, Queen Square, London, more recently I have been working at Young Epilepsy in Lingfield, Surrey. I do about nine or ten gigs each year but not in the professional sense. I still enjoy my music very much."[12]

Addendum 1: *The Applejacks on film*
Just for You *was a 63-minute colour feature film made at Shepperton Studios and released in the UK on 28 June 1964. It was later released on 1 June 1966 in the USA but with a new title,* Disk-O-Tek Holiday.
Swinging UK *was a 27-minute short released to cinemas on 28 September. The presenters were Alan Freeman, Brian Matthew and Kent Walton.*

Addendum 2: *The Applejacks reform*
Past glories were re-lived for the Applejacks and their fans when some 40 years later, on 11 December 2010, the original line-up re-formed for a one-off charity concert in St Mary's Church, Solihull where they used to rehearse and which was by then in need of refurbishment.

Addendum 3: *Megan appears at Burtonfest*
On Sunday 1 and 2 June 2019, Megan was one of a host of music stars from the Birmingham area, including Roy Wood, Chris 'Ace' Kefford, Andy Fairweather Low, Emma Jonson, the Steve Gibbons Band and Raymond Froggatt, who came together for 'Burtonfest', a benefit concert performed for Birmingham music legend Trevor Burton (co-founder of the Move). Very sadly Trevor had become seriously ill and as a result forced to retire from playing. (On the occasion of the benefit concert the Trevor Burton Band did perform but without Trevor.)

1, 4, 7, 10,12 & 13 Megan Davies in conversation with the author.
2 Don Gould in conversation with broadcaster Spencer Leigh, 2008, at Radio Merseyside.
5 *Paul McCartney, Many Years from Now*, Barry Miles (Vintage, 1998) p. 82–83.
6 '*The Beatles – All These Years: Volume One: Tune In*, Extended Special Edition, Mark Lewisohn (Little, Brown, 2013) p.1018.
8a, 8b *Disc* music weekly, edition 324, 6 June 1964, 'Singles with Don Nicholl', p.10.
9 *Beat Merchants* by Alan Clayson, (Blandford,1995) p.137.
11 BrumBeat.net

Chapter 72:
1964, BILLY J. SEEN … FROM A WINDOW

Throughout 1964, as the whole wide world turned on, tuned in and went completely crazy, so it was that the Beatles became unstoppable.

In the wake of the Beatles' meteoric rise, new groups and artists were springing up everywhere. As previous chapters have detailed, artists other than their Liverpool cohorts also began to benefit from the remarkable songwriting talent of John Lennon and Paul McCartney. New acts to grace the charts, Peter and Gordon from London and the Applejacks from Solihull, both scored heavily with Lennon-McCartney songs.

The songs gifted to Peter and Gordon and the Applejacks show that John and Paul were not averse to dig deep into their past to revive tunes they had either composed when they were just starting out or which no longer featured in the Beatles' repertoire. They may have been written several years earlier, but John and Paul still believed in their worth.

At other times when the request was made, Paul in particular would often agree to provide a song even though he knew he did not actually have one immediately to hand to spare or hidden away in the locker. In those instances he would simply sit down and see what he could conjure.

And so it was that in 1964, Brian Epstein, John Lennon and Paul McCartney happily obliged new acts like Peter and Gordon, the Applejacks and the Strangers with Mike Shannon with original Lennon-McCartney product that was both old and new.

When asked for tunes for Billy J. Kramer and Cilla Black they composed custom-built tunes especially for them.

The first was Billy J.

When Billy J. had resisted Brian Epstein's entreaties *not* to record 'Little Children', there is no doubt that Brian, who took what he perceived as slights very personally, felt put out. He remonstrated with Billy J. that he was effectively turning down two of the world's greatest songwriters. Kramer felt Epstein's response was an over-reaction, but even so by the time he entered the studio with the Dakotas to record 'Little Children' he had already agreed with Brian that his follow-up to this *would be* a new Paul and John song. It was entitled 'From a Window'.

Undoubtedly a Paul tune in its inception, McCartney has described how usually when he and John were approached by Epstein for a new song for Billy, "We would sit down at rehearsal and grab a couple of hours somewhere and just with a pen and a bit of paper, scribble the lyrics down."[1]

In this instance, however, 'From a Window' was Paul's work alone which John acknowledged years later by commenting, "That's Paul's. That's his artsy period with Jane Asher…"[2]

BILLY J. KRAMER with THE DAKOTAS
FROM A WINDOW (1:55)
(Lennon-McCartney)
Northern Songs Ltd
Parlophone R 5156
Recorded: 29 May 1964 in Studio 2, Abbey Road

Paul McCartney attended the recording and can be heard at the very end of the song, harmonising on the final word. Kramer was thrilled that Paul was there to do so: "I had a cold that day and had trouble hitting the end-note, so Paul sang it with me to strengthen the sound. It was the only record that I ever went back on. I recorded it but when I took it home I got on to George Martin and said it isn't right. When he asked me 'Why?' I said it was because Paul had a particular feel on the piano and to me it was the ingredient that we'd missed. So we went back into the studio and put it right."[3]

B-side: Second to None (2:20)
(Robin MacDonald)
MacDonald, the composer of the B-side, was of course rhythm guitarist with the Dakotas.
Recorded: 7 May 1964
Both sides produced: George Martin
Engineers: Norman Smith and Geoff Emerick
Released: 17 July 1964

'From a Window' entered the UK Top 20 chart on Thursday 23 July 1964. peaked at number 10 on 26 August 1964 and was on the chart for 8 weeks in total.

Released in the USA on Imperial 66051 on 12 August 1964, it charted for 10 weeks on *Billboard*'s Hot 100, peaking at number 23 on 3 October 1964. This was a creditable achievement and was Billy J. and the Dakotas' fourth US Top 40 hit within five months, but hits-wise it was also the endgame. Billy J. never enjoyed any further stateside chart successes, although he remains a popular concert draw there, as he does in Europe and back home in the UK.

In the UK, the comparatively 'moderate' success of 'From a Window' compared to Billy J's four previous chart-topping/Top Five singles was a harbinger of things to come.

At the time it was released, however, the music papers were impressed. *Disc* reviewer Don Nicholl was typical and rated it as a tune likely to spin to the top, giving it his highest accolade – a 'DNT' (5 stars). Lest anyone was not aware he began his review by mentioning that "Billy J. has another Lennon and McCartney composition to sing … 'From a Window'. Double-tracking, he places the easy ballad comfortably and should find more big sales." However, the Dakota's Robin MacDonald would have been even happier with what Nicholl had to say about the B-side, 'Second to None', which he'd written for Billy: "I prefer the B-deck actually, Kramer seems to be in better voice and the song is forthright and effective."[4]

His follow-up was a Kenny Lynch song, the ironically titled 'It's Gotta Last Forever', which did not enter the Top 50. His fortunes revived briefly with his next single, a fine version of Burt Bacharach's 'Trains and Boats and Planes' which became a number 12 hit for Billy J. in the summer of 1965. After this success, however, with or without the Dakotas, Billy J. Kramer did not chart in the UK again.

After their difference of opinion regarding 'Little Children', Billy was fully aware of a change in the way Brian Epstein felt about him: "From the middle of 1964 ... we were no longer like family. Maybe it was because the Beatles were becoming so hugely popular and he was just busy with them. I don't know ... I went on to make other records, but they didn't sell as well as the earlier ones had. I'd express my feeling to Brian, explaining that the Dakotas did not always want to work on the songs as we had done with 'Little Children'. He would just close the discussion down, saying they were an excellent band and he thought they were doing a great job. I think what he meant was that he was beginning to lose interest in me. I didn't help matters by drinking like a lunatic and taking pills. I started to let myself go..."[5]

And so it was. The gradual decline in his closeness to Epstein and the downturn in his recording career found Billy J. Kramer fading from the scene that, along with the Beatles, Gerry and the Pacemakers and Cilla Black, he had only recently dominated. Seven more singles followed during the Sixties including, in 1968, Billy's version of 'A World without Love' which was released on the NEMS label. None entered the charts and with 1969's 'Colour of My Life' Billy was no longer a contender as far as the UK hit machine was concerned.

Despite everything, Brian retained a professional loyalty towards Billy J.: "My relationship with Brian wasn't over because of 'Little Children'. Some things I never spoke about when my recording deal with EMI was up for renewal but Brian was in the process of forming the NEMS label and he asked me to make a record with Robert Stigwood who managed the Bee Gees and Cream. I recorded a Bee Gees song before they were known called 'Town of Tuxley Toy Maker Part 1' which really upset the Dakotas."[6]

Indeed, in 1967 Brian Epstein had new ideas for Billy's future: "Brian hadn't lost interest. In mid-July 1967, shortly before he died, I was appearing at the Shakespeare Theatre in Liverpool for a week and Brian came to see me on the Monday night. We talked about starting a new recording project when he returned from the States. (Brian was due to visit the USA in early Autumn.) I was on the road shortly afterwards and was in Stockton-on-Tees when I turned on the TV in my hotel room to find out that Brian had passed. I was immediately in shock ... I felt depressed because in spite of everything I had lost a true friend."[7]

When Brian had come to see Billy at the Shakespeare Theatre, Billy had thought Brian looked healthy and seemed very together and so the news hit hard. "When I was screwing up, Brian was the first one to come and see me about it. When I was overweight, he showed me the damage I was doing to myself ... there was a human side to Brian that most people didn't know. He took me a long way from a guy who worked on the railway to a guy who topped the charts."[8]

In the aftermath of Brian's passing, Billy says, "I discussed my future with Brian's brother Clive. I recorded the Harry Nilsson song '1941' before Harry was known by the Beatles, it was a record I was very proud of. NEMS Enterprises, Brian's company, was like a family to me, when he passed I thought it would never be the same. Although I liked Clive as a person and he offered me a five-year contract with NEMS, I just thought NEMS could never be the same without Brian and so I left and signed with Ken Ashcroft who had worked for NEMS, and in the early days had been my road manager..."[9]

In the 2010s, Billy became a vocal champion of Brian Epstein and formed a 'Liverpool Rock and Roll Justice for Epstein Campaign', which called for the Beatles manager to be inducted into the non-performers' section of the Rock and Roll Hall of Fame. In support of Brian's contribution to popular music, Billy J. composed his acclaimed song 'To Liverpool with Love' which appeared on his 2014 album *I Won the Fight*. Billy's efforts helped ensure that this long overdue accolade finally happened when, on Thursday 10 April 2014, Brian Epstein was posthumously inducted (by Peter Asher) into the Rock and Roll Hall of Fame.

One thing Billy J. Kramer has certainly never been is a quitter, and although the hits dried up and 'life', in the shape of alcohol and drugs, took Billy to places he would rather not have gone, he never gave up making music and in turn he has always had an audience who want to hear him sing.

These days Billy is enjoying a revival. His first marriage to Ann Ginn broke down and he relocated to the USA where he fell in love with Roni whom he married and their relationship became the enduring rock on which he battled his demons and rebuilt his career. He has stopped drinking and taking pills. He continues to tour (sometimes as the headline act on the popular 'Solid Sixties' package tours) and became re-energised. In 2013, Billy J. returned to the recording studios to cut *I Won the Fight*, an album of new material (mostly his own self-penned tunes), that won him critical and fan acclaim and placed him firmly back in the spotlight. Since then he has followed with *Unplugged* (2017) and *Raw Influences* (2018).

In 2016, Billy J. published his autobiography entitled *Do You Want to Know a Secret?* This memoir is a very candid, straightforward account of his life that pulls no punches and again, like his new songs, it has won praise from critics and fans alike (this author included). It has been *the* invaluable source of information for all I have written about him in these pages.

Coronavirus defined the year 2020. As for everyone, it was a challenging one for Billy but he used it to embark upon a new project that fulfilled a long held ambition. "On November 8 I went to Nashville to make a Country record. I was really excited to be doing so because I've always enjoyed Country music. Country, or 'Country and Western' as it was known back in the Fifties in Liverpool, was really popular when I was growing up. There were lots of homegrown Liverpool Country singers and bands and clubs back then. In the Sixties I actually suggested making a Country album to George Martin but nothing came of it. I'm proud to say that The Alessi Brothers have written the songs especially for me for my new record and that's something I'm really happy about. They are so talented."[10]

Indeed they are. The Alessi Brothers are legends of the American music scene having scored hits on *Billboard*'s Hot 100, such as 'Put Your Love Away' (1982) and before that in 1976 they made the UK Top 20 with 'Oh Lori'. Famously, their song 'Savin' the Day' featured on the original soundtrack album for the *Ghostbusters* movie in 1984. During what is now a lengthy career they have arranged, written and produced releases for artists such as Sir Paul McCartney, Frankie Valli, Olivia Newton John, Richie Havens and Christopher Cross. Significantly they provided backing vocals for the John and Yoko album *Milk and Honey*. As songwriters they are very much in demand and have written tunes for artists such as Rick Springfield and Peter Frampton …

For the boy from Bootle it's been a long, and at times hard road but thankfully Billy J. Kramer is still out there, not a rock casualty but a talented survivor.

Author's note: Very sadly while completing this book in October 2021 I learned that Roni had passed away. I first met Roni during a visit she made with Billy to 'Mendips' where I was proud to be their host. She and Billy made me very welcome at his gigs at the Cavern and Philharmonic and we enjoyed fun times along the way. The bond between them was strong and loving and there for all to see. She was indeed his rock.

ADDENDUM: *A Pocket History of the Dakotas*

Brian Epstein's choice to back Billy J. Kramer were the Dakotas, an already established Manchester-based group. They were ambitious and although they were backing lead vocalist Pete MacLaine at the time Epstein approached them, they eagerly accepted his invitation and parted company with Pete. From the outset, the Dakotas felt they were a good enough act to be signed in their own right, not simply as a 'backing group', and so, eager to preserve their own professional identity, the Dakotas were always billed as Billy J. Kramer 'with' the Dakotas, not Billy J. Kramer 'and' the Dakotas. Apparently this was also on Brian's insistence.

On linking Kramer with the Dakotas, Epstein sent the new combination to Hamburg to 'perfect' their act. As we have learned from Billy, they never quite managed this because from the very start Billy J. felt the Dakotas distanced themselves from him.

As Billy J. readily acknowledges, "The Dakotas were excellent musicians and I can't knock them in the studios, they were never fazed by anything they were asked to do."[11]

The Dakotas issued singles in their own right, the first being their most successful. It was 'The Cruel Sea' (written by the Dakotas' own Mike Maxfield who also wrote the B-side, 'The Millionaire'). Released on Parlophone R 5044 on 5 July it entered the UK charts on 11 July 1963, peaked at number 18 and remained on the charts for a very creditable 13 weeks. In the USA it was released as 'The Cruel Surf' but was not a hit. It was later covered by American group the Ventures and was the B-side of that group's 1964 USA number 8 hit, 'Walk Don't Run '64' (which had already been a number 2 hit for them in 1960, although this single was a new version of that tune).

The Dakotas issued two further singles. The first was 'Magic Carpet' (written by George Martin), the B-side of which was 'Humdinger' written by Mike Maxfield and Robin MacDonald of the group. The third single was 'Oyeh', a tune penned by 'legendary' guitarist Mick Green (who had joined the Dakotas in 1964) and band-mates Mike MacDonald, Mike Maxfield and Tony Mansfield. The B-side was 'My Girl Josephine', written by Domino and Bartholomew. When issued, neither of these singles troubled the charts. Later, in 1975, 'Oyeh' was covered by Dr. Feelgood on their Down by the Jetty album.

In 1964, after an argument with Brian Epstein, bassist Ray Jones left the Dakotas. Robin MacDonald switched to bass and that's when and why Mick Green – formerly of Johnny Kidd and the Pirates – took over on lead. Mike Maxfield quit the group in 1965 to focus on songwriting. Another ex-Pirate, Frank Farley, joined the Dakotas in 1966 to replace Mansfield on drums.

Kramer finally split from the Dakotas in 1967 and was briefly backed by the Remo Four with whom he enjoyed a far more convivial rapport.

MacDonald, Green and Farley went on to join Cliff Bennett's backing band. (In August 1966, Bennett enjoyed a number 6 UK hit with a cover of Lennon and McCartney's 'Got to Get You into My Life'.)

---

1 Paul McCartney, Many Years from Now by Barry Miles (Vintage, 1998) p.181.
2 All We Are Saying: The Last Major Interview with John Lennon and Yoko Ono, conducted by David Sheff (Sidwick & Jackson, 2000) p.172.
3, 6, 7, 9,10 & 11 Billy J. Kramer interview with the author, 19 October 2020.
4 Disc music weekly, edition 329, 11 July 1964, 'Singles with Don Nicholl', p.8.
5 & 8 Do You Want to Know a Secret? The Autobiography of Billy J. Kramer, by Billy J. Kramer with Alyn Shipton, (Equinox, 2016): p.48, p.74 and p.107–8.

Chapter 73:
THIS ONE'S FOR YOU CILLA!

By the time John and Paul gifted Cilla with a brand new, 'especially written for her' song, she had enjoyed back-to-back consecutive number 1 hit singles. Like fellow Liverpudlian Billy J. Kramer, under Brian Epstein's mentorship Cilla Black's career had taken off spectacularly. Almost before she had had time to draw breath she was at the very top of the tree.

The 1-2 knockout success of 'Anyone Who Had a Heart' and 'You're My World' occurred just as Brian Epstein booked Black into a short season at the prestigious London Palladium, where she was support on a show called *Startime* to popular headliner singer Frankie Vaughan and comedian/magician Tommy Cooper. Alongside Cilla, in a supporting role, were the Fourmost. This was the very show during which the Fourmost came into conflict with Epstein over the fact he had not negotiated a 'get-out' clause in their contract. The show was so popular that it ran from May until December 1964, during which time Cilla says she did 13 shows a week, a total of over 400 performances.

The stunning success of 'Anyone Who Had a Heart' and 'You're My World', which had collectively clocked up some 34 weeks on the chart, left everyone – Cilla included – wondering if she could repeat the trick for a third time with her next release. As she began to contemplate cutting a follow-up, she was told by George Martin that her next A-side was to be another Lennon-McCartney song written especially for her.

Paul recorded a version of the song for Cilla, accompanying himself on piano, which he cut onto a standard 7-inch vinyl Dick James Music Limited Demo Disc. Under the title, the disc did not carry his name, in the space for the artist's name it simply said, 'Demo'.

Paul's demo was sent to the Palladium and on the disc Paul sang 'It's for You' as a waltz. As Cilla told Bob Harris, "That's when Paul talks about my 'big voice'. He wanted a 'Big Band' arrangement on it, which was the Johnnie Spence* band with Kenny Clare on drums, who was my favourite drummer of the time. To be in the studio with a big jazz band took me back to when I used to listen to the Della Reece records. Not only did I love rock and roll but I loved all the old standards."[1]

(*Johnnie (aka 'Johnny') Spence later became Tom Jones's personal musical director. Just who actually came up with the jazzy arrangement for 'It's for You' is open to conjecture. In her 2009 interview with Bob Harris, Cilla resolutely referred to Johnnie Spence, but the booklet notes that accompany the 1997 triple CD release, Cilla 1963-1973: The George Martin/Abbey Road Decade (Zonophone), says of 'It's for You': "Beautifully arranged by Johnny Scott this jazz feel proved very comfortable for Cilla and she delivered one of her finest vocal performances receiving rave reviews..."

In a 1964 interview with Disc *music weekly*, Cilla referred to "George Martin's fabulous arrangement."

Both Spence and Scott worked on Cilla Black records alongside George Martin. Spence was the musical director for Cilla's debut TV series, Cilla, which first aired in 1968.)

Paul McCartney had been present in the studio when Cilla recorded her breakthrough hit 'Anyone Who Had a Heart' (which was also her first number 1). Apparently Paul told Cilla that he and John had composed 'It's for You' using 'Anyone Who Had a Heart' as their template, although Cilla said, "For my money, 'It's for You' is nothing like 'Anyone Who Had a Heart'."[2]

George Martin said of 'It's for You': "It's a great song and when Paul wrote it I think he had Cilla in mind. It was custom-built for her in the same way 'Step Inside Love' was written specially for her. He knew by this time what her voice was capable of. 'It's for You' is a very good song, it was very successful."[3]

The recording session for 'It's for You' was an exciting and memorable occasion for Cilla: "When I got into the studio I was just so excited. The boys (John and Paul) came down to the studio which was fantastic … it gave me an extra boost. They never interfered – Paul tends to – but I suppose the maestro was there: Johnny Spence was doing the arrangement which was awesome."* 4

(*As previously noted, in 1964 itself Cilla enthused about George Martin's arrangement of the tune and the original record label refers to the 'accompaniment directed by George Martin'.)

John and Paul had only just returned from Australia and so it was a great compliment to Cilla that after such a mammoth journey they made the effort to attend. The finished recording was described by Cilla as "a sort of jazz waltz". 5

When asked by Bob Harris if Paul McCartney played piano on 'It's for You', as some commentators have suggested, Cilla replied, "He might have dropped in later. By that time we were on twin track, we could even have been on four track by then. They were in the box, where the big stairs are at Studio 2, I could see them in the box. I would take a bet that Paul *didn't* play, not whilst I was there."[6]

Back in 1964, in an interview with record reviewer Don Nicholl for his 'Behind the Singles Scene' column in *Disc*, Cilla commented: "Paul himself came along to the session and contributed a few ideas about how it should be done. But actually there were very few changes made to George Martin's fabulous arrangement. Paul stayed to the end and said he thought it sounded great."[7]

Nicholl's interview noted that 'It's for You' was a Lennon-McCartney composition "but one which swings away from Cilla's till now ballad style." The change in style was something that clearly excited Cilla, who told Nicholl, "And that's good, 'cos I don't wish to be typed as a singer of lovely sorrowful songs."[8]

CILLA BLACK
IT'S FOR YOU (2:20)
(Lennon-McCartney)
Northern Songs Ltd
Parlophone R 5162
Recorded at Abbey Road on 29 June 1964
Accompaniment directed by George Martin
Piano: Johnny Pearson (who had played on all Cilla's A-sides to date and in 1966 became leader of BBC TV's 'Top of the Pops Orchestra'.
Guitar: Judd Proctor (a highly regarded player who had played the lead guitar on 'You're My World')
Drums: Kenny Clare (an esteemed drummer who during his career played with – among others – Jack Parnell, Johnny Dankworth, Dudley Moore, Ted Heath…)

According to Cilla, when she spoke with Don Nicholl in 1964, she didn't have long to rehearse the song before the recording session and that it was on tape within an hour. Nicholl also likened George Martin to film producer Alfred Hitchcock, in that just as 'Hitch' always turned up in his own pictures, "so George pops up in his recordings." This time "he's to be heard with some piano effects added when everyone else had gone home."[9]

B-side: He Won't Ask Me (Willis)
'with Instrumental Accompaniment'
Both sides produced George Martin

Released in the UK on 31 July 1964, 'It's for You' attracted 200,000 advance orders and just one week later on 8 August 1964 entered the UK chart at number 25. Its progress into the Top 10 was swift and by 4 September it had reached number 7. But that was to be it.

At that point the brakes went on and what had seemed an irresistible climb to number 1 ended: 'It's for You' exited the chart with even greater alacrity than it had entered. In total it spent 10 weeks on the UK chart, some seven weeks less than either 'Anyone Who Had a Heart' or 'You're My World'. Cilla was "gutted" that it failed to make the top spot and become her third consecutive number 1.

The song was her second release in the USA following on from 'You're My World' which had peaked at number 26 in the *Billboard* Hot 100 on 1 August 1964. The portents were good for Cilla's stateside follow-up 'It's for You'. But when it was issued in September 1964, 'It's for You' peaked disappointingly at number 79 in the *Billboard* Hot 100 on 3 October 1964 where it camped for just 2 weeks. (It fared better in the *Billboard* Adult Contemporary Chart where earlier on 26 September it reached number 15.)

This briefest of successes for Cilla in the USA came despite Paul doing his level best to promote her record: "I wrote it for Cilla. That's not a bad little song, I remember when we … went over to America plugging it to all these DJs we used to talk to endlessly: 'Look, there's this girl singer in our stable and you should listen out for this song.' It didn't do very well…"[10]

'It's for You' fared better in Australia where it reached number 17.

Critical reception had certainly been strongly in favour of 'It's for You'. *Disc* was typical. In the week it was reviewed (1 August 1964) it was only one of three tunes to receive a 'DNT' with Don Nicholl extolling its virtues as, "A first class song by Lennon and McCartney, 'It's for You' gives Cilla a complete change from the type of ballad she has recorded previously. Under George Martin's direction the tempo has a quirky waltz pattern that comes close to Brubeck." High praise indeed! And so the review continued: "It's slow, compulsive material and Miss Black sings it very well … Strings glide in the background, but there's also an up-front rhythm section … I applaud this exciting getaway into something different … Cilla and George Martin are about to prove you don't need to play safe to reach the Top 10."[11]

The story of this great single does not quite end here. Shortly after Cilla's death a remarkable postscript was added:

Whatever happened to Paul's original demo of 'It's for You' remained a mystery until 2016 when it came up for auction at the annual Liverpool Beatles Memorabilia Auction on 27 August. Prior to this it was generally believed the item had been lost. Thankfully this was not the case, in fact it had been kept safe and sound for over 50 years by Cilla's younger brother, Allan. In a letter of Provenance written by his son, Simon White on 19 August 2016, Simon described how it had been found completely unexpectedly inside a brown cardboard sleeve on the cover of which had been handwritten Cilla's name and the song title. Immediately recognising the writing to be that of his father Simon believed Cilla must have given it to him sometime in 1964 when his father would have been 18 years old. Cilla knew her younger brother was a keen record collector who took great care of his collection and would welcome such a unique addition to his collection. Apparently he made the protective cardboard sleeve himself before writing the disc's title and Cilla's name on it and placing it in his collection where it had remained safe and sound ever since. Having discovered this disc – but still completely unaware that it wasn't Cilla singing on the demo – Simon had taken it along with 21 other such acetates from his father's collection to be valued at the legendary 'Beatles Shop' on Mathew Street in Liverpool. It was at this point that shop manager Stephen Bailey played the disc and was immediately stopped in his tracks when he recognised it was Paul singing on the demo, not Cilla as written on the sleeve. Stephen knew this was a major and amazing discovery for all concerned. At the subsequent annual Beatles Auction in Liverpool it fetched a reported £18,000. As the story unfolded Cilla's family also discovered that Sir Paul McCartney had not kept a copy of his demo for himself and as "a courtesy and as a gesture of respect" the family allowed him to make a copy to add to his personal archive. [12]

After 'It's for You', it would be some two and a half years and eight hit singles later before

Cilla was to be gifted another original Lennon-McCartney song.

Cilla achieved a higher chart placing in the UK with her follow-up to 'It's for You' when her cover of 'You've Lost That Lovin' Feeling' rocketed to number 2 on 30 January 1965 and seemed destined to provide her with her third number 1. It didn't, for she was ultimately denied the top slot by the Righteous Brothers' own, original version of the song which has been described as the 'ultimate pop record'.[13]

Indeed, Cilla was the recipient of some outrage in Britain for having the audacity to record a cover of 'Lovin' Feeling', such was the awe and esteem in which UK hipsters (especially in London) held the Righteous Brothers' original.

Rolling Stones manager Andrew Loog Oldham was one such purist. A friend of Phil Spector's who had written and recorded the song with the Righteous Brothers, Loog Oldham went so far as to take out an advert in *Melody Maker* that voiced his huge support for their version. Oldham had been moved to such action by his righteous disdain for the fact Cilla's version was leading the race up the charts and his letter was an attempt by one buddy to support fellow buddy Phil and his artists.

"This advert is not for commercial gain, it is taken as something that must be said about the great new PHIL SPECTOR Record, THE RIGHTEOUS BROTHERS singing "YOU'VE LOST THAT LOVIN' FEELING". Already in the American Top 10, this is Spector's greatest production, the last word in Tomorrow's sound Today, exposing the overall mediocrity of the Music Industry.
Signed,
Andrew Oldham"

1, 4, 5 & 6 Cilla Black in conversation with Bob Harris OBE for the BBC Radio 2 Documentary *The Songs the Beatles Gave Away*, 2009, written and narrated by Bob Harris, produced by Bob Harris and Trudie Myerscough-Harris for WBBC.
2 *What's It All About*, Cilla Black, (Ebury Press, 2003) p.113.
3 Sir George Martin in conversation with Bob Harris OBE and Colin Hall for the 2009 BBC Radio 2 documentary *The Songs the Beatles Gave Away*, written and narrated by Bob Harris, produced by Bob Harris and Trudie Myerscough-Harris for WBBC.
7, 8 & 9 *Disc* music weekly, edition 332, 1 August 1964, 'Behind The Singles Scene' by Don Nicholl, p.10.
10 *Paul McCartney, Many Years from Now* by Barry Miles (Vintage, 1998) p.181.
11 *Disc* music weekly, edition 332, 1 August 1964, 'Singles with Don Nicholl', p.8.
12 www.beatlesauction.co.uk > 2016/07 > rare-lost-beatles-demo
13 *Encyclopedia of Great Popular Song Recordings, Volume 2*, Steve Sullivan, (Scarecrow Press, 4 October, 2013).

Chapter 74:
1965 AND A CHANGING OF THE GUARD

1964 ended with the Beatles once again ensconced at number 1. 'I Feel Fine' was their sixth consecutive UK chart topper and on 10 December it had toppled the Rolling Stones' 'Little Red Rooster'. As a result, the Beatles were still sitting on top of the pile when the first singles charts of 1965 was published.

For Mersey Beat and Brian Epstein's stable of stars, the final UK Top 20 singles chart of December 1964 suggested that just maybe the Mersey Beat bubble had punctured. The only other Liverpool group who featured on that final December '64 chart were the Searchers with their superb, ethereal version of Malvina Reynolds' folk song, 'What Have They Done to the Rain' and, of course, the Searchers were not a NEMS/Brian Epstein act.

THE UK's TOP 20 CHART FOR 26 DEC 1964 ACCORDING TO *RECORD MIRROR*
01 I Feel Fine: The Beatles
02 Petula Clark: Downtown
03 Gene Pitney: I'm Gonna Be Strong
04 Val Doonican: Walk Tall
05 Freddie and the Dreamers: I Understand
06 Roy Orbison: Pretty Paper
07 The Bachelors: No Arms Could Ever Hold You
08 The Rolling Stones: Little Red Rooster
09 Cliff Richard: I Could Easily Fall
10 P.J. Proby: Somewhere
11 Elvis Presley: Blue Christmas
12 Twinkle: Terry
13 Sandie Shaw: Girl Don't Come
14 Adam Faith: Message to Martha
15 The Supremes: Baby Love
16 The Searchers: What Have They Done to the Rain
17 Georgie Fame: Yeh Yeh
18 Jim Reeves: There's a Heartache Following Me
19 The Kinks: All Day and All of the Night
20 Matt Monro: Walk Away

A year earlier and 1963's final Top 20 had featured records by the Beatles ('I Want to Hold Hour Hand' and 'She Loves You'), Gerry and the Pacemakers ('You'll Never Walk Alone'), Billy J. Kramer with the Dakotas ('I'll Keep You Satisfied') while the Searchers' 'Sugar and Spice' had only recently exited the Top 20 earlier in December).

The full Top 100 of all 1964's biggest-selling chart records was more encouraging with six Liverpool acts occupying ten places in the Top 30, but pop music is a fickle beast and somehow the feeling was growing that the circus was pulling up stakes.

THE TOP 30 MOST POPULAR RECORDS OF 1964

01 Jim Reeves: I Love You Because
02 Jim Reeves: I Won't Forget You
03 Roy Orbison: It's Over
04 Roy Orbison: Oh Pretty Woman
05 The Beatles: A Hard Day's Night
06 Cilla Black: You're My World
07 Cilla Black: Anyone Who Had a Heart
08 The Searchers: Needles and Pins
09 The Honeycombs: Have I the Right?
10 Manfred Mann: Do Wah Diddy Diddy
11 Herman's Hermits: I'm into Something Good
12 Dave Clark Five: Glad All Over
13 The Bachelors: Diane
14 The Rolling Stones: It's All Over Now
15 The Beatles: Can't Buy Me Love
16 Billy J Kramer and the Dakotas: Little Children
17 The Bachelors: I Believe
18 The Beatles: I Want to Hold Your Hand
19 Julie Rogers: The Wedding
20 Peter and Gordon: World Without Love
21 The Four Pennies: Juliet
22 Millie Small: My Boy Lollipop
23 Brian Poole and the Tremeloes: Someone, Someone
24 The Swinging Blue Jeans: Hippy Hippy Shake
25 Sandie Shaw: (There's) Always Something There to Remind Me
26 The Kinks: You Really Got Me
27 The Searchers: Don't Throw Your Love Away
28 The Supremes: Baby Love
29 Gerry and the Pacemakers: I'm the One
30 The Supremes: Where Did Our Love Go

Below number 30, Liverpool acts closely associated with Mersey Beat occupied nine of the 70 remaining places. The Beatles featured twice at numbers 34 and 53 respectively with 'I Feel Fine' and 'She Loves You' while the Merseybeats were at number 39 with 'I Think of You', the Searchers were at number 49 with 'When You Walk in the Room', the Swinging Blue Jeans at number 61 with 'You're No Good', the Fourmost at number 73 with 'A Little Loving', Gerry and the Pacemakers at number 81 with 'Don't Let the Sun Catch You Crying', Cilla Black at number 89 with 'It's for You', and at number 100 were the Mojos with 'Everything's Alright'.

Throughout 1965, the Beatles remained in the ascendant with three more number ones ('Ticket to Ride', 'Help!' and the double A-side Christmas hit 'Day Tripper / We Can Work It Out') but the pendulum continued to swing farther away from Liverpool as fewer of its Mersey Beat stars made chart showings.

Here's a run-down of the acts for whom 1965 was going to be a big, pivotal year:

The Kinks scored five hits (including a second number 1 with 'Tired of Waiting for You') and in terms of weeks on the singles chart were second only to the Beatles.

The Rolling Stones had by now established themselves as major chart rivals to their good friends the Beatles with three straight Jagger- and Richards-composed number ones: 'The Last Time', '(I Can't Get No) Satisfaction' and 'Get off My Cloud'.

The Hollies cemented their position as Sixties chart regulars with four hits including their one and only number 1 during the Sixties: 'I'm Alive'. Their final hit of 1965 was a cover of George Harrison's 'If I Needed Someone' which peaked at number 20 and gave George his first Top 20 hit as a composer. However, he was not impressed with their rendition. George criticised their interpretation: apparently the word 'rubbish' was used and he likened the Hollies to session men going through the motions of making a record. John Lennon also chipped in to support George's assessment. The Hollies, particularly Graham Nash, were obviously unhappy with such derisory comments and believed George and John's negative responses affected the sales and ultimate success of the record. A war of words broke out in the music press but, with the passage of time, peace broke out and later George and Graham became friends.

Beyond the Beatles, Kinks, Rolling Stones and Hollies, the UK singles chart was alive with new names, several of whom were destined like the Beatles, Stones and Kinks to become legends in their own lifetimes:

Bob Dylan scored five chart hits including 'The Times They Are a-Changing' (number 9), 'Subterranean Homesick Blues (number 9), 'Like a Rolling Stone' (number 4) and 'Positively Fourth Street' (number 8).

The Who enjoyed three hits including the incendiary 'My Generation'.

The Walker Brothers announced their presence with the magnificent 'Make It Easy on Yourself'.

Van Morrison made himself heard for the first time on the UK charts as lead singer with Them and their two classic singles: 'Baby Please Don't Go' (which had the amazing Morrison-composed 'Gloria' as its B-side) and 'Here Comes the Night'.

Next to zoom into focus were the Yardbirds with three Top 3 singles in succession: 'For Your Love', 'Heart Full of Soul' and the double A-sided 'Evil Hearted You' / 'Still I'm Sad'.

Others who made significant chart debuts in 1965 included Joan Baez, Donovan, and the Seekers.

Cliff Richard remained a glued-on chart presence with four hits including the number 1, 'The Minute You're Gone'. The Shadows also enjoyed four hits in their own right.

Elvis had become a remote presence, but his singles still made the Top 20 and in June he pulled the rabbit out of the hat yet again to score another UK number 1 with 'Crying in the Chapel'.

Those for whom the bell tolled chart-wise were Billy J. Kramer and the Dakotas and Brian Poole and the Tremeloes. Billy J. enjoyed his last UK chart hit in May 1965 with 'Trains and Boats and Planes' (number 12), Brian Poole bowed out with two hits, 'Three Bells' (number 17 in January) and 'I Want Candy' (number 25 in July). (Undaunted, without Brian, the Tremeloes continued in their own right and went on to great success, beginning again in 1967 with three consecutive Top 10 hits including a number 1 with 'Silence Is Golden'.)

The Searchers continued to make the charts in 1965, but after a number 4 with 'Goodbye My Love' there were to be no more Top 10 hits. The following year they bowed out of chart contention for good with the appropriately questioning 'Have You Ever Loved Somebody?'. Peaking at number 48, the record's success was a mere shadow of former glories. As a live act, however, they would be forever in demand.

After her January number 2 with 'You've Lost That Lovin' Feeling', Cilla only troubled the charts once more in 1965, albeit with an underrated gem entitled 'I've Been Wrong Before' (number 17 in May). However, this proved to be but a mere hiatus, time in which to catch her breath. Ms. Black returned to the charts in 1966 and in the years ahead also became a major, hugely popular TV personality.

Liverpool's most successful chart presence other than the Beatles during 1965 was the King of Knotty Ash, Ken Dodd. The zany comedian could also hold a tune better than most, and his plaintive 'Tears' was number 1 throughout October clocking up an incredible 21 weeks in the UK Top 20.

Elsewhere, 'Protest' music was the in-vogue lyric trend. Barry McGuire's 'Eve of Destruction' was one of the most memorable hits of the year (number 3 in October). Hedgehoppers Anonymous scored a number 5 hit in November with the ironic 'It's Good News Week'. Donovan's impressive cover of Buffy Sainte-Marie's anti-war song 'Universal Soldier' was the title track of his successful EP released in August '65 which reached number 5 on the singles chart. Manfred Mann included a version of Bob Dylan's anti-war 'With God on Our Side' on their June 1965 EP entitled *The One in the Middle* (the EP was a number 2 hit on the singles chart). When he first emerged on the scene Dylan was classed as a 'protest' singer *par excellence* as well as the most important folk singer of his generation.

For the Beatles, beyond the hit singles, 1965 was another year spent in constant demand and in the full glare of the spotlight. Their every move was international news. As in 1964 a punishing schedule of filming, touring and recording accounted for most of their relentless workload.

After the conclusion of the successful 'Another Beatles Christmas Show' season at the Odeon Cinema in Hammersmith, on Saturday 16 January, the group took time out before entering Studio 2 at Abbey Road on Monday 15 February 1965 where they began the day by recording 'Ticket to Ride', their follow-up single to 'I Feel Fine'. In total they spent six days ensconced inside Studio 2 recording a B-side for 'Ticket to Ride', plus several tunes for their second feature film, *Help!*. The pressure to come up with the songs for their second film was intense, for shooting was scheduled to begin in the Bahamas on Tuesday 23 February. No one could ever say the Beatles did not work hard to achieve and maintain their success.

During that six-day stint in the studio, the Beatles cut not only 'Ticket to Ride' and its B-side 'Yes It Is', but also a slew of brand new tunes intended either for inclusion in the film *Help!* itself or on the non-soundtrack side of the album: 'Another Girl' (a Paul song), 'I Need You' (a George composition), 'The Night Before' (another Paul tune), 'You Like Me Too Much' (George again), 'You've Got to Hide Your Love Away' (a John song, his performance of which clearly revealed he had been listening to Bob Dylan), 'If You've Got Trouble' (a John and Paul rocker especially penned for Ringo but not used in the film or on the non-soundtrack side but left in the vault), 'Tell Me What You See' (another Paul tune), 'You're Going to Lose That Girl' (John) and 'That Means a Lot' (a John and Paul co-write especially for the film). Eleven songs in total and amongst them a song they could not capture to their satisfaction and which they would eventually 'give away'.

Filming was a different matter to *A Hard Day's Night*, for *Help!* went into production with a much bigger budget behind it. Shot in glorious technicolour and in locations such as the Bahamas and Austria, the filming schedule occupied the group's attention more or less non-stop until Wednesday 16 June.

Originally the film's director Richard Lester had it in mind to call the new film *Beatles 2*, but this was before Ringo suggested *Eight Arms to Hold You*. By mid-April, however, the title changed again and *Help!* had been agreed. Once more John came up with a song to fit the title which was recorded during the evening of Tuesday 13 April in Studio 2 at Abbey Road.

It was in early May, at Twickenham studios, during the filming of *Help!* that Brian Epstein informed the Beatles that the British prime minister (Harold Wilson) and HRH The Queen had awarded them each an MBE. This was a prestigious medal awarded by Her Majesty for services to the country. The initials stood for the 'Most Excellent Order of the British Empire'. Unsure as to what it actually was, Epstein informed them to a somewhat muted response. John was the most unimpressed (and would indeed return his MBE amidst a flurry of personal protest and, in some quarters public outrage, in November 1969). In 1965 some members of the public got very hot under the collar that mere 'pop stars' should receive an award for simply selling records ('exports') while for others it was deserved and to be applauded. However reluctant he was to accept it, John joined the others at a ceremony at Buckingham Palace on 26 October 1965 in which the Queen bestowed them each with their medal. It was a measure of how huge their success was and the income they were earning for the UK from exports that the prime minister felt he could justify honouring them in this way and thus able to stave off accusations that he had simply done so to gain much needed support from young voters within the electorate.

Whilst filming was ongoing, the Beatles made brief excursions to attend to other business. On Sunday 28 March they taped a personal appearance on *Thank Your Lucky Stars*, in which they mimed to 'Eight Days a Week', 'Yes It Is' and 'Ticket to Ride'. This was their final appearance on the show that had been the launch-pad for them on UK national TV in January 1963.

Similarly, time was taken on 10 April to record mimed performances of both 'Ticket to Ride' and 'Yes It is' for broadcast on BBC's *Top of the Pops*. It was to be the last time they filmed a mimed performance exclusively for *TOTP*. It was also the first time that the group wore the fawn-coloured, military-style jackets (replete with epaulettes) that would become forever associated with their 15 August 1965 performance at Shea Stadium, Queens, NYC. (The jacket became a popular fashion item of Beatles memorabilia for fans and these *Help!* style jackets continue to sell well into the 2020s at the 'Hard Day's Night Shop' in Liverpool and other worldwide emporiums dedicated to the sale of Beatle-related merchandise.)

The very next day after the *TOTP* taping, the group played the *NME* Annual Poll Winners' All-Star Concert, before appearing live on that evening's ABC TV's *The Eamonn Andrews Show*.

John and George turned up on the 16 April edition of *RSG!* (called *Ready Steady Goes Live!* at this time). Among the other artists on the show that evening was a singer from the USA called Doris Troy. Doris had enjoyed a Top 10 hit in the USA in 1963 with 'Just One Look', which had been covered by the Hollies in the UK in 1964 where it became a number 2 hit for them. Earlier in January '65, Troy herself had spent five weeks on the lower regions of the UK chart with a song called 'What'cha Gonna Do About It'*.

*(*Doris peaked at number 38 with 'What'cha Gonna Do About It', but her tune should not to be confused with the Small Faces' debut UK hit 'Whatcha Gonna Do About It' which reached number 14 in October '65. They were two different tunes.)*

Just a short while down the road from meeting each other on *RSG!*, George and Doris would further pursue their friendship to a mutual musical and creative advantage.

Maybe the most significant of these rare days taken out from filming was Monday 14 June. On this day, inside Studio 2, the Beatles recorded three songs emanating from Paul: 'I'm Down', a blistering Paul-in-Little-Richard-rocker mode, Paul's skiffle style 'I've Just Seen a Face' and last, in the evening between 7 and 10.30pm, Paul McCartney recorded two takes of 'Yesterday' accompanying himself on acoustic guitar.

By any stretch of the imagination that was an incredible day's work. The stylistic differences in the songs recorded perfectly illustrates Paul's musical genius and with 'Yesterday' his absolute mastery of melody. He returned to add finishing touches to this song, but on this day he laid down the vocals on one of the most enduring, most recorded, most cherished and most loved songs of all time. The tune originally came to him in his sleep one night in May 1965 during the filming of *Help!*. He awoke, way up in his attic bedroom of 57 Wimpole Street, and immediately sat down at the piano where he played it back to himself. However, before recording it for release by the Beatles, it was a song he offered to other singers, including Billy J. Kramer who passed on it because he was looking for something more 'rocky'.[1]

The next day in Studio 2, the Beatles recorded 'It's Only Love', a John song which continued in the semi-acoustic style of several songs on the *Help!* album. On 17 June, the Beatles were back in the studio to record Ringo's lead vocal on the song that had been chosen for him to sing on the *Help!* album. John and Paul's 'If You've Got Trouble' had been jettisoned and instead country music fan Ringo had chosen to sing 'Act Naturally', which was a cover of a Buck Owens tune already much loved by the drummer. The group also recorded a brand new John and Paul collaboration entitled 'Wait', which did not make the cut for *Help!*, but which was there for inclusion on *Rubber Soul*.

Just three days later after this flurry of recording activity, the Beatles were on stage in Paris for the start of a European tour that concluded in Barcelona on 3 July.

Their return afforded them but a brief respite from the treadmill, for by 14 August the group were back in the USA taping a performance for *The Ed Sullivan Show*. This was screened on 12 September and joining them on the very same edition was Cilla Black, whose appearance had been filmed on the same day as her pals John, Paul, George and Ringo.

From 15 August until 31 August, the Beatles were on the road across America. It was their third visit to the USA and their second full concert tour. It was a monumental success, the screaming and hysterics as loud and as fever-pitched as ever.

On their return home, the Beatles enjoyed an unprecedented (in recent years) six weeks' break. When they did return to work it was to fulfil a contractual obligation to Parlophone, by which they were bound to record two long-playing records a year. They had already recorded *Help* and needed to cut the second to fulfil the demands of that contract. The record had to be completed and in the shops by the beginning of December. For the project, John and Paul were compelled to come up with a dozen or so new songs. In addition, such was the norm that had been set, they would also cut two sides for their next single, neither of which would be included on the album. The date they stepped into Studio 2 to begin this challenging task was Tuesday 12 October. It is credit to their industry and artistry that just one month later on Monday 15 November the album and single were complete: *Rubber Soul* and the double A-sider 'Day Tripper' / 'We Can Work It Out'.

Significantly they interrupted the sessions for *Rubber Soul* to spend two days in Manchester (1 and 2 November) filming a TV special for Granada TV entitled *The Music of Lennon and McCartney*, which was screened in mid-December. This one-off programme was a direct celebration of John and Paul's songwriting talent. In an early December edition of *Melody Maker*, in which the special was announced, journalist Mike Hennessey penned an article describing the Beatles as "a pop music phenomenon which may very well never recur on such a monumental scale", before adding that, "unquestionably the biggest single factor in their unprecedented success is the superb songwriting partnership of John Lennon and Paul McCartney."[2]

Once the new album and song were in the bag, the Beatles had just about time to draw breath before embarking on what was destined to be their last ever UK tour. Beginning in Glasgow on 3 December the group played nine venues around Britain (two shows per venue) ending in Cardiff at the Capitol Cinema on 12 December. The Beatles never performed outside London again. Their famous Apple rooftop appearance aside (30 January 1969), the group's last ever onstage performance in the UK was at the annual *NME* Poll Winners' Concert in London, 1 May 1966.

The Beatles declined to participate in a Christmas show at the end of the year as they had done in 1962–3 and 1963–4: living in the eye of the storm was beginning to take its toll on John, Paul, George and Ringo.

1966 was to be even more rigorously demanding in terms of their energy and psyche, but by the end of 1965 the era of the Beatles as 'mop top' idols was already showing significant signs of drawing to a close.

---

1 Billy J. Kramer from an interview with Spencer Leigh and featured in the 2009 BBC Radio 2 music documentary *The Songs the Beatles Gave Away*, written and narrated by Bob Harris OBE and produced by Bob Harris and Trudie Myerscough-Harris for WBBC.
2 *Melody Maker*, 4 December 1965, 'Sing Me A Beatle Song' by Mike Hennessey.

Chapter 75:
BEING A SHORT DIVERSION INTO 'YESTERDAY'

1965
Was the year when ... the USA announced it had 190,000 troops in Vietnam ... 34 people died in the Watts ghetto riot ... 32,000 people participated on the 54 mile 'freedom march' from Selma to Montgomery' ... Malcolm X was assassinated ... Bob Dylan went 'electric' at the Newport Folk Festival ... The Beatles played Shea Stadium, the first rock band to play a stadium concert ...

As established songwriters, John and Paul's output of 'giveaways' almost dried up during 1965 as their partnership yielded only one such song. Called 'That Means a Lot', it had not been penned originally as a 'giveaway' but with the Beatles in mind for possible inclusion on the *Help!* album. Despite several attempts the group failed to record what they considered a suitable version of their own and passed on it.

'Giveaways' did not necessarily dry up after this, but 'That Means a Lot' was the last on which John and Paul specifically collaborated. And of course, in its inception they had not intended to gift it to another artist.

From this point on the sole source of Lennon-McCartney giveaways was Paul, although the songs he wrote specifically for others continued to carry the 'Lennon and McCartney' imprimatur.

By now the urge and ambition to become the UK's 'Goffin and King' was a box ticked, an ambition realised. In an hour-long, one-off BBC radio special broadcast between 4:30 and 5:30pm on Bank Holiday Monday 29 August 1966, and entitled *The Lennon and McCartney Songbook*, John and Paul were still referencing Gerry Goffin and Carole King. They described the American duo as "the kind of writers we set out to be..." John went on to detail exactly why they found the couple's songs so appealing: "They are always commercial, easy to sing but never horrible, never sickly, always interesting as songs." The only problem he and Paul apparently had was in deciding which of them "would be Carole..."[1]

By the end of 1965, going in to 1966, their songwriting solely for the Beatles had more than ensured John and Paul's reputation as songwriters *par excellence.* As a result of this, John was simply no longer enthused to write for others, although Paul continued to be interested. For John the songs he and Paul had already composed and would continue to compose specifically for the Beatles provided a treasure trove into which other artists could delve if they wanted to try for a hit with a Lennon-McCartney tune. He was not moved to write more.

In the same 29 August 1966 BBC Radio special, John seemed to suggest the reasons he and Paul wrote less for others was that they were too busy writing for the Beatles: "We used to write in the early days, when we had more time, for other people, that's the only time ... those days were the only ones we really wrote for other people, we thought we had some (songs) to spare."[2]

N.B. As examples of songs they had written for others, Paul said, "We wrote one for Helen Shapiro and Kenny Lynch did it." John added, "We wrote one for Cliff and we did it ... and Billy J."[3]

Paul, however, as a songwriter, was cut from different cloth to John. He delighted in the traditional 'Tin Pan Alley' role of songwriting, of providing hits for others. And so he continued supplying songs for those who asked. To do so he either wrote freshly minted tunes or continued to draw from the recesses of his memory …

Individually, during 1965, Paul did write a song *specifically* to be sung by another act and not by the Beatles. It was a completely solo effort on his part. More to the point it was the first tune either he or John had written that was not credited to the partnership of 'Lennon and McCartney'. Scrutiny of the label on the single in question did not even credit Paul McCartney as the writer. Instead it was credited to a previously unheard of composer called Bernard Webb. More of whom later …

For Lennon and McCartney, the well of commercially unreleased songs written when they were teenagers dreaming of musical success had almost dried up. It had not been very deep in the first place, just over 20 or so songs, of which three had become sizeable popular hits in the UK when later 'gifted' to Peter and Gordon, the Fourmost and the Applejacks. Those early tunes may have been the work of youngsters learning their craft, but what they make totally apparent is that from the get-go, Lennon and McCartney had all that it took to write hits.

By 1965 it had become the norm for new Beatles albums to be routinely scoured by fellow artists looking for precious Lennon-McCartney gems to 'cover'. Thus songs they had already written for, and had recorded as the Beatles, were providing plenty of material that other artists were falling over themselves to cover. Neither John nor Paul were under any pressure to further their reputation or boost their income by writing additional tunes specifically for others. So massively profitable was Beatles product alone, the need to 'write a swimming pool' by penning additional material had become unnecessary. By the mid-Sixties, by simply writing exclusively for the Beatles, John and Paul *were* in effect also writing and providing material for others.

When, on Saturday 6 August 1966, broadcaster and interviewer Keith Fordyce and BBC producer Derek Chinnery went to interview Paul and John at Paul's London home for *The Lennon and McCartney Songbook* radio special, the show opened with a version of 'She Loves You' as recorded by the Irish Guards. As the music faded, Fordyce commented that it was just one on a list of over 300 covers he had made of Lennon-McCartney songs produced in the UK alone.

A spike in what had already been a fast growing number of Lennon-McCartney 'covers' occurred in the wake of a Granada UK TV variety special, entitled *The Music of Lennon and McCartney*, broadcast eight months before the radio show. The brainchild of producer Johnnie Hamp, who had championed the Beatles as far back as 1962, a year before they became nationally famous, the one-off TV show had been devised as a tribute to the duo's songwriting partnership. Although Paul did comment that the show wasn't 'really our thing', the Beatles agreed to participate out of loyalty to Hamp. Introduced or 'compered' by the two songwriters themselves, the show featured 15 artists performing/miming Paul and John songs, including the Beatles who mimed to both sides of their then current single, 'Day Tripper' and 'We Can Work It Out'. Although John and Paul appeared ill-at-ease when delivering their scripted links, the show nevertheless presented an impressive musical smorgasbord of how Beatles songs could be interpreted and in turn it sparked a rush on the Northern Songs catalogue by other artists eager for material to 'interpret' and put before the public. However much it may *not* have been the Beatles' 'thing', Hamp's tribute certainly helped to consolidate John and Paul's position on the musical map beyond being just 'pop' stars and on a par with the likes of Gershwin as writers.[4]

No wonder John no longer felt the need to write specifically for others, especially as, at the same time, he appeared unimpressed by most of the covers he had heard. He told Mike Hennessey from *Melody Maker* that: "There are only about a hundred people in the world who really understand what our music is all about … The reason so many people use our numbers and add nothing at all to them is that they do not understand the music. Consequently, they make a mess of it."[5]

Fortunately, John singled George and Ringo out as being amongst the select group who *did* understand it.

In *The Lennon and McCartney Songbook* BBC Radio special, John said much the same again when he disagreed with Paul who began the programme by saying he liked most of the versions of their songs that people did. However, when prompted by John's difference of opinion, Paul corrected himself to say what he meant was that he preferred versions by solo artists such as Peggy Lee (Fordyce had just played Lee's version of 'A Hard Day's Night') who didn't simply copy the Beatles' style but brought something of their own to the song. On hearing this John then quickly concurred with his partner. Paul: "When solo artists like Peggy Lee do them they do them different and it's probably a bit better because it's different…"[6]

Two songs alone from Lennon and McCartney's 1965 songbook and released by the Beatles underline just *how* redundant the need to write for others had become.

First is the presence of 'Yesterday' on the non-soundtrack side of the *Help!* long player. Second was 'Michelle', track 7 on side 1 of *Rubber Soul*.

From the instant both tunes were released they underlined the amazing level of success Lennon and McCartney as composers were enjoying.

Any other artist in the world would have rush-released 'Yesterday' as a sure-fire hit single. However, in 1965 neither Paul McCartney nor the Beatles could be classed as 'any other' artists.

Although recorded for inclusion on *Help!*, George Martin and Brian Epstein debated whether the song should *even* be issued as Beatles product, but instead released separately and credited simply to Paul. Epstein's fear was that if they did this it could split the group. The Beatles themselves recognised 'Yesterday' was something completely different for them as a group and had not participated in recording it, although George had been present during the recording of the basic track which suggests the original intention may have been to include the others. As a result of such considerations they would not sanction its release as a single by the group in the UK.[7]

Of course, the Beatles' decision not to release 'Yesterday' as a single did not prevent others from 'covering' it. Consequently, George Martin's old friend Matt Monro was first out of the blocks with his version of 'Yesterday' which he took into the UK Top 10 during the autumn of 1965. Munro's alacrity rewarded him with a UK number 8 on 10 November 1965, thus becoming the first artist to release and enjoy a hit with this wonderful song. He was to be the first of many, many more to follow …

Things were a little different in the USA where Capitol were not quite as in thrall to the group's whims as Parlophone was in the UK. Stateside, 'Yesterday' was released as a single with Ringo's version of 'Act Naturally' on the B-side. Released on 13 September 1965, within four weeks it had reached the top of the *Billboard* Hot 100 where it remained for four weeks. In total it spent 11 weeks in the Hot 100. It also climbed to the top of the *Cashbox* singles chart. According to *Billboard*, within five weeks 'Yesterday' had amassed over a million US sales.

In the UK, 'Yesterday' won the prestigious Ivor Novello award as the 'Outstanding Song of 1965'. Despite this it came second to 'Michelle' as the 'Most Performed Work of the Year': as contests go this must have been an incredibly close-run thing!

'Michelle' was another mostly Paul-inspired Lennon-McCartney credited composition. Like 'Yesterday' it became another massive selling song by both the Beatles as well as other artists.

In its origins, 'Michelle' was yet another piece from very early in Paul's writing career but which, along the way, had some input from two others: John Lennon and Jan Vaughan. As a teenager back home in Forthlin Road, he'd composed the tune on his then new Zenith guitar. It wasn't until 1965, however, that he returned to the tune to develop it into a completed work ready for inclusion on *Rubber Soul*.

That he did so was at John's suggestion, who remembered it as "a good tune" Paul used to play at all-night parties held by Austin Mitchell, one of John's lecturers from art school.

Thus, in 1965, Paul followed up John's suggestion to complete the song, but when it came to putting lyrics to it he enlisted the help of Jan Vaughan, the wife of his best friend Ivan, Paul's close friend from his days at the Liverpool Institute. Paul asked Jan for some French words to rhyme with 'Michelle' and she came up with 'ma belle'. She also provided the line 'Sont les mots qui vont très bien ensemble' as a translation for 'these are words that go together well'. Jan also taught Paul how to pronounce the words. To complete what was by now something of a collaborative effort, Paul turned to John Lennon for help with the 'middle eight'. In 1980 John told author David Sheff that it was he who came up with the distinctive and plaintive 'I love you, I love you, I love you', having himself being inspired by hearing Nina Simone singing these words in 'I Put a Spell on You'.

'Michelle' was included on *Rubber Soul*, the Beatles' second album of the year, and immediately upon its release became popular with Beatles fans. Likewise, two UK recording artists immediately recognised 'Michelle's' 'hit potential' and almost fell over each other in their eagerness to secure a studio in which to record cover versions of their own.

The Overlanders released theirs on 31 December 1965 in the UK where, by the end of January 1966, it had reached number 1. George Martin produced a rival version cut by David and Jonathan which also made the Top 20, peaking at number 11 at the same time as the Overlanders were enjoying their second of three weeks at number 1 (5 February 1966). The success enjoyed by the Overlanders and David and Jonathan proved to be only just the beginning for 'Michelle'.

In 1999, BMI placed 'Yesterday' third on their list of most performed songs with some 7 million plays on American radio and television during the twentieth century. Back in the UK, also in 1999, a BBC Radio 2 poll voted 'Yesterday' the 'Best Song of the 20th Century'.

Initially 'Yesterday' failed to match its Ivor Novello glory in the UK and was pipped in the USA for the 1966 Grammy for 'Song of the Year' by Tony Bennett's 'The Shadow of Your Smile'. Indeed 'Yesterday' was nominated for six Grammys in total that year while *Help!* and its namesake album were nominated in a further four categories. After neither song or the Beatles failed to win any of the ten awards for which they were nominated, the head of Capitol Records, Alan Livingstone, officially protested about the results with the words, "'Yesterday' being passed over for the 'Song of the Year' makes a mockery of the whole event."

There is no doubt it was an amazing oversight and it was not until 1997 that Paul's song was eventually inducted into the Grammy Hall of Fame.

Despite appearing to diss on the tune in the barbed lyrics to his 1971 song 'How Do You Sleep', in 1980, shortly before his death, John Lennon described Paul's masterpiece to journalist David Sheff with the words, "We know all about 'Yesterday'. I have *so* much accolade for 'Yesterday'. That's Paul's song and Paul's baby. Well done. Beautiful – and I never wished I'd written it."[8]

As significant as any words said, written or sung about 'Yesterday', in 2012 the BBC reported that it remained the fourth most successful song of all time in terms of royalties paid, having by then amassed a staggering total of £19.5 million in payments. John Lennon may not have wished he'd written it but, by gum, whenever he received his bank statements he must have been exceedingly pleased that Paul had!

As Matt Monro enjoyed Top 10 success in the UK in November 1965 with his cover of a Lennon-McCartney song from the non-soundtrack side of the *Help!* album, another singer was watching his 'gift' of a Lennon-McCartney *reject* from the *Help!* soundtrack falter and stutter before plummeting down the chart.

That other singer was P.J. Proby, and the song was 'That Means a Lot', the *only* collaborative Lennon-McCartney 'giveaway' of '65. On 10 November 1965 it slipped from its peak at number 30 to number 34: the very same date Monro took 'Yesterday' into the Top 10.

Addendum 1: *The Music of Lennon and McCartney*
Granada Television
Producer: Johnnie Hamp
Filmed at Granada Studios in Manchester on 1 and 2 November 1965
Northern UK television premiere: 16 December 1965 between 21:40 and 22:35 on Granada.
It was broadcast by the rest of the Independent Television network on the next evening, 17 December 1975.
The list of artists in the order they performed on the show, hosted by John and Paul:
Part 1
The George Martin Orchestra ('I Feel Fine')
Peter and Gordon ('A World without Love')
Lulu ('I Saw Him Standing There')
Alan Haven and Tony Crombie ('A Hard Day's Night')
Fritz Spiegel's Barock and Roll Ensemble (medley)
The Beatles ('Day Tripper')
Part 2
Paul McCartney / Marianne Faithfull ('Yesterday')
Antonio Vargus ('She Loves You')
Dick Rivers ('Ces Mots Qu'on Oublie un Jour') *
Billy J. Kramer with The Dakotas ('Bad to Me')
Cilla Black ('It's for You')
Part 3
The George Martin Orchestra ('Ringo's Theme (This Boy)')
Henry Mancini ('If I Fell')
Esther Phillips ('And I Love Him')
Peter Sellers ('A Hard Day's Night')
The Beatles ('We Can Work It Out')
* 'Things We Said Today'

The filmed sequences of themselves performing 'Day Tripper' and 'We Can Work It Out' for Granada gave the Beatles the idea of making their own film clips of themselves performing these tunes for use on other TV shows. Consequently, they were filmed by the Intertel company at Twickenham on 23 November 1965 and it was these promos that were used by shows such as *Top of the Pops* and others. (The ones filmed by Granada were not shown outside of *The Music of Lennon and McCartney* TV special.)

    The Beatles had requested that Esther Phillips be flown over from the USA especially so she could perform on the show.

    Marianne Faithfull sang 'Yesterday' in a different key to Paul. (A sign of the times: Marianne was seen only from her shoulders upwards because she was pregnant at the time of filming.)

    Peter Sellers' performance was pre-recorded because of his film commitments.

    The harmonium played by John on 'We Can Work It Out' was that used by Granada TV in the TV soap opera *Coronation Street*, when it would be seen in the home of one of the show's first great stars, the redoubtable Ena Sharples (played by Violet Carson) who occasionally played it.

    It took two months of negotiations to insure the participation of the Beatles, who that year turned down an invitation to appear at the *Royal Variety Show* and refused Brian Epstein's entreaties to reprise the Beatles Christmas Shows of 1963-64 and 1964-65.

The show was not aired again until December 1985 when it was broadcast as part of Channel 4's celebrations of 30 years of Granada Television.

Addendum 2: *The Lennon and McCartney Songbook*
BBC Radio, the Light Programme
Producer: Derek Chinnery
Host: Keith Fordyce
Featuring: Paul McCartney, John Lennon
Recorded at 7 Cavendish Avenue, London, between 4pm and 6pm Saturday 6 August 1966
Broadcast: Bank Holiday Monday 29 August 1966 between 4:30 pm and 5:30 pm
The programme featured 'cover' recordings of 15 Beatles songs by artists including Peggy Lee, the Band of the Irish Guards, the Mamas and Papas, Matt Monro, Frankie Vaughan and Ella Fitzgerald.

The programme also featured an impromptu performance by Paul's pet dog, Martha of 'Martha My Dear' fame. An Old English Sheepdog, she was a seven-week old puppy at the time and can be heard off-mic in another room vigorously complaining about being left alone.

A 13-minute edited version (without any music) of the programme was pressed on vinyl and sent to overseas radio stations by the BBC's Transcription Service and renamed Songwriters Extraordinary – Lennon and McCartney.

1, 2, 3 & 6 Comments taken from *The Lennon & McCartney Songbook*, BBC Radio, The Light Programme, 29 August 1966. Produced by Derek Chinnery, Presented by Keith Fordyce: John Lennon and Paul McCartney in conversation with Keith Fordyce.
4 *The Music of Lennon & McCartney*, Granada Television UK, Variety Special,16 December 1965. Producer: Johnnie Hamp. A tribute to the songwriting of John Lennon and Paul McCartney.
5 *Melody Maker*, 4 December 1965, 'Sing Me A Beatles Song' by Mike Hennessey, John Lennon.
7 Dave Ravenscroft & *The Beatles Anthology 2* 1996, Disc 1, Track 7, (Apple): Track 7 is Take 1 of the song, the only alternate studio recording of 'Yesterday'. (Take 2 was the version released on disc although Paul did transpose two lines from this version in to that.) Paul performs solo, voice and guitar. Before he begins to play he is heard talking to George Harrison. During the exchange George asks in what key the song is. Paul explains that he was playing a G chord but that it would be in F for George. Paul's guitar was detuned a tone so that although he was playing a G chord, it was actually in F. George does not however appear, according to the Anthology's accompanying booklet, "to be musically evident" on the tape. However George's presence and his brief conversation with Paul suggests it had not been finally decided that the others would not at some stage be included and that this would be a solo Paul recording.
8 *All We Are Saying: The Last Major Interview with John Lennon and Yoko Ono*, conducted by David Sheff (Sidwick & Jackson, 2000) p.172 (Originally published in *Playboy*, 1981) p.177.

Chapter 76:
A MAN IN NEED OF A DECENT TAILOR

American rock 'n' roller P.J. Proby (born James Marcus Smith on the 6 November 1938 in Houston, Texas, USA) arrived in the UK in 1964 as an unknown. By re-locating to the UK, Proby was ready to seize an opportunity that had come his way to re-launch his career as a recording artist. In the USA, Proby, aka Jett Powers, had attracted the attention of established American songwriter Sharon Sheeley who, aged 18 in 1958, had penned 'Poor Little Fool' for Rick Nelson. The song became Nelson's first US number 1 and the first number 1 on the *Billboard* new Hot 100 Chart.

Sheeley had, of course, been Eddie Cochran's partner who survived the car crash that killed him. During their relationship she had written several songs for him including 'Cherished Memories', 'Lonely' and (written with Eddie's brother Bob) his big hit, 'Somethin' Else'. Back home in the USA after Eddie's death Sheeley clocked Powers as a formidable singer equally at home rockin' it up like Elvis or emoting it to the max in the mode of a heartbreaking balladeer. Shelley got Jett a recording contract with Liberty Records and a song-writing deal with the label's publishing house, Metric Music. He composed under his real name, James Marcus Smith and significantly, among others, penned 'Clown Shoes' for Johnny Burnette (released in the UK in 1962) and 'Ain't Gonna Kiss You' which, as recorded by the Searchers, became the dynamic title track for their equally dynamic debut EP of 1963 that hurtled to the top of the UK's EP charts. Sheeley changed Powers' name to P.J. Proby (apparently after an old flame of hers from high school) and recommended him to UK TV producer Jack Good who, at the time, was working in the USA producing the hit pop music TV show *Shindig!* (and also scouting for new talent). On seeing and hearing Powers, Jack Good recognised that the combination of his considerable vocal gifts and 'Presleyesque' good looks, made the singer an artist with everything in his favour but who, up to that point in time was tantalisingly just one hit tune away from fame and success.

Sharing Sheeley's enthusiasm, Good believed Proby could well find the elusive break he needed in the UK and so when, in 1964, he was commissioned to produce the Beatles TV special *Around The Beatles* he brought the Texan over to appear on the show. It was a stroke of genius. A complete unknown before the show, the moment it was aired and he stepped in front of the camera Proby became the next 'big thing'. The millions of Beatles fans who tuned into the show on Wednesday evening 6 May 1964 were treated to a sensational performance. The singer had not only been re-named but attention had been paid to his image: he didn't come on looking like the other be-suited long hairs of the day. A pony tail (tied in a bow) had been added, as had tight trousers and a flowing open neck shirt very much in the style of something the swashbuckling Errol Flynn might have worn in one of his big-screen piratical portrayals. Such sartorial flamboyance immediately caught the eye and instantly established Proby's individuality. He became the talk of the show, an instant critical and popular success.

In front of the adoring eyes of millions of British teens a star had been born.

Before the dust settled on his performance, Proby cut the irresistibly frenzied 'Hold Me' – a crazed three-minute burst of manic melodic power pop – as his first UK single. Within a month of appearing on *Around the Beatles*, on 3 June his debut UK single entered the UK Top 50 at number 44 and by 15 July it was at number 3. In considerable style, Proby had arrived.

Already signed by Brian Epstein to NEMS Enterprises, as a follow-up to his sensational debut, Proby recorded 'Together', another soaring, sonic masterpiece that again cracked the UK Top 10 at number 8. (On both records Proby benefitted from the incredible session-

PJ Proby live on stage in 1965 at the peak of his popularity in the UK.
(Trinity Mirror / Mirrorpix / Alamy Stock Photo)

guitar work of a young Jimmy Page.)[1]

As 1964 drew to a close, Proby had reached the UK Top 10 for a third time with his melodramatic rendition of Leonard Bernstein and Stephen Sondheim's 'Somewhere' from the hit musical *West Side Story*. It eventually climbed to number 6. After proving his worth as a rocker, Proby had set out his stall as dramatic romantic balladeer.

Not long after he'd appeared on *Around the Beatles*, Proby's electrifying effect on a 'live' audience was proven beyond doubt when his energetic full-on performance, as support for Adam Faith at the Albert Hall in London, had caused screaming fans to rush the stage. Proby's act was a taste of what was to come when James Brown later rolled into town for the very first time. With fans desperate to get close to him, P.J. had to be escorted from the theatre as the mania continued unabated.

Further appearances only confirmed Proby's incendiary effect on audiences and it became absolutely apparent that the sensation from *Around the Beatles* had the stage act to provoke (and promote) mayhem.

Proby was not only a great singer, but he was also an all-American Texan boy who took both his stage show *and* his private life to the limit. Drinking more than was maybe good for him and partying to the max were high on his agenda. If, as a result, trouble came his way, Proby didn't step aside. His presence on the 'pop' scene took the rock 'n' roll lifestyle to another level and as a consequence he soon gained the notice and censure of both the UK media and the country's 'moral majority'.

For 1965 'conservative' Britain, there was no doubt that P.J. Proby presented a challenging presence. As a 'pop' star he had a huge following of young people, especially girls, and for many disapproving adults this made him a serious cause for concern. Someone to be watched and kept in check.

As 1965 dawned and 'Somewhere' was keeping Proby's star in the ascendant, Brian Epstein decided it was time to put the American in front of a baying public beyond the capital. A package tour was arranged on which Proby and Cilla Black co-headlined. Performance-wise it represented a stark difference in styles, but vocally this was a dynamite coupling. Beginning on Friday 29 January in Croydon, the tour was scheduled to run for 22 nights before ending on Sunday 21 February at the Empire, Liverpool. Fifteen of the 22 venues were ABC cinemas. Amid much anticipation it was on the opening night at the ABC in Croydon that, for Proby, it all started to unravel.

Thanks to going on tour wearing a pair of crushed purple velvet trousers (one of 12 he had especially made for the extravaganza) that were simply too tight for him, P.J. immediately provided the moral majority with exactly the kind of fuel they needed to feed their insatiable ire. Already fearing that the current wave of long-haired pop stars was undermining the moral fibre of British youth, Proby now provided them with clear evidence of the level of debauchery to which rock 'n' roll could descend.

On stage that night in Croydon, Proby's enthusiastic cavorting caused his trousers to split. Some say it was just at the knee, others say they ripped from crotch to knee. One report declared that the rip exposed 'the most intimate part of Proby's anatomy' (which begs the question, was he not wearing underpants?). (A photo of the time depicts Proby on stage, lying on his back, his right leg bent and his trousers split at the knee, while behind that leg it's clear the left trouser leg has split on the inside from knee upwards. Nothing untoward whatsoever is revealed in this photograph.) Nevertheless, such behaviour was considered outrageous for the time – here was a man whose moral standards were clearly and absolutely beyond the pale! Whatever had been revealed, it was simply *too* much.

Proby professed his innocence and declared the trouser-splitting to be an accident, but such was the furore it had provoked he was only allowed to continue on the tour after promising it *wouldn't* happen again. But, of course, Proby simply could not help himself: he'd got 12 pairs exactly the same and so, inevitably, his contortions soon pushed another to the limit of their endurance and sure enough he split a second pair two nights later in Luton.

By now the press were primed and believed without a doubt that the trouser-splitting was staged. (He himself insisted in a front-page article in the *Daily Mirror* on Tuesday 2 February that it was "Not a publicity stunt ... but that when I had the suits made, I just hadn't allowed for the way I moved on stage."[2] And so it was that three nights later on Monday 1 February in Northampton in anticipation of Proby repeating the trick yet again, the press had gathered in number within the theatre and were well placed to report any calamity that Proby might conjure. They were not disappointed. Proby's act not only brought the curtain down but it also got him arrested on stage for performing an act of 'public lewdity'.

In that era of package tours and hordes of screaming, highly excited fans it had become standard practice for there to be a police presence within theatres and so there was on this particular occasion. The reckless behaviour of fans meant there were huge public safety concerns surrounding package tours. Artists, theatre staff and fans were all aware of the dangers they faced. A police presence was accepted/welcomed as essential. They were needed not just for Proby but for most teenage pop shows at which it had become the norm for fans to rush and climb onto stages to reach and grab hold of their idols while outside venues they would attempt to stop or climb onto vehicles ferrying artists to and from the theatres: going on tour involved considerable physical risks for the performers and required strategic planning by the police to prevent foreseeable accidents.

Ironically, that evening in Northampton the chief security and arresting officer on duty was one PC Bryn Harris, the father of none other than future rock 'n' roll UK broadcasting legend 'Whispering' Bob Harris.

In the aftermath of his arrest in Northampton the press ripped into Proby like a pack of wild dogs. Acting as self-declared defenders of the moral standards of decency in public life, popular newspapers like the *Daily Mail*, *Daily Express* and *Daily Mirror* loved nothing better than to become morally outraged on behalf of the nation. Proby presented an easy target with whom to become enraged and flex their muscles.

The *Daily Mirror* was typical of the times when it proclaimed Proby was a "morally insane degenerate" and strongly advised parents not to allow their children to attend his concerts.

Proby was also an early target for social activist and watchdog Mary Whitehouse who actively and vocally opposed, as she perceived it, the growing social liberalism of the Sixties. Deemed a reactionary by the proponents of social liberalism, in particular she was a thorn in the side of the BBC which Whitehouse believed was actively promoting the growth of a permissive society in Britain. She declared Sir Hugh Greene, the Beeb's Director General, to be "the devil incarnate" and in January 1964 with Norah Buckland had established the 'Clean Up TV Campaign', which was succeeded by 'The National Viewers and Listeners' Association' in November 1965. (It is now known as Mediawatch UK.)

To Whitehouse, Proby's 'thrusting' movements on stage were obscene and she immediately called for him to be banned. Proby denied the accusations but no one was listening, especially the press: it simply would not have been in their interests to do so. The British dailies had got their teeth into a good story and were too busy arousing public indignation which they could then actively milk and actively champion. They were deaf to any protestations of innocence. As Proby himself declared: "I was Britain's Errol Flynn, the rough mother of pop. I was Jimmy Dean all busted up. I was Marlon Brando. They wanted rid of me."

Within the ranks of the press it was clear something had to be done to quash this moral degenerate and so it was: a sledgehammer was applied to crack this particular nut. After Northampton, Proby was banned from appearing in ABC's major chain of UK theatres (not good for an artist for whom touring was a major source of income). The ban was extended to their own ABC-owned major UK TV Channel. Huffing and puffing with outrage like all the others, the BBC TV boarded the bandwagon and banned Proby from appearing on their screens. Altogether this was not good for any performing artist out there trying to promote themselves and their product.

Although he never intended it, Bryn Harris's order to bring the curtain down on Proby's act that night in Northampton effectively brought the curtain down on Proby's subsequent career.

Already primed, watching and waiting in the wings to take Proby's place was another up-and-coming singing sensation: Tom Jones and the Squires. No stranger himself to tight pants and on-stage gyrations, unlike Proby, Jones had the nous to know where to draw the line. The moral committee had got their way. Jones was a terrific talent who kept his kecks on and so avoided their wrath (although, ironically, it became a feature of his later stage shows for women in his audiences to remove their panties and throw them at Jones as he performed).

Commenting, many years later in her autobiography of 2003, Cilla said that Proby's trousers were "so weakly sewn at the seams" and consequently "used to split open during his act."[3]

Thus, bad boy Proby was replaced. He effectively became yesterday's man, a clear example of what lay in store for all those within the rock 'n' roll community who thought they too could fly in the face of public decency and the Establishment.

Even so, the hits continued throughout 1965 – somewhat appropriately Proby's next single was 'I Apologise' which peaked at number 11 on 24 March, but with one exception, 'Maria' (number 8, 22 December 1965), P.J. Proby never seriously troubled the charts again and spent the next 50-plus years lurching from comeback to comeback without ever again being a serious chart contender.

THE TOP 20 MOST POPULAR RECORDS OF 1965

01 Ken Dodd: Tears
02 The Seekers: I'll Never Find Another You
03 The Beatles: Help!
04 Elvis Presley: Crying In The Chapel
05 The Hollies: I'm Alive
06 The Seekers: The Carnival Is Over
07 The Beatles: Ticket To Ride
08 The Rolling Stones: The Last Time
09 Sonny & Cher: I Got You Babe
10 Tom Jones: It's Not Unusual
11 Sandie Shaw: Long Live Love
12 The Byrds: Mr. Tambourine Man
13 The Walker Brothers: Make It Easy On Yourself
14 The Rolling Stones: (I Can't Get No) Satisfaction
15 The Seekers: A World Of Our Own
16 The Rolling Stones: Get Off Of My Cloud
17 Andy Williams: Almost There
18 Roger Miller: King Of The Road
19 Cliff Richard: The Minute You're Gone
20 Unit 4 + 2: Concrete And Clay

1 www.jimmypage.com/discography/sessions)
2 *Daily Mirror*, Tuesday 2 February 1965, front page article entitled 'Teenagers Mob P.J Proby'.
3 *What's It All About*, Cilla Black, (Ebury Press, 2003), p.118.

Chapter 77:
P.J. GETS A LITTLE HELP FROM HIS FRIENDS

While the furore around PJ and his splitting trousers continued to define his reputation, Proby exercised some damage limitation to keep his suddenly flagging career alive. His ban from performing 'live' in many major theatres and subsequent ban on appearing on TV limited the exposure his music could receive and the income he could earn. Throughout 1965 he made sure there was enough music out there to avoid going unnoticed. His singles continued to sell in sufficient quantities to maintain a presence on the UK singles chart, albeit with generally lower chart placings than before. As mentioned, Proby managed a late resurgence at the close of the year when his version of 'Maria', another track from *West Side Story*, made it into the Top 10 for a solitary week. He never made it back.

His follow-up to 'Somewhere', the appropriately titled 'I Apologise', charted for eight weeks and peaked at number 11 (24 March). After that came a cover of a song first released by Ben E. King in 1964 entitled 'Let the Water Run Down', which like its predecessor was on the charts for eight weeks, sneaking into the Top 20 at number 19 (4 August) at its highest.

And then came a little help from his friends. Paul (no doubt at the behest of Brian Epstein who was still managing the errant American and undoubtedly fearing for his wayward star's future) gifted Proby 'That Means a Lot'.

Mainly written by McCartney but deemed a Lennon-McCartney collaboration, the song was an outtake from the *Help!* sessions of 20 February 1965 when the Beatles had spent five hours in Abbey Road trying to cut an acceptable version of it for themselves. John and Paul's original assessment of the tune had been that it was a contender for the film's soundtrack album.

After rehearsing the tune four times they set about recording it. With McCartney on vocals and piano, Lennon and Harrison playing guitars and singing backing vocals and Starr on drums, the rhythm track was recorded in just one take. Next they over-dubbed more guitars and vocals. The arrangement was unlike anything the Beatles had attempted before, heavy with tape echo and vibrato it was more Phil Spector than George Martin. However, despite spending so long on the tune, the group were not satisfied with the final 20 February version and returned to the studio on 30 March to try again. Over two sessions and in excess of 20 takes the Beatles never did find what they were looking for and consigned 'That Means a Lot' to the vaults. It was never released during their lifetime as a working/recording band, but eventually that discarded 20 February version turned up on *Anthology 2* in 1996.

Back in 1965, not long after these abandoned takes, a somewhat reluctant Paul McCartney was persuaded to offer 'That Means a Lot' to PJ Proby. His own group's experience of trying to record a version suitable for themselves had left him wary. Even so the American was keen to have a Beatles 'original' in his portfolio despite Paul's obvious lack of enthusiasm for it: "You know sometimes when you'd write a song you'd get ones that didn't work out and so then you'd move on and write something that did work out ... PJ Proby was one of those ... He asked me if I had a song and I said, well not really (as I was kind of loathe to give people these not very good songs) but there is this one called 'That Means a Lot', but I'm not awfully keen on it."[1]

And so it was that within the space of just eight days 'That Means a Lot' went from being a contender for a song on a Beatles soundtrack album to PJ Proby recording it as the

A-side for his next single.

Proby was not deterred by Paul's lack of enthusiasm: the Beatles may have been unable to make 'That Means a Lot' work to their satisfaction, but Proby was a man in need and had faith in his ability to turn it into something, especially when he knew he'd be working in tandem with George Martin on the song.

PJ PROBY
THAT MEANS A LOT (2:31)
(Lennon-McCartney)
Northern Songs Ltd
Liberty LIB 10215
Producer: Ron Richards
Strings arranged and conducted by George Martin
B-side in the UK: My Prayer
(Boulanger-Kennedy)
Recorded at Abbey Road On 7 April 1965
Jimmy Page on guitar, John Paul Jones on bass

Speaking to Ron Tennant for the PJ Proby Fan Forum, Proby seemed to recall that it was very likely, but "doesn't know for sure", that 60s UK session drummer Bobby Graham drummed on the track.[2]

Although recorded shortly after the Beatles had toyed with the song, Proby's slightly slower take was not released until 17 September 1965. It entered the UK Top 40 at number 39 on 6 October and became Proby's sixth consecutive UK Top 30 hit when it peaked at number 30 on 3 November 1965. Its stay on the chart was brief, just 6 weeks. On the *NME* chart 'That Means a Lot' attained a higher placing, climbing to number 24.

In the USA, the single was released on the Liberty label F-55806 during June 1965. It had a different B-side ('Let the Water Run Down') to its UK counterpart but made neither the *Billboard* nor *Cashbox* charts.

A minor hit by Proby's standards of the time, but a hit nonetheless that kept him in the game a while longer.

In an interview for *NME* in 1965, John Lennon remarked that, "The song is a ballad which Paul and I wrote for the film but we found we just couldn't sing it. In fact, we made a hash of it, so we thought we'd better give it to someone who could do it well."[3]

John's remark was quite a compliment for Proby, and Paul also respected Proby's version of 'That Means a Lot', telling Bob Harris and myself many years later that, "PJ's version was not that bad actually, he made something of it. I thought it was horrible, the song, not his version."[4]

As 1966 broke, Proby was at number 12 as 'Maria' made its way down the UK chart. From then on the hits were minor and the singer's popularity declined. Not even a duet with Marc Almond on a version of 'Yesterday Has Gone' in 1996 could restore him to the higher echelons of the chart. It entered the chart on 28 December 1996 at number 58 but went no further, thereafter plummeting down and out of the listings. In total it spent just four weeks on the UK Top 100.

Despite the lack of chart success, and following a cardiac arrest in 1992 – after which he learned to talk and walk again – Proby's career as a singer did not end. Later in the 1990s, he performed in Bill Kenwright's stage shows *Good Rockin' Tonight*, *Only the Lonely*, and *Elvis: The Musical*. By 1996, he was touring the USA and Europe with The Who as the Godfather in the group's stage production of their rock opera *Quadrophenia*.

Despite his experiences in the UK, Proby has remained resident in the country. In 2019, he announced a final 'farewell' UK tour, an occasion intended to celebrate not only his

80th birthday but also his retirement from performance.

It was not to be. History repeated itself. Almost as soon as it had been announced the whole tour was cancelled.

Once again, Proby was the agent of his own professional pratfall. Towards the end of March 2019, and while promoting the tour, he gave what turned out to be an ill-judged interview to a freelance journalist in which he made comments about his views on marriage: "I won't marry a girl I can't raise from the age of 12, 13 or 14. I like that they're young and fresh-looking and don't come with baggage – nobody's messed with their heart and broken it. They're still in school so I can have a hand in their education and make sure their grades are all right, make sure the way they think about religion is all right, and what is and isn't proper."[5]

Not surprisingly, the interview was quickly circulated and became a feature in major UK tabloids such as the *Mirror* and the *Daily Mail*. In the wake of their publication public reaction was instant, horrified and followed immediately by the cancellation of his farewell tour.

Proby apologised and denied he held such views, claiming that he had been misquoted and misconstrued in the *Mirror*, *Daily Mail* and other newspapers. On 30 March 2019, he published an online letter to his fans saying that he had chosen "my words wrongly" and that he had "never been guilty of these accusations of lust nor the inflammable headlines that preceded them".

In an effort to clear his name, in August 2019 he made an official complaint against the *Daily Mirror* to the Independent Press Standards Organisation (IPSO) claiming that in an article published on 27 March 2019 the tabloid gave a "distorted impression" of comments he made during his interview with the freelance reporter. Proby went further and asserted that the *Mirror* had been in breach of the IPSO Editors' Code of Practice in publishing the article.

The regulatory body's Code Committee ruled against Proby's assertion that the *Mirror* had been in breach of the Code's Clause 1 (accuracy).[6]

Proby was unwavering in his denials. Even after allegedly making such unacceptable comments – comments that would more often than not end an artist's career – PJ Proby seemed to weather this reputation-shredding storm, taking part, in 2021, in a 33-date 'Sixties Gold Tour' alongside legendary artists of the era.

1, 4 Sir Paul McCartney in conversation with Bob Harris and Colin Hall for the March 2009 BBC Radio 2 music documentary *The Songs the Beatles Gave Away*, narrated by Bob Harris and produced by Bob Harris and Trudie Myerscough-Harris for WBBC.
2 PJ Proby to Ron Tennant from the PJ Proby Fan Forum, 7 October 2020.
3 John Lennon as reported in the *New Musical Express*, 1965.
5 *Daily Mirror* (online), from an article by Frances Kindon, 'Showbiz Features Writer' published on 29 March 2019.
6 www.pressgazette.co.uk › singer-pj-proby-loses-ipso-complaint-over-...

Chapter 78:
BERNARD WEBB LENDS A HAND

As 1965 drew to a close, Paul McCartney was becoming a tad sensitive to the occasionally aired view that the 'Lennon and McCartney' songwriting tag virtually guaranteed a song chart success, regardless of how good it actually was. With this in mind he decided to test the theory and set about writing a song under a pseudonym that would be recorded by his friends Peter and Gordon. They would release it as a single but without any reference to his contribution to the single.

The song was to be the first A-side Paul had written for the duo since 'I Don't Want to See You Again' in early 1964. After the stunningly successful 'A World without Love', and contributing the A-sides for their follow-up singles 'Nobody I Know' and 'I Don't Want to See You Again', Paul had stepped back and the duo had turned to other writers for songs. Their success had continued with their cover versions of the Buddy Holly and Phil Spector tunes 'True Love Ways' and 'To Know You Is to Love You' that kept them high in the UK Top 10 at number 2 and number 5 respectively during 1965.

Peter Asher: "Paul had written 'Woman' for us and asked if we wouldn't mind trying an experiment because people were saying that anything with the Beatles name or his name on it would automatically be a hit regardless of quality. He thought that was weird and that suggestion probably annoyed him and so he asked if we might try putting it out as if it had not been written by him. We were fine with that, so we invented a pseudonym and a cover story. The cover story only lasted about three or four weeks but that was long enough to prove that it was a hit regardless what name was on it even when it was Bernard Webb."[1]

'Woman' was recorded at Abbey Road during December 1965 sometime after the Beatles completed their final UK tour (Sunday 12 December). Peter Asher commented that while none of the Beatles had previously attended the recording of any of Peter and Gordon's singles, Paul did attend one of the first sessions for 'Woman'.

PETER AND GORDON
***WOMAN* (2:21)**
(Webb)
Northern Songs, NCB
Columbia DB 7834
Produced by: John Burgess
Arranged and conductor: Bob Leaper
Recorded EMI Studios, Abbey Road, December 1965.
B-SIDE: Wrong from the Start (Asher-Waller)
Accompaniment directed by: Geoff Love

Released in the UK on 11 February 1966 it entered the UK singles chart on 2 March 1966 at number 44 and peaked at number 28 on 23 March. It spent a total of 7 weeks on the chart, its last position in the Top 50 being number 43 on 13 April.

Later that year, in June, writing in *Disc* and *Music Echo*, reviewer Mike Ledgerwood said of Peter and Gordon's latest UK album: "They are much more at home on songs with meaningful lyrics. Best tracks here are … 'Woman' (great, of course), their own composition 'Morning's Calling' and 'Homeward Bound'"[2]

'Woman' had been released a month earlier in the USA on Capitol 5579 on 10 January 1966 where it enjoyed a higher chart placing. It spent 12 weeks on the *Billboard* Hot 100 peaking at number 14 on 2 April and a few places lower at number 17 on the *Cashbox* Top 100. (On some early pressings in the USA the name 'A. Smith' was used as the writer's name instead of Bernard Webb.)

On 22 January 1966, just less than two weeks after it had been released in the USA, 'Woman' received a favourable review in *Billboard*'s newsweekly. On the paper's 'Spotlight Singles' page it featured as one of that week's records predicted to make the Top 60 of the Hot 100. Short and to the point the reviewer opined: "The duo offers a power ballad featuring strings, cellos in the baroque fashion and with an easy beat in strong support. Should prove a chart item."[3]

In Canada, 'Woman' did even better where it reached number 1 in the *RPM* Top Singles. In New Zealand it broke into the Top 10 to reach number 7.

Seen in the light of its international success and not just from the perspective of its more modest UK chart position, it is clear 'Woman' was a considerable international hit for Peter and Gordon and undoubtedly reassured Mr. Webb that he did not need the 'Lennon and McCartney' tag to score a hit.

According to Peter Asher (who most definitely should know) the version of 'Woman' that was released as a single was not the version Paul had wanted to be issued: "There were a couple of different versions of it but Paul and our producer John Burgess didn't quite agree on how the record should be done. This was the only one of our recordings Paul *did* get involved with in the studio in any way. He wanted the song to be 'smaller' but John Burgess got the arranger Bob Leaper to turn Paul's ideas into something 'bigger'. Paul did not come back after that. There is a much less arranged version somewhere out there but John Burgess, as our producer, wanted the big Bob Leaper version and that's what came out. In retrospect Paul was right. We could have made a better record, it was a great song."[4]

Despite 'A World without Love' being his duo's first hit and worldwide success, Gordon Waller retained a special affection for 'Woman'. For him it was his favourite of their records and captures the essence of Peter and Gordon: "You can sing it without any music, you can sing it with one guitar, you can sing it with a band, or you can sing it with a bloody orchestra. I think it envelops a lot of our other songs from that period, which were basically all love songs."[5]

During the 1969 *Let It Be* sessions Paul briefly returned to the song and expressed his preference for Peter and Gordon's earlier take of 'Woman' musing whether or not Peter Asher still had the Beatles acetate of the song.

'Woman' gave its name to an American album (Capitol ST 2477) released by Peter and Gordon on 7 March 1966 and was also included on an American Capitol Starline *Best of Peter and Gordon* compilation (ST 2549) released on 5 July 1966.

Peter Asher was to feature greatly in the Beatles story in the future when he became an integral part of 'Apple': "I had produced records before Apple and Paul was part of some of that, he played on one of the records I produced. Paul was aware of my ambitions to produce and of my ability to do so, so in that context he initially asked if I wanted to produce some records at Apple and then asked if I wanted to be A&R for the label. The first full album I produced for Apple was James Taylor and I was involved in the signing of other artists to Apple including Mary Hopkin, Jackie Lomax, the Iveys/Badfinger. As the head of A&R, I was overall responsible for all the sessions even if George or someone else was producing. George's sessions were fun to visit because, as on the Jackie Lomax and Doris Troy records, he put together such great bands."[6]

1, 4 & 6 Peter Asher in conversation with the author in 2019.
2 *Disc and Music Echo*, 18 June 1966, 'New albums', Peter and Gordon review by Mike Ledgerwood, p.12.
3 *Billboard*, The First International Music-Record Newsweekly, 22 January 1966, 'Spotlight Singles', p.16.
5 *Echoes of the Sixties*, Marti Smiley Childs & Jeff March (2011), Davis CA: EditPros LLC.

Chapter 79:
1966, Part 1 – BLOODY TRIBAL RITES

1966
Was the year when ... the USA announced it had 400,000 troops in Vietnam ... the First Acid Test was conducted at the Fillmore in San Francisco ... the TV series Star Trek *debuted in the USA ... Bob Dylan broke his neck in a motorcycle accident and 'disappeared' for a year ...*

The Beatles spent the last two weeks of 1965 and the first three of 1966 at number 1 in the UK chart with their double A-side single 'Day Tripper' / 'We Can Work It Out'. They also ended the year with *Rubber Soul* at number 1 in the LP chart where it stayed for the first seven weeks of 1966. It permanently left the Top 20 on 27 August when it slipped to number 24.

In the USA on 6 December 1965, 'Day Tripper' / 'We Can Work It Out' was released three days after it had been in the UK. 'We Can Work It Out' individually made the number 1 position on the *Billboard* Hot 100 in the early weeks of 1966, while 'Day Tripper' peaked at number 5 on 22 January. (How they worked these different placings out was surely an intricate science!)

Also on 6 December in the USA, a shorter, differing version from its UK counterpart of *Rubber Soul* was released. *Rubber Soul* in the USA was only 12 tracks long compared to 14 in the UK. The US version lost 'Drive My Car', 'Nowhere Man', 'What Goes On' and 'If I Needed Someone', and gained 'I've Just Seen a Face' and 'It's Only Love' from *Help!*. The changes made for a softer, more folksy record which did not prevent it from becoming a huge hit. By 8 January 1966 it was at number 1. It remained on *Billboard*'s album chart for a total of 70 weeks, six of them at number 1.

Those looking at the time for evidence of the first signs that the Beatles' popularity was beginning to wane would have been hard pressed to find any.

The demands for the Beatles' time on stage, on radio, on TV, on film, on record were as unrelenting as ever. For John, Paul, George and Ringo the most disappointing element of it all was what had happened to their concerts. It seemed that no one came along any more to *hear* the Beatles. They could have performed unplugged for all their audiences knew or really seemed to care. The fans came for a communal event: to see the group, scream at the group, to be in their presence, *but*, listening to the group, had it been possible through the cacophony, was not what attending a Beatles concert was primarily about and it hadn't been for a long time now, it was incidental. As John Lennon would remark later in 1966: "Beatles concerts are nothing to do with music anymore. They're just bloody tribal rites."[1]

In just a few succinct words, John had nailed the situation on the head.

Something had to give. The Beatles had tired of the whole crazed shenanigans of touring, individually they felt mentally stressed and physically at risk. Ringo had become bored with the whole scene. George hated flying.

Significantly, once their 1965 UK tour ended (Sunday 12 December at the Capitol Cinema, Cardiff) the Beatles removed themselves almost entirely from the fray. They needed to escape the circus and catch up with whom and what they had become as individuals during the unprecedented and unremitting craziness of Beatlemania.

1965 ended with the Beatles still firmly ensconced in the eye of the storm. They were at number 1 again in the UK and around the World. They were still being celebrated as newly honoured Members of the British Empire when in mid-December a further accolade was bestowed upon John and Paul for their talent for writing songs in the form of a one-off UK television special entitled *The Music of Lennon and McCartney*.

Significantly, however, they had refused to appear in a third consecutive Christmas show, a sure sign the tide was beginning to turn as the Beatles no longer felt compelled nor had any interest in treading the well-worn path taken by most pop stars into the realms of variety and all-round entertaining.

It was not until Wednesday 6 April 1966 that they reconvened at Abbey Road to make music once more. Ensconced inside Studio 3 from 8:00pm until 1:15am, they began work on their next album, *Revolver*. They did so by laying down the rhythm track to the most mind-blowing tune they had ever recorded, the John Lennon conceived and composed 'Tomorrow Never Knows'. The choice of material was almost prescient. This mesmeric track alone, never mind the album for which it was destined, was unprecedented in its scope, sense of derring-do and joyous invention.

Revolver was not just another album, it re-wrote the book of popular music and in doing so it freed its makers from the conventions of the day to voyage into a future of infinite possibilities.

In the heads of John, Paul, George and Ringo they were no longer 'mop tops'.

Emancipated from the treadmill of Beatlemania, the near-four months of relaxation they had enjoyed prior to recording *Revolver* meant that when they entered the studio to do so they were on a creative high bursting with invention and ideas.

Unfortunately for them the last remaining elements of that former manic life had not gone away, it was impatiently waiting for them a little further along the road. Maybe they were all just a little bit too relaxed and off-guard (Brian Epstein included) for when they *did* re-enter the mêlée it bit back in ways to which they were not accustomed and was to exact an even greater toll than ever before on their collective group resilience.

1966 became the defining moment in their career, the point at which all that they had experienced as Beatles coalesced to convince them that if they were to retain their sanity they had to step away from the physical maelstrom of mass popularity, never to engage with it so intimately again. Unfortunately, it proved impossible for them to step away unscathed.

Work on Abbey Road continued virtually unabated throughout the rest of April, all of May and most of June (the final mono and stereo mixes were made in Studio 3 during the evening of Wednesday 22 June). The group poured their heart and soul into these sessions. Included in the recording schedule for the album, the Beatles also recorded two extra tracks that were to become their new single. Work on Paul's 'Paperback Writer' began on Wednesday 13 April and was completed and mixed by 8:00pm the following day, immediately after which they began work on John's 'Rain'. Friday was a rest day for the group, but by the end of Saturday 16 April (and after 11 uninterrupted hours of work) 'Rain' was in the can.

In his marvellous *The Complete Beatles Chronicle* (1992) Mark Lewisohn superbly caught the essence of the high level of creativity and invention that lay at the heart of the sessions for *Revolver*, when he described the recording of 'Rain' as being "full of all the latest technological advancements: limiters, compressors, jangle boxes, Leslie speakers, ADT ('Artificial Double Tracking'), tapes played backwards, machines deliberately running faster or slower than usual, and vars-speed vocals."[2]

In the same tome Lewisohn also reminds us that ADT had been invented by Abbey Road technical engineer Ken Townsend directly at the Beatles' request. It was first used on *Revolver* and "saved the Beatles the chore of manually double-tracking their voices or instrument, an effect they so frequently sought."[3] Thereafter ADT was in use in studios around the world.

The spirit of joyous invention at work during *Revolver* and the Beatles' love of

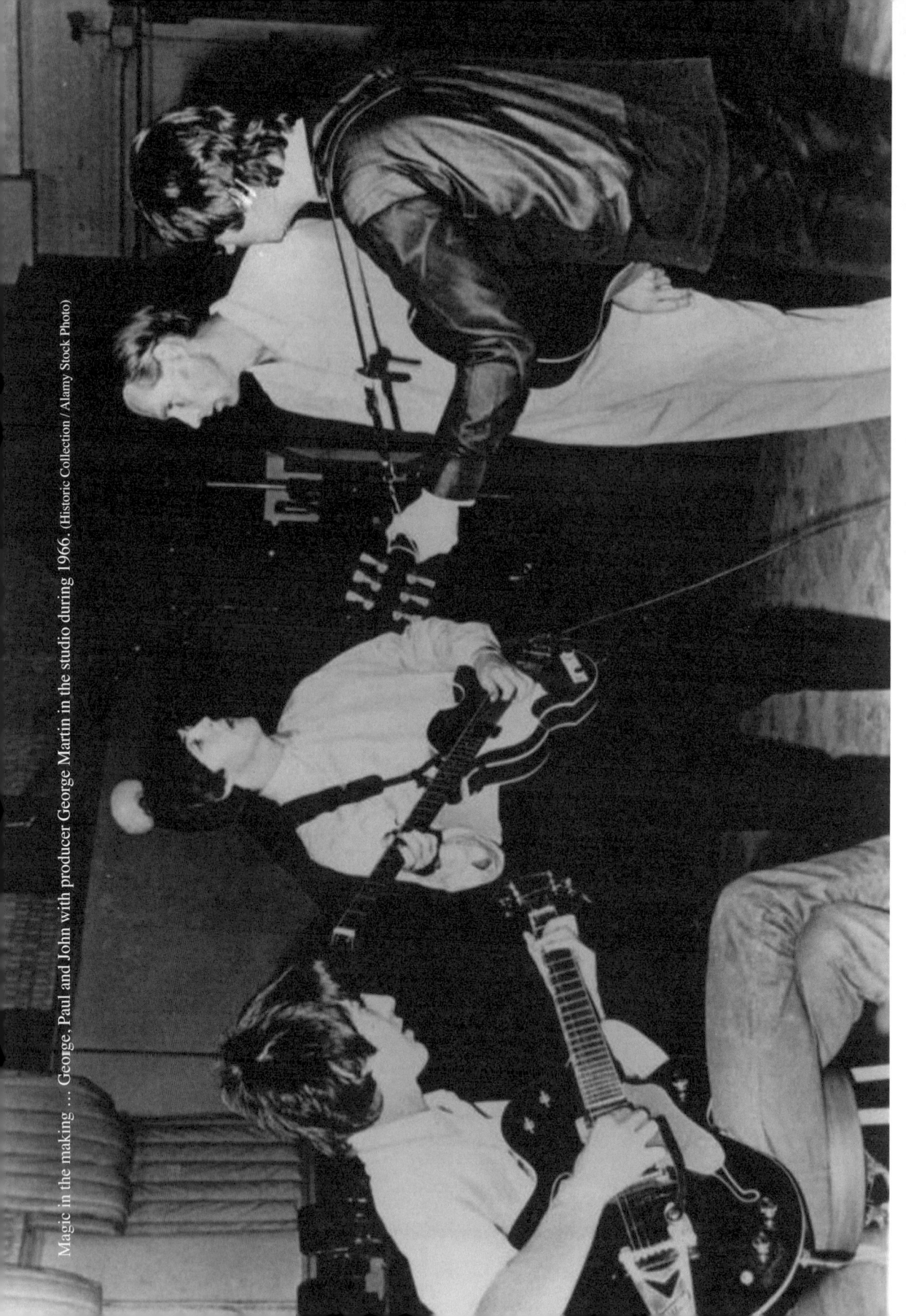

Magic in the making … George, Paul and John with producer George Martin in the studio during 1966. (Historic Collection / Alamy Stock Photo)

experimentation was, in part, possible because of their growing mastery of all the latest studio devices and techniques (all either introduced to them or championed of course by their brilliant producer, George Martin).

Another aspect of their lives that most definitely fired their creative juices on *Revolver* was their intake of drugs.

An integral aspect of their lives as both musicians and seriously famous people, drugs helped the Beatles both endure the pressures their lifestyle laid upon them while, at the same time, the use of 'recreational' drugs, be they legal or illegal, could and did stimulate their creativity.

During the Sixties this aspect of their lives (and that of other pop musicians) came to hold endless fascination for the media. This was because during the decade the social use of drugs (other than alcohol) became more widespread, especially among the young. As a consequence, it triggered a wide-ranging public debate on the negatives and positives of smoking marijuana or taking hallucinogenic drugs such as lysergic acid diethylamide (LSD). Mostly the debate focused on the horrors of drug use and the popular press loved nothing more than to report lurid stories of 'pop' stars and rock musicians discovered in the act of taking these substances or behaving badly while 'under the influence'.

When it suited them, the British press, police and judiciary deemed 'pop' stars to be 'role models' for young people and, as such, drug-induced debauched behaviour did not receive a sympathetic hearing, especially as what they were doing was often also illegal. Illegality could not be countenanced under any circumstances. Principal demons of the pop world whom the media particularly loved to name, shame and demonise, included Rolling Stones' Brian Jones, Mick Jagger and Keith Richards, 'wild man' Jimi Hendrix, while the Pretty Things always provided good copy for a suitably juicy shock-horror public dressing down. It took a strong character to ride out such persistent hounding and bad publicity. The press sensed that Brian Jones in particular was not strong and easily broken and so he became a popular victim for their focus and bile.

At first the media appeared to look the other way as far as the Beatles and their 'bad habits' were concerned. But any perceived amnesty that might have been in place was merely temporary and illusory. Scenting success and looking for bigger targets to fell 'the Establishment's' craving to teach the upstarts of the pop world a lesson that they and their fans would not forget knew no bounds. Working in tandem, the press and the police soon had the Beatles in their sights.

From their teenage days in Hamburg, the Beatles had learned the use they could make of ingesting drugs to keep them awake on stage for the hours on end that they were contracted to perform. Their drug of choice back then was Preludin which gave them what appeared to be limitless energy. When the effects began to wear off they simply took some more. Consequently, by 1966 the Beatles and drugs were by no means strangers. They may have stopped taking Preludin, but had not stopped taking drugs and had also learned of additional benefits that taking specific drugs could provide. As writer Charles Moss so sagely observed: "If *Rubber Soul* was known as the pot album, then *Revolver* would be known as the LSD album. It would be foolish to attribute the innovative surge the group experienced during the *Revolver* sessions to LSD alone, but it certainly didn't hurt when it came to opening up their minds to musical possibilities that might not have been seen otherwise."[4]

---

1 *The Beatles Anthology*, (Cassell & Co, 2000), p. 229.
2 & 3 *The Complete Beatles Chronicle*, by Mark Lewisohn, (Chancellor Press, 1992) p.218 and p.216.
4 'How the Beatles' 'Revolver' Gave Brian Wilson a Nervous Breakdown', The magic behind rock & roll's artistic revolution of 1966, Charles J. Moss, August 4, 2014, *medium.com> cue point*

Chapter 80:
1966, Part 2 – MAKING PROMOS

One brief and significant excursion from the studios during the recording of *Revolver* was made on Thursday 16 June. That evening the Beatles decamped to the BBC's Television Centre to appear live on that evening's edition of *Top of the Pops*. Despite many requests during previous years from the show's producer Johnnie Stewart for the group to appear 'live' on the show this was the one and only time the Beatles obliged.

John, Paul, George and Ringo were most definitely 'live' in the studio for the broadcast, but of course they only mimed to both 'Paperback Writer' and 'Rain', they did not perform either song 'live'. Their acceptance of Stewart's invitation was hugely appreciated by the producer and with the exception of their appearance on the worldwide networked *One World*, on which they performed 'All You Need Is Love' on 25 June 1967, it was the group's last live appearance on a musical TV show in the UK.*

The mayhem and mania that accompanied the Beatles' appearance anywhere meant every visit anywhere had to be highly organised and co-ordinated, planned well in advance almost like a military campaign in which many people were pledged to secrecy. This was not only time-consuming and costly but tedious for the group to endure. As a result, the Beatles decided they would cut back on visits to TV studios to 'promo' their records, from then on they removed the hassle from the process by staying put and making their own short promotional film clips to distribute in the promotion of new product.

As George Harrison explained, "We thought we can't go everywhere. We're stopping touring and we'll send these films out to promote the record. It was too much trouble to go and fight our way through all the screaming hordes of people to mime the latest single."[1]

It was a simple idea that made eminently good sense and so began another innovation courtesy of the Beatles that everyone else adopted: the idea heralded the birth of 'the music video' from which came the concept of non-stop Music TV …

(*It did look very much as if the Beatles were playing 'Hey Jude' live on the David Frost on Saturday Show in early September 1968, but this was thanks to some skilful editing. The clip had actually been filmed several days earlier on Wednesday 4 September at Twickenham. As George explained, "We made a film in front of an audience. They had brought people in for 'Hey Jude'. It wasn't done just for David Frost, but it was shown on his show and he was actually there when we filmed it."*)[2]

Another brief excursion from the *Revolver* sessions was made on Sunday 1 May when the group performed live at the *NME* Poll Winners' Concert which was held at the Empire Pool, Wembley. Four songs and just 15 minutes in duration it was the Beatles' final advertised British live appearance. The Beatles were filmed receiving their awards (John also received an individual award) but regrettably due to a contractual dispute between NEMS and ABC Television the group's actual performance was not, and so lost for posterity.

A further break from recording came on Thursday and Friday 19 and 20 May when the group were video-taped miming to both 'Paperback Writer' and 'Rain' for broadcast on various TV shows. These included clips taped in colour for *The Ed Sullivan Show* in the USA and a black and white clip for the very last edition of *Thank Your Lucky Stars* which was appropriately titled *Goodbye Lucky Stars*.

1, 2 George Harrison quoted in *The Beatles Anthology*, (Cassell & Co, 2000), p. 214 and p. 298.

Chapter 81:
1966, Part 3 – BACK ON THE ROAD AGAIN

Two days after the recording and mixing of *Revolver* (which at that time did not have a title) had been completed, the Beatles stepped back into the maelstrom of playing a concert tour. Despite no prior rehearsals whatsoever, by Friday 24 June 1965 they were in Munich to perform two concerts at Circus-Krone-Bau, Marsstrasse. According to Mark Lewisohn, somewhat incredulously, the Beatles performed 'Yesterday' as a group number replete with electric guitars and drums!

The visit to Germany was very brief, just three days: after playing two shows in Essen on the 25th they travelled to Hamburg to play two shows. It was their first time back in Hamburg since their New Year's Eve show at the Star-Club on 31 December 1962. Astrid Kirchherr and other old friends were there to spend time with them. Mark Lewisohn described the Beatles' level of performance in Germany (and on their subsequent ventures to Japan, the Philippines and the USA) as having reached "its absolute nadir ... their repertoire numbered a mere 11 songs and they murdered each in turn with off-key, out-of-time singing and playing."[1]

The brief excursion to Germany was to prove the lull before the storm of an unhappy world tour that took the Beatles first to Japan for five concerts in Tokyo from Thursday 30 July until Saturday 2 July, after which they flew directly to the Philippines.

Even before they arrived the portents for what was their first and only visit to Japan had not been good. Demonstrations and protests had broken out in Tokyo because local promoter Tatsuji Nagashima had booked the group to perform at the Nippon Budokan, which was believed by many in Japan to be a sacred place suitable only for the presentation of Japanese martial arts.

It can only be surmised just what Nagashima had been thinking when he chose this as the venue in which to present the Beatles. Even more puzzling is that the Japanese authorities in charge of the Budokan agreed to let him do so. To stage wild Western rock 'n' roll shows at the Budokan was an outrageous and utterly baffling decision.

As a result of the protests, and determined that no harm whatsoever should come to the Beatles whilst in Japan, the authorities engaged a huge police presence (plus a further 35,000 security staff) to surround and protect the group. Apart from when being escorted to and from the Budokan, for their entire stay in Japan, the Beatles were essentially imprisoned in their hotel suite at the Tokyo Hilton.

The Beatles' first performances at the Budokan were filmed in colour. Unfortunately, the footage does nothing to challenge Lewisohn's comments about the standard of their performances at this time.

If Japan had been formidable and fraught, the Philippines was to prove downright hellish.

On Sunday morning 3 July, the Beatles flew out of Japan headed for Manila International Airport, stopping only briefly in Hong Kong for their plane to re-fuel. On arrival in Manila the group were greeted at the airport by 5000 fans. From there the Beatles were driven in a police motorcycle escorted cavalcade to the Philippine Navy Headquarters for the obligatory press conference.

From the outset, nothing in the Philippines went to plan. Inadvertently they did themselves no favours at the press conference by not taking it seriously. (Which poses the question, whenever had they taken a press conference seriously? The whole point surely was *not* to take them seriously!) Thus press conferences held on arrival in a different country were usually lighthearted affairs and by now the questions put to them had long become over-familiar and trite, a ritual to be endured rather than enjoyed.

Unfortunately, Philippine reporters had never been party to this ritual and, not surprisingly, took it all very seriously. Local reporters were quick to note (and irked and insulted by the fact) that the Beatles seemed to know very little about the Philippines. They could not have known that this was not an unusual situation for John, Paul, George and Ringo given that Beatles world tours had become not so much tours of different countries but tours of different airports, hotels, dressing rooms, concert halls and screaming fans. Tourists they were not. These were not holiday trips on which they were embarked. Sightseeing was not on the itinerary. As a result, it had become very hard for the group to show interest any more in places they were never going to get to see or visit. Again, the Philippine press were also not up to speed on this fact of Beatle-life.

Immediately after the press conference the Beatles were taken to a private yacht owned by a wealthy Filipino newspaper owner, one Don Manolo Elizalde, a friend of local concert promoter Ramon Ramos Jr. At first Tony Barrow, the Beatles press officer, says this arrangement went down well with John, Paul, George and Ringo: "They were enjoying the thought of being cut off from the world for 24 hours…"[2]

What unsettled them, however, was the sight of armed police patrolling the deck.

The Beatles' initial pleasure at this brief period of seclusion was further diminished when they discovered that, so tight was the security surrounding them, that they would be landed the next afternoon not long before they were due on stage, which did not suit their purpose. The desire by their Filipino hosts to keep the group safe through an elaborate security regime failed to take into account the group's own requirements and schedule for staging a show. As Barrow noted: "They had no idea of the group's lengthy pre-show routine, including the preparation of stage suits and instruments."[3]

What should truly have set alarm bells ringing among the Beatles and their personal entourage, was not so much the tightness of the police security plan, but a report featured in the 3 July edition of the *Manila Sunday Times*. Published just one day ahead of the group's scheduled concerts at the Rizal Memorial Football Stadium, the article described forthcoming events of which they should already have been fully aware and prepared … but weren't.

Herein lay the proud announcement that President Ferdinand Marcos of the Philippines and his formidable First Wife, Imelda would be guests of honour at one of the shows. Much more to the point, the report declared that Imelda believed the Beatles would be attending both a reception and a luncheon she was going to host in their honour and at which they would personally meet her and her children.

Imelda's prestigious reception at the Malacañang Palace was scheduled for 11am on Monday 4 July, to be followed at 3pm by a luncheon.

Unfortunately, the Beatles were entirely ignorant of any of this. They and Brian had not entered into any agreement with anyone to be anywhere on 4 July other than at the Rizal Memorial Football Stadium.

Unknown to them, in his original tour schedule which he *had* presented to Brian Epstein, local concert promoter Ramon Ramos Jr had included a 'drop-in' at the Palace at 3pm on 4 July. What Ramos had apparently failed to do was impress upon Epstein the utmost importance of the Marcos invitation, inferring instead that it was an option to attend and certainly not a set-in-stone, ignore-at-your-peril agreement. As a consequence, Brian rejected it immediately because the reception clashed with the Beatles' scheduled time of arrival at the Rizal Memorial Football Stadium. As was their practice when on tour, the group insisted on arriving at any venue two hours ahead of their performance time to afford them sufficient time to prepare.

Ramos had apparently been forced into making the arrangement to attend the Marcos reception by the palace, but for some reason had not pushed Epstein on the matter, fearing Brian would refuse it because it was so close to their expected time on stage.

Instead of insisting on negotiating a response from Brian, he simply left the problem to resolve itself and informed neither the Palace nor Imelda that their invitation had been declined.

Tony Barrow has confirmed that as a result of all the chaos aboard the yacht on which they were staying, Ramon Ramos Jr's tour itinerary for the Beatles was never discussed properly between himself, Epstein and the others in the party. In fact, Barrow seriously doubted that Brian read the itinerary thoroughly and, as a consequence of not having his attention drawn to this crucial issue, failed to pick up on the crucial implication of ignoring the lines that suggested the Beatles '*might* call in on' the First Lady, the president's wife, Imelda Marcos, at three o'clock on Monday afternoon, after which they would proceed directly from the Malacañang Palace to the stadium in time for the first concert.

As Barrow notes, by using the word 'might' Ramos had made the group's attendance appear optional, as if they had a choice: it did not read as – and he did not impress upon Epstein – that it was in effect a direct command from the President's office to be there, which in fact it undoubtedly was.

Thus Epstein and Barrow had no inkling of the seriousness or depth of shit that was coming their way.

Such an important detail in the Beatles' schedule was not something Epstein would ever have allowed Ramos to agree to without first fully informing him and gaining his personal response.

As Tony Barrow, who accompanied Epstein throughout the whole sorry episode notes: "If Ramos had raised the invitation with him directly, Epstein would have turned it down on the boys' behalf, knowing that with an afternoon show to perform they would have wanted to be safely installed in their dressing room by three o'clock at the latest. Plus, the Beatles hated meeting dignitaries of all types, from small-town mayors up to heads of state, and would have been only too pleased to use their matinee commitment as a get-out."[4]

Consequently, the Beatles did not show and Imelda was left looking like a fool in front of her children and the Filipino press. The Beatles might as well have spat in her face. If, as the quotation says, 'Hell hath no fury like a woman scorned', here was a perfect moment for Imelda Marcos to prove its validity. And prove it she did: all hell did let loose. Imelda had been publicly insulted and embarrassed on her own turf. As a matter of honour, vengeance against the Beatles now had to be exacted and done so with great alacrity *before* they left the country.

The concerts went ahead as scheduled, both were very successful and enjoyed by the 90,000 fans fortunate enough to obtain a ticket (some estimates claim the combined attendance for the shows was actually double the official figure published).

But from the moment they left the stadium, the Beatles' visit to the Philippines descended into the stuff of nightmares. Reports on TV and in the *Manila Times* and *Manila Daily Mirror* all boasted headline features accusing the Beatles of 'snubbing' the First Lady and her three children. An official delivered a tax bill to Brian Epstein for immediate payment of the tax due on the Beatles' fee. Suddenly all service and assistance at the hotel and airport was withdrawn. The news reports ensured a very hostile, aggressive attitude towards the group was rapidly whipped up within the general public.

Whilst Epstein attended to the tax bill, the prime aim of the entire Beatles entourage was to get the group and themselves safely out of the country. To this end press officer Tony Barrow and NEMS employee Vic Lewis went directly to the airport to check-in. They arrived to find the atmosphere was already toxic and getting worse by the minute. Barrow: "When the Beatles joined us, Filipino thugs, some in military uniform, closed in on our party from all sides. Guns were brandished and fired into the air, makeshift cudgels and coshes were waved in our faces ... There was no alternative but to run the gauntlet of the menacing mob."[5]

Barrow says members of the Beatles entourage were physically assaulted: Brian Epstein was punched in the face and kicked in the groin, while roadie Mal Evans was kicked in the ribs and tripped up and left to hobble unaided across the runway to the airplane with blood streaming down one leg.

It was a tense and terrifying experience in which Barrow says they all feared for their lives: "We did our best to shield John, Paul, George and Ringo from direct blows. Vic Lewis and I were the last to go. He held an open hand across his back saying it might protect his spine from a sniper's bullet."[6]

Finally, amid much holding of breath and a dread of last-minute delays, at 16:45 on Tuesday 5 July 1966, the Beatles flew out of Manila International Airport. Take-off was accompanied by a round of spontaneous applause from all on board.

For the Beatles this was the last straw: they were not enamoured by anything that they had experienced in either Japan or the Philippines, most especially the latter. The visits had done nothing to change, only enhance, the group's increasingly negative view towards touring. The debacle in the Philippines left them none too happy with Brian either.

To compound the group's disaffection, an intended 'relaxing' stop-over in New Delhi was marred by crowds of fans descending on their hotel.

Eventually the group returned home to London Airport on Friday 8 July where, in response to a reporter's inquiry as to what was next for the Beatles, George replied by saying, "We're going to have a couple of weeks to recuperate before we go and get beaten up by the Americans."

As he spoke these words he could never have realised how prescient they were.

1 *The Complete Beatles Chronicle*, by Mark Lewisohn, (Chancellor Press, 1992) p.210.
2 & 3, 4, 5 & 6 *John, Paul, George, Ringo & Me*, by Tony Barrow, (André Deutsch, 2005) p. 192, p.193, p.197.

Chapter 82:
1966, Part 4 – ON BEING MORE POPULAR THAN JESUS

On Thursday 11 August, the Beatles flew from London to Chicago (via Boston). The very next day they kicked off a 14-date tour of the USA and Canada by playing two shows at the International Amphitheatre in Chicago.

It was unlike any of their previous tours of North America. And it was to be their final tour, ever. After the concluding concert at Candlestick Park in San Francisco, the Beatles returned to the UK never again to set out on the road together for a concert tour.

The final tour was a sour and scary expedition that left George declaring on the flight from San Francisco to Los Angeles, immediately after their show in Candlestick Park, "Well, that's it, I'm not a Beatle anymore."[1]

The reason why this tour in particular proved so odious was because of an interview John Lennon had given to UK journalist Maureen Cleave. Published in the Friday 4 March edition of the *London Evening Standard* (some five months prior to the Beatles' tour of the USA) and entitled 'How Does a Beatle Live? John Lennon Lives Like This', Cleave's article was destined to become forever famous for John's comment: "We're more popular than Jesus now".

His words were part of a longer comment in Cleave's article in which John opined: "Christianity will go. It will vanish and shrink. I needn't argue about that; I'm right and I'll be proved right. We're more popular than Jesus now; I don't know which will go first – rock 'n' roll or Christianity. Jesus was all right but his disciples were thick and ordinary. It's them twisting it that ruins it for me."[2]

Her Lennon interview was the first in a series of five features Cleave penned about the individual Beatles and their manager. They all appeared in the *Evening Standard* during 1966, each under the collective title of 'How Does a Beatle Live?' Ringo was featured on Friday 11 March, George on Friday 18 March, Paul on Friday 25 March and Brian on Friday 1 April.[3]

In the UK the articles passed without undue comment. The general reaction was that they provided interesting comment, but taken in context they provoked no outcry whatsoever.

It proved an entirely different matter in the USA. The trouble started on 29 July 1966 when liberal American teen-orientated magazine *Datebook* published both Paul and John's *Evening Standard* interviews in full. It did so in a special 'Shoot-Out Issue' dedicated to encouraging debate around what were then controversial youth-orientated themes: drugs, sex, religion, long hair and the war in Vietnam.

Prior to this, and to no significant response, John's interview, and extracts and references to it, had appeared in a March edition of *Newsweek* and the May edition of *Detroit Magazine*. On 3 July the *New York Times Magazine* published all four of Cleave's Beatles interviews as a five-page feature under the title of 'Old Beatles – A Study in Paradox'.

It had been Beatles press officer Tony Barrow who had suggested the articles to *Datebook*. He recognised the magazine was a forum for older teenagers that addressed issues relevant to their lives and times and which was not just concerned with what the pop stars ate for breakfast or what they looked for in a girlfriend. This was an opportunity to appeal to the more mature Beatles fans who would appreciate a more in-depth conversation with John and Paul. Editor Art Unger eagerly agreed to publish the features. He recognised that both articles provided comment likely to arouse interest and spark a lively response, if not controversy, among his readership.

Unger believed it was Paul's comments which provided the most likely content to provoke controversy and so it was Paul's photograph that appeared on the cover. At the side of Paul's cover-picture, under the headline 'SHOOT-OUT ISSUE', Unger printed a series of quotations and taglines intended to spark interest and further investigation from his readers. Each quotation was printed in differently coloured boxes.

The first was from Paul: "It's (the USA) a lousy country where anyone black is a dirty nigger!"

Then came John's: "I don't know which will go first – rock 'n' roll or Christianity."

Next came quotes from Len Barry ("English groups won't last. There is no longevity in dirt!"), Scott Walker ("Pop music can warp your sense of values about Life"), Bob Dylan ("Message songs are a drag"), Mike Brian ("Inter-racial dating must follow school integration"), Tim Leary ("Turn in, tune in, drop out").[4]

Datebook's weighty 'Shoot Out Issue' certainly did spark controversy: controversy that went beyond anything Unger had contemplated. It caused a national furore.

Somewhat surprisingly it wasn't Paul's comment that caused the uproar, it was John's. The magazine's re-published Cleave *Evening Standard* interview evoked a response that was unprecedented. Christian fundamentalists were at first outraged and then very quickly mobilised. In their eyes John Lennon had blasphemed, and for a blasphemer the only way back was to repent their sins (or possibly be burned at the stake).

Radio stations and newspapers, mainly in the southern states of the USA, promoted protest and encouraged people to attend organised bonfires of Beatles records and memorabilia in order to display their outrage, sully Lennon's name and force him to repent. Simultaneously, the Beatles' music was banned by 22 radio stations in Alabama alone.[5]

Ahead of the Beatles' forthcoming tour, Brian Epstein attempted to calm the storm but his words had little effect. The situation grew uglier with each passing day and with the protests came death threats against the Beatles and their families. With the assassination of President Kennedy still fresh in the memory, such threats were not taken lightly. The safety of the Beatles in the USA was in serious jeopardy.

It was inevitable that John would have to personally and publicly explain his comments. And so, on arrival in Chicago, he appeared in front of the press and did just that. Not only did he explain his comments but he also apologised. His words and personal demeanour in front of the cameras was such that the situation was largely deflated to the point calm was mostly restored and the planned bonfires were cancelled. The press conference was unlike any the Beatles had faced before, especially in the USA. It was uncomfortable for all the Beatles, but most especially it was unsettling for John.

The incident underlined just how under the microscope the Beatles were, how their every word, their every action was scrutinised, dissected and interpreted. They were not perceived in the same way as their contemporaries. For their every utterance to be so picked apart was alarming for them. In their minds they were first and foremost musicians not seers. The media, however, had now positioned them as 'role models' for young, vulnerable people and, as such, their every move, their every utterance and action were under surveillance to ensure they upheld this exalted position of moral exactitude. And of course that same media were just waiting to record and publicise any perceived fall from grace …

All those years ago, when they had first plugged in at the Cavern to play their beloved rock 'n' roll, this was not what they had envisioned the future to be. Even if successful, death threats and hate were not part of the deal. Popularity, success and wealth, yes, but when crammed into lousy accommodation in Hamburg and elsewhere, while imagining their collective future at the 'Toppermost of the Poppermost', what they had envisioned had not looked remotely like this.

Within that close-knit brotherhood of the Beatles something had to give.

And it did.

The tour of America was a very tense, largely disagreeable and ugly affair, marred by the lingering unpleasantness of the whole 'bigger than Jesus' debacle. From the very start it was something for the Beatles to get through, not to be enjoyed. Physically and emotionally it became a trawl through assassination threats, protests by the Ku Klux Klan, pitch invasions at stadiums, being trapped inside an armoured truck for two hours surrounded by fans, bad weather, having to play a short half-hour set of songs of which they had personally long ago grown tired. They were unable to play anything from *Revolver* and venues like Shea Stadium had not sold out. Wherever they performed they did so always surrounded by police and heavy security. At Candlesticks Park the group performed encaged inside a six-foot wire fence. It was a metaphor for how they perceived their life on the road, and in the spotlight, had become.

Psychologically, for the moment, the Beatles needed some time out.

1 George Harrison: words attributed to George and apparently spoken/announced by him on the Beatles' flight home from the USA , 29 August 1966.
2 John Lennon quotation from 'How Does A Beatles Live? John Lennon Lives Like This', an article by Maureen Cleave in the *Evening Standard*, published Friday 4 March 1966.
3 Steve Hoffman Music Forums.
https://forums.stevehoffman.tv/threads/beatles-1966-interviews-with-maureen-cleave.331741/
4 All quotations taken from the front cover of USA teen-magazine *Datebook* 'Shoot-Out Edition' published 29 July 1966, edited by Art Unger.
5 *The Complete Beatles Chronicle*, by Mark Lewisohn, (Chancellor Press, 1966) p.212.

Chapter 83:
1966, Part 5 – INDICA

Candlestick Park was an ending. The Beatles did not tour again: the return to Britain on 31 August 1966 was, for all of them, a blessed relief that ushered in a period of downtime and escape in which the individual members of the group were freed of group commitments to recuperate and pursue their own interests and activities.

John accepted Richard Lester's invitation to play the supporting role of Private Gripweed in the film *How I Won the War* and so disappeared to Spain.

Paul pursued a new, solo musical venture by turning his hand to composing a film score. For some time, he and Jane had been becoming more closely acquainted with London's emergent 'underground' cultural scene, largely because of her brother Peter's close association with the Indica Gallery: "In the mid-Sixties, when Swinging London was just about the hippest city on the planet, Indica, the capital's first conceptual art gallery, was just about the coolest place to be..."[1]

Situated in Mason's Yard, Mayfair, the Indica was the brainchild of its three founders: Barry Miles, John Dunbar and Peter Asher, three well-known young hipsters around town who in turn knew an awful lot of groovy people. The Indica enjoyed two fabulous years from when it opened in November 1965 until its closure at the end of the 'Summer of Love' in November 1967.

In London on 14 October 1966, the first edition of the *International Times* newspaper (aka *IT*) was published. This was the mouthpiece of the UK's 'underground' scene. Based in London it reported on the doings of what by then was becoming a fast-moving social and cultural revolution among many young people up and down the land. Three pages into the first edition it served notice of a one-person art show of 'Instructional Painting' by Yoko Ono that was to be held at the Indica Gallery from November 9 to 22, 1966. The piece featured a photograph of Yoko Ono in performance of her *Cut Piece in the Destruction of Art Symposium* and noted that this would be the very first time her works had been shown outside Japan and the US.

The very next evening after *IT* was available on the streets, for the very first time Paul attended its launch party at London's Roundhouse Theatre in Chalk Farm. Coincidentally the *IT* party was the venue's debut gig. Suitably it was an all-night affair (or 'rave' as such events were being heralded) and described as a 'pop-op-costume-masque-drag ball'.

Invitees were invited to 'bring their own poison' which would have included grass and acid. The events lined up for the evening included readings, screenings and music which were described as 'happenings'. Dressed as an Arab and along with 2,500 other devotees, who included Mike Jagger and Marianne Faithfull (dressed as a nun), McCartney experienced first-hand how the rock scene was changing in terms of how the music was being presented on stage and how the groups and audience interacted with each other in a psychedelic 'experience' that incorporated loud music, lights, screens, standing, sitting, free form dance and drugs. Emergent bands the Soft Machine and Pink Floyd performed that night.

For the UK, Pink Floyd's 'liquid light show' was stunningly revolutionary in the way it mingled mind, sight and sound. This was a true 'happening'. At one point some partygoers could be found rolling in a huge jelly that had been made by Biddy Peppin, "but Syd Barrett and Pink Floyd's roadie Po accidentally destroyed it by removing a piece of wood that was holding the whole structure in place. Gallons of jelly splashed all over their Kings Road clothes, but there was still plenty left for people to roll in."[2]

As far as the story of the Beatles is concerned, the party was most probably the first time any one of the four had seen, heard or become aware of a woman who was to make a huge impact on their lives individually and therefore collectively.

As Daevid Allen of Soft Machine recalled, the launch party for the *International Times* "was our first gig as a quartet. Yoko Ono came on stage and created a giant happening by getting everybody to touch each other in the dark, right in the middle of the set. We also had a motorcycle brought onto stage and would put a microphone against the cylinder head for a good noise."[3]

(John returned from filming just in time to attend a preview of Yoko's exhibition, to which, of course, he was invited.)

Meanwhile, to return to what each Beatle did in the immediate aftermath of that last tour of the USA ...

George relocated to India to study its music and culture. Already a devotee of Ravi Shankar and his sitar music, George was on a journey that would have profound effects not only on him, his music and his outlook on life, but also on his fellow Beatles and Western popular music as a whole. He was opening doors through which what we now call World Music could pass and receive a greater and more appreciative audience. George Harrison was creating a musical revolution of his own, but one which initially reached the ears of many millions through the music of the Beatles.

Ringo immersed himself in home and family matters.

Brian had been seriously afflicted by the stress of the previous months to the point he spent time in hospital suffering from depression which had caused him to attempt suicide.

'Escape' for all these men was, however, only a word, a tantalising promise but never a reality: the press never let them out of their sights. They were forever there, quietly observing, keeping an eye on what was going on. With very little actually happening for the Beatles as a group and noting that the Beatles were each 'doing their own thing', the media surmised that they had, in effect, broken up. When articles and news bulletins appeared suggesting this was the case, from the supposed sanctuary of his hospital bed, a poorly Epstein denied them as best he could.

The Beatles had, of course, not split but they had certainly changed. Visually they dressed individually: the distinctive former group attire of matching suits was no longer necessary as they would no longer be touring. (Although they did don suits one more time as Sgt. Pepper's Lonely Heart Club Band.) The familiar conveyor-belt pattern of life demanding a new single every few months, followed by a new album, supporting tours, and numerous TV and radio appearances was no longer how it would be.

From now on they were musicians and writers making music for themselves to share with the public on record alone. The stage would no longer confine or define their musical ambition or output. They could compose music and make albums without having to worry how it could be performed 'live'.

Their return to recording occurred on Thursday 24 November when the four musicians assembled in Studio 2 at Abbey Road to begin work on a new album. The song that engaged them for that entire session and many more thereafter was a song John had written on location in Santa Isabel, near Algeria in southern Spain. It was a blissful hallucinogenic evocation of his childhood in Woolton that he called 'Strawberry Fields Forever'.

From its simple acoustic origin, the Beatles would transform John's song into something shimmering and wondrous, surely one of the most groundbreaking and greatest pop songs ever recorded.

Their wondrous opus of 1966, *Revolver*, had set the precedent for what came next. The Beatles may have not been together for nearly three months, but their reunion not only heralded the beginning of a new experimental phase in their career, it also heralded the beginning of work on an album that would turn popular music on its head and inside out.

Not for the first time in their career, the Beatles were plotting a new direction others would soon be eagerly attempting to follow.

Work on 'Strawberry Fields Forever' continued throughout the few remaining days of November and through most of December, although the Beatles also recorded 'When I'm Sixty-Four' during this time. Fittingly, the last working day in the studio of 1966, Friday 30 December, focused not only on 'When I'm Sixty-Four' and 'Strawberry Fields Forever', but also on a Paul song they had recorded called 'Penny Lane'.

Rumours (aided and abetted by the world's media) suggesting that the Beatles were on the verge of breaking up, or had already possibly done so, prompted all four Beatles to attempt to put such stories to bed. Hence, on Tuesday 20 December, they agreed to be interviewed individually by reporter John Edwards for British Independent Television News' weekly in-depth news magazine, *Reporting '66*. Each Beatle talked about the group's exploits in the studio where they were recording new material. Entitled *End of Beatlemania*, the 25-minute programme was screened nationally over 28 and 29 December and, while its title presaged something had definitely changed, its actual content did much to allay fans' fears that the Beatles were no more.

1 'Where John met Yoko: The gallery that broke the mould', Terry Kirby, Tuesday 21 November 2006. www.independent.co.uk
2 *Early Days of the London Underground Scene* by Barry Miles, 29 Sep 2016, featuring previously unpublished text from 2002, https://lux.org.uk › writing › early-days-of-the-london-underground-scene…
3 *Wrong Movements: A Robert Wyatt History*, Michael King, (SAF Publishing, 1994).

Chapter 84:
1966, Part 6 – WHAT PAUL DID ON HIS HOLIDAYS

For Paul, making music and writing songs was his life and so, when the Beatles took a break in 1966, he could not just stop composing. However, by then he no longer wished to simply confine himself to writing 'pop' songs. Instead he set himself the musical challenge of composing the theme for a film. This endeavour marked the very first time that either he or John had ever composed music intended to be used *outside* the remit of the Beatles.

Almost immediately prior to setting off for their fateful final tour of the USA, on Saturday 6 August, while sitting together in Paul's London home to record *The Lennon and McCartney Songbook* radio programme, John and Paul had happily extolled the virtues of writing together although they had both made it clear it *wasn't* an imperative.

Further to this, when asked if they felt their individual talents were dependent on each other, both Beatles said that they weren't.

John: "No, not really, but it helps a lot, you get a better point of view as well."[1]

Paul concurred by commenting, "We can do them on our own…", but added that, when they did so, quite often there would be a verse or a word that as the writer they felt did not work or was "corny", and at such times it was always useful to be able to seek the other's advice.[2]

Another big plus of working together that John noted was that songs got finished: "You … get so involved with somebody you finish it, but if you are on your own you haven't got the energy to go over it."[3]

Asked if, as songwriters, they thought alike or differently, Paul explained: "We think nearly alike but pretty differently at the same time. We can write a song like 'Day Tripper' where we've *got* to write one and … be thinking the same thing about it, but if you wrote it individually it would be a completely different song."[4]

Explaining that he and John had begun composing as youngsters "apart then together", Paul had added, "I think George didn't write any because he thought we could write the songs and the other two couldn't and Ringo still thinks it. But I think anyone can write songs probably."[5]

Asked specifically if 'And I Love Her' had been written for anybody in particular while not revealing that person's identity, and after a long pause, Paul replied: "Yes," before adding, "Probably most of the songs are … I think so, in a way."[6]

John provided an insight into the Lennon-McCartney writing habits by saying they weren't particularly night-writers and that writing as a team could happen "any time really when you're awake. Not too near the morning when you are half asleep and not when you're tired. So it doesn't matter what time it is, just the period when you feel quite healthy."[7]

Pinpointing the piano or guitar as being their instruments of choice on which to compose, but that 'anything' would do, John commented, "I'm just finding I don't know enough chords to write them on guitars … I'm going to have to get some old fellah to come in and play to me."[8]

When it came to taking a break after the trauma of the USA, one of the ways Paul chose to relax was to write some music on his own, and specifically this was to be the theme tune for a motion picture. The film Paul chose was *very* much of its time: it was a very British endeavour and very 'Sixties' in its theme.

Towards the end of the Fifties and the beginning of the Sixties, three groundbreaking films, *Room at the Top* (1959), *Saturday Night and Sunday Morning* (1961) and *The Loneliness of the Long Distance Runner* (1962) heralded a 'British New Wave' of filmmaking. Adapted from novels written by British writers Alan Sillitoe and John Braine, the films were shot in stark black and white, taking as their theme 'class and realism'. Taken together they ushered in a new genre of film known as 'kitchen sink dramas'. Typical of the genre, they were set in northern English working-class communities (Sillitoe was from Nottingham, Braine from Bradford). Sillitoe and Braine, along with other writers such as John Osborne and Kingsley Amis, were described as 'angry young men', although they personally did not encourage the use of this title. It came from the content of their work which, in the Fifties and early Sixties, focused on the prevailing feeling of disillusionment within certain sectors of post-war Britain. Novels such as *Saturday Night and Sunday Morning* especially dealt with the lack of opportunities available for the country's working-class population.

At the heart of these works were young working-class anti-heroes (Joe Lampton, Arthur Seaton, Colin Smith), who were themselves 'angry' and who railed against their respective lots in life. This style of leading male had first been given voice by John Osborne's character, Jimmy Porter, in the 1956 play *Look Back in Anger*. Such young 'rebels' would typically be in conflict with their elders, bosses and supposed 'superiors', while sex (still very much a taboo subject at the time) across the marital and class borders was a major component of the storyline of both *Room at the Top* and *Saturday Night and Sunday Morning*. What 'love' there was in such dramas was usually doomed, hard fought for and decidedly unromantic.

During the Sixties, this genre of gritty, sharply observed social drama not only reflected the emergence of working-class culture as a wellspring for creativity, but it also placed the north of England itself as the ideal setting for a series of realistic dramatic motion pictures with 'something to say'.

It was from this wellspring of working-class dramas that the film for which Paul McCartney wrote his first theme tune came.

In an article penned by journalist Andy Gray in a late December edition of the *New Musical Express*, Paul explained how he had become involved in the project: "It was most unglamorous really. I rang our NEMS office and said I would like to write a film theme, not a score, just a theme. John was away filming so I had time to do it. NEMS fixed it for me to do the theme for *The Family Way*."[9]

Gray's article was entitled 'Paul's Film Music Causes a Panic' and was published to coincide with the release of two separate single versions of Paul's music from the film: 'Love in the Open Air' is backed with 'Theme from The Family Way'.*

(*Much later in an interview for The Beatles Anthology, *Paul gave a slightly different explanation for how his involvement in the film came about: "I got an offer through the Boulting Brothers for him (George Martin) and me to do some film music for* The Family Way. *I had a look at the film and thought it was great. I still do. It's very powerful and emotional, soppy, but good for its time."*)[10]

Although he was away in Spain filming, there is no doubt John Lennon was fully aware of Paul's intended project and had a decidedly different take on how the composing for *The Family Way* was going to pan out.

Long before Paul spoke to *NME*'s Andy Gray in December '66, on 29 October 1966, USA DJ, Fred Robbins, visited John Lennon in Carboneras, Spain. There, on the set of *How I Won the War (not Way)*, he recorded a 14-minute interview for broadcast in the USA. During their conversation Robbins inquired if John knew when the Beatles would be doing another tour, to which Lennon replied: "No idea. I know we've got music to write, as soon as we get back. And Paul's just signed *us* up to write the music for a film. So I suppose it's off the plane and into bed and – knock knock knock, 'Get up and write some songs'."[11]

John's comments were supported by an article in an October 1966 edition of *NME*:

"When he returns from filming in Spain next month, John Lennon will help his songwriting partner Paul McCartney to score the new Hayley Mills film, All in Good Time *[the stage play title for* The Family Way*] … The picture's alternative working title of* Wedlocked *has now been dropped, the producers having settled on* All in Good Time. *Paul is believed to* *be already working on the music."*[12]

Of course, by the time John returned to the UK, Paul *had* already begun work on the music. He'd 'written' the film's titular theme tune. That he had gone ahead and done so without him quite upset John Lennon, although at the time he did not say so directly to Paul. Apparently it became an early wedge (as perceived by John) between the two Beatles, of which Paul only became fully aware long after John's death. "I was told recently by Yoko that one of the things that hurt John over the years was me going off and doing *The Family Way*."[13]

Instead of voicing his hurt at the time, John had simply held back and said nothing. As Paul reflected: "He would have had his suit of armour on and said: 'No I don't mind.'"[14]

At the time Paul felt it was a great opportunity for himself – one not to be missed – and very much in the prevailing spirit of them both doing their own things outside the Beatles. "My reasoning would be that at exactly the same time he went off to make a film. He wrote his books ... It was in the spirit of all that. But what I didn't realise was that this was the first time one of us had done it on songs. John would write a book and I was supposed not to be jealous, which I wasn't ... But I didn't realise he made a distinction between all those solo things and actually writing music because this was the first time one of us had done it in film scoring. I suppose what I should have said was: 'I'd like to write it with John,' and then that would have been ok."[15]

Based on an original TV play written by Bolton-based author Bill Naughton, *The Family Way* was a warmer, more reflective, humorous piece of work than its other grittier 'kitchen sink' northern counterparts. The leading male character Arthur Fitton (Hywel Bennett) is more sensitive than angry. In essence it is a comedy of manners, a love story full of northern wit and wisdom whose characters are well grounded and earthy. The film's theme also reflected (albeit largely through double entendre) the decade's changing, more 'open' attitude towards sex, as it contrasted the differing outlooks on life and love of those who found themselves on opposite sides of the generation gap.

The Family Way, Feature Film
The Boulting Brothers' Production THE FAMILY WAY
Directed by: Roy Boulting
Screenplay by Bill Naughton after his stage play *All in Good Time*
Adapted by Roy Boulting and Jeffrey Dell
Programme content copyright 1966 Janbox/Boulting Brothers
Although most of the location filming took place in Rochdale, additional scenes were shot in Bolton and Slough and some indoor scenes were filmed at Shepperton Studios.
Duration: 1 hour, 55 minutes
Colour: Colour by Eastman Colour
Genre: Comedy/Drama/Romance
Country: UK
Language: English
Made at: Shepperton Studios, Surrey
Certification: X
Music: Composed by Paul McCartney
Music: Supervised and Orchestrations Arranged by George Martin
Recorded in November 1966 at CTS (Cine-Tele Sound) Studios, 49–53 Kensington Gardens Square, Bayswater, City of Westminster, Royal Borough of Kensington and Chelsea, central London.
UK Premiere: Sunday 18 December 1966 at London's Warner Theatre
UK General Release: 6 January 1967
USA Release: 28 June 1967 (New York City, New York)
Awards: Ivor Novello Award for Best Instrumental Theme 1967: Paul McCartney

National Film Critics Awards for Best Supporting Actress 1967: Marjorie Rhodes
Cast (principal characters):
Hayley Mills as Jenny Piper
Avril Angers as Liz Piper
John Comer as Leslie Piper
Wilfred Pickles as Uncle Fred
John Mills as Ezra Litton
Marjorie Rhodes as Lucy Fitton
Hywel Bennett as Arthur Fitton
Murray Head as Geoffrey Fitton
Barry Foster as Joe Thompson
Liz Fraser as Molly Thompson
Setting: A town in Lancashire
Storyline: After the wedding and wedding reception, newly weds Arthur Litton and Jenny Piper want nothing more than to be alone. They have just one night to spend together at home before winging their way to a much anticipated honeymoon in Spain. That one night is spoiled by a practical joke that misfires. This calamity is followed immediately by another when the trip to Spain is cancelled, leaving the young couple with no choice but to stay with Arthur's parents (Ezra and Lucy) in their small house where privacy and intimacy do not coincide. The couple's wish to consummate their marriage is not only interrupted but their failure to do so soon becomes common knowledge beyond the home. The film traces Arthur and Lucy's attempts to deal with this embarrassing and difficult situation while fending off the attention and not always well-intentioned advice of family and friends.

All details re: The Family Way available on the BFI organisation website

1 2, 3, 4, 5, 6, 7 & 8 John Lennon and Paul McCartney recorded on Saturday 6 August 1966 speaking to Keith Fordyce for the BBC Light Programme special *The Lennon & McCartney Songbook,* broadcast on 29 August 1964.
9 Paul McCartney interviewed by Andy Gray for the *New Musical Express*, published week ending Saturday, December 24, 1966.
10 *The Beatles Anthology*, the Beatles, (Cassell & Co, 2000), Paul McCartney p.234.
11 John Lennon, interview w/ Fred Robbins. (October 29th, 1966), 'Somewhere In Spain'
Transcript: 'The Beatles Ultimate Experiences', www.beatlesinterviews.org
'a moral to this song' -amoralto.tumblr.com
12 John Lennon quoted in the New Musical Express, October 1966.
13, 14 & 15 *McCartney: Yesterday and Today*, Ray Coleman (Boxtree, 1995) p.102–3.

Chapter 85:
1966, Part 7 – GEORGE MARTIN AND THE SAGA OF THE TUDOR MINSTRELS

Paul has never hidden his admiration for what he describes as the 'craft' of great songwriting partnerships, such as Rodgers and Hammerstein, or solo composers such as Cole Porter, who could turn their gift to writing music for a variety of forms such as musicals and film scores.

It was therefore no surprise that he had been drawn to writing a film score, especially as he could call on the great talent of George Martin to write and orchestrate what he could hear but which Paul himself was unable to transcribe.

Paul composed the opening 'Theme from *The Family Way*' on piano, but because he could not write music (which he compared to being like 'Braille') he turned to George Martin for help to transcribe the notes and arrange the melody. "He is the interpreter, I play themes and chords on piano or guitar. He gets it down on paper. I talk about the idea I have for instrumentation then he works out the arrangement."[1]

The initial theme Paul played to Martin on piano comprised just 15 seconds of music. Martin then went away to arrange this simple piece of work for a variety of instruments. In an *NME* article, w/ending 24 December 1966, entitled 'Paul's Film Music Causes a Panic',* Martin explained to writer Andy Gray his role in the recording of the score: "I jotted the notes down and then got to work on the arrangements. I brought in, as Paul agreed, a church organ, a bit of a brass band with tuba to the fore, a string quartet flavour, and percussion, and merged the lot to play the 'Theme of *The Family Way*'."[2]

(*In the same article Andy Gray described Paul's 'Theme From The Family Way' as possessing "a dour mournful dirge like dignity to it which is quite catching".)

George Martin: "We worked together on this. Paul couldn't score but he had very good ideas. It was a Northern town film, a domestic drama. He wanted to use the sound of a northern band and was thinking in terms of a brass band. The opening titles were of this ilk. We had a little march which I scored for brass band."[3]

Paul particularly wanted brass-band music to feature in his score for *The Family Way*. Although he and the Beatles were experimenting with many forms of music, he considered brass band was, as he expressed it, "a little too Northern and 'Hovis'" for them. Nevertheless, Paul's love of brass bands had not abated from his childhood when his father Jim had played trumpet in a dance band. *The Family Way* provided him with a perfect opportunity to create music that carried echoes of the music of his childhood … and in doing so he enjoyed himself immensely.

Paul's family affiliation with and affection for brass bands would surface again when, in 1968, he would be asked to compose a theme tune for a TV series set in Yorkshire. Paul's father James had played trumpet ('until his teeth gave out'), his brother Jack played trombone and grandfather Joe McCartney played E-flat bass (a large brass tuba-like instrument). "My dad would take us to brass band concerts in the band shelter in the park, and we would sit and listen, and I would always like that. It was very northern."[4]

The composing and recording processes of Martin and McCartney for *The Family Way* came to a temporary halt when George embarked on a cruise aboard the *Queen Mary* to New York, while Paul went on vacation to France where he linked up with Mal Evans from where the two drove through Spain and from there went on safari in Kenya.

(Whilst away 'solo' on vacation and to liberate himself from fan recognition, Paul adopted various disguises which proved quite successful. While flying home with Mal from Nairobi to London, he began to work on the concept of 'disguise' to incorporate the group as a whole. If, Paul contemplated, they each adopted a different disguise it may open up the Beatles to new ideas and opportunities. On board the plane, as this germ of an idea took shape, Mal briefly forgot what the S and P stood for on the small salt and pepper sachets served with the airline meal, to which Paul joked back 'Sergeant Pepper'…)

Two weeks later, on Paul's return to London, George Martin told Andy Gray of *NME*, "I realised we needed a love theme for the centre of the picture, something wistful. I told Paul and he said he'd compose something. I waited, but nothing materialised."[5]

As time was of the essence and the release date for the film was fast approaching, Martin was compelled into action to persuade Paul to deliver the love theme: "'Love in the Open Air' was the love theme … and he didn't give it to me. I got very frustrated because I had a deadline to meet. I remember going round to the house in St. John's Wood where he was working with John on another song. I said, 'Paul, I need this and I need it now!' I said, 'If you don't give me what I'm looking for I'll write something myself and I'll put it in'. He looked at John and said, 'I'd better do something, hadn't I?', and there and then he wrote the basic theme of 'Love in the Open Air'. It was beautiful, wistful, it just came out of him. We put it in the film and I made a single out of it. It was very successful. It was a very poignant film and quite unlike most of the things the Beatles did. I enjoyed it, it was great."[6]

Despite the impending deadline and while, at the same time, working with the Beatles at Abbey Road on the recording of 'Strawberry Fields Forever' over five sessions that spanned some three days and nights, George also scored Paul's new film melody at CTS Studios in London. (CTS studios is where, earlier that year, the Beatles had taped overdubs for the Shea Stadium recordings.)

McCartney and Martin arranged the music together in styles that encompassed a brass band and Duane Eddy-style guitar. In these different styles the theme is heard throughout the film.

Martin completed his recordings of the film's music just two weeks ahead of its premiere: Sunday 18 December 1966 at London's Warner Theatre.

THE FAMILY WAY (Original Soundtrack Album)
The George Martin Orchestra
Music composed by: Paul McCartney
Produced by George Martin
Recorded: November 1966 at CTS Studios, London
Released in the UK in both mono and stereo: 6 January 1967 on Decca SKL 4847
Released in the USA: 12 June 1967 on London MS 82007
Both in the UK and USA the OST albums failed to chart
Side One (13:09)
cut one: 2:07
cut two: 1:10
cut three: 1:00
cut four: 1:28
cut five: 3:26
cut six: 3:58 'Love in the Open Air'
Side Two (11:10)
cut one: 2:09
cut two: 1:19
cut three: 1:03
cut four: 1:46
cut five: 1:00
cut six: 2:51
cut seven: 1:02

Twenty-four minutes, 19 seconds of music in total.

For most Beatles fans and historians George Harrison's film soundtrack album *Wonderwall Music* released in 1968 represents the first 'solo' release by a Beatle, despite *The Family Way* preceding it (it had been recorded and released in 1967). The distinction is arrived at because, despite Paul composing the themes for the music of *The Family Way*, and the prominence of his name on the album cover, Paul himself did not appear on the album. He and Martin arranged the pieces, but the production and conducting had been done by George Martin. On the other hand, George Harrison not only directed and produced *Wonderwall Music*, he also performed on some tracks.

For this reason, *Wonderwall Music* is considered more of a 'solo' piece than *The Family Way*.

For the purposes of this book this distinction allows Paul's music for *The Family Way* to therefore be considered as a Beatle's 'giveaway'.

Paul summed up his work on *The Family Way* soundtrack with these words: "The George Martin thing, 'Love in the Open Air', I was asked to do some music for a Boulting Brothers film. They were very famous directors/producers of British films, Elstree/Pinewood kind of thing. They had Hayley and John Mills and Hywel Bennett in a film … and so they asked me to do it. I enlisted George Martin because I couldn't have actually scored it, but I could make the tunes up and add the inspiration. So I did this thing called 'Love in the Open Air' which was for a love scene in the middle of the film where they're walking around the town, the young couple, and it's a nice little scene. It actually got an Ivor Novello for Best Film that year."[7]

Paul was particularly pleased to win a prestigious Ivor Novello award for the score. (He also let on that 'Love in the Open Air' could have had lyrics when he commented: "Johnny Mercer was nearly going to put lyrics to it, but I didn't know who he was. Later I realised, 'Oh, that Johnny Mercer! You mean the greatest lyricist on the planet!' I should have done that. Never mind – it fell through – but it was good fun doing the music." Oops! [8]

After all the work and creative energy George Martin poured into *The Family Way*, it must have been somewhat galling for him to see Paul walk away with the award and garner all the acclaim while he was not personally acknowledged for his huge contribution to the work. This lack of music industry recognition followed an earlier oversight Martin had endured concerning his contribution to the recording of the music for the soundtrack. A debacle surrounding the release of a single culled from the film's soundtrack album that did not sit right with him …

In the first instance, George received a 'Conducted and Produced' credit for the music for the original soundtrack album for Tudor Films, the Boulting Brothers company which made the picture and who had assured George the recordings would only be issued on LP.

With this in mind, Martin had decided he would release a single under his own name as the 'George Martin Orchestra' featuring music he had recorded for the soundtrack.

Unfortunately for George, this agreement changed significantly when the Decca company bought the music rights from the Boulting Brothers and had different ideas on how the music from the soundtrack was to be marketed, promoted and released.

To cash in and coincide with the London premiere of the film, Decca decided that they *would* issue a single comprising 'Love in the Open Air' backed by 'Theme from *The Family Way*' which they would release under the name of 'The Tudor Minstrels. These were the musicians who had recorded the soundtrack and had been conducted by George Martin. On the album sleeve, however, they had been credited as 'The George Martin Orchestra', which was not now going to be the case on the single.

With good reason, Decca's decision irritated, wrong-footed, and upset George Martin and his plans to release (on the United Artists label) his own single version of 'Love in the

Open Air' with a B-side featuring 'Theme from *The Family Way*'.

His justifiable ire stemmed from the fact that the very orchestra he had conducted would reap the acclaim for any success the single gained, but by being called 'The Tudor Minstrels' any mention of his name was excluded. Importantly this effectively denied him from sharing in any financial success the Decca single might accrue from physical sales, even though he was responsible for it. (He would, of course, have received a fee for his production and conducting work.)

Not only that, but Decca could move very quickly to release a single because the Tudor Minstrels' versions were already in the can courtesy of George Martin, whereas George himself had not even started his intended recordings with his own orchestra. As a result, Martin protested to Decca and had the copyright delayed. This action effectively thwarted their intention to release the Minstrels' version to coincide with the very day of the film's premiere, but it did so only by a week.

For Martin this was all he required: he sprang into action, speedily recorded his own versions of the tunes and his single, released under his own name, was in the shops on the very same day (23 December 1966 on the United Artists label) as the Tudor Minstrels' version also hit the counters. A battle for chart success had begun!

It was to this situation that the word 'Panic' referred in Andy Gray's *NME* headline. His report explained how, for the first time in his career, George Martin found himself in the embarrassing position of being in competition with himself as two rival labels released records, both of which he had arranged, conducted and produced and which featured the very same tunes, but only one of which would possibly benefit him financially (other than his session fee) if it became a hit.

When Gray had inquired of Martin why he had felt the need to release his own single, George explained, "The film soundtrack music fitted the visual film, but wasn't quite commercial enough to be issued as a single."[9]

As a consequence, Martin explained that on his own version he had speeded the music up a bit to make it more acceptable to buyers.

In the same interview Martin also candidly said that he hoped his version would prove more popular than the Tudor Minstrels' soundtrack version, because it was going out under his name and he would receive more money which, to most people, seemed perfectly reasonable considering all the work he had done on these tunes.

In support of his mentor, Paul expressed surprise at Decca's decision while at the same time pointing out he had no say in the matter and never interfered with the business side of things.

As it came to pass, neither single made any impression on the record charts anywhere, but at least George had made his point.

GEORGE MARTIN AND HIS ORCHESTRA
LOVE IN THE OPEN AIR **(2:18)**
(from film *The Family Way*)
(Paul McCartney)
Northern Songs, NCB
United Artists UP 1165
B-side: ***THEME FROM THE FAMILY WAY*** **(2:05)**
(from film *The Family Way*)
(Paul McCartney)
Northern Songs, NCB

Both sides: Produced by A.I.R. (London) i.e., George Martin

Recorded: During the morning of 15 December 1966 at EMI Studios, Abbey Road, London
Released in the UK: 23 December 1966
Released in the USA: 24 April 1967 on United Artists UA 50148 with a different B-Side: 'Bahama Sound'

THE TUDOR MINSTRELS
LOVE IN THE OPEN AIR
(The soundtrack theme from *The Family Way*)
(Paul McCartney)
Northern Songs
Decca F.12536
B-SIDE: *A THEME FROM THE FAMILY WAY*
(Paul McCartney)
Northern Songs
Both sides: Supervised and Orchestrations Arranged by George Martin
Recorded at CTS Studios, London, November 1966

Released in the UK: 23 December 1966 (delayed a week from 16 December 1966) but did not chart

Despite the spat that preceded the release of these singles, neither charted in either the UK or the USA (nor anywhere else for that matter).

In the end-of-year edition of the new-look *Disc and Music Echo* on 31 December 1966, in her review of that week's latest singles, reviewer Penny Valentine had this to say of George Martin's and the Tudor Minstrels' versions of 'Love in the Open Air': "Two versions of the pretty misty Paul McCartney music for the Hayley Mills film. A delicate piece of music like wet leaves and warm forests. George Martin's version is clearer and really rather better arranged than the other which is pretty but too muzzy."[10]

'Muzzy'?

A week earlier in the same publication, in his review of the *The Family Way* itself, film critic Mike Ledgerwood opined, "All the accolades must undoubtedly be poured on the head of John Mills, Hayley's father-in-law in this parochial parody of young married life in a Northern industrial town…"[11a]

Ledgerwood applauded not only John Mills' performance, but admired Hayley in her first major adult role and the script which he described as "excellent".[11b]

Of the music he had this to say: "One can't help feeling that Paul had an easy time composing the music … the score isn't the most instantly noticeable thing about it. No doubt it will become an extremely popular and much-requested theme as the film does the rounds, but it had a definite undercurrent of that lilting melody 'Nature Boy' with which Bobby Darin* had a lot of success."[11c]

(*Bobby Darin had reached number 24 in the UK singles chart with 'Nature Boy' in the summer of 1961.)

The lack of interest in either George Martin's or the Tudor Minstrels' singles was not quite the end of the story, however …

ADDENDUM 1: *The Singular Adventures of 'LOVE IN THE OPEN AIR'*
George Martin and the Tudor Minstrels were not the only ones who believed that 'Love in the Open Air had the potential to become a hit single, especially as it possessed the 'magic' of a Paul McCartney tagline and neither side had been recorded either by him or the Beatles. Plus, it was a tune that was receiving much attention as it was the theme from a brand new film, The Family Way that had opened in both the UK and North America. Thus it proved irresistible for other chart hopefuls, and so it was that later in 1967 both

George Martin's and the Tudor Minstrels' versions were joined by other contenders looking for a hit ...

**SOUNDS SENSATIONAL
with THE MIKE SAMMES SINGERS**
LOVE IN THE OPEN AIR **(2:31)**
(film *The Family Way*)
(McCartney)
HMV POP 1584
B-SIDE featuring only SOUNDS SENSATIONAL:
Night Cry
(Woodman)
Both sides producer: Walter J. Ridley
UK release: 3 March 1967. It did not chart.

Walter J. Ridley was one of the great UK record producers of the Fifties and Sixties. He was appointed by EMI to build the HMV ('His Master's Voice') label from being purely a classical music outlet to embrace a wider range of British artists. His first notable signing was Alma Cogan (who became a good friend of John Lennon). In 1959 he signed Johnny Kidd and the Pirates for whom he produced the sensational 'Shakin' All Over' which reached number 1 in the UK. Another notable hit that he produced was the Swinging Blue Jeans version of Chan Romero's classic 'Hippy Hippy Shake' which spent 17 weeks on the UK singles chart peaking at number 2 in late January 1964 and at number 24 on 4 April 1964 in the USA.

(Food for thought: of all the singles that were recorded by groups from Liverpool, the Swinging Blue Jeans' version of 'Hippy Hippy Shake' is most probably the most redolent of the the 'Mersey Sound' or 'Mersey Beat' and one of the most enduring popular tunes of the mid-Sixties.)

The Walter J. Ridley-produced, Mike Sammes Singers version was also released in the USA in July 1967 on Capitol 5957, but with 'Someday Soon' (Head) on the B-side performed by Murray Head and the Blue Monks. This hybrid single was released by Capitol in Canada during early July 1967. Neither track was included in the London soundtrack album and so this was a unique 'soundtrack' 45 created especially for the Canadian market. Both sides had received individual releases in the UK, but here they were united as both sides of the same disc. Head's 'Some Day Soon' had earlier been released as the A-side of a single released on Columbia DB 8102 on 13 January 1967 and the Sammes Singers' had been issued on 3 March 1967.

Murray Head played the part of Geoffrey Fitton in The Family Way, the younger brother of main character Arthur Fitton played by Hywel Bennett. Head sang in the film (fronting the rock band who perform at the wedding reception) performing his self-penned song 'Someday Soon' (the third UK Tim Rice-produced single) in a style similar to the Zombies singer Colin Blunstone. Although he appeared in the film singing this song, it did not appear on the soundtrack album. www.idmb.com/thefamilyway

Almost at the same time, in the USA popular exponents of the 'Now Sound', the Brass Ring, felt the same way and gave 'Love in the Open Air' a loose-limbed, hip makeover and released it with an eye on the Hot 100.

**THE BRASS RING
featuring PHIL BODNER**
b. 13 June 1917, Waterbury, Connecticut, USA
d. 24 February 2008, New York City, New York, USA
***LOVE IN THE OPEN AIR* (2:39)**
(Paul McCartney)
Comet Music Corp. (ASCAP)
Dunhill D-4090
B-SIDE: Wait for Me
(Sid Cooper)
(From the Dunhill LP *The Dis-Advantages of You* – D-50017)
Both sides, Producer: Phil Bodner
Released: June 1967 in the USA where it failed to chart.

The Brass Ring were a group of American studio musicians led by Phil Bodner. In the New York Times obituary for Bodner, published on the 27 and 28 February 2008, they described him as "The musician's musician, master of twelve woodwind instruments. Virtuoso to the stars including Sinatra, Fitzgerald, Torme and many others..."

In the early 1950s, Bodner had played with Benny Goodman's small combo and would record with him in 1958. In the same year, Bodner recorded with Miles Davis and Gil Scott.

The excellent 'Space Age Pop' website (www.spaceagepop.com)[12] calls Bodner "the busiest reed man of the Space Age Pop era", noting that with the Brass Ring, Bodner "successfully adapted Herb Alpert's hugely successful Tijuana Brass sound by giving the melody to the reeds and loosening the rhythm to a light swing groove." This, the site says, resulted in what became the 'signature' sound of "the mid-late 1960s instrumental sound known as the 'Now Sound'".

In the mid-Sixties, the Brass Ring and Bodner scored several hits on the Billboard Adult Contemporary Chart and two on the Hot 100: 'The Phoenix Love Theme (Senza Fine)' spent nine weeks on the chart, peaking at number 32 on 7 May 1966 and 'The Dis-Advantages of You' reached number 36 on 11 March 1967 and spent seven weeks on the Hot 100.

Possibly the most obscure 1967 single release of 'Love in the Open Air' was by the **Casino Royales** (London Records HLU 10122) with a B-side written by Italian lyricist Alberto Testa and Italian composer Tony Renis, entitled 'When I Tell (That I Love You)'. Released in the UK on 31 March 1967 it also failed to ignite the singles chart here ... or anywhere else.

ADDENDUM 2: *George Martin, Paul McCartney and Harry Saltzman*
It seems appropriate that the last word on 'Love in the Open Air' should go to Sir George Martin: "When we did 'Love in the Open Air' if Paul had had the training he could have done the whole thing, I wouldn't have been needed. I said to him that he really ought to think about taking lessons in writing – and he did actually for a short time – and then gave it up. I said to him you have the imagination for orchestration but he said well I don't need to do it if I've got you. When it came to a later film, the Bond feature *Live and Let Die*, he wrote just the beginning of the song and that was it as far as he was concerned. I had to do the rest of the 55-minute score and I tried to persuade him to come down and meet the producer Harry Saltzman which he never did and which was a shame because it was a good film."*[13]

(*Sir George speculated that Paul's lack of interest in meeting Saltzman was because, on hearing the score, Saltzman had suggested the title song should be sung by Aretha Franklin.)

1 Paul McCartney, from *The Sunday Times*, 1969, Chip Madinger, sleeve notes for *The Family Way* CD release, Varése Sarabande, 2011.
2 & 9 George Martin as quoted in the *New Musical Express* feature 'Paul's Film Music Causes A Panic' by Andy Gray in the edition w/ending December 24, 1966.
3, 6 & 13 Sir George Martin in conversation with Bob Harris OBE and Colin Hall for the 2009 BBC Radio 2 documentary *The Songs the Beatles Gave Away*, written and narrated by Bob Harris, produced by Bob Harris and Trudie Myerscough-Harris for WBBC.
4 *Many Years from Now*, Barry Miles (Vintage, 1998) p.24.
5 George Martin as quoted in the *New Musical Express* feature 'Paul's Film Music Causes A Panic' by Andy Gray in the edition w/ending December 24, 1966).
7 Sir Paul McCartney in conversation with Bob Harris OBE and Colin Hall, *The Songs the Beatles Gave Away*, BBC Radio 2 (March 2009), written and narrated by Bob Harris produced by Bob Harris and Trudie Myerscough-Harris for WBBC.
8 *The Beatles Anthology*, the Beatles, (Cassell & Co, 2000) Paul McCartney, p.234.
10 *Disc and Music Echo*, 31 December 1966, Penny Valentine singles review, p.11.
11a, b, and c *Disc and Music Echo*, 24 December 1966, Mike Ledgerwood film review of *The Family Way*, p.16.
12 www.spaceagepop.com

Chapter 86:
1966, Part 8 – YOU CAN'T PLEASE EVERYBODY …
PAUL ON TRYING TO KEEP IT IN THE FAMILY (WAY)

According to Yoko Ono Lennon, the misunderstanding surrounding Paul's decision to work individually on the film score for *The Family Way* continued to niggle John Lennon for a considerable while after the event. Yoko informed Paul that by saying next to nothing to him at the time about what he apparently interpreted as a slight, John had brooded on it instead and allowed it to form a wedge between him and his co-writer and friend.

At the very time he was working on the score, it seems Paul was aware that his decision to compose the score on his own had created some tension between John and himself to the point he insisted on sharing the money he earned from doing so with John.

In a 1969 interview in *Melody Maker*, John told writer BP Fallon: "I copped money for *Family Way*, the film music that Paul wrote while I was out of the country making *How I Won the War*." John further elaborated: "I said to Paul, 'You'd better keep that,' and he said, 'Don't be soft.' It's the concept. We inspired each other so much in the early days. We write how we write now because of each other … I wouldn't write like I write now if it weren't for Paul, and he wouldn't write like he does if it weren't for me."[1]

Many years after her husband's death, Yoko Ono Lennon picked up on the perceived slight felt by John and talked to Paul about it. That Paul failed to see beyond Lennon's defensive passivity at the time and recognise he was upset and wished to be included was ultimately what, according to Yoko, upset John. Apparently John was secretly hoping Paul would have a change of heart and ask him to join him in the work.

There seems little doubt that the two friends did talk about it at the time, but equally it seems John kept his guard too high. For once the usually assertive Beatle covered up, allowing Paul to take his acceptance at face value.

Paul's inclusion of John on the royalty payment cheque surely signals that words had been passed and that Paul felt he needed to affect some sort of reconciliation with John over the matter. From what Yoko said, it appears the gesture did not heal the hurt. "It's funny because talking to Yoko recently, you know, you talk about all these things that happen way back in history. It turns out John was not pleased; but I didn't know 'til a year ago that he wasn't pleased. He always told me, 'Fine.' 'Cause he'd been acting in a film, he did a film called *How I Won the War*, so we started to do little solo things, just for a change, just for a break, and so I assumed, I asked him, 'Is it okay with you?' He said, 'Yeah, fine, fine'."[2]

Paul: "For me it was very interesting, because it allowed me to do something of my own … Because with the Beatles, it was a bit like a marriage. So it was quite good to just get away, do something of my own. I think that if I'd known John was disturbed by it, I would have just asked him to join me. We could have done it. It would have been no problem."[3]

Coming towards the end of 1966, and what had been a tumultuous and remarkable year for the Beatles as a group and as individuals, the premiere of *The Family Way* allowed Paul to publicly end the year in some style when he, his fiancée Jane Asher and George Martin, attended the star-studded premiere on Sunday 18 December 1966 at the Warner Theatre, London.

As has been mentioned, for Paul the icing on this first venture into the world of solo musicianship came in 1967 when he won an Ivor Novello Award for best film score. Maybe at the time this was just salt in the wound, another reason for John to feel miffed at

Paul for not having included him … whatever, the incident highlights the competitive edge between the two old friends when it came to writing music.

The Family Way apart … for all the psychological pounding, hurly-burly and bad vibes of touring the Philippines and the USA, ultimately 1966 caught the Beatles cresting a creative wave the like of which the world of pop music had never before experienced.

1966 was the year the long player record (LP) came into its own as the palette on which 'pop' musicians could express themselves beyond the confines of the three-minute single. Up to this point the single was a pop musician's key modus operandi, while LPs took a definite second place. 'Pop' singers and 'pop' groups were about hit singles, long players were more or less a marketing opportunity to milk extra income from the hits one more time. An LP was viewed by the record companies as a mere collection of one or two recent hits or A-sides, plus their B-sides accompanied by eight to ten other tunes that comprised an artist's stage favourites, covers or songs written simply to 'fill' the space ('fillers') on the record. In the main, a long player record was a unit shifter that stood firmly in the shadows of the money-minting hit single. Fans did not really expect the quality of the supporting material on an LP to match the quality of the hits: had they done so they would have been issued as A-sides in their own right.

From the start, the Beatles as recording artists had challenged the premise that the quality of the fillers on their LPs need not match that of the hits. Their long players were full of quality songs that could have been stand-alone hit singles for them and because of this, almost from the word go, their LPs were raided by other artists for exactly that reason.

Even by the Beatles high standards 1966 was a game changer. *Revolver* was their most accomplished and inventive LP to date. A superbly sequenced collection of memorable songs that simply took the breath away the album was inspired and, in itself, complete. A natural and seamless progression from the previous year's marvellous *Rubber Soul*, as such it left mere singles as a means of artistic expression in the shade.

That they had risen to such heights had a great deal to do with the influence of the principal songwriter/composer of leading American harmony group, The Beach Boys: Brian Wilson. Wilson's *Pet Sounds* and his incredible melodic gifts had upped the album as a canvas on which to express a group's music sufficiently enough for Paul McCartney to want to emulate them. Elsewhere the recently 'gone electric' former folkster Bob Dylan had released the incredible game-changing double album *Blonde On Blonde*. A rollercoaster of imagination, intoxicating lyricism and stunning tunes it served notice on three minutes as the norm for the length of a 'pop' song while its mind-blowing literacy called time on simple rhyming 'moon in June' love song-style lyrics as the staple fare for a 'pop' record. From the start Dylan had revolutionised the subject matter of song lyrics to show they could be about something more than girls, boys, cars and blue suede shoes. The Beatles were already devotees.

The Rolling Stones proved themselves well attuned to the prevailing zeitgeist when they released *Aftermath* in April 1966 several months ahead of *Revolver*. All the songs on this, their fourth UK long player, had been composed by Mick Jagger and Keith Richards and showed that stylistically the duo were well capable of pushing the envelope, although lyrically, in some instances, the attitude towards women made for uncomfortable if not unpleasant reading and listening, such as 'Under My Thumb'.

From now on, the prevailing jargon in popular music also changed. The Beatles, the Rolling Stones, Kinks, Bob Dylan, and Jimi Hendrix were no longer strictly 'pop stars', but were morphing into 'rock musicians'. This change in artistic title was key, for it signalled the seriousness with which their music was now held. 'Pop star' was fast becoming a label used to describe artists for whom the hit single remained their focus, the Top 10 remained their market, younger teens their audience, the journey into 'all-round entertainers' most likely their goal. 'Pop stars' by definition were lightweight, throwaway, whereas 'rock music' and 'rock musicians' were something altogether more serious and meaningful.

Rock musicians were viewed as more musically gifted, virtuosic, and possibly (in some cases, not all!) more lyrically demanding. What pop stars sold was of the moment, while rock musicians were producing something more substantial … or so the theory went. One thing for sure was it bred elitism and gave ageing teens an extended adolescence in which to indulge their dedication to the cause of rock and roll. As this distinction evolved, so LPs became 'albums' not merely 'LPs'. It was a subtle change in name that signified an artist's ascendance into producing a serious body of work of greater artistic consequence than singles. Rock musicians looked now towards the album chart to better reflect their importance and relevance and success as artists and, in turn, albums began to sell in much greater numbers.

Whether this was a good or bad thing depends upon your point of view or of the artist under discussion. For some, the 'album' became an indulgence on which all manner of musical misdemeanours could be committed in the name of 'art', while others soared, clearly liberated from the confines of the 'single'. Brian Wilson, Ray Davies and Bob Dylan were prime examples of those who soared. Whatever, it changed the dynamic of the music industry and gave most artists greater musical freedom.

Never let it be said, however, that composing and creating great 45s is easy – it isn't. If it was we'd all do it and be number 1. It is an art form in itself. Take a moment to think of your favourite all-time hit single, play it loud and allow yourself to be blown away all over again.

This shift in importance from singles to albums (in terms of revenue generated) would be *the* defining element of Seventies popular music culture.

THE UK'S TOP 30 MOST POPULAR RECORDS OF 1966
01 Jim Reeves: Distant Drums
02 Frank Sinatra: Strangers in the Night
03 The Beatles: Yellow Submarine / Eleanor Rigby
04 The Four Tops: Reach Out I'll Be There
05 Nancy Sinatra: These Boots Are Made for Walkin'
06 The Walker Brothers: The Sun Ain't Gonna Shine Anymore
07 Tom Jones: Green Grass of Home
08 The Kinks: Sunny Afternoon
09 Troggs: With a Girl Like You
10 Manfred Mann: Pretty Flamingo
11 Herb Alpert & the Tijuana Brass: Spanish Flea
12 The Beach Boys: Good Vibrations
13 The Beatles: Day Tripper / We Can Work It Out
14 The Beach Boys: God Only Knows
15 The Spencer Davis Group: Keep on Running
16 The Beatles: Paperback Writer
17 The Mindbenders: Groovy Kind of Love
18 Chris Farlowe: Out of Time
19 The Small Faces: All or Nothing
20 The Beach Boys: Sloop John B
21 The Spencer Davis Group: Somebody Help Me
22 Dusty Springfield: You Don't Have to Say You Love Me
23 The Overlanders: Michelle
24 The New Vaudeville Band: Winchester Cathedral
25 Dave Dee, Dozy, Beaky Mick and Tich: Hold Tight
26 Roy Orbison: Too Soon to Know
27 Los Bravos: Black Is Black
28 The Who: I'm a Boy
29 Dave Dee, Dozy, Beaky, Mick and Tich: Bend It!
30 The Rolling Stones: Paint It, Black

1 John Lennon, interview with B.P. Fallon for *Melody Maker*,1969, source: *The Beatles Press Reports* by W. Fraser Sandercombe (Collector's Guide Publishing, Inc., 2007).
2 Paul McCartney, interview w/ Michel Laverdière. (23 May 1995), source: 'a moral to this song' – amoralto.tumblr.com
3 Paul McCartney film clip from 1998 sourced/entitled 'A&E: Paul McCartney's Musical Ways',
(1998) amoralto.tumblr.com 'a moral to this song' .

Chapter 87:
1967, Part 1 – 'SERGEANT PEPPER' AND FRIENDS

1967 took the musically liberating vibe of '66 and upped the ante several notches. It was the year that the doors came off their hinges as musicians seized the opportunity to liberate themselves, their minds and their music. From now on everything was possible.

To keep that creative flag waving and ensure their 'hip' credentials, artists took mind-expanding drugs in copious amounts. Grass and cocaine had always been part of the music scene, but now they were joined by the decade-defining hallucinogenic 'LSD' (lysergic acid diethylamide). The time had arrived for rock music to take a trip inside its own head to discover just what lay there and turn any cosmic revelations and visions experienced therein into great, inspirational music or, in some cases, the pretentious ramblings of someone out of their depth with nothing much to say of any interest or substance in the first place.

The Beatles were never out of their depth and they never stopped making great singles and albums.

As 1967 broke, they found themselves free to experiment and explore. Their teeny-bop image had finally been cast aside and with great aplomb they had successfully navigated the tricky transition from 'pop' stars to serious artists/rock musicians. Along the way their fans did not desert them. Revered by their peers, critics and fans, they remained 'cool' and 'hip' and hugely popular. Since 1963, they were the kings of their world, one step ahead of the rest: where they led, others followed.

As ever, Mark Lewisohn says it best: "They were now four self-possessed and financially secure young men, and they spoke for youth because they were a part of youth themselves. In January, as they set about continuing the recording of their next album, John and Ringo were still only 26, Paul 24 and George 23."[1]

Of course, the album they were working on as 1967 dawned would become the one and only *Sergeant Pepper's Lonely Hearts Club Band*. On release it almost instantly became the most celebrated music album (any genre, any artist) of all time. Just sitting at home listening to it in the privacy of your own living room was an event. From the astonishing artwork by Peter Blake that adorned its cover, to the final lingering power chord of 'A Day in the Life', *Sergeant Pepper* revolutionised popular music. It felt like the beginning of a new world.

It would not be a record that they ever toured or played 'live' in front of an audience. They had transcended the need to always 'promote product' by going on the road or appearing on TV. In turn, this liberated the group to become more adventurous in the arrangements they wanted for their new songs. They did not have to concern themselves with how a song could be played 'live' or toured … because it wasn't going to be.

In the ten years from being Quarry Men to becoming members of Sergeant Pepper's Lonely Hearts Club Band, from playing simple homemade and acoustic instruments, to calling upon orchestras, sitars and synthesisers to colour and texture their songs, the Beatles had made a quantum creative leap.

1967 has gone down in history as the epitome of what the Sixties was all about (which in itself is the subject for unending debate). As a whole, the year itself will forever be associated with the flowering of psychedelia, LSD, grass, taking a trip, hippies, the continuing war in Vietnam, San Francisco, the Monterey Pop Festival and the 'Summer of Love'.

Musically, *Sergeant Pepper* towered above all else that was released that year, but it wasn't the only record released in 1967 that caused ears to pop and heads to turn. Album-wise, 1967 was notable for some other *very* remarkable, groundbreaking releases, including:

'The Doors' The Doors, 'Between The Buttons' The Rolling Stones, 'The Supremes Sing Holland–Dozier–Holland' The Supremes, 'Miles Smiles' Miles Davis, 'Surrealistic Pillow' Jefferson Airplane, 'More Than A New Discovery' Laura Nyro, 'Younger Than Yesterday' The Byrds, 'Hello, I'm Dolly' Dolly Parton, 'A Hard Road' John Mayall & The Bluesbreakers, 'Images' The Walker Brothers, 'I'm A Lonesome Fugitive' Merle Haggard, 'I Never Loved a Man the Way I Love You' Aretha Franklin, 'Matthew And Son' Cat Stevens, 'The Velvet Underground & Nico' The Velvet Underground & Nico, 'King & Queen' Otis Redding & Carla Thomas, 'The Grateful Dead' The Grateful Dead, 'Nina Simone Sings The Blues' Nina Simone, 'James Brown Sings Raw Soul' James Brown, 'Mellow Yellow' Donovan, 'Waylon Sings Ol' Harlan' Waylon Jennings, 'The Electric Prunes' The Electric Prunes, 'Tim Hardin 2' Tim Hardin, 'Electric Music For The Mind And Body' Country Joe and the Fish, 'Are You Experienced' The Jimi Hendrix Experience, 'Headquarters' The Monkees, 'Absolutely Free' The Mothers Of Invention, 'Small Faces' Small Faces, 'Make Way For Willie Nelson' Willie Nelson, 'Moby Grape' Moby Grape, 'Evolution' The Hollies, 'Super Psychedelics' The Ventures, 'Bee Gees' 1st' Bee Gees, 'The 5000 Spirits or the Layers of the Onion' The Incredible String Band, 'Canned Heat' Canned Heat, 'Reach Out' The Four Tops, 'The Sound of Wilson Pickett' Wilson Pickett, 'The Piper at the Gates of Dawn' Pink Floyd, 'Big Brother and the Holding Company' Big Brother and the Holding Company, 'Born Under a Bad Sign' Albert King, 'Vanilla Fudge' Vanilla Fudge, 'Something Else by The Kinks' The Kinks, 'Scott' Scott Walker, 'Smiley Smile' The Beach Boys, 'Blowin' Your Mind!' Van Morrison, 'Procol Harum' Procol Harum, 'Safe as Milk' Captain Beefheart, 'Soul Men' Sam & Dave, 'Where Am I Going?' Dusty Springfield, 'Chelsea Girl' Nico, 'Ten Years After' Ten Years After, 'Gorilla' Bonzo Doo-Dah Dog Band, 'Wildflowers' Judy Collins, 'Forever Changes' Love, 'Days of Future Passed' The Moody Blues, 'Disraeli Gears' Cream, 'Axis: Bold as Love' The Jimi Hendrix Experience, 'Mr. Fantasy' Traffic, 'The Trip' Electric Flag, 'Their Satanic Majesties Request' The Rolling Stones, 'The Who Sell Out' The Who, 'John Wesley Harding' Bob Dylan and 'Songs of Leonard Cohen' Leonard Cohen.

That's a comprehensive list of sorts, one that someone else may write very differently, but I hope it captures the flavour and sheer diversity of the year. As can be seen, 1967 saw significant new artists such as Jimi Hendrix, Pink Floyd and Leonard Cohen making their debut.

Despite the ascendance of the 'album', singles had not gone away and the worldwide big hit singles of 1967 were *very* big indeed. They included 'A Whiter Shade of Pale' by Procol Harum, 'I'm a Believer' by the Monkees, 'All You Need Is Love' by the Beatles, and 'Light My Fire' by the Doors. In the UK, it was notably the year of two great summer hits: 'Waterloo Sunset' and 'Itchycoo Park' by the Kinks and Small faces, respectively. Meanwhile, songs that, in different ways, caught the zeitgeist of the USA's 'Summer of Love' were 'San Francisco (Be Sure to Wear Flowers in Your Hair)' by Scott McKenzie, 'White Rabbit' by Jefferson Airplane and 'San Franciscan Nights' by Eric Burdon and the Animals. The UK's growing love affair with soul music and Tamla Motown included the hits 'Bernadette' by the Four Tops, 'Jimmy Mack' by Martha Reeves and the Vandellas, Arthur Conley's 'Sweet Soul Music', Sam and Dave's 'Soul Man' and 'I Second That Emotion' by Smokey Robinson and the Miracles, while the title of the Supremes' 'The Happening' seems well in touch with the dominant vibe of the year, but in truth was more a reflection on a broken love affair than any acid-induced experience.

And for those who weren't there … it truly was as mind blowing as it reads.

---

1 Mark Lewisohn, *The Complete Beatles Chronicle* (The Chancellor Press, 1996) p.236.

Chapter 88:
1967, Part 2 – MUSIC THE BEATLES RECORDED AND GAVE AWAY NEVER TO BE HEARD AGAIN …

1967
Was the year when … Rolling Stone magazine was founded … China announced it had the H-Bomb … The 'Human-Be-In' took place in Golden Gate Park in San Francisco which heralded the start of the 'Summer Of Love' … not long after Hippies were seen on the streets of Liverpool … Afghan coats, loon pants, tie-die grandad vests, sandals, beads and bells become fashion statements … the first heart transplant operation was carried out in South Africa … Muhammad Ali refused military service … Elvis married Priscilla … LSD was declared illegal in the USA … the Boston Strangler was convicted … in the UK the NHS Family Planning Act was passed which resulted in the oral contraceptive pill becoming more widely available …

For all that the success of the past four years had bestowed upon the Beatles, even by their own amazing standards, 1966 had been stupendous. 1967 beckoned with infinite possibilities. True to their serious work ethic, by Thursday 5 January the group were back in the studio working on a new song about their hometown: 'Penny Lane'.

The very next day, however, they turned their combined creative talents to something new and most definitely out of the ordinary. Paul's links to the burgeoning 'underground' had led him to accept an invitation to provide an 'effects tape' for the movement's 'The Million Volt Light and Sound Rave', aka 'The Carnival of Light Rave', an art festival organised by Binder, Edwards and Vaughan as a showcase for electronic music and light shows

This latest 'happening' was scheduled to take place at the Roundhouse over two Saturdays: 28 January and 4 February 1967. The posters for the event proclaimed Paul would be providing some specially composed music, as would 'Unit Delta Music Plus' (a group of 'early electronic music pioneers', whose numbers included Delia Derbyshire, Brian Hodgson from the BBC Radiophonic Workshop and fellow electronic artist Peter Zinovieff).

When designer David Vaughan had painted a psychedelic design on a piano owned by Paul, the Beatles had agreed to provide an experimental montage of sound for the forthcoming event.

Thus the Beatles gathered between 7pm and half past midnight at Abbey Road, so that Paul could supervise his bandmates as they assisted him in his sonic creation for the Carnival of Light Rave. It was a bizarre recording, utilising tapes and loops, voices, drums and electronic noises (think 'Revolution 9'). The complete piece lasted just less than 14 minutes and its composition in terms of what sounds it incorporated is well detailed and described by Mark Lewisohn (one of the few to have actually heard the piece) as "the longest uninterrupted Beatles recording to date, and it was the combination of a one-take basic track plus numerous overdubs, so that by its end it included distorted, hypnotic drum and organ sounds, a distorted lead guitar, the sound of a church organ, various effects (water-gargling was one) and, perhaps most intimidating of all, John and Paul screaming dementedly and bawling aloud random phrases like 'Are you alright!' and 'Barcelona!'"[1]

In 2008, Paul himself recalled his instructions to John, George and Ringo as to what he was after that evening in Abbey Road: "I said, 'All I want you to do is just wander around all the stuff, bang it, shout, play it, it doesn't need to make any sense. Hit a drum, then wander onto the piano, hit a few notes and just wander around' … So that's what we did and then put a bit of an echo on it. It's very free."[2]

Inspired by the experimental composers, John Cage and Karlheinz Stockhausen, to this very day Paul retains an affection for the track: "I like it because it's the Beatles free, going off-piste."[3]

Satisfied he had captured what he was after, later that same evening Paul delivered this asylum of sound to the organisers under what has, along the way, gained the title of, 'Carnival of Light Rave'.

Ravers at the original Carnival of Light Rave were no doubt either too stoned to fully comprehend just what they were hearing, and how privileged they were to do so, or possibly just took another toke to make it more bearable. However much it was appreciated on the night, it has lain dormant ever since.

McCartney has occasionally suggested its time had come again, most notably that it should be included in the *Anthology* series because it revealed how the group were expanding their horizons to work with avant-garde concepts. George (in particular), Ringo and Yoko did not agree, and so it did not make the final cut. (It would be interesting to know what Yoko's misgivings were.)

His bandmates' negativity towards their journey into the avant-garde is reflected by Paul's long-time friend from the Indica and his official biographer, Barry Miles. He is someone who, like Lewisohn, has heard the piece and despite his closeness to Paul has dismissed it as "really dreadful", saying that, "It doesn't bear being released. It's just masses of echo. It sounds like they put it through twice. It was the same thing that everybody was doing at home."[4]

The master tapes still exist, no doubt Paul has his own copy and the original will no doubt be somewhere inside the vaults at Abbey Road. Thus the odds are that it will someday receive a commercial release. When it does it may well prove revelatory, a piece that invokes the spirit of '67 and further enhances the Beatles' creative reputation.

There again … it may not.

---

1 *The Complete Beatles Chronicle* by Mark Lewisohn, (Chancellor Press, 1996 edition) p.240.
2, 3 'Mythical' Beatles song confirmed, BBC News, 16 November 2008.
4 *The Act You've Known for All These Years: The Life, and Afterlife, of Sgt. Pepper*, Clinton Heylin, (Canongate Books, 2007) p.70.

Chapter 89:
1967, Part 3 – 'OUR WORLD'

The recording of *Sergeant Pepper's Lonely Hearts Club Band* occupied most of January, all of February and March. On Saturday 1 April the group assembled to record 'Reprise' of the title track. To do so was Paul's idea: the album was, in the loosest of terms, 'a concept album', but the only truly discernible theme or concept running through the record was that it was a show recorded by the one and only Sgt. Pepper Band. To close the show, Paul thought the Peppers should re-visit the title song, so setting the scene before the final, majestic encore of 'A Day in the Life' that would actually draw proceedings to a close. No band could follow that.

With 'Reprise' in the can, on 3 April Paul McCartney flew to the USA for ten days. Of the remaining Beatles, George Harrison had the most left to do in the studio to ensure the recording of *Sgt. Pepper's Lonely Hearts Club Band* could be wound up. Working alongside George Martin, eight violinists and three cellists, on Monday 3 April he completed the recording of 'Within You, Without You'. The next day (courtesy of library effects tapes at Abbey Road) he added the laughter that ends the track.

Apart from preparing stereo mixes of the completed album (which the Beatles left to George Martin and Geoff Emerick, although the group always attended mono mixes), once George had added the strings and burst of laughter to 'Within You, Without You', work on *Sgt. Pepper's Lonely Hearts Club Band* was apparently over. Or so they thought.

Listening to the record, the Beatles decided that it should not just fade out as the final climatic piano chord played out. The previous tunes had all bled into each other and so it would be with 'A Day in the Life'. And so on Friday 21 April at Abbey Road, the Beatles recorded strange voices and gobbledygook that could be heard right at the very end of the fading piano chord where it would play (on non-automatic hi-fi systems) repeatedly until the arm was moved. For good measure John suggested that for the benefit of dogs everywhere the sound of a high-pitched dog whistle should be recorded and inserted at the end of the piano chord immediately ahead of the strange voices. It was then, and only then, that they considered the recording to be finally complete.

After the marathon recording sessions that accompanied *Sgt. Pepper* (some 700 hours in total, according to Geoff Emerick) it might seem reasonable that the Beatles would be ready for a break, but it was not to be the case.

While in the USA, Paul McCartney had come up with another project into which he believed the Beatles could immerse themselves. This time it was an idea for a TV film. He had drawn a circle which he divided into four sections, each to be filled with songs and sketches. The basic premise being the film would follow the Beatles as they participated as passengers on a 'Magical Mystery Tour' coach trip. Paul's vision was somewhere along the lines of a sort of British seaside version of California's Ken Kesey and his Merry Pranksters odyssey around the Golden State, in which the travellers expounded upon the wonders of acid. The main difference being that Paul's film would not be for hipsters and 'Heads', but for British Christmas TV and the largely family audience it attracted. And so instead of acid it was intended that the Beatles would promote having fun, albeit an occasionally bizarre and a tad surreal sort of fun …

Work on the titular soundtrack song began on Tuesday 25 April.

It was not the only film upon which the Beatles would focus their energies and attention over the next few months. They would also be writing and recording songs for a full-length animated feature film that was in production based on their own 'Yellow Submarine' and which would feature at least three especially composed original Beatles tunes.

As the Beatles turned their thoughts to the Blue Meanies and mystery tours over the next month, *Sgt. Pepper* was released on Thursday 1 June*.

(*On page 6 of its 27 May edition, Disc and Music Echo *reported that the release date had been brought forward to the 27th itself, while 'A Day in the Life' had already been banned by the BBC because "it might encourage a permissive attitude towards drug-taking."*)

The release of *Pepper* was the undoubted music highlight of the year. The acclaim and commercial success was unprecedented and, from a creative perspective, fully justified their decision to stop touring. Brian Epstein's fear that the Peter Blake cover, filled with images of people each of the Beatles admired, could prove a legal minefield was receiving critical acclaim rather than falling foul of any litigation (although 'A Day in the Life' had been banned by the Beeb, and in the USA before it was even released there).

During the summer, the Beatles appeared on a groundbreaking worldwide TV extravaganza entitled *Our World*, an ambitious project that had been conceived by the BBC and was televised live on Sunday 25 June when satellites spinning above the earth linked together to broadcast the first ever global television programme. The Beatles had agreed to participate and were seen in the studio recording a song composed especially for the occasion. This was an ambitious project for the group and was several days in preparation.

With George Martin at the helm, the song was performed by the Beatles and an accompanying orchestra conducted by former Manfred Mann saxophonist Mike Vickers, who later taught the Beatles how to play the Moog synthesiser. In turn this mighty musical ensemble were supported by a welter of technicians, studio engineers and a gaggle of specially invited partygoers, as the group had decided to be filmed in celebratory mode.

The song they sang was John's 'All You Need Is Love'. If ever a song fitted the bill it was this one. Lyrically it conveyed the message that lay at the heart of the 'Summer of Love' and its words were simple enough to be understood and sung by viewers around the world (which was John's intention when writing them). Musically it was joyous, catchy and conveyed a warm feeling of love and bonhomie. In all respects it was the perfect evocation of what the programme was about. To avoid any hitches on the night, in the days before the event, George Martin had pre-recorded a rhythm track that would be played during the broadcast, while the vocals, Paul's bass, the lead guitar solo, Ringo's drums and the orchestra were all 'live' on the night.

For the show, the Beatles (with the exception of Ringo behind his drums) sat on high stools surrounded by family and friends who mostly sat cross-legged on the floor. The studio was decorated with balloons, streamers, humorous placards and at the end some of the guests danced the conga around the studio. Among the guests were Jane Asher, Mike McCartney, Pattie Harrison, Hunter Davies, Mick Jagger, Marianne Faithfull, Keith Richards, Keith Moon, Eric Clapton, Gary Leeds and Graham Nash (and his former wife Rose Eccles).

The programme proved a great success, especially for the Beatles, whose single release of 'All You Need Is Love' became synonymous with the programme and the summer of 1967. Released in the UK on 7 July 1967, it topped the singles charts not just in the UK but also Australia, Austria, Canada, West Germany, Ireland, the Netherlands, Norway, Sweden and the USA.

They may not have been touring, but fans were nevertheless the recipients of much great Beatles music throughout the year:

Three singles: 'Penny Lane' / 'Strawberry Fields Forever' (number 2), 'All You Need Is Love' (number 1), 'Hello, Goodbye' (number 1).

A six-track EP: 'Magical Mystery Tour' that peaked at number 2 in the UK singles chart (December 1967).

An international bestselling number 1 album: *Sergeant Pepper's Lonely Hearts Club Band*.

Not only that but there was the bonus of a Christmas TV special and after that the promise of an animated film in production.

Ultimately, the colourful Christmas extravaganza, *Magical Mystery Tour*, fizzled where other Beatles films sparkled. Filmed in colour but screened in black and white it disappointed fans and critics alike. Showing it at prime time on Boxing Day was a big mistake. Even so, at least there was 'Yellow Submarine' to look forward to …

Brian Epstein had been very enthusiastic about the concept of the *Magical Mystery Tour*. Unfortunately, just what he would have made of its ultimate realisation was never known.

The sense of adventure and exploration evident in both *Sgt. Pepper* and *Magical Mystery Tour* was pervasive throughout 1967. If you were young there was a palpable feeling that for those living in the West there had never been a better time to be alive. The world seemed full of infinite possibilities. Institutes of further education welcomed more young people than ever before and the notion of taking time out to travel the world was seized upon by growing numbers of young explorers keen to broaden their horizons. Freedom and opportunities abounded. Drugs and sex had never been so available. Sex had simply never been so 'out there' before. Not only was there by now a readily available (NHS) contraceptive pill, but in 1967 the NHS Family Planning Act gained royal assent (the formal approval from the Queen that establishes an act of parliament). The effects these changes had on society and sexual relationships were profound: "This combined with the introduction of the pill and changes in societal attitudes resulted in LHA-funded family health clinics being explicitly allowed to give contraceptive advice to unmarried women, on both medical and social grounds."[1]

This is not to say that 1967 was fuelled by pure hedonism. *But*, the good times were getting more indulgent and, since having sex was not the huge risk it used to be, so the kids were very keen to make love not war.

Scrape beneath the surface, however, and you would find war, nuclear terror, racism, bigotry, sexism, diseases, drought, famine and poverty: the world was in its usual sad and sorry state.

Around the world, opposition to the American war in Vietnam (against communism) was growing to the point that for one incandescent moment it seemed possible that the current post-war generation of young people fuelled up on rock music, long hair, drugs and sex might be the one to declare war null and void for ever and establish love, peace and understanding as the basis on which to conduct human affairs everywhere around the globe.

During the Sixties, anti-war demonstrations in both the USA, UK and Europe became a regular feature of, and on, the news. The way in which it was reported was new and shocking with images direct from the frontline appearing on the evening news bulletins: Vietnam was one of the first wars to be televised as it happened. For those at home it gave the fighting a shocking immediacy that war had not previously had. Seeing people shot in front of your eyes while you ate your tea was terrifyingly real. Young people in the USA who faced the very real prospect of conscription could see exactly what lay ahead should they be called up. It was horrifying and brutal and not somewhere any young person would wish to be. Images of villages being bombed and burned and the civilian casualties incurred were horrifically shocking. Whatever your politics, what was going on was just plain wrong. Increasingly it felt very much that this was a war in which the USA had become entangled unnecessarily and in which it should extricate itself as soon as possible.

Unfortunately, the politicians did not see it this way and so the conflict was ramped up in desperate efforts to effect a swift ending that just didn't come. And so, as the body count grew, so did the opposition to it.

Within this context, during the mid-to-late Sixties, among the USA's counterculture something called the 'hippie' movement emerged. Acid-fuelled, it was a movement made up mostly of young people that quickly spread worldwide. The movement was characterised by a rejection of 'straight' or traditional values, it opposed war, promoted non-violence, peace, smoking dope and dropping acid. A central figure of the counterculture was American psychologist, writer and star-turn Timothy Leary, who advocated a philosophy of 'think for yourself and question authority' and advised people to 'turn on, tune in and drop out'. As the counterculture gained prominence and more young people adopted some or all of the hippie ethic, it placed the achievement of world peace seriously on the agenda. All its supporters needed to do was turn the music up high, get enough people loaded and out on the streets at exactly the same time …

The soundtrack for this revolution was rock 'n' roll and 'All You Need Is Love' caught the prevailing zeitgeist perfectly. Here was the anthem on which hippies everywhere could march to peace.

1 'The contraceptive pill was introduced to the UK in 1961…' navigator.health.org.uk

Chapter 90:
1967, Part 4 – A CATCALL FROM THE PAST

A trumpeter and trombonist who had largely helped to popularise traditional jazz within British jazz circles, Chris Barber was already a legend when in 1967 he became the fortunate recipient of a song from Paul McCartney.

Barber had encountered the Beatles way back in the Fifties at the Cavern when it was still principally a jazz club. Lonnie Donegan had been a member of Chris Barber's Jazz Band when he recorded 'Rock Island Line'. The song had been typical of the material with which Donegan would entertain audiences when the rest of the band took a break. He called it 'skiffle'. On the recording Donegan is the named artist – 'The Lonnie Donegan Skiffle Group' – and he is credited with providing the vocals and playing guitar, Chris Barber with the bass and Beryl Bryden with playing washboard. Lonnie's single was released in the UK on 14 November 1955 and its subsequent Top 10 popularity gave birth to the 'skiffle craze' from which almost all else in this book followed.

Barber and his jazz band enjoyed Top 10 success themselves when they took the million-selling 'Petit Fleur' into the UK charts in 1959 for a total of 24 weeks, including three weeks at number 3 during April and May. Since first fronting his Jazz Band in 1954, Barber's career never stalled. He was an active fan of blues and gospel music and in the 1960s he brought many legendary performers to the UK. These included Sonny Terry and Brownie McGhee, Muddy Waters, Louis Jordan, Sonny Boy Williamson and Sister Rosetta Tharpe. Notably, in 1958, together with Harold Pendleton, Barber opened the celebrated Marquee Club in London where groups such as Alexis Korner's Blues Incorporated and the Rolling Stones were showcased.

Barber's appetite for 'live' performance was prodigious and only after a fall and 65 years of leading his band did he finally announce his retirement in August 2019 aged 89. Sadly, Chris died in 2021 but, in accordance with his wishes, his Big Chris Barber Band (which had come into existence in 2000), was set to continue performing.

By 1967 Paul was ensconced in his new London home and thoroughly enjoying life at Cavendish Avenue. He began thinking of it as his 'bachelor pad' although his relationship with Jane was still in place. "There would be lots of people around there. If you wanted to hang out, and you were living in London and couldn't think of anything to do, you'd ring me and say, 'What you doing?' So quite a strange assortment of people came through here. Some of my relatives would be staying upstairs, then there might be Mick and Marianne, just because it was a good place to hang. It was cool."[1]

With John, George and Ringo now residing out of London, Paul was the only Beatle left in the city and as such proved to be a very sociable one. As Marianne Faithfull commented, Paul was "accessible" but John wasn't. It was as simple as that.

Earlier in the year Paul and Jane had accompanied the other Beatles to study meditation in India but, since their return from Rishikesh, Paul and Jane's social lives had inevitably drifted apart as Paul became immersed in the recording of *Sergeant Pepper* and was spending long evenings in the studio. Not long before the sessions for *Pepper* ended (April 21) Jane had gone on tour to the USA with the Bristol Old Vic and apparently Paul harboured the idea of Jane possibly giving up the theatre and focusing her time and energy on him. (It appears that even for one as hip or as liberated as Paul McCartney was in the 1960s, like most men he still harboured the old entrenched male attitudes of the 'little woman at home': attitudes which took some breaking down.) Jane had no such intentions. And why would she? In their own fields they were at the peak of their success.

The price of success for the couple, however, was that it did keep them apart at a crucial point in their lives and relationship. Not only that, but drugs had become a part of the social life Paul was embracing, especially LSD, whereas Jane was not into drugs at all. Despite this they were very close and wanted their relationship to work and so when she returned from the USA, the couple were determined to make an all out effort to ensure it survived.

Indeed, prior to her return, immediately the sessions for *Pepper* ended, Paul had flown to the USA as a surprise for Jane for her 21st birthday. Officially her birthday had been on 5 April at which time she was on tour with the Old Vic Theatre company, but as ever in matters of the heart it's the thought that counts if not the date.

Ironically, it was on his return home from this trip and back in the studios, recording songs for both the *Magical Mystery Tour* TV film and the *Yellow Submarine* animated film, that one night during a break from recording Paul met Linda Eastman for the very first time. The date was 15 May 1967 and the venue was the Bag O'Nails Club. Linda was there with her friends the Animals, whom she had photographed in New York. They both remembered the evening because it was the first time that they and most of the people in the club had ever heard the record 'Whiter Shade of Pale' and everyone present was speculating as to just who it was singing. Stevie Winwood was most people's choice, but of course it was Gary Brooker and the group were Procol Harum. The couple flirted and ended up at Cavendish Avenue, along with Lulu and Dudley Vaughan who had painted Paul's piano. Four days later their paths crossed again when Linda was one of a dozen photographers who attended an exclusive launch party for *Sergeant Pepper's Lonely Hearts Club Band* at Brian Epstein's pad, number 24 Chapel Street, Belgravia. Not long after, Linda flew home to be with her four-year-old daughter, Heather.

Jane returned from her trip to the USA with the Bristol Old Vic in June 1967 and was to comment that Paul had changed. Most probably it was LSD to which she was referring and they both remained committed to making their relationship work.

Chris Barber and his wife Ottilie were friends of Paul's who coincidentally had a connection with his new home. On 13 April 1965, Paul had bought 7 Cavendish Avenue, a three-storey Regency townhouse in St. John's Wood, just behind Lord's Cricket Ground and a short walk to the EMI Studios on Abbey Road, for £40,000. After some renovations he moved in late March 1966. Paul's role model for Cavendish Avenue was Wimpole Street, except his new home was more spacious. He loved the idea of entertaining his friends in his own place and from the moment he moved in dinner parties, lunch and afternoon tea were features of social life that both Paul and Jane eagerly embraced.

Paul had bought Cavendish Road from a somewhat eccentric physician named Desmond O'Neill and it turned out that Ottilie had been a patient of his. On learning this Paul invited Chris and Ottilie to see the house and see what he had done to it. Paul had heard stories that the doctor – clad just in a pair of shorts – would paint his house in mid-winter. This unusual behaviour appealed to Paul's sense of the absurd and so he invited Chris and Ottilie to his new home to hear what stories she may have to tell about its previous occupant.

Paul had always liked Chris Barber not only because he was an excellent musician but because he was also good company. Unlike many jazz musicians that Paul had encountered in the early days, Barber had never been patronising towards the younger generation of rock and rollers. He could remember how some of those older jazz musicians had acted as if they were a cut above, giving off the vibe that unlike rock musicians they were 'real' musicians who could read music and knew more scales. Consequently, they could be a tad sniffy but Chris Barber had never had that attitude.

Somewhere along the line, Barber asked Paul if he had any songs that he had written but which had not been used. At the time Paul did not have any 'new' tunes but from the back of his mind he came up with 'Catswalk' (aka 'Cat Call') a jazz styled instrumental from his Quarry Men days he'd originally composed in 1959.

This, of course, was not Paul's first attempt at getting someone else to record his tune.

Chris Barber and his wife Ottilie Patterson circa 1964. Friends of Paul McCartney and Jane Asher. Paul, Jane and Ottilie all featured in the 'outro' of Chris's recording of Paul's instrumental, 'Catcall'. (Pictorial Press Ltd / Alamy Stock Photo)

The Beatles had played the number in the early days when instrumental tunes were very popular and artists such as Duane Eddy, the Tornados, the Shadows and others were enjoying big hits. Although the Beatles had not made a studio recording of Paul's tune, they had recorded a version during a rehearsal at the Cavern in late 1962, and while they were not considering releasing it commercially themselves, Paul thought Dick James might find a home for it elsewhere and so had cut a demo of it with the Beatles. He himself had guitarist Bert Weedon in mind … but Bert's label passed on it as a possibility for the British guitar ace.

Never one to miss an opportunity, Paul now believed that finally, in Chris Barber, he had found the very person for whom 'Cat Call' had been waiting.

Paul: "When I was growing up, before I actually met John, I was playing around on guitar and I did have a couple of little things which were more instrumentals. There is one which made it onto the Beatles *Anthology* called 'Cayenne', or something like that. They were just little tunes which I knocked up and stuck a title on them. So there were very early things I'd done and I seem to remember 'Cat Call' was one of them. I used to see Chris down some of the London clubs like The Bag O'Nails or the Marquee ... we'd go to those after a gig because you had to unwind and by then you couldn't go to a pub or a restaurant as they were closed, so you'd go down the clubs and it was a great scene, we'd play lots of great records. So I got to know Chris quite well, and you know, one evening we were just chatting and he asked, 'Have you got anything I could do?' and I said, 'Well, let me have a think about it,' and I remembered this old song called 'Cat Call'. I rang him up and said, 'What about this tune?' and he said, 'Yeah, ok,' and he liked it. So that's how those things came to be, you know, just out of a late-night conversation."[2]

Barber first recorded a version of the tune during sessions at one of his studios at his Marquee Club in London with Paul in attendance. Barber's Marquee recording cast the tune as a more or less straight jazz piece, but when Paul heard the playback he stepped in with a broader view of the number, envisioning it as a much more spirited number.

Barber recalled that, "McCartney decided the song should be done in a more lighthearted 'big production number with catcalls as a sort of joke song or put-on'."[3]

As a result of Paul's view of how the song should be presented, recording relocated to Chappell Studios and was conducted under Paul's supervision. Brian Auger played organ on the track and he and Chris Barber recall that Paul was very much involved in the production of the tune. Auger also remembered that McCartney played piano on the recording.

Towards the end of the Chappell Studios session, those present were invited to contribute vigorous catcalls and whistles. Among the eager participants was Jane Asher who was back from the USA and had accompanied Paul to the session with Chris and Ottilie. As well as contributing catcalls, Paul can clearly be heard calling for the band to 'Please play slower' just before the half-speed coda and then leading a brief chorus of 'for he's a jolly good fellow'.

It was at this session that the song's title was changed from 'Catswalk' to 'Cat Call'.

CHRIS BARBER'S BAND
Chris Barber, OBE (awarded in 1991 for his services to music)
born: Donald Christopher Barber in Welwyn Garden City, Hertfordshire, England on 17 April 1930
died: 2 March 2021

CAT CALL **(3:00)**
(Lennon-McCartney)
Northern Songs Ltd
Marmalade 598-005
B-SIDE: Mercy, Mercy, Mercy (Zawinul)

On the occasion of the recording of 'Cat Call', the Chris Barber Band was expanded by several friends and so the full personnel in the studio consisted of:
Chris Barber, trombone
Pat Halcox, trumpet
Ian Wheeler, alto saxophone
John Slaughter, guitar
'Stu' Morrison, banjo
Jackie Flavelle, bass
Graham Burbidge, drums
Brian Auger, organ and 'catcalls'
Barry Jenkins, 'catcalls'
Vic Briggs, 'catcalls'
Viv Prince, cymbal dropping and 'catcalls'
Paul McCartney, keyboard, yell, 'catcalls', backing vocals
Jane Asher, 'catcalls'
Madeleine Hirsiger, 'catcalls'
John Ryan, 'catcalls'
Ottilie Patterson, 'catcalls'
Gustav Karl Lorenz Schneeweiss-Moody, backing vocals and 'catcalls' *
Giorgio Gomelsky, voice
Producer (both sides): Giorgio Gomelsky
A-side recorded: Thursday 20 July 1967 at Chappell Recording Studios, 52 Maddox Street, London.

(*Gustav Karl Lorenz Schneeweiss-Moody? I'm not sure just who 'Cat Caller' Gustav Karl Lorenz Schneeweiss-Moody is. My best efforts suggest he could have been responsible for/had something to do with the picture cover of the single or the album cover on which 'Catcall' was a featured track (Battersea Rain Dance). The only info I have uncovered is that he was responsible for the typography on Heavy Prog Rock band Stray's 1970 eponymous album (released by Transatlantic), the cover of which featured just their name written in very distinctive lettering.)

Released (UK): 20 October 1967
Despite the good time had by all at the session, 'Cat Call' failed to make the charts.

Two days after the session, Paul and Jane joined the other Beatles and their wives on a trip to Greece, the purpose of which was for the group to possibly invest some money by purchasing some islands on which they could all live and work.

On paper or in conversation it was no doubt a good idea and felt even better when the sun was shining, but ultimately it did not pan out, especially when they realised it could rain in Greece as well as Liverpool.

George Harrison recalled that when they stepped ashore on an island they were considering buying a storm broke, lightning flashed and the rain began to bucket down. Spirits dampened, the Beatles boarded the yacht they had hired and sailed away never to return.

The trip to Greece and an already burgeoning group interest in spiritual enlightenment (inspired by George and Pattie) found the Beatles sharing much during the summer of 1967. Anyone who still believed the group were on the verge of splitting would not have been supported by the evidence provided by their adventures of that summer.

1 *Paul McCartney: Many Years from Now*, Barry Miles (Vintage, 1998) p. 431.
2 Sir Paul McCartney in conversation with Bob Harris OBE and Colin Hall for *The Songs the Beatles Gave Away*, BBC Radio 2 (March 2009), written and narrated by Bob Harris, produced by Bob Harris and Trudie Myerscough-Harris for WBBC.
3 *Beatles Undercover*, Kristofer Engelhardt (Collector's Guide Publishing Inc., Ontario, 1998) p.41.

Chapter 91:
1967, Part 5 – THE MAHARISHI MAHESH YOGI AND TRANSCENDENTAL MEDITATION

"When George heard Indian music ... it was like a bell that went off in his head. It not only awakened a desire to hear more music, but also to understand what was going on in Indian philosophy. It was a unique diversion."[1]
Olivia Harrison

The part played by Maharishi Mahesh Yogi and Transcendental Meditation in the lives of the Beatles during 1967 reflects the growing influence of George Harrison within the group. It also highlights the growth of the Beatles as individuals and the distance that they had already put between themselves and the hurly-burly of Beatlemania.

The Maharishi's emergence as a figure of importance to them, as well as to other rock musicians and young people around the world, weaves seamlessly into the rich tapestry of cultural interplay and exciting new possibilities that were introduced into Western consciousness during 1967. Never before had spiritualism played such a major role in popular music.

Just how the Beatles turned onto Transcendental Meditation sprang from George Harrison's disillusionment with fame and his growing disillusionment with the acid and psychedelic 'scene' and the corresponding interest in meditation of Pattie Harrison and her sister Jennie Boyd.

George and Pattie had married on 21 January 1966 and lived in 'Kinfauns', a bungalow on the Claremont Estate, Esher, Surrey, that George had bought in 1964. It was through Pattie that George tuned into Transcendental Meditation. Jenny Boyd, Pattie's younger sister, may have been into Transcendental Meditation ahead of her sister Pattie, but whichever of them became aware of it first it was undoubtedly an interest they closely shared.

A useful reference/song for how George perceived the acid experience is 'It's All Too Much', a tune he had begun recording with John, Paul and Ringo at Abbey Road on 25 May 1967 and which was destined for the *Yellow Submarine* film soundtrack. Its lyric expresses how acid had impacted on George's wider consciousness. Lines such as:

'The more I go inside, the more there is to see'
'All the world is birthday cake, so take a piece but not too much'
'*It's All Too Much*'

Such words married the depth of wonder a trip unleashed within a user alongside the everyday experiences of life that person continued to experience while still tripping. George would later explain that 'It's All Too Much' was "written in a childlike manner from realisations that appeared during and after some LSD experiences and which were later confirmed in meditation."[2]

It was during the summer of 1965 that Beatles' dentist, John Riley, turned George and the other Beatles on to their first acid trip when (without first informing them) he spiked their coffee at a dinner party held at his house. The result was that the Beatles, their spouses and girlfriends experienced a disconcerting 12-hour trip. There is no doubt the experience altered George's consciousness. It was illuminating in that it brought into blinding focus all the doubts and questions he was experiencing about his life as a Beatle

The Beatles, accompanied by the Maharishi and Mick Jagger, arriving at Bangor railway station in Gwynedd, North Wales on 25 August, 1967. (Bob Hewitt)

just at the very moment he and the others were growing tired of life inside the bubble of Beatlemania. The insanity of that life was wearing all of them down and their shared acid trip was an awakening to the important, deeper things in life.

Although he initially enjoyed the enlightenment acid brought, George was not enamoured by the burgeoning acid/drug/psychedlic scene, especially as he experienced it in the USA on Monday 7 August 1967. George was already in the USA on this day when he and his party of Pattie, Neil Aspinall, Derek Taylor and new Beatle associate (some may say, 'hanger-on') Alexis 'Magic Alex' Mardas, flew to San Francisco, to visit Pattie's sister Jenny who was already there with Joe Massot. As soon as they arrived they decided to walk around the hippy district of Haight-Ashbury which was the very epicentre of the counterculture. And so it was that, at the height of the 'Summer of Love', George just happened to take a stroll through the LSD capital of the world.

In comparison, the acid scene in the UK was a more refined and genteel affair, certainly it was more eccentric than threatening, more Edward Lear and *Alice in Wonderland* than in the USA where the emerging counterculture/psychedelic movement had become heavy and politicised. Many young people had become caught up in anti-Vietnam war protests and the ongoing struggles of the Civil Rights movement. The hippie scene and the burgeoning drug culture provided release and rebellion from that war and their potential part in it as conscripts: refined and genteel the American 'youth revolution' most certainly wasn't.

George's stroll around Haight-Ashbury was not what he expected. By the time George arrived, this perceived epicentre of the hippie/acid/pot smoking/free love scene was no longer the 'nirvana' it might once have been. For George there was not much spiritual or questing about it at all. Instead what he saw and encountered was dark, dirty, ugly and hostile, more aggressive than "groovy". In his own words, all he found were "a lot of bums – spotty youths".

No wonder that Pattie's growing fascination with TM stepped in to fill the void left by George's rapid disenchantment with the acid scene. Meditation provided him with the true way forward towards enlightenment. Thus it became the direction George's spiritual journey took and in his quest he was joined by his fellow Beatles.

George's interest in Indian music and culture had inspired Pattie to undertake lessons in the dilruba (a bowed Indian instrument) and in Indian dance. It was whilst pursuing her studies she had picked up on Transcendental Meditation and in February 1967 had become a member of the Spiritual Regeneration Movement and received her mantra.

George was quickly swept up by Pattie's enthusiasm for TM and in turn so were Paul, John and Ringo, to the point that George bought them all tickets (priced 7/6d each) to attend a lecture by the Maharishi at the Hilton Hotel in London on Thursday 24 August 1967. Their attendance at this talk set in motion a sequence of events that had far-reaching effects on the Beatles and their lives.

Immediately after the lecture the Maharishi spoke to the Beatles privately for over an hour and invited them to his ten-day conference at Normal College (now part of Bangor University) in Bangor, North Wales. It was an invitation they readily accepted.

(Significantly, another person who attended the Maharishi's lecture – independently – was Yoko Ono. After the event, much to John and Cynthia's amazement, Yoko got into their chauffeur-driven Rolls Royce with them and asked to be dropped off on the way home.)

The very next day after the lecture, Friday 25 August, the group took the 15:50 *Daily-Mirror*-dubbed 'Mystic Special' from Euston to Bangor. Mick and Marianne came along too.

At this point it is highly probable that the Maharishi was not aware just who the Beatles were, or at least not aware of the extent of their international popularity. His immersion in TM and spreading 'the word' was total, but very quickly the Maharishi's own personal horizons would be broadened to comprehend just how popular the Beatles were and the massive influence they wielded. As Ringo sagely noted: "We all went to Wales to meet Maharishi. He didn't know who we were then, which was really fabulous. Only when we got off the train and he saw all the kids running, I think then he may have felt, 'Wow, things are looking up for me.' They ran right past him and were looking in our faces, and I think ho realised that these boys could get his message across real fast."[3]

For Cynthia Lennon the chaos surrounding the Beatles' departure from Euston Station became symbolic of the state of her marriage. Caught in the crowds as she struggled with the bags while John surged ahead, Cynthia missed the train. Although this is how it had always been, Cyn trailing behind while John moved fast to escape, always expecting someone else to sort the fine details for him, on this occasion as she stood on the platform watching the train pull away without her aboard it felt different, prophetic: a sign of what lay ahead.

Cynthia remembered being comforted at the time by Brian Epstein's assistant Peter Brown who had come to see them all off. It was a powerfully embarrassing moment for Cynthia as she stood exposed to the barrage of inquiring press photographers and reporters. Brown immediately offered to drive Cynthia to Bangor.

What Peter Brown nor anyone could have realised was that Cynthia's tears were falling not because she had missed her train, they were falling because she knew she was losing John: "I was crying because the incident seemed symbolic of what was happening to my marriage. John was on the train, speeding into the future, and I was left behind."4

As it turned out it was Neil Aspinall who drove her to Bangor, but Cynthia's intuition was to prove correct.

As the Beatles began their studies in Bangor they were a man short. Their guide, mentor and manager Brian Epstein was due to join them on Monday 28 August (Bank Holiday Monday) but he never did. Instead a terrible accident occurred: on 27 August, Brian Epstein, aged just 32, was found dead at his house in London. The subsequent inquest found he had succumbed to a fatal build up of the sleeping pill/barbiturate Carbitral in his system and his death was declared an accidental overdose.

The Beatles were, of course, devastated: at the very moment they believed they may have found their spiritual guide the Beatles had lost their earthly anchor.

The cessation of touring had left Epstein concerned as to just where within the group dynamic his role would reside in the future. He was a troubled man. Nevertheless, at the moment of his death he was still very much part of their inner circle, a close friend, much loved and a trusted colleague. Brian had been their champion, their crucial guide to, and negotiator with, the boring but essential world of finance and business that lay beyond the walls of the recording studio and concert hall. His loss was a mighty blow that they felt dearly.

The Beatles did not attend Epstein's funeral, which was held on 29 August 1967 at the Greenbank Drive Synagogue in Wavertree. They did so to preserve some privacy for the family which they knew would not be possible if they were present. Epstein's body was carried from the synagogue and buried in section A grave H12, Long Lane Jewish Cemetery, Aintree, Liverpool. (The Bee Gees' 1968 song 'In the Summer of His Years' was written and recorded as a tribute to Epstein.)

The chief executive of NEMS Enterprises, Geoffrey Ellis, recalled that the day before the funeral, on behalf of all the Beatles, George Harrison had handed a single chrysanthemum flower wrapped in a newspaper to Nat Weiss, Epstein's good friend and confidant. The group wanted the flower to be a final farewell to Brian and asked Weiss, who himself was Jewish, to place it on Brian's coffin. What they did not realise was that flowers are forbidden at Jewish funerals and burials. Weiss did not wish to disappoint the Beatles and had discussed his predicament with Ellis. Fortunately for both men the dilemma was resolved when they noticed two men at the cemetery beginning to shovel earth onto Brian's casket. Weiss took this opportunity to cast the flower, still wrapped in newspaper, onto the coffin top where it was soon covered by soil.5

On 17 October 1967, at the New London Synagogue in St John's Wood (near Abbey Road Studios), a memorial service was held for Brian with the Beatles in attendance.

After Brian's death, the Beatles informed the media that although Brian could never be replaced things would continue as normal. Their words disguised the fact that if things did not change pretty damn quickly they would be landed with an income tax bill for several million pounds from HM Government. Consequently, things could not be allowed to carry on as normal for any longer than necessary. Epstein himself had been fully aware of the problems that lay ahead and at the time of his death had been in the process of initiating changes he believed were necessary to avoid catastrophe.

---

1 *George Harrison: Behind the Locked Door*, Graeme Thomson (Omnibus Press, 2013) Olivia Harrison as quoted on p.114.
2 *I, Me, Mine* by George Harrison, The Extended Edition (Genesis Publications, 2016) p.104.
3 *The Beatles Anthology*, the Beatles, (Cassell & Co, 2000), Ringo Starr p.261.
4 *John* by Cynthia Lennon, (Hodder & Stoughton Ltd, 2005) pp. 263–4.
5 *I Should Have Known Better: A Life in Pop Management*, Geoffrey Ellis (Thorogood, 2004) p.133.

Chapter 92:
1967, Part 6 – BRIAN EPSTEIN AND APPLE

During 1967, Brian Epstein was struggling to comprehend the entangled web that the Beatles' financial empire had become and set things on a surer footing for the future. His accountants told him that the group desperately needed to diversify and invest in other things if they were to avoid the huge tax bills that were looming on the horizon. In response, Brian set up a small publishing company in an office on Baker Street, London. Terry Doran was employed to run it and it was called 'Apple Publishing'.

(On the back cover for *Sergeant Pepper's Lonely Hearts Club Band* can be found the first public acknowledgement of what was in the pipeline: just below the Parlophone and EMI logos are the words 'Cover by M C Productions and The Apple'.)

And so it was that Apple arose from the desperate need for the Beatles' financial affairs to be put into better order ...

Beatles writer Pete Doggett summed up the dilemma facing them at the time Epstein died: "During late 1966 and early 1967 the Beatles' manager was undergoing a process of psychological disintegration fuelled by his drug use, his chaotic sexual habits and his fear that by quitting live performance the group were slowly moving beyond his control..."[1]

To assist him in righting a ship that was in serious danger of capsizing, Brian recruited a partner: the producer and entrepreneur Robert Stigwood. Stigwood was a man on a mission and did little to hide his desire to assume complete control of NEMS Enterprises.

In March 1967 he came close to achieving this ambition when Brian nearly succumbed and was contemplating selling Stigwood a 51% holding in NEMS, but the deal did not materialise.

At the same time Epstein and Stigwood were collaborating, Brian had begun work to change the company known as 'The Beatles Ltd' into a new corporation called 'Apple Corps' in an attempt to change the Beatles' tax liabilities from income to corporation tax and so avoid that looming tax bill.

Unlike Brian, however, the Beatles were not enamoured in any way with Stigwood. Paul McCartney could not have made this any clearer to Brian when he said that if Epstein ever sold the Beatles to his new partner the group would "only ever record out-of-tune versions of 'God Save the Queen'."[2]

Just why they were facing such a massive tax bill resulted from the fact that the group were four individuals sharing their income from 'The Beatles Ltd', a company formed in 1963 to hold their collective income (excluding songwriting). They did so only after Brian's NEMS organisation had received its 25% management share (the norm was 10%). Once Brian's 25% was taken out, the remaining money was owned in equal 25% shares by the individual members of the Beatles. The group had never realised at the time the implications of signing such a deal, but in the wake of Brian's demise they were being rapidly brought up to speed.

The financial mess into which their affairs had fallen was complex. Leading the haemorrhaging of cash were some of the following deals they had been persuaded to sign:

Their earnings from the Recording Contract they signed with EMI in 1962 gave 25% of their lifetime earnings away to Brian (even if their relationship broke down).

A different company, Northern Songs, controlled John and Paul's songwriting interests, the income from which passed to the holding company Maclen Ltd (of which Brian took director's fees as well as his subsequent 25%).

George's songwriting income went into Harrisongs and was subject to financial demands similar to Northern Songs.

Both Northern and Harrisongs were run by George Martin's publishing associate, Dick James.

Subafilms Ltd (established in 1964) looked after the Beatles' filming concerns.

Brian Epstein allowed lawyer David Jacobs to control merchandise. In turn Jacobs gave exclusive rights to these for just 10% to Nicky Byrne who set up Seltaeb Inc in the USA and Stramsact in the UK. (Realising his error, Brian did somewhat redress the balance of this dreadful deal when in August 1964 he renegotiated a commission of 49%.)

Also on 27 January 1967, Brian had signed a new worldwide 9-year recording deal with EMI for the Beatles. This new deal outran his own management deal with the Beatles which was due to expire in October 1967. The new contract considerably improved their income from record sales, but even so it earned them less than it should have done because he failed to use the correct wording. For reasons best known only to himself, Epstein insisted on the percentage figures the Beatles would earn being based on 'wholesale' sales instead of 'retail' sales and further insisted on the word 'wholesale' being the word written into the contract. 'Wholesale' was the price EMI sold to record shops, 'retail' price was the price at which record shops sold the records to the public. 'Wholesale' was 20% lower. 10% of the retail price is what he should have gone for.

Once signed it meant that in the future in the UK they earned 10% of 'wholesale' sales for up to 100,000 singles, after which the percentage increased to 15%. Similarly, they earned 10% for sales of up to 10,000 EPs or 30,000 albums, after which it increased to 15% for LPs. In the USA they received 10% of 'wholesale' price of the first 100,000 singles and 30,000 LPs, which increased to 17.5% for sales over this number. In the USA, for LP sales in excess of 30,000 the percentage rose to 17.5%.[3]

As part of the new contract the group could choose their producer, control artwork and track listings. They received quarterly statements outlining the number of sales achieved and the royalties due from these.

After Brian's death it fell to his younger brother Clive to negotiate the group's way out of their imminent liability as co-owners of The Beatles Ltd for £3 million in income tax bills. As previously noted, Brian had begun to do this in April. Clive completed the process. Thus, John, Paul, George and Ringo changed from being co-owners of The Beatles Ltd to becoming four employees of a new corporation entitled 'The Beatles & Co', of which they would each own a 5% stake. The remaining 80% would be held by The Beatles Ltd as the holding company which would be renamed 'Apple Music Ltd' in 1967, and then in January 1968 it would change again to 'Apple Corps Ltd'. This meant that the individual Beatles' earnings would be subject to corporation tax rather than income tax (which then stood at 94% for high earners such as John, Paul, George and Ringo). They could also claim back personal living expenses from Apple.

Clive did this because he was part of NEMS, and on Brian's death the responsibility to do so initially fell to him. He assumed control of NEMS because he had no other option, *not* because he had any inclination whatsoever to take over Brian's role as manager long term.

John Lennon acknowledged that although Apple became the Beatles' responsibility and 'brand' it had originally been conceived by the Epsteins and NEMS as a means to avoid paying heavy taxes. John reflected that Clive had told them that if they did not create a business enterprise along the lines of Apple most of their money would disappear in taxes. In essence it was a *fait accompli* that none of them wanted, but having realised they had no choice, John said they decided to make Apple something of which they could approve, live with and enjoy …

John: "It's a business concerning records, films and electronics and, as a sideline manufacturing or whatever … The aim of this company isn't really a stack of gold teeth in the bank. We've done that bit. It's more of a trick to see if we can actually get artistic freedom within a business structure…"[4]

Paul: "We're in the happy position of not really needing any more money, so for the first time the bosses aren't in it for the profit. We've already bought all our dreams, so now we want to share that possibility with others."[5]

George: "I had very little to do with Apple … It was basically John and Paul's madness – their egos running away with themselves or with each other. There were a lot of ideas, but when it came down to it, the only thing we could do successfully was write songs and be Beatles."[6]

Ringo: "The idea was that artists would come and see us and tell us their ideas and their schemes, and if any one of us felt it was ok, we'd give them the money … we always felt that we'd had to beg a little in the early Sixties, and so we didn't want people begging from us."[7]

The Apple company logo was inspired by René Magritte's painting *Le Jeu de Mourre* ('The Guessing Game') which was one of the artist's last works and owned by Paul. Magritte completed the work in 1966 and it had been sent immediately from his dealer to Paul's friend and gallery owner Robert Fraser in London who, one day during the summer of that year, had left it propped up on Paul's table at 7 Cavendish Avenue as a surprise for Paul to discover. When Fraser had turned up with the painting Paul was not inside the house but out in the garden busy filming with Mary Hopkin. Not wishing to disturb them, Fraser left it for Paul to discover as a surprise.

George Harrison declared the enterprise a 'bad idea' born out of Brian's death. The Beatles knew they needed to do something and not wishing someone like Robert Stigwood or Clive Epstein to run the show, they decided to do it themselves. Fuelled by their own youthful energy, the prevailing hippie ethic and their own egos, they sincerely believed that they could not only do things differently, but more ethically. There would be no more ripping people off, no more making artists 'beg', but giving them opportunities and money to create without the usual corporate compromises that acquiring a record or publishing deal involved. Apple in its original incarnation incorporated the idealism of the Sixties that the Beatles wholeheartedly embraced. And, of course, the Sixties were nothing if they were not about forging new ways of doing things and better ways of treating people. The old order was on the run, change was in the air, the feeling that anything was possible was almost palpable and no one felt this more keenly than the Beatles.

Four days after Brian's death, on Tuesday 5 September 1967, the Beatles met at Paul's London home to decide their immediate plans. What quickly became apparent was that, for the foreseeable future, as a group they would manage themselves.

What we know now is Brian's passing effectively presaged the break-up of the band. No one person could have managed them single-handedly in the way he had. Only Neil Aspinall and Mal Evans were as close as he was to, or understood the Beatles as Brian did. The bond he shared went way beyond words on a contract. In 1967 Brian was the fifth Beatle. He may have made mistakes but critics have the benefit of hindsight. In his time he was walking on unchartered paths no manager in the UK had ever navigated before. Every day presented incredible challenges; difficult decisions had to be made in next to no time … and he'd done it all with impeccable class and style. He was an honourable man who loved the Beatles. They were lost without him. Managing themselves was never going to work.

Initially, the idea of putting all their affairs into one company and doing everything they had always wanted to do held great appeal. It meant there would be no one around to say, 'No, you can't do that.' No wonder that such artistic freedom drew initial enthusiasm from the group. However, as Paul McCartney noted, although at the start there was much enthusiasm, things fell apart very quickly because there was no one in charge: ideas were born and acted upon without weighing the consequences or costs. The inevitable result was that from the outset Apple leaked money.

At their first meeting after Brian's death, eager to keep the group focused and productive, Paul ensured his *Magical Mystery Tour* project was confirmed. In fact, there was no hesitating at all, the project started rolling immediately: they began serious recording sessions that very same evening by making a start on 'I Am the Walrus' and by Monday 11 September they began five days of filming for the film.

This Paul-conceived project was without a real script and when finally aired at 8:35pm on BBC 1 on Boxing Day, Tuesday 26 December 1967, it bombed. On the black and white UK TV screens of 1967, what was always conceived as a 'colour film' looked awful and appeared very amateurish, a made-up-on-the-spot venture with no real plot beyond observing a bizarre bunch of folk embarked upon a coach trip with no idea where they were bound or what they were about. (Colour TV had arrived on BBC 2 in 1967, but everything on BBC 1 was still seen in black and white until the end of 1968.)

The general public perceived it as pretentious and pointless, a clear indication that the Beatles were getting above themselves (or taking too many drugs, or both). The film's saving grace was always going to be the original music and film of the group performing these tunes. Even so, these elements alone could not prevent the film from receiving a critical mauling, so much so that Paul appeared on TV the night after it was aired to try and calm the troubled waters.

For the British press, the *Magical Mystery Tour* was the first time they felt emboldened enough to knock the Beatles. It gave the media a chance to remind the Beatles of their power and let the group know that this time they had gone too far. It was typical of the UK press who love to adopt the role of arbiters of good taste and morality. As ever the papers made a meal of their disdain. They cast the Beatles as celebrities who had grown too big for their boots and who thought they could foist any old rubbish on the British public. It was time to take the wind out of their sails.

Viewed in hindsight, it was undoubtedly a mistake to allow the film to be screened in black and white and not colour, for which it was intended, especially when sequences such as that for the instrumental tune 'Flying' feature a backdrop of changing colour clouds which lost all impact in monochrome. It should have gone out on BBC 2. Despite this, the film certainly has its moments. As Paul noted it was daring for the time, John's dream scene in which he shovels spaghetti onto a fat lady's plate is inspired, as is the Beatles' one and only performance of 'I Am the Walrus'.

At the same meeting at which Paul was promoting *Magical Mystery Tour* to his fellow Beatles, George had been urging them all to locate to India to study 'at length' with the Maharishi at his ashram in Rishikesh. Somewhat inevitably, it was Paul who got his way (the Beatles' schedule did not allow for delay, for the film was sold specifically for broadcast over the Christmas holiday of 1967). George was unhappy at having to wait and as a result never fully engaged in the film project. His dirge-like song for the film, 'Blue Jay Way' is about being bored, waiting for friends to arrive who are lost in the fog. It stands as a metaphor for his prevailing mood during the entire venture.

Years later, George was to reflect on his participation in *Magical Mystery Tour* with the words: "It was very flimsy, and we had no idea what we were doing. At least I didn't. I had no idea what was happening … my problem, basically, was that I was in another world … I didn't really belong: I was just an appendage."[8]

Unsurprisingly, given George's disconnect with *Magical Mystery Tour*, when American film director, Joe Massot (a friend of Jenny Boyd's with whom she had worked on a previous film of his) asked George to write the music/soundtrack for his new film, *Wonderwall*, George jumped at the chance.

THE UK'S TOP 30 SELLING RECORDS OF 1967
01 Engelbert Humperdinck: Release Me
02 Engelbert Humperdinck: The Last Waltz
03 Scott McKenzie: San Francisco (Be Sure to Wear Some Flowers in Your Hair)
04 Procol Harum: A Whiter Shade of Pale
05 Engelbert Humperdinck: There Goes My Everything
06 Sandie Shaw: Puppet on a String
07 The Monkees: I'm a Believer
08 The Bee Gees: Massachusetts
09 Nancy Sinatra and Frank Sinatra: Somethin' Stupid
10 The Beatles: All You Need Is Love
11 Tom Jones: I'll Never Fall in Love Again
12 The Tremeloes: Silence Is Golden
13 The Foundations: Baby Now That I've Found You
14 Petula Clark: This Is My Song
15 Anita Harris: Just Loving You
16 Keith West: Excerpt from 'A Teenage Opera'
17 The Mamas and the Papas: Dedicated to the One I Love
18 Tom Jones: Green Green Grass of Home
19 Vikki Carr: It Must Be Him (Seul Sur Son Etoile)
20 Vince Hill: Edelweiss
21 The Move: Flowers in the Rain
22 Traffic: Hole in My Shoe
23 Long John Baldry: Let the Heartaches Begin
24 The Beatles: Penny Lane / Strawberry Fields Forever
25 Frankie Vaughan: There Must Be a Way
26 The Monkees: Alternate Title
27 The Beatles: Hello Goodbye
28 The Turtles: She'd Rather Be with Me
29 The Kinks: Waterloo Sunset
30 Harry Secombe: This Is My Song

1 *You Never Give Me Your Money*, Pete Doggett, (Bodley Head, 2009) p.27.
2 *The Beatles Anthology* by The Beatles, (Cassell & Co, 2000) p.268.
3 *Beatles for Sale*, John Blaney, (Jawbone Press, 2008) p.83.
4, 5, 6 and 7 *The Beatles Anthology*, by The Beatles (Cassell & C0, 2000) p. 287.
8 *The Beatles Anthology* by The Beatles (Cassell & Co, 2000) p. 272.

PART 4

APPLE

Chapter 93:
WONDERWALL

"John and Paul chose to work with each other and let's face it, each of them were infinitely better songwriters than anybody else you could imagine at that time and George was conscious of that. He didn't have the encouragement or the response of someone to work with him, he had to do it by himself. Consequently, his first songs weren't very good, I didn't think anyway, and I had enough on my plate with the others, I couldn't spend too much time with him. The first time I really thought he'd got something great was in 'Here Comes the Sun'. That, I thought, was terrific. 'My Sweet Lord' and those ones were very derivative, but with 'Here Comes the Sun' he did something quite special. And then, of course, the final coup de grace was 'Something'. You couldn't write a better song than that. Frank Sinatra said it was the best love song ever written. It was an astonishing achievement for the underdog."
George Martin, 2009

While *Wonderwall Music* does not strictly count as a 'Beatles giveaway', it is undoubtedly a swathe of music written by a Beatle during the group's lifetime that was not intended to be performed by the group and which George composed specifically for another venture. Just as Paul had 'given' his themes for *The Family Way* to others to record and release, so George 'gave' this music to someone else. The difference between the two was that George actually performed on the resulting album, whereas Paul hadn't.

Its significance in this story is that *Wonderwall Music* heralds George's growing confidence in himself as a composer and his emergence from the huge shadows cast by Lennon and McCartney as the songwriters within the group. He had always written songs, only for a handful to appear on Beatles albums, but now it was different. It was as if a psychological dam wall had broken and tunes began flowing from George and his guitar for which he needed an outlet.

As 1968 dawned, George not only completed his recording of *Wonderwall* but provided a B-side for a Beatles single and led the group on their pilgrimage to India. From then on, within the group, George grew as a major creative force in terms of his compositions. Not only that but he flourished as a producer and writer for the newly established 'Apple Records' label. He and Paul wrote for other artists in a way that John chose not to. For that reason, a detailed look at *Wonderwall* seems appropriate.

It had been with the film's director Joe Massot* that Jenny Boyd had been staying with when George and Pattie visited her during their fateful trip to Haight-Ashbury.

Massot (born NYC 1933, died London 4 April 2002) had arrived in London in the mid-Sixties and in 1965 met the Beatles on the set of *Help!* Massot's short 1966 film *Reflections on Love* included footage of the Beatles at London Airport on 13 August 1965. Jenny is also seen at various points throughout the film.

(*Joe Massot directed Led Zeppelin's The Song Remains the Same (1976), although he was removed from the project when the producer became unhappy with the progress he was making. He was replaced by Peter Clifton. Joe also made Dance Craze in 1980 about the new Ska movement featuring, among others, Madness, the Specials and the Selecter.)

Wonderwall, the movie, stars Jane Birkin (as Penny Lane) and Jack MacGowran (as Professor Oscar Collins) and tells the story of a man escaping from the boredom of 'straight' society into the colourful world of psychedelia. As such it could not have been more in tune with the spiritual zeitgeist of the times. George wrote the music and the resulting soundtrack album became the first solo Apple release by a Beatle. The costumes and the 'Wonderwall' itself were designed by a group of talented entrepreneurial artists known as 'The Fool', who by this time had painted the psychedelic designs on George's Mini Cooper car and fireplace at 'Kinfauns'. They also designed clothes for the Beatles and later ran the Apple Shop where Jenny Boyd also helped out.

George's fascination with Indian music and Indian spiritualism began in the Bahamas (February and March 1965) during the filming of *Help!*. Whilst there, on his 22nd birthday, he was approached by Swami Vishnu-Devananda, a 37-year-old Indian guru and teacher of Sivananda Yoga, who was preaching its wider message throughout North America. He had opened a yogic ashram on Paradise Island in the Bahamas and was able to give George a copy of his book, *The Complete Illustrated Guide to Yoga*, which George not only read but apparently saw as 'a sign'.

Later, back in England, filming scenes for *Help!* at Twickenham Film Studios on 5 and 6 April, George heard the sitar for the first time when it was played by Indian musicians brought in to perform in the movie's Rajahama Indian restaurant scene. He was immediately fascinated. As he and the other Beatles waited to shoot a scene in which a chap is thrown into the soup, George recalled, "There were a few Indian musicians playing in the background. I remember picking up the sitar and trying to hold it and thinking, 'This is a funny sound.'"[1]

After finishing *Help!*, during the 1965 Beatles USA tour, Roger McGuinn of the Byrds was with George when the Beatle took his second acid trip. It happened in the bathroom of 2850 Mulholland Drive, Beverly Hills, the former home of Zsa Zsa Gabor, where the Beatles were living for a week. Having met the Byrds a month earlier in Blaises, a London nightclub, they invited the Americans to join them for an evening at 2850 Mulholland Drive and together they dropped acid. A guitar was being passed around and McGuinn played something for George that sounded like sitar music. George was intrigued and asked what it was. McGuinn explained what it was and also spoke of his interest in the real sitar music of Ravi Shankar. The Byrds had access to Ravi's records because McGuinn and David Crosby had recorded for World Pacific and had become aware of his music. Crosby and McGuinn were both big fans and the latter believes this was the first time George had heard about or became aware of Shankar. He suggested George should listen to Ravi's album *Portrait of Genius*.

That was exactly what George did and what he heard changed his life. "I put it on and it hit a certain spot in me that I can't explain, but it seemed very familiar to me. The only way I can describe it was: my intellect didn't know what was going on and yet this other part of me identified with it. It just called to me."[2]

Speaking of his trip to India after the ill-fated Beatles tour of the USA, George Harrison commented: "My heart was still in India. That was the big thing for me when that happened in '66. After that everything seemed like hard work. It was a job, like doing something I didn't really want to do. I was losing interest in being fab, at that point."[3]

Over time, George became very close to Ravi and by the time the Beatles flew to Rishikesh in 1968 to meditate with the Maharishi, Ravi had already visited George at 'Kinfauns' and begun teaching him to play the sitar. Likewise, George had already visited Ravi in India and toured some of the country with Ravi.

WONDERWALL MUSIC
The soundtrack was composed by George Harrison who, like Paul before him, had never composed a film soundtrack. Massot knew this but was happy to have Harrison collaborating and was willing to work around it. When George aired his trepidation about writing a film score, Massot simply assured him that anything he wrote would feature in the film and so it was on this understanding that George proceeded.

Fired by his new passion, George made the soundtrack a simple anthology of Indian music, towards which end he recorded a series of short ragas at EMI's recording studio in Bombay between 9-13 January 1968 after flying there on the 7th. For George, Bombay was the *very* source of the music and so he called upon local musicians to play on the recordings which reflected both his immersion in the music and his dedication to the project.

The pieces recorded in Bombay were credited to George Harrison and Band/Indian Orchestra.

While recording in Bombay for *Wonderwall Music*, George also recorded the instrumental music for 'The Inner Light'. His vocals were added back in London on Tuesday 6 February 1968 and the song became the B-side for 'Lady Madonna' (released 15 March 1968).

The single was recorded specifically to be released while the Beatles were away in India. At the time, 'Lady Madonna' was heralded as a departure from the Beatles' more psychedelic ventures of late and a return to a more basic rock 'n' roll sound. Apparently Paul had in mind the piano style of Fats Domino when he recorded 'Lady Madonna', although the driving piano phrase on the record bears a striking resemblance to the piano riff on trad jazz king Humphrey Lyttelton's 1956 hit single 'Bad Penny Blues', released on Parlophone not long after George Martin had become the label's head.

George mixed his recordings from India with pieces he composed in rock/pop and other Western musical styles and which he recorded in London prior to flying to India. George timed each segment of music with a stopwatch as he watched the unfinished film. The result was a varied musical programme that was released on Apple as the soundtrack album, *Wonderwall Music*.

George asked classical pianist and arranger John Barham to work with him on the project. George and John had first met at 'Kinfauns' when Ravi Shankar had visited George and Pattie at their home to perform a recital of Indian music for them. Barham accompanied Shankar to George's home that evening as his assistant and was therefore the more natural choice to work alongside the Beatle on the project than George Martin. On *Wonderwall Music* he contributed the musical arrangements. George would sing his melodies to Barham who then transcribed them onto manuscript.

GEORGE HARRISON and BAND/INDIAN ORCHESTRA
WONDERWALL MUSIC
(Original Soundtrack Album)
Produced: George Harrison
December 1967, EMI Studios, Abbey Road, London
Musicians:
Sarod: Aashish Khan
Tabla, pakavaj: Mahapurush Misra
The Remo Four:
Guitar, steel guitar: Colin Manley
Piano, jangle piano, organ, Mellotron: Tony Ashton
Bass: Philip Rogers
Drums: Roy Dyke
Piano, flugelhorn: John Barham
Piano, guitar: George Harrison
Harmonica: Tommy Reilly
Guitar on 'Ski-ing': Eddie Clayton aka Eric Clapton
Drums on 'Ski-ing': Richie Snares aka Ringo Starr
January 9-13, 1968, HMV Studio, Bombay (now Mumbai), India
Sitar: Shambhu Das, Indri Bhattacharya
Tabla: Shankar Ghosh

Surbahar: Chandrasekhar Naringrekar
Shehnai: Sharad Kumar, Hanuman Jadev
Taar-shehnai: Vinayek Vora
Harmonium: Rijram Desad
Tabla-taran: Rijjram Desad
Santoro: Shivkumar Sharma
All songs composed by 'Harrison'.
Album sleeve designed by: Bob Gill, John Kelly, Alan Aldridge
Photo of George by Astrid Kemp (nee Kirchherr)
Side One
Microbes 3:39
Red Lady Too 1:53
medley:
Tabla and Pakavaj 1:04
In the Park 4:04
medley:
Drilling a Home 3:07
Guru Vandana 3:07
medley:
Greasy Legs 1:27
Ski-ing and Gat Kirwani £:06
Dream Scene 5:27
Side Two
Party Seacombe 4:34
medley:
Love Scene 4:16
Crying 1:14
Cowboy Museum 1:27
medley:
Fantasy Sequins 1:49
Glass Box 2:21
On the Bed 1:05
Wonderwall to Be Here 1:24
Singing Om 1:54

The original soundtrack album *Wonderwall Music* was released in the UK on 1 November 1968 by Apple Records as SAPCOR 1 and as such was Apple's first LP. This is the catalogue number of the stereo version and there is also a very rare mono version – APCOR 1.
Released in the USA on 2 December 1968 as Apple ST 3350
Wonderwall Music appeared on compact disc in 1992, during reissues of the Apple catalogue, and was reissued again in 2014.*
   (*The 2014 CD release had three additional tracks recorded at the same time as the original sessions: 'Almost Shankara' and 'The Inner Light' (alternative take instrumental) both from the Bombay sessions. 'In the First Place' was recorded in London by the Remo Four, composed by Colin Manley and Tony Ashton and produced by George Harrison.)

1, 2 & 3 George Harrison as quoted in the *Wonderwall Music*, 2014 CD re-issue booklet, from the essay by Kevin Howlett.

Chapter 94:
1968 – BLUE MEANIES IN SIGHT

"The universal and ever-present urge to self-transcendence is not to be abolished by slamming the current popular Doors in the Wall. The only reasonable policy is to open other, better doors in the hope of inducing men and women to exchange their old habits for new and less harmful ones." **Aldous Huxley from The Doors of Perception and Heaven and Hell**

1967 had been a momentous year for the Beatles. 1968 was to be another.

Despite the poor critical reception their TV film *Magical Mystery Tour* received, they concluded 1967 and began '68 in total control of the UK charts. They were still by far and away the most popular group around. In the singles chart 'Hello Goodbye' was rooted at number 1 from 12 December until 23 January 1968, the *Magical Mystery Tour* EP spent 12 weeks on the singles chart and was at number 2 for three of those (2–16 January 1968). Meanwhile, in the album chart, *Sergeant Pepper* returned to the number 1 spot for the final weeks of December '67. That initial chart run clocked up a total of 52 consecutive weeks from 3 June 1967 until 25 May 1968, 27 of them at number 1.

Even so, as the year ended, change was once more in the air for the Beatles.

On 7 December, the Beatles became retailers in their own right when they opened the Apple Boutique at 94 Baker Street, London NW1, after a launch party on the 5th. Apple and its various business offshoots would dominate their working lives up to and beyond the group's demise in 1970.

On 16 December, John and George joined the Maharishi to attend a UNICEF gala in Paris.

Meanwhile, Paul and Jane spent the first three weeks of December at Paul's getaway farmhouse on the Mull of Kintyre before announcing to Paul's family that they had become engaged. The announcement was almost like a self-agreed 'now or never/do or die' moment for a couple whose relationship some observers believed (because of their personal career demands) had faltered earlier in the year.

Unknown to his fellow Beatles as 1968 dawned, John Lennon was at a similar crossroads in his personal life.

As 1967 drew to a close, Cynthia Lennon was becoming increasingly aware of John's growing fascination for the seemingly bizarre Japanese avant-garde artist who had cheekily hitched a ride with them after the Maharishi's lecture at the Hilton Hotel in London in August.

Previously, on 7 November 1966, John had attended a private preview of Yoko Ono's exhibition entitled *Unfinished Paintings and Objects*, which opened at the Indica Gallery on the 8th, and ever since Ono had gradually become a presence in his life. Not long after that first encounter Yoko sent him a copy of her book *Grapefruit* which he read in bed at night as he lay beside Cynthia. A stream of letters and postcards from her began to arrive at their home in Weybridge. She once visited their home when they were both out and had been allowed inside by their housekeeper on the pretext of needing to make a telephone call. After that she would call him on the phone at home.

Yoko's unconventional entrance into John and Cynthia's domestic life coincided with John having confided to Cyn in early 1967 that he had not been faithful to her. Whilst John's confession took her by surprise the content of what he revealed didn't. Their relationship was, by Cynthia's own admission, no longer at the peak of the intense passion they had enjoyed during their student days and by the time John confessed his infidelity it had become more of a friendship. She had always been aware of the temptations of pop stardom and was actually happy that finally he had been able to talk to her about these issues.

Despite this welcome openness, the rift between them caused by his increasing consumption of LSD remained of great concern to Cynthia throughout 1967. It was one of many things she could not share with him even though she had made an attempt to do so. John became irritable at home when she cautioned him against its effects. In particular, she did not like him taking acid when Julian was around.

When Cynthia confronted John about Yoko and her weird behaviour she was rebuffed as John insisted that Ono was just "another nutter wanting money for all that 'avant-garde' bullshit."[1]

Publicly, cracks such as these in the Beatles' private lives were not apparent.

On 18 October, John and Cynthia attended the Motor Show at Earl's Court and in the evening all four Beatles, accompanied by Cynthia, Jane, Pattie and Maureen, attended the London premiere of *How I Won the War* at the London Pavilion. After the film they all moved on to a celebration party held for them by Cilla Black at her London apartment.

Another public engagement on 19 November found Paul and Jane at Brian Epstein's Saville Theatre on Shaftesbury Avenue where they attended a concert featuring the Bee Gees, the Bonzo Dog Doo-Dah Band, the Flowerpot Men, and Tony Rivers and the Castaways. Significantly, most of Tony Rivers et al. had been signed by Brian and on December they became the second* group to be signed to the newly formed Apple Publishing (Apple did not have its own record label at this time) albeit under their new name of 'Grapefruit'. The new name came courtesy of John Lennon and the title of Yoko Ono's book that he had been reading. (The lack of a record label of its own meant that in the UK Apple licensed Grapefruit's records to RCA Records and to Equinox in the USA.)

(*The first group signed by Terry Doran to Apple Publishing in September 1967 were Focal Point from Liverpool.)

Of course, John had not been totally honest with Cynthia about his feelings for Yoko. How could he have been when he was unsure of almost everything in his life at that time? Throughout 1967 he was at a crossroads. His biographer Ray Coleman noted that John's 'physical flings' were an indication of issues that ran deeper within him. He had no desire to hurt Cyn, but was restless for some new 'milestone' in his life, something or someone new to fire his imagination. Living the life of a family man in the relative seclusion of a big house had lost its appeal: "He did not feel comfortable in his Weybridge mansion in the stockbroker belt … The roller-coaster of Beatlemania had lost its attraction for him. Drugs were increasing their hold over him and the continuing clashes with Cynthia over his use of LSD rocked their marriage still further."[2]

Yoko Ono's entreaties fed directly into John's troubled psyche and gradually what had at first appeared bizarre became inspirational and exciting. As 1967 ended and a trip to India with the other Beatles beckoned, John felt the pull of opportunities opening in his life that he no longer wished to resist. Cynthia would accompany him to Rishikesh, but Yoko's presence was ever present for whilst there he remained (secretly) in touch.

---

1 & 2 *Lennon: The Definitive Biography*, by Ray Coleman (Pan, The Anniversary Edition 2000) pages 450 and 445.

Chapter 95:
A NEW SONG FOR CILLA

1968
Was the year when ... Martin Luther King Jr. was assassinated ... Richard Nixon was elected President of the USA ... Robert Kennedy was assassinated ... the musical Hair *opened on Broadway ... Saddam Hussein seized power in Iraq ...*

1967 had been a challenging year for the Beatles and as 1968 dawned much remained to be resolved within and without the Beatles.

Similarly, for Cilla Black 1967 had not been easy as she had felt increasingly neglected by Brian Epstein. Her feelings of unease had begun in November 1966 when she was starring alongside comedian Frankie Howerd at the Prince of Wales Theatre in a review entitled *Way Out in Piccadilly*. Brian dutifully attended the opening night on 3 November, but whereas once he would have made weekly visits to view her stage performances, her once ever-attentive manager made only sporadic visits during its nine-month run, at one point letting a whole month pass without attending.

Cilla's youthful ego was deeply hurt and she began to feel it was time to seek out a new manager. As time passed she began to think it would be best if she left Brian and NEMS altogether and allowed her boyfriend Bobby to take control of her affairs. When Bobby relayed her decision to Brian, the latter became immediately distraught. Despite being in the midst of health and personal crises (which by staying away he had successfully kept from Cilla) Epstein knew he had been inattentive and was desperate not to lose his most treasured artist after the Beatles. At a hastily convened lunch for Cilla and Bobby at his Belgravia home, the deeply remorseful Epstein broke down in tears and pleaded with her not to leave him. All three ended up in tears and made up.

Epstein moved swiftly to prove to Cilla that she was uppermost in his thoughts. He had always envisaged her as an all-round entertainer whose career would endure long after her hits became fewer and so he negotiated with the BBC to give Cilla her very own TV show. Within days of their lunch at Chapel Street he had secured the deal. Unfortunately, it came with a condition: the corporation wanted her to sing for Europe on the show. Black refused this condition outright, telling Epstein, that it was her strongly held belief that because Sandie Shaw had won it the year before with 'Puppet on a String' it was inconceivable that another British girl would win it again the very next year. Not only that but Cilla made it abundantly clear to Brian she simply did not want to, and would not, sing a Eurovision song.

With her refusal ringing in Brian's ears, Cilla and Bobby left for a holiday with Tom Jones in the Algarve, Portugal. Acting quickly Epstein returned to the negotiating table with the BBC and on 25 August 1967 secured the deal she wanted: her own TV series that was not tied to a condition to perform songs for the Eurovision Song Contest. Brian was thrilled with his news and was excited to tell Cilla. He tried to contact her by phone to personally break the news to her but had been unable to do so. A busy weekend lay ahead: he was seeing his friends Geoffrey Ellis and Peter Brown in Kingsley Hill and from there travelling to Bangor, North Wales, to join the Beatles and the Maharishi in Bangor. And so he left a note for his secretary Joanne Newfield to find on her return to work after the weekend: "Joanne, Please send suitable cable to Cilla requesting she calls me (Sussex or here) S.A.P. as I've tried to contact her but impossible. Urgent matter".

Cilla never received Brian's intended telegram: instead, on holiday in Portugal, she learned of Brian's tragic passing as she sat with Bobby in a nightclub overlooking the Gulf of Cadiz.

When Brian's body was discovered in his bedroom, among the items laying next to him was the contract for *Cilla* the TV series about which he had been so excited to tell her. Cilla was convinced that the presence of the contract by his side was clear evidence that Brian's tragic death was a dreadful accident.

In accordance with Jewish law, Cilla was not allowed to attend Brian's funeral, but unlike the Beatles she did attend the service in the synagogue. Epstein's death had utterly devastated her and it took many months for her to feel able to return to work. By the time she did, Bobby had become her personal manager and set her up for a week in cabaret at the Variety Club in Batley, Yorkshire. Of Bobby and his management skills Cilla commented, "He cut his teeth on *Cilla*".

Of course, Bobby became so much more than Cilla's manager, he also became her 'talisman' and 'security blanket' roles previously performed on her behalf by 'my Eppy', as she had dubbed Brian.

For a long time after his death, memories of Brian would come unexpectedly into Cilla's mind. She said it could be on stage, in a television studio, or when recording. A particular instance of this was the first time she saw her own 'mugshot' on the cover of the *Radio Times* advertising her forthcoming TV series. As she saw her own face and read the words 'Cilla Black in her own show on BBC1' she experienced a 'Brian moment'. She knew how excited he would have been to see the cover on display in his local newsagent's and that he would have telephoned her immediately to ask if she had seen it yet, and if not, not to worry because he had bought a dozen copies.

Cilla was a series of eight shows broadcast live from the BBC Theatre, Shepherd's Bush, London, beginning on 30 January, 1968. Among her many guests on the show were friends, singers and musicians, Ringo Starr, Cliff Richard, Lulu, Sandie Shaw and Henry Mancini, comedians Les Dawson, Frankie Howerd and Spike Milligan.

It was as she rehearsed for the series that, just like he had done in the past, Paul stepped in to lend a helping hand by donating a song he had written especially for her.

Cilla was the youngest female entertainer to host such a series, but producer Michael Hurll had detected that she wasn't comfortable with the big brassy opening numbers she was being asked to sing. As a consequence, Hurll wondered if Paul could help out: "I was approached by her producer Michael Hurll … they came to see me for this little meeting and they said that they would like me to write a song that Cilla could open the show with. So, I mean, having been a great mate of Cilla's and admirer of her voice, 'cos you know in the early days she used to do a lot of Dinah Washington stuff – she's a great belter old Cilla – she used to do a lot more bluesy stuff than she became known for later. So I was pleased to have a stab at it and came up with 'Step Inside Love', which was kind of custom-made for her to invite a TV audience in and she did a great job on that I think."[1]

Cilla herself admitted: "I was in a dilemma. By this time my career had really soared through the roof and Bill Cotton Jnr. decided to give me my own TV series, the youngest girl to present that type of big show and it was a bit daunting. They were giving me all these 'Billy Cotton big openers' … all this razzamatazz, very big openers. I was going through these songs in my living room when I got a phone call from Paul. He said, 'I know what they're doing, they are giving you all of those 'Billy Cotton Band Show type openers. I know that's not you, that's not your image. You shouldn't be going into their living rooms, you should be inviting them into yours.' And I thought, 'You know what, you're absolutely right,' and he said, 'I'm going to write one for you. I haven't written it all yet, it's called 'Step Inside Love'."[2]

It's interesting to speculate that with the gift of 'Step Inside Love' Paul himself was maybe, in some way, subconsciously responding to Brian's recent death. The situation is so redolent of what Brian Epstein would have done in the early days of Mersey Beat, especially for one of his dearest Liverpool acts. Realising Cilla was in need of a song, Brian's first instinct would surely have been to turn to Paul and John to see if they could help. And of those two Paul was the most likely to have something stowed away in his locker or to sit down right away and compose a brand new tune. While, by 1967, John was less moved by the challenge of writing for others than he had been, it still appealed to Paul. He still enjoyed the buzz of hearing a Lennon-McCartney 'original' gracing the charts and airwaves.

Hurll and Cilla were both thrilled with Paul's idea and Cilla loved Paul's song. "And of course 'Step Inside Love, let me find you a place', it was really great *and* it still had the big beat. We went for a try out, just Paul and I with George (Martin) in some studios off Bond Street ... it wasn't in my key ... and he was struggling to find the chords to put it in my key. But it was great and it just felt really good."[3]

The demo recording with Paul took place on 21 November 1967 at Chappell Studios and an edited version featuring some brief studio banter, Paul on acoustic guitar and Cilla singing was released in 1997 on the second disc of her three CD set *Cilla Black 1963-1973: The Abbey Road Decade*. The accompanying booklet notes researched and annotated by Ted Carfrae confirm Cilla's comments about the key in which she sang on that day: "Recorded before the final keys were set, we hear Cilla singing in a lower, warmer register. McCartney can be heard humming over the bridge giving Cilla an idea of the song's structure and arrangement."[4]

The same three-set CD compilation also contains the 'First Take' recorded at the same session on 21 November, but as the booklet notes: "This fully orchestrated version differs remarkably from the more commercial sounding single release recorded some three months later. The most obvious difference is the Bossa Nova rhythm behind the verses, the instrumental bridge and ending."[5]

The chorus, however, is very similar to how it is on the single that was eventually released in March 1968.

When the series was first aired on 30 January, Cilla had not released a finished version of the song and when it was time to go live in front of the cameras not everything went to plan: "Everything was live and I was full of nerves, you know I'd got telegrams from everybody, everybody except the Queen actually – you name them, I got a telegram from them, even Gracie Fields! So, I opened my mouth to sing, 'Step inside love', and the brain went blank, but I knew I had to do another line and I put in 'Nice to see you again'. Of course, I hadn't seen them before anyway! Paul was sitting at home watching it, thinking Michael Hurll has made me change the lyrics and he's furious. I said, 'No, no, I take the blame, I just forgot the words on the opening night, it was live, what could I do – the show must go on!' He (Paul) came down to Shepherd's Bush in the afternoon for the dress rehearsal just to make sure that the song was ok. It's unbelievable."[6]

Such was the success of the series, Cilla was called into the studios in February 1968 to record a finished version of 'Step Inside Love' for release as a single. It is remarkable that she had not done so before the first programme had been broadcast. The finished product was a re-recording of the version she had cut at Chappell Studio in November 1967.

CILLA BLACK
***STEP INSIDE LOVE* (2:20)**
(Lennon-McCartney)
Northern Songs Ltd
Parlophone R 5674
Recorded at Abbey Road on 28 February 1968
Producer: George Martin
Arranged by Mike Vickers
B-side: I Couldn't Take My Eyes off You (Willis/Westlake)

It is highly unlikely that any of Paul's acoustic guitar from the original demo appeared on the single and he could neither attend nor contribute any more to the February session in Abbey Road because by that time he was in an ashram in India meditating with the Maharishi.

The success of Cilla's groundbreaking TV series meant her new single was rush released on 9 March 1968. Ten days later on 19 March it entered the UK Top 40 chart at number 35. It spent a total of 9 weeks on the chart, peaking at number 8 on April 13.

('Step Inside Love' was released in the USA on 6 May 1968, but failed to make the *Billboard* charts. It was also released in Ireland where, in April 1968, it reached number 15.)

In the UK, 'Step Inside Love' was a critical as well as a commercial success. Writer Penny Valentine of *Disc and Music Echo* was one of many who liked it and headlined her review with the words 'Cilla with McCartney magic: so good!' Penny called it, "Definitely the best record Cilla's made for a long time". Duly noting it was written by Paul, she wrote, "a lot of the actual form is very Bacharach-like." This was praise indeed and from then on Valentine's enthusiasm for the record was irresistible: "It starts in a Latin American style and then bursts into a big tambourine and backing chorus and then descends back into guitar and trumpet." Calling it "sophisticated", Penny notes it was "an odd mixture of sweet and sour" which "Cilla handles ... superbly", before concluding, "it's an ancient thought ... but isn't it odd how it takes the McCartney magic to make something so good?"[7]

N.B. *Cilla also recorded an Italian version of 'Step Inside Love' in 1968, produced by George Martin at Abbey Road, entitled 'M'Innamoro'. This was not unusual, many artists would record their hits in other languages. These would not be released in large numbers and the Italian version of 'Step Inside Love' was also released in a (now very collectable) full cover picture sleeve. (It is also available on Cilla's 1997 three-CD set* Cilla 1963-1973: The Abbey Road Decade *(Zonophone, EMI Records Ltd).*

M'Innamoro (Step Inside Love)
(McCartney-Lennon-Mogol*)
Ricordi International SIR 20.080
Recorded at Abbey Road
   (*Mogol was the name of the writer who translated the lyrics into Italian. His real name was Giulio Rapetti (b.1936). In 1961 he had written the song 'Uno Del Tanti' (English: 'One Among Many') which was rewritten in 1963 by Jerry Leiber and Mike Stoller for Ben E. King as 'I (Who Have Nothing)'. Released in June it peaked at number 29 on the Billboard Top 100 chart. Shirley Bassey covered this in the UK. Her version peaked at number 6 in the UK where it enjoyed a 20-week run on the charts that began on 26 September 1963. King's version did not chart in the UK. During his very successful career as a writer, Mogol would go on to translate the lyrics of songs by Bob Dylan and David Bowie, among many others.)
B-side: Non c'e´ domani (Where Is Tomorrow) (Umberto Bindi-Luciano Beretta)
Produced by George Martin
Umberto Bindi, the co-writer of this B-side had, together with Gino Paoli, co-written 'Il Mio Mondo' – Cilla's second number 1 'You're My World'.

'Step Inside Love' also appeared on Cilla's third solo studio LP *Sher-oo!*. Released on the Parlophone label on 6 April 1968, 'Step Inside Love' was the first single released from the album. The album itself reached number 7 in the UK album chart. During the Seventies, *Sher-oo!* was re-issued on EMI's budget music label MFP (Music for Pleasure) when it was re-titled 'Step Inside Love' and given a different cover.

In her 2009 BBC interview with Bob Harris for the BBC Radio 2 documentary, *The Songs the Beatles Gave Away*, Cilla revealed that when it was first released 'Step Inside Love' had been banned in South Africa: "The stories go on about 'Step Inside Love', it was actually banned on the radio in South Africa because of its sexual connotations, you know,

'Step inside love, Let me find you a place'. It made me sound like a prostitute, they said! But that was South Africa at the time."[8]

In 2002, as a fun way of celebrating her 60th birthday, DJ Tommy Sandhu persuaded Cilla back into the studio to re-record 'Step Inside Love'. (The studio was Ronnie Wood's home studio.) Sandhu mixed this new version and 3000 white label copies were sent to British clubs under the name 'TS vs CB' (White Label 12" / Burn 'Em Records). The 12-inch charted at number 3 on *Music Week*'s Club Chart.

The relationship between Sandhu and Black began when he was a contestant on *Blind Date*, Cilla's long-term and massively popular TV dating game show. Later for the final series Sandhu replaced 'our Graham' the original announcer. He also produced the theme music. A maxi single of Sandhu remixes was released to download worldwide on 30 November 2009: Track 1 'Step Inside Love' (Original Mix 6:29), Track 2 'Step Inside Love' (Vacation Dub 4:53), Track 3 'Step Inside Love' (All Burnt Out Mix 4:20).

Tommy Sandhu's club remix of 'Step Inside Love' (All Burnt Out Mix) was released on 22 September 2003 as a 'hidden track' on Cilla Black's 15th studio album entitled *Cilla Beginnings: Greatest Hits and New Songs*. This compilation comprised 11 new tracks recorded by Black and produced by Ted Carfrae together with nine remastered versions of her George Martin-produced hit singles. Among the remastered George Martin singles were two of the tunes John and Paul had written exclusively for her: 'It's for You' and 'Step Inside Love'. Consequently, 'Step Inside Love' appeared twice on the record: the remaster of George Martin's version and Tommy Sandhu's 'hidden' remix version closed the album.

Not long after the CD version of *Cilla Beginnings: Greatest Hits and New Songs* was deleted in 2008 it received a digital download release. That was not the end of the story, however, for on the 3 August 2009 it received another digital download EMI release, this time as a repackaged edition simply called *Beginnings: Revisited*. This version celebrated what was then Black's 45th year in show business and included only the 2003 Ted Carfrae recordings (plus many previously unreleased tunes from those sessions), none of the remastered hit singles were included in this repackage, although the 'Tommy Sandhu All Burnt Out club remix' version of 'Step Inside Love' was.

Also in 2009, as a digital download, K-Tel issued all Sandhu's original remixes of the song, plus one especially commissioned new Sandhu remix. They were released as *Cilla Black – Step Inside Love: Tommy Sandhu Remixes*: 1 Step Inside Love (2009 The Stunner Mix 3:32); 2 Step Inside Love (2002 Club Mix 6:37); 3 Step Inside Love (2002 Vacation Dub 4:59); 4 Step Inside Love (2002 Club Mix – Radio Edit 3:10); 5 Step Inside Love (2002 All Burnt Out Mix 4:29).

(N.B. *The Beatles cut a spontaneous one-off recording of 'Step Inside Love', on 16 September 1968 in Abbey Road, during a session to record 'I Will', when Paul responded to John and Ringo's request to 'jam'. Paul played acoustic guitar with the other two providing percussion. It was very much off-the-cuff and never intended for anything more than a bit of downtime fun in the studio. It remained unissued until 1996 when it was unearthed for Volume 3 of the Anthology series.)*

1, 2, 3, 6 & 8 Cilla Black in conversation with Bob Harris OBE for *The Songs the Beatles Gave Away*, BBC Radio 2, March 2009, written and narrated by Bob Harris, produced by Bob Harris and Trudie Myerscough-Harris for WBBC.
4, 5 *Cilla Black 1963–1973 The Abbey Road Decade* (Zonophone, EMI Records Ltd.) 3 CD compilation, Cilla as quoted in the accompanying booklet written by Ted Carfrae.
7 *Disc and Music Echo*, 9 March 1968, 'Penny Valentine – Britain's Top Singles Reviewer Spins This Week's New Discs', p.23.

Chapter 96:
CILLA AND THE SONGS GEORGE AND RINGO WROTE FOR HER

Cilla Black is possibly the only artist for whom all four Beatles wrote or offered songs that *initially* they were not thinking of recording themselves. The songs discussed in this chapter are not strictly songs the Beatles gave away because the offers came after the Beatles had split and John, Paul, George and Ringo were recording/performing/releasing records strictly as solo acts. Nevertheless, it is interesting to note the affection and respect with which she was held as a friend and fellow musician.

During her interview with Bob Harris for the 2009 BBC Radio 2 documentary *The Songs the Beatles Gave Away*, at one point Cilla's memory turned to a week in 1971 that she and Bobby had spent in Cannes where they attended the famous Film Festival. Principally they were there to attend the screening of two films John and Yoko had made: *Erection* and *Imagine*. Not surprisingly, Ringo was there as well for the same reason. He was aboard the SS *Marala*, a yacht he'd hired for the week. His shipmates included his wife Maureen, George and Pattie, Roger Shine and his fiancée Christine, Marc and June Bolan. He invited Cilla and Bobby to join them. The launch that Ringo sent to ferry them to the yacht was impressive enough for Cilla, it was not small and put her in mind of the Mersey ferries. On boarding she asked the uniformed officer who welcomed them where Ringo was, only to be told he and his party were waiting for them aboard the yacht moored out in the harbour. When she looked seawards she saw the *Marala* and was quite stunned to see a huge three-decked yacht which at the time was the sixth largest private vessel in the world. It was owned by Princess Marie de Savoy and boasted a crew of 22 and three dining rooms. A step up from a Mersey ferry in anyone's book.

Naturally, given the number of musicians on board, the guitars came out and in her 2003 autobiography *What's It All About?*, Cilla comments that George decided to write a song for her and so all the assembled musicians sat down to work on it together. The song that emerged was called 'Photograph', to which she contributed some lyrics (which she couldn't remember) as did Ringo's friend Roger Shine. On her return to the UK she inquired about the tune only to be told by Ringo that he had decided to record it himself, which he did, and as Cilla wryly commented, "The bugger had a hit with it too!"[1]

Cilla also recalled that, "George also wrote for me 'Back Off Boogaloo', but by then I was doing too many ballads, the career chose me. In the early days I would have done it, I loved the rock and roll."[2]

Cilla was mistaken about who originally offered her 'Back Off Boogaloo'. It was Ringo, not George. It was a song he and George had written together although in the main it was a Ringo composition he recorded in September 1971 at the Apple Studio in London. George Harrison produced and it was released as an Apple single on 17 March 1972. Ringo's good friend Marc Bolan had supplied the title and was the original inspiration for the tune, indeed Ringo's version was very much in the Glam Rock style so popular at the time. 'Back Off Boogaloo' was Ringo's follow-up to 'It Don't Come Easy', and on release the songwriting credit was credited to just 'Richard Starkey' (as was the B-side 'Blindman'). It wasn't until 2017 that George Harrison was credited as the co-writer, as he had added some chords and finished the melody. George also played slide guitar on the single.

For a tune he almost gave away it proved immensely successful for Ringo Starr as a solo artist: it climbed to number 2 in the UK where it remains his highest-charting single.

In Canada and in the USA it snuck into the *Billboard* Hot 100 Top 10 to peak at number 9.

Of course it was the Starkey-Harrison credited 'Photograph' on which Cilla had set her heart and which became Ringo's follow-up to 'Back Off Boogaloo'. In 1973, Ringo took it to number 1 in both the *Billboard* and *Cashbox* charts in the USA, as well as to number 1 in Australia and Canada, whereas in the UK it peaked at number 8. Either way, Cilla most certainly missed out!

George had not forgotten Cilla, for a year later he invited her into the Apple Studio to record two songs: 'You've Got to Stay with Me' and 'I Still Love You'. (The latter was originally titled 'Whenever', but when it was copyrighted to Harrisongs in 1972 it was by the title 'When Every Song Is Sung'.)

George enrolled a stellar house band for the session with Cilla, including Ringo on drums, Klaus Voormann on bass, Eric Clapton and himself on guitars. Cilla spoke to both BBC Radio Merseyside broadcaster Spencer Leigh and Bob Harris about the session, telling Bob: "I'd come down from Blackpool where I'd been working to go and see a dentist. I arrived at Apple with a very swollen mouth ... the lyrics of the song are, 'When every song is sung, When every bell is rung, when every picture's hung up, I'll still love you'."[3]

As a result of her discomfort, the session did not realise a finished product. She did make a second recording between 1974–75 with producer Dave Mackay. As with the George-produced version, Cilla was still not completely happy with her second attempt:"(The song) didn't have the magic it deserved. It should have had a 'Yesterday'-type arrangement."[4]

As a consequence, the Dave Mackay version also remained in EMI's vaults until it was finally released in May 2003, as 'I'll Still Love You (When Every Song Is Sung)' as part of her three-CD compilation, *Cilla: The Best of 1963–78*.

According to author Keith Badman, sometime over Christmas, 1982, Harrison and Black met in a London restaurant to discuss completing their recordings from ten years earlier, but nothing came of the idea.[5]

George Harrison's original handwritten lyrics for 'When Every Song Is Sung', aka 'Whenever', aka 'I Still Love You', appear in the extended version of his autobiography *I, Me, Mine*, alongside his personal reflections on the tune in which he says he made several attempts to record it with artists such as Ronnie Spector (Phil Spector's wife), Cilla Black, Leon Russell and Leon's wife Mary, and that he had even started producing it as a single for Cilla, but that they never finished it. In the end it was Ringo who recorded and released the first finished version of the song on his 1976 album, *Ringo's Rotogravure*.

Another major name associated with the song is Shirley Bassey who had recorded a hit version of Harrison's 'Something', after which it had been suggested maybe George should start writing songs specifically for her in the manner of Burt Bacharach and Dionne Warwick. It was not an idea with which George was overly enamoured, and so it is humorous to note at the top of his original handwritten lyrics (in brackets) for 'When Every Song Is Sung', next to the title 'Whenever', somewhat tongue-in-cheek, George had written 'by Shirley Bassey', commenting that he thought it would be a good one for her.[6]

Similarly, in George's annotated handwritten lyrics included in *I, Me, Mine*, he says of 'The Light that Has Lighted the World' that it came about at the same time he was trying to record 'When Every Song Is Sung' with Cilla Black. Apparently he had it in mind as the B-side. Working on 'The Light that Has Lighted the World' prompted him to consider how he related to Cilla. First there was the Liverpool connection. Like himself, Cilla had left the city to pursue a career as a singer/recording artiste. After that, George recalled how success initially pleases everyone, but once someone leaves their hometown people start to say they have changed, which is what people said of Cilla and himself. With that experience in mind, he got the idea for the lyric which in turn became 'The Light that Has Lighted the World', by which time he'd forgotten about the Cilla single and so he used it on his own 1973 album, *Living in the Material World*. (A wonderful acoustic version of this song can be heard on the posthumous compilation album issued in 2012, entitled *Early Takes: Volume 1*.)

1 *What's It All About?*, Cilla Black (Ebury Press, 2003) p. 217.
2, 3 Cilla Black in conversation with Bob Harris OBE for *The Songs the Beatles Gave Away,* BBC Radio 2, March 2009, written and narrated by Bob Harris, produced by Bob Harris and Trudie Myerscough-Harris
4 *George Harrison*, Alan Clayson, (Sanctuary, 2003) p. 332.
5 *The Beatles Diary Volume 2: After the Break-Up 1970–2001*, Keith Badman, (Omnibus Press, London, 2001).
6 *I, Me, Mine* by George Harrison, (Genesis Publications, 2016) p. 246.

Chapter 97:
RINGO, EMMANUEL AND A GIRL CALLED CANDY

As 1967 drew to a close, Ringo was not left sitting at home twiddling his thumbs. He was also actively pursuing a solo venture. Following on from the critical acclaim he had received from his acting performances in both *A Hard Day's Night* and *Help!*, NEMS had been on the alert for a suitable solo film role for him. And so it was that they landed a cameo for him in a movie being made of Terry Southern and Mason Hoffenberg's acclaimed satirical novel *Candy*. As a result, between 3–17 December 1967, Ringo found himself in Rome filming his role as a Mexican gardener by the name of Emmanuel. The film boasted an incredible cast including Marlon Brando, Richard Burton, James Coburn, John Huston, and Ewa Aulin in the title role. (Anita Pallenberg played Nurse Bullock.)

Directed by Christian Marquand, it was released first in the USA on 17 December 1968 and in the UK on 20 February 1969.*

(*Wikipedia notes: Candy *"opened to mixed box office, but later became a cult classic from the psychedelic years of film. It was the 18th highest grossing film of 1968. According to* Variety, *the film earned North American rentals of $7.3 million, but because of costs (including over $1 million paid out in participation fees), it recorded an overall loss of $25,000. It was the 12th most popular movie at the UK box office in 1969.)"*[1]

Despite its success as a novel (American author Terry Southern was a much respected and highly successful writer in the Sixties, noted for his 'distinctive satirical style') depending on your point of view, *Candy* the film was either a sex farce that satirises pornographic stories or an utter waste of its hugely talented cast's time. Given the benefit of hindsight, it now seems a disappointing, if not dire, start to Ringo's solo film career.

Acting-wise things looked up when Ringo accepted a second co-starring role, this time alongside Peter Sellers. It was a big screen adaptation of another Terry Southern satirical novel entitled *The Magic Christian*. Filmed in London over 13 weeks during 1969, it was a much more appropriate vehicle for Ringo's acting abilities.

Satire was big in the Sixties: check out *That Was the Week That Was*, 1962/63 – produced and directed by Ned Sherrin and presented by David Frost. Southern was a renowned exponent. A highly regarded novelist, screenwriter, essayist and lecturer, he was a key figure of the 1950s and '60s. Hugely respected by the Beat writers of Greenwich Village by the Sixties he was at the heart of 'Swinging London'. Apart from *Candy* and *The Magic Christian*, he also wrote the dialogue for *Dr. Strangelove* (1965), *The Cincinnati Kid* (1965), and co-wrote with Peter Fonda and Dennis Hopper the script for *Easy Rider* (1969).

An advert for *Candy* published in the 12 April 1969 edition of *Disc and Music Echo* carried the following newspaper quotes: "It's eroticism without parallel ... the most controversial movie perhaps of this generation" (*Evening Standard*); "Candy makes the mind boggle" (*Daily Mail*); and "A pornographic eyeful. Hilariously funny, a blazing satire on current vogues" (*The People*).[2]

As ever you paid your money and took your choice ...

---

1 en.wikipedia.org › wiki › Candy_(1968_film).
2 *Disc and Music Echo*, 12 April 1969, advertisement for the film *Candy*, p.9.

Chapter 98:
1968, GIVING IT ALL AWAY: BUSINESS BITES FROM THE APPLE AND BEYOND

By 1968, Apple was integral to the lives and careers of the Beatles. The business sides of this venture and the opportunities with which they provided them to either sign, champion and write for, or work with, other artists is interesting to note. As 'businessmen' not clad in suits here is a snapshot of tasks/ventures/enterprises that came along to occupy some of their time:

September 1967: Apple Music Publishing signed its first group (coincidentally, also from Liverpool) called Focal Point.

November 1967: The Beatles & Co was established. This was a new corporation created to avoid the individual Beatles having to face huge income tax bills. From now on, each Beatle held a 5% stake in The Beatles & Co (and paid corporation tax) while the remaining 80% was held by The Beatles Ltd.

7 December 1967: The Apple Boutique, 94 Baker Street, London, opened.

11 December 1967: Apple Music Publishing signs its second group, Grapefruit. (A party was held on 28 January 1968 to welcome them to Apple.)

12 January 1968: The Beatles officially founded Apple Corps. Ltd, a multi-faceted corporation which replaced The Beatles Ltd. It was a conglomerate or holding company with several different businesses operating under a corporate name. At the same time, the Apple trademark was registered in 47 countries. The chief division within Apple Corps Ltd was Apple Records which it launched later that year.

February 1968: Apple Corps Ltd registered Apple Electronics, Apple Films Ltd, Apple Management, Apple Music Publishing, Apple Overseas, Apple Publicity, Apple Records, Apple Retail, and Apple Tailoring (Civil and Theatrical), which represented the five focal points of its business: records, electronics, film, publishing and retailing.

30 July 1968: The Apple Boutique closed. It had not been profitable, thanks in part to the shoplifting it had incurred. (During the evening prior to the shop's closure, the Beatles and their friends helped themselves to what they wanted. When the doors of the shop were opened the next day members of the public were allowed to help themselves to any remaining stock. Even the carpets went.)

The little remembered second boutique that the group had opened on 22 May at 161 King's Road, Apple Tailoring (Civil and Theatrical), was also closed. The Beatles generously gave it to its manager.

If 1967 found the Beatles largely enjoying the freedom that being their own bosses gave them, 1968 found them less and less enamoured with their newfound roles as businessmen. It was not what they had signed up to be way back in 1962. Nevertheless, they began the new year, despite the loss of Brian Epstein, still buoyed by the fact that they were no longer bound by the rigours and restrictions of touring. The artistic freedom of not touring had already inspired them to new heights, and the time spent together in the studio creating *Sergeant Pepper* had been a bonding experience, while Transcendental Meditation appeared to be a further sign of their close group unity.

The harmony such group activity suggested to the public disguised the fissures that had actually opened in their once rock-solid group bond. Both John and George had become disenchanted with being Beatles. George was increasingly unhappy that he was still not encouraged to provide more tunes to Beatles records. As a result, he had begun to bond with musicians beyond the Beatles camp while his work for *Wonderwall Music* coincided with his growing confidence and maturity as a writer. Meditation, Indian music and Indian culture were further informing his outlook on life.

Reflecting on George's interest in the sitar and meditation, Roger McGuinn of the Byrds noted: "Indian music is inspired by transcendence, so it all did fit together."[1]

John, also no longer enamoured with 'Beatlemania' was hiding within an acid haze, but no amount of tripping could suppress his burgeoning desire to break out from the stultifying confines of life as he was living it. He was desperate to break free and try something new. As the Beatles' trip to India loomed ever closer he was convinced that within the intriguing persona of Yoko Ono he had found the door to the new reality he so craved to explore. While all the Beatles could have done without the responsibilities of being 'businessmen that Apple thrust upon their shoulders all four were open to the freedom the corporation appeared to present for them to do what they wanted as musicians.

As 1968 began, on 7 January George flew to India to record the Indian music for *Wonderwall*, but by Thursday 25 January he was back in London alongside his fellow Beatles filming an appearance that was to be included at the very end of the *Yellow Submarine* animated film. (*The film received its world premiere later that year at the London Pavilion cinema on Wednesday 17 July at which the Beatles were present. It was not released in the USA until November. It was a critical success.*)

At this moment in time George was managing to successfully combine his Beatles chores with his solo ventures.

For all of the group the journey to Rishikesh to study at the feet of the Maharishi offered a golden opportunity to strengthen any faltering bonds, and to truly escape the strains and stresses of running their own company, which were already beginning to reveal themselves and which already felt like huge burdens.

Unfortunately the visit to India did not go to plan. The group had set aside two months of their time to be there.

George, Pattie, Jenny Boyd, John and Cynthia flew out to Delhi on 15 February 1968. Mal Evans met them at the airport, having flown out ahead to organise transport for them from Delhi to the Maharishi's ashram in Rishikesh where they were to study with him. The ashram lies approximately 150 miles from Delhi (halfway to Tibet) in the foothills of the Himalayas. Four days later, Paul, Jane, Ringo and Maureen arrived in Delhi to make the same long, dusty and bumpy journey. Among others present with the Beatles in Rishikesh at various times were Neil Aspinall, Apple employee Alex 'Magic' Mardas, actress Mia Farrow and her sister Prudence, singer-songwriter Donovan and his friend Gypsy Dave, flautist Paul Horn, and Beach Boy Mike Love.

From the start Ringo and Maureen felt ill at ease. Maureen became obsessed with the flies. Ringo didn't like the local cuisine. They also missed their children. And so after 11 days, on 1 March, they returned home. After five weeks, on 26 March, Paul and Jane also left ahead of schedule. It was not, so they stressed, that they had become disillusioned, rather that five weeks was enough. They enthused that it had been a rewarding experience and never deviated from that point of view.

Arriving late to the party had been Beatles hanger-on and already director of 'Apple Electronics Ltd', one Alexis 'Magic' Mardas. He had wormed his way into John's inner circle promising to produce all manner of wonderful electronic devices and inventions. Unfortunately Mardas was jealous that he had apparently been superseded as John Lennon's go-to guru by the Maharishi, to whom Mardas believed John was now more attentive. As a result Mardas arrived not in the mood to dedicate himself to meditation, instead he was determined to regain John's attention and was directly instrumental in bringing the whole shebang to a premature close. He did so by airing some made-up tittle-tattle about the Maharishi and his designs on Mia Farrow.

Without offering the clueless Maharishi a chance to defend himself against Mardas's accusations, the remaining Beatles simply upped and left on Friday 12 April 1968. That was that, the visit was over, there would be no more mention of the Maharishi. The Beatles as a group were done with him (but not with Transcendental Meditation). George, Pattie Harrison and her sister Jenny did not return directly to the UK. Instead they headed south to visit Ravi Shankar in Madras and stayed there until 21 April 1968.

Pattie: "George didn't want to go straight from two months of meditation into the chaos that was waiting for him in England – the new business, finding a new manager, the fans and the press. Instead we went to see Ravi Shankar and lost ourselves in his music."[2]

Another positive outcome, other than their deeper understanding of Transcendental Meditation, that John, Paul and George brought back from India was a wealth of new songs they had written whilst there. Around 40 songs were composed at Rishikesh and sometime during the third week of May 1968 all four Beatles gathered at George's home, 'Kinfauns', to tape demos of 23 of these. Most would be re-recorded for inclusion on that year's double album *The Beatles* (otherwise known as the *White Album* because of its brilliant white cover on which the group name was embossed).

Included in these tunes there was a song a Beatle would give away: George's marvellous 'Sour Milk Sea'.

Of the 23 tunes recorded at 'Kinfauns' (usually referred to as 'The Esher Demos') 11 were John songs, 7 were by Paul, 5 by George. They were essentially solo compositions. Of these songs composed in India, 9 of John's made the *The Beatles* 30-track double album, 6 of Paul's and 2 of George's.

The Esher Demos
The songs were:
Cry Baby Cry (John)
Child of Nature (John, later, in 1971, given a new lyric and a new title, 'Jealous Guy')
The Continuing Story of Bungalow Bill (John)
I'm So Tired (John)
Yer Blues (John)
Everybody's Got Something to Hide Except Me and My Monkey (John)
What's the New Mary Jane (John)
Revolution (John)
Julia (John)
Dear Prudence (John)
Sexy Sadie (John)
While My Guitar Gently Weeps (George)
Circles (George)
Sour Milk Sea (George)
Not Guilty (George)
Piggies (George)
Blackbird (Paul)
Rocky Raccoon (Paul)
Back in the USSR (Paul)
Honey Pie (Paul)
Mother Nature's Son (Paul)
Ob-La-Di, Ob-La-Da (Paul)
Junk (Paul)

Sessions to record what became *The Beatles* album were booked to start on 20 May right through until 26 July 1968, but it was not until Thursday 30 May that these actually began when work on John's 'Revolution' kick-started the sessions. Such were the number of songs the Beatles had ready to record that the new record grew into a double album.

Ringo also had a song up for consideration that he had begun writing many years before these sessions began, the one and only … 'Don't Pass Me By'!

Sessions continued well beyond the end of July right through into October when, as the deadline for a November release loomed ever closer, the album was finally completed over the 16, 17 and 18 of that month. (In addition to the material for *The Beatles* they still had stereo mixes to complete for the tunes they had recorded specifically for the *Yellow Submarine* soundtrack album.)

In the interim between returning from Rishikesh and beginning recording 'Revolution' three significant events had happened:

a) On 11 May, John and Paul (accompanied by Neil Aspinall and John's new best friend 'Magic' Alex) had flown to the USA for four days to unveil 'Apple Corps' to their American fans via a series of interviews with the press and TV appearances.

b) While they were in New York, Linda Eastman was able to contact Paul again and he invited her to ride with them to the airport to take some photographs. Linda later recalled sitting in the limo with her camera bag in between John and Paul during which time she says she and Paul got to know one another a bit more …

c) Within a few days of their return to London, while Cynthia was away on holiday abroad, John invited Yoko Ono to Kenwood, his house in Weybridge, Surrey. John and Yoko spent an evening recording an album of strange sound effects entitled *Unfinished Music No 1: Two Virgins* and from that point onwards were united: John's marriage to Cynthia was effectively over, as was Yoko's to film-maker Terry Cox. Within months both couples had divorced their previous spouses and on 20 March 1969 John and Yoko married in Gibraltar (near Spain).

During the summer as work progressed on *The Beatles*, John, Paul, George and Ringo would not always be together in the same studio as each other and, as recording continued, on some occasions one or two Beatles might not even be in the country. For example, 'Revolution 9' was almost exclusively John's work with some input from Yoko Ono and George, and while they worked on that Paul was working solo in another studio recording a song entitled 'Blackbird'.

One time when they *were* all together was for the recording of their follow-up single to 'Lady Madonna'. This was a Paul song (although John worked with him to help complete it) entitled 'Hey Jude'. Rehearsed, recorded and mixed between 29 July and 7 August the single broke the unofficial 'three-minute' rule for the length of a 45rpm by clocking in at 7 minutes 11 seconds. They weren't the first to break the rule – actor Richard Harris had done so earlier in April 1968 with his 7 minute 21 second version of Jimmy Webb's 'MacArthur Park' which had made it to number 4 in the UK chart and number 2 in the USA's *Billboard* Hot 100. Released on 26 August in the UK, 'Hey Jude' topped the charts in at least 20 countries worldwide including both the UK and the USA.

---

1 *George Harrison: Behind the Locked Door*, Graeme Thomson (Omnibus Press, 2013) Roger McGuinn as quoted on p.114.
2 *Wonderful Today*, Pattie Boyd, (Headline Review, 2007) p.118.

Chapter 99:
APPLE RECORDS AND OL' BLUE EYES

Ringo: "The records Apple made were exciting. It started with Mary Hopkin, and then George brought Jackie Lomax and later Billy Preston. I put John Tavener on the label. His brother was working for me as a builder … and said, 'Would you like to hear my brother's tape?' I loved it. We were very open to all different kinds of music, so we thought we'd put it on Apple."[1a]

Paul: "Anyone in the Beatles who wanted to show up and produce as much as he wanted was welcome to do so. Everyone was involved, but people didn't all do the same amount. I lived in London so I was there more…" (As a caveat to this comment Paul added these words: "Apple was quite a nice little record company, if that had been what we wanted to do. But, once the business hassles came in, we thought, 'Who needs a record company? I'd rather just have my freedom.'")[1b]

Owning their own recording label gave the Beatles artistic licence, the like of which they could only have dreamed when they first signed to Parlophone in 1962. Apple Records was not only to be their group 'home' but a home to artists the Beatles liked and wanted to help get their music in front of the public.

It certainly gave them the opportunity to encourage and mentor new talent by working alongside them in the studio. They would often produce other artists' records and write songs with or for them. The establishment of a second label, Zapple, promised to give a voice to niche artists who otherwise may have not found it easy at all to access audio outlets for their work. Thus the establishment of Apple Records heralded a fresh surge in Beatles 'giveaways'.

In hindsight the whole Apple venture can be seen as one mass 'giveaway' by the Beatles, not only of their money but of their songs, talents, time, facilities, studios, contacts, media exposure, outlets and opportunities to further other artists' careers that individually they would otherwise have struggled to do. The Beatles removed some of the barriers artists usually faced, especially those who were less well known and whose work was considered to be more 'esoteric'.

Paul McCartney and George Harrison (whatever misgivings he may have expressed about Apple) in particular enjoyed the freedom to step beyond the confines of the Beatles to work with other musicians, and in the case of a singer such as Mary Hopkin, Paul went beyond the music and helped direct her early career by providing opportunities she might not otherwise have been able to access so easily. (He never became her manager.)

Apart from introducing John Tavener to the label ('underground classical music') Ringo enjoyed and supported the ethos of the label. He made himself readily available to drum on many sessions for artists signed to Apple.

John Lennon was not active in adding to the list of other artists who became signed to Apple. His focus in life at this time was Yoko, as he was to her, and to that end he particularly enjoyed the ready availability the label provided to release his own, Yoko's own and his and Yoko's solo product to the world (some of which might – by nearly every other label – have been considered most definitely 'esoteric' and which otherwise would have found it problematic to secure a release).

Apple, Zapple and the Beatles' endeavours to use the company to help other artists with their careers was a unique enterprise for the time. Ultimately it was short-lived but they have to be applauded for attempting to give back to other artists when others may have sat back and just counted their money. They knew how hard it had been for them when they were starting out and they wanted to make it easier for others in an industry where the focus was always on profit and taking risks was not really an option. They were doing their bit to overcome the dilemma of 'Art versus Commerce'.

'Lady Madonna' was the last Beatles record to be released on the Parlophone label and 'Hey Jude' their debut Apple single. From then on, in both the USA and the UK, all Beatles records were issued on the Apple label. The copyright for these records remained with EMI and so Beatles records continued to use Parlophone and Capitol catalogue numbers.

John, Paul, George and Ringo always viewed Apple Records as something more than just a conduit for their own releases, but as a 'proper' label, a home for others as well. When other artists released records their copyrights were (in the main) held by Apple Corps Ltd and their releases had Apple catalogue numbers, e.g., Apple 3, Apple 4, etc. Thus the numbering on the first four commercially released UK Apple singles was as such:

The Beatles, 'Hey Jude', Apple (Parlophone) R 5722, UK release: Friday, 30 August 1968

Mary Hopkin, 'Those Were the Days' (Apple 2), UK release: Friday, 30 August 1968

Jackie Lomax, 'Sour Milk Sea' (Apple 3), UK release: Friday, 6 September 1968

John Foster and Sons Ltd Black Dyke Mills Band, 'Thingumybob' (Apple 4), UK release: Friday, 6 September 1968

(In the USA all four records were released on the same day, Monday 26 August 1969.)

APPLE 1

Because 'Hey Jude' could not be catalogued as 'Apple 1', missing from the list of four above is a single numbered 'Apple 1'. That is not because a record with that catalogue number does not exist or was not issued, it does and it was. Apple 1 is 'The Lady Is a Champ' as sung by none other than Frank Sinatra to the melody of the Richard Rogers composition 'The Lady Is a Tramp'. It was a special one-off recording (on which Frank was accompanied by just a piano) never intended for commercial release but made especially for Ringo Starr's wife Maureen on the occasion of her 22nd birthday. (Lorenz Hart had written the lyrics to the original version but for Frank's Apple recording Sammy Cahn penned new words.) Legend has it that only one copy was cut (others suggest maybe a few more) after which the master tape was destroyed to preserve the uniqueness of the gift. Despite its rarity it has been available to hear on YouTube since 2010. The lyrics contain words such as: 'She married Ringo and she could have had Paul, That's why the lady is a champ' and 'So I whistle and stamp, Because the lady, The charming lady, Mr. Ringo's lady is a champ'.

Beyond the first four commercial releases detailed above, the Apple Records catalogue boasted a wide-ranging list of artists that reflected its owners' diverse musical tastes as this list of acts signed to the label between 1969 and 1973 shows:

Badfinger (formerly the Iveys)
John Foster & Sons Ltd Black Dyke Mills Band
Brute Force (Stephen Friedland)
Elephant's Memory
Chris Hodge
Mary Hopkin
Jackie Lomax
Modern Jazz Quartet

Billy Preston
Radha Krishna Temple
Ravi Shankar
Ronnie Spector
James Taylor
John Tavener
Trash (formerly White Trash)
Doris Troy

1a & 1b *The Beatles Anthology*, by The Beatles (Cassell & Co, 2000) page 289.

Chapter 100:
'Z' IS FOR ZAPPLE

Apple Records was not the only record label the Beatles launched. There was a second, called 'Zapple'. Its formation in part came out of the frustration they had faced from EMI over the cover for *Sergeant Pepper*. The company got very wound up about legal concerns such as, 'Would the people featured on the cover object and take legal action?' and if they did, 'How much was that going to cost?' The negativity coming from the people in charge had convinced the Beatles that something had to change, they felt EMI was out of touch not only with them as artists but with the young people who bought their records. Thus the formation of Zapple was seen as a way of breaking free of the usual restraints and conventionality of being signed to a major label.

John came up with the name. In essence Zapple was a continuation of an experimental demo studio Paul had established in 1966 in a flat belonging to Ringo that the drummer was not using at the time. In Paul's mind Zapple would be the link between Apple and the Indica Bookshop, especially as he and John entrusted Barry Miles to also manage the label.

Miles, along with John Dunbar and Peter Asher had formed a company to open (in the same premises) the Indica Books and Gallery in Mason's Yard, off Duke Street, St. James's. (For the name think 1960s and 'cannabis indica'…) On the day the bookshop opened Paul turned up with a large heavy package in the back of his Aston Martin. It was a present for the bookshop: 5000 sheets of wrapping paper for the shop which he had personally designed and had printed. Paul's design was very Sixties in concept and comprised his own hand-lettered name and the address of the shop in black and white which he had drawn in the shape of a Union Jack. It was a very thoughtful and amazing gift that saved the day, for Asher, Dunbar and Miles had forgotten to order wrapping paper.

At the time the Indica opened Paul had been living in the same house as Peter Asher and he was their first customer. As well as providing practical support by helping prepare the premises ready for opening and donating the wrapping paper, most importantly Paul generously supported the venture financially.

The gallery played a crucial role in the romance of John Lennon and Yoko Ono, for it was there that the couple first met. Later the Bookshop moved to a separate address in Bloomsbury. Sadly the Gallery closed in 1967 but the Bookshop hung on until 29 February 1970 when it also closed. As well as his work for and at Indica, Barry Miles was also a director of the *International Times*, Europe's first underground newspaper. Appropriately the *IT* was first published in the basement of the Indica Bookshop. Paul was a great supporter of *IT* and encouraged his friends in the music business to be interviewed for it.

"When John was living out in the suburbs by the golf course with Cynthia and hanging out there, I was getting in with a guy called Miles and the people at the Indica. I used to be at his house a lot of nights, just him and his wife, because he was just so interesting, very well-read. So he'd turn you on to Burroughs and all that. I'd done a bit of literature at school, but I never did anything modern."[1]

Of the impetus behind the second label, Barry Miles wrote: "Apple was seen as a way of controlling their own 'brand' as it would now be called. All along they had wanted to release more controversial and experimental material – John and Yoko's *Two Virgins* being the best example, which EMI had refused point-blank to distribute – and the Zapple division was created specifically to do this."[2]

The official launch of Zapple was 3 February 1969. An American press release explained the raison d'être behind the new label in these words:

"It will emphasise a series of 'spoken word' albums and some music releases of a more wide-ranging and esoteric nature." The same press release explained that some releases would be at a budget price and that Barry Miles, "a British writer-intellectual in his late 20s" would be supervising the 'Zapple program'."[3a]

Specifically it also announced that:

"The first three releases on the Zapple label are now being pressed".[3b]

Earlier than this a British press release/advertisement written by Derek Taylor announced the formation of Zapple in the UK and provided specific details of its first three albums:

"One's by John Lennon and Yoko Ono. It's called *Life with the Lions: Unfinished Music No. 2*. The other's by George Harrison. It's called *Electronic Sound*. This is a new thing for George. It's all done on a machine called the Moog Synthesiser. One side's called 'Under the Mersey Wall'. The other's called 'No Time or Space'. The third Zapple album will be by American poet Richard Brautigan. It'll be called *Listening to Richard Brautigan*. We're hoping to release it soon along with one other, which we've yet to decide on."[4a]

Taylor's press release was a far more engaging read than its dour American counterpart, going out of its way to prepare readers/listeners for how different Zapple releases were going to be from the more mainstream Apple label records: "We want to publish all sorts of sounds. Some of these sounds will be spoken, some electronic, some classical. We'll be producing recorded interviews too. Some of the people we put on record will be well known, some not so well known. This means you'll get plenty of variety. We don't want Zapple to become a one-track record label. We'll publish almost anything providing it's valid and good." Reassuringly Taylor added: "We're not going to put out rubbish, at any price."[4b]

Further, Taylor emphasised the 'budget' nature of the label's prices and that Zapple product (which Taylor dubbed 'Zapples') would be available from 'leading record shops and some bookshops'.

Just in case anyone reading the press release was unsure as to what a 'leading record shop' was or where one could be found, Taylor's release provided a coupon on which people could complete their details, send to Zapple, which by return would send out a list of stockists!

Tantalisingly, the American press release gave a list of writers and poets who had committed to Zapple releases, which included Lawrence Ferlinghetti, Michael McClure, Kenneth Patchen, Charles Olson and Allen Ginsberg. It also stated that the Beatles themselves would record 'discussion sessions among themselves' which would be released in the autumn, confidently explaining, "It is the hope of Apple Corps Ltd that the new label will help pioneer a new era for the recording industry equivalent to what the paperback revolution did to book publishing."

These were big ambitions.

Ahead of the American press release announcing this brave new Beatles venture, on 29 January 1969, Barry Miles arrived in New York to record sessions with Ken Weaver (one of the Fugs) and poet Charles Olson. It was one of two visits he made to the USA as he worked tirelessly recording and preparing material for future recordings.

Sadly the plans both the Beatles and Miles had for Zapple did go awry, for it became an immediate victim of the Beatles' internal divisions and inability to function efficiently as businessmen. Apart from George's and John and Yoko's albums nothing else was released by the label.* They were issued (not at a budget price) simultaneously in the UK on 9 May 1969 (26 May in the USA), the day after Paul had refused to sign a contract appointing Allen Klein as his manager which, of course, John, George and Ringo had already signed.

Zapple was not the only victim of Klein's extreme 'streamlining' of Apple. Klein was appointed business manager of Apple on 21 March 1969 and soon after heads began to roll. Some, like Alistair Taylor (Brian Epstein's long-time go-to man) and Ron Kass, Head of Apple Records, were simply sacked (both on the same day 8 May 1969), others like Peter Asher, Head of A&R at Apple, and Denis O'Dell, Head of Apple Films, saw the way the wind was blowing and by June 1969 had both resigned.

(*The Brautigan album later surfaced on EMI-Harvest in 1970.)

1 Sir Paul in conversation with Barry Miles, 4 November 1993. Quoted in *The Zapple Diaries: The Rise and Fall of the Last Beatles Label*, Barry Miles (Peter Owen Publishers, 2015) pp 44–45.
2 *The Zapple Diaries*, Barry Miles, (Peter Owen Publishing, 2015) p.17.
3 a, b: Extracts from The American press release announcing the Zapple label sourced from *Paul McCartney: Many Years from Now*, Barry Miles (Vintage, 1998) p.474.
4 a, b: Extracts of Derek Taylor's UK Apple advertisement sourced from *The Zapple Diaries* by Barry Miles (Peter Owen Publishing, 2015) pp. 21, 22, 23.

Chapter 101:
LIVERPOOL SLIM

The development of Apple Corps coincided with George Harrison's growing influence within the Beatles. George's exquisite guitar playing had always been a major creative element of the group's recordings, fans could sing his solos, they were as integral to each composition as the words, existing as an instrumental verse or chorus within the song.

Now, just as he was presenting more of his own compositions for consideration for inclusion on Beatles records, so he was also enjoying playing with other musicians such as Eric Clapton. This not only enhanced George's reputation but also provided him with an outlet with which to further enjoy his freedom from the burdens of Beatlemania and touring. Sharing music and listening to other people's tunes was integral to his life as a musician. When, in 1967, (on John Lennon's recommendation) former Mersey musician/ Cavern contemporary Jackie Lomax was employed by Apple Publishing as a songwriter, so his and George's paths were destined to cross almost as regularly as they did when, as younger men, they were playing music in venues on the Liverpool circuit. It was, most definitely, a relationship ripe for development and opportunity.

JACKIE LOMAX
b. John Richard Lomax on 10 May 1944 in Wallasey on the Wirral Peninsula, Cheshire (nowadays Wallasey is included as part of Merseyside).
d. 15 September 2013 in Wallasey whilst on a visit from his home in Southern California to attend his daughter's wedding.

Jackie's life as a performer began as guitarist with Dee and the Dynamites whom he left in 1962 to join popular Mersey Beat combo, the Undertakers. Like Jackie, although originating from Wallasey, the Undertakers were stalwarts of the Liverpool scene and hugely popular down the Cavern, Iron Door and other venues, in part because they offered a little more in terms of content than other, more textbook groups, around them.

Jackie Lomax recalled it was around '61 his group and the Beatles crossed paths: "The Undertakers were playing in Liverpool just about the same time John, Paul, George, Stuart and Pete made the transition from 'The Silver Beatles' to 'The Beatles'. We used to see them at the Cavern, we used to be on the same bill sometimes. We went through the Hamburg scene and all of that. We ran across each other a lot."[1]

Jackie particularly recalled a Liverpool habit which both bands shared with many of their contemporaries from the Cavern: "After a show we always used to go to Joe's Café for curried chicken. All the bands used to go there."[2]

Like all the other groups they could play the bread-and-butter American rock 'n' roll that fans demanded very well indeed, but the presence of saxophonist (which was unusual for the time) Brian Jones (no relation to the Rolling Stone) within their number allowed them to play a soul influenced big band style of R&B. Added to this heady mix was the ear-busting level of sound they generated. They were so serious about their music and the sound they made that they invested the money made from playing into buying equipment. Not only were they reputed to be the first group in the country with an all-Gibson guitar line-up, but they were also the first to use a 100-watt PA system. This gave them a very distinctive sound and locally they were described as 'hard rockers'.

Added to this heady sonic mix was the utterly distinctive 'white soul' vocals of singer Jackie Lomax. Regarded as one of the best singers on the Mersey scene (comparable to

Signed to Apple as a songwriter and solo recording artist, success was surely just a heartbeat away …
(Pictorial Press Ltd / Alamy Stock Photo)

the Animals' Eric Burdon) Jackie gave them yet another edge over the competition.

It was during the summer of 1962 that the Undertakers' reputation on Merseyside found them graduating to Hamburg. Musically their residency at the Star-Club was a godsend for them, for performing at the venue at the same time were Ray Charles and Little Richard. The Undertakers were in seventh heaven and paid very close attention to what they heard.

For all their excellent musical pedigree and promise, ultimately the group's Achilles heel was that they lacked their own in-house songwriter. For all their musicality and (for the time) distinctive 'black' sound they were essentially, like most of the other beat groups in Liverpool, a covers band, albeit their covers were a tad different to those of their Scouse contemporaries. They succeeded in giving fans a brilliant night's entertainment but failed to harness their unique sound into producing their own, self-written compositions, and so they were reliant for their repertoire on songs already recorded and written by others.

Of course, this was no barrier to Brian Epstein, who could overcome this deficit because he had his own songwriting team to hand. He was aware of both the Undertakers' popularity and the esteem in which they were held by other local groups of the time, so when they returned from Hamburg he tried to sign them to his management company, NEMS. Amazingly he was rebuffed and instead the Undertakers signed with Ralph Webster who had connections with many Liverpool venues. By the spring of 1963 they had signed to Pye Records with songwriter Tony Hatch as their producer. Not part of Epstein's 'stable' then, but nevertheless they seemed set for chart success.

Unfortunately, Hatch chose the wrong songs to cut with the group and they had none of their own tunes with which to counter his choices. As a working partnership Hatch and the Undertakers never quite gelled and in his attempts to cut that one all-important commercial big-hitting single with them he never truly captured on disc the essence of what made the group so special on stage.

Four singles were cut for Pye. Their debut July 1963 release 'Everybody Loves a Lover' (formerly a hit for Doris Day in 1958) failed to chart at all and was more memorable for its B-side, 'Mashed Potatoes'. (Author's note: this song is often referred to as 'The Mashed Potato' or '(Do the) Mashed Potato', but on the record label it is written 'Mashed Potatoes').

A memorable clip of film* exists of the group performing this particular tune in which they are all dressed in the black frock coats and top hats associated with undertakers. It still rocks and had it been promoted as the A-side it may well have secured them a sizeable hit, thus securing their place in the history of UK pop music as leading exponents of a major dance craze … Maybe.

(*The film clip referred to here comes from a BBC documentary entitled The Mersey Sound *which was the first serious attempt to investigate what was then a 'new' phenomenon. It was broadcast on 9 October 1963.)*

Their second 1963 single released in September was the Hatch-chosen 'What About Us' (a Leiber-Stoller rock 'n' roll number that had been a hit in the USA by the Coasters). This choice of A-side ran contrary to the group's wish to have their version of 'Money' as the topside but which Hatch relegated to the B-side. Like its predecessor this single made no impression on the chart. The band's version of 'Money' was much more in tune with the zeitgeist and they must have been galled (as well as proven right) when two months later the same song became a UK Top 20 hit for Bern Elliott and the Fenmen. (On 21 November 1963, Elliott and his Fenmen entered the UK charts at number 43 with 'Money' and during a 13-week chart run took it all the way to number 14 on 19 December.)

The Undertakers' one and only UK 'chart' single came with their third 45, a spirited version of 'Just a Little Bit', which had first been recorded on 1 September 1959 by American blues singer-songwriter Rosco Gordon. Released in November 1959, by early 1960 Gordon was climbing the USA's *Billboard* R&B Chart with the song. The Undertakers accompanied their version of his tune with a fine version of soul man Solomon Burke's 'Stupidity' gracing the B-side. This was much more like it. For the first time they had been allowed to choose the A-side. However, the single's chart success was brief in the extreme. On 9 April 1964, the Undertakers and 'Just a Little Bit' had squeezed into the UK Top 50 at number 49 … but that was it … a week later they were gone, never to return.

For the song itself, however, it was just the beginning of a long career. The Undertakers' version was just the second 'cover' of 'Just a Little Bit' in what became a veritable landslide. Them featuring Van Morrison released a version on their 1965 album The Angry Young Them *and, as time has passed, many more 'covers' of this tune have been recorded including those by Roy Head, the Liverpool Five, Tony Worsley and the Blue Jays, Etta James, Elvis Presley, Mitch Ryder and the Detroit Wheels, the Mindbenders, Little Milton, T-Bone Walker, Steve Miller, Slade, Joe Louis Walker, Rory Gallagher, and so the list goes on …*

For Jackie Lomax and the Undertakers in the UK there was to be just one more shot at the charts with Pye.

Deeming their name to be too gloomy it was reduced to just 'The 'Takers'. Sartorially they were also given a makeover: out went the presence of a coffin on stage, the mournful looks and the undertaker garb, and in came more modern, stylish attire and some smiles. As the 'Takers the label released their fine version of another Lieber and Stoller tune, 'If You Don't Come Back'. The image and name change seemed to have worked when the 'Takers secured a spot on *Thank Your Lucky Stars*, but sadly it proved all too late.

'If You Don't Come Back' showed initial signs of enjoying a chart run but Fate intervened to deny them the success they deserved. In this instance they were boyond unlucky. Apparently after the initial run no more copies of the single were pressed because the factory pressing the vinyl shut for its annual holidays and by the time they resumed work the group's moment had gone.

Understandably miffed at having effectively missed out on the chart success others artists from Liverpool had enjoyed during the 'Mersey Beat' boom and wondering how to move forward The Undertakers/'Takers accepted work in the USA. And so it was (without rhythm guitarist Geoff Nugent who elected to stay at home) that in 1965 the group decamped to New York City.

Guitarist Chris Huston had initiated this move after he saw an advertisement in a magazine by a promoter called Bob Harvey inviting groups to come to the States where he would record them with a view to promoting their career in the USA. The Undertakers were not the only ones to fall under the sway of Harvey's advert so had Pete Best. And so, on arrival in the Big Apple, the group found themselves unexpectedly thrown together with their old friend from the Cavern.

The promised recordings (produced by Bob Gallo) did take place but the trip was a disaster. The band did not have the right visas and so live work in the USA was problematic which in turn meant ready income was in short supply. Only one single ever emerged at the time,* a cover of 'I Fell In Love (For The Very First Time)' a song co-written by Robert Bateman who had also co-written 'Please Mr. Postman'. The B-side was significant because finally the Undertakers - as they had reverted to calling themselves - cut a tune that was actually written by one of them, a Jackie Lomax original called 'Throw Your Love Away Girl' - his first original song to make it onto a record.

(*The rest of their New York recordings plus the tracks they cut for Pye eventually emerged in 1996 on an album entitled Unearthed by Jackie Lomax and the Undertakers. Released on the Ace label it is still available to this day and well worth the price of entry.)

On the Ace Records website alongside the album's details Lomax succinctly details the more than disappointing New York sojourn endured by he and his group: "The promoter was Bob Harvey, whose idea was, he'd get Pete Best over there and promote him as the ex-Beatle suing for $8 million, and make a fortune. He didn't care about us."[3]

After initially housing them in a sleazy motel, Lomax recalled that when the money ran out the Undertakers were reduced to sleeping in the cockroach infested recording studio. To make some money while ensconced in the studio they played a lot of sessions and cut their own versions of tunes they liked by the Shirelles, Miracles and others. Harvey finally abandoned them after a performance in Canada saying (not for the first time) that he had run out of money. This most probably did not come as too much of a surprise to the boys in the group but after this setback the individual members started to get gigs on their own in order to survive. Inevitably this situation could not continue and Lomax recalled that, "The band really split up when Brian went home that Chistmas 'cos he was missing his mum."[4]

While Lomax, guitarist Chris Huston and drummer 'Bugs' (Warren) Pemberton toughed it out in New York, back home in Liverpool, Brian Jones reunited with Geoff Nugent to form 'The New Undertakers'.

Unable to find work together in New York the three remaining 'Takers began playing separate gigs. Chris linked up with the Young Rascals while, after a few adventures with a band based in Queens called the Mersey Lads, Lomax and Pemberton settled into a band called 'The Lost Souls' who were a 'quasi-Beatles' outfit and regulars on the scene in Greenwich Village. Once Lomax and Pemberton were on board the Lost Souls merged into more of an R&B outfit, eventually morphing into the 'Lomax Alliance'. The line-up comprised bassist Tom Caccetta (aka 'Peters'), guitarist John Cannon (guitar), drummer Bugs Pemberton and Jackie Lomax on guitar and vocals.

When, in 1966, Brian Epstein was in town with The Beatles for their gig at Shea Stadium on Tuesday 23 August, Lomax and the Alliance hung out with them in the Warwick Hotel where John, Paul, George and Ringo stayed for two nights prior to their concert. They also accompanied them to the show.

It was at this point that Brian Epstein renewed his interest in Lomax and offered to manage him, this time as a solo artist: "Epstein wanted to take me back to London as a singer, but I told him to listen to the whole band, and the entire Lomax Alliance went back to London..."[5]

---

1 & 2 Jackie Lomax in conversation with the author, Colin Hall, for *The Songs the Beatles Gave Away*, BBC Radio 2 (2009) written and narrated by Bob Harris OBE, and produced by Bob Harris and Trudie Myerscough-Harris for WBBC.
3, 4 & 5 Information/comments on the Undertakers and their recordings have come from the author's own interview with Jackie Lomax and also the following invaluable source: ace records.co.uk > unearthed

Chapter 102:
APPLE 3, A SONG FROM RISHIKESH

At the time of their return to the UK, the Lomax Alliance were already signed to CBS and plans were in place for an album and single to be recorded and produced by John Simon. To this end some tracks had already been cut in NYC at the Columbia Studios where they had been engineered by Roy Halee of Bob Dylan and the Byrds fame. Epstein arranged for Simon to oversee more recordings to be done in London where the engineer was Dave Siddle who had worked with the Animals and Donovan. On 6 May 1967 the first single by the Lomax Alliance was released in the UK: 'Try As You May' / 'See the People'. It did not chart. The A-side was a Jackie Lomax composition, the B-side was a 'Cannon, Caccetta' tune.

Epstein's death brought the project to a premature end and no more Alliance material under that name was released in the UK, but by then they were a NEMS act and on Brian's death they were passed on to Brian's then partner, Robert Stigwood. Unfortunately, Stigwood was more fully engaged with the Bee Gees* and in promoting their career and so interest in the Alliance lapsed.

(*Not so engaged however that Stigwood didn't recognise the Alliance as suitable candidates to assist him in his promotion of the Bee Gees by getting them to record a Robin, Barry and Maurice Gibb tune entitled 'One Minute Woman'. The single was eventually released by CBS on 20 October 1967 and the B-side featured another track from the Alliance's UK sessions entitled 'Genuine Imitation Life'. The single was credited as 'A Robert Stigwood Production' with Bill Shepherd responsible for Musical Direction on both sides. 'Genuine Imitation Life' was written by Jake Holmes and while lyrically in tune with the times being a reflection on the shallowness/fakery of 'ordinary' people's lives and society itself, in which the singer – as narrator – can clearly see through. Jackie gave the song his best, but its overly stern, pompous and dour tone destined it and its A-side for the bargain bin.)

Once again what had initially seemed like a good career move was all-too quickly thwarted and so Lomax and the Alliance returned to the States where they split soon after. Lomax returned once more to the UK leaving Cannon, Caccetta (Peters) and Pemberton in the USA where they worked as a trio, called 'One'. Under this name they released a single on Columbia, both sides of which had been previously recorded by the Lomax Alliance: the A-side 'Hey Taxi' was a Lomax, Cannon collaboration from the New York sessions while the B-side Cannon's 'Enter Into My World' had been recorded in London. Jackie sang and played on both tracks.[1]

Back in London, Lomax approached the Beatles once more for some advice and it was John who set him on the path to become a paid songwriter for Apple. "You have to understand, none of this was anticipated. I didn't plan to do any of what happened and I don't think anybody else did. It was a matter of 'right place at the right time' when someone's looking for something and you happen to be there. It was actually John who told me to go and see Terry Doran at Apple Publishing which I did and I got signed as a writer. All this had happened before they'd even launched the (Apple) record label."[2]

As Lomax says Apple's Music Publishing predated the label's record company, but apparently he was not the first songwriter signed to the company, for in September 1967 Apple Publishing had signed two songwriters, also from Liverpool. They were Paul Tennant and David Rhodes to whom Paul offered a contract after he met them in Hyde Park. Brian Epstein and John Lennon liked their demos and Epstein offered to manage them under the name 'Focal Point'. Brian's premature demise prevented this from happening, but Terry Doran at Apple Publishing stepped in to become their manager, landing them a contract with Deram Records while from early 1968 Apple published their songs. As all this was happening and Jackie Lomax was signing to the Publishing division of Apple, so were a group called Grapefruit. As they extricated themselves from Northern Songs, George and Ringo also signed to Apple Publishing before going on to establish their own publishing companies.

Apple Publishing was situated in the attic above the Apple boutique on Baker Street. For any songwriter the deal Jackie had landed was very impressive: Apple paid him for every song he wrote. It turned out to be just the beginning of something extraordinary because not long after George became personally involved in the story.

"George really surprised me by listening to some songs that I'd taped onto a two-track in the attic that passed for Apple publishing. This was before the record company was open, even before they'd bought the building in Savile Row. I was up there with the two-track putting songs down, playing everything myself, tambourine, the drums – real primitive! Maybe half a dozen songs I thought I was writing for other artists, but then George Harrison came in one day and said, 'I really like this stuff, would you like to do an album, me producing?'"[3]

Jackie Lomax had not seen this coming and such was the casual 'oh, by the way, I'm not sure what you'll think about this' manner in which George made his offer, in the moment Jackie was left almost speechless. "My insides went down like an elevator, but outside, being Liverpool I was just casual 'yeah, we're cool, that would be great George'. Inside, my head was exploding because I never even anticipated that."[4]

Despite being on an immediate high, Jackie had to then immediately temper his excitement and urge to get started: "For then George went to India and got me really worried that he'd never come back."

When, in 2008, as he related his story to the author, it was at this precise moment Jackie experienced a fit of the giggles. It was as if the nerves he'd originally felt way back in 1968 were still there having remained hidden just beneath the surface waiting for just such a moment in which to escape. The tenterhooks he must have endured at the time were made particularly vivid when with a genuine sigh of relief – almost as if he didn't believe it himself – he said, "You know ... he *was* the last to come back! I thought oh no, he's found a guru and a cave all to himself and would remain there meditating for the rest of his life!"[5]

And wait Jackie had to, for George was indeed the last of the Beatles to return from India. Once back in town, however, it was clear George's commitment to Jackie's cause had not waned: "Thankfully he didn't stay, he came back, much to my relief, and we started work."[6]

The only song on Jackie Lomax's George Harrison-produced Apple album not penned by Lomax himself was on Side One, Track 5: 'Sour Milk Sea'. This was, of course, a George song from Rishikesh, and it became the A-side of Jackie's debut Apple single.

Lomax was thrilled to be gifted what he considered a great tune by George, but was initially unsure as to what it was actually about: "George had written 'Sour Milk Sea' in India while he was with the Maharishi. I profess I didn't know what he really meant by that title or phrase because it's part of the Tantric teachings with which I was not familiar."[7]

Of course it wasn't long before George enlightened Jackie: "In a vague sense what he told me was the song's lyric talks about the ages of the Earth and which the Earth goes through every so many thousands of years, and then it 'shudders' and shakes things off and starts again, it's cyclic. In India the 'in-between part' of the different stages is called 'sour milk sea' and you can't do anything with sour milk sea. Nobody wants sour milk and a whole sea of it would be harder to deal with, so getting rid of it is a good idea."[8]

In his autobiographical work, *I, Me, Mine*, George Harrison provides a more detailed description of where he got the unusual title for this song (which he recorded as part of the 'Kinfauns demos')* by saying, as Jackie Lomax mentioned that it is based on Vishvasara Tantra from Tantric art ('What is here is elsewhere, what is not here is nowhere'). George says: "It's a picture, and the picture is called 'Sour Milk Sea', 'Kalladadi Samudra' in Sanskrit, 'the origin and growth of Jambudvita, the central continent, surrounded by fish symbols, according to the geological theory of the evolution of organic life on earth. The appearance of fishes marks the second stage. Well that's the origin of the song title."[9]

(*When, in 2018 the boxed set version of *The Beatles* aka *The White Album* was issued, a different demo of 'Sour Milk Sea' was released to the one that had been available for many years on bootleg, which suggests George had at least two goes at recording it himself.)

As for the meaning of his lyrics he continued by saying they were really about meditation.
'If your life's not right
Doesn't satisfy you,
You don't get the breaks,
That some of us do
Better work it out
Find where you've gone wrong'

Again, in *I, Me, Mine*, of lines such as these George comments, "I used 'Sour Milk Sea' as the idea of, if you're in the shit, don't go around moaning about it: do something about it…"[10]

JACKIE LOMAX
SOUR MILK SEA **(3:51)**
(George Harrison)
Apple Publishing Ltd
APPLE 3
B-SIDE: The Eagle Laughs at You
(Lomax)
Both sides Produced by: George Harrison

Both sides were recorded between: 24–26 June 1968 at Abbey Road during a break from the Beatles' protracted sessions for *The Beatles* double album aka *The White Album*.
John, with help from Yoko Ono, was busy elsewhere inside Studio 2 completing work on 'Revolution 1' and 'Revolution 9', while Paul was on a short trip with his old school friend Ivan Vaughan and Tony Bramwell to the USA. Paul and his cohorts had flown out on 20 June to Los Angeles to address a Capitol Records Sales Conference (Capitol was going to distribute Apple records in America). Ahead of his American trip Paul had called Linda in New York and invited her to join him for a couple of days at the Beverly Hills Hotel in LA, which she did.
With his Beatles buddies either elsewhere or otherwise occupied, George took advantage of this natural hiatus in recording for *The White Album* to begin work with Jackie Lomax on 'Sour Milk Sea'.
Jackie Lomax: "I first did the song with George singing it acoustic and I played bass, just to get the idea of it. We did this in his house in Esher at that time."[11]
When I spoke with Jackie in 2008 it was clear that he remained in awe as to what was happening to him at this time in his life. He elaborated on his visits to 'Kinfauns' and how he dealt with and navigated his way around what he had become part of. "I found a bootleg of that 'Sour Milk Sea' session and at the same time John Lennon had obviously also come over to Esher and started playing 'Bungalow Bill', which is also about India, right? And on that bootleg I'm singing the chorus with John. That kind of thing happened at Esher: people came over and jammed and recorded a little bit on George's four-track. It was very interesting for me, for you have to understand I was the new kid on the block and the Beatles were the biggest thing in the world (and in my opinion they still are).
"In their presence it was almost like you were afraid you were just going to stand in the corner and not say anything. It was difficult for me because I was kind of shy when normally I'm not shy … but in that situation I was, sort of, 'don't say much, don't stand in

the way, the Beatles are talking, you're not privy ... to join in'. It was an interesting thing for me and George was magnanimous in his hospitality ... he was taking me under his wing, if you like."[12]

Clearly George and Pattie were great hosts and reached out to visitors and friends, especially those whom they understood might find socialising in such company quite thrilling but also quite challenging. Being thrust into the inner circle of the Beatles may have been what every fan on Earth fantasised about at the time, but the reality of it was something else.

The recording for 'Sour Milk Sea' started in Studio 3 at EMI Studios, on Abbey Road, London, but moved to Trident on Wardour Street to take advantage of that studio's superior eight-track recording equipment. Recording was completed on 26 June.

On why George cut Jackie's album simultaneously with his own work on *The White Album*, Jackie commented: "The reason for that is that George would wait for the Beatles to finish and then start with my stuff. It was a matter of changing wheels, setting it up balance-wise and then doing some work. He *didn't have to* do that, *he wanted to* do it. I thought it was great. I just came up with all these songs myself, some of which I hadn't written ahead of the album but during the album."[13]

As Paul had returned from LA on 25 June, he was able to play bass on the 'Sour Milk Sea' sessions held at EMI.

The personnel for 'Sour Milk Sea' comprised:
Jackie Lomax: vocals
George Harrison: acoustic and electric guitar
Eric Clapton: guitar
Nicky Hopkins: piano
Paul McCartney: bass
Ringo Starr: Drums

George and Eric shared lead guitar duties: George's solo follows Eric's lead break approximately two minutes into the song.

One look at the ensemble who played on this recording clearly reveals how George had pulled out all the stops for Jackie. The band he assembled for those sessions was stellar in the extreme. "'Sour Milk Sea' was the first thing that we did. Ringo, god bless him, played for 12 hours on that, over and over again and just got better and better. And you got people like Eric Clapton, it just kind of blows your mind, this guy is so good and he would always say, 'Well I can do it better'. And I'd be like, 'What? Better than *that*?!' Nobody could!"[14]

Jackie had previously witnessed Eric's perfectionism when he was present during the Beatles recording of 'While My Guitar Gently Weeps': "George asked him, 'Can you make it cry Eric?' The first take floored me because I mean he really did make it cry and weep and wail all the way through that solo. *But*, I had to bite my tongue in the studio control room because they started about 'dropping in' in the middle of the solo because of one part and another part, asking 'is it still smooth?' ... and they lost that first take. On the other hand, when they did the tribute to George in the Albert Hall, Eric only had one take and he did it like that again, he made it cry again. He's brilliant for that. Those experiences to me were like I was really honoured to be there."[15]

Singing in front of three Beatles was a daunting experience for Jackie Lomax. As he stood at the mic, the three faces staring back at him from inside the control booth were those of George, Paul and Ringo. It became even harder when George slipped him a curved ball he had not seen coming: "When you get to the 'Sour Milk Sea' sound track it was much higher than George sang it in his sort of 'medium' voice. I used to have a reputation of singing high and so when I was walking out to do the vocal George said to me, 'Are you sure you can sing it this high, Jack?' I was like suddenly thrown, I swallowed my voice … gulp, now I was thinking I can't sing at all! But I did it and I think I did a good job."[16]

As a postscript to this story, when Jackie spoke with the author in 2008 it was not long after he had re-recorded 'Sour Milk Sea', and of his vocals on his new version he commented: "I recorded it a little lower in key … it's just better a little lower now that I'm older and I can hit the note properly and am not trying to guess at it."[17]

The personnel on 'The Eagle Laughs at You':
Jackie Lomax: rhythm guitar, bass
George Harrison: lead guitar and 'a couple of overdubs'
Tony Newman (Sounds Incorporated): drums
Overdub: cornet.

Another fascinating insight from the 'Sour Milk Sea' / 'The Eagle Laughs at You' sessions concerned the cornet on the B-side, 'The Eagle Laughs at You', which Jackie recalled was played by the person employed to clean the studio. Somehow they had discovered he could play the instrument, recorded him and over-loaded it to the point "it sounds like a bloody elephant screaming through the place."
UK Release: 6 September 1968
USA Release: 26 August 1966 as Apple 1802
Neither release charted although in the USA 'Sour Milk Sea' enjoyed two weeks on the 'Bubbling Under' listings of *Billboard*'s Hot 100 Chart, peaking at 117 while the B-Side 'The Eagle Laughs at You' peaked separately at number 125. In Canada 'Sour Milk Sea' peaked at number 29 in the RPM chart.
'Sour Milk Sea' was released for a second time in the USA on 21 June 1971 as Apple 1834, this time with '(I) Fall Inside Your Eyes' as the B-Side, but once more it did not make the charts.

Just why such an excellent record as 'Sour Milk Sea' did not cause a stir, pick up lots of airplay and present Jackie Lomax with his first major hit, is difficult to fathom. Certainly it seems there was no major promotion of the single or its stellar cast. The problems that were building up within Apple impacted directly on its chances of success (the boutique had gone west by the date of the single's release and it was already recognised that the whole Apple venture was leaking money). Consequently, the long reach of Allen Klein affected nearly every act signed to Apple Records. Jackie Lomax was no exception. Budgets to release product were tightened, never mind budgets to *promote* records.

Although no doubt mightily disappointed at the time, in later years Jackie became philosophical about his single's lack of success, commenting in 2008 that, "Of course I was disappointed the single and album didn't chart, but if you look at the facts, how could I get radio play back then? If you've got Mary Hopkin and 'Those Were the Days' going on and you got 'Hey Jude', the first seven-minute single, they are pretty big competition, and both on Apple, and nobody played my record or that brass band thing* … because the other record companies would be offended if you played three records from one company and not three from theirs. So there was 'politics' involved in that. And it seems to me that nobody took any notice of my album or single until six months after their release, and then the deejays had started looking around for what else has Apple had out and I started to get radio play, but by then it was way too late to coincide with promotional photos or any of the original promo."[18]

(*In the UK only three of those first four were released together on the same day, 30 August, the "brass band thing" to which Jackie refers was released on its own a week later, 6 September. All four singles were released simultaneously in the USA on 26 August.)

There is no doubt that at that time the Beatles and Mary Hopkin were the current darlings of the press in the UK. They generated their own promo. The press came to them eager for copy. The razzamatazz around any new Beatles single, especially one that was over seven minutes long and the first on their own brand new record label, was always destined to attract massive media attention. Hopkin's record was also very big news even before it was released because she was already so much in the public eye because of her winning appearances on the hugely popular TV talent show, *Opportunity Knocks*. Paul had signed her to Apple after seeing her on the show and so the press were busy weaving quite a fairytale around that.

In comparison Jackie did not have such a compelling story with which to attract the press and public's attention to his cause.

Apple did secure him an unmissable full front-page picture and advert ('Apple Rock') on the 14 September 1968 issue of *NME*. Even so the cover also promoted an inside story (just above Jackie's cover picture) entitled 'Paul's Startling Hope for Mary'. But that was it, inside there was not another word about Jackie Lomax or his single, not even a review. Consequently, despite the good reviews in the music press his record did pick up, it quietly slipped out of sight.

Apple also secured Jackie a nationwide TV appearance on the *David Frost Show*, but even this failed to provide a breakthrough for him, although it might have done so if the show had lifted the veil in front of which he performed to reveal his back-up band on the night: "I did the *David Frost Show* and it was live so they put me up on a little stage to sing as a solo singer. I had a curtain behind me and behind the curtain, playing live, were Ringo, Klaus Voormann, Eric Clapton and Nicky Hopkin, but because of the curtain nobody ever saw them! I'd love to have a copy of that but it was not kept. Singing all by myself alone knowing that band is there was very strange. I wasn't really a lead singer I used to be a bass player/lead singer, I'm not used to being without an instrument. I tried it for a while at Apple and it worked out pretty good." (Although he sang, Jackie did not play an instrument on the recording of 'Sour Milk Sea').[19]

The lack of the song's success must have bothered George as well, especially after all the work he'd invested in it and the faith he had in Jackie as a superb singer, musician and writer.

Between mid-October 1968 and January 1969 work continued on Jackie's album *Is This What You Want?* with George producing. The sessions began in Abbey Road but some tracks were recorded at Trident and Marquee Studios. It was eventually completed over seven weeks in LA at Sound Recorders Studios after George and Jackie decamped to California in November 1968. While there, George gathered the cream of LA's session men to work with them, including Larry Knetchel (piano), Joe Osborn (bass), Hal Blaine (drums) and George's long-time friend from Hamburg, Klaus Voormann on bass. Apart from 'Sour Milk Sea', the other ten tracks on the original album release were Lomax compositions.

Commenting on *Is This What You Want?* Jackie had these words to say in 2008: "I am proud of it, I cut some real ground there and had access to great musicians. We went and did seven tracks in Los Angeles. Sitting round the pool in Los Angeles, George played me the beginnings of 'Something'. I said, 'That's a wonderful song George, if you finish that we'll put it on the album!' I think he realised it was an important song and that it should go on a Beatles album and it never came up again! It was one of those little windows of opportunity that just closed. A related story is about James Taylor who came into the studio one day in London and played me the first verse and chorus of 'Fire and Rain', which is all he had at that point. I said, 'Oh James that's a great song, if you finish that I can put it on the album'. He finished it off all right, but flew off to the States with it!"[20]

Finally, on 21 March 1969, *Is This What You Want?* (Apple SAPCOR 6 (LP)) received its UK release. (In the USA it was issued on 19 May 1969 with the same title and with one extra track, another Lomax song called 'New Day' featuring Ringo on drums and produced by Jackie and Mal Evans.)

Like its promo single 'Sour Milk Sea', Jackie's wonderful, star-studded album failed to sell enough copies to make the UK or American charts, but Jackie always appreciated what George Harrison had done for him: "It was a great honour for me to be around George and all of that and watch their technique in the studio. It was really unbelievable that they had so much time in the studio where most bands at that time got a block of three hours and had to get it all done and get out because there was somebody else coming in. EMI just gave them free rein.

"From my career point of view, it didn't make me famous, it didn't hit the big time all at once, but it got my name everywhere. People were familiar with the name but maybe they didn't know what I did … a sort of familiar name but in what context they don't know. So it got me started. It got me signed to Warner Brothers and to live in Woodstock where I did two albums. I didn't stop writing, I didn't just throw up my hands and say that's it. Apple's closed, I'm done. No, George had inspired me enough to keep going and writing and writing better for the right reasons too – integrity and creativity and ever since I always try and better myself."[21]

It may not have charted but 'Sour Milk Sea' *is* remembered to this day. It has lasted the course and for many fans and music critics alike it is *the* great George Harrison song he never cut for himself as a Beatle. It was certainly a stand-out track that he brought back from India. George would have surely known that. Thus, to give it away was an act of selfless generosity that reveals not only the measure of the man, but of how dearly he wanted success for his friend Jackie Lomax, an artist for whom he had the greatest respect and love.

Jackie Lomax, in 2008: "It was a very uptempo, hard rock 'n' roll track that the Beatles hardly ever did at that time and I think that's why it has lasted – it's got personality that has lasted. Especially, it has Ringo, he's a brilliant drummer. He was the best drummer in Liverpool and that's why he got the job. He was not just a great drummer, he was a Beatles-type, he fitted in."[22]

1 The Lomax Alliance and CBS Records 1966-1967 – Jackie … www.jackielomax.com › story
2, 3, 4, 5, 7, 8,11, 12, 13, 14, 15, 16, 17, 18, 19, 20, 21 & 22 Jackie Lomax in conversation with Colin Hall in 2008 for the 2009 BBC Radio 2 documentary *The Songs the Beatles Gave Away*, written and narrated by Bob Harris OBE and produced by Bob Harris and Trudie Myerscough-Harris for WBBC.
9 & 10 *I, Me, Mine*, George Harrison, (Genesis Publications, Extended Edition, 2016) p.140.

Chapter 103:
THE FURTHER ADVENTURES OF JACKIE LOMAX

The break-up of the Beatles, and the inevitable diversion of their energies into negotiating all this right then and for a good time thereafter, signalled the end of Jackie Lomax's association with Apple. The arrival of Allen Klein meant that most people associated with the Beatles were either being shown the door, directed towards it, or had already made their own way out.

Before he too left the label, Jackie released two more singles in the UK on the Apple Label:

'New Day'
(Lomax)
APPLE 11
Produced by Jackie Lomax and Mal Evans
Some sources cite that Ringo Starr played drums and Eric Clapton guitar on this track but Lomax says they didn't. He says George played guitar.
B-side: '(I) Fall Inside Your Eyes' was
Produced by George Harrison
Previously released as track two, side one on *Is This What You Want?*
UK Release: 9 May 1969 Apple 11
USA Release: 2 June 1969 Apple 1807
In the States, 'New Day' was issued but with a different song as the B-side which was Leiber, Stoller's 'Thumbin' a Ride' which had originally been done by the Coasters. It was recorded on 11 March 1969 and produced by Paul McCartney

'How the Web Was Woven'
(Clive Westlake, David Most)
APPLE 23
Produced by George Harrison
Recorded Mid-November 1969
B-side: 'Thumbin' a Ride'
(Lieber, Stoller)
Produced by Paul McCartney

Jackie recalled that it was Paul McCartney's idea for him to record 'Thumbin' a Ride' and that Paul produced it because George Harrison was away at the time.

It was apparently recorded on sessions at Apple on both 11 and 12 March. Paul had found the tune tucked away on a B-side of a Coasters record he had in his collection. Interestingly the 15 March 1969 issue of the *NME* reported that on 11 March within hours of announcing he was to marry Linda Eastman, on 12 March Paul was apparently in Apple's basement studio playing drums with George Harrison (there is a photo of Paul on drums and Lomax on bass in the 2010 CD re-issue of *Is This What You Want?*).

Remarkably, after marrying Linda and attending the reception, Paul returned to the studio on the 12th to continue working on 'Thumbin' a Ride'. George had been in London during the day (to attend Paul's wedding) but Pattie was home when the police, led by the infamous Sergeant Pilcher*, raided Kinfauns. The officers claimed to have 'found' a block of hashish. George returned home (he'd earlier asked Pete Shotton to go to Kinfauns to keep Pattie company) and on his arrival he and Pattie were taken to Esher Police Station to be charged with possession of cannabis resin. Outwardly George remained calm throughout, but on the inside was seething. Pilcher's intervention in his and Pattie's life certainly delayed their arrival at Paul and Linda's wedding reception at the Ritz. As Pattie would later recall they were both formally charged but released on bail. When they returned home both she and George felt very down and so decided to lift their spirits by going out to Paul and Linda's wedding reception party.

(**N.B.** *Neither Ringo and Maureen nor John and Yoko attended either the wedding or the reception.*)

Whether or not George stayed to sit in with Paul and Jackie to complete the recording of 'Thumbin' a Ride' later that evening is unclear, but as Paul was credited as the producer it seems possibly not and this would support Lomax's view that George was "away at the time".

UK Release: 6 February 1970
USA Release: 9 March 1970, Apple1819 with Jackie's own song 'Fall Inside Your Eyes' from *Is This What You Want?* as the B-side.

(***Sergeant Norman (aka 'Nobby') Clement Pilcher of the Drug Squad became something of a celebrity of sorts towards the end of the Sixties for his high-profile arrests of several prominent 'pop' stars on charges of possessing drugs. These included Mick Jagger, Brian Jones, and Keith Richards of the Rolling Stones and Donovan, after which he was ready to grab himself a Beatle or two. (He almost nabbed Eric Clapton but the quick-thinking guitarist beat a hasty retreat via the back door when he heard Pilcher knocking at the front.) Pilcher (with the assistance of seven officers including himself and two sniffer dogs, Yogi and Boo-Boo) first arrested John and Yoko on 18 October 1968 for the unauthorised possession of cannabis before turning his attention to George and Pattie a few months later. His dubious methods, amongst which was a reputation for 'planting' evidence and his penchant for tipping off the press to ensure maximum publicity were bound to catch him out, and in 1973 it did. Pilcher was imprisoned for perjury that related to a drugs case in which he had been involved. It is widely believed that the 'Semolina pilchard' who ascended the Eiffel Tower was an undercover name for the offending officer.*)

None of Jackie's Apple singles made the charts in either the UK or USA.

In 2008, Jackie Lomax mentioned a second song to the author that was recorded and produced by Paul around the same time as 'Thumbin' a Ride'. It was called 'Going Back to Liverpool' and Jackie said, "It was a song originally recorded at Apple but never released. I was unsure why not for I thought it was an obvious tune not only for the fact that it mentioned 'Liverpool' which at the time not many did although it was relevant. I thought it would have made a good single. At the time I thought I've got a hit here, but no! It was not released."[1]

Jackie's most bizarre release on Apple Records was as one of four artists featured on a promotional disc issued by Wall's Ice Cream:

WALL'S ICE CREAM
Various Artists
UK Special Business Promotion
APPLE CT 1 (EP)
Side 1
'Storm in a Teacup' (Tom*) … The Iveys** (Produced: Mal Evans)
'Something's Wrong' (James Taylor) … James Taylor (Produced: Peter Asher)
Side 2
'Little Yellow Pill' (Jackie Lomax) … Jackie Lomax (Produced: George Harrison)
'Pebble and the Man' (Donovan) … Mary Hopkin (Produced: Paul McCartney)
*Tom Evans ** Soon to become Badfinger
Released: 18 July 1969

(During their tenure at Apple, Jackie Lomax and Doris Troy co-wrote 'I've Got To Be Strong'. The song closed the first side of Troy's George-Harrison-produced Apple album, entitled Ain't That Cute. *What Lomax was too modest to say was that Doris earned her co-credit on the song by making just a one-word change to the title ... Doris's album was released in both the UK (11 September 1970) and the USA (9 November 1970). Despite nicking a writing credit, Jackie enjoyed Doris's version of his song for its combination of soul and R&B replete with horns.)*

Whilst recording with George at Apple, Jackie was invited to attend Beatles sessions for the *White Album*. He was recruited to provide hand claps and backing vocals on 'Dear Prudence'. He also said he turned down John's offer to record 'Across the Universe': "The Beatles were very close-knit and very hard to get in on and that's why I was terrified and shocked when I was in Trident Studio and the Beatles were doing 'Dear Prudence' and I'm just sitting there just loving the beautiful three-part harmonies. The track was already done and John called me into the studio and asked if I wanted to sing on it. I almost lost my lunch, I mean where do I sing on this? I mean shall I elbow out John and do the lead part? That doesn't sound right! I could have sung high like Paul McCartney but that wouldn't have been right. George was on the lower third part, I wasn't going to take that over either because they had the perfect blend. So I went on the bottom with this deep voice and I think it's the only Beatles track that has that kind of sound on it because they never did four-part harmony. If I was going to do something it had to be away from them because my voice is very distinctive, it would have stuck out ... I couldn't ad-lib over 'Dear Prudence', that would have been sacrilege, musically speaking. To hear it years later, it's just gratifying, like – 'Wow, did I actually do that?' People often ask if it is me and when I say yes most people don't believe me or that I'm just saying it, where's the proof? And I say I don't need the proof – just listen to it?"[2]

On 6 December 1969, *NME* announced that Jackie had joined a band called Heavy Jelly along with former Animals drummer Barry Jenkins. As Heavy Jelly, Jackie recorded an album but the proverbial 'contractual difficulties' that artists tend to encounter when making records kicked in. Lomax found his existing contract with Apple Records meant his Heavy Jelly record could not be released. This was a shame, for Lomax had recruited some formidable musicians to play on the record: alongside himself and drummer Barry Jenkins, there was Alex Dmochowski and John Morphed, both of whom had been in the Aynsley Dunbar Retaliation, Badfinger's Pete Ham and Tom Evans and Rolling Stones wind section of Bobby Keys and Jim Price. Frustrated by this impasse, by the end of 1970 Lomax signed to Warner Brothers and relocated once more to the USA where he lived in Woodstock, Ulster County, New York State.

Since Jackie's death in 2013, the problems with Apple Records have been resolved and Angel Air Records officially released his Heavy Jelly opus on 10 March 2014.

In Woodstock he re-united with drummer Bugs Pemberton and bass player Tommy Caccetta to cut his second solo album, *Home Is in My Head* (Warner Brothers). Recorded in 1970 and released in 1971, unfortunately, despite being highly regarded it did not make the charts. His second album for Warner and his third solo record was also recorded in Woodstock. He called it *Three* and it was produced by John Simon, but like its predecessors the critical acclaim it received was not accompanied by any subsequent chart action.

In 1973 Jackie once more returned home where he joined a band called Badger that had been formed by ex-Yes keyboard player Tony Kaye. To anyone listening to the album Badger recorded with Jackie, *White Lady* was very much a Jackie Lomax record. A potent blend of R&B and soul it followed in the vein of *Three* and as such was a marked departure from Badger's previous album. Allen Toussaint produced, Jackie wrote all the songs and sang them while Jeff Beck contributed the guitar solo on the title track.

Jackie's return to the UK and his engagement with Badger did not go according to plan: "It was my album ... they had no songs. I had 33 songs, and said, 'Pick the ones you want.' There was a great lack of motivation in that band. I went back to England to do that, but nobody showed much enthusiasm. I had to go to New Orleans and explain that to Allen Toussaint, who'd done horn and background vocal arrangements. It turned out much better than I thought it would, but I had to mix it myself. When I did, the band fell apart..."[3]

Somewhat inevitably Lomax returned to the USA to pick up his solo career. This time he stayed put and in 1975 signed to Capitol for whom he made two albums, *Livin' for Lovin'* (1975) and in 1977 *Did You Ever Have That Feeling?* (cover designed by Klaus Voormann). Once his Capitol contract had expired he moved to Los Angeles, California, where in the late 1980s Jackie made Ojai, Ventura County his home.

Among his many adventures in the USA (right into the 90s) Lomax played bass for the Drifters, the Diamonds, the Coasters and the Shirelles. His move to Ojai in the late 1980s re-connected him to playing the six-string guitar instead of the bass, very much enjoying the fact that audiences like to hear lead guitar solos much more than they do bass solos.

Life in Ojai seemed to suit the former Undertaker down to the ground, but first and foremost he was a Liverpool lad at heart and in 1996 was very much involved in the Big Beat release of the Undertakers' CD. This featured all of the group's Pye singles as well as an American single and unreleased material from the mid-60s. He also continued to perform, playing his beloved R&B, blues and soul at venues such as the Café Voltaire in Ventura, the Coconut Teaser on Sunset Strip and Libby Park in Ojai itself.

When in 2008 Jackie commented to this author about what he gained from George, he said, "George ... inspired me enough to keep going and writing and writing better for the right reasons too – integrity and creativity – and ever since I always try and better myself."

His personal proof that he had done just this lay in what he was doing right then in that very moment: "I think I've achieved it because as my new album, *The Ballad of Liverpool Slim*, shows I can play guitar and I can be funky, it's not just straight rock 'n' roll, which is kind of old-fashioned to me now. When you played rock 'n' roll in the Sixties it was all Chuck Berry and Little Richard, very simple three-chord stuff. Well, I graduated from that and that would be because of the inspiration from George, because if he hadn't said let's make an album I might have just faded away and left it that I was a songwriter once at Apple Publishing and that was it. But I didn't! I was inspired and I wanted to go forward and at this moment in time I have 10 CDs out all over the world because I've done them. I never expected them to come out again but there's a new revival of my career and it's astonishing to me. I thought I won't be playing music after 40 and here I am playing music after 60! It doesn't make sense..."[4]

As the new millennium had dawned, prior to our meeting in 2008, Jackie was already very focused on ensuring his musical legacy was either available or would become available for those who wished to tune in, not only to *The Undertakers Unearthed* CD, but to all his releases past and present, and so in 2001 he established the website: www.JackieLomax.com

Thankfully during the 2000s many of his official albums have enjoyed re-releases. It has been a gradual process, but as this book was being written everything by Jackie Lomax was available again.

He himself had never been forgotten and the new millennium found him much in-demand as a performer. He particularly enjoyed his annual sorties to Liverpool to play shows both as a solo artist or with the re-united Undertakers. These began in 2003 when he made a triumphant return to play the Cavern. In 2006 he contributed two tracks to the Undertakers' new album *Resurrection*, and began recording a new album with his long-time friend and bandmate, Brian Jones.

In 2001 he recorded a new solo album, *The Ballad of Liverpool Slim*. (The name came from his pool playing name as part of the Grumpy Old Men team in Ventura County.) It finally received a worldwide release in 2009 on Angel Air Records as *The Ballad of Liverpool Slim ... Plus* because of the addition of two extra 'live' cuts not on the original release, one

Jackie Lomax with the author in Liverpool in 2000. Jackie is standing in front of a photograph of his younger self taken in Hamburg in 1968 by Astrid Kirchherr.

of which was a 1976 concert version of 'Sour Milk Sea'. (Hence in his conversation with me in 2008 he referred to *The Ballad of Liverpool Slim* as his 'new' record.)

In 2012 Jackie performed as a solo artist and also with the Undertakers at the 50th Anniversary of the Star-Club in Hamburg.

In 2013 he completed his new solo record – the collaboration with Brian Jones begun in 2006 – *Against All the Odds*, which was released by Angel Air Records on 14 January 2014. This, sadly, proved to be Jackie's final album. He and Brian were in as good form as ever and it stands as a tremendous tribute to two of Liverpool's greatest but all too often unsung heroes.

Very sadly in 2013, on 15 September, while on a trip back home to the Wirral, Merseyside, to be with his family, Jackie Lomax passed away. He was 69 years old.

1 & 2 Jackie Lomax in conversation with the author in 2008 for the 2009 BBC Radio 2 documentary *The Songs the Beatles Gave Away*, produced Bob Harris OBE and Trudie Myerscough-Harris for WBBC by WBBC.
3 & 4 www.jackielomax.com

Chapter 104:
APPLE 4, PAUL GOES TO YORKSHIRE

On Tuesday 25 June 1968, Paul McCartney returned from Los Angeles where he had been addressing a Capitol Records Sales Conference. The trip had been brief, just five days, and took place in the midst of recording sessions for *The White Album*. On his arrival home he just had time to play bass for Jackie Lomax on 'Sour Milk Sea' before he was off on his travels once more.

This time he was headed north, to Saltaire in Yorkshire to record a tune he had specifically written as the theme for a new TV series. He had also specifically written it to be performed by a brass band. Not just *any* brass band mind, but Yorkshire's best: the Black Dyke Mills Band.

The tune was called 'Thingumybob'.

'Thingumybob' the word has many spelling variations including 'thingamabob', 'thingymebob', 'thingmebob' and 'thingummibob'. According to *Green's Dictionary of Slang*, it is a word used to describe items/people whose name you can't remember or which don't actually exist.[1]

The word was an appropriate choice because not only is it strongly associated with the north of England, but the series for which Paul had been commissioned was set in Yorkshire. In addition to that the title word directly referenced the show's ageing principal character, one 'Bob Bridge' who was to be played by the renowned actor Stanley Holloway who, coincidentally, both off camera and in rehearsals, had a habit of using the word 'thingumybob' as a name to call people and things whose actual names he could not recall.

Thingumybob was an eight-part comedy TV series written by Kenneth Cope, produced by David Askey and alongside Stanley Holloway starred Rose Hill as Fay Bridge, John Junkin as Bert Ryding and Stella Tanner as Mrs. Green. Earlier in his career Junkin had played 'Shake' in the Beatles' 1964 debut film, *A Hard Day's Night*. London Weekend Television (which had just been awarded the franchise by ITV) commissioned Paul to write the series' theme tune.

Unfortunately, *Thingumybob* the series appears to be lost, certainly as this book was being written no episodes were to be found on any site. The first episode was aired on London Weekend Television on 9 August 1968, the second on 18 August. The programmes were broadcast in black and white and ran for 45 minutes (commercial breaks would have extended the viewing time).

Of course, it wasn't the first time Paul had been asked to provide a theme tune for a drama set in the North and, as with *The Family Way* (1966) it wasn't the first time he had composed music to be played by a brass band. On that occasion the music he came up with had been supervised, orchestrated and arranged by George Martin and had featured a brass band. This time however the Beatle was more or less on his own.

From being a young boy growing up in Liverpool, Paul had always enjoyed brass band music. A genre closely associated with the 'North', for any young person growing up in the north of England brass bands were part of the musical soundtrack to their life, especially redolent of visits to the park in summer where more often than not a brass band would be sitting in the sunshine (although the odds are it must have rained sometimes) underneath the canopy of the bandstand serenading appreciative audiences and casual passersby. Brass band music was certainly very much a part of the McCartney family story. You could say it was in his blood. Paul and Michael's grandfather Joe had worked for Cope Brothers

Paul McCartney accompanying himself on trumpet and backed by the Black Dyke Mills Brass Band. Photo taken in Saltaire, near Bradford in West Yorkshire in June 1968. Accompanying Paul is Martha, his Old English Sheepdog.
(Trinity Mirror / Mirrorpix / Alamy Stock Photo)

& Co, importers of tobacco, for nigh on 50 years and described by Mark Lewisohn as, "a quiet and likeable man, teetotal, he blew the huge E-flat bass in his works brass band … Joe was the first in a still continuing line of male McCartney musicians to perform in public."[2]

Consequently, when Paul was asked to write the theme tune for the new TV series, he was more than happy to do so.

Before approaching the Black Dyke Band to record the instrumental, McCartney had attempted to record a version of 'Thingumybob' in a club in London with a brass ensemble, but as cornet player with the Black Dyke Mills Band, John Clays recalled, "They could not deliver the 'big brass sound' Paul was so keen to capture."[3]

Shortly after this failed attempt, Paul, John and their friends Derek Taylor and Neil Aspinall were enjoying a night out together in New York at Nat Weiss's* apartment when Paul was reminded of an old song called 'Alexander's Ragtime Band' (a very popular, much-recorded tune composed in 1911 by Irving Berlin). Paul was so reminded because for the enjoyment of all those present he was playing a demo of the brass ensemble's version of 'Thingumybob' on Weiss's record player.

(*Nat was a New York attorney and close friend of Brian Epstein with whom in 1966 he and his stepson Shaun Weiss had co-founded the management company, Nemperor Artists.)*

What happened next was later recalled in some detail in Derek Taylor's acclaimed memoir (published in 1974), *As Times Goes By*. It appears that those assembled felt that there was something missing from the version Paul had played them. It sounded too 'ordinary'. Noting Paul's dissatisfaction with the version he had already recorded, Taylor himself remarked, "Seems to me the only way to get a brass band sound on gramophone record, is to use a brass band."[4]

Paul's attention was further drawn (no doubt by Taylor) to the line in Irving Berlin's first major hit song (1911) 'Alexander's Ragtime Band' that describes Alexander's band as 'the best band in the land'. And so Paul was fired with the notion that in order to achieve that elusive 'big brass sound' he so desired he should record 'Thingumybob' with the best brass band in the land and it so happened that that band was none other than Yorkshire's legendary Black Dyke Mills Band.

So enthused, McCartney engaged the redoubtable Derek Taylor to connect him with Geoffrey Brand, the professional conductor of the Black Dyke Mills Band.

And as a consequence, on Saturday 29 June, Paul found himself headed north to Bradford aboard his own chauffeur-driven black Rolls Royce on a mission to cut 'Thingumybob' with the best brass band in the UK.

He did not travel alone, but was accompanied by Peter Asher, Derek Taylor and Tony Bramwell. Also along for the trip was Martha, Paul's much loved Old English Sheepdog. The personnel accompanying Paul reflects the fact that the Beatles had left Parlophone and established Apple, for Paul's travelling companions were not only his good friends but were all also working for Apple in one capacity or another. Peter Asher was, of course, Jane's brother, the one and only Peter of Peter and Gordon, who was now not only a producer at Apple but also head of the label's A&R. At the time he headed north with Paul, Peter was already working with a young, unknown singer-songwriter signed to Apple called James Taylor.

The party did not arrive at their hotel in Bradford until midnight.*

(*On the return journey to London this travelling party was expanded by Alan Smith, the then editor of NME. Smith had travelled independently to Saltaire to report on Paul's trip. Smith was well known to the Beatles and a colleague of Taylor's from back in the early days when Taylor was a writer on the* Liverpool Daily Post *and Smith on the* Birkenhead News. *Of all the songs given away by the Beatles it appears that Paul's 'Thingumybob' is the most well-documented of all.)*

1 *Green's Dictionary Of Slang*, by Jonathan Green, (Chambers Harrap Publishers, 2010).
2 *The Beatles – All These Years: Volume One: Tune In*, Mark Lewisohn (Little, Brown 2013) p.19.
3 John Clay of the Black Dyke Mills Band in conversation with Colin Hall, 2019.
4 *As Time Goes By*, by Derek Taylor, (Abacus, 1974) p.68.

Chapter 105:
A DAY OUT IN SALTAIRE

The following account of Paul's working visit to Saltaire is based on conversations between the author and John Clay who played cornet and flugelhorn with the Black Dyke Mills Band and participated in the recording of 'Thingumybob' (2 January 2019). Peter Asher also kindly contributed his memories of the day.

From the age of 14-and-a-half in 1958 until he was 29 in 1973 John Clay played both cornet and flugelhorn with the historic, much-loved and hugely acclaimed Yorkshire-based (in Queensbury, close to Bradford) Black Dyke Mills Band.

Of the band's name John comments, "The Band originated in 1855 and its official title until the early 1970s was the Black Dyke Mills Band. John Foster & Sons Ltd was the name of the band's sponsor and his family were the original owners of the Black Dyke mills themselves. The firm's name was added for a few years but eventually dropped."

During his 15 years with them, John proudly played all of the cornet positions that there are in a brass band and for three months in 1962 he held the prestigious position of principal cornet.

During 1964, John says, "I changed from cornet to flugelhorn and so it was as a flugelhorn player that in 1968 I participated in the John Foster & Son Black Dyke Band's recording of Paul McCartney's instrumental tune 'Thingumybob' which Paul also produced."

As John comments, "At the time Geoffrey Brand was well known beyond being our *professional* conductor and in the brief time we had been together we had already won the National Championship in 1967. Under Mr. Brand we went on to win the British Open Championship in September '68. With him as conductor we won both competitions again in 1972 and the World Championship in 1970."

John says, "Before joining us Mr. Brand had enjoyed a long and successful musical career. He had been a very successful professional trumpet player who had played for the Royal Philharmonic, the Philharmonia and Covent Garden orchestras. As a producer for the BBC's Third Programme from 1955 to 1967 he worked closely with military and brass bands during which time he gained a reputation as one of the leaders of modern band music. Geoffrey promoted the work of composers such as Aberdeen-born Martin Dalby (1942-2018) and Edinburgh-born Thea Musgrave (b.1928). During 1967, Mr. Brand invited the Black Dyke Band to London to perform Dalby's 1962 piece 'Music for a Brass Band' and Musgrave's 'Variations for Brass Band' which she had written in 1966 as a commission from the Scottish Amateur Music Society for the National Youth Brass Band of Scotland."

Clay says that Brand made an immediate impression on them: "We, the Black Dyke Band, were so impressed with Geoffrey Brand both as a person in his own right and his style of conducting that he commanded our instant and ever-lasting respect. So much so that on the coach home that night we took a vote to invite him to join us as our professional conductor. It was an invitation he kindly accepted."

John's respect for Geoffrey Brand was such that he says he only ever called him 'Mr. Brand' and describes him as, "Being out of the same mould as the great George Willcocks. Major Willcocks had been the professional conductor of the Black Dyke Mills Band from 1957 until 1961. It was clear to us that Mr. Brand had studied hard and knew exactly what he wanted from a piece of music and the band who were or would be performing it. He was a real gentleman who had respect for all the players with whom he worked, both as musicians and as individuals."

Paul intended his theme tune 'Thingumybob' to be recorded for Apple Records who would release and promote the piece as a single. He not only asked Geoffrey Brand to expand his arrangement of 'Thingumybob' but to also create an arrangement for *Yellow Submarine* which was to be the record's B-side. Brand agreed to do so and arranged the latter tune as a march.

Just three weeks later Paul McCartney was in Saltaire ready to record with the Black Dyke Mills Band. John Clay clearly remembers the occasion: "The location chosen for the recording was the Victoria Hall in Saltaire near Bradford. The session was booked for Sunday morning, 30 June. It had to be in the morning because we had a booking that same day to play in the afternoon at Thorne Park, near Doncaster. We were booked to play twice, from 3pm to 5pm and from 7pm to 9pm. In those days *before* motorways it took at least an hour to get there from Saltaire and being a Sunday we anticipated it would be likely to be busy on the roads and delays highly likely, consequently we could not be late leaving."

Paul and his travelling companions arrived in Yorkshire on Saturday 29 June and stayed overnight at the Midland Hotel in Bradford.

Whether John Clay would have been aware that Peter Asher was a 'pop' star in his own right or had ever heard Peter and Gordon's hit tune 'A World Without Love' is a moot point: "In my home my parents had made sure I focused on classical music as I grew up, so I was not really aware of the pop scene, even so in the 1960s *everyone* had heard of the Beatles and so I was very excited to be meeting and working with Paul. Everyone in the Black Dyke Band was, despite the early call!"

It was not the first time the Black Dyke Mills Band had recorded in the Victoria Hall. "We assembled in the Victoria Hall between 8 and 8.30am. As we had recorded there before we set up in the middle of the hall, not on the stage itself. Recording on the stage was too difficult because it was too cramped for us and too difficult to place the microphones correctly. Consequently, we were in the middle."

The actual recording gear used on the day was very simple: "A portable recording unit was used to tape our performances. Mr. Brand already knew which songs were to be performed: 'Thingumybob' and 'Yellow Submarine' and he had already arranged them for us and was going to be the conductor for the session, so once we had set up we were raring to go. I think 'Yellow Submarine' had been chosen as the B-side of the single because the cartoon film of the same name was being released later that year."

Peter Asher recalls that, "The portable recording unit we used was already there, it was provided. As I recall it was the way the Black Dyke Mills Band had made their own records previously. In making a plan for the day I'd asked them about this. They had already made many records and when I asked how they did it, I was told they liked to work in this particular hall, it sounded really good and they used a remote set-up from somewhere local. I said, 'Great, we'll do that.' I remember getting there early just to check the set-up and meet the guy running the remote, but the idea was to record it just the way the Black Dyke Mills Band recorded themselves customarily."[1]

Of the day Asher says, "Paul was the producer, Paul was working with the musicians, telling the band how he wanted them to play 'Thingumybob'. I was making sure that it was recorded properly, I was just being an attentive A&R guy making sure the session went smoothly and that everything got recorded."[2]

As far as John Clay recalls, "We recorded 'Thingumybob' about six or seven times but Paul was not satisfied with any of them. I think the problem was that because the Hall was empty there was too much echo. He wasn't getting that full sound he was after. As 'Thingumybob' was just short of two minutes long each recording had been very short and the playbacks had been as equally brief. Even so time was of the essence. It was approaching 10:30/11am and getting close to when we would have to leave for Doncaster. Nevertheless, it was at this point that Paul decided we should move to record outside on

Exhibition Road to try for a good take in the open air."

The move to make some recordings outside actually emanated from Peter Asher: "I did make one suggestion, we had recorded it inside but this had produced a 'roomy' sound so we set the band up outside in the open air and recorded it that way. I'm not sure which version was used, but I wanted to have one *without* the 'room sound', just in case."[3]

By now, of course, 'word' had got round Saltaire that there was a Beatle in the village. There had been sightings and rumours but now it was fact for there, parked outside the Victoria Hall, was Paul's glossy, chauffeur-driven black Rolls Royce.

As John explains: "A Rolls Royce was something to behold in those days. We didn't see many of those in Yorkshire and in itself it would have been something to see. That it was Paul McCartney's Rolls Royce and that he was there in person was something very special indeed. About 200 people, including at least 40 children, had assembled outside waiting to catch a glimpse of him. Paul did not let this bother him and so we set up in the street and this time Paul was delighted. Finally he'd got the brass band sound on 'Thingumybob' for which he was searching. Outside we also cut our version of 'Yellow Submarine' and Paul got the children to participate: when he gave them the signal they had to shout out 'Land Ahoy!' and clap and whistle. You can hear them on the recording that was issued. We recorded both tunes two or three times each."

John remembers that, "to add to the atmosphere on 'Yellow Submarine' some guests who were there that day were asked to join in. Our 2nd Horn player Kevin Wadsworth's father Maurice played a ship's bell. Alan Bailey, who played for the Fire Service Band, played klaxon and a homemade wind machine devised by Geoffrey Brand was operated by his son Michael!"

The session went right to the wire, but finally it was done and dusted and everyone was happy. The Black Dyke Band could not hang around, however, for almost as soon as the final take of 'Yellow Submarine' was in the bag they packed up very quickly and boarded the coach that was waiting to take them on their journey to Thorne Park.

During the recordings John Clay remembers that everyone was excited and happy. He also remembered Martha: "Both inside and outside the Victoria Hall, Martha was generally very well behaved, she just sat down and listened although once she did howl and had to be taken outside."

John says, "Paul later sent a letter of thanks to the band and we all received a 45 rpm record. I still have mine!"

John also recalls Paul chatting with some of the Black Dyke's principal players on the day while he himself politely asked Paul to sign his autograph book. It's a volume he cherishes for inside are signatures of other musical greats he has had the pleasure to know, such as Sir John Barbirolli and Sir Malcolm Sargent. So Paul is in truly august company, his autograph a reminder of the day a Beatle came to Bradford to make a record with the one and only Black Dyke Band.

Of the day, Derek Taylor was to write that after he, Paul, Peter and Tony had eaten breakfast, "We went off to the Victoria Hall where the Black Dyke Mills Band were waiting on hard wooden chairs, looking bloody marvellous and real…"[4]

A memorable day had been enjoyed by one and all.

The quotations used throughout this chapter are the words of John Clay who played clarinet for the Black Dyke Mills Band and are taken from his conversation with the author in 2019.
In addition to John's memories are words from Peter Asher and Derek Taylor as noted here:-

1, 2 & 3 Peter Asher in conversation with the author, Colin Hall, 2019.
4 *As Time Goes By*, by Derek Taylor, (Abacus, 1974) p.71.

Chapter 106:
JOHN FOSTER AND SONS LTD
BLACK DYKE MILLS BAND

JOHN FOSTER AND SONS LTD BLACK DYKE MILLS BAND
'THINGUMYBOB' (1:51)
(Lennon-McCartney)
Northern Songs Ltd
Apple 4
B-SIDE: Yellow Submarine (2:54)
(Lennon-McCartney)
Northern Songs Ltd
Both sides Produced by: Paul McCartney
Both sides Arranged and Conducted by: Geoffrey Brand
Recorded: Sunday 30 June 1968 in Saltaire, near Bradford, Yorkshire

Members of Black Dyke Mills Band who performed on 'Thingumybob' and 'Yellow Submarine'

Professional Conductor	Geoffrey Brand	2nd Horn	Kevin Wadsworth
Resident Conductor	Roy Newsome	1st Baritone	John Slinger
Soprano Cornet	Thomas Waterman	2nd Baritone	Colin Hardy
Principal Cornet	James Shepherd	1st Trombone	Frank Berry
Solo Cornet	David Pratt	2nd Trombone	Derek Southcott
Solo Cornet	William Gibson	Bass Trombone	Ian Copeland
Solo Cornet	Jack Brooke	Solo Euphonium	John Clough
Repiano Cornet	David Horsfield	2nd Euphonium	Brian Broadbent
2nd Cornet	David Pogson	EEb Bass	Peter Wells
2nd Cornet	Malcolm Turton	EEb Bass	Derek Robinson
3rd Cornet	Fred Ellis	BBb Bass	Peter McNab
3rd Cornet	Eric Bland	BBb Bass	Derek Jackson
Flugelhorn	John Clay	Percussion	Harry Burnley
Solo Horn	Brian Wood	Percussion	Len Haley
1st Horn	Alan Holdsworth		

Guests: Maurice Wadsworth, ship's bell
Alan Bailey, klaxon
Michael Brand, homemade wind machine

UK Release: Friday 6 September 1968 APPLE 4
USA Release: 26 August 1968 Apple 1800
'Thingumybob' was written by Paul McCartney but is credited on the record label to 'Lennon - McCartney.
'Thingumybob' (Apple 4) shared the same UK (6 September) and USA (Monday 26 August) release dates with Jackie Lomax's 'Sour Milk Sea' (Apple 3)
In the USA 'Thingumybob' became the B-side to 'Yellow Submarine' (catalogue number Apple 1800)
  This reversal of the A-side in the USA was most probably down to the fact that American

audiences may not have understood the meaning of the word 'Thingumybob' but would have already been familiar with the Beatles' version of the song 'Yellow Submarine'. The cartoon feature film *Yellow Submarine* was also on its way: released in the UK on 17 July 1968 it was due for release in America on 13 November 1968. For both reasons it was the more obvious choice for the A-side in the States.

A tad confusingly, while the centre labels on the discs use the name 'John Foster & Son Black Dyke Mills Band', picture sleeve editions such as those released in the Netherlands used the shorter version 'Black Dyke Mills Band'.

Sadly, 'Thingumybob' did not chart on either side of the Atlantic.

N.B. *The Black Dyke Mills Band worked with Paul McCartney on a second occasion when they performed on the last ever Wings studio album, Back to the Egg. Released on 8 June 1979 it climbed to number 6 in the UK and number 8 in the USA album charts. The Black Dyke Band played on side two, track 11, a medley entitled 'Winter Rose/Love Awake'.*

Addendum: *The Return from Saltaire*
At the end of their busy but thoroughly enjoyable day in Saltaire it was a case of all aboard Paul's Rolls Royce for the return trip home to London. For this journey Paul, Martha and their companions Peter Asher, Tony Bramwell and Derek Taylor were joined by the NME*'s Alan Smith. It was a journey well-documented by Derek Taylor in his 1973 memoir,* As Time Goes By. *Told in Taylor's inimitable style the trip had clearly created an indelible impression on his memory. Taylor recalled he was as high as a kite on acid and dressed appropriately (Mexican white shirt, red corduroys, beads and an Indian scarf). A merry diversion was decided upon when, keen to enjoy what had become a perfect summer's evening, the party were in total accord with Taylor's suggestion that they make a pit-stop. They were in Bedfordshire at the time and elected to visit the nearest village with the most beautiful name. After consulting the AA book Peter Asher proposed 'Harrold' as their destination and so Harrold it was. His choice found the group soon paused in the centre of an idyllic English village just on opening time. It truly was a blessed day!*
What happened next is related by Taylor in an idiosyncratic and trippy psychedelic prose this writer could never match. Best for all concerned that they seek As Time Goes By *for the full experience! In the meantime here is a nutshell version of the story ... Needless to say once inside the pub Paul was recognised and all of his companions were befriended by the inquisitive and generous locals. After much supping an excursion was made within the village to the home of the local dentist where, after more supping and feasting, Paul performed a new song for the dentist and his family that he had only just written, a tune called 'Hey Jude'. Not long after this the party returned once more to the pub which, having just closed, was immediately re-opened in their honour and where like father, like son, Paul was soon ensconced at the piano entertaining everyone as the night rolled on ... Much merriment later, at three in the morning, the by now very merry pranksters resumed their journey home!*

List of the Black Dyke Mills Band's personnel on the recording of 'Thingumybob' and 'Yellow Submarine' courtesy of John Clay.

Chapter 107:
1968 ... THOSE WERE THE DAYS ...

1968 was a tumultuous year packed with important Beatles events that with hindsight (and despite the continued massive worldwide success of their music) can be seen as signposts towards the disintegration of the group.

It was also a year in which Paul continued to write for and produce emerging talent on the Apple Records label while George was looking beyond the group to fulfil his creative drive.

For Paul in particular his talents as a performer and writer combined with his experience as a performer came together to shape and guide the career of an emerging singing star with whom the nation had fallen in love after her appearances on national TV.

Paul's adventure began on 5 May when his good friend, the famous Sixties UK teen model, Twiggy drew Paul's attention to that of a young Welsh singer called Mary Hopkin who had recently won over the nation's hearts and minds by winning the very popular national TV talent show, *Opportunity Knocks*.

By mid-July Paul had signed Hopkin to Apple Records where she was looked after by his good friend Peter Asher, the label's A&R. As they sought to capitalise on Hopkin's current and huge national popularity by finding a song suitable for her to record and release as the A-side of her first single, fortuitously for all concerned Paul recalled a song he'd heard one night down the Blue Angel cabaret club in Berkeley Square. Sung by amateur American duo, Gene and Francesca Raskin, it was called 'Those Were the Days' and McCartney was convinced it would be ideal for Hopkin to record as her debut single, which she did. The B-side was a no-brainer: Hopkin cut her version of 'Turn, Turn, Turn', which she had sung so successfully on *Opportunity Knocks* and which was recorded in just one take.

This fine brace of songs became Apple 2 and was released in the UK on the same day as 'Hey Jude'. Mary's single followed 'Hey Jude' to the number 1 position in the UK chart, toppling Paul and his pals from the top slot.

This was a particularly busy period in the lives of the Beatles as can be evidenced by all that happened to them both as a group and as individuals:

Just after Paul's attention had been drawn to Mary Hopkin's TV talent show performances, on 11 May he and John (plus 'Magic' Alex) had flown to New York to launch Apple in the USA where Linda Eastman joined them for their car journey back to the airport on 15 May.

On 17 May *Wonderwall* received its World premiere at the Cannes Film Festival at which George, Pattie, Ringo and Maureen were in attendance.

20 June: Paul returned to the USA. He was accompanied by Tony Bramwell and Ivan Vaughan. The three flew to Los Angeles where Paul attended the Capitol Records Sales Conference. Prior to doing so he had invited Linda Eastman to join him there, which she did.

June was a very busy and productive month for both George and Paul during which they both worked on songs they had decided to 'give away': on the 24th Harrison began recording 'Sour Milk Sea' with Jackie Lomax while just a few days later on the 30th McCartney was in Yorkshire recording 'Thingumybob' with the Black Dyke Mills Band.

Immediately prior to the premiere of *Yellow Submarine* on 16 July, Abbey Road studios engineer Geoff Emerick quit working with the Beatles. Apparently he no longer felt as at ease within the group's working environment as he had done previously, this was possibly an early sign that all was not well within the Beatles.

The world premiere of *Yellow Submarine* was held on Wednesday 17 July at the London Pavilion in Piccadilly Circus when fans turned out *en masse* at the front of the cinema to catch a glimpse of the group. John and Yoko, Ringo and Maureen were in attendance as was Paul, although surprisingly he turned up on his own. Also in attendance that evening was Paul's protégé Mary Hopkin who, just ahead of the premiere, had recorded 'Those Were the Days'.

Paul's solo appearance at the *Yellow Submarine* film premiere gained clearer perspective when on Saturday 20 July Jane Asher appeared on the BBC TV show, *Dee Time* and informed host Simon Dee that Paul had broken off their engagement.

On Monday 29 July the Beatles attended Abbey Road to begin recording 'Hey Jude'. On the next day the Apple Boutique closed, a portent of the struggles to come for Apple Corps.

By Tuesday 20 August relationships between the Beatles had reached such a low point that Ringo quit. The straw that broke Ringo's resolve was a fluffed tom-tom fill for which he had been taken to task by one of the others. To escape the tension he flew to the Mediterranean and spent two weeks aboard his friend Peter Sellers' yacht. During the trip he wrote, 'Octopus's Garden'.

Thursday 22 August marked the day Cynthia filed for divorce on the grounds of John's adultery with Yoko. John did not contest her claim.

In the USA on Monday 26 August, the first four Apple Records singles, 'Hey Jude', 'Thingumybob', 'Those Were The Days' and 'Sour Milk Sea' were released. This momentous occasion was followed in the UK when on Friday 30 August 'Hey Jude' and 'Those Were the Days' and were released. 'Sour Milk Sea' and 'Thingumybob' followed a week later on Friday 6 September.

After spending some healing time away from his bandmates, on Tuesday 3 September Ringo returned to rejoin the Beatles. He found his drum kit smothered in flowers. On his return to the fold Ringo let it be known just who had upset him when he described Paul as the greatest bass guitarist in the world, but at the same time noted his friend's great determination and by saying Paul could be dogged, persisting with something until he got his own way. Diplomatically Ringo commented that while this could be a positive it could also produce musical disagreements within the group.

Significantly, on 6 September at Abbey Road, at George's request, Eric Clapton recorded his solo for George's 'While My Guitar Gently Weeps'.

For original British Beatles fans still alive today, and therefore old enough they will recall Sunday 8 September 1968 was a very memorable day, for on that evening a film clip (aka 'video') of the Beatles performing 'Hey Jude' was premiered on the LWT show *Frost on Sunday*. We hadn't seen too much of them of late and so their appearance was a big deal, especially as they were debuting a new song. To teenagers like myself it looked as if they were live with Frost on the actual show, but we learned later that their appearance had been pre-recorded. Whatever, it didn't matter, for as far as we were concerned the Beatles were still together and 'Hey Jude' was proof positive that they were still making incredible records and that this one was surely one of their very best.

The Beatles' position as cultural icons was confirmed, on 30 September, when *The Beatles: The Authorised Biography* by Hunter Davies (William Heinemann Limited) was published. To this day it stands as a unique publication, for it is the only authorised biography of the group written during their lifetime as a working band. The access Davies was given to John, Paul, George and Ringo was equalled only by that given just a few years earlier to Michael Braun. As such both books remain essential reads for not just fans but anyone wishing to gain an insight into the Sixties and the cultural revolution that was afoot.

An event that was to become a real thorn in John Lennon's side later in his life occurred when on Thursday 10 October he and Yoko were remanded on bail re: charges of unauthorised possession of cannabis.

For Paul, however, three weeks later on 31 October, an event occurred that was to fill his life with great happiness and joy: Linda Eastman and her daughter Heather moved to live with him in his London home.

Friday 1 November saw the release of what became recognised as the first Beatle's 'solo' record when *Wonderwall Music* (Original Soundtrack Album) by George Harrison and Band/Orchestra was issued – in Stereo – in the UK on Apple as SAPCOR 1. (A mono version was also released, catalogue number 'Apcor 1'.) The record was issued in the USA on 2 December.

On 8 November, Cynthia Lennon was granted a *decree nisi*. Just three days later on Monday 11 November, *Unfinished Music No.1: Two Virgins* by John Lennon and Yoko One was released in the USA as Apple T 5001. Because of the photograph of a nude John and Yoko on the front cover, Capitol refused to distribute it and so upstepped a tiny spoken-word label Tetragrammaton who did, but not before placing each copy in a plain brown paper sleeve with a cut-away hole at the front, out of which John and Yoko's faces peeped.

Also concealed inside brown paper bags *Two Virgins* was released in the UK on 29 November as Apple SAPCOR 2. (Like *Wonderwall* before it there was a mono version of the album with the catalogue number 'Apcor 2' prepared, although it was supposedly withdrawn and never issued although very rare copies do occasionally turn up at auction.)

Trauma struck John and Yoko when on 21 November Yoko miscarried her and John's baby. This tragedy had no doubt been brought about in no small measure by the stress she suffered by being arrested on drugs offences.

Significantly, on Friday 22 November *The Beatles* (aka *The White Album*) double album was released in the UK. (It came out on 25 November in the USA.)

Another small but ominous portent for Apple happened on 24 November when Grapefruit, the first band to be signed to Apple, left the label with their manager Terry Doran. Doran was reported as saying he liked the Beatles as friends but not as bosses, commenting that, "There's too much driftwood at Apple."[1]

An example of the unusual if not bizarre goings on at number 3 Savile Row, the home of the Apple offices, occurred on Wednesday 4 December when via an office memo George informed Apple staff that 12 Hell's Angels, "who may look like they are going to do you in but are very straight and do good things", were coming to stay. Apparently, so George's memo also informed everyone at Apple, the Angels were stopping by on their way "to straighten out Czechoslovakia." This must be the one and only time in the history of the Hell's Angels that they have been likened to/mistaken for an international peacekeeping force.[2]

Within the story of 1968 it was just a footnote at the time, but has since proved to be a significant one, for on 6 December James Taylor's eponymous (Peter Asher-produced) album was released as Apple SAPCOR 3. It was the acorn from which a mighty oak would grow. In 1968 it did not set the charts alight but it announced the arrival of an artist who, alongside one half of John and Paul's former songwriting heroes Goffin and King, Carole King, would shape the way the record industry plied its product in the Seventies to make more money than anyone could ever have dreamed of.

In a spontaneous moment of madness on 11 December, Paul, Linda and her daughter chartered a jet to fly to Praia da Luz in the Portuguese Algarve to holiday with Beatles' 'official' biographer Hunter Davies and his family who were already there and had invited them over.

Elsewhere on 11 December, John, his son Julian and Yoko were at Wembley Studios where John and Yoko filmed an appearance for *The Rolling Stones' Rock and Roll Circus* TV special. They performed together in an ad hoc band called 'The Dirty Mac' featuring John on guitar and vocals, Yoko Ono on vocals, Eric Clapton on guitar, Keith Richards on bass, Mitch Mitchell on drums and the Israeli virtuoso violinist Ivry Gitlis who played alongside Yoko on 'Whole Lotta Yoko'. (The Stones, for whom this was Brian Jones's last live appearance, were reportedly dissatisfied with their own performance on the night and consequently mothballed the project. It remained locked away for many, many years until, as part of the New York Film Festival, on 12 October 1996 it received its belated premiere at the Walter Reade Theater, NYC. Not long after it was shown on TV (6 December) and later released on CD and DVD).

With Christmas on the immediate horizon more madness filled the Apple offices when on 23 December Apple held its first Christmas Party at which John and Yoko turned up dressed as Father and Mother Christmas. Apple's new singing sensation, Mary Hopkin, also attended as did the Hell's Angels who were still in town. Adding to this wacky festive melée were members of a Californian hippie commune who, being in town, were on the guest list too. It's impossible to imagine, as festive gatherings go, just how much more bizarre it could have been.

As the year closed, although relations between the Beatles were not as close as they once had been, commercially they were every bit as successful as ever. For the first time in years they did not have a Christmas single on the charts but their tenth studio album (if you include in that list the *A Collection of Beatles Oldies* compilation) and first on their own Apple label, *The Beatles* aka *The White Album*, had gone straight to number 1 in the UK, and as 1968 closed it remained ensconced at the top. By then worldwide its sales had topped 4 million copies which at the time was a record for a double album.

Even so, despite its phenomenal worldwide record sales there was no way Apple could continue spending money as it was and the Beatles could no longer pretend to be businessmen. They weren't. Something had to give … the largesse had to stop.

As a group the internal tensions that had begun to make themselves felt during the year, partly as a result of the pressure of being businessmen, were not about to disappear. The group bond that had always been so strong and had always kept them sane during the utter insanity of Beatlemania had begun to unravel.

Fans were aware all was not well, for although The White *Album* was a superb feast of great songs, it could not detract from the fact that many of them were almost solo efforts. And, of course they were. The most solo track of all was on side four, a 'Lennon and McCartney' (so it said on the cover) composition entitled 'Revolution 9'. Unfortunately, however many times a fan may play this (and not too many of them do after hearing it once), it never sounded any different: to their ears it was the most alien-sounding track ever released by the group. There wasn't very much Beatles about it, but they could hear an awful lot of John and Yoko. Fans didn't need to be told the dynamic within the group had shifted: they could hear it in this track and, for most of them, what they heard didn't sit right at all …

THE UK'S TOP 30 MOST POPULAR SINGLES OF1968
01 Louis Armstrong: What a Wonderful World / Cabaret
02 Mary Hopkin: Those Were the Days
03 Des O'Connor: I Pretend
04 Hugo Montenegro: The Good, the Bad and the Ugly
05 Union Gap: Young Girl
06 Tommy James & the Shondells: Mony Mony
07 The Beatles: Hey Jude
08 The Equals: Baby Come Back
09 Esther and Abi Ofarim: Cinderella Rockefella
10 Tom Jones: Delilah
11 Love Affair: Everlasting Love
12 The Bee Gees: I've Gotta Get a Message to You

13 Casuals: Jessamine
14 Engelbert Humperdinck: A Man Without Love
15 The Scaffold: Lily the Pink
16 Crazy World of Arthur Brown: Fire
17 Manfred Mann: The Mighty Quinn
18 Leapy Lee: Little Arrows
19 Cliff Richard: Congratulations
20 The Rolling Stones: Jumpin' Jack Flash
21 1910 Fruitgum Company: Simon Says
22 Herb Alpert: This Guy's in Love with You
23 The Beach Boys: Do It Again
24 Bobby Goldsboro: Honey
25 Tom Jones: Help Yourself
26 Dave Dee Dozy Beaky Mick and Tich: Legend of Xanadu
27 OC Smith: Son of Hickory Holler's Tramp
28 John Rowles: If I Only Had Time
29 Solomon King: She Wears My Ring
30 Joe Cocker: With a Little Help from My Friends

1 *The Beatles: A diary*, Barry Miles (Omnibus Press, 1998) p. 279.
2 *The Complete Beatles Chronicle*, Mark Lewisohn (Chancellor Press, 1996 edition) p.278 .

Chapter 108:
1969, GETTING BACK

Despite the success of *The White Album*, group unity was at a low ebb when on Thursday 2 January 1969 the Beatles gathered at Twickenham Film Studios to begin filming rehearsal sessions towards a TV special performance they had agreed to make in lieu of touring.

The new project was largely Paul's 'baby' because of the four it was he who most wanted a return to performing live and he believed the former bonds between them could be restored if they 'got back' to doing what they first got together to do as teenagers: play live!

As might be expected, George in particular had no desire to do this. A special one-off concert filmed for TV was the compromise solution. Par for the course, group decisions at this time aimed at deciding on the venue for such a venture proved tricky. In turn this inability to agree led to another compromise.

Ringo was due to begin filming at Twickenham Film Studios with Peter Sellers on February 3 in an adaptation of another Terry Southern novel, *The Magic Christian*. Before then, a suggestion came from Apple Film's director Denis O'Dell, who had booked the sound stage at Twickenham from that date for the filming of Ringo's movie, that the group could use it as a space to rehearse for the TV concert. Better still, he suggested why not film the rehearsals themselves and use some of the footage for a TV documentary entitled *Beatles at Work* that could accompany the proposed TV show.

O'Dell's compromise was agreed but with reluctance on the part of some participants.

The fractures that had appeared during the protracted sessions for 'The White Album' quickly revealed themselves once the group convened at Twickenham.

And so it was that things began amidst a very edgy atmosphere in which it was clear that George did not want to be there. There were a number of things unsettling him, including the constant presence of Yoko Ono, which he resented. To be fair, so did others. By now John was on heroin and as a result had become a largely silent presence for whom Yoko did the talking which also did not go down well. It wasn't just George who found this challenging; Paul was also uncomfortable with the situation.

Mostly such tensions simmered below the surface and the sessions proceeded smoothly with only an occasional falling out. One such occasion was when George fell out with Paul and declared that the group should split up, however almost before the dust settled on that particular tiff George fell out even bigger-time with John when he believed Lennon had been demeaning about his songwriting. George was incensed.

Meltdown occurred on 10 January when the simmering resentments within George erupted. The fracas kicked off as he and Paul started to snipe at each other, but then George seriously clashed with John who chided him for not contributing to, or showing interest in, the sessions. It was at that point George decided he had heard enough.

Quietly informing the others that he'd see them "round the clubs," he promptly quit the set and walked out. (Somewhat symbolically he immediately drove back to where he once came from: Liverpool, to his mum and dad's house.)

Stunned, speechless, and with no idea what to say to each other, the three remaining Beatles plus Yoko simply carried on by returning to the sound stage where they backed Yoko as she (adding insult to injury) sat on George's blue cushion and screamed full tilt. Once it was over they left. Through it all not a word between them had been spoken.

Life, of course, carried on. The day after George quit the group the *Wonderwall* film opened. Three days after this on January 13 the *Yellow Submarine* (Original Soundtrack Album) was released in the USA (it came out on 17 January in the UK). Despite the absence of their lead guitarist the others continued somewhat aimlessly to gather at the film studio.

On Wednesday 15 January George returned to the Beatlefold from his self-imposed exile and, during a protracted five-hour meeting at Twickenham, reconciled his position within the group. Most importantly, he and John made up.

George's return was not without conditions: he only agreed to do so after the others agreed to drop the idea of a live show. In return, however, George let it be known he *was* prepared to make a film of them as a group recording a new album. Being all agreed on this revised plan George seized the moment to further persuade John, Paul and Ringo to abandon the cavernous and impersonal film studios of Twickenham for the more intimate confines of their own Apple recording studio.

George's suggestions produced positive outcomes. Once The Beatles settled into filming at Apple, they became more relaxed and relationships between them became much more harmonious and they made good music.

N.B. *When they made the decision to switch from Twickenham to Apple the group believed that their friend and head of Apple Electronics 'Magic' Alex Mardas had, in this capacity, been busy building a mega-state-of-the-art, space-age 72-track recording studio in the basement of number 3 Savile Row. He hadn't. Quickly discovering that this was far from being the case, as on previous occasions, they turned to trusty George Martin to save their day. George brought over two four-track recording machines from Abbey Road and by 22 January they were up and running, and recording began.*

George, full of good ideas at this point, and keen to further heal the wounds between him and the others, asked an old friend of the group from their Hamburg days to join them in the studios. And so it was that ace keyboard player Billy Preston began to sit in with the Beatles. George's reasoning here was that Preston's presence could well provide the melioration needed to help improve relationships within the group and keep them focused on making music: he was spot on in his analysis.

On return to Apple the idea of a *Beatles at Work* half-hour TV documentary morphed into the idea of a full-length motion picture project. It also gained a title which was intended to be the same as the album: *Get Back*.

Requiring a focal point for the film's conclusion, on Sunday 26 January director Michael Lindsay-Hogg convened a meeting where it was mooted that the Beatles should perform live in which they would play some of the songs they had been filmed rehearsing. To nip opposition to this idea in the bud it was suggested (most probably by Lindsay-Hogg) that the roof of 3 Savile Row could be a suitable location for this live shoot. It was a wise suggestion for it involved no travel, no crowds and as little hassle as possible, thus making the logistics positive and painless for the players (especially George).

Initially the decision was not unanimous, for while John, Paul and Ringo supported the notion, George was not much in favour saying he'd do it if he had to but wasn't keen about going on the roof … Thankfully he was persuaded otherwise and on 30 January 1969 they all turned up to perform a 42-minute lunchtime concert on the roof of the Apple building. The sound of their music brought traffic on the road below to a standstill as crowds gathered to listen and look up towards its source. The event was concluded just as several somewhat reluctant police officers arrived on the scene to restore 'order'. At the point officers arrived, the Beatles had actually played all of the songs they had intended to perform and were in the process of repeating a couple for the purposes of the film. It was dropping quite cold and so the arrival of the police provided a very convenient excuse to retreat back inside to the warmth of the studio. Conveniently the police intervention also provided a better, more dramatic ending to the film, rather than just letting it fizzle out as the group returned inside. The ending became famous not only for the police intervention but most especially for John's concluding quip, "I hope we passed the audition".

It was the last time the group played together in public.

Filming was completed the next day, but production dragged from that point on and it was over a year before the finished product reached the screen.

Turning the songs they had cut as they filmed into 'finished product' proved to be a dispiriting affair. Producer Glyn Johns who had been working with The Beatles on the project from its inception came up with a 'fly on the wall' idea for an 'audio documentary' style album for which he made an acetate with which the group were not enamoured. Later they requested John return to his idea and he produced another mix of the songs/material but once again they shelved the finished product. Eventually they enlisted the services of ace American producer Phil Spector to 'rescue' the *Get Back* album so that it could be released in a form that met with their approval. Spector almost achieved this but Paul in particular never liked Spector's realisation of the record. (His dissatisfaction with what Spector produced lingered until in 2003 when the group issued *Let It Be ... Naked* which Paul felt came closer to the 'stripped down' rock 'n' roll performance they had originally been after.)

Two days before that legendary rooftop concert took place, John Lennon and Yoko Ono had met with Allen Klein in the Dorchester Hotel and had been so impressed John instantly made Klein his personal advisor. Not only that but without hesitation Lennon wrote to Sir Joseph Lockwood of EMI to advise him that Klein would be handling all his business from then on.

On 3 February the Beatles met with Allen Klein and Lee Eastman (Linda's father) at which it was decided Klein was to be appointed the Beatles' business manager and tasked with examining their finances and preventing NEMS from taking a quarter of their income. Paul had been hoping the Beatles would appoint Linda's father Lee and brother (John) as their representatives and was very uneasy about Klein's appearance on the Beatles' scene. It was in deference to Paul that Lee and John and Eastman were appointed to Apple's General Council to act as a check on Klein's wheelings and dealings.

For the group the rift caused by Allen Klein's arrival in their world became mighty. Although, ostensibly still working together as a team (or at least in tandem), Klein's presence in their midst caused the battle lines to be drawn that would eventually tear the Beatles apart.

During the fallout between Paul and the other three Beatles about who would ultimately manage their affairs, NEMS Enterprises was bought out by a firm of merchant bankers which most crucially meant the Beatles lost control of Northern Songs and with that went Paul and John's control of their own publishing copyrights.

While everything else appeared to be going down the pan, amazingly, artistically, all was not lost and the Beatles enjoyed one last hurrah as a creative entity in the studio.

In July, maybe intuitively driven by the need *not* to leave *Get Back* as possibly their last body of work recorded together, they re-grouped for the recording of a new album. Untitled at first it became their swan song, *Abbey Road*. Fittingly it was cut under the tutelage of their long-time, most talented and most trusted mentor: George Martin.

Making records (particularly with George Martin in the control room) were what the Beatles had always been brilliant at doing and what they achieved at Apple Records was no exception. As Apple Corps Ltd faltered during 1969 its most successful division, Apple Records, continued to flourish. And it was not just the Beatles' own product that made the charts and garnered success and acclaim. As we have learned, other artists whom they signed and mentored also had moments of considerable national and international success (that also made a lot of money for the label).

Released by the label, after 'Hey Jude' itself, Apple 2, was an old Russian folk song entitled 'Those Were the Days'. Sung by Welsh singer Mary Hopkin it was one of the label's most incredible successes. It toppled 'Hey Jude' from the Number 1 spot in the UK, climbed to Number 2 in the USA, and became a worldwide hit that sold in excess of 8,000,000 copies.

Paul had signed Hopkin to Apple and not only chose the song but had produced it as well.

Chapter 109:
FOR MARY HOPKIN OF PONTARDAWE, SOUTH WALES …

OPPORTUNITY KNOCKS!

Mary Hopkin was born Mary Elizabeth Blodnen Hopkin on Wednesday 3 May 1950 in Ystradgynlais, near Swansea, South Wales. Her story has a distinct touch of the stuff from which 'dreams are made', that is, 'An unknown pretty young girl with an equally pretty voice (from humble origins, of course) is 'discovered' by a handsome and famous prince of pop who then whisks her away to turn her into a star…'

Mary's family were Welsh-speaking and she grew up in Pontardawe, Neath Port Talbot, Wales. Her parents had been quick to recognise her musical talent and paid for her to have weekly singing lessons. By her teens she was performing in the local clubs as both a solo act and as part of a folk band called the 'Selby Set and Mary'. Before long she had recorded an EP for local record label Cambrian on which all four tracks were sung in the Welsh language. This limited its chances of airplay as at that time there were no local radio stations, nevertheless, locally, it sold well.

Such modest, local success could in no way have prepared her or her family for what happened next …

Aged just 17, Mary Hopkin's life changed, almost in the blink of an eye, when on Saturday 4 May 1968, she appeared on popular entertainer Hughie Green's even more popular TV talent show *Opportunity Knocks*. Singing a beautiful version of 'Turn, Turn, Turn', her winning performance caused a sensation … especially when she won again the next week … and then the next.

Among the television audience glued to their screens keenly following Mary's progress was Paul McCartney's good friend Twiggy. Dubbed 'The Face of 1966', by 1967 Twiggy had become an international supermodel and fashion icon … and good friend of the Beatles. Like nearly every one who saw and heard Hopkin on *Opportuniy Knocks* she was very impressed by Mary's performance. Fortunately, Twiggy also knew that Apple was on the lookout for new artists to sign.

On Sunday 5 May 1968, Twiggy and her manager Justin de Villeneuve were Paul's dinner guests at his father's house in Heswall on the Wirral where, over pudding, the conversation turned to TV talent-discovery shows, during which Paul pondered whether the winners of such shows ever really did make it beyond just winning the show, that is, did they stay 'discovered'? It was at this point Twiggy drew Mary Hopkin to Paul's attention. His curiosity was so engaged that the very next week he tuned in to the show to hear her sing for himself. Once again Hopkin turned in a winning performance of 'Turn, Turn, Turn' and Paul was taken with what he both heard and saw.

Young, blonde, pretty, and with a wonderful voice, Paul knew intuitively that given the right song Mary Hopkin could have the world at her feet.

Suitably enthused, Paul decided she should make a record for Apple and called her at home, later telling *Melody Maker* that: "This beautiful little Welsh voice came on the phone and I said: 'This is Apple Records here; would you be interested in coming down here to record for us?' She said: 'Well, er, would you like to speak to my mother?' and then her mother came on the line and we had a chat, and two further telephone conversations later that week Mary and her mum came to London."[1]

As she kept winning, Hopkin continued to appear on *Opportunity Knocks*, but now she was also recording with Paul McCartney. There is a clip available on YouTube that shows her performing 'Turn, Turn, Turn' on the show. It is from July 1968 and at the end of her performance she is interviewed by Hughie Green who notices she has a new guitar and is informed by Mary that it was a gift to her from George Harrison. She also informs Green that she has recorded a single and remarks that as the guest of the Beatles she had attended the premiere of *Yellow Submarine* held on Wednesday 17 July. From her performance preserved on this clip it is clear just why viewers kept voting her back and just what Twiggy and Paul had seen and heard in her as a potential recording artist.

Mary seems to remember she got the invite to record for Apple via telegram, for as she told Bob Harris, "They sent a telegram from Apple Records and brought me up to London to sing for Paul."[2]

There may be doubts as to precisely how she received the invitation but there is no doubt that, within days, accompanied by her mother, Mary travelled to London for her audition with Paul. Paul was sensitive to the fact that for anyone, never mind such a young artist as Mary, arriving in London to go straight into a studio to sing for him would be a daunting experience, and so not to drop her in at the deep end, but to help her relax and get to know her and her mother a little, Paul first took them out for a meal. "He took us out to lunch, my mum and I. We had a nice steak at the Angus Steakhouse on Oxford Street, and then we went off to Dick James. I sang a couple of folk songs, Donovan songs and things and then I went back to Wales. The next visit was when Paul played a lovely song called 'Those Were the Days' to me."[3]

Once in the studio, despite the pressure others might have felt in the same situation, as she began to sing Hopkin remained calm: "I was very shy and quite in awe of Paul as I had been a Beatles fan since I was 13 years old. So it was very exciting, but singing for him didn't faze me very much, although I did stand with my back to him: he was up in the control room. I didn't feel particularly nervous singing for him, I do remember breaking a guitar string halfway through though."[4]

The 'new' song Paul sang to Mary was a very typical McCartney choice. All through the stories of *The Songs the Beatles Gave Away* Paul's marvellous memory for tunes has been apparent. Several of his compositions as performed by other artists that found their way into the charts were early tunes he recalled from his formative days as a composer living in the family home on Forthlin Road in Liverpool ... 'World Without Love', 'Cat Call', 'Tip of My Tongue', 'Like Dreamers Do' ... It seems once heard/written Paul never forgets a tune, however fragmentary, and can keep it locked inside his memory until the right moment or artist comes along for whom it may fit. 'Those Were the Days', although *not* one of his own compositions, was another example of a tune Paul had stored inside his head just waiting for the right voice to come along. Inside his own mind Paul could hear exactly how it should sound and now, with Mary standing in front of him, he firmly believed he had found the artist who could do it justice and make it into the hit he believed it could be.

As Hopkin explains: "Apparently it was a Ukrainian folk song melody and it was sung by Gene Raskin, an American architect and his wife Francesca, who used to do the clubs in London where Paul had heard them at the Blue Angel. He loved the song and hung onto it for quite a few years. I think he offered it to people like Donovan and a band called the Limeliters. Nothing happened with it and then I came along and Paul thought it suited my voice."[5]

Hopkin is correct about Paul suggesting it to Donovan but not about the Limeliters. Paul sang it to Donovan when they were in India meditating together. Donovan liked it but never did anything with it. Paul also suggested it to the Moody Blues (via singer Denny Laine), who likewise did nothing with it. The Limeliters were an American folk trio and they had actually recorded 'Those Were the Days' several years before Hopkin sang it. Both they and Paul McCartney got the song from the same source: one Gene Raskin.

The Limliters had included the song on their 1962 album, *Folk Matinee*. During the height of the folk boom in the USA, in 1962 the Limiters were a successful group who got the song from Gene Raskin of the folk duo 'Gene and Francesca'. At that time Gene and Francesca were performing in Greenwich Village but by the mid-Sixties they had re-located to, and were regulars on, the London club circuit. The song was not a Raskin original. It was a Russian tune to which Gene had written new English lyrics, and as such they were *not* a literal translation of the original Russian lyrics: the original lyrics had been penned by the poet Konstantin Podrevsky. The original song was entitled 'Dorogoi dlinnoyu' ('Дорогой длинною') which translates literally to 'By the long road', and had been composed by one Boris Fomin (1900–1948). Not only did the Limliters record the Raskin arrangement 'Those Were the Days' replete with his new lyrics, they also recorded a Raskin original entitled, 'That's Just the Way It Goes'.[6]

Having already recognised the 'hit' potential of 'Those Were the Days', Paul believed he had now found the right artist to perform it. And so he played it to Mary who liked it, very quickly picked it up and understood how Paul thought she should sing it. A song of this nature could have been problematic for such a young artist as Hopkin to deliver, for it was essentially a nostalgic tune for which the words had been written as if they were those of an older person reflecting on their lives from the vantage point of being old. Despite such concerns Hopkin's youthfulness presented no barrier to her grasp of the nature of the lyrics and her delivery perfectly captured the wistful heart of the song.

Paul's instinct for a hit was bang on the money. 'Those Were the days' was a massive success and everyone did very well out of it, except maybe original composer Boris Fomin (who, to be fair, had died in 1948) whose name was not credited on original copies because Eugene Raskin claimed full composer credits. From his writer's royalties (according to Wikipedia) Raskin was able to purchase a home in Pollensa, Mallorca, a Porsche Spyder and a sail boat, none of which, of course, would have been much use to poor old Boris by that time.

Paul recorded Mary singing the song in several languages including French *(Le temps des fleurs)*, Italian (*Quelli erano giorni*), Spanish (*Qué tiempo tan feliz*) and German (*An jenem Tag*). It reached the number 1 spot in a total of 16 countries worldwide, although in Italy, despite her Italian language version of the tune, it only managed to reach number 15.

Paul was not the only one to consider 'Those Were the Days' to be hit material. On the day Mary's version was issued, and on which she made the front page of *Disc and Music Echo*, it was announced that top UK singer Sandie Shaw had also recorded the song and was rush-releasing it in direct competition with Hopkin. Shaw's opportunism wasn't quick enough: her version came out in early September shortly after Mary's, but there was no competition: by then Mary was on her way to the top and Shaw's version sank without trace.

The success of 'Those Were the Days' inspired Paul. He was convinced that with careful guidance Mary Hopkin could go on to become an international star. Further, he understood that if she did achieve global success this in turn would help establish Apple Records internationally.

Such was his determination to assist Hopkin achieve this level of success he produced her debut album, *Post Card*. Recorded over several months (mid-November 1968 to mid-January 1969) and released on 21 February 1969, it was an eclectic collection intended to broaden Mary's appeal beyond that of 'just' a folk singer. Paul was determined that the album should highlight her ability to perform a wide range of material and so it was a diverse collection combining new, contemporary tunes alongside well-known 'standards'. The songwriting credits reflect the eclectic nature of the album and include Donovan Leitch ('Lord of the Reedy River' and two others), Harry Nilsson ('The Puppy Song'), Ray Noble ('Love Is the Sweetest Thing'), Irving Berlin ('There's No Business Like Show Business'), Ira and George Gershwin ('Someone to Watch over Me') and George Martin who contributed a tune entitled 'The Game' as well as conducting the orchestra and playing piano. To further strengthen the album's 'international' appeal, Paul also recorded Mary singing two non-English tracks: one in her native tongue called 'Y Blodyn Glyn' (E.J. Hughes, R.H. Jones) and in French on 'Prince En Avignon' (Jean Pierre Bourtayre).

The producer-artist relationship between Paul and Mary worked well during the recording of *Post Card*: "When we recorded the album he was very sensitive, if I wasn't sure how to approach a song he was very helpful … he was great to work with."[7]

The McCartney 'determination' of which Ringo had commented was very much in evidence during the making of *Post Card*: Paul not only chose all the songs, produced and played on the album, but he enlisted Linda to take the front cover photograph of Mary while he provided a handwritten set list (as if written on the back of a postcard) for the back cover.

All the whistles and bells he could think to pull out of the hat were included in his efforts to make *Post Card* fly. Given that at the time he was in the midst of the meltdown of the Beatles (and the fractious recording sessions for *Get Back*), he was enormously generous with his time and energy. The only problem with this approach, however, was that ultimately the album was more about Paul McCartney's vision of Mary Hopkin than it was about Mary Hopkin's vision of herself: as artists there was more of him invested in it than her.

Despite such artistic imbalance, *Post Card* was a huge success in the UK where it reached number 3 and, significantly, it made the Top 30 album charts in both the USA (number 28) and Canada (number 26). Surprisingly the hoped-for success in countries where 'Those Were the Days' had been a number 1 hit proved strangely elusive.

Despite her reservations at the time about its song content, recording *Post Card* provided Mary with many magical memories, one in particular which stands out: "A wonderful memory for me, we were sat in Abbey Road doing two or three Donovan songs. So I was sitting in the middle on a stool with Donovan's handwritten lyrics in a beautiful leather-bound book in front of me and I was reading/singing the songs whilst Paul and Donovan sat either side of me with acoustic guitars and played … I was too shy to utter a word (other than to sing), I just listened to the two of them conversing through the session and then to hear them playing together was wonderful."[8]

Donovan's tunes were to be her favourites from the album, no doubt because of their folk style with which she felt a closer artistic kinship.

The one thing Paul had not done on the album, somewhat surprisingly, was to record Mary singing a Lennon-McCartney tune. This situation was rectified with her follow-up single and in doing so Paul helped Mary to achieve another massive worldwide hit: "It was about a year after 'Those Were the Days' Paul wrote 'Goodbye' for me."[9]

Mary has a clear memory of how Paul introduced his new song to her (and how he came to compose it). "Well, the same way as he sang 'Those Were the Days' to me, for that he just sat in a chair and strummed, it was the same with 'Goodbye'. And then he made a little demo for me to take home, and I loved it. I felt very privileged to have a song especially written for me. Apparently he wrote it in a delightful little Italian restaurant where everyone used to go to from Apple – it no longer exists – called 'The Capri' in Ayer Street. Apparently Paul was there with some friends one evening for a meal. He used to take his guitar along and strum and he came up with this idea and thought 'Mary needs a song' and apparently he wrote this in a matter of minutes, which only he can do!"[10]

As Mary says, prior to her recording 'Goodbye', Paul recorded a home demo of the song for Mary and arranger Richard Hewson. Featuring just Paul and his guitar he cut an acetate at Abbey Road for them to familiarise themselves with the tune. Paul's demo finally received a Beatles release as one of the 'sessions' tracks included in the 2019 'Anniversary Edition' of *Abbey Road*.

Paul McCartney and Mary Hopkin, 1968
… those were the days. (United Archives
GmbH / Alamy Stock Photo)

MARY HOPKIN
GOODBYE (2:23)
(Lennon/McCartney)
Northern Songs Ltd
APPLE 10
Arranged by Richard Hewson
Recorded on 1 March 1969 in Morgan Studios, Willesden, north west London
Mary Hopkin: vocals, acoustic guitar.
Paul McCartney: solo acoustic guitar introduction, bass, lap-slapping, drums and percussion.
Richard Hewson overdubbed backing vocals, horns and strings.
The session was filmed by Tony Bramwell of Apple and the footage was intended to be used for a promotional clip but never was. It featured Mary and Paul working on the song, talking and singing.
A second clip of colour film of Mary (alone) exists in which she sits on the ground amid buttercups singing and playing her guitar. It was shot in the back garden of Paul's house in St. John's Wood with Paul's dog, Mary first sitting behind her and then rolling about in front of her. Despite Martha's best efforts to derail her performance Mary never misses a beat!
B-SIDE: Sparrow
(Gallagher and Lyle)
Recorded: 2 March 1969.
Mary: vocals, guitar
Paul: maracas
A session musician played upright bass
Richard Hewson added a choir part.
Producer (both sides): Paul McCartney
Arranger (both sides): Richard Hewson

Mary's memory of recording 'Goodbye' and 'Sparrow' was that the recordings took place on the same day. "Paul produced 'Goodbye' ... at Morgan Studios ... and I believe on the day we recorded a double A-side. We recorded 'Sparrow' by Bernard Gallagher and Graham Lyle* as well. They were writing for Apple at the same time, so I think we recorded them both on the same day.

"I remember sorting out a little guitar riff that Paul came up with and we sat side by side playing that together, then Paul put this wonderful thigh slap on – you can hear it quite clearly, it's him slapping his thigh, so that runs through the song which is quite novel."[11]

'Goodbye' was the first Apple single to be released in a picture cover.

(*Benny Gallagher and Graham Lyle were a songwriting duo from Scotland signed to Apple Publishing. In 1970 the duo joined McGuiness Flint and penned the group's debut UK hit 'When I'm Dead and Gone' and its follow-up 'Malt and Barley Blues'. They penned 'A Heart in New York' for Art Garfunkel which he so memorably performed in September 1981 at 'The Concert in Central Park' (with Paul Simon). They also scored hits in their own right including 'Heart on My Sleeve'.)

Released in the UK: 28 March 1969, 'Goodbye' climbed to #2 on 22 April, dropped to #3 the following week before regaining the #2 position for two more weeks in early May. It stayed on the charts for 14 weeks. Mary Hopkin was denied a second successive number 1 by her mentor's band when, from the end of April through most of May, the Beatles took up a four-week residency at number 1 with *Get Back*.

Released in the USA: 7 April 1969 APPLE 1806, 'Goodbye' peaked at number 13 on the *Billboard* Hot 100 and number 6 on their Easy Listening Chart.

In the booklet notes that accompanied the 2010 CD compilation album *Come and Get It: The Best of Apple Records*, of 'Goodbye' it says, "Apple had high hopes for the single, and issued it in around 35 different countries."[12] These hopes were realised in 1969 when

'Goodbye' made the upper echelons of the charts in the following countries:

Belgium: 7
Canada: 15
Denmark: 3
Netherlands: 1
Finland: 4
France: 9
Ireland: 1
Israel: 5
Norway: 3
Poland: 4
Sweden: 3

Many years later Paul received a warm commendation for the song that he much appreciated when, on a boat trip from the north of Scotland to the Orkney Islands, the skipper told him it was his favourite song. Paul reckoned this was because it was "a leaving-the-port song."[13]

Paul writes at length about the composition of 'Goodbye' in his two-volume autobiographical *The Lyrics* published in 2021, describing it as being "in the tradition of the 'I'm leaving, but I'll be back soon' kind of song you used to hear when you were a kid. They'd be requested on the radio …"[14]

He continues by commenting that what is of particular interest to him in the lyric is a device that he doesn't think he's ever used "before or since" and that is "the use of the same word over and over." And so it is 'late' is repeated three times in the first verse, 'leave' twice in the second and 'lonely' twice in the third. He comments that usually he would try and find another word but "I think repetition, sometimes, is effective." [15]

1 Paul McCartney, *Melody Maker*, 1968.
2, 3, 4, 5, 7, 8, 9, 10 & 11 Mary Hopkin in conversation with her cousin Bob Harris OBE for the 2009 BBC Radio 2 music documentary *The Songs the Beatles Gave Away,* written and narrated by Bob Harris, produced by Bob Harris and Trudie Mysercough-Harris.
6 *Gene Raskin – Singer, songwriter and architectural scholar*, by Pierre Perrone, *Independent*, 18 June 2004.
12 *Come and Get It: The Best Of Apple Records* (2010), 21 digitally re-mastered track CD compilation, booklet notes by Andy Davis.
13 *Abbey Road*, 2019 De Luxe 50th Anniversary CD Edition, accompanying book, p.63.
14 & 15 *The Lyrics*, Paul McCartney (Allen Lane, 2021) p.238.

Chapter 110:
MARY HOPKIN BIDS APPLE GOODBYE

For Mary Hopkin her time at Apple were heady days indeed. Aged just 17 when she signed to the label, almost overnight she became an international star.

Accompanying such a high profile there soon came numerous personal appearances on TV and radio, concert tours, interviews, photo shoots, film offers, invitations to this and invitations to that. In the blink of an eye she embarked on a fabulous journey that so many crave but few ever achieve. For one so young this was an amazing change of lifestyle to both encounter and, even more importantly, to survive.

Through it all Mary worked hard and stayed focused when at times her life must have felt not quite her own. Such was her personality and family background she never lost the plot, always aware of who she was and what she really wanted from life.

As a young singer under the tutelage of those more experienced than her in the world of 'entertainment' she would occasionally chafe at the direction in which she was being drawn, but although she could do little to change what was happening, through quiet determination she retained her artistic integrity and, ultimately, control of her destiny.

It must have taken great inner strength not to succumb to the temptations and persuasions that the music industry placed in front of her. And yet, she did: by staying true to herself she emerged as the artist she always wanted to be, singing the songs she felt were right for her, a musician for whom her peers have the greatest respect.

Reflecting on her time at Apple for Bob Harris, Mary recalled a moment of horror that still haunts her: "One memory that stirs me and gives me the chills is that Paul and Linda and Ringo and Maureen came to see me at the Savoy Hotel where I was doing the most dreadful cabaret. It was not at all my idea and they came to the opening night which was very, very sweet of them. I was totally humiliated as I was doing some awful songs."[1]

Despite this difficult moment nothing could ever take away from Mary the magic of those days spent singing and playing guitar with and for Paul McCartney: "While we were working we worked closely every day on the album (*Post Card*). It was an amazing time and I feel very privileged to have been part of that at the beginning of my career. I mean, you tend to work with gifted people like that way into your career. I was straight out of school and working with Paul McCartney!"[2]

After her dream start at Apple she continued to record for the label and continued to enjoy UK chart success with: 'Temma Harbour', a number 6 hit in February 1970, and 'Knock Knock Who's There' a number 2 in April 1970.

Later, on 31 October 1970, she entered the chart with 'Think About Your Children' which eventually peaked at number 19.

Her final Apple hit was 'Let My Name Be Sorrow'. Released in July 1971 it spent only one week in the Top 50 at number 46.

The perceived wisdom is that after 'Goodbye' Mary and Paul did not work together again, but they did. In early August 1969 Paul produced what was intended to be Mary's follow-up single to 'Goodbye'. He wanted this to be another catchy pop song that would both keep the momentum going and further establish Hopkin's international chart status. To this end he chose the Oscar Academy-winning Jay Livingston and Ray Evans' pop classic 'Que Sera, Sera (Whatever Will Be, Will Be)'. This well-known song had originally been recorded in 1956 by film star and singer Doris Day who sang it in the film *The Man Who Knew Too Much*. Doris Day had enjoyed huge international success with the song: it was a number 2 in the USA and a number 1 in the UK and quickly became Day's signature tune.

Unfortunately for Paul, 'Que Sera, Sera' was a step too far in the direction Mary no longer wished to go. During the recording of 'Que Sera, Sera', she asserted herself artistically, letting it be known she did not want to record the song. Despite Hopkin's reluctance McCartney was unmoved. (For the B-side, Mary recorded another Gallagher and Lyle tune entitled 'The Fields of St. Etienne'.)

Even though Paul and Ringo apparently played on both tracks, Hopkin's strong dislike of the record prevailed and it was not released in the UK. As Apple 16 it was released in France on 19 September 1969 but was not a hit. A year later on 15 June 1970 the single received a USA release (catalogue number Apple 1823) where it was a modest hit, reaching number 77 on the *Billboard* Hot 100, number 7 on the US Adult Contemporary Chart, while in Canada it climbed to number 47. It was also a hit in Japan, Australia, New Zealand, and Zimbabwe. From this commercial perspective it has to be said Paul's instincts were sound.

However, the recording of 'Que Sera, Sera' *did* mark a turning point in her career and in her artistic relationship with Paul. Mary's reaction to recording 'Que Sera, Sera' made clear her discomfort with the direction in which such a song would take her: artistically she wished to stem the flow of catchy, commercial 'pop' songs being put in front of her and move more towards singing folk orientated material, songs in which she could believe. Paul was not so interested in producing that kind of material and so the working relationship fizzled.

The irony of this is that she continued to score UK hits with catchy tunes. As she and Paul were no longer in tandem as a working partnership, renowned producer Mickie Most was brought in to produce her next two singles: 'Temma Harbour' and 'Knock, Knock Who's There?'. Both were catchy, both were big hits, the latter being the UK's 1970 Eurovision song contest entry (Mary came second to Ireland's Dana and 'All Kinds of Everything'). For Mary, however, they continued in the direction she no longer wished to go. She particularly disliked 'Knock, Knock Who's There' and found singing it an ordeal.

(A career outcome from her Eurovision adventure was that she received her own peak-time TV series on BBC1. The shows were another step towards becoming an 'all-round entertainer' which was anathema to Hopkin. Entitled *Mary Hopkin in the Land of ...*, the series comprised six half-hour shows that were broadcast in 1970. Each show focused on a different aspect of storytelling through music and dance as Hopkin journeyed through six 'fantasy' lands: film, legend, theatre, books, rhymes, and pantomime. In each show she sang about six songs and as she did so she was followed by a cast of children. While its target audience seems to have been children, it was broadcast at 8:30 in the evening. Book-casing the series, Mary appeared in two pantomimes: one in 1969 with Tommy Steele in *Dick Whittington* in London, and *Cinderella* in Manchester 1970. Her TV series was repeated in 1971.)

Hopkin also expressed her unhappiness with Terry Doran whom Apple had appointed as her manager and on 3 October 1969 a piece appeared in the UK music newspaper *Disc*, announcing that Doran had been replaced by Carole Hopkin as Mary's personal manager.

In a telling interview with Chris Connelly, published in 1985 in *Rolling Stone*, Mary reflected on her career at Apple, commenting that at the time the label seemed as embarrassed as her with the twee 'pop' image she was gaining but did little to alter it and, if anything, in her view, exaggerated it. Clearly she felt pigeon-holed as an artist, unable to express herself sincerely. In the *Rolling Stone* article she commented that, "I was pushed into doing cabaret, doing dreadful songs that nobody cares about. They (the business people) don't understand that you're trying to express yourself. They don't give a damn."[3]

Fortunately, for Hopkin, working as a producer for Apple at this time was American, Tony Visconti. He had been assigned to a band Mal Evans had introduced into Apple called the Iveys (who were to change their name to Badfinger) and he also became Mary's producer.

In Visconti, Mary found a producer more attuned to her personal musical vision. Their relationship marked the beginning of a move away from what she perceived as her 'cute pop star' image singing lightweight songs.

Mary had first encountered Visconti when he recorded her singing a Welsh-language version of 'Sparrow' (the B-side of 'Goodbye') and it was he who took over the production of Hopkin's final Apple recordings, including her final hits: 'Think About Your Children' (number 19, October 1970), and 'Let My Name Be Sorrow' (number 46, summer 1971).

During 1971, Visconti worked with Hopkin to produce her second album for Apple, entitled *Earth Song, Ocean Song*, taking time and care over song selection to ensure it was the album she really wanted to make. They succeeded, for the album has endured and is acclaimed by many critics as her career-best. Within the canon of Apple album releases, beyond the label's classic Beatles records, *Earth Song, Ocean Song* is regarded as one of the best of all the Apple long players. A bright mixture of folk-pop tunes, Mary sings beautiful versions of songs written by Gallagher and Lyle, Cat Stevens and Ralph McTell. Either side of the record closes with songs written by Liz Thorsen, the title tracks, 'Earth Song' and 'Ocean Song'. Released by Apple on 1 October 1971, artistically it is a more satisfying record than *Post Card*, although it did not match its predecessor's commercial success.

A single lifted from the album, 'Water, Paper and Clay' (APPLE 39), in November '71 was her final Apple 45 and in March 1972 Mary Hopkin announced that she had left the label.

By the time *Earth Song, Ocean Song* was released, Mary Hopkin and Tony Visconti were not simply engaged in an artist-producer relationship, they had fallen in love and married. Her departure from Apple was a case of perfect timing as she took time out from recording and show business to have a family (Delaney aka Morgan, born in 1972 and Jessica born in 1976).

In 1972, Apple released a compilation album entitled *Those Were the Days*, which included 'Goodbye' and, somewhat inevitably, that Paul-produced-'lost'-single 'Que Sera, Sera'. (The compilation was released in the UK on 24 November (Apple SAPCOR 23) and in the USA on 25 September (Apple SW 3395.)

Somewhere along the way during her career at Apple, Mary sang backing vocals on 'Hey Jude' and backing vocals on 'Let It Be'. Linda McCartney thought that while both she and Mary were *meant* to sing on the latter, by the time the group got round to actually recording it Mary had gone home, however Hopkin is adamant this was not the case.

She also possibly sang backing vocals on 'Govinda', a George Harrison-produced single by the Radha Krsna Temple on the Apple label. George Harrison apparently offered her his song 'I'll Still Love You' aka 'When Every Song Is Sung'. Certainly it was a tune George offered around at the time and cut versions of it with Cilla Black, Ronnie Spector and Leon and Mary Russell, so it seems entirely likely Mary would have been included in his list of potential interpreters.

Much water and many adventures later, relations between Paul and Mary are good, with the former Beatle describing Hopkin as 'an old friend'.

In *The Lyrics*, Paul McCartney comments, "I was very happy to produce Mary, but she wanted to be a folk singer pure and simple. I said, 'Well that's great ... but I myself wouldn't be that into it.' So I did an album with her, but it wasn't folk: it was songs we agreed we liked, but it wasn't the style she wanted to follow."[4]

Mary Hopkin may have quietly slipped out of the limelight when she left Apple to become a mum, but she never stopped recording and performing. At the time of her departure her manager Jo Lustig said she was considering offers from three major record labels to sign a recording contract, but nothing materialised, although she did record and release a 1972 Christmas single for Regal Zonophone entitled, appropriately, 'Mary Had a Baby'. Earlier in the year, on 29 July, she had starred in her own, one-off TV special for

BBC1, called *Sing Hi, Sing Lo*, which was billed – that dreaded anathema again – as 'light entertainment starring Mary Hopkin'.

Her husband Tony Visconti famously produced not only Badfinger but also David Bowie, T.Rex, Thin Lizzy, Sparks, Bert Jansch and many more. Under the name Mary Visconti, she sang backing vocals on many of these Visconti-produced records (most notably with Brian Eno on Bowie's *Sound and Vision*). She also made occasional personal appearances, such as guesting on the 16 February 1974 edition of *The Cilla Black Show* to perform a beautiful version of the John Kongos song, 'Shamarack', and to also duet with Cilla on Joni Mitchell's 'Both Sides Now'. In August 1977 she accompanied Bert Jansch on stage at the Cambridge Folk Festival.

In 1976 she returned to the UK Top 40 when, under the name Mary Hopkin, she released a single on Visconti's Good Earth label. 'If You Love Me' entered the Top 40 on 20 March 1976 and spent four weeks on the chart, peaking at number 32. A follow-up 'Wrap Your Arms Around Me' did not chart, but significantly the B-sides of both singles were Hopkin's own tunes, 'Tell Me Now' and 'Just a Dreamer'.

Her marriage to Visconti ended in 1981 and not long after she briefly joined a group called Sundance who issued just one single in the spring of 1982, entitled 'What's Love?'. On the back of this they toured with Dr. Hook but Hopkin left soon after. The single was a hit in South Africa …

In the mid-Eighties, Hopkin responded to a request from Peter Skellern to join him and Julian Lloyd Webber in a band called 'Oasis', a kind of 'easy listening' supergroup.

Oasis recorded two singles and an album for WEA. They took their name from the closing-Peter-Skellern-composed track on side one of the record. The album was a number 23 hit on the UK chart where it enjoyed a 14-week run. It remains an acclaimed album in its genre and has had CD releases. Things ground to a halt for the Hopkin-Skellern-Lloyd Webber 'Oasis' when a proposed tour was pulled because of Hopkin's ill health.

The pattern of Mary's career following Oasis has been to carefully engage only with projects that appeal to her and this has provided her with a highly entertaining, diverse CV.

Among the many memorable appearances Mary has made was one in 1988 in the role of Rosie Probert in George Martin's production of Dylan Thomas's *Under Milk Wood*. The TV Arts programme, *The South Bank Show*, filmed a special edition of the show showing Martin rehearsing and recording this album. Hopkin's duet with Freddie Jones ('Captain Cat') on 'Love Duet' was a particular highlight of the TV Special which was screened on 13 October. On 12 December 1992, to benefit the Prince's Trust, the original cast reunited in the presence of Prince Charles, to revisit their performance as a tribute to Thomas.

Among her many appearances with other artists, on 12 December 1983 she sang with Ralph McTell at the London Palladium. On 17 June 1991 she again attended the Palladium to appear as a guest of the Chieftains, with whom, during May 1999, she appeared on the British dates of their world tour.

Her occasional association with Ralph McTell continued in 2002 when she sang his tune 'Wales' as the title track for the TV series *Billy Connolly's World Tour of England, Ireland and Wales*. She also contributed a Welsh-language song to the series called 'Bugeilio'r Gwenith Gwyn'.

Significantly, during 2005, daughter Jessica founded 'Mary Hopkin Music' which opened the door for Mary to release music from her personal archives. This project began that year with *Live at the Royal Festival Hall 1972*. From this source she has since released a treasure trove of great albums: *Valentine*, *Recollections* and *Now and Then*, featuring unreleased material recorded with Tony Visconti.

Mary has also worked alongside Jessica and Morgan on their own music.

Notably, on 31 August 2018, the three collaborated on a 50th anniversary commemoration of her Apple debut. Together they cut a new, stripped-down version of 'Those Were The Days' for which Mary should be given due credit for ensuring it carried the songwriting credit 'Gene Raskin/Boris Fomin'. (Something that the track listing in the accompanying booklet for the *Come and Get It: The Best of Apple Records* 2010 remastered CD release had not done.)

1 & 2 Mary Hopkin interviewed by Bob Harris OBE for the 2009 BBC Radio documentary *The Songs the Beatles Gave Away*, 2010, written and narrated by Bob Harris, produced by Bob Harris and Trudie Mysercough-Harris.
3 *Rolling Stone* music newspaper, 12 September 1985: Interview feature 'Where Are They Now: Mary Hopkin', by Christopher Connelly.
4 *The Lyrics*, Paul McCartney (Allen Lane, 2021) p.238.

Chapter 111:
GEORGE STEPS OUT

The friendship between Eric Clapton and the Beatles began in late December 1964. At that time Clapton was playing with the British R&B band, the Yardbirds, who were one of the support acts on the Beatles' 'Another Beatles' Christmas Show' at the Hammersmith Odeon. Eric became friends with all four Beatles, but it was with George that he formed the closest bond.

1968 and '69 were watershed years in the story of the Beatles. Tensions (as well as creativity) ran high as personal and musical differences arose within the group. The old unity of the Beatlemania days was fracturing. George wanted more of his songs on albums. Paul was not particularly impressed by George's material. John, George and Ringo did not like Paul songs like 'Maxwell's Silver Hammer' and 'Ob La Di, Ob La Da' and didn't really want them released as Beatles tracks. George, John and Ringo found Paul too pushy. Paul wanted the Beatles to be more pro-active and return to live performance. He believed this would help bring them all closer again. For George the scars of Beatlemania and touring ran deep and he did not want a return to this way of life. George, Paul and Ringo found the constant presence of Yoko Ono in the studio irritating to say the least. Apple was a constant headache. All four had quickly learned they weren't businessmen but they could not agree who they wanted to manage them in place of the now deceased Brian Epstein. John, George and Ringo wanted Allen Klein. Paul wanted Lee (his father-in-law) and John (his brother-in-law) Eastman ... and so on it went, day after day, irritations and disagreements mounted. Ringo left, Ringo came back, George left, George came back. John simmered. Paul pushed.

As ever it was the music that bonded them.

When George walked out on 10 January 1969 during the contentious early sessions for *Get Back*, John Lennon went so far as to suggest that maybe they could recruit Eric Clapton to take his place ...

By the time of George's falling out with John, Eric had already recorded with the Beatles in Abbey Road when, on 6 September 1968, at Harrison's request, he attended the sessions for 'While My Guitar Gently Weeps'. John was not actually there on that very day, but Ringo, Paul and George were and it was in their presence that Eric added his amazing guitar solo.

George and Eric's friendship flourished further when Harrison and Jackie Lomax decamped to LA for seven weeks in December '68 to do some recording. Harrison took the opportunity to get together with Clapton who was out there with his band, Cream. When they met socially George and Eric liked to play guitar and so it was only natural that out of that relationship an original tune might evolve ... and it did. (In the 20 December 1969 edition of *Melody Maker*, George was quoted as describing Eric as, "one of those people I get on so well with it's like looking at myself".)[1]

In the mid-Sixties, Cream were one of, if not the first, 'supergroup' to emerge from the UK beat and R&B scene. A powerhouse trio with a formidable live reputation prior to forming Cream, each member had earned a reputation as a virtuoso on their instrument: Ginger Baker on drums, Jack Bruce on bass, Eric Clapton on guitar. Previously Clapton had played in John Mayall's Bluesbreakers and, before that with the Yardbirds. Clapton had met and been impressed by Bruce when the bassist had joined the Bluesbreakers to record a 'live' album that was ultimately shelved. Ginger Baker had led the Graham Bond Organisation when Bruce played with them on bass, harmonica and piano. Famously, Baker and Bruce fought like cat and dog on and off stage. As Clapton would only join Cream, which was Baker's brainchild, if Bruce was in the band, Baker and Bruce agreed

Cream. One of the first powerhouse supergroups of the Sixties. A dynamic trio of instrumental virtuosos but with a toxic internal dynamic between drummer Ginger Baker and bassist Jack Bruce that proved to be their undoing. Left to right: Ginger Baker (drums), Jack Bruce (bass, vocals), Eric Clapton (lead guitar, vocals). (Pictorial Press Ltd / Alamy Stock Photo)

to put their differences aside and work for the common good. For a while it worked and they became hugely successful, particularly in the USA.

Cream were mainly considered as an 'albums act' (*Fresh Cream* (1966), *Disraeli Gears* (1967) and *Wheels of Fire* (1968)) but scored a couple of hit singles in the UK with 'I Feel Free' (1966) and 'Strange Brew' (1967). It was *Disraeli Gears*, with its distinctive Martin Sharp-designed psychedelic collage cover, that established them in the USA as a major headline act. It reached number 4 in the *Billboard* chart (number 5 in the UK). 1968's *Wheels of Fire* took Cream to the top in the USA, Canada and Australia and to number 3 in the UK. It was the world's first platinum-selling double album. Their live performances were renowned for their instrumental solos and sheer loudness. (Ginger Baker said playing with Cream permanently damaged his hearing.)

Despite their success, by mid-1968 tensions within the group proved too difficult to withstand and just ahead of the release of *Wheels of Fire* they announced they were going to split. As their swan song they went out on the road from 4 October to 4 November 1968 to play a final tour of the US, comprising 22 shows in addition to which they added a two-night stand at London's Royal Albert Hall on 25 and 26 November 1968.

The trio also marked its departure by releasing a fourth album (in early February 1969), the appropriately entitled *Goodbye* which comprised six tracks: three live recordings culled from a concert at the LA Forum plus three new individually composed tunes: Ginger Baker wrote 'What a Bringdown', Jack Bruce (in collaboration with Pete Brown) 'Doing That Scrapyard Thing' and Eric Clapton, in collaboration with George Harrison, came up with 'Badge'.

In their respective autobiographies, *I, Me, Mine* by George, and *Eric Clapton: The Autobiography*, both have described the origin of the composition of 'Badge': Eric had been tasked to write a song for the valedictory Cream album, *Goodbye*. He had come up with a fragment of a melody, at which point he turned to George to help him complete it, which George did. Harrison also wrote the words.

It was while they were working on the song that Eric and George, accidentally, arrived at its title. Harrison had handwritten the lyrics on a piece of paper and when he had reached the middle part of the tune he wrote the word 'bridge' to describe that section of a song. Sitting opposite each other in the studio, Clapton could see George's words, but they were upside down and he mis-read 'bridge' as 'badge'. On inquiring what George meant by 'badge' and being duly informed, Eric was amused by his error and decided to call the song 'Badge'.

George recalled that Ringo Starr also made a contribution to the lyrics. Having got to the line, 'I told you not to drive around in the dark', Ringo appeared on the scene. George described Ringo as being 'plastered', but nevertheless able to provide the next line about 'the swans that live in the park'. (This begs the question, 'If Doris Troy could get a co-writing credit on a Jackie Lomax song for merely changing just one word in its title, surely Ringo deserved one here for providing an entire line?')

As the song was originated by Eric Clapton expressly for Cream, clearly George never intended 'Badge' as a song for the Beatles. It is included here as a 'giveaway' to reflect George's emerging talent as a songwriter and his enjoyment in collaborating with other artists, which in turn encouraged him to direct his creative energies elsewhere beyond the Beatles.

CREAM
Eric Clapton, b. Eric Patrick Clapton, 30 March 1945 in Ripley, Surrey, England:
Lead guitar, lead vocals
Ginger Baker, b. Peter Edward Baker, 19 August 1939 in Lewisham, South London, England.
Died: 6 October 2019 (aged 80) in Canterbury, Kent, England:
Bass guitar, backing vocals
Jack Bruce: b. John Symon Asher Bruce, 14 May 1943 in Bishopbriggs, Lanarkshire, Scotland.
Died: 25 October 2014 (aged 71) in Sudbury, Suffolk, England

BADGE (2:45)
(Clapton-Harrison)
Dratleaf/Harrisongs
Polydor 2058-285

'Badge' was the only song by Cream to feature *five* musicians. On this track Eric, Jack and Ginger were augmented by Felix Pappalardi on piano, mellotron, and L'Angelo Misterioso on rhythm guitar. (L'Angelo was, of course, George Harrison, who for contractual reasons at the time could not be credited as himself. It is Italian and means 'The Mysterious Angel'.)

'Badge' was recorded at the Wally Heider Studios, Los Angeles, California, USA, under George's supervision in early November* 1968, although the very reliable 'The Beatles Bible' website assuredly dates the session as 21 November.[2]

(Jack and Ginger's songs were also recorded during Cream's Heider Studio sessions but George did not participate in those recordings. Final overdubs and mixing of the three tracks was done at International Broadcasting Company aka IBC Studios, 35 Portland Place, London in late November/early December. George was still in LA at that time and so could not have participated in those sessions either.)

(*Nailing the exact date for when 'Badge' was recorded is not easy. Initial confusion stemmed from a mis-reading of dates written on tapes because Americans write the date in a different sequence to Brits. Whereas Brits write 08/09/1968 for 8 September 1968 Americans would enter the month first followed by the day and so this would read 09/08/1968, i.e., 8 September 1968.)

On 'Badge' Eric ran his guitar through a Leslie speaker cabinet in order to achieve a distinctive swirling sound. Designed for organ the Leslie contained a rotary wheel and many rock guitarists experimented with it. According to Martin Mocha, rather than playing his Gibson Firebird, Clapton used his newly acquired secondhand Gibson ES-335 on this recording having purchased it two weeks earlier from Jerry Donahue at the Selmers store in London.[3]

B-SIDE: What A Bringdown
(Baker)
Both sides produced by: Felix Pappalardi by arrangement with Robert Stigwood.
Engineer: Damon Lyon-Shaw
Released in the USA: 17 March 1969
Released in the UK: 3 April 1969
Reissued in the UK: 21 September 1969 ahead of the UK release of a *Best of Cream* compilation.
In the UK 'Badge' spent ten weeks on the singles chart in 1969, peaking at number 18 on 13 May.
It received a re-release in 1969 on 21 September to promote the imminent release of a 'best of' Cream album compilation in October, but on this occasion it did not make the charts.
It was re-released as a single for the third time in the UK on 13 October 1972 as part of Polydor's 2058 re-release series (258) and retained 'What a Bringdown' as its B-side. It spent four weeks on the chart, peaking at number 42 on 28 October.
On release in the USA the single fared less well, spending only five weeks on *Billboard*'s Hot 100, peaking at a lowly number 60 on 3 May 1969 and stalling on *Cashbox*'s Top Singles chart at number 65.
Worldwide 'Badge' enjoyed chart action, achieving the following chart positions:
Australia: 43
Austria: 18
Canada RPM: 49
Germany: 29
Netherlands: 14
Prior to its release as a single 'Badge' appeared as cut 2, side 2 on Cream's farewell album *Goodbye*, released in the USA on ATCO SD 7001 on 5 February 1969 and in the UK on Polydor 583-053 on 28 February 1969. On the album the song was only credited to Eric Clapton although this had been corrected by the time the song was released as a single.
Cream's back-to-back sets at London's Royal Albert Hall on 25 and 26 November 1968 were their official 'farewell' performances. On the 25th Eric played his Gibson Firebird and on the 26th his Gibson ES-335.

Support on both nights came from prog rockers Yes and Taste, the latter being a three-piece from Ireland featuring Rory Gallagher on lead guitar.

The London performances were filmed by Tony Palmer and screened on BBC TV on 5 January 1969. When it was first screened the editing of the film was criticised for it showed Eric playing both guitars on the same songs and Ginger Baker wearing different clothes while playing his drum solo.

'Badge' has also been included on Cream compilation albums, most notably:

Best of Cream, the release of this record in the USA on ATCO SD 33-291 on 7 July 1969, and in the UK on Polydor 583-060 on 24 October 1969 most probably explains the re-release of the single in that year on 21 September.

Heavy Cream, a double album, (USA Polydor PD 3502 released 9 October 1972, UK RSO 2659-022 released 27 April 1973)

The Very Best of Cream, (UK Polydor 523 752-2) 1995

Addendum: *CREAM Reunions*

Despite splitting from Cream, Baker and Clapton were not long in getting back together again when they formed another supergroup called Blind Faith. However, it would not be until 1993 that the three again shared a stage together as Cream to perform a three-song set to mark their induction into the Rock 'n' Roll Hall of Fame.

Twelve years later memories had possibly mellowed (unlikely but true apparently) and they reunited for what was the last time when they played a series of concerts at the Royal Albert Hall in London on May 2, 3, 5 and 6, 2005 (for which the tickets for all four shows sold out within an hour) and at Madison Square Garden 24-26 New York City. Baker would later claim he'd been talked into doing the shows by Clapton, and Clapton would agree he had been the one to initiate the idea in the belief that the passage of time would have laid the old animosities to rest. However, by the time they played the shows in the USA it was apparent Clapton had misread the situation.

The accompanying double CD and double DVD releases of the 2005 shows included a performance of 'Badge'. The album peaked at number 59 on the Billboard 200 album chart on 22 October 2005 and the DVD made it to number 1 in the American Top Music Video listings.

Apparently, according to Jack Bruce, a Cream reunion/tour was in the pipeline for 2013/14. Certainly not long before his death in October 2014, Bruce had gone public in Rolling Stone to say it had all been agreed but claimed Ginger Baker said or did something to upset Eric Clapton, causing the idea to be dropped.[4]

Jack's claim was totally at odds with an interview with Eric Clapton that appeared not long after in the UK's Uncut music magazine's June 2014 edition, in which the guitarist said there had been no dialogue between him and the other two since the reunion concerts of 2005. He also told the magazine that he found touring 'unbearable' and that after the concerts of 2005 he knew they (Cream) had gone as far as they could "without someone getting killed", adding that, in the interim, nothing had occurred to change his perspective.[5] Sadly, Bruce died in October 2014 and Baker in October 2019.

---

1 *MelodyMaker* 20 December 1969 edition.
2 www.beatlesbible.com
3 www.songfacts.com
4 *Rolling Stone*, Jack Bruce interview with Kory Grow, 15 April 2014.
5 *Uncut* music magazine, Eric Clapton interview, June 2014 edition.

Chapter 112:
THE CONTINUING ADVENTURES OF GEORGE AND ERIC, 1969

1969
Was the year when ... The Woodstock Music and Art Fair was held at Yasgur's Farm near Bethel, New York between 15 and 18 August at which an estimated 500,000 people heard 32 acts perform ... the film Easy Rider *was premiered ... astronaut Neil Armstrong became the first man to walk on the moon ... Charles Manson and his followers embarked on a brutal murdering spree in Los Angeles, California ... John Lennon returned his MBE 'as a protest against Britain's involvement in the Nigeria-Biafra thing', the UK's 'support of America in Vietnam' and 'against 'Cold Turkey' slipping down the charts' ... Monty Python's Flying Circus debuted on BBC TV ... the Altamont Free Concert was held in northern California ...*

George and Eric famously remained close friends for the rest of George's life. In the tumultuous days surrounding the break-downs and eventual break-up of relations within the Beatles, his relationship with Eric no doubt allowed Harrison to see a life beyond the fraternity of the Beatles. Like George, Eric did not feel entirely comfortable in the spotlight of superstardom, for them it was the enjoyment that playing brought that fired their ambitions and imaginations. George was, in some ways, the emergent talent within the Beatles as they disintegrated. He was certainly seeking greater individual recognition and expression in a group where Lennon and McCartney had always taken poll position. Mixing with musicians of the calibre of Clapton and Ravi Shankar allowed George to experience the respect with which he was held beyond the fraternity of the Beatles.

In the immediate demise of Cream, Eric Clapton and Ginger Baker formed a new 'supergroup' together with Steve Winwood, formerly of Traffic, and Ric Grech, formerly of Family. Calling themselves Blind Faith, much was expected of them. The venture was to become a case of too much expectation too soon. Indeed, after recording their debut album and touring in Sweden and the USA, they split up. On stage the band's lack of original material meant that they had to supplement their sets with Cream and Traffic numbers. This pleased the audiences who in many cases preferred these old favourites to the group's new material. For Clapton, however, it was unfulfilling and ran contrary to what he felt Blind Faith was meant to be. Significantly, during the tour of the USA, Clapton started to show more interest in the support group, Delaney and Bonnie with whom he would appear on stage, preferring to play a supporting role with them.

The final gig of the Blind Faith tour was in Hawaii on 24 August 1969, after which the band folded.

For Clapton, being thrust into the spotlight with Blind Faith clearly came too soon after the demise of Cream and as a consequence he made sure his next two projects were away from the spotlight by performing as a sideman: first with the Plastic Ono Band, with whom he appeared on stage at the Toronto Rock and Roll Festival, and then with the Delaney and Bonnie Band.

Plastic Ono Band was John and Yoko's group, formed at the time Lennon was becoming more and more disenchanted with the Beatles. By the time of the Toronto festival in September 1969, John had privately decided he wanted what he called 'a divorce' from the Beatles but did not divulge his decision to the other Beatles until he met with them *after* Toronto on 20 September. The occasion was primarily to sign the new, much-improved contract between the Beatles and EMI/Capitol as negotiated on their behalf by Allen Klein.

Even after signing John agreed with Klein and his fellow Fabs that he would not announce his decision to leave the group publicly and so it remained a 'secret'.

Lennon had initially been invited to attend the festival in Toronto as a principal guest (ticket sales weren't good) but surprised the organiser John Brower (of local company Brower Walker) by saying he would not only attend but bring a band (the Plastic Ono Band) with him and perform (once this was made public the tickets sold out).

A recording exists of the moment the call came through to John and Yoko at Apple, after which they began to put a band together (initially wondering if George might be able to put it together for them). The role John believed they were being offered at the Festival is described by him in this quote from *The Beatles Anthology*: "We got a call on a Friday night ... they were inviting us as king and queen to preside over it, not play." He continues by saying, "I didn't hear that bit. I said, 'Just give me time to get a band together' and we went the next morning."

John *did* approach George Harrison to join him for the gig (but not to form a band for him). George declined the invitation (because he believed it would be an *avant-garde* band which he didn't wish to join). In his place John recruited Eric Clapton with whom he'd already played in the Dirty Mac (December 1968), the band he'd put together to perform on the still-to-be-televised Rolling Stones' *Rock and Roll Circus* TV special. After Yoko and Clapton, for his Toronto band, on bass John brought in his old friend from Hamburg, Klaus Voormann and to complete the line up he invited teenage drum sensation Alan White. So quickly had Lennon assembled this version of the Plastic Ono Band the only rehearsal they managed before treading the boards in Toronto was on the plane immediately ahead of the gig. The set they played on the evening of Saturday 13 September 1969 comprised three of John's favourite rock 'n' roll standards, three of his own compositions (including a brand new tune he'd written called 'Cold Turkey') while Yoko rounded off the group's performance with a couple of her numbers, 'Don't Worry Kyoto (Mummy's Only Looking for Her Hand in the Snow)' and the protracted wail-along 'John, John (Let's Hope For Peace)'. John told the audience before singing 'Give Peace a Chance' that 'peace' was the reason why he and the band had come to play the festival, hence the name given to the resulting 'live' album.

The band's Toronto performance was not only recorded but was also filmed by D.A. Pennebaker who in 1965 had filmed the much acclaimed and admired Bob Dylan documentary *Don't Look Back* (released in 1967).

Live Peace in Toronto became the debut Plastic Ono Band album and enjoyed a simultaneous 12 December 1969 Apple Records release in the UK and USA (Apple CORE 2001 and Apple 1815 respectively). It reached number 10 in America but failed to chart in Britain.

The Pennebaker film of the festival (*Sweet Toronto*) became beset with contractual problems, culminating in a delayed 1971 release that did *not* include the Plastic Ono Band performance. The John and Yoko sequence was not released commercially until 1989 when it was broadcast on TV and made available on VHS video and laserdisc.

Back in London in late September and early October, John quickly recorded, produced and mixed studio versions of 'Cold Turkey' and 'Don't Worry Kyoko' for release as the A- and B-sides of the Plastic Ono Band's second* single (Apple 1001, on 17 October in the UK and as Apple 1813 in the USA on 24 October). It was a number 14 hit in the UK and peaked at number 30 in the USA. The personnel for the studio recording remained the same as for the Toronto gig, except for Alan White who was replaced by Ringo Starr on drums. White would return to the drum seat for Plastic Ono's third single, 'Instant Karma' and also for the sessions for the *Imagine* album, including playing drums on the title track.

(*The Plastic Ono's debut Apple single in both the UK and the USA released in July 1969 had been 'Give Peace a Chance'. It reached number 2 in Britain and number 14 in America.)

After performing with John and Yoko in the Plastic Ono Band in Toronto, Eric took another sideman's job, this time in the Delaney and Bonnie Band with whom he'd been so

Delaney & Bonnie & Friends. Backstage photograph taken at Birmingham Town Hall on Thursday 4 December, 1969. Left to right: Eric Clapton, Bonnie Bramlett, Delaney Bramlett, George Harrison. George joined the ensemble for his first tour since playing with the Beatles in 1966. (Trinity Mirror / Mirrorpix / Alamy Stock Photo)

taken when they had supported Cream in the USA. During the first half of December 1969 he accompanied them on their 'Delaney and Bonnie and Friends UK tour' and was joined on stage by his good friend George Harrison. (Their itinerary included a gig in Liverpool.) George had himself encountered the Delaney and Bonnie band in Spring 1968 when he had heard them play at a private party. So impressed was he, he took tapes of the group back to the UK with the intention of signing them to Apple Records. The record that was set for release was called *The Original Delaney and Bonnie – Accept No Substitute*. It was assigned the catalogue number SAPCOR 7 and a release date of 23 May 1969, but in the end it was withdrawn and released on the Elektra label in the USA.

After Delaney and Bonnie's UK dates ended, George, Eric and Billy Preston also performed with the group on all three nights of their Copenhagen, Denmark residency at the Falconer Theatre on 10, 11, 12 December, the latter show of which was filmed. George's association with Eric and the Delaney and Bonnie Bramlett band is further evidence of his stepping out and giving of his time and talent to the benefit of other artists.

Three days after this both Eric and George performed as part of John and Yoko's expanded Plastic Ono Band at a benefit concert held for the charity Unicef at the Lyceum Ballroom on 15 December 1969. Suitably the concert was entitled 'Peace for Christmas'. Other members of that extended version of the Plastic Onos on that memorable occasion were Tony Ashton, Eric Barrett, Neil Boland, Delaney and Bonnie Bramlett, Jim Gordon, Bobby Keys, Keith Moon, Billy Preston, Klaus Voormann and Alan White.

By spending time in each other's company George and Eric clearly found much that helped them assuage the pressures and problems of being 'superstars' forever in the limelight. In addition, their relationship no doubt provided a relief and release from the tempestuous relationships within their own bands. Famously George wrote, 'Here Comes the Sun' at Eric's house when he was 'sagging off' a recording session with the Beatles.

And, of course, later, Eric fell for Pattie and she for him ... but that *is* another story.

N.B. *Delaney and Bonnie's European and UK tour provided them with their biggest selling album which they entitled On Tour with Eric Clapton which they released in March 1970. It had been recorded on 7 December 1969 over the two sets the group performed at the Fairfields Hall, Croydon which featured George Harrison. The track 'I Don't Want to Discuss It' is a recording from the first show in Bristol. (The On Tour album was re-issued in 2010 as a four-disc box set on the Rhino label.)*

Addendum: *Billy Preston and 'My Sweet Lord'*

During his sojourn in Copenhagen with Delaney and Bonnie, George began writing the song that became known as 'My Sweet Lord'. George's new tune was initially inspired by the Edwin Hawkins Singers' 'Oh Happy Day'. On his return to London in January 1970, where he was co-producing a second album for Billy Preston at Olympic Studios – and with input from Preston himself – George completed his new tune. Intended as a 'multi-faith devotional song' Preston's background in gospel music was the perfect foil for assisting George with this. And so it came to pass that George then gifted it to Preston for inclusion on his new album, Encouraging Words, *and together they recorded it with the Edwin Hawkins Singers who conveniently happened to be in town at the time. Recorded in January, in the UK Preston's album was not released until 11 September 1970 (catalogue number Apple SAPCOR 14) and in the USA until 9 November (Apple ST 3370). By then the Beatles had officially broken up. Preston's version of 'My Sweet Lord' preceded his UK album release when, as Apple 29, on 4 September it was released as the album's lead-off single. (In the USA George Harrison's own version was not released as a single until 23 November 1970 and it was 15 January 1971 before it was issued in the UK.)*

Chapter 113:
PAUL AND LINDA ENJOY A WINTER BREAK

As the mayhem at Apple raged, and just a week after George Harrison's 4 December 1968 memo to all at Apple that his peace-keeping pals from Hell (out of California) were about to descend upon the office, Paul literally whisked Linda and her daughter Heather off to Praia da Luz in the Algarve, Portugal, for a winter break. This sudden gesture came in response to a postcard Paul had received from Hunter Davies, the Beatles' official biographer who was already there on holiday with his family, in which Davies invited Paul to join him. So spontaneous was Paul's decision there was no time to take a regular flight and so he hired a private jet … and late in the evening on 11 December the three last-minute holidaymakers knocked on Hunter's door along with a taxi driver who needed money for his fare because in Paul's haste to make the trip he had no Portuguese escudos on him.

Of course the arrival of a private jet carrying a Beatle on board did not escape the notice of the local press and the next day Paul gave an interview on the beach in return for a promise to thereafter be left to holiday in peace.

The locality in which Paul, Linda and Heather were holidaying is renowned for its golf and is home to some excellent courses, none more so than the Penina Hotel and Golf Resort. Set in 360 acres it is renowned for being 'where golf started in this southern corner of the Iberian Peninsula' and especially for its 18-hole Sir Henry Cotton Championship Course designed by the said Sir Henry himself, one of Britain's most successful players.

The luxurious hotel became the setting for Paul's most spontaneous gift of a song to a fellow artist.

Some 48 years after the event Paul explained the circumstances of how he came to write and give away this rarest of McCartney tunes to Bob Harris and the author with these words: "It was late one night, I was on holiday in Portugal and ended up in a bar in a quite well-known golf club … And for some reason, I was not in full possession of my senses … I think I was drunk. I got on the drum kit, I wanted to get on that drum kit! So I got up there and I grabbed the mic near me and started making up this song about the name of the golf club, La Penina or something … and I'm making up this terrible song but someone must have recorded it and passed it over to Carlos (Mendes). I got a phone call, 'You know that night?' 'Well I don't really remember it but yeah' … They said, 'We've got the tape of that, can we let Carlos have it?' And I said, 'Oh yeah, definitely – as long as you don't put my name on it.' But it got found out I had done it."[1]

Paul's recollection tells only half the story for it was to the hotel band who were playing in the bar when he and Linda walked in late at night (around two in the morning) to whom he originally offered the song, not Carlos Mendes (who was not present). The band was a Portuguese quartet called 'Jotta Herre', and all of the boys in the band were students from Porto. Their leader (and main songwriter) was Annibal Cunha.

Whatever a Beatle did in those days could never be kept secret for long and the news that while on holiday Paul had 'given' his hotel's resident band a song was first disclosed not long after he had returned from Portugal. The *Get Back* rehearsals had already begun when, in the 9 January 1969 edition of the *Daily Express*, renowned columnist William Hickey published a story entitled, 'Beatle Paul Writes a £20,000 Holiday Tip'. Hickey's piece said McCartney had enjoyed listening to the resident band playing and had given them the tune by way of 'a tip'. Hickey described Paul's tune as no more than 'a few bars' and quoted Derek Taylor as saying that what Paul had actually given the group was 'not a whole song' but 'more a riff'. Hickey also noted that Paul had played the drums in the hotel

Jotto Herre, the house band at the Penina Hotel in the resort of Praia da Luz in the Algarve, Portugal in 1968. Paul was on holiday at the hotel and sat in with the band on the evening of 18 and early morning of 19 December 1968.

bar. Furthermore, the journalist was well informed enough to know the name of the bandleader as 'Anibal Cuna' (slightly different spelling), although he did not quote the actual name of the 'resident band'.[2]

Several months (six ... seven) later after encountering Paul in the bar, Jotta Herre were back at the Penina Hotel for the launch of their own recording of the song that Paul had especially gifted them. The story had grabbed the attention of the world's press and so along with Portuguese radio and TV, journalists from Amsterdam, Lisbon, London, Madrid and Paris were also on hand to get the background story ...

A newspaper clip dated August 1969 entitled 'Paul McCartney's Penina, International Fame for Portuguese Group with First Disc?' penned by one of those journalists present for the launch provided more details of what happened that night Paul played drums with Jotta Herre.[3]

(Unfortunately neither the newspaper's name or the writer's byline are to be seen on the clipping and so I am unable to credit them.)

Apparently, late on the night of Wednesday 18 December/early hours of the morning of Thursday 19, a very tired Linda and an inebriated Paul wandered into the luxurious bar of the Penina Hotel which overlooks a fabulous swimming pool. While Linda fell asleep on a couch, Paul joined Jotta Herre on stage. Bandleader Cunha says the band were just about to leave when Paul and Linda arrived and although she wanted to go to bed Paul was in the mood to play. Jotta Herre could not believe their luck for here they were, four unknown Portuguese musicians on stage with a Beatle who was asking *them* to play music with him. Any ideas of going home were quickly banished from their minds. Cunha says together they 'improvised' on some Beatles tunes but Paul was more interested in playing Portuguese music, which, with them guiding the way, he soon picked up.

And so as the wee small hours ticked away, Paul and his fellow bandmates played on. It was at about six in the morning, around sunrise, with Linda still soundly asleep on the couch, that things finally began to draw to a close and Paul gifted Jotta Herre the song. Cunha suggests he wrote it while seated at the piano rather than at the drums. The lyric reflected exactly what was happening, 'Time has come, Time has gone, Forgive my friends, Take my arm girl, Let's go home.'

For Jotta Herre this must have been the most incredible evening of playing music they had ever experienced. To cap it all Paul had made it even more special by spontaneously gifting them an original composition.

They should be so lucky ...

Unfortunately for Jotta Herre, Paul's generosity came to the attention of his British lawyers who were employed to protect the copyright of John and Paul's songs. In particular, it alerted solicitor Michael Eaton at Stephenson Harwood and Tatham who acted for them and Northern Songs. Although Paul failed to inform Eaton that he had written and given away a song while on vacation, Eaton was quick to find out and equally quick to inform Jotta Herre that Paul couldn't just give a song away like that. There were ramifications ... not least that, as William Hickey had pointed out in his piece for the *Daily Express*, the merest scrap of a tune by Paul would fetch at least £20,000, and in most cases a whole lot more ... Anything Paul wrote, even a fragment, the copyright was owned by

Northern Songs and its shareholders who would not countenance tunes being given away for nothing as they expected to earn dividends from their investments.[4]

In the end, after considerable negotiations, Jotta Herre were able to release 'Penina'. Finding a specific release date for when this was has not proved easy. The date of the unidentified newspaper article telling their story is not specific, just 'August 1969', and as it would obviously have had to be written in advance of that publication date this would seem to indicate that its Portuguese/European release, could/would have been earlier, maybe in July, maybe earlier. It was issued in the major record-buying countries of Europe and the existence of a copy of a Chilean release suggests it enjoyed a release well beyond Europe. Hopes were clearly high within Jotta Herre themselves, but they were never realised for sadly their version of 'Penina' was not a hit.

The newspaper article from August 1969 also claimed that Paul McCartney sent Jotta Herre a letter wishing them "all the best of British luck".

However, as Paul's interview with Bob Harris and the author indicates, Jotta Herre weren't the only Portuguese act to release a version of 'Penina'. So did singer Carlos Mendes.

By the time of Paul's visit to the Algarve, Mendes was already a well-known singer in his home country, having represented Portugal earlier in the year in the Eurovision Song Contest where, with a song entitled 'Verão', he came 11th out of the 17 entrants. Prior to this Mendes had been the bass player and vocalist in the country's top group the Sheiks. Active between 1963 and 1967, the Sheiks were from Lisbon and known as Portugal's 'answer to the Beatles'.

The Sheiks had recorded for Parlophone in Portugal and would certainly have been in a good position within the Portuguese recording industry to know Paul had given a song to Jotta Herre. He most probably requested permission to record it himself and already being on Parlophone was well placed to be allowed to do so. It is from these connections no doubt that Paul became aware that Mendes cut a version of his song. No accurate records of the release dates for singles seem to have been kept and while some commentators say Mendes released his version in March 1969 ahead of Jotta Herre, July seems to be the more favoured date. Whatever the story, like Jotta Herre, he failed to earn a hit with the song.

Mendes went on to enjoy a successful career as a singer, composer and television actor in Portugal. In 1972, after winning the Portuguese Song Festival with 'A Festa da Vida' ('The Party of Life'), he represented Portugal in the Eurovision Song Contest for a second time. This time he came 7th. After a 19-year break from recording, in April 2018 Carlos released a career retrospective entitled *A Festa da Vida* for which he recorded new versions of his most popular and successful tunes, including 'Penina'.

The Beatles never recorded a version of the song, but not long after he had returned from Portugal, during the very early *Get Back* rehearsals at Twickenham, Paul and the other Beatles did play a spontaneous, rough version of the song. Bootleg tapes of those rehearsals are 'out there'. These include one on YouTube dating from 9 January 1969 in which Paul can be heard (but not seen) reacting to Hickey's article as he slips into a slow, bluesy rendition of 'Penina'. It is proof that however slight he considers a piece to be that he composes, Paul McCartney will nevertheless retain a precise memory of how it goes and in this instance a good recall of the words. On the clip he sings: 'Been to Albufeira, Had a few drinks there, Now I'm on my way home, I really don't care, La Penina … Hotel'. The other Beatles provide accompaniment but in less than a minute it's all over and they are ready to move on.

Many years later in a 1994 interview for his *Club Sandwich* fan magazine, McCartney said he doubted if he ever would record a version himself.

For Paul and Linda, most probably the happiest memory of their winter break in Portugal, by far eclipsing the saga of 'Penina', was that it was while there he proposed to her and Linda also realised she was pregnant with their first child, Mary.

JOTTA HERRE
Anibal Cunha
Rui Pereira
Carlos Pinto
Giuseppe Flaminio
PENINA (3:00)
(Paul McCartney)
B.I.E.M.
Philips 369 002 PF
B-SIDE: North
(C. Pinto/R. Pereira)
Released in at least Portugal, Germany, Spain, Italy, France, Holland ... and Chile ... circa June/July 1969.

As already mentioned an actual release date has been difficult to pin down. My estimate based on the newspaper article I traced would suggest a release in Portugal sometime in late June/early July 1969, ahead of Carlos Mendes's version. No doubt it would have been released simultaneously in Spain, Italy and the Netherlands, etc. In all territories it appears to have been issued in a picture sleeve showing a black and white photo of Jotta Herre (superimposed over a photo of the hotel) along with the words 'Paul McCartney's Penina'.

CARLOS MENDES
PENINA (2:34)
(Paul McCartney)
PM 144
BIEM
Parlophone PM 144 BIEM
B-SIDE: Wings of Revenge
(Joao M. Pereira - Nuno da N. Fernandes)
Released: 18 July 1969

Released in Portugal in a picture sleeve depicting an uncredited colour painting of a man leaning on a white wall looking down on a small harbour scene depicting a flotilla of small boats, and single sail yachts in the foreground. On the wall in black cursive writing are the words 'Carlos Mendes, Penina, Paul McCartney'. (Carlos's version was also released elsewhere in Europe.)
It also failed to chart.

---

1 Sir Paul McCartney in conversation with Bob Harris OBE and Colin Hall for the 2009 BBC Radio 2 music documentary *The Songs the Beatles Gave Away*, written and narrated by Bob Harris, produced by Bob Harris and Trudie Myerscough-Harris for WBBC.
2 'Beatle Paul Writes A £20,000 Holiday Tip', written by William Hickey for the 9 January 1969 edition of the *Daily Express* newspaper.
3 'Paul McCartney's Penina, International Fame For Portuguese Group With First Disc?' newspaper article from August 1969, source and writer unknown.
4 *Northern Songs*, Brian Southall with Rupert Perry (Omnibus Press, 2006) p.31–32.

Chapter 114:
MORTIMER AND THE ILL-FATED STORY OF APPLE 16

1969 had certainly been a fractious but creative year for the Beatles.

Beginning with the acrimonious *Get Back* rehearsals at Twickenham on 2 January, these switched to the Apple Studios at Savile Row, London, on Wednesday 22 January where the mood improved. By then the idea of either a film or TV show being made of a one-off Beatles concert had been ditched and the idea was that the group would be filmed as they recorded a new album. The resulting sessions at Apple were well documented. Largely produced by Glyn Johns rather than George Martin, whose role in the project remains somewhat vague, (he says he "hated" the *Get Back* album) the sessions were protracted, rambling, unfocused affairs. Along the way on Wednesday 22 January, after George had spotted him at Apple, they were joined by Billy Preston which produced greater accord and focus during which the five musicians recorded 'Get Back' and 'Don't Let Me Down'. Two days later the group, with Billy Preston on keyboards, filmed the (now legendary) Apple Rooftop Concert. Mixing the tracks for *Get Back* lingered on into February, although filming had concluded on Friday 31 January. It was in early March that Lennon and McCartney met with Glyn Johns to finally hand over the many reels of tape from the drawn-out sessions and invited him to compile them into an album …

Johns came up with two versions neither of which passed muster, which in turn led to Phil Spector being engaged to try his hand at producing something acceptable, which he did. The Spector-enhanced version emerged in May 1970 as a boxed record (replete with an accompanying glossy book) entitled *Let It Be (Original Soundtrack Album)*. The back cover credited Phil Spector for reproducing for the disc "the warmth and the freshness" of a Beatles live performance and extends thanks to George Martin, Glyn Johns, Billy Preston, Mal Davies, Peter Bown, Richard Hewson and Brian Rogers.

Elsewhere, and as already mentioned at other times, in 1969 Ringo filmed *The Magic Christian* with Peter Sellers (3 February to 2 May), Paul recorded Mary Hopkin singing 'Goodbye' on 1 March and married Linda on Wednesday 12 March, as George and Pattie were simultaneously being busted for possession of illegal substances. On Thursday 20 March, John and Yoko got married in Gibraltar, near Spain, before honeymooning in Paris and then moving to Amsterdam where, ensconced in the Hilton Hotel, they held the first of their famous bed-ins devoted entirely to promoting their message of peace.

On Friday 11 April, the Beatles' first single in eight months, 'Get Back', notably accredited to 'The Beatles with Billy Preston', was released. Another number 1 hit for the group, it clocked up 13 weeks on the UK chart.

On Monday 14 April, John and Paul recorded a new John song at Abbey Road called 'The Ballad of John and Yoko'. George Martin produced the session. Because of his filming commitments Ringo was not available and so Paul played drums on the record. George was, apparently, out of the country and also unable to attend. Backed by George's 'Old Brown Shoe' the song was released as the next Beatles single on Friday 30 May even though 'Get Back' was still at number 1. 'The Ballad of John and Yoko' was the Beatles' final UK number 1. (Neither future singles 'Something' nor 'Let It Be' reached number 1, peaking respectively at numbers 4 and 2.)

Just as it seemed the Beatles would never again be united as a recording entity inside Abbey Road, the seemingly impossible happened. On Tuesday 1 July Paul entered Abbey Road to dub a vocal onto a new song of his, entitled 'You Never Give Me Your Money'. It was a track on which he, John, George and Ringo had begun work on Tuesday 6 May at

Olympic Studios. George, Ringo and John were not present for the 1 July session (John was in hospital in Scotland having crashed the car he was driving in which Yoko, her daughter Kyoto and John's son Julian were passengers) but it was a significant return to Abbey Road, for it marked a commitment by the Beatles to return to record together in the 'old way'. This time out there would be none of the shambolic approach they'd fallen into for *Get Back*; this time they were all committed to adopting a more structured, organised approach with George Martin as producer. They already had a bevy of songs they had recorded post *Get Back* which included 'Something', 'I Want You', 'Oh! Darling', 'Octopus's Garden' and 'On Our Way Home'…

Most of July and August 1969 saw extensive Beatles studio action at Abbey Road: the group block-booked the 2:30-10:00pm slot in studio 2 every weekday from 1 July until 29 August. (During July Geoff Emerick returned to the Beatles' side as their chief balance engineer.)

The resulting album, the last the Beatles recorded, became known as *Abbey Road*.

Early in his relationship with Linda one of their favourite things to do to escape the pressures of his recording schedules and being a business man for Apple Corps was to jump in Paul's car (with Martha the sheepdog on the backseat) and head out of London and go wherever the road took them. It was both liberating and great fun. During one such road trip Paul was inspired to write 'On Our Way Home' about his adventures with Linda and which he later re-titled as 'Two of Us'. It was a song Paul introduced to the Beatles on the first day they began work at Twickenham Film Studios and which was quickly embraced by his fellow Beatles.

Always intended as a tune for the Beatles to record, this Everly-style close harmony song was a perfect fit for John and him but which he also donated to a New York-based harmony rock trio called 'Mortimer' who had recently signed to Apple … Still called 'On Our Way Home' when he did so it is not a 'giveaway' as such but is a good story and a great example of how the Beatles would reach out to young artists looking to break into the record industry.

MORTIMER

By early 1968 Mortimer were a highly regarded punchy, acoustic soft-rock/harmony trio playing venues in New York.

Mortimer had evolved from a 'garage rock' style four-piece group called the Teddy Boys: Tom Smith and Bob Ronga both on vocals and guitar, Anthony Van Benschoten on bass and vocals, Guy Masson on drums.

They had issued several singles under that name on both MGM ('Jezebel' b/w 'It's You' in May 1966) and Cameo-Parkway (in October 1966 their own version of Ray Davies' 'Where Have All the Good Times Gone' backed by their own 'It's You'). These were followed in December 1966 by their take on Bo Diddley's 'Mona' backed by their own 'Good Morning Blues'. (There had been an earlier Teddy Boys single in 1964 entitled 'Don't Mess with Me', written by Van Benschoten and Robert Ronga.)

By the time they had cut enough tunes to release a debut Teddy Boys album, the one and only Allen Klein had bought a controlling share of Cameo-Parkway and proceeded to do what Allen Klein did: manage the books and make some money. His handiwork was garnering him a name with which to be reckoned within the music industry but this was often at the cost of emerging talent. And so it was at Cameo-Parkway, to help cut the costs Klein promptly axed the intended Teddy Boys' long player.

Down but certainly not out, by February 1967 the Teddy Boys morphed into Pinnochio and the Pirates and released a single on the Mercury label. Both sides were heavy guitar instrumentals, the proto-psychedelic A-side 'Fusion' and the twangy B-side 'Cowboys and Indians'. Most significantly both tunes were group compositions credited to 'Robert Ronga, Smith, Van, Masson'. From this incarnation of the original Teddy Boys the acoustic trio Mortimer emerged: Anthony Van Benschoten (guitar), Tom Smith (guitar) and Guy Masson (percussion).

The Teddy Boys/Mortimer had spent nearly four and a half years living in New York's bohemian Chelsea Hotel perfecting their act and writing songs during the day, playing clubs such as Max's Kansas City at night. Tony Van Berschoten recalls that fellow hotel residents included legendary personalities as Viva, Edie Sedgwick and Nico.

Eventually the trio found themselves managed by one Daniel 'Danny' Secunda, brother of successful UK pop manager Tony Secunda (Moody Blues, Motörhead, Steeleye Span, Marianne Faithfull – briefly, Chrissie Hynde, etc) and became the house band at 'Arthur' Sybil Burton's hip Manhattan nightclub. Hopes for the group were so high they were installed in a flat where they were encouraged to write new material which they did as they also developed Mortimer's acoustic and melodic style. A record deal was secured with Philips and in May 1968 the label released Mortimer's eponymous debut album from which a couple of singles were lifted. These included the album's catchy opening track 'Dedicated Music Man' which proved very popular with New York's pop music radio stations. Despite all this *and* an appearance on *American Bandstand* the album and single did not chart.

Given Mortimer's healthy album sales, radio play and live popularity during the summer of 1968, Secunda directed the trio to England to test the waters there where he felt they could well make a commercial breakthrough. (In doing so Mortimer were following a trail already blazed with some success by the likes of P.J. Proby, the Walker Brothers and Jimi Hendrix.) Sleeping on the floor of Secunda's flat the trio secured some dates at the Marquee and other London clubs in Soho and Mayfair, often playing several gigs a night.

Time passed and although Mortimer were getting bookings little had happened to further progress the trio's recording career. As a result it was decided they should return to the USA.

Fortuitously, just before they did so, they heard someone on the radio say that Apple Records were looking for songs for Mary Hopkin. Mortimer had plenty of songs that they thought could be suitable for her and so hotfoot they beat a path to number 3 Savile Row to volunteer their goods.

On arrival the lady at the front desk explained that what Apple actually wanted were tapes of songs not the writers in person. Seizing the moment the group explained that they did not have any tapes and as they were due to return to the USA the very next day they had no time to record any. Tony Van Benschoten then went one further and asked if they could simply perform them for someone at the offices.

Mortimer were in luck for the person in Apple Publishing that the lady in reception contacted was Mike O'Connor. She could not have spoken to anyone better: amazingly O'Connor had not only heard of Mortimer but actually had a copy of their Philips' album which had been given to him by none other than John Lennon.

John had acquired Mortimer's album from Nat Weiss, the Beatles' attorney in New York. Nat Weiss had acquired his copy from Guy Masson himself earlier in the summer of 1968. Masson had put the album in Weiss's hands when he'd learned that John and Paul were staying in New York in Weiss's apartment just a few blocks down from where Masson himself was living. Encouraged by a friend and armed with a copy of the Mortimer album the two of them visited Weiss's apartment block where they somehow managed to gain entrance to the building. Once inside they knocked on the apartment door which was answered by Weiss himself and into whose hands they deposited the album. Leaving them at the door Weiss disappeared back inside his apartment where they could hear that a party was in full flow. Moments later Weiss returned to inform Masson and his friend that he had put the album directly into John Lennon's hands and that the Beatle had promised to listen to it. (You can't make this stuff up!)

Now, waiting with his fellow bandmates in the foyer at Apple, Masson knew John Lennon

On Our Way Home was released on the RPM label (RETRO987) and is a remastered version of the original album replete with two extra tracks recorded by the group at the same time. It comes replete with an illustrated booklet which includes more of Peter Asher's photographs of the trio. Recommended.

had done exactly as he had promised. He had not forgotten their album and furthermore had ensured it reached Apple Publishing in London for consideration.

Mike O'Connor dropped what he was doing to join Mortimer in reception and took them into a room where they sat on a couple of sofas and began playing a song from their Philips album entitled 'Life's Sweet Music'. All was going better than they could have imagined when remarkably it suddenly got a whole lot better: midway through their performance, a door opened and in came a 'waltzing' George Harrison. Unfazed, somehow Mortimer kept on playing as a clearly impressed Harrison danced his way across the room pausing only briefly to say, 'Sign them up,' before continuing to dance his way out of the room.

A (no doubt) suitably gobsmacked Mortimer had hit gold.

Immediately the trio's departure to the USA was cancelled and within a few days they had agreed to sign to Apple Records and Apple Publishing. On 30 November 1968 a three-year contract with an option for a further year was signed.

As winter drew close the trio recorded demos from which they selected the songs they would record at Trident Studios in February 1969 for their forthcoming Apple long player. The album was produced by Apple's A&R main man Peter Asher with extra arrangements by Richard Hewson and was finally mastered during April 1969.

These were undeniably heady times for Mortimer. Every day it seemed there was something new and incredibly exciting to write home about. First one dream would come true … and then another. Amazingly things were to crank up several more notches when, after Peter Asher played him the Mortimer master tape of their proposed album, Paul McCartney began to take an active interest in the group. The ultimate was reached when Paul dropped in on a Mortimer session just after they had recorded a tune that they and Peter Asher thought had the potential to be the album's lead single. It was called 'You Don't Say You Love Me', and although McCartney liked the song he wasn't convinced it was single material. However, by coincidence, Paul *did* have thoughts on a tune he proposed Mortimer *might* like to record for inclusion on their record.

Paul and John had just recorded a demo of an acoustic/Everly Brothers-style tune Paul had penned and which he now thought perfectly suited Mortimer's acoustic, harmony style*. There and then in the studio Paul played them the acetate and immediately offered it to them: it was called 'On Our Way Home' (later re-titled by Paul as 'Two of Us').

(*'On Our Way Home' was only recorded during the sessions for the Let It Be film and it was a rough mix of one of the takes that was given to Mortimer as a demo.)

Mortimer duly went back to Trident with Peter Asher and on 1 May 1969, with a little help from Mike Vickers on synthesiser, recorded and mastered their version of 'On Our Way Home'. They were never completely happy with their own version believing it didn't capture the warmth of the original demo they had been given but this was a Beatles song personally gifted to them by Paul, there was no way they could (or would) pass on it!

In the end it not only made the cut for Mortimer's debut Apple album but was chosen as the opening and title track. Even more than that it was chosen to be their first Apple single release just ahead of the LP and was pencilled in with the catalogue number of 'Apple 16'.

The scheduled release date for *'On Our Way Home'*, both single and album, was the summer of '69, immediately after the debut release of another new signing to Apple Records and Publishing, a group calling themselves the Iveys.

Over in the USA the President of Apple Records, Ron Kass was particularly taken with Mortimer and was predicting big things for both them and their album.

Mortimer's whole Apple trip must now have seemed to them to be truly blessed, the very stuff from which dreams were fashioned. Everything that had happened since they walked through the front door of Apple seemed almost too good to be true …

… Unfortunately, it was.

Someone somewhere must have pinched someone very hard right at this very moment, for not long after experiencing such euphoria Mortimer woke up to a harsh reality in which happy endings cost more money than, all of a sudden, the Beatles were deemed to have.

Tragically the glittering future that appeared to be waiting for them on the horizon never happened: at the very point of lift off, *'On Our Way Home'* – both album and single – along with the group themselves, were dropped. The dream was over.

Fate, in the ruthless shape of Allen Klein, intervened and Mortimer became yet another victim of his determined efforts to tighten every belt he could in order to staunch the flow of cash from Apple Corps. As a result Ron Kass and Peter Asher had not only left Apple but Mortimer's record was immediately consigned to the vaults where it was to remain for nearly 50 years.

The group did not survive this crushing blow to their hopes and dreams: they split.

At the time everything was falling apart, Guy Masson managed to get within the same room as Klein at Apple where a brief confrontation took place. While Guy did his best to ask what was going on, Klein remained impassive. Unfortunately the 'meeting' yielded no joy, instead Guy ended up being 'escorted' from the Apple Offices without any word of explanation from the erstwhile 'Robin Hood of Pop'.

Back in New York, Masson played on Van Morrison's sessions for 'Moondance' but Tom and Tony did not cut any more records.

Belatedly, but good to report, on 17 March 2017, Mortimer's *On Our Way Home* album achieved a mightily belated release on the RPM* label under its original title and with its intended cover photo that Peter Asher had snapped. Asher's picture (prophetically perhaps) depicts the three musicians adrift in a small rowing boat on a small lake. Peter had photographed Mortimer in several locations, including Regents Park and inside his parents' home, 57 Wimpole Street, before eventually settling on a picture he had taken of them in the grounds of his home.

---

*The story of Mortimer's Apple adventures has been gleaned, in part, from: *On Our Way Home* by Mortimer (RPM Retro 987), 15 track CD, booklet notes by Stefan Granados, 2016.

Chapter 115:
ENTER THE IVEYS ...

On Thursday 24 July 1969, a day after recording 'The End' with John, George and Ringo, Paul went back into Studio 2 to cut a demo of a new song he had written and which he intended to give to a new group signed to Apple Records called the Iveys. The song was 'Come and Get It'.

Whispered one night into a home tape recorder as Linda lay asleep upstairs in bed, McCartney's razor sharp instincts told him from the moment he penned 'Come and Get It' that it was a sure-fire hit. Of this he was abundantly sure.

Never destined for the Beatles, 'Come and Get It' became the hit that kickstarted the career of a group who at the time were struggling to get airborne.

Paul gifted the Iveys his brand new song at the moment they believed they were destined to be forever known as Apple's best kept secret. Signed in July 1968 their November '68 debut single, Apple 5, 'Maybe Tomorrow', had not troubled the charts in either the UK or the USA (peaking Stateside at a lowly number 67) and the LP they had recorded with the same title was not released in either territory. Material that the Iveys had recorded since had not received a favourable response from the Beatles and a growing sense of frustration had set in within the group.

Before signing to Apple Records, the Iveys had had a chequered history. It was something that did not change even after they changed their name to Badfinger.

Originating in Swansea in 1961 the group went through several names (the Black Velvets, the Wild Ones, etc) before settling on the Iveys in 1964. The name derived from Ivey Place, a street in Swansea. Highly regarded in their home town, the group came to the notice of Bill Collins the father of Lewis, the actor and bass player in Mersey beat combo 'The Mojos'. Lewis was also a good friend of Paul's younger brother, Mike McGear.

After they had enjoyed a Top 10 hit with 'Everything's Alright' in April 1964, Bill had moved to London taking the Mojos with him. The early promise shown by the group did not produce any more major hits, although they enjoyed two Top 30 singles later that year with 'Why Not Tonight' (June) and 'Seven Daffodils' (September). Consequently, by 1966 Collins was on the lookout for another act to manage. It was then that he happened upon the Iveys who, in December 1966, joined Bill and the Mojos to live in his now crowded house in Golders Green.

The Iveys were a very proficient covers act who soon established themselves on the London club circuit. Pete Ham and Ron Griffiths of the band had a way with a song and so the group soon attracted record label interest. In January 1967, the Kinks' Ray Davies produced a four-track recording of the group which unfortunately came to nothing and by August original member Dai Jenkins left the band (not by choice), his place being taken by Liverpool guitarist Tom Evans.

The ever-enterprising Bill Collins' next move was to invite Beatles minder/go-to-man Mal Evans and Apple A&R Peter Asher to attend the Marquee Club on 25 January 1968 expressly to hear the Iveys perform. Evans and Asher were duly impressed, Evans in particular. Mal pushed their cause with each individual Beatle ensuring that they each received demo tapes of the Iveys. (Apparently John and Paul were the hardest to convince.) Finally, on 23 July 1968 they became the first group after the Beatles to be signed to Apple Records. Evans, Gibbins, Griffiths and Ham were also signed individually to Apple Publishing.

The Iveys' early Apple recordings were recorded and produced by either Mal Evans himself or Tony Visconti.

The first Iveys single, the Visconti-produced 'Maybe Tomorrow' (Apple 5), received a worldwide release on 15 November 1968, but despite being a number 1 in the Netherlands, and reaching the Top 10 in some other European countries and Japan, achieved only very modest success in the major market of the USA (67 in the *Billboard* Hot 100, 51 in the *Cashbox* Top 100) and even more disappointingly *none* at home in the UK. The follow-up, also produced by Visconti, a Ron Griffiths song called 'Dear Angie' (Apple 14) was prepared for worldwide release on 18 July 1969, to coincide with the release of their debut Apple album (on which the single featured). Before this could happen, however, Allen Klein had taken the reins at Apple Corps and would only sanction a limited release for both the single and LP, limiting their release to only territories where 'Maybe Tomorrow' had been a hit, that is, Europe and Japan. Therefore, neither the single nor the album received a UK or American release. (Even so, the Iveys fared better than label-mates Mortimer whose imminent releases were axed completely.)

As can be imagined this situation did not go down well with the Iveys who made their displeasure known. Ron Griffiths went so far as to tell British pop music weekly *Disc and Music Echo* that the group felt "a bit neglected" at Apple and were finding the label/Beatles "very hard to please!" Griffiths commented that, "We keep writing songs for a new single and submitting them to Apple, but the Beatles keep sending them back saying they're not good enough."[1a]

Lest they sounded *too* ungrateful, Tom Evans took care to mention that apart from not releasing a new single the Beatles had been very generous towards the Iveys: "We've had a lot of things that most groups could not expect. The Beatles bought our gear for us, all the equipment and the group van, and we've had all sorts of concessions…"[1b]

Evans also pointed out that the group remained determined to succeed: "We're going to keep on writing, and we're determined to come up with something the Beatles like. At first we were adamant about not recording anything but one of our own songs, but now we'd record anything, so long as it was good." Tellingly he added, "No, the Beatles haven't offered us any of their songs, but then we're not really expecting them to…"[1c]

Such criticism rang loud and clear and had a galvanising effect on Paul McCartney who determined to rectify the situation.

Possessed of a new song he believed had 'hit' written all over it, instead of recording it with the Beatles, Paul donated 'Come And Get It' to the Iveys, confident that it would provide them with their long-sought-after breakthrough chart debut.

Paul's generosity went beyond just giving the Iveys a song he believed to be a guaranteed hit, he also passed on to them a commission he'd accepted to contribute a total of three tracks for the soundtrack to Ringo's film, *The Magic Christian*.

(**N.B.** *Paul had not been the only pop musician invited to provide material for* The Magic Christian. *The 27 September 1969 edition of* NME *reported that in addition to John Sebastian (The Lovin' Spoonful) who was writing the 'incidental score' for* The Magic Christian, *ex-Move bassist Trevor Burton and ex-Moody Blues singer Denny Laine "had been commissioned" to write six songs for the film. For whatever reasons these commissions did not materialise, John Sebastian was replaced by Ken Thorne who had written the score for the Beatles movie,* Help!)[2]

Almost out of nowhere the Iveys were back in business. Before they knew it they had recorded 'Come and Get It' and written and performed the two other songs required for the soundtrack: 'Carry On Till Tomorrow' (aka *'Carry On To Tomorrow'*) written by Pete Ham and Tom Evans and 'Rock of All Ages'* penned by Pete Ham, Tom Evans and Mike Gibbins).

Paul's mighty generous gesture had literally pulled the group back from the brink.

(*Paul co-produced 'Rock of All Ages' with Mal Evans and helped with the writing of the song, although this was not credited at the time. He also contributed piano and a guide vocal to Tom Evans's lead vocal (although this was eventually replaced by a second vocal from Tom). The song became the B-side to 'Come and Get It'.)

During the summer of 1969, when the Iveys worked on tracks for *The Magic Christian* sound track, bassist Ron Griffiths was still a member of the group, but as time progressed he became increasingly estranged from the other members. Ron was the only married Ivey. He and his wife had had a child and with the onset of his responsibilities as a family man he found himself no longer enamoured with the rock 'n' roll lifestyle in which his fellow bandmates still expected him to indulge. What especially concerned him were the ever-present supplies of drugs and drink. By not participating in such habits, distance developed between him and the others. Ron was also struggling to support his family financially because at this point in their career the Iveys had not made any money from their music. Not long after recording 'Come and Get It' he contracted chicken pox and so only made a limited contribution to the recording of the additional material they contributed to the *Magic Christian Music* album. His bass parts were played by Tom Evans.

Inevitably the friction that arose between Griffiths and the other Iveys led to him being dismissed from the band in October. (At which time the group recruited a second Liverpudlian guitarist into the band, one Joey Molland, while Ron's place on bass was taken by Tom Evans.)

Meanwhile back inside the Apple, Paul thought that one of the reasons the Iveys were struggling was that their name was too old hat. He believed they needed something more striking. Pete Ham concurred especially as the band would often be asked if they were the old 'Ivy League'.

Paul and John suggested 'Home' and 'The Prix' (guess who suggested which) but they settled on 'Badfinger' which was a Neil Aspinall's suggestion which emanated from his memory of the working title for 'With a Little Help from My Friends' which had been 'Bad Finger Boogie'. This had derived from the fact that at the time of writing the song with Paul, John was hampered by an injured forefinger and was reduced to playing the piano by using just his middle finger. (Somewhat more amusingly George Harrison told the tale differently suggesting that the name originated from a Beatle memory of a stripper they had encountered in Hamburg who went by the name of 'Helga Fabdinger'.)

On Thursday 24 July, Paul McCartney entered Studio 2 in Abbey Road with just John Lennon for company and in one incredible hour between 2:30 and 3:30pm he recorded a demo of his new song, 'Come and Get It' to give to the Iveys.

John remained patiently in the control room while Paul went into the studio to perform the song. He first recorded himself singing and playing the piano. To this vocal he overdubbed/double-tracked a second while at the same time playing maracas. On separate tracks he overdubbed first drums and then bass. Joining John and engineer Phil McDonald in the control room a stereo mix was made from which an acetate was cut for Paul to pass on to the Iveys. (Paul was not done for the day for he then returned to work, joining John, George and Ringo in Studio 2 to record two new John songs, 'Sun King' and 'Mean Mr. Mustard'. The work ethic of the Beatles was truly quite something.)[3]

Nine days later Paul returned to Abbey Road with the Iveys, now aka Badfinger, where they recorded their version of his new song.

BADFINGER
COME AND GET IT (2:21)
(Paul McCartney)
Northern Songs Ltd
Apple 20
Recorded at EMI Studios, London on 2 August 1969
Produced: Paul McCartney (who also played percussion on the track)
Engineer: Tony Clark
Badfinger's personnel on the recording comprised:
Tom Evans, (b. Thomas Evans Jr, 5 June 1947, Liverpool; d. 19 November 1983, Richmond, Surrey), on lead vocals, rhythm guitar
Pete Ham, (b. Peter William Ham, 27 April 1947 Swansea, Wales; d. aged 27 on 24 April

The Iveys photographed in December 1968. Signed to Apple the Iveys became Badfinger and changed personnel but before they did these were the musicians who recorded 'Come and Get It'. Standing, from left to right: Peter Ham (lead guitar, vocals), Tom Evans (rhythm guitar, vocals), Mike Gibbins (drums, vocals). Seated: Ron Griffiths (bass, vocals).
(Pictorial Press Ltd / Alamy Stock Photo)

1975 in Surrey), backing vocals, piano
Mike Gibbins, (b. Michael George Gibbins 12 March, 1949 Swansea, Wales; d. aged 56 on 4 October 2005 in Florida, USA), drums, percussion
Ron Griffiths*: (b. Ronald Llewellyn Griffiths, 2 October 1946, Swansea) bass, backing vocals
   (*As already noted Ron Griffiths left Badfinger before 'Come and Get It' was released but his picture was featured along with the other members of the group on the single's picture sleeve. Replaced by guitarist Joey Molland (Joseph Charles Molland, born 21 June 1947, Edge Hill, Liverpool), it was this new line-up of Ham, Evans, Molland and Gibbins (1969–74) that became Badfinger's best known.)

   More than happy to gift Badfinger with 'Come and Get It', before doing so Paul laid down one very important condition: they had to promise to record it absolutely faithfully, note for note as per his arrangement on the demo he gave them: "Please don't change this. I can guarantee it's a hit."[4]

   Although Badfinger had some ideas of their own that they wanted to incorporate, Paul was adamant, insisting that it would be a hit if they adhered absolutely to his arrangement. He was so sure of the song he had made gifting Badfinger the task of writing the other songs for *The Magic Christian* soundtrack conditional on them not changing his arrangement one bit. And so they bowed to Paul's judgement, no changes whatsoever were made and as he had predicted they scored their first UK Top 10 hit.

   The recording of 'Come and Get It' proved to be protracted: Ron Griffiths said it took "around thirty takes"[5] to nail a version that met with Paul's satisfaction. During this time, Pete, Tommy and Ron all attempted the vocal, but in the end it fell to Tommy to take the lead.

   Paul's original demo recorded with John present in the control room was one of the many highlights of the Anniversary Edition box set of Abbey Road *released in 2019. Track 3 on CD Three – 'Sessions'.*

B-SIDE: Rock of All Ages*
(Tom Evans, Pete Ham, Mike Gibbins)*
(*Paul also helped co-write this song but was not credited.)
Recorded IBC Studios, London on 18 September 1969
Produced: Paul McCartney and Mal Evans
Both songs were written and recorded specifically for The Magic Christian original soundtrack.
Released in the UK: 5 December 1969, 'Come and Get It' entered the singles chart at number 33 on 10 January 1970. It peaked at number 4 on 31 January, spent the next two weeks at number 5 and 11 weeks on the charts in total.
Released in the USA as Apple 1815: 12 January 1970 it became the record that broke Badfinger in the USA when it became a Top 10 hit in both the Billboard Hot 100 (number 7) and the Cashbox 100 (number 6).
Although not a critical success, The Magic Christian drew a considerable audience which helped Badfinger enjoy enormous success beyond the prime markets of the UK and USA with 'Come and Get It':
Australia: 14
Canada: 4
New Zealand: 1

The single had done exactly what Paul said it would and went on to become one of the biggest selling singles on the Apple label.

The Magic Christian starred Peter Sellers and Ringo Starr. Based on Terry Southern's novel of the same name, Southern co-wrote the screenplay with the film's director, Joseph McGrath. In the UK it was released by Commonwealth United Corporation on 12 December 1969 and in the USA on 11 February 1970. Described as a 'satirical black comedy' the film featured performances (some uncredited) from, amongst many others, John Cleese, Graham Chapman, Raquel Welch, Richard Attenborough, Roman Polanski, Christopher Lee, Yul Brynner, Wilfred Hyde-White, Hattie Jacques, Clive Dunn, Peter Graves, Dennis Price, Patrick Cargill, Alan Whicker, Michael Aspel, John Le Mesurier, Jimmy Clitheroe, Harry Carpenter, David Lodge and Spike Milligan. Impressive in the extreme, but even so not enough to prevent The Magic Christian from being ultimately overbearing and hard going.

Critical reaction to the film was somewhat negative, typical of which were these words from the American magazine Variety: "a spotty uneven satire ... there's a great dismal feeling of self indulgence as of a picture created merely to please an assorted bunch of chums. Much of it is too 'clever' by half."

The Badfinger album Magic Christian Music (Apple SAPCOR 12 in the UK, Apple ST 3364 in the USA) was confusingly not the official soundtrack album release. Their album was released in the UK on 9 January 1970 and 16 February 1970 in the USA and featured a mixture of tracks including the three Badfinger had contributed to the film plus other additional tunes they had recorded for Apple which included their first two singles, some remixed tracks from their debut Apple album as the Iveys and four previously unreleased songs. The band personnel on all 14 album tracks was therefore the same as for the 'Come and Get It' single.

The Magic Christian Official Soundtrack album by Ken Thorne and Orchestra was released on Pye International NSPL 28133 in the UK, but not until 10 April 1970 where it did not chart.

In the USA it was released on the somewhat obscure Commonwealth United Records label 6004 on 11 February 1970 where it also did not chart.

Apart from Ken Thorne's incidental music for the film this 'Official' soundtrack album featured tracks by Badfinger: 'Come and Get It' (plus a 25-second reprisal of this), 'Rock of All Ages', 'Carry On Till Tomorrow', plus Thunderclap Newman's 'Something in the Air' (which had been a number 1 hit in the UK during the summer of 1969), a version of Noel Coward's 'Mad About the Boy' featuring Peter Sellers and Norbert Scultze's 'Lilli Marlene', which is actually Sellers reciting the 'There was a young lady from Exeter' limerick followed by an uncredited performance of 'Lilli Marlene' which was heard in the film under dialogue.

While they remained on Apple Records, Badfinger scored two more UK Top 10 hits: 'No Matter What' (written by Pete Ham, produced by Mal Evans and re-mixed by Geoff Emerick) which was a number 5 in January 1971, and a year later they hit number 10 with 'Day After Day' (written by Pete Ham, produced by George Harrison).

In the USA and Canada they also enjoyed Top 10 hits with these tunes: 'Day After Day' which soared to number 2 in the Canadian Top 10 while in the States it reached number 4 in the *Billboard* Hot 100 and number 3 in the *Cashbox* Top 100 and 'Baby Blue' (produced by Todd Rundgren) their fourth big hit in these territories reaching number 7 in Canada, number 14 in the USA's *Billboard* Hot 100 and number 9 in *Cashbox*'s Top 100. This song was not released in the UK as a single.

After this, however, the hit singles dried up.

However, it wasn't the end of the story for Badfinger. Most notably Pete Ham and Tom Evans wrote the epic heartbreak ballad 'Without You' which Paul McCartney described as the 'killer song of all time'. Originally recorded by Badfinger themselves on 15 and 29 July 1970 for their 1970 Apple album *No Dice* it was produced by Geoff Emerick and released 9 November 1970. The song became one of the biggest hits of the Seventies, but not by Badfinger themselves – it became an international sensation when American singer Harry Nilsson recorded and released it in 1972. For Nilsson, 'Without You' was a global hit that reached number 1 in Australia, Canada, Ireland, the UK and the USA. So successful was it that it went on to win Ham and Evans the 1972 Ivor Novello Award for 'Best Song Musically and Lyrically'.

Since Nilsson's version it has been recorded by over 180 artists, the most successful of which was by Mariah Carey. Mariah recorded it in 1993 and released it as a single in 1994. Like Nilsson's, her version became an international hit reaching number 1 in 15 charts worldwide (but not in the USA where it peaked at number 3 in the *Billboard* Hot 100).

During Badfinger's time at Apple they also became involved in other artists' recordings, most notably George Harrison for whom they provided acoustic guitar and percussion accompaniment for his triple album *All Things Must Pass*. This included playing on such tracks as 'My Sweet Lord', 'Isn't It a Pity' and 'What Is Life'. George produced half of Badfinger's 1971 album *Straight Up*. They also appeared alongside Harrison at 'The Concert for Bangladesh' on 1 August 1971. Molland and Evans did session work on two tracks on John's *Imagine* album and Ham and Evans sang backing vocals on Ringo Starr's single 'It Don't Come Easy'. These were heady days indeed for the group called Badfinger.

That things went wrong for them is an understatement. The very title 'Come and Get It' now seems prophetic. While success and fame had, at last, become Badfinger's to enjoy, the song's title now reads like an open invitation to others to help themselves to the very fruits of their labour.

And so it was, as the world became their oyster it was also the signal for one very unscrupulous person in particular to ruthlessly rip them off. As their career at Apple took off they signed a management deal with an American businessman by the name of Stan Polley. Polley was powerful and persuasive but ultimately not good for the band. Some might say he was toxic. Others a heartless crook. As a businessman he operated outside the law. He signed them up to dubious deals that turned out to be profitable for him but always left the group inexplicably short of cash.

In 1972, Badfinger began work on *Ass*, their last album for Apple. Released in the USA on 26 November 1973 and in the UK on 8 March 1974, the cover painting by Peter Corriston (whose other notable covers include Led Zeppelin's 'Physical Graffiti' and the Rolling Stones' 'Some Girls') was unintentionally prophetic. It represented Badfinger's feelings about their Apple experience depicting, as it does, a loosely tethered donkey looking longingly towards a gigantic hand-held carrot in the sky.

It was the last original album released on Apple Records not by an ex-Beatle. From then on only the solo Beatles released records on the label.

After leaving Apple, Badfinger signed an apparently financially rewarding ($3 million) but ludicrously demanding deal with Warner Brothers which demanded six albums over three years. Within a year of signing to Warners the group began to realise that Stan Polley was not all he had promised to be. Their second album for Warners, *Wish You Were Here*, had been released to critical acclaim and healthy sales, but then it all went wrong. Speaking to *REBEAT* digital magazine in 2017, Joey Molland described exactly what happened: "Warner Brothers discovered that a huge escrow account had been gotten into somehow, and that all the money was gone. This money was hundreds of thousands of dollars in advances that we were supposed to get as we released our albums. They found out that Polley had somehow gotten into the account ... they filed a lawsuit against the band, suing us for the missing money."[6]

Polley would not reveal where the money had gone. Alongside the lawsuit, Warners pulled *Wish You Were Here* from the shops and terminated their publishing deal with Badfinger.

Within the group, lack of money and personal frictions caused Pete Ham to quit but he returned in time for a UK tour only for Molland to leave once it had been completed (December 1974) by which time Warner Publishing had filed a lawsuit against Polley and Badfinger in the LA Superior Court. This legal action prevented the group from releasing *Head First*, which was the third album they had completed for Warners.

Things became increasingly desperate for the group, especially when in March and April 1975 the individual members of the group did not receive their salary cheques. For Pete Ham things were more than desperate. He had a new house in Surrey to pay for, his girlfriend was pregnant and he was mired in drawn-out legal actions with no immediate income.

On 23 April a phone call from the American Justice Department informed him that all his money had disappeared. Ham was utterly devastated. He called Tom Evans and together the two bandmates went to the pub where Ham imbibed a lot of whisky. Later, in the early hours of 24 April, he hanged himself. He was just 27 years old. Pete Ham's suicide note, which was addressed to his girlfriend Anne Herriot and her son Blair, expressed his love for them and blamed Stan Polley for his state of utter despair (calling the American "a soulless bastard"). A month later Anne gave birth to their daughter Petera. At the same time, Warner Bros terminated its contract with Badfinger causing the band to dissolve. Coincidentally, Apple deleted all the group's albums.

A Molland-inspired reunion with Tom Evans began in 1978 and continued into 1981 when the two parted company to form separate bands, both operating under the name 'Badfinger'. After a disastrous US tour, Evans became entangled in a multi-million-dollar legal battle with his manager, American businessman John Cass (which was not resolved until 1985, some two years after Tom's death in 1983, and which Cass won).

By 1983 Evans and Molland together became immersed in unresolved negotiations over income being held by Apple but still owed to Badfinger. On another front Molland, Mike Gibbins and former manager Bill Collins were unhappy over the royalties Evans was receiving from 'Without You' believing that they were entitled to a share.

On 18 November 1983, Tom Evans and Joey Molland spoke on the telephone about the financial issues facing the members of Badfinger which included Pete's widow and former manager Bill Collins. In a 2020 interview with the online magazine *Guitar World*, Joey spoke about his conversation with Tom: "It was very complicated. I had an argument the night before he died; he was talking about getting that money ... We had to all sit down ... and agree how it was going to be divided, and then we had to get lawyers involved. Pete's heirs had to be involved, too. All of us had to agree to it. Tommy wanted it done a certain way, but I wanted it to be done the way we had agreed it originally. So did the others. Tommy had his reasons for it, but they weren't our reasons. He told me that night he was going to kill himself. It was surreal. It had nothing to do with Pete dying, as some have suggested. It was eight years later."[7]

The burden of woe had clearly become too much for Tom. Years of constant litigation and being let down had left him despondent and depressed. He could see no end to the lawsuits and protracted negotiations that had blighted his career and tragically taken the life of his friend Pete Ham.

On the morning of 19 November, Tom hung himself in his garden in Richmond, Surrey. He was cremated in Woking on 25 November.

ADDENDUM: *The Continuing Saga of Badfinger*

Since that dark, dark day various issues have been resolved within the group, including re-issues of the Badfinger back catalogue and releases of albums recorded but not released.

In the USA, Joey Molland has kept the band name alive as an on-going concern where they tour under the name 'Joey Molland's Badfinger'. In 2016 he released a solo album of brand new songs entitled Be True to Yourself. Produced by Mark Hudson, who had previously worked with Ringo Starr, it featured guest appearances from (among many others) Julian Lennon, Micky Dolenz and Christopher Cross. Molland described his new tunes as "fresh catchy rock songs, with many ... reminiscent of Badfinger's sound".

In the UK (pre-Covid) a former member of a 1970s line-up of Badfinger, Bob Jackson toured the UK as 'Bob Jackson's Badfinger' with original bassist Ron Griffiths in their ranks.

According to Wikipedia's Badfinger webpage, "By 2013, the issue of royalty payments had been resolved in court. The main songwriter receives 32 percent of publishing royalties and 25 percent of ASCAP royalties. The other band members and Collins share the rest. Revenue from album sales is shared equally with 20% going to each member as well as Collins. (For example, in 1994, the year in which Mariah Carey covered the song "Without You", the royalties for Ham's estate spiked up to $500,000 USD.)"[8]

This desperately late resolution of Badfinger's entangled business affairs, while undoubtedly welcome for all concerned, seems only to enhance the tragedy of their collective tale.

Former manager Bill Collins died in 2002, aged 89.

On 4 October 2005, Mike Gibbins died in his sleep in his home in Florida, aged 56.

Joey Molland's wife Kathie passed away in 2009.

Stan Polley died on 20 July 2009 in California.

An official blue plaque commemorating the achievements of Pete Ham was unveiled in Swansea on 27 April 2013 and the opening ceremony was attended by former members of both the Iveys and Badfinger.

1a, 1b and 1c *Disc and Music Echo*, 5 July 1969, 'Iveys Find It Hard To Please Beatles', p.16.
2 *New Musical Express*, 27 September 1969.
3, 4 & 5 *Abbey Road*, the Beatles, Anniversary Super Deluxe Edition, released 27 September 2019, from page 71 of the accompanying hardback book *Track By Track* by Kevin Howlett: details of Paul's demo, Paul quote re: not changing his arrangement, Ron Griffiths quote re: the number of takes it took to get the vocal right.
6 *REBEAT* digital blog/magazine, 2017, www.rebeatmag.com > finding-good-badfinger-history 'Finding the Good in Badfinger's History, A Conversation with Joey Molland'.
7 *Guitar World*, 21 October 2020, www.guitarworld.com > joey-molland-looks 'Joey Molland looks back on Badfinger's tumultuous, remarkable career – 50 years on', interview by Joe Bosso.
8 en.wikipedia >> Badfinger, Section 4 '1984 – The Present'.

Chapter 116:
AND, IN THE END

Abbey Road was the last long player record that the Beatles recorded, but not the last they released. *Let It Be* was largely recorded before* *Abbey Road* but became such a protracted endeavour it was not released until May 1970 some nine months after *Abbey Road*.

(*Several tracks heard on Let It Be *were actually finished by Paul, George and Ringo in 1970. George's song 'I Me Mine' was recorded from scratch as it had been heard in the film only briefly when George plays it to Ringo and so a full take had not been recorded.)*

Six days after Paul cut 'Come and Get It' for Badfinger (2 August 1969), the famous zebra crossing cover for *Abbey Road* was photographed just outside the studios. By Wednesday 20 August the record was finished. All four gathered at Abbey Road to listen to the tracks they had recorded which were played back in the order it was proposed to release them. Unknown to them at the time, it was the last occasion on which they would all be together in the studios that they had made globally famous.

The next day they met together again, but this time at Apple Corps, 3 Savile Row for the corporation's first annual general meeting. And on the following day, Friday 22 August 1969 they convened at John and Yoko's home, Tittenhurst Park for what was their final photo session, although, once more, they did not realise this then.

And so it was, unknown to them at the time, the Beatles as a recording entity would soon be no more. As a group their job was done, the last songs had been sung and, apart from some final mixing, *Abbey Road* was ready to be released.

As the Beatles left the photo session at Tittenhurst, they still believed they had a future together.

That this was the case was revealed in 2019 in a newly discovered tape recording of a meeting between John, Paul and George held on 8 September 1969 which offers a vital and fresh insight (and some re-writing of history) into ideas being explored within the Beatles to ensure their future together just prior to the release of *Abbey Road*. The tape recording was a revelatory feature of Mark Lewisohn's excellent 2019 UK tour entitled 'Hornsey Road' in which the acclaimed Beatles historian celebrated the Fiftieth Anniversary of the release of *Abbey Road*.[1]

The tape is hugely illuminating (and especially tantalising for Beatles fans). It appears that on the same day Ringo was taken into hospital with an intestinal illness (8 September 1969) the other three Beatles met to consider the group's future plans. The meeting was recorded by John especially for Ringo in his absence so he could listen in to what they had been talking about and, significantly, *had* apparently agreed.

Despite all that has been written that *Abbey Road* was recorded knowingly as their last hurrah, the conversation preserved on the tape suggests very strongly otherwise.

John appears to lead the discussion which focuses on plans for their *next* album and even the release of a Christmas single. This is utterly surprising in itself for, at the time, Lennon was the one who appeared the most tired of the Beatles and was looking for an 'out'. The first suggestion John proffered was that they should each bring in a tune for consideration as a Christmas single. (As we know he did have a new song appropriately entitled 'Cold Turkey' but despite the seasonal suitability of its title it was as lyrically far from a festive celebration as is possible to get.)

On the tape, Lennon then addressed one of the underlying reasons for George's dissatisfaction with being a Beatle: his gripe that he isn't afforded a look-in with the song-writing because of the domination of the 'Lennon, McCartney' monopoly. With this in mind for the *next* album, Lennon detailed a more equitable division of labour: this was that John, Paul and George should each bring in four songs (Ringo can bring two if he wished to contribute). In this way Lennon was clearly indicating that the 'Lennon, McCartney' partnership was defunct: from now on John says each would be individually credited for their songs. This ending of that iconic songwriting combo would at the time have been revolutionary stuff to the greater public, but within the group itself it only acknowledged the truth of what had been a reality for a long time. The elevation of George to equal status with Paul and John, as proposed by Lennon, was the radical departure here.

As John outlined his master plan, Paul remained calm but when he spoke his words, as heard on tape, were to the point, quietly asserting that until Abbey Road Harrison's songs weren't good enough. (Paul's comment is obviously spontaneous and not at all thought through because by inference he's dissed on 'While My Guitar Gently Weeps' and 'Taxman'.) George did not rise to the bait and simply commented that Paul's view was 'a matter of taste' and that people had always enjoyed his tunes.

John came to George's defence by pointing out that he, George and Ringo did not like Paul songs such as 'Maxwell's Silver Hammer' and that he should give such material to other artists such as Mary Hopkin. John even suggested that Paul most probably didn't even like the song himself. In response Paul simply said that he *did* like it.

Such comments and criticisms by and between Paul and John must have raised the tension in the room, but by the time they left the meeting there had been no falling out. They didn't leave to contemplate the dissolution of the band but, instead, it was to consider John's template for *the continued way forward* of the group and to plan for the next album, the follow-up to *Abbey Road*.

The tape confounds much of the perceived wisdom on the subject of the recording of *Abbey Road*. Ever since the group broke up over 50 years ago, it has been believed that *Abbey Road* was made by the Beatles *knowingly* as their swan song, that after the acrimony of *Let It Be*, they had wanted to get together to make a record 'in the old way': George Martin at the helm, the Beatles at ease with each other, working collectively and cohesively as a bonded group for the last time.

Now, the evidence of the tape suggests, they made *Abbey Road* more to assuage the bad vibes that had bedevilled *Let It Be* rather than to draw a line under their career together.

George Harrison: "I didn't know at the time that it was the last Beatle record that we would make ... I remember liking the record and enjoying it, but I don't recall thinking that was it because there was so much going on all the time."[2]

George Martin: "Nobody knew for sure that it was going to be the last album…"[3]

Sadly, however much the recommendations arrived at on 8 September might have suggested a possible way forward, it was not to be, they simply became a last, lost opportunity …

Within days of the meeting John, Yoko and their hastily convened Plastic Ono Band flew off to appear at the Toronto 'Rock 'n' Roll Revival Concert' (Saturday 13 September 1969). Despite the ideas discussed on the 8th, during this trip John resolved to move on and leave the Beatles. Immediately upon his return he attended a meeting held on Saturday 20 September to sign the sparkling, new and improved royalty-rate recording contract with EMI/Capitol negotiated by Klein on their behalf. It was during this meeting that John informed Paul and Ringo that he'd had enough and was leaving the Beatles. In effect, new deal or not, the group was over.

George was not present at the meeting of the 20th to sign the new contract and so not privy on that occasion to John's startling revelation. He was away from London visiting his sick mother. No doubt he heard about it very soon after! His signature on the new contract was added a few days later when he returned.[4]

Of course, when he had presented the new EMI/Capitol contract to the group, Allen

Klein already knew of John's decision. In the light of this advantageous new deal and the imminent UK release of *Abbey Road*, Lennon was prevailed upon by an anxious Paul, Ringo and Klein not to go public. John was loyal enough to the cause and savvy enough to bow to their wishes.

And he didn't, good to his word he remained silent. In his official biography Paul recalled the moment John dropped his bombshell: "Everyone went, 'Gulp!' The weight was dropped, our jaws dropped along with it, everyone blanched except John, who coloured a little..."[5]

From that moment on John simply pressed ahead with his solo career: on 25 September he and Yoko ensconced themselves in Abbey Road to work on a Plastic Ono Band album release featuring their performance in Toronto. Later that same day he cut a studio version of 'Cold Turkey', the new song he'd premiered in Toronto (and, as already mentioned had suggested, surely ironically, to the other Beatles as a possible 'Christmas single').

And so it was, as they came to terms with John's news, all the individual members of the Beatles became focused on solo endeavours.

Throughout all the machinations regarding Apple and the future of the Beatles as businessmen, the group had fallen into two camps, John, George and Ringo were represented by Allen Klein, while Paul was represented by his in-laws John and Lee Eastman. This division was the source of much friction and distress among the former bandmates, stretching friendships to the limit.

It also contributed towards John and Paul losing their songs.

The death of Brian Epstein had initially caused shares in Northern Songs to fall, but although they rallied, without Brian there to protect the interests of John and Paul, "It left the company vulnerable to hostile takeovers."[6]

It was in March 1969, with Allen Klein newly installed (3 February) as the Beatles business manager by John George and Ringo, but with Lee Eastman (Linda's father) representing Paul, in place specifically to keep a watchful eye on Klein's wheeling and dealing, disaster struck.

Unknown to them all, having observed the tensions between John and Paul in particular, and bothered as to what was happening inside Apple, Dick James became exceedingly concerned as to financial security of Northern Songs and his investment in the company. He was worried that the two composers had not yet signed an extension to their Northern Songs contract. As a result he felt less secure about his business relationship with the group. Since the death of Epstein, Peter Brown, an Apple director, observed that Dick James's links with the group had become less close: "He wasn't in the loop about how things had developed as we built Apple and became less a part of the group. He was never part of the inner circle ... there was no feeling of a relationship between them and him."[7]

He was also well aware that his old show-biz friend from ATV, Lew Grade, had previously shown an interest in becoming a shareholder of the company but had not succeeded ... And so, with this in mind, and fearing the worst for the future of Northern Songs should the Beatles cease to be, in 1968 Dick James secretly approached Grade with a view to selling his and Charles Silver's shares in the company to ATV.

He did so without approaching either John or Paul as to what he was doing, reasoning later that secrecy was essential to avoid the press getting wind of what was going on and scuppering the deal. Significantly he also did not inform Northern Songs' other major shareholder, NEMS Enterprises.[8]

James's fears for the future relationship between John and Paul and the continued existence of the Beatles were based on what was happening at the time. He had sound reasons to fear the worst. As their publisher he (and his son Stephen) had worked extremely hard over many years to promote their music and get other artists to cover their songs. There is no doubt he had been hugely influential in their success. In return he had become very successful through his work for them. However, by 1968/9 there is no doubt he had noticed what he and others around the Beatles felt was the toxic influence of Allen Klein. He could see the way the American worked. It was clear John and Paul had different ideas as to who should manage their affairs. He feared the way the wind was blowing. As Peter Brown commented: "I think he was terrified that Klein would accuse him of ripping off the Beatles and was running scared so he ran in the direction of someone he knew and would be a big guy to defend his situation – Lew Grade."[9]

And so it was James must have felt very nervous about the future and therefore compelled to act to save the personal fortune he had wrapped up in Northern Songs.

His failure to take his concerns to John and Paul and inform them of his intentions was nevertheless a grave error of judgement on his behalf. Secrecy always suggests deceit and in this instance it has left Dick James as the villain of the piece.

And so it was that the covert negotiations reached fruition and were announced on 28 March 1969: ATV had bought Dick James and Charles Silver's 32% holding in Northern songs (for approximately £3 million).

In legal terms James had not acted wrongfully, there was no clause in their contract with Northern Songs that John and Paul (nor Brian) should be given first refusal to buy the company should it ever be offered for sale.[10]

However, in moral terms, it is hard to avoid the conclusion that Grade's failure to consult John and Paul was deceitful in the extreme. That he waited until John and Paul were out of the country before doing so (John was in Amsterdam, Paul in the USA) compounds the fact that he knew he was not acting as he should.

James attempted to justify his secrecy by saying, "What I did I did in their interests as well as mine … I was not acting behind their backs. I believed I was acting for them and the future good of the company…" (He also believed his actions were in the best interests of the 3,000 independent shareholders in Northern Songs.) "Over the years I've resisted thousands of offers … but the ATV bid seemed to make good sense … I really thought I was acting for them … I have great faith in the boys, but I felt that, as magnificent songwriters as they are, I had to relieve them of the responsibility for the company's future affairs … I think I acted for the best."[11]

His words would do little to persuade an independent observer to James's point of view. His comment that he did what he did to "relieve (John and Paul) of the responsibility for the company's future failures", is surely disrespectful and condescending to say the least.

The eventual loss of their songs had been made a distinct possibility several years earlier when quarter of the 5 million shares in Northern Songs had been sold on the Stock Market. Of the remaining shares Dick James and his partner Charles Silver received 937,300 each which gave them a controlling interest in the company, John and Paul 750,000 each and NEMS 375,000, (George and Ringo received 40,000 each). By floating the company on the Stock Market in this way its shareholders made huge sums of tax-free money, but left Northern Songs open to takeover bids. Effectively, from that point on, John and Paul's control of their songs had slipped from their grasp.[12]

Feeling betrayed, Lennon and McCartney tried valiantly to avoid what they regarded as a personal catastrophe. They were determined to seize control of Northern Songs. By 27 April 1969 they owned 27% of the capital in Northern Songs but still needed a further 23.1% to take control. They were hampered in their attempts to raise the cash (£2,000,000) to do so by the fact that at the same time as they needed money to secure Northern Songs for themselves, the Beatles were also attempting to buy NEMS Enterprises. One way or another they were being mightily stretched financially.[13]

The negotiations continued for months but were not helped by the fact that John and Paul were represented by different people. Allen Klein and Lee Eastman neither liked nor trusted each other. For them to make a joint decision was never likely nor straightforward. (Adding to the tension was the fact that, unknown to John, Paul had been secretly buying shares for himself as a way "of investing in myself.")[14]

Complicating matters was the emergence of a consortium of investors who together owned 15% of the shares in Northern Songs. Both ATV and the Beatles did their best to get the consortium to sell to them ... To cut a complicated story short, the consortium eventually sold to ATV which meant that by September 1969 Lew Grade owned 54% of Northern Songs ... and the Beatles had lost control of the company originally set up to secure their finances for the future. From this point on they had no choice but to sell their shares to ATV. Klein and Eastman continued to disagree and as a consequence of this a last-minute deal that would (among other things) have allowed John and Paul to re-sign with Northern Songs, Harrison and Starr to switch from Apple Music to Northern Songs and give Apple sub-publishing rights for the USA never happened. With no other alternatives available to them, for £3.5 million in ATV loan stock, the Beatles had no option but to sell their shares in Northern Songs. By December 1969, ATV owned 92% of Northern Songs ...[15]

And so it was and so it goes ... it was a highly damaging time for all concerned and just the beginning of various attempts post-Beatles by Paul and/or Paul and Yoko to buy back Northern Songs ... none of which were successful. Most famously Michael Jackson acquired ATV and Northern Songs in August 1985. By 1995 Jackson was himself in financial difficulties and merged ATV with Sony Music for $110 million. (It didn't end his money problems but that's another story.) The merger with Sony meant Northern Songs was dissolved and became part of Sony/ATV Music Publishing, the name of which was rebranded in 2021 to Sony Music Publishing, (replete with a new logo).

Meanwhile, back in 1969 ... Individually the now *ex*-Beatles worked hard throughout the remainder of the year on solo projects:-

George produced the Radha Krishna Temple's single 'Hare Krishna Mantra'.

Billy Preston's album *That's the Way God Planned It* produced by George Harrison was released in the UK on 22 August.

George also signed American soul music legend Doris Troy to Apple Records and began to work alongside her on cutting a debut album for the label.

As noted earlier, during December George toured the UK (and travelled to and performed in Copenhagen) as sideman in Delaney and Bonnie and Friends.

John did record and release a Plastic Ono single, 'Cold Turkey' for which Yoko provided the B-side. It was issued in October.

As the Plastic Ono Band, John and Yoko released 'Live Peace in Toronto'.

As John Ono Lennon and Yoko Ono Lennon they released their album *Wedding Album*.

On 25 November, John famously returned his MBE to the Queen in protest against British support of the USA's involvement in the Vietnam War and the British involvement in the Nigerian-Biafran War. (He also said his gesture was 'against 'Cold Turkey' slipping down the charts'.) His Aunt Mimi who had up to then proudly displayed the award in her bungalow in Sandbanks was not impressed.

In December as the year drew to a close, John and Yoko were very busy with various projects promoting their message of peace including the display of huge billboards in 11 cities around the world proclaiming 'War Is Over! If You Want It. Happy Christmas from John and Yoko.' During December, John and Yoko travelled to Canada where they met with Prime Minister Pierre Trudeau to discuss their campaign for world peace. They spent New Year in Denmark with Yoko's former husband Anthony Cox, his new wife Melinda and Anthony's and Yoko's daughter, Kyoko.

From the end of October to 26 December, Ringo recorded what would become his debut solo album, *Sentimental Journey*. Further recordings were made between mid-January and 6 March 1970 before the record was released on the Apple label in the UK on 27 March 1970, and in the USA on 24 April. It reached number 7 in the UK album chart and number 22 in the USA.

In between his work on his album Ringo had been making himself available for promotional duties for *The Magic Christian* and together with Maureen, John and Yoko attended the world royal premiere of the film in London on 10 December.

On a personal level these were tough times indeed for John and Paul in particular:

Tragically four days after being admitted to the King's College Hospital, London, on 12 October, Yoko miscarried hers and John's expected baby.

Unusually for a productive and active artist such as himself, Paul lay low during the whole period following John's 20 September private declaration that he wanted "a divorce" from his fellow Beatles. He took Linda, Heather and new baby Mary to live in his High Park farm in Kintyre, Campbeltown, Scotland where he sank into an alcohol-fuelled depression. Suddenly he had lost the band and friends who for so many years had, and still did, define him as an artist. He was hit hard by the break-up of his beloved Beatles and was particularly hurt by the division that had opened between himself on one side and John, George and Ringo on the other as a result of the faltering fortunes of Apple Corps Ltd.

This was a desperate time not only for Paul but for Linda who witnessed the suffering he endured. It was during these dreadful times that the heinous rumour was spread that Paul had died and replaced by a lookalike.

It was with Linda's support that Paul grew stronger as he gradually came to see that there could be a life after the Beatles. As part of the healing process, just as when his Mother had passed away, Paul immersed himself in music to help find a path through his pain, he began to write some tunes and just ahead of Christmas he and his family returned to London where he began to record these 'solo' songs that later, in April 1970, became his first solo album release, *McCartney*.

Paul and Linda joined George and Pattie as guests of Ringo and Maureen at their New Year's Eve party in Highgate, London.

THE UK'S TOP 30 MOST POPULAR RECORDS OF 1969

01 Archies: Sugar Sugar
02 The Beatles with Billy Preston: Get Back
03 The Rolling Stones: Honky Tonk Women
04 Peter Sarstedt: Where Do You Go To (My Lovely)
05 Jane Birkin and Serge Gainsbourg: Je T'Aime … Moi Non Plus
06 Marvin Gaye: I Heard It Through the Grapevine
07 Creedence Clearwater Revival: Bad Moon Rising
08 Fleetwood Mac: Albatross
09 Frank Sinatra: My Way
10 Bobbie Gentry: I'll Never Fall in Love Again
11 Dean Martin: Gentle on My Mind
12 Zager & Evans: In the Year 2525
13 Elvis Presley: In the Ghetto
14 Marmalade: Ob-La-Di Ob-La-Da
15 The Beatles: The Ballad of John and Yoko
16 Tommy Roe: Dizzy
17 Robin GibB: Saved by the Bell
18 Thunderclap Newman: Something in the Air
19 Mary Hopkin: Goodbye
20 Fleetwood Mac: Oh Well
21 Desmond Dekker & the Aces: The Israelites
22 Kenny Rogers & the First Edition: Ruby Don't Take Your Love to Town
23 Donald Peers: Please Don't Go
24 The Bee Gees: Don't Forget to Remember
25 Plastic Ono Band: Give Peace a Chance
26 Fleetwood Mac: Man of the World
27 Amen Corner: (If Paradise Is) Half as Nice
28 Lou Christie: I'm Gonna Make You Mine
29 Karen Young: Nobody's Child
30 The Scaffold: Lily The Pink

---

1 'Hornsey Road' Mark Lewisohn's 2019 Autumn Tour in celebration of the 50th Anniversary of the release of *Abbey Road* + the *Guardian* newspaper, 11 September 2019, in which Mark Lewisohn was interviewed by Richard Williams: 'This Tape rewrites everything we knew about the Beatles'.
2 & 3 *The Beatles Anthology*, by The Beatles (Cassell & Co, 2000), George Harrison p.343, George Martin p.342.
4 *The Beatles: A Diary* by Barry Miles (Omnibus Press, 2007) p.301.
5 *Paul McCartney, Many Years from Now* by Barry Miles (Vintage, 1998) p.561.
6, 8, 12 & 13 *Beatles for Sale* by John Blaney (A Genuine Jawbone Book, 2008) pp.118,119, 114–4, 120.
7, 9, 10 & 15 *Northern Songs* by Brian Southall with Rupert Perry (Omnibus Press, 2006) pp.72, 70, 73 and p.80.
11 *The Beatles Off the Record* by Keith Badman (Omnibus Press, 2000) p.432.
14 Paul McCartney quotation from *Northern Songs* by Southall with Perry (Omnibus, 2006) p.75.

Chapter 117:
GEORGE AND DORIS

1970
Was the year when ... the USA invaded Cambodia ... Jimi Hendrix and Janis Joplin died ... the World's population reached 3.63 billion ... Edward Heath (Conservative) replaced Harold Wilson as Prime Minister ... Concorde made its first supersonic flight of 700mph ... the National Guard killed 4 protestors at Kent State University, USA ... in Washington DC 100,000 people demonstrated against the war in Vietnam ... the 'Nuclear Non-Proliferation Treaty' was ratified ... a cyclone in Bangladesh killed 500,000 people

Doris Troy grew up in Harlem, NYC. Her father was a Pentecostal minister who moved to Harlem from Barbados, and so it was that as a member of her father's choir Doris was brought up listening to and singing gospel songs. At home, music such as R&B was condoned and so it was only a matter of time before it became part of her life, especially when, aged 16 (1953), she got a job as an usherette in the Apollo Theatre ('The Soul of American Culture') and was 'discovered' by James Brown. Along the way she started to write songs and called herself Doris Payne, having adopted the surname of her grandma. In 1959, as Doris Payne, she co-wrote (with someone called 'F. Augustus') 'How About That' which became a number 33 hit on the *Billboard* Hot 100 and a number 10 hit on the *Billboard* Hot R&B Chart for American soul singer Dee Clark.

Doris worked as a backup singer for Atlantic Records and was an original member of the Sweet Inspirations alongside Cissy Houston and her nieces Dee Dee and Dionne Warwick. She adopted the stage name of Doris Troy, naming herself after Helen of Troy. Among the artists for whom she sang backup were the Drifters and Solomon Burke.

For a young, aspiring singer and songwriter, Troy's early experiences were most instructive as well as impressive.

During the early 1960s, Troy sang in a quartet called the Halos that had been put together by soul singer, songwriter and music producer Gregory Carroll. It was with Carroll that in 1963 she co-wrote (as Doris Payne) 'Just One Look'.

With Troy as the lead vocalist, Carroll produced a demo of the song which, after being rejected by Sue Records, was picked up by Jerry Wexler at Atlantic. Wexler immediately recognised the quality of the song as he heard it on that original demo. Without attempting to re-record, Weller released the Carroll-produced demo exactly as it was. Wexler's instincts were proved to be absolutely on the money when 'Just One Look' became an international hit, charting in Canada (number 1 on the famous Toronto CHUM radio station's 'CHUM Chart') and New Zealand (number 8) as well in the USA (number 10 on the *Billboard* Hot 100, number 3 on the *Billboard* Hot R&B Singles Chart and number 9 on the *Cashbox* 100).

With 'Just One Look', Doris Troy the singer and songwriter had truly arrived. The song became not only an R&B classic but also a classic 'pop' song, especially when in February 1964 the UK, beat and harmony group the Hollies took their cover of the Troy-Carroll song to number 2 in the British singles chart.

Strangely, Troy did not make the charts in the USA again despite releasing some excellent soul and R&B singles including, in 1964, another co-write with Gregory Carroll entitled 'What'cha Gonna Do About It'*. This excellent song became her only UK hit when in November it entered the UK Top 50 and stayed on the chart for seven weeks, peaking at number 37 before re-entering the Top 50 in January '65 for a further five weeks when it peaked at number 38. Not a massive hit for sure, but solid enough for her to have made

Doris Troy photographed in 1970. Doris was an early favourite singer and songwriter of the Beatles. For George in particular, signing Doris to Apple was a no-brainer. (United Archives GmbH / Alamy Stock Photo)

a mark and earn a trip to the UK to promote her music.

(*Troy's 'What'cha Gonna Do About It' is not the same song as the Small Faces' debut UK hit, 'Whatcha Gonna Do About It?'. They just shared the (almost) same title. The Small Faces record charted in September 1965 and was a number 14 hit. It had been penned by Brian Potter and Ian Sawmill around an original melody from Small Faces' Ronnie Lane and Steve Marriott who said they were inspired by Solomon Burke's 'Everybody Needs Someone to Love'.)

During her first promo visit to the UK on Good Friday 16 April 1965 Troy attended Studio One of commercial TV Redifusion's Wembley Studios for an appearance on their groundbreaking teen music programme *Ready Steady Go!* which by then was going out as *Ready Steady Goes Live!*. Broadcast that evening, as its new title suggested, live from 18:08 until 19:00 the other guests on the show included Adam Faith, the Kinks (performing 'Everybody's Gonna Be Happy'), Herman's Hermits (performing 'Wonderful World'), the Yardbirds (performing 'For Your Love'). Also on the show, as non-performing guests, were John Lennon and George Harrison who were there to chat with the show's presenter, Cathy McGowan, about the Beatles' new single 'Ticket to Ride'. When, later, Adam Faith performed 'I Need Your Lovin'', other guests on the show, including Troy, John and George, joined in.

Troy's initial visit to Britain was the beginning of a two-way love affair between Troy and her UK fans that, a visit or two later in 1969, found her residing in London where she was already friends with American-born singers Marsha Hunt and Madeline Bell. Together with Bell, Liza Strike and Nanette Workman, Doris became part of a highly sought after group of backing singers who worked with artists such as Eric Clapton, Joe Cocker, Billy Preston and Stephen Stills.

It was at a Billy Preston session for his debut Apple album that Troy became part of the Apple organisation. Invited to a session by Madeline Bell who was singing backup for Billy, Troy was not only invited to join Bell to sing on the album but she also contributed a song she co-wrote with Preston called 'Everything's Alright'. George Harrison was producing Billy's album and during the sessions Troy was flattered to learn that George was a fan of hers and owned copies of her single 'Just One Look' and her 1963 solo Atlantic album *Doris Troy Sings Just One Look and other Memorable Selections*.

Having ascertained that Troy had no immediate plans or contracts, Harrison offered to sign her to Apple Records. Not one to hold back, Troy apparently told him that she wanted to be a writer, producer and artist. Unfazed by her request, George had Doris sign three contracts with the label, just as she had asked for. Not only that but she was given her own office at Apple at 3 Savile Row, London, in which a piano was installed.

Troy's office was on the top floor just next door to Apple's A&R chief, the one and only Peter Asher. Both George and Ringo wrote songs with her in this office as did other visitors to Apple. As for the songs for her own album, several were composed 'in the moment' during the actual studio sessions themselves. She also worked on other material for her album at George's home in Esher.

The only snag in this generous deal was that by the time Troy joined Apple the business was in free-fall, the Beatles were slowly disintegrating and the very unpopular Allen Klein (amongst Apple staff) was asserting himself within their ranks. As a consequence, Doris Troy would not be a part of Apple for too long, but long enough to write, co-write and produce her own album and release two singles. She benefitted from George's desire to encourage musicians whom he admired and as a result found many of his friends and other Apple artists volunteering their support for her project. Ringo Starr, Billy Preston, Klaus Voormann, Eric Clapton and Jackie Lomax all contributed, as did Peter Frampton, Stephen Stills, Leon Russell, Alan White, Bobby Keys and Liza Strike. The list of luminaries did not end there: Delaney Bramlett plus members of the Delaney and Bonnie and Friends touring band Carl Radle, Jim Gordon and Jim Price all participated as did her own ex-pat friends Madeline Bell and Nanette Workman.

The word for this kind of ensemble is, of course, 'star-studded', but even that seems inadequate to describe the array of talented musicians Troy and Harrison assembled to work on her recordings. It also makes for some uncertainty as to exactly who played on the tracks that were released. For instance, on the lead single from the album *Aint That Cute*, the guitar solo is sometimes credited to Eric Clapton while in fact it was actually played by Peter Frampton.

Exactly when recording sessions began on Doris's Apple album is unclear, although some suggest June 1969, others opt for September, October or even November. Most probably, given George's commitment to Billy Preston's debut Apple album, autumn seems most probable, especially as Doris Troy's initially intended stand-alone single, 'Ain't That Cute' (released in the UK in February 1970) was recorded in October, but an exact date for that session is not available. As sessions for the album progressed the decision for 'Ain't That Cute' to be a stand-alone 45 was rescinded and it was decided that the song would be included on Troy's eponymous (and, as it proved, *only*) Apple album, the sessions for which stretched right through until June 1970. The album was released later that year on the 11 September in the UK and the 9 November in the USA.

'Ain't That Cute' was a song co-written by Doris and George. As such (like 'Badge') it wasn't strictly a Beatles 'giveaway' because by this time the Beatles were at the point of no return. George never intended the song as a potential tune to offer his own band to play because by the time it was recorded (December 1969) John had already informed his bandmates of his intention to leave the Beatles (September 1969).

Nevertheless, it is included here because by this time in the story George and Paul were very pro-active with artists they signed to Apple Records. They helped in a variety of roles that included producing, arranging, recording and writing with the artists concerned. Ringo was also an active participant in sessions produced by George and, along with Doris, George and Steve Stills he also received a co-writer's credit on one song on Doris's album: 'Gonna Get My Baby Back'. Despite their incredible fame and great wealth, Paul, George and Ringo were not living remote lives in some inaccessible house, out of touch and cut off from everyone, they were accessible, 'very hands-on' and living in the moment.

There was a very strong element of 'giving' about what they were doing at Apple. Paul, George and Ringo were gifting artists not only songs but the facilities and opportunities to write and record they might otherwise not have had. Just as generously, the three Beatles were also gifting their own talent, time, playing, money and attention. (John, while not such an active participant in Apple recording sessions for others, as a director of the company would have to agree all that happened at Apple Records.)

'Ain't That Cute' is a great example of George riding high, an artist acclaimed not only within the Beatles but also without.

DORIS TROY
b. Doris Elaine Higginsen on 6 January 1937 in the Bronx, New York, USA
d. 16 February 2004 in Las Vegas, Nevada, USA

AIN'T THAT CUTE
(Harrison/Troy)
Harrisongs/Apple Pub. Ltd
APPLE 24
Recorded: December 1969 at Trident Studios, Soho, London
Produced by: George Harrison
Personnel (from):

Doris Troy: vocals
Peter Frampton: lead guitar
George Harrison: rhythm guitar
Alan White: drums *
Daryl Runswick: bass **
Bobby Keys: saxophone
Jim Price: trumpet

Reg Powell: piano
Billy Preston: keyboards
Delaney Bramlett: backing vocals
Madeline Bell: backing vocals
Liza Strike: backing vocals
Nanette Workman: backing vocals

(*In correspondence with the author in 2020, drummer Alan White recalled: "At that time I was being booked for individual sessions with numerous artists in the London music scene including many for the Apple label. One of these Apple artists was Doris Troy and another was Jackie Lomax. I recorded the song 'Ain't That Cute' along with other songs on Doris's album at Trident Studios under the direction of George Harrison. Another recording done at that studio around that time was the 'Hari Krishna' song with the Hari Krishna troupe. George produced and played guitar on that record.)"[1]

B-SIDE: Vaya Con Dios (May God Be with You)
(Larry Russell/Inez James/Buddy Pepper)
Recording location: Trident (possibly Apple, possibly Abbey Road)
Recording date: Most likely October 1969
Personnel:

Doris Troy: vocals
George Harrison: guitar
Billy Preston: keyboards

Reg Powell*: keyboards
Bill Moody: drums
Daryl Runswick**: bass

Produced by: Doris Troy
(**In 1969 the Reg Powell Trio featuring Daryl Runswick on double bass regularly played the Pickwick Club, a London nightclub that George knew well as did one of his closest friends and fellow musician, Klaus Voormann. In 1965, Klaus played the Pickwick Club "a lot" with his band 'Paddy, Klaus and Gibson'. He described the Pickwick to the author in these words: "It was one of those very posh clubs where people used to go after the theatre or such. They all came down: Princess Margaret, John, Paul, George, Ringo, even Brian Epstein. It was after seeing us play there that Brian decided to sign us up.")[2]
Released in the UK: 13 February 1970
Released in the USA: 16 March 1970

For George Harrison the writing of 'Ain't That Cute' was, at the time, a unique experience. It was not one that he or Doris had written and brought into the studio already composed and arranged, ready to go, but a pure studio creation, a song made up in the moment, on the spot. For George writing from scratch in the studio was a new experience, not something he did in normal circumstances.

In the liner notes for the 2010 CD re-issue of *Doris Troy*, George specifically notes that it was Peter Frampton who played guitar on the session. Frampton himself also has specific memories of playing the solo on the record. He was just 19 years old at the time and already a former 'teen idol', the 'Face of '68' no less (as bestowed by *Rave* magazine). As a member of pop/rock band, the Herd, Frampton had scored two Top 10 successes in 1967 and '68, but by the time he joined George and Doris in the studio he'd left the Herd to try and establish himself as a more seriously respected musician and was part of Humble Pie, a band he'd formed in early 1969 with former Small Face, Steve Marriott. By the time Frampton recorded his solo on 'Ain't That Cute' Humble Pie had already enjoyed UK chart success with their debut single, the Steve Marriott-composed 'Natural Born Bugie', which had reached number 4 in September 1969 and their debut album *As Safe as Yesterday Is* was on the chart (number 16 in the UK album chart).

Despite his own current fame and success, Frampton was nevertheless thrilled to be playing alongside a Beatle. He said it was his first meeting with George and he "was walking on air". He remembers walking into the control room at Trident Studios where George looked him straight in the eye and asked if he wanted to play. When Frampton replied in the affirmative, apparently George handed him a Les Paul guitar, but when Frampton proceeded to play rhythm George immediately stopped him said that he himself was going to play rhythm and he wanted Frampton to play lead. "That's when I developed the lead riff for 'Ain't That Cute'; that's not Clapton, that's me! Eric wasn't there when I was."[3]

Unfortunately, despite strong reviews, 'Ain't That Cute' failed to chart in either the UK or the USA. Even so it made enough of an impact on the UK's record-buying public for the readers of *Melody Maker* to vote it 'Soul Record of the Year'.

Addendum: *What Doris Did Next*
Originally recorded as a stand-alone single, 'Ain't That Cute' eventually kick-started Doris's eponymous Apple solo album as its opening track.

As already mooted, recording for the album most probably began during the autumn of 1969, not long after Doris and George cut 'Ain't That Cute' and sessions on the record continued until 7 June 1970 when George completed the final mix. (Mal Evans took the cover photo.)

Doris Troy was released on 11 September 1970 in the UK as Apple SAPCOR 13 and on 9 November 1970 in the USA as Apple ST 3371.

Thirteen tracks long, George and Ringo played on most of the album sessions which included one other Harrison-Troy co-write, 'Give Me Back My Dynamite',* and together they co-arranged the traditional song 'Jacob's Ladder'. A further two tunes on the record were credited to the songwriting team of 'Harrison-Starkey-Doris Troy-Stephen Stills', namely 'Gonna Get My Baby Back' and 'You Give Me Joy Joy'. The aforementioned 'Starkey' was, of course, none other than the one and only Ringo Starr.

(*This song is not included here as a Beatles 'giveaway', for unlike 'Ain't That Cute', by the time of the composition of 'Give Me Back My Dynamite', the Beatles had officially split.)

Although they worked together on production, Doris was named as the album's sole producer with the exception of the opening track, 'Ain't That Cute', for which George received the credit.

Klaus Voormann told the author that he did not play on 'Ain't That Cute' but remembered Trident Studios and some of the other sessions, in particular the one for 'So Far' which was a song he had written. Echoing Jackie Lomax's* experience before him, Klaus commented, "I wrote and recorded this song with the whole Delaney and Bonnie band. Doris wrote three words for 'So Far' and got half the royalties!"4

(*Doris had been given a co-write credit for the Jackie Lomax song 'You've Got to Be Strong' because for the purposes of her version she changed the word in the title from 'You've' to 'I've'!)

The 'star-studded' ensemble gathered by George and Doris to play on the album included:
Vocals: Doris Troy
Backing vocalists: Madeline Bell, Delaney Bramlett, Liza Strike, Nanette Workman
Bassists: Carl Radle, Klaus Voormann, Daryl Runswick
Drummers: Jim Gordon, Barry Morgan*, Ringo Starr, Alan White
Guitarists: Eric Clapton, Peter Frampton, George Harrison, Stephen Stills
Horns: Jim Price
Saxophone: Bobby Keys
Keyboards/piano: Reg Powell, Billy Preston, Leon Russell, Gary Wright
Orchestral arrangements: John Barham

(*Barry Morgan drummed with the British band Blue Mink who formed during 1969. Roger Cook was lead singer and Madeline Bell was also a member of the group. 'Melting Pot' in 1970 was their biggest UK hit (of seven). It was written by Cook and his songwriting partner Roger Greenaway who were employed by Apple as songwriters ... it's a small world.)

A week before Doris Troy the album was released in the UK a follow-up single to 'Ain't That Cute' was issued as promo for the album: 'Jacob's Ladder' was the A-side and Doris's version of 'Get Back' was the B-side. The A-side was a 'traditional' song 'arranged by Doris Troy and George Harrison'.

Like its predecessor it failed to make an impression on either the UK or US charts.

Despite its impressive credentials and cast (who amazingly were not mentioned on the album sleeve) and largely positive reviews, the impact of Allen Klein's cost-cutting activities affected the potential success of the album. By now firmly in control at Apple and wishing to economise, like many Apple albums around this time by artists other than the Beatles, Doris's album did not receive the promotion it deserved and consequently failed to make the charts in either the UK or USA.

Like those around her, Troy recognised that things were falling apart at Apple and that it was time to leave, and so she did.

Her credentials meant she was in demand as a backing singer (amongst many others she can be heard on 'You Can't Always Get What You Want' by the Rolling Stones, Carly Simon's 'You're So Vain' and on Pink Floyd's album Dark Side of the Moon). She formed a group called the Gospel Truth and signed to Polydor Records for whom she cut the album Rainbow Testament in 1972, and in 1974 she released Stretching Out on the People Records label. Neither record sold well and by 1974 Troy had returned to the USA where she lived in Las Vegas and sang back-up for Lola Falana's stage show as well as working as a session singer.

In 1983 a stage musical based on Troy's life, entitled Mama I Want to Sing, opened at the Heckscher Theatre in East or 'Spanish' Harlem. Co-written first as a play in 1979 and then published as a book by Troy's sister Vy Higginsen (a popular radio personality in

NYC) and her husband Ken Hydro (they also wrote the lyrics for the show) it took much persuading and battling before they finally got their musical onto a stage. Indeed, to do so Higginsen and Hydro had had to invest their life-savings to hire out the Heckscher Theatre. In the original production Queen Esther Marrow played Troy's mother, Geraldine, but was succeeded in the role from 1983 until 2000 by Doris herself. The musical's success was outstanding. Within four years of opening it had played to over 3 million people in the USA, Europe and Japan and grossed over $62 million.

In 2009 it was made into a feature film starring Ciara Harris-Wilson, Lynn Whitfield, Patti LaBelle and Billy Zane. Among the other actors are Ahmaya Knoll (Vy and Ken's daughter) and Vy herself plays a 'cameo'. Production difficulties saw the film's premiere delayed on three occasions until it was finally released 'direct to video' on 14 February 2014.

Sadly Doris became beset with breathing problems during the 1990s and in 2004 succumbed to emphysema at her home in Las Vegas, Nevada, aged 67.

THE UK'S TOP 30 MOST POPULAR RECORDS OF 1970
01 Elvis Presley: The Wonder of You
02 Mungo Jerry: In the Summertime
03 Freda Payne: Band of Gold
04 Simon & Garfunkel: Bridge over Troubled Water
05 Rolf Harris: Two Little Boys
06 Lee Marvin: Wand'rin' Star
07 Norman Greenbaum: Spirit in the Sky
08 England World Cup Squad: Back Home
09 Free: All Right Now
10 Christie: Yellow River
11 Edison Lighthouse: Love Grows (Where My Rosemary Grows)
12 Smokey Robinson & the Miracles: Tears of a Clown
13 Dave Edmunds: I Hear You Knocking
14 Matthew's Southern Comfort: Woodstock
15 Dana: All Kinds of Everything
16 Deep Purple: Black Night
17 Andy Williams: Can't Help Falling in Love
18 Mr Bloe: Groovin' with Mr Bloe
19 The Kinks: Lola
20 Shirley Bassey: Something
21 Hotlegs: Neanderthal Man
22 Clarence Carter: Patches
23 Desmond Dekker: You Can Get It If You Really Want
24 Kenny Rogers & the First Edition: Ruby Don't Take Your Love to Town
25 The Beach Boys: Cottonfields
26 Jimi Hendrix Experience: Voodoo Chile
27 Peter Paul & Mary: Leavin' on a Jet Plane
28 Canned Heat: Let's Work Together
29 Glen Campbell: Honey Come Back
30 The Tremeloes: Me and My Life
And … elsewhere:
36 Mary Hopkin: Knock Knock Who's There
57 The Beatles: Let It Be
66 Badfinger: Come and Get It
83 John Lennon and Yoko Ono with the Plastic Ono Band: Instant Karma
88 Mary Hopkin: Temma Harbour

Drummer, human being extraordinaire Alan White with the author at Mendips, Liverpool, 10 July 2010. Alan drummed most famously for Yes but early on in his career he played with John and Yoko in the Plastic Ono Band, most notably at Live Peace in Toronto and the *Imagine* album. He also drummed for George on the *All Things Must Pass* LP as well as playing on Doris Troy's Apple single, 'Ain't That Cute' and numerous other sessions for the label.

Sadly Alan passed away on 26 May 2022 at his home in Newcastle, Seattle, Washington State, USA where he lived with his beautiful wife and soulmate, Gigi.

1a & b Alan White in correspondence with the author, Colin Hall, 23 May 2020.
2 & 4 Klaus Voormann in conversation with the author Colin Hall, 25 November 2019.
3 Peter Frampton's memories are from the Andy Davis compiled booklet that accompanied the 2010 APPLE CD re-issue of the original 1970 Apple Records album *Doris Troy*.

Chapter 118:
SORRY, BUT IT'S TIME TO GO

George Harrison's work with Doris Troy on 'Ain't That Cute' and her Apple long player concludes the story of the songs the Beatles gave away.

The dissolution of the group as a recording entity was finally made public when Paul promoted the release of his solo album, *McCartney*.

Paul had been rocked by John Lennon's announcement in September 1969 that he was quitting the Beatles. The demise of the group was kept secret but from this moment on Paul knew this really was the end.

The Beatles had had little or no time to respond to the possible way forward set out by John Lennon himself in a meeting held on 8 September that had been specifically convened to attempt to agree a future for the Beatles as a creative and recording entity. Despite the ideas set out during this meeting for them each to take away and consider, none of them had responded by the time of the meeting of 20 September. John's departure for Toronto just a few days after that 8 September meeting suggests that an immediate response was not expected, especially as Ringo had been in hospital when it was convened.

Consequently, John's declaration just 12 days later that he was leaving was an unexpected bombshell that neatly kicked those ideas into touch.

Devastated by the implications of the split, Paul fell into a depression but with Linda's help he fought his demons and gradually came to terms with a life without the Beatles as his anchor. As when his mother, Mary, had died when he was just 14 years old and music had helped him find a way through the darkness of that awful tragedy, so once more it came to his rescue. In this time of emotional crisis, he wrote some new tunes and recorded his first solo album, *McCartney*.

McCartney was released on 17 April 1970, but a week earlier Paul had finally let the Beatles' secret out of the bag. To promote and accompany his new album, on 9 April, Paul produced and issued a press release composed in the form of an interview in which he answered pre-prepared questions by Peter Brown at Apple.

In simple, straightforward answers, Paul said things no Beatles fan had ever wanted to hear.

Q. "Are you planning a new album or single with the Beatles?"
A. "No."
Q. "Is this album a rest away from the Beatles or the start of a solo career?"
A. "Time will tell. Being a solo album means it's 'the start of a solo career...' and not being done with the Beatles means it's just a rest. So it's both."
(The phrases "it's just a rest" and "so it's both" are cagey ... open to interpretation as to whether the group had split.)
Q. "Is your break with the Beatles temporary or permanent, due to personal differences or musical ones?"
A. "Personal differences, business differences, musical differences, but most of all because I have a better time with my family. Temporary or permanent? I don't really know."
(Any comfort Beatles fans might have drawn from those words "I don't really know", that just maybe the group was not finished yet, were pretty much quashed by the next Q&A.)
Q. "Do you foresee a time when Lennon-McCartney becomes an active songwriting partnership again?"
A. "No."

It does not come more unequivocal than that. However much his previous answers possibly hedged about a split, this one did not. It sounded loud and clear, the fans knew all they needed to know: the dream was over. How could there possibly be a Beatles without the Lennon-McCartney songwriting partnership?

The long-delayed release of *Let It Be* on 8 May 1970 did little to lift the spirits. Boxed within a funereal-looking black sleeve with no group picture on the cover, the four individual portrait photographs that did adorn it only served to reinforce the notion that the Beatles were now separate entities. The sense of joy and good humour that permeated *Abbey Road* was not present in the production and presentation of *Let It Be*. The title itself was resigned, and perceived by most observers as an acceptance by the group itself that this was it, they were resigned to the fact that there would be no way back.

And there wasn't. On 31 December 1970 Paul attended the High Court of Justice in London to initiate proceedings to wind up the Beatles ...

Q & A selections taken from the 'Apple Press Release' for the *McCartney* album published 9 April 1970.

POSTSCRIPT:
WE LOVE YOU BEATLES – OH YES WE DO!

Inevitably the demise of the Beatles as a business enterprise was protracted as the lawyers, those dreaded 'men in suits', took control to sort out their confused, complicated and contentious affairs. It was more ugly than it needed to be, but beneath the newspaper headlines and court decisions the love between John, Paul, George and Ringo never died (although at times it has to be said they worked hard to keep it well hidden).

What is sure is that music fans everywhere have never lost their love for the Beatles.

As the third decade of the 21st century begins, and a major worldwide life-threatening pandemic has afflicted the world, the Beatles remain as popular as ever: their music remains relevant, constantly played, an inspiration. It has more than stood the test of time.

Although there will never be any new songs, each re-mastered, super-deluxe, bonus track-bedecked and boxed-up, re-packaged, limited edition re-release of the singles, long player records and EPs that everyone has already bought at least three times before, defy logic and sell in the millions. The appetite for product, most of it recycled, seems insatiable. As individuals, each Beatle is loved and revered. As a group the Beatles will never grew old and 50 years after their break-up they continue to walk on water.

A fresh perspective on the *Get Back* project was provided in November 2021 by a new three-part documentary film directed by Sir Peter Jackson entitled *The Beatles: Get Back*. Aired over three nights on the Disney TV Channel after a delay of a year because of the coronavirus pandemic and using footage originally shot by Michael Lindsay-Hogg for his documentary film *Let It Be* (which originally had the working title of *Get Back*) visually it looks much brighter and presents a distinctly more upbeat, warmer and harmonious view of the still-extant friendship between the four Beatles. In doing so it challenges the long-held notion that the project was all stress and strained relationships. Very clearly it wasn't. Once the music kicks in something intangible transcends proceedings, it's beyond words and how we wish they had never stopped. Crucially the sound is much more dynamic.

As might be expected McCartney and Starr thoroughly approved of this corrected version of events believing that it provides a more balanced and truer insight into the events of the time. In a press release to announce the project Ringo Starr enthused: "I'm really looking forward to this film. Peter is great and it was so cool looking at all this footage. There was hours and hours of us just laughing and playing music, not at all like the version that came out. There was a lot of joy and I think Peter will show that. I think this version will be a lot more peace and loving, like we really were."

Peter Jackson is euphoric: "Working on this project has been a joyous discovery. I've been privileged to be a fly on the wall while the greatest band of all time works, plays and creates masterpieces."

Paul McCartney is equally thrilled that, at last, the truth will out: "I am really happy that Peter has delved into our archives to make a film that shows the truth about the Beatles recording together. The friendship and love between us comes over and reminds me of what a crazily beautiful time we had."

The Songs the Beatles Gave Away has been my attempt to tell their story from a slightly oblique angle. While they remain centre circle, this is very much the story of others who were touched by the creative genius of this marvellous band of bands. The stories related here capture ephemeral, but nevertheless dazzling moments in the history of both the Beatles and of 1960s 'pop' music in general.

Some individual stories haven't always ended happily or successfully for the artists concerned, but theirs were nevertheless than an interesting, usually exciting, if not at times exhilarating, journey. For each of them it was a never-to-be-repeated experience that, in the main, they are usually very happy and proud to have experienced.

What Billy J. Kramer with the Dakotas, Cilla Black, the Fourmost, Tommy Quickly, the Applejacks, Peter and Gordon, the Strangers with Mike Shannon, P.J. Proby, the Black Dyke Brass Band, Jotta Herre, Mary Hopkin, Jackie Lomax, Badfinger and Doris Troy received was something unique: a genuine 'Lennon, McCartney' or 'Harrison' 'original'. As such this was pure gold, a gift from the 'gods'. Not every 'giveaway' was successful in terms of the charts, but each tune has assured the individual artists not only a place within the story of the Beatles but also within the annals of the popular music of the Sixties.

Billy Hatton said it best when he commented: "Only after many, many years has it registered just how significant it was being gifted Beatle-written songs written at the height of Beatlemania. At the time it was a job. It's like a joiner, if he wants to make a wonderful cabinet, he has to start with a half decent piece of wood. We were given that piece of wood by the Beatles. How we shaped it, was up to us. At the time everything was so new, we realised it was important because they were so big and their talents could help you get a record. But many, many years later, now I'm an older man, when I look back and find out how many others entered our club, given songs that the Beatles wrote that they never recorded but wrote specifically for us, it's a very small, very private club and we're proud to be members."[1]

Colin Hall, November 2021
Menlove Avenue, Woolton, Liverpool

---

[1] Billy Hatton of the Fourmost in conversation with the author, 2009.

"After the Beatles I think Paul missed John and John missed Paul because together they were invincible, they were still marvellous by themselves, much more marvellous than most people but there was something lacking when they didn't have that collaboration. Individually they each wrote some good stuff on their own solo albums but nothing like what they did when they were together."

George Martin, 2009

Sources

Re: Original 45rpm singles UK & USA chart details, timings
The core information in my book re: the original singles, their release dates, playing time, label information, sleeves and chart successes (or otherwise) have been drawn from my personal copies of the records themselves and from the following invaluable sources:
'Official Charts, Official Singles' compiled by 'The Official UK Charts Company' www.officialcharts.com/
The Guinness Book of British Hit Singles by Jo & Tim Rice with Paul Gambaccini & Mike Read (1977 edition)
20 Years of British Record Charts 1955–1975, with commentary by Peter Jones & Tony Jasper, edited by Tony Jasper, (Queen Anne Press, 1976)
All Together Now: The First Complete Beatles Discography 1961–1975 by Harry Castleman & Walter J. Podrazik (Ballantine Books, New York, 1976)
An online invaluable source of information re: 'Twist And Shout' is the www.jpgr.co.uk website

TV series, TV programmes and Film details
The invaluable source is IMDb, the amazing online database, check it out via: imdb.com

Bibliography (in alphabetical order)
The volumes of literature out there to which I have turned to assist me in my research would fill a small library. (Then there is the mountain of old newspapers, magazines, fanzines, pamphlets and websites!)

In particular, during the course of writing this tome my copies of works by Mark Lewisohn, Barry Miles, Ray Coleman, David Sheff and Spencer Leigh have gone from being in 'good' condition to 'well beyond well-thumbed' aka 'falling apart'. Anything these authors publish is to be highly recommended.

However, **all** the books noted below come very highly recommended and are hugely informative, entertaining and in many cases mind-bogglingly well researched and informed. My huge appreciation goes out to all the authors for their work and the time and sheer diligence that has gone into writing/researching them. It has been my joy to delve into all of them.

A Cellarful of Noise, by Brian Epstein, (Souvenir Press, 1964)
A Twist of Lennon, by Cynthia Lennon, (Star, 1978)
All Together Now: The First Complete Beatles Discography 1961–1975, by Harry Castleman & Walter J. Podrazik, (Ballantine Books, New York,1976)
All We Are Saying: The Last Major Interview with John Lennon and Yoko Ono, interviews conducted by David Sheff for *Playboy*, (Sidgwick & Jackson, 2000)
All You Need Is Ears, by George Martin and Jeremy Hornsby, (Macmillan,1979)
Apple to the Core, by Peter McCabe & Robert D. Schonfeld, (Sphere Books Limited, 1973)
As Time Goes By, by Derek Taylor, (Abacus, 1974)
Beat Merchants, by Alan Clayson, (Blandford, 1995)
Beatle!: The Pete Best Story, by Pete Best and Patrick Doncaster, (Plexus Publishing Limited, 1989)
Beatles for Sale, by John Blaney, (Jawbone, 2008)
Beatles Undercover, by Kristofer Engelhardt, (Collector's Guide Publishing Inc., 1998)
Brian Epstein: The Man Who Made the Beatles, by Ray Coleman, (Penguin Books, 1990)
Do You Want to Know a Secret?: The Autobiography of Billy J. Kramer, by Billy J. Kramer with Alyn Skipton, (Equinox Publishing, 2016)
Echoes of the Sixties: Intimate Profiles of 43 of the Musical Composers and Performers Who Influenced an Entire Generation, by Jeff March & Marti Childs, (Billboard Books, U.S., 2000)
Encyclopedia of Great Popular Song Recordings, Volume 2, by Steve Sullivan, (Scarecrow Press, October 4, 2013)
George Harrison, by Alan Clayson, Sanctuary, (London, 2003)
I, Me, Mine, The Extended Edition by George Harrison, (Genesis Publications, 2016)
Imagine This: Growing Up with My Brother John Lennon by Julia Baird, (Hodder & Stoughton, 2007)
John, by Cynthia Lennon, (Hodder & Stoughton, 2005)
John Lennon, by Ray Coleman, (Futura Publications, 1984) aka *Lennon: The Definitive Biography, Anniversary Edition*, by Ray Coleman (Pan Books, 2000)
John Lennon in His Own Words, compiled by Miles, (Omnibus Press, 1980)
John Lennon in My Life by Pete Shotton, Shotton & Nicholas Schaffer, (Stein and Day, 1983)
Johnny Gentle & the Beatles First Ever Tour, by Johnny Gentle & Ian Forsyth (Merseyrock Publications, 1998)
Love Me Do: The Beatles' Progress, Michael Braun, (Penguin Books, 1964)
McCartney: Yesterday and Today, by Ray Coleman (Boxtree, 1995)
Northern Songs, by Brian Southall with Rupert Perry, (Omnibus Press, 2006)
Paul McCartney: Many Years from Now, by Barry Miles, (Vintage, 1998)
Pre:Fab!, by Colin Hanton with Colin Hall, (The Book Guild Limited, 2018)
Step Inside, by Cilla Black, (J.M. Dent & Sons, 1985)
The Act You've Known for All These Years: The Life, and Afterlife, of Sgt. Pepper, by Clinton Heylin, (Canongate Books, 2007)
The Beatles – All These Years: Volume One: Tune In, Extended Special Edition, by Mark Lewisohn (Little, Brown 2013)
The Beatles Anthology, by The Beatles, (Cassell & Co. 2000)
The Beatles As Musicians: The Quarry Men through Rubber Soul, by Walter Everett, (Oxford University Press, USA, 2001)
The Beatles Diary Volume 2: After the Break-Up 1970–2001, by Keith Badman, (Omnibus Press, London, 2001)
The Beatles from A to Zed, by Peter Asher, (Henry Holt and Company, 2019)
The Beatles Off the Record, by Keith Badman, (Omnibus Press, 2007)
The Beatles: The Authorised Biography, by Hunter Davies, (Heinemann, 1968)
The Best of Fellas: The Story of Bob Wooler, by Spencer Leigh, (Drivegreen Publications Ltd In association with Jim Turner, 2002)
The Complete Beatles Recording Sessions, by Mark Lewisohn, (The Hamlyn Publishing Group Limited, 1988)
The Complete Beatles Songs, by Steve Turner, (Seven Oaks, 2016)
The Gospel According to John Lennon, by Alan Clayson, (Sanctuary Publishing, 2007)
The Guinness Book of British Hit Singles, by Jo & Tim Rice with Paul Gambaccini & Mike Read (1977 edition)

The Liverpool of Brian Epstein, text by Jeremy Deller, drawings by Paul Ryan (Published by Tate Liverpool on the occasion of the 'Creative Universe: Liverpool and the Avant-Garde, 2007)
The Lyrics: 1956 to the Present, by Paul McCartney (Allen Lane, 2021) Edited by Paul Muldoon
The Paul McCartney Encyclopedia, by Bill Harry, (Virgin Books, 2002)
The Perfect Storm Part 3 – 1960, by Spencer Leigh, www.spencerleigh.co.uk/2013
The Unreleased Beatles, by Richie Unterberger (Backbeat Books, 2006)
The Zapple Diaries, by Barry Miles, (Peter Owen Publishing, 2015)
Walking Back to Happiness, by Helen Shapiro, (Harper Collins, 1993)
What's It All About, by Cilla Black, (Ebury Press, 2003)
Wonderful Today, by Pattie Boyd with Penny Junor, (Headline Review, 2007)
Wrong Movements: A Robert Wyatt History, by Michael King, (SAF Publishing, 1994)
You Never Give Me Your Money, by Pete Doggett, (Bodley Head, 2009)

Discography (Selective)

My discography does not include the original individual single releases as written about in the text as they and all the details appertaining to their release, labels, success or otherwise are more or less fully detailed therein.
Abbey Road by the Beatles (Apple/Universal) 2019, 3CD & Blu-Ray Audio disc Anniversary Edition.
Disc 2, Track 2 features Paul's home demo of 'Goodbye'; Disc 3, Track 3 features Paul's studio demo of 'Come And Get It'
John Barry: The Hits & the Misses by Various Artists, (Play It Again/EMI), 1998 PLAY 007, a 2 CD 50 track compilation of music arranged and conducted by John Barry.
Disc Two, Track 2 features 'I've Just Fallen For Someone' as performed by Darren Young (aka John Askew aka Johnny Gentle) and written by Askew with a little help from John Lennon. Track 3 of side 2 of this compilation features what was the A-side of that song, 'My Tears Will Turn to Laughter' which was also written by John Askew.
The Beatles by the Beatles, (Apple/Universal), 2018 6 CD: Blu-Ray Anniversary Edition.
Disc 3 - 'Esher Demos', Track 16 'Sour Milk Sea', George sings the song he eventually gifted to Jackie Lomax.
The Beatles Anthology 1 by the Beatles, (Apple/EMI), 1995 2 CD, 60 track compilation.
Features Beatles recordings/demos of 'Like Dreamers Do' and 'Hello Little Girl'.
The Beatles Anthology 2 by the Beatles, (Apple/EMI), 1996 2 CD, 45 track compilation.
Features a Beatles recording of 'That Means a Lot' that the group never used/released at the time of recording.
The Beatles Anthology 3 by the Beatles, (Apple/EMI), 1996 2 CD, 49 track compilation.
Features Paul singing 'Step Inside Love' and the demo John and Paul made of 'Two of Us' aka 'On Our Way Home' as played by Paul to Mortimer.
The Beatles Live at the BBC by the Beatles, (Apple), 1994 2 CD, a compilation of 56 songs and 13 tracks of dialogue.
Disc 1, Track 7 'I'll Be On My Way' is the only recording by the group of this song that they gave to Billy J. Kramer with the Dakotas. which they released as the B-side of their first single and has the distinction of being the first of the Beatles' 'giveaways'.
Cilla 1963 - 1973: The Abbey Road Decade by Cilla Black, (Zonophone), re-mastered 1997 3CD set, 65 track compilation.
CD 3, Track 12, 'Step Inside Love', is the original demo version featuring Paul on acoustic guitar and Cilla on vocals.
Come and Get It: The Best of Apple Records by Various Artists, Apple, 2010 re-mastered 21 track CD compilation.
Includes the singles 'Thingumybob' by the Black Dyke Mills Band, 'Sour Milk Sea' by Jackie Lomax, 'Goodbye' by Mary Hopkin, 'Come And Get It' by Badfinger and 'Ain't That Cute' by Doris Troy. (There's also 'God Save Us' by Bill Elliot & The Elastic Oz Band, a song John gave away not long after the Beatles were no more.)
The Very Best of Cream, Cream, (Polydor), remastered 1995 20 track CD compilation.
Track 20 is 'Badge' featuring George Harrison on rhythm guitar.
Doris Troy by Doris Troy, (Apple Records), 1992 re-mastered CD release featuring 'Ain't That Cute' and five additional recordings.
The Family Way, Original Soundtrack Recording, Music Composed by Paul McCartney, Supervised and Orchestrations Arranged by George Martin, (Varése Saraband), 2011 CD release.
Tracks 6 and 14 are bonus tracks featuring the Tudor Minstrels' versions of 'Love in the Open Air' and 'Theme from The Family Way'.
Is This What You Want? by Jackie Lomax, (Apple Records), 2010 re-mastered CD release produced by George Harrison
Features 'Sour Milk Sea'.
Let It Be by the Beatles (Apple/Universal), 2021, Super Deluxe 6-Disc Edition.
The deluxe edition features all-new mixes by Giles Martin and Sam Okell. Includes the *Get Back* album 1969 mix by Glyn Johns, *Let It Be* EP and a 100-page hardback book. Various takes of 'Two of Us' appear throughout.
On Our Way Home by Mortimer, RPM Records (under licence to Cherry Red Records Ltd), 2017 re-mastered release of the group's unissued Apple album.
Features their version of Paul's song which, of course was not – in this tome's definition of the word – ever destined to be a 'giveaway', but which demonstrates Paul's willingness to give an aspiring group a helping hand with first go at an original 'McCartney-Lennon' tune.
Wonderwall Music by George Harrison Original Soundtrack, George Harrison, (Apple) 2014 re-mastered CD featuring three additional recordings.

Out there somewhere are three albums which feature the songs the Beatles gave away. One is a compilation of the records I've written about (more or less) and two feature collections recorded by independent artists.
The Songs Lennon and McCartney Gave Away by Various Artists, (EMI, NUT 18), 20 track vinyl album released 18 April 1979.
The album includes 19 of the tracks featured in this book. They are all songs written by John and Paul (including Paul as 'Bernard Webb' writer of 'Woman'). All the tracks are by the original artists. The odd one out, as far as the remit of this book goes, is the 20th track. It opens side one and is 'I'm the Greatest' by Ringo Starr, an album track from 1973 written for Ringo by John.
Off the Beatle Track by Apple Jam (Roseta Productions) 2009 15 track CD.
This indie album was recorded in Seattle and featured the tunes John and Paul gifted to acts such as Peter & Gordon, Billy J. Kramer, Cilla Black, Tommy Quickly, The Fourmost and The Strangers with Mike Shannon. Apple Jam took these giveaways and skilfully arranged and recorded them in the style of the Beatles circa 'With The Beatles'/'A Hard Day's Night'. Hence 'A World Without Love' recalls the semi-acoustic lilt of 'And I Love Her', the big band blast of Cilla's 'Love of the Loved' becomes something altogether more Mersey Beat and for good measure the set includes a take on the 'lost' George Harrison song, 'You Know What to Do' which neatly provided Apple Jam with their very own original Beatles 'cover'. It was/is a winning formula that made for an enjoyable collection of some rarely heard Lennon-McCartney and Harrison songs.
Northern Songs by Revolver (Rox Recordings) 1979 17 track vinyl album.
The Lennon & McCartney compositions the Beatles never issued.
An independent recording of Beatles 'giveaway' songs produced by David Crosby (no relation) in Liverpool.

Thank you

The Songs the Beatles Gave Away has been what feels like a lifetime in the making.

In 2007 I was lucky to work with my long-time friend and legendary broadcaster, Bob Harris on *The Day John Met Paul*. We made the radio documentary for the production company 'The Whispering Bob Broadcasting Company' he had formed with his wife, Trudie Myerscough-Harris. Aired on BBC Radio 2, it won a Sony Award. Not long after, when Bob was looking for other programme ideas, I suggested, *The Songs the Beatles Gave Away*. Luckily for me WBBC ran with the idea and so it was that Bob, Trudie, Neil Myners, Genevieve Willis and myself became the team that built the final programme. Once again BBC Radio 2 liked it and it debuted on 28 November, 2009.

We had so much fun making the programme we sometimes had to pinch ourselves that what we were doing was actually 'work'. I mean, our diaries included visiting Sir Paul at MPL in London, spending time with Sir George and Lady Martin in their Oxfordshire home, myself talking with Jackie Lomax and Billy Hatton at Mendips ... Bob chatting at length with Cilla Black and his cousin Mary Hopkin. When all is said and done it wasn't a bad way to earn a living!

Bob Harris and Trudie Myerscough-Harris

It fell to Bob and Neil to listen (over and over) to, and then edit, the hours of interview tape we had accumulated, into the hour-long programme that was finally aired. Along the way Bob wrote and narrated the script. Behind the scenes Trudie pulled all the strings, made all the calls and sent all the emails. Her trusty helper at WBBC, Genevieve, transcribed all the hours of interviews we accumulated.

I was in awe of just how much work everyone did, and, always to such high standards and with such great attention to detail. I was humbled and inspired to work alongside such consummate professionals. The sense of achievement that I believe we all felt when the programme went out was very special indeed.

So, my thanks start here with Bob, Trudie, Neil and Genevieve. Your friendship, inclusivity and professionalism were inspiring and, on both programmes, provided a great learning curve and the perfect environment for a novice such as myself in which to work.

Having 'released' the programme we were all aware that the interview tapes now locked away in the vaults at WBBC were loaded with many more stories than those that made the final cut and so it became my goal to revisit these and turn them into the book that hopefully nestles in your hand right now as you read these words.

However, before I could put pen to paper I became seriously ill with a mysterious illness called Guillain Barre Syndrome which literally stopped me in my tracks for a year or more. I was simply not able to stand, sit up, or even walk, let alone contemplate writing a book. Without the NHS and the incredible people who work within that amazing organisation I would most probably not be here now. I struggle to find the words that are adequate to convey the depth of gratitude I feel for those remarkable people and the amazing work they do: miracles large and small performed each and every day within the blink of an eye and with no expectation of any kind of fuss or celebration being made. Remarkable, awe-inspiring people.

As I began to find my feet, along came another interruption in the shape of Colin Hanton of the Quarry Men. Colin made me an offer I simply could not refuse: the chance to co-write his memoir (*Pre:Fab!*) about his life and times as the original drummer in the Quarry Men. And so it was to be another three very enjoyable years before the decks were finally clear and I could return to write *The Songs the Beatles Gave Away*.

As with *Pre:Fab!* I am the writer but, as with that previous tome, *The Songs the Beatles Gave Away* also owes its existence to the support, generosity, input and assistance of other kind folk without whom it would not, and could not, have reached fruition. And it is to those marvellous people who have supported me and/or contributed to this venture along the way that I now offer my sincere gratitude.

First, foremost and forever to my beloved family. Love always to my amazing, beautiful wife Sylvia for her unwavering support, kindness, patience, sense of humour and her ability to listen when I may well have been 'on repeat' just one too many times! Sylvia is the former National Trust custodian of both 20 Forthlin Road (nine years) and before that Mendips for two seasons whilst I drove the National Trust mini-bus because the original driver suddenly left. It was she who had the idea to always leave the bedroom light on overnight in John's bedroom at Mendips each December 8 to commemorate his passing. For nine years of my working life as custodian at 'Mendips', Sylvia performed the same job at 20 Forthlin Road, the former home of Sir Paul and Mike McCartney BEM. Sylvia and I also lived-in at Mendips for nine years which was a unique experience. Working at 'Mendips' and Forthlin as its 'custodians' was always a privilege, and inevitably became more than just a 'job': especially when we were living in the house, it became our home as well. In 2017 when we were chosen as 'Tourism Stars Of The Year' for the Liverpool City Region we were immensely proud. It was very special. All I know is that without Sylvia I would achieve nothing, she is my inspiration, my driving force.

To my incredible, intelligent and beautiful daughter Hannah for her constant support, enthusiasm and belief in her Dad to get the job done. Hannah was hugely instrumental in helping me traverse the labyrinth that had become the doorway to the record companies of yesteryear. She is always there for me, my best friend who offers great advice when I need it most.

To my brilliant son-in-law Toby Clark, for his friendship, technological/computer wizardry, support and masterful photographic skills. Toby took all the pictures of the 45rpm records from my collection which are featured on the cover and throughout the book.

To Bob and Trudie – beyond the working environment of WBBC – your friendship, massive enthusiasm, belief and support both practical and psychological have been the rocks that have inspired me to fashion this written version of the original radio documentary. Your permission to access all the interviews we recorded to make that programme is the keystone that locked everything into place. Bob has also contributed a marvellous 'Foreword' for which I am very grateful. Quite simply: Bob and Trudie, you are the best!

Next up is Dave Ravenscroft whose supreme knowledge and insight into the lives and times of the Beatles has been immensely helpful (to say the very least). Dave's generosity of spirit (and time) has helped me keep the faith whenever I began to doubt the worth of the whole project. To have him riding shotgun, has been like playing alongside Virgil van Dijk: occasional factual errors may get past me but never past him. I am very fortunate. Dave: you are the man, thank you so much.

To Freda Kelly whose friendship I value enormously. Her eyewitness account of the lunchtime sessions 'down the Cavern' that she has contributed is just one example of her legendary kindness and generosity. Your support in this – and other Beatles-related ventures in which we have participated – means more than I can say. Thank you so much, Freda.

To Billy J. Kramer who not only spoke to me at great length but kindly contributed a wonderful 'Preface'. Billy also took time out to read sections of the book before it went to print. Indeed, his generosity with both his time and enthusiasm for the project in general speaks volumes for what a helpful, thoughtful man he is.

Thanks in abundance go to my mightily patient publisher, guitar ace and designer supreme, the one and only Mr. David Burrill of Great Northern Books, who could be forgiven at times for believing *The Songs the Beatles Gave Away* was but a figment of my imagination. David is a good listener, gives generously of his time and provides sound advice. He's all that a good friend should be. There could not have been a better publisher for *The Songs the Beatles Gave Away*. I am a lucky man. He believed in the book from our very first phone conversation. Plus, he digs Billy J. ... in my book, no more need be said.

Ross Jamieson from Great Northern is not only hugely insightful and very, very good at what he does, but deserves the award for the most patient man on the planet (after David B!) as he guided me through the first-read through of my original manuscript ... without the need to resort to violence ... and to the point Great Northern could prise my fingers away from it. His support has been monumental.

My heartfelt gratitude goes to the true stars at the heart of the show: the hugely talented artists who contributed insightful interviews either for the original radio documentary, for the book itself or, in some instances, who had talked to me about the Beatles before either documentary or book were even contemplated. Altogether, let's please hear it for: Peter Asher, Cilla Black OBE, John Clay, Megan Davies, John Askew aka Johnny Gentle, Colin Hanton, Billy Hatton, Mary Hopkin, Freda Kelly, Arthur Kelly, Astrid Kirchherr, Billy J. Kramer, Jackie Lomax, John Duff Lowe, Sir Paul McCartney, Sir George Martin, Chas Newby, Klaus Voormann, Nigel Walley and Alan White.

I am particularly moved to remember Billy Hatton and Jackie Lomax who were my guests at Mendips and have since passed away. All too briefly Billy became a friend who would occasionally drop in at the house for a chat or we'd bump into each other at various Beatles-related events in Liverpool. His sense of humour and kindness of spirit were ever present. Like Jackie, he is mightily missed.

To Mark Lewisohn, a marvellous and generous friend whose reputation, in mine and many people's minds, as the world's leading Beatles historian, is unassailable – thanks always. In order to put together *The Songs the Beatles Gave Away* I have leaned mightily on the brilliant collection of books Mark has painstakingly researched and authored (none more so than his classic *Tune In*). In doing so I have become amazed all over again at what an incredible historian and archivist he is and such a great writer to boot. It's a rare combination and one to be cherished. The Beatles, their fans and the city of Liverpool are very fortunate to have Mark documenting their history as accurately and eloquently as he has done and continues to do.

To Spencer Leigh, Liverpool's very own legendary and amazing broadcaster, journalist, author and musicologist supreme, who allowed me to raid his considerable collection of Beatles books and access tomes I did not know existed and which contain valuable long-forgotten nuggets of information, some of which now also grace these pages. Thank you yet again, Mr. Leigh!

As with Mark Lewisohn, Liverpool is very fortunate indeed to count Spencer Leigh among its most significant historians and writers when it comes to accurately recording, preserving and interpreting the story of Liverpool, its musicians and their fans in, particularly, the decades of the Fifties and Sixties of the 20th century.

Spencer's lively biography of Bob Wooler (*The Best of Fellas*) is just one example of how he gets to the very heart of the matter: an indispensable resource for any Beatles fan, and for me it was an absolute delight to re-visit it for the purposes of researching *The Songs the Beatles Gave Away*.

Thanks to Gavin Askew, a real kindred spirit, who provided the act of generosity I never saw coming. Gavin not only contributed to the design of the ace cover that graces the front of this book but he also opened up his collection of pop memorabilia and photographs for me to use for *The Songs the Beatles Gave Away*. What a gift! Gavin's act of kindness was very special and pulled many strands together for me in that he is also the son of John Askew aka Johnny Gentle!

To those whose friendship and encouragement in all my Beatles/Liverpool-related activities has been constant and much appreciated even though they may not have always been aware of it: Liam Bailey, Eric & Mary Ann Brace, Paul Brady, Jackson Browne, Jon Byrd, Patrick Burke, Mike and Lynda Cadwallader, Jean Catharell, Dick and Diane Cvitanich, Rod Davis, Peter & Gabi Davies, Jo and Kev Delaney, Lori Fletcher, Steve Forbert, Neil Lochiel, Ingrid and Uwe Franke, Sam and Sofia Genders, Debbie and Nigel Greenberg, Chris Hall, Jennifer Kelly, Donna Jackson, James Kaplan, Roni Kramer, Jamii Layton, Bob Hewitt, Mike McCartney BEM, Tom McConnell, Sandy McMillan, Colin Maddocks, Helena Mulhearn, Willie Nile, Sylvia O'Malley, Dave and Ellen Pegg (who so kindly put me in touch with Megan Davies), Michael and Andrea Ramage, Danny and Hannah Scott, Jackie Spencer, Chris Stanley, Frankie Tibbles, Dave Upton, Jan Vaughan, Iain Walker (Beatles enthusiast and record collector extraordinaire), Gary and Rachel Watson, Alan and Gigi White ...

To those whose knowledge of the way (legal) things work and what belongs to whom and thus (hopefully) helped me avoid unnecessary legal collisions: Iain Connor and whomever I spoke to at the Intellectual Property Office (they wouldn't tell me their name).

The Songs the Beatles Gave Away is neither 'authorised', 'endorsed' nor in any way associated with either Yoko Ono Lennon or the National Trust but as their employee/representative at 'Mendips' for over 18 years I would hope they like my book. I certainly wish to acknowledge how my work for them has helped me connect with people who have contributed to this tome. To all the visitors to 'Mendips' from here, there and everywhere around the world who, since 2004, have toured the property with me as their host: on a daily basis your energy and enthusiasm for all things John Lennon/Paul McCartney/Beatles has never ceased to amaze and sustain me. I am a very fortunate man to have met you all. Peace and love always to all of you who remember me ... and to those who don't!

To Dr. Winston O'Boogie: living and working in your childhood home in Liverpool has been inspirational, an absolute honour, great fun ... an incredible journey. To my friends and I as young boys and girls growing up in Liverpool and its environs you and your group were our heroes. Your music was, and still remains, the best. It never failed us and neither did you.

Every day at 'Mendips' I see and hear how massively John as an individual is missed, how much he is loved by each and every one of those who come to say hello, shed a tear, sometimes sing and always to remember.

To the Beatles collectively, thank you: like so many teenagers in the Sixties I bought all your records, saving my pocket money for the big event, eagerly awaiting every release date ... tuning in to every TV and radio appearance ... you were inspirational, 'the band of bands'. You still are.

Colin Hall
Menlove Avenue, Woolton, Liverpool
Spring, 2022

Photographs

My sincere thanks to the following for their kind permission to use their personal photographs:
Rod Davis for use of his father James L. Davis's priceless photograph of the Quarry Men aboard a truck in Woolton on 6 July 1957 as part of the procession that preceded the crowning of the Rose Queen and the opening of the St. Peter's Annual Church Garden Fete.
The Quarry Men for their brilliant photograph of the group in performance at the Wilson Hall, October 1957 with John and Paul fronting the line-up.
Ursula L. Wilding for her evocative photograph of the Cavern 1965.
Eddie King for his marvellous picture of himself and Peter Asher on tour in Japan.
Bob Hewitt for his historic and exclusive photograph of the Beatles with the Maharishi and Mick Jagger in Bangor, North Wales, 1967.